P9-BZR-775

Peterson's

MASTER THE

GED® TEST

2014

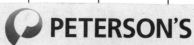

PETERSON'S

FENNVILLE DISTRICT LIBRARY
400 W. Main P.O. Box 1130
FENNVILLE, MI 49408

About Peterson's

Peterson's provides the accurate, dependable, high-quality education content and guidance you need to succeed. No matter where you are on your academic or professional path, you can rely on Peterson's print and digital publications for the most up-to-date education exploration data, expert test-prep tools, and top-notch career success resources—everything you need to achieve your goals.

Visit us online at www.petersonsbooks.com and let Peterson's help you achieve your goals.

For more information, contact Peterson's, 3 Columbia Circle, Suite 205, Albany, NY 12203-5158; 800-338-3282 Ext. 54229; or find us online at www.petersonsbooks.com.

By printing this book on recycled paper (40% post-consumer waste), 914 trees were saved.

Contents

PART I: THE GED® TESTS—THE BASICS

PART II: DETERMINING STRENGTHS AND WEAKNESSES

PART III: REASONING THROUGH LANGUAGE ARTS

Contents

PART IV: THE SOCIAL STUDIES TEST

Contents

Credits

Excerpts from "The Fortieth Door," by Mary Hastings Bradley

Obesity and Cancer Risk, National Cancer Institute website (www.cancer.gov)

Mystery of the Missing Waves on Titan, Science@NASA website (science.nasa.gov)

Adam's Needle, U.S. Department of Agriculture website (www.usda.gov)

Lead in the Environment, U.S. Environmental Protection Agency, Office of Superfund Remediation and Technology Innovation website (www.epa.gov)

Passage about "Migrant Mother" excerpted from No Caption Needed: Iconic Photographs, Public Culture, and Liberal Democracy, "Migrant Mother," by Robert Hariman and John Louis Lucaites; University of Chicago Press website (http://www.press.uchicago.edu/Misc/Chicago/316062.html).

Excerpts from *The Game*, by Jack London

Excerpts from *Journey to the Center of the Earth*, by Jules Verne

Hero Tales from American History, Chapter 1 "Washington," by Henry Cabot Lodge and Theodore Roosevelt

Excerpts from *Patrick Henry*, by Moses Coit Tyler

Excerpts from *The Age of Innocence*, by Edith Wharton

Excerpts from *Robert Kennedy and the Cuban Missile Crisis A Reinterpretation*, by Mark White

Excerpts from *The Awakening*, by Kate Chopin

Before You Begin

You've decided to get your high school diploma by preparing to take the 2014 GED® test. This is a great step! By now, you know that a high school diploma is a very important document to possess. With your diploma, you will be able to take advantage of training and educational opportunities beyond the high school level and increase your earning potential.

You want to do your best on the 2014 GED® test, and that's why you purchased this book. Used correctly, this self-tutor will show you what to expect while giving you the most effective practice with subjects you can expect to see on the actual exam. Peterson's *Master the GED® Test* provides you with the necessary tools to make the most of the study time you have, including:

- **Top 10 GED® Test-taking Tips** lists the ten most important tips to help you score high on the GED® test.

- **Part I** is essential reading if you are preparing to take the 2014 GED® test. You'll find out about the overall structure of the new GED® test, what each section of the test covers, the scoring and passing requirements, scheduling and testing procedures, and what you need to do to get ready to take the exam.

- **Part II** allows you to dip your toes into the 2014 GED® test waters by taking a Diagnostic Practice Test. Use the results of this Diagnostic Test to determine where you need to focus your GED® test preparation.

- **Parts III–VI** review the subject matter for each test area of the GED® test—Reasoning Through Language Arts, Social Studies, Science, and Mathematical Reasoning—and offer you powerful strategies for attacking every question type you'll encounter in the actual exam.

- **Part VII** consists of 2 full-length Practice Tests, with answer explanations for each question. Each test contains a similar number and mix of question types you'll encounter on the actual exam. To accurately measure your performance on these Practice Tests, be sure to adhere strictly to the stated time limits for each section.

- **Word List** in the Appendix offers you a great tool to help boost your vocabulary for ALL of the sections of the 2014 GED® test.

THE DIAGNOSTIC PRACTICE TEST AND PROCESS

The Diagnostic Practice Test does more than give you testing experience. It helps you recognize your strengths and pinpoint areas that need improvement. By understanding your "testing profile," you can immediately address your weak areas by working through the relevant review chapters, learning the pertinent test-taking tips, and studying the numerous examples and explanations provided.

The Review Sections

The Reasoning Through Language Arts section provides an opportunity to improve your language skills, which are necessary for good performance in reading, writing, and in all other academic areas. The reading selections consist of a wide range of reading matter, from nonfiction to a scene from a novel to business memos and e-mails. Writing questions will examine usage, organization, and mechanics skills in a variety of situations.

The Social Studies review covers history, civics and government, economics, and geography. The review will help you sharpen your comprehension, analysis, evaluation, and application skills for the actual exam.

The Science section reviews those subjects that will appear on the actual GED® exam: life science (biology), earth science (geology and oceanography), space science (astronomy), and physical science (chemistry and physics). The review will help you with your ability to recall and understand information, draw inferences and conclusions, evaluate data, and apply concepts and ideas to other situations.

The Mathematical Reasoning section provides user-friendly explanations of math processes in recognition of the particular difficulty that many students have in this area. The review, examples, and answer explanations will help you better comprehend the difficult concepts in the tested areas of numbers, number sense, and operations; data, statistics, and probability; algebra, functions, and patterns; and geometry, and measurement.

THE PRACTICE TESTS

When you have completed your reviews, take the Practice Tests under simulated test conditions to further sharpen your skills. Find a quiet place where you won't be distracted or interrupted, set a timer for the required time, and work through each test as though it were test day.

SPECIAL STUDY FEATURES

Overview

Each chapter begins with a bulleted overview listing the topics that will be covered in the chapter. You know immediately where to look for a topic that you need to work on.

Summing It Up

Each review chapter ends with a point-by-point summary that captures the most important items. The summaries are a convenient way to review the content of the chapters.

Access Two New GED® Tests Online

Peterson's is providing you with access to two additional practice tests for the 2014 GED® test. The testing content of these two practice tests was created by the test-prep experts at Peterson's. The Peterson's online testing experience resembles the testing experience you will find on the 2014 GED® test. You can access these two practice tests at petersonspublishing.com/GED. You will be asked to enter your e-mail address, and Peterson's will e-mail you an activation code and the link needed to access the online practice tests for the 2014 GED® test.

WORD LIST

Vocabulary *as such* is not tested on the 2014 GED® test; however, there are plenty of indirect and hidden vocabulary questions throughout the exam. The broader, more varied, and more accurate your vocabulary knowledge, the better your chances of answering questions quickly and correctly. To help you with this task, we've put together a list of about 500 commonly used words on the 2014 GED® test, including hundreds of related words—words that are variants of the primary words or words that share a common word root. You'll find the Word List in the Appendix. Use it to enhance your vocabulary study for all parts of the 2014 GED® test.

YOU'RE WELL ON YOUR WAY TO SUCCESS

Remember that knowledge is power. By using Peterson's *Master the GED® Test*, you will be studying the most comprehensive test-preparation guide available for the 2014 GED® test, and you will become extremely knowledgeable about the new GED® test. We look forward to helping you pass the GED® test and obtain your GED® test certificate or diploma. Good luck!

GIVE US YOUR FEEDBACK

Peterson's publishes a full line of resources to help guide you. Peterson's publications can be found at high school guidance offices, college libraries and career centers, your local bookstore or library, and online at www.petersonsbooks.com. Peterson's books are also available as ebooks.

We welcome any comments or suggestions you may have about this publication.

Peterson's, a Nelnet Company
3 Columbia Circle
Suite 205
Albany, NY 12203-5158
E-mail: custsvc@petersons.com

PART I

THE GED® TESTS—THE BASICS

All About the GED® Test

Congratulations on taking the first step to advancing your academic career. Whether you are taking the 2014 GED® test to prepare for college entrance or looking for the career opportunities that become available after completing the GED® test, you are not alone. Since 1943, more than 20 million people have earned their GED® credential. It is estimated that in the United States today 1 out of every 7 high school students will complete their education by taking the GED® exams. In fact, in 2009, more than 418,000 individuals were awarded their high school credential.

This book was designed to assist you in successfully passing all four of the individual tests in the 2014 GED® test. The lessons in this book will help you develop skills essential to passing each test, and the individual subject reviews will help you become comfortable with the knowledge areas covered on the tests. The example questions provided throughout the lessons, along with the book's Diagnostic and Practice Tests (including access to two online tests), afford you plenty of practice with just the types of questions you will encounter on the real 2014 GED® test.

THE 2014 GED® TEST

You probably already know that the 2014 GED® test is a brand-new test—a test that's different in many ways from its predecessor, which was created in 2002. You probably also know that if you didn't complete all of the old GED® tests, you need to begin again with the new GED® test.

According to the GED® test-makers, the new GED® test "measures the college- and career-readiness skills students need, and [it] prepares them with a basic level of computer literacy to compete in today's job market." The biggest change is that the

chapter 1

2014 GED® test is now given entirely on the computer in official GED® test centers. You'll learn more about the computer-based test later in this chapter. Here are some of the other differences between the old and new GED® test:

- **Scheduling the Test:** Previously, students called or visited multiple centers to schedule their tests; now all information is available on MyGED™.

- **Taking the Practice Test:** The 2002 GED® practice test provided limited feedback for a student to act upon; the 2014 GED® practice test (GED Ready™) offers personalized, actionable feedback and comes with targeted study recommendations to improve scores.

- **Taking the Test:** The 2002 GED® test required students to take certain exams on certain days; the 2014 GED® test allows you to take the exam you want when you want to take it.

- **Getting Your Scores:** It took four to eight weeks to receive the 2002 GED® test scores; the 2014 GED® test scores are available the same day.

- **Requesting Transcripts:** The 2002 GED® test usually required students to request transcripts in person, and it took two to three weeks. You can request your 2014 GED® test transcripts through MyGED™, and you'll have them the same day.

- **Transitioning Post-GED® Test:** The 2002 GED® test offered limited post-test options; the 2014 GED® test provides college and career transition resources through its program.

The new GED® test is aligned with Common Core Standards, a national set of standards designed to help students attain their highest potential. Many of the questions on the 2014 GED® test require you to show *how* you got the answer—not just filling in a correct multiple-choice bubble. On the new GED® test, you will need to type, click on graphs, use a "drag-and-drop" feature, and more. But don't worry—Peterson's *Master the GED® Test* has just what you need to help you succeed on this important new test.

WHAT IS THE GED® TEST?

The **Tests of General Education Development,** or **GED® test,** are standardized tests that measure skills required of high school graduates in the United States and Canada. The ultimate goal in passing these exams is a certificate that is equivalent to a high school diploma. A GED® certificate can be useful for gaining admission to college, for obtaining certain vocational licenses, or for finding employment in the many types of jobs that require a high school diploma or its equivalent.

The battery of four GED® tests are designed and administered by the GED® testing Service® of the American Council on Education® in partnership with Pearson. This new organization formed in 2011 to represent a public-private partnership. These tests were originally developed to help veterans returning from service in World War II regain academic skills and complete an education that had been interrupted by the war. Many returning veterans used this additional education to obtain civilian jobs. Since the

1940s, the emphasis of the GED® tests has gradually shifted from knowledge required for industrial jobs to the kinds of knowledge and skills needed for today's information-driven world. In 2014, the test was revised to not only provide adults with a diploma equivalency, but also measure career- and college-readiness skills. This test is fully computer based and includes "technology-enhanced items" in addition to traditional multiple-choice and extended-response essay questions. One thing has not changed, though: millions of motivated men and women like you have earned their high school credential by completing the GED® battery of tests.

THE FOUR GED® TESTS—AT A GLANCE

In order to pass the GED® tests and earn a GED® certificate, for each subject area you must demonstrate a mastery of skills and knowledge at least equal to 40 percent of high school graduates. The test measures a foundational core of knowledge and skills, ensuring that adults are prepared for college and careers. Each of the four tests is designed to gauge the same four broad skills:

- Comprehension (understanding and interpreting information)

- Analysis (drawing specific inferences and conclusions from information)

- Synthesis and evaluation (characterizing, generalizing from, and making judgments about information)

- Application (using information in ways other than those presented)

Of course, each of the four tests measures these skills in its own unique way. And to be successful on the GED® tests, in addition to exercising this skill-set, you must apply your common knowledge and your common sense, both of which are acquired through everyday experiences and observations, as well as through rudimentary education.

The 2014 GED® Test Structure

The GED® tests consist of four individual tests, all of which must now be taken on a computer-based testing platform, which allows for richer interactive test items. Each test covers a different component of standard high school curriculum, and it is aligned to Assessment Targets derived from the Common Core State Standards and similar standards in Texas and Virginia. The following table shows the various areas that each test covers, along with the number of questions available and the time limit for each test.

TEST	CONTENT AREAS	NUMBER AND TYPES OF QUESTIONS	TIME LIMIT
Reasoning Through Language Arts	Reading comprehension Informational (75%) Literature (25%) Writing Editing	49 questions multiple choice drop-down fill-in-the-blank drag-and-drop extended response (1)	150 minutes†

Social Studies	U.S. history (20%) Civics and government (50%) Economics (15%) Geography and the world (15%)	34 questions multiple choice drop-down fill-in-the-blank drag-and-drop hot spot extended response (1)	90 minutes[†]
Science	Life science (40%) Earth and space science (20%) Physical science (40%)	30 questions multiple choice drop-down short answer fill-in-the-blank drag-and-drop hot spot	90 minutes
Mathematical Reasoning	Quantitative Problem Solving (45%) Algebraic Problem Solving (55%)	37 questions multiple choice drop-down fill-in-the-blank drag-and-drop hot spot	90 minutes

[†]This time includes a 10-minute break and a strict 45 minutes to write the extended-response essay.

The tests include multiple-choice items, technology-enhanced items, short answers, and extended-response essays. The multiple-choice items have four answer choices consisting of one correct answer and three distractors. The technology-enhanced items are drop-down, fill-in-the-blank, drag-and-drop, and hot spot items. A drop-down item will have a drop-down menu embedded into a passage or statement, and you need to choose the correct answer from this menu. A fill-in-the-blank will have a blank box in which to write the correct answer. A drag-and-drop will be an interactive task; you will move pictures, words, or numbers to drop targets on the computer screen. A hot spot is a graphic image with sensors to mark your answer to a question. The Science test has short answer items that allow you to give a brief response to open-ended questions. There are two extended-response items on the GED® test: one is in the Reasoning Through Language Arts Test and the other is in the Social Studies Test. Both require you to analyze source texts and produce a writing sample that meets the items in the appropriate rubrics.

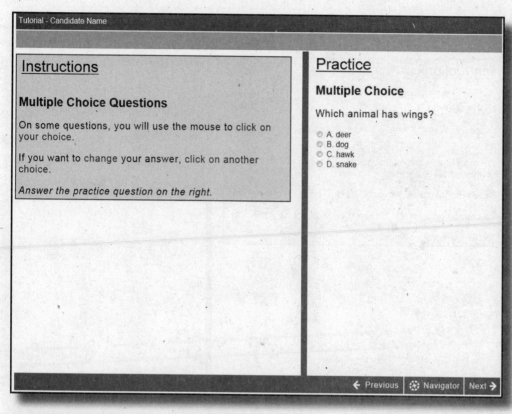

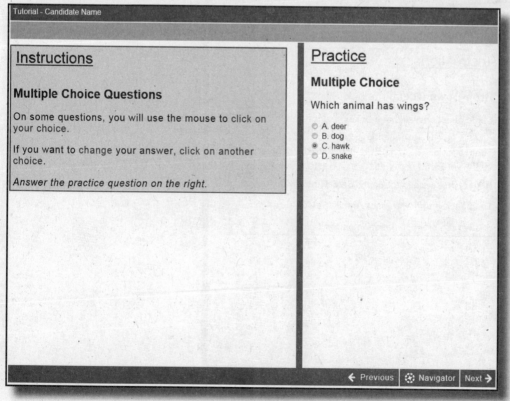

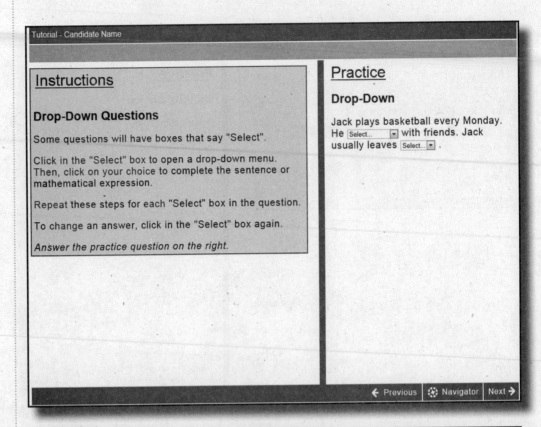

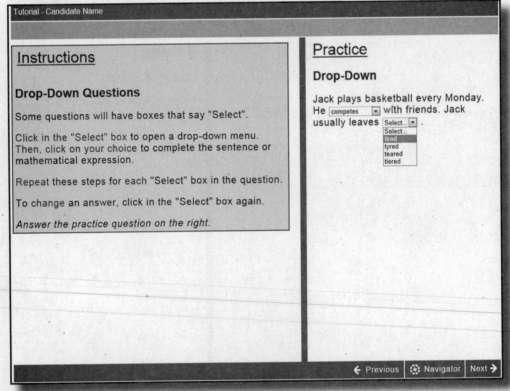

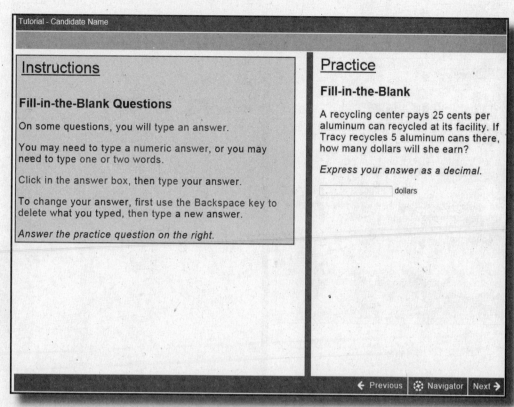

Tutorial - Candidate Name

Instructions

Fill-in-the-Blank Questions

On some questions, you will type an answer.

You may need to type a numeric answer, or you may need to type one or two words.

Click in the answer box, then type your answer.

To change your answer, first use the Backspace key to delete what you typed, then type a new answer.

Answer the practice question on the right.

Practice

Fill-in-the-Blank

A recycling center pays 25 cents per aluminum can recycled at its facility. If Tracy recycles 5 aluminum cans there, how many dollars will she earn?

Express your answer as a decimal.

[   ] dollars

← Previous   ⚙ Navigator   Next →

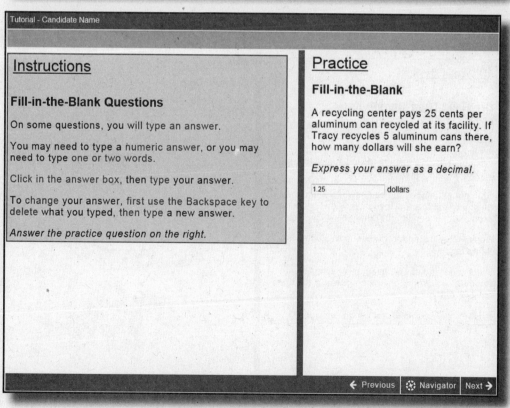

Tutorial - Candidate Name

Instructions

Fill-in-the-Blank Questions

On some questions, you will type an answer.

You may need to type a numeric answer, or you may need to type one or two words.

Click in the answer box, then type your answer.

To change your answer, first use the Backspace key to delete what you typed, then type a new answer.

Answer the practice question on the right.

Practice

Fill-in-the-Blank

A recycling center pays 25 cents per aluminum can recycled at its facility. If Tracy recycles 5 aluminum cans there, how many dollars will she earn?

Express your answer as a decimal.

[1.25   ] dollars

← Previous   ⚙ Navigator   Next →

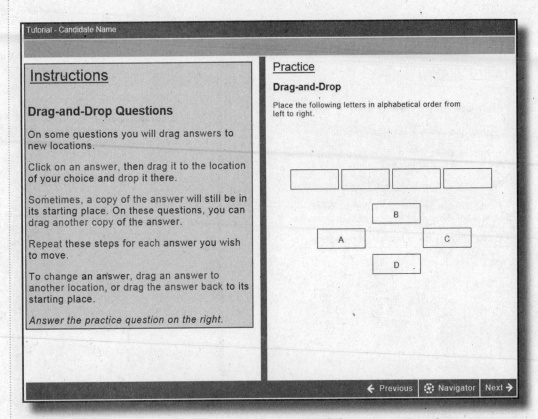

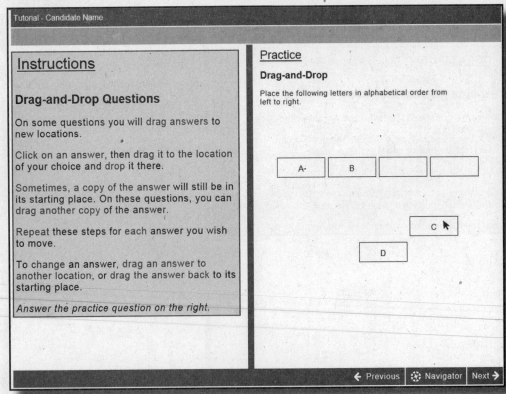

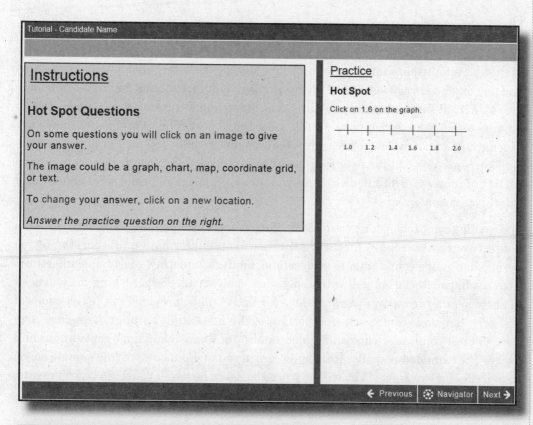

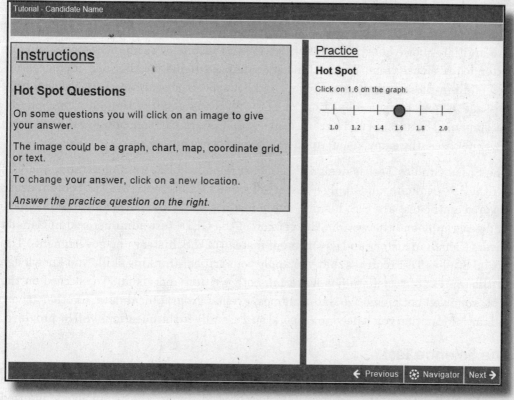

The Reasoning Through Language Arts Test

The Reasoning Through Language Arts Test consists of 49 questions. The majority of these are multiple-choice questions, but there are also technology-enhanced items and one extended-response item. The technology-enhanced items for this test include drop-down, fill-in-the-blank, and drag-and-drop. Some questions are presented in groups—each group based on the same selection of text. The reading selections vary in length (400–900 words for reading comprehension, 350–450 for language comprehension, and 550–650 for extended-response passages) and are drawn from a wide variety of sources, including fiction and nonfiction, such as informational articles and workplace documents.

The reading comprehension portion of the Reasoning Through Language Arts Test does *not* test your knowledge of literature or other factual information. Rather, the test is designed to gauge your ability to understand, analyze, and draw reasonable inferences from reading material, as well as to apply what you've read. So everything you will need to know in order to answer the questions correctly will be provided in the selections of text. The language comprehension portion of the Reasoning Through Language Arts Test will test your knowledge and understanding of English language conventions and usage. The extended-response item will require you to produce a writing sample based on paired source passages. You will be scored based on how well you analyze arguments, provide evidence, organize thoughts, and write fluently.

The Social Studies Test

The Social Studies Test consists of 34 multiple-choice questions. The majority of these are multiple-choice questions, but there are also technology-enhanced items and one extended-response item. The technology-enhanced items for this test include drop-down, fill-in-the-blank, drag-and-drop, and hot spot. Each question is based on a brief passage of text, a visual depiction, or both. As many as 20 of the questions may be accompanied by a visual (a diagram, table, graph, chart, cartoon, or other illustration). In some cases, the same visual applies to two or more questions.

The Social Studies Test is designed to measure your ability to understand, analyze, synthesize, evaluate, and apply a variety of social studies concepts. The content areas covered on the test are U.S. history, world history, civics and government, economics, and geography and the world. (The version of the GED® test administered in Canada covers Canadian history and government instead of U.S. history and government.) The Social Studies Test requires that you apply your critical-thinking skills and knowledge in the context of social studies material, both written and visual. To succeed on the test, you need not memorize dates, names, events, geographical data, or other trivia. All the information you'll need to respond successfully to the questions will be provided.

The Science Test

The Science Test consists of 30 questions. The majority of these are multiple-choice questions, but there are also technology-enhanced items. The technology-enhanced items for this test include drop-down, short answer, fill-in-the-blank, drag-and-drop, and hot spot. Each question is based on a brief passage of text, a visual depiction, or both. Many of the questions are accompanied by visuals (diagrams, tables, graphs, charts, and illustrations). In some cases, the same visual applies to two or more questions.

The Science Test is designed to gauge your ability to understand, analyze, synthesize, evaluate, and apply basic high school science concepts. The content areas covered on the test include life science, earth and space science, and physical science. The Science Test is primarily a critical-thinking skills test rather than a knowledge test. Most of what you need to know to respond successfully to the questions will be provided. However, the test does presuppose the basic level of science knowledge that most people have acquired through their everyday observations and experiences.

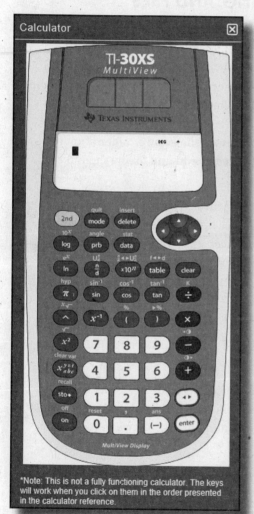

*Note: This is not a fully functioning calculator. The keys will work when you click on them in the order presented in the calculator reference.

The Mathematical Reasoning Test

The Mathematical Reasoning Test consists of 37 questions. The majority of these are multiple-choice questions, but there are also technology-enhanced items. The technology-enhanced items for this test include drop-down, fill-in-the-blank, drag-and-drop, and hot spot.

Mathematical Reasoning Test questions cover two areas: quantitative problem solving and algebraic problem solving. Some questions are based on visuals such as geometry figures and data presented in graphical format (tables, charts, and graphs).

On-screen calculators are provided for two areas: quantitative problem solving and algebraic problem solving but there will be 5 items that you need to answer without the use of a calculator. The items that allow use of the calculator emphasize number operations and calculations, while the ones where you can't use it place greater emphasis on math concepts, estimation, and "mental math."

GED® TEST SCORING AND PASSING REQUIREMENTS

For each GED® test, the more questions you answer correctly, the higher your score. No penalties are assessed for incorrect responses. Extended-response answers will be evaluated by an automated scoring engine that replicates human scoring. Each extended response will be scored based on a three-trait rubric. These traits identify the qualities of the writing that will be evaluated. The Reasoning Through Language Arts answers are scored on a six-point scale and each trait is worth up to two points, so the final raw score is twelve points. The Social Studies answers are scored on a four-point scale. The first trait is worth up to two points, and the other two are worth one point each. This score is then doubled to represent eight raw score points overall for the Social Studies test. Your scores for each extended response will be combined with your score for the rest of the scoring module for that subject.

The 2014 GED® test is scored with a "standard score" system in which the number of correct answers on each GED® test is converted to a 1100–200 scale. To pass the 2014 GED® test, a minimum score of 600 must be achieved across the four-test battery with a minimum score of 150 for each separate test.

GED® TEST AVAILABILITY, SCHEDULING, AND FEES

The GED® battery of tests is administered in every state of the United States, in every Canadian province, and in more than 100 international locations. The tests are offered in English, French, Spanish, large print, Braille, and even audiotape format. Special testing accommodations may be available for test-takers with a diagnosed learning disability, Attention Deficit/Hyperactivity Disorder, emotional/mental health conditions, physical/chronic health disabilities, or any other condition that may interfere with a test-taker's ability to fully demonstrate what he or she knows under standard testing conditions. For more information, visit www.acenet.edu and follow the links to the GED® test and accommodations for disabilities.

Currently, there are more than 3400 testing centers throughout the United States and Canada, as well as internationally. Testing centers are typically located at adult-education and community-education facilities. Some centers are located at military installations. Finding a convenient testing center should not be difficult if you live in a populous state. California, for example, boasts over 200 testing centers altogether, across every county in the state.

Local testing centers in the United States and Canada can be found by calling the toll-free hotline at 800-626-9433 (800-62-MY GED®). To find an international testing center, visit http://securereg3.prometric.com/.

GED® testing is scheduled through MyGED™. Each of the four GED® tests can be taken separately, at any time based on the test-takers preferences, scheduling, and readiness. (The total GED® testing time is over 7 hours, not including breaks between tests—far too long for a single testing day.)

The number of times the GED® tests are administered each year varies from one testing center to another. Each center establishes its own schedule. Centers in urban areas may offer testing every day, whereas centers in remote, rural areas may offer testing only once or twice a year. The GED® testing service charges testing jurisdictions $30 per module, making it $120 for the complete test. Testing jurisdictions will set their own price for test-takers and the overall price will vary from state to state.

It is important to note that while the GED® tests are taken on the computer, they cannot be taken online outside a certified testing center. Test officials strongly warn of fraudulent online programs that offer high school equivalencies for a fee.

RETAKING ALL OR PART OF THE GED® TEST

Once you receive your GED® test transcript (see "Score Transcripts and Your GED® Test Certificate"), you will be eligible to retake any or all of the individual GED® tests for which you did not meet the minimum passing score. Most testing centers charge an additional fee for retaking all or part of the GED® test. You may retake the same test no more than three times during the same calendar year.

At the time of retesting, you will be given a different version of the exam, which means that you will not be tested on the same questions you worked with previously. Multiple scores for the same test (for example, the Mathematical Reasoning Test) are *not* averaged. Only your highest score for each test is considered in determining whether you have attained the minimum passing score for that test.

SCORE TRANSCRIPTS AND YOUR GED® TEST CERTIFICATE

You will be able to access your scores online approximately 3 hours after your test is completed. Official and unofficial transcripts provide scaled scores, but they do not provide the number of correct or incorrect answers for any of the four tests. However, you will receive a comprehensive assessment of strengths and weaknesses along with a college- and career-readiness evaluation. Once you receive your scores, you may present it to a college-admissions office or as proof for employment purposes that you have met all GED® test requirements.

The GED® test certificate is a separate document issued by the state where you took the GED® tests. (Some states refer to this document as a diploma.) GED® test certificates are generally mailed. However, most states require that you reach a minimum age before the certificate is issued to you. It is important to keep your certificate in a safe place because some states will issue only one to you.

GETTING READY FOR THE GED® TESTS

Be sure to give yourself plenty of time to prepare for all four of the GED® tests. Many GED® test candidates find that taking a course with an instructor gives them the needed structure to accomplish their goal. Others have the self-discipline to study on a regular basis without the structure of a class. Regardless of which method you use, GED® test counselors often recommend spreading out GED® testing—rather than taking all the GED® tests in a short period of time—to allow plenty of time to prepare adequately for each test.

Setting and Sticking to a Study Schedule

If you're preparing for the GED® tests on your own, set up a regular review and practice schedule, which ideally should begin several weeks before each exam. Use the Practice Tests in this book, along with the supplemental online practice tests, to apply the skills and knowledge you learn throughout the lessons in this book. If you have time, supplement this book with one or two other GED® test-prep books, scheduling additional Practice

Testing from those books. You should also take the 2014 GED® practice test through GED Ready™. That will give you the feedback you need to determine if you're all set to take the test or if you still need additional preparation. Try to stagger, or spread out, your Practice Testing evenly rather than waiting until the last few days—or even the last week—before the exam. This way, you will experience steady improvement over time, which will instill confidence that will motivate you and help boost your scores.

Getting ready for the GED® tests is a bit like training for an athletic event. The more you practice under exam-like conditions, the better you'll perform during the actual exam. So be sure to take your Practice Tests under simulated testing conditions. Avoid interruptions and distractions, sit at a desk in a quiet spot, and adhere strictly to the time limit imposed during the actual test. Try to take each Practice Test from beginning to end in one sitting, just as you will during the actual test. Do not underestimate the role that endurance can play during the test. Be sure to thoroughly review each test after taking it, so you can identify your weaknesses and focus on them in further study.

Using Other Resources to Prepare for the Tests

Tap online and offline sources of local, national, and international news. Read articles from reputable magazines and websites focusing on current topics in science, economics, and politics. As you read, try to distinguish main ideas from supporting details, fact from opinion, and well-supported conclusions from poorly supported ones.

Examine charts, tables, and graphs provided in newspapers and magazines. Read a good daily newspaper and analyze its editorial cartoons (you'll see editorial cartoons on the GED® Social Studies Test). Ask yourself what ideas these various types of graphics are attempting to convey, what conclusions you can draw from them, and whether they are presenting information in an objective manner or from a certain slant or perspective.

Don't forget about textbooks and subject-review books, whether written for high school students or for a more general audience. At your library, you'll find basic introductory books on math, biology, physics, chemistry, earth science, astronomy, economics, history, civics, and geography. Multi-volume works such as the Time-Life book series contain easy-to-understand information relevant to the GED® Social Studies and Science Tests.

In short, spending time between now and test day to sharpen your reading and critical-thinking skills will serve you well during all of the GED® tests.

The Day Before the Test and the Day of the Test

The day before your actual test, avoid studying or practicing for it. In fact, try to avoid even thinking about the test. Consider this day your day off to relax by seeing a movie or spending time with friends. Take some pressure off yourself, and your mind will be fresher on exam day. The night before the test, eat a good dinner and get a good night's rest. On the morning of the test, eat a good breakfast and arrive at the testing center early so that you have time to unwind a bit before the exam. Chat with other test-takers about anything other than the test itself.

As you enter the testing room, try not to be nervous about taking the GED® tests. Remind yourself that these tests are practical measures of knowledge that you have gained through study and your life experiences. In addition, find reassurance in the hard work and hours of preparation you have invested in this endeavor. As the testing clock starts to run, tackle your test with confidence and enthusiasm—knowing that you have done your best to prepare for it.

OBTAINING MORE INFORMATION ABOUT THE GED® TEST

For locations and dates for GED® testing in your area, contact your state's GED® testing Service or a nearby GED® testing Center. For general information about the GED® tests, including information about future test changes, contact General Educational Development or consult the organization's official GED® test website:

General Educational Development
GED® Testing Service
American Council on Education
One DuPont Circle, NW
Washington, D.C. 20036
800-626-9433 (toll-free)
www.acenet.edu

If you're interested in enrolling in a GED® test-prep course, try contacting the adult-education or continuing-education department at your local community college or university. For additional self-study, you can utilize a variety of other GED® test-prep books and GED® test websites.

TOP 10 GED® TEST-TAKING TIPS

The general strategies and tips provided here apply to all four of the GED® tests (except for the Extended Response portion of the Reasoning Through Language Arts and Social Studies Tests). Be sure to look over this Top-10 list again just before exam day—you'll be glad you did.

1 Use your erasable white board to make notes.

Using your provided erasable white board can help you organize your thoughts, keep key ideas straight in your mind, and prevent careless errors. When reading a passage of text, consider jotting down words and phrases that are essential to understanding the passage's ideas. For lengthy or confusing text passages, write notes or make brief outlines on your erasable white board (which will be provided). During the portion of the Mathematical Reasoning Test for which a calculator is not allowed, perform all but the simplest computations on your erasable white board.

2 When answering a question based on visual information, size up the visual first.

Many questions on the Mathematical Reasoning, Science, and Social Studies tests contain visual information (graphs, charts, illustrations, diagrams, and so forth). Inspect any such "visual" carefully. Try to understand what the visual involves and what its overall intent and meaning is. Be sure to read any title or caption, which may provide clues for answering the question at hand.

3 Make sure you understand the question.

Read each question carefully so you know exactly what it is asking. Pay attention to key words such as *true, accurate, supports, probably,* and *most likely.* These words tell you the features to look for in the correct answer choice. Also look for words in capital letters such as NOT, LEAST, EXCEPT, and CANNOT. These capitalized words tell you that the question is being asked in the negative. (Note that these and other key words may also appear in **boldface.)** If a question is based on a passage of text, read the question stem (the question itself, apart from the answer choices) before you read the passage so you have an idea of what to look for in the passage.

4 Attempt to answer the question in your own words before reading the answer choices.

If you can formulate your own answer to a question, by all means do so. Then you can simply look for the answer choice that best matches what you already know is correct. What's more, you'll waste less time trying to understand the other choices, which can often be confusing and even nonsensical.

5 Read all the answer possibilities carefully.

The first answer choice you read might appear to provide a good answer, but by reading further you may discover that there is a better choice. Never select a final answer before reading and carefully considering all choices. For drop-down items, be sure to read each option as it fits into the sentence, and do not just read it on its own.

6 Select an answer choice that answers the question being asked.

This may seem obvious, but you should be careful not to choose an answer merely because it provides accurate information or a true statement, or because it is supported by information given in a passage of text or a visual. If the answer does not respond to the question, eliminate it.

7 Try to eliminate as many incorrect answer choices as possible.

Many questions will come with answer choices that are wrong because they provide the opposite of what the question asks for. For instance, a question that asks which statement is best supported by the text will probably come with at least two choices that are *contradicted* by the text. Some wrong-answer choices might be *off topic,* meaning that they convey ideas that are not relevant to the specific topic or the question. If you're paying attention, you can easily spot these sorts of answer choices and eliminate them to improve your odds of answering the questions correctly.

8 Apply common sense and common knowledge to your advantage.

Many questions may involve concepts and topics that are unfamiliar to you. You can use your real-life, practical knowledge and common sense to help you answer many such questions—or at least to narrow the answer choices.

9 **Answer every question, even if you need to guess.**
Your score on each of the four tests is determined by the number of questions you answer correctly. You won't be penalized for incorrect answers, so you should never leave a question unanswered. If you don't know the answer, just guess—you have nothing to lose and everything to gain.

10 **Pace yourself to leave enough time for reviewing your answers.**
Don't be a constant clock-watcher, but do check the time every so often to make sure you are on pace to read and answer all questions within the time allowed. Try to maintain a pace that leaves you at least 5 minutes to return to those questions you were unsure about and reconsider them.

SUMMING IT UP

- The Tests of General Education Development, or GED® tests, are standardized tests that measure skills required of high school graduates in the United States and Canada. The ultimate goal in passing these exams is a certificate that is equivalent to a high school diploma.

- The 2014 GED® test is the brand-new GED® test available on January 2, 2014. More than five years in the making by experts with a seventy-year history in high school equivalency, the test is aligned with current high school standards (including grade 12 standards) and is designed to ensure career and college readiness.

- The 2014 GED® test is delivered solely on the computer at official testing centers. The new test offers same-day scoring on all four parts—including the new score report for reporting and remediation. There are two score levels:
  - GED® test Passing Score: at or higher than the minimum needed to demonstrate high school equivalency-level skills and abilities
  - GED® test Passing Score with Honors: at or higher than the minimum needed to demonstrate career- and college-readiness (CCR)

- The four GED® tests can be taken in any order, separately, and at any time based on the test-taker's preferences.

- The tests that make up the GED® test battery are Reasoning Through Language Arts, Social Studies, Science, and Mathematical Reasoning. These tests consist of multiple-choice, drop-down, fill-in-the-blank, drag-and-drop, hot spot, and short-answer items. The Reasoning Through Language Arts and Social Studies Tests each include one extended-response item.

- For each GED® test, the more questions you answer correctly, the higher your score. No penalties are assessed for incorrect responses. The GED® test Extended Responses (included in the Reasoning Through Language Arts and Social Studies Tests) are evaluated by an automated scoring engine that replicates human scoring, and this score is combined with your score for the remainder of the corresponding test.

- In order to earn your GED®, you must attain a minimum average of 600, with a minimum of 150 on each separate test.

- Getting ready for the GED® tests is like training for an athletic event. The more you practice under exam-like conditions, the better you'll perform during the actual exam. Be sure to review each test after taking it, so you can identify your weaknesses and focus on them in further study.

- For general information about the GED® tests, consult the official GED® test website: www.acenet.edu.

PART II

DETERMINING STRENGTHS AND WEAKNESSES

CHAPTER 2   Practice Test 1: Diagnostic

Practice Test 1: Diagnostic

DIRECTIONS FOR TAKING THE DIAGNOSTIC TEST

Directions: The GED® Diagnostic Test has four separate subtests: Reasoning Through Language Arts, Mathematical Reasoning, Science, and Social Studies.

- Read and follow the directions at the start of each test.

- Stick to the time limits.

- Enter your answers to the multiple-choice questions on the tear-out Answer Sheets provided. You will answer so-called technology-enhanced questions —like fill-in-the-blank, hot spot, drag-and-drop, and drop-down questions— directly in the test.

- When you have completed the entire test, compare your answers with the correct answers given in the Answer Key and Explanations at the end of this Practice Test.

- Remember to check the "Are You Ready to Take the GED® Test?" section to gauge how close you are to mastering the GED® test.

diagnostic test

ANSWER SHEET PRACTICE TEST 1: DIAGNOSTIC TEST

Reasoning Through Language Arts

1. Ⓐ Ⓑ Ⓒ Ⓓ   18. Ⓐ Ⓑ Ⓒ Ⓓ   35. Ⓐ Ⓑ Ⓒ Ⓓ

2. _____   19. Ⓐ Ⓑ Ⓒ Ⓓ   36. Ⓐ Ⓑ Ⓒ Ⓓ

3. Ⓐ Ⓑ Ⓒ Ⓓ   20. Ⓐ Ⓑ Ⓒ Ⓓ   37. _____

4. _____   21. Ⓐ Ⓑ Ⓒ Ⓓ   38. Ⓐ Ⓑ Ⓒ Ⓓ

5. Ⓐ Ⓑ Ⓒ Ⓓ   22. _____   39. _____

6. Ⓐ Ⓑ Ⓒ Ⓓ   23. Ⓐ Ⓑ Ⓒ Ⓓ   40. Ⓐ Ⓑ Ⓒ Ⓓ

7. Ⓐ Ⓑ Ⓒ Ⓓ   24. Ⓐ Ⓑ Ⓒ Ⓓ   41. Ⓐ Ⓑ Ⓒ Ⓓ

8. Ⓐ Ⓑ Ⓒ Ⓓ   25. Ⓐ Ⓑ Ⓒ Ⓓ   42. Ⓐ Ⓑ Ⓒ Ⓓ

9. Ⓐ Ⓑ Ⓒ Ⓓ   26. Ⓐ Ⓑ Ⓒ Ⓓ   43. Ⓐ Ⓑ Ⓒ Ⓓ

10. Ⓐ Ⓑ Ⓒ Ⓓ   27. Ⓐ Ⓑ Ⓒ Ⓓ   44. Ⓐ Ⓑ Ⓒ Ⓓ

11. Ⓐ Ⓑ Ⓒ Ⓓ   28. _____   45. Ⓐ Ⓑ Ⓒ Ⓓ

12. _____   29. Ⓐ Ⓑ Ⓒ Ⓓ   46. Ⓐ Ⓑ Ⓒ Ⓓ

13. Ⓐ Ⓑ Ⓒ Ⓓ   30. Ⓐ Ⓑ Ⓒ Ⓓ   47. Ⓐ Ⓑ Ⓒ Ⓓ

14. _____   31. _____   48. Ⓐ Ⓑ Ⓒ Ⓓ

15. Ⓐ Ⓑ Ⓒ Ⓓ   32. Ⓐ Ⓑ Ⓒ Ⓓ   49. Ⓐ Ⓑ Ⓒ Ⓓ

16. _____   33. Ⓐ Ⓑ Ⓒ Ⓓ

17. Ⓐ Ⓑ Ⓒ Ⓓ   34. Ⓐ Ⓑ Ⓒ Ⓓ

ANSWER SHEET PRACTICE TEST 1: DIAGNOSTIC TEST

Mathematical Reasoning

1. _____

2. Ⓐ Ⓑ Ⓒ Ⓓ

3. Ⓐ Ⓑ Ⓒ Ⓓ

4. Ⓐ Ⓑ Ⓒ Ⓓ

5. _____

6. Ⓐ Ⓑ Ⓒ Ⓓ

7. Ⓐ Ⓑ Ⓒ Ⓓ

8. Ⓐ Ⓑ Ⓒ Ⓓ

9. Ⓐ Ⓑ Ⓒ Ⓓ

10. Ⓐ Ⓑ Ⓒ Ⓓ

11. _____

12. Ⓐ Ⓑ Ⓒ Ⓓ

13. Ⓐ Ⓑ Ⓒ Ⓓ

14. Ⓐ Ⓑ Ⓒ Ⓓ

15. _____

16. _____

17. Ⓐ Ⓑ Ⓒ Ⓓ

18. _____

19. Ⓐ Ⓑ Ⓒ Ⓓ

20. Ⓐ Ⓑ Ⓒ Ⓓ

21. _____

22. _____

23. _____

24. Ⓐ Ⓑ Ⓒ Ⓓ

25. _____

26. Ⓐ Ⓑ Ⓒ Ⓓ

27. Ⓐ Ⓑ Ⓒ Ⓓ

28. Ⓐ Ⓑ Ⓒ Ⓓ

29. Ⓐ Ⓑ Ⓒ Ⓓ

30. _____

31. _____

32. Ⓐ Ⓑ Ⓒ Ⓓ

33. Ⓐ Ⓑ Ⓒ Ⓓ

34. Ⓐ Ⓑ Ⓒ Ⓓ

35. _____

36. Ⓐ Ⓑ Ⓒ Ⓓ

37. Ⓐ Ⓑ Ⓒ Ⓓ

answer sheet

ANSWER SHEET PRACTICE TEST 1: DIAGNOSTIC TEST

Science

1. Ⓐ Ⓑ Ⓒ Ⓓ   11. Ⓐ Ⓑ Ⓒ Ⓓ   22. _____

2. Ⓐ Ⓑ Ⓒ Ⓓ   12. Ⓐ Ⓑ Ⓒ Ⓓ   23. Ⓐ Ⓑ Ⓒ Ⓓ

3. Ⓐ Ⓑ Ⓒ Ⓓ   13. Ⓐ Ⓑ Ⓒ Ⓓ   24. Ⓐ Ⓑ Ⓒ Ⓓ

4. Ⓐ Ⓑ Ⓒ Ⓓ   14. Ⓐ Ⓑ Ⓒ Ⓓ   25. Ⓐ Ⓑ Ⓒ Ⓓ

5. Ⓐ Ⓑ Ⓒ Ⓓ   15. Ⓐ Ⓑ Ⓒ Ⓓ   26. Ⓐ Ⓑ Ⓒ Ⓓ

6. _____   16. Ⓐ Ⓑ Ⓒ Ⓓ   27. _____

7. _____   17. Ⓐ Ⓑ Ⓒ Ⓓ   28. _____

8. _____   18. Ⓐ Ⓑ Ⓒ Ⓓ   29. Ⓐ Ⓑ Ⓒ Ⓓ

9. _____   19. _____   30. Ⓐ Ⓑ Ⓒ Ⓓ

10. Ⓐ Ⓑ Ⓒ Ⓓ   20. Ⓐ Ⓑ Ⓒ Ⓓ

21. _____

ANSWER SHEET PRACTICE TEST 1: DIAGNOSTIC TEST

Social Studies

1. Ⓐ Ⓑ Ⓒ Ⓓ   13. Ⓐ Ⓑ Ⓒ Ⓓ   24. Ⓐ Ⓑ Ⓒ Ⓓ

2. Ⓐ Ⓑ Ⓒ Ⓓ   14. Ⓐ Ⓑ Ⓒ Ⓓ   25. Ⓐ Ⓑ Ⓒ Ⓓ

3. Ⓐ Ⓑ Ⓒ Ⓓ   15. _____   26. Ⓐ Ⓑ Ⓒ Ⓓ

4. Ⓐ Ⓑ Ⓒ Ⓓ   16. _____   27. _____

5. Ⓐ Ⓑ Ⓒ Ⓓ   17. Ⓐ Ⓑ Ⓒ Ⓓ   28. Ⓐ Ⓑ Ⓒ Ⓓ

6. Ⓐ Ⓑ Ⓒ Ⓓ   18. Ⓐ Ⓑ Ⓒ Ⓓ   29. _____

7. Ⓐ Ⓑ Ⓒ Ⓓ   19. Ⓐ Ⓑ Ⓒ Ⓓ   30. Ⓐ Ⓑ Ⓒ Ⓓ

8. Ⓐ Ⓑ Ⓒ Ⓓ   20. Ⓐ Ⓑ Ⓒ Ⓓ   31. Ⓐ Ⓑ Ⓒ Ⓓ

9. _____   21. Ⓐ Ⓑ Ⓒ Ⓓ   32. Ⓐ Ⓑ Ⓒ Ⓓ

10. _____   22. Ⓐ Ⓑ Ⓒ Ⓓ   33. Ⓐ Ⓑ Ⓒ Ⓓ

11. _____   23. Ⓐ Ⓑ Ⓒ Ⓓ   34. Ⓐ Ⓑ Ⓒ Ⓓ

12. _____

answer sheet

Essay

_____

_____

_____

_____

_____

_____

_____

_____

_____

_____

_____

_____

_____

_____

_____

_____

_____

_____

_____

_____

_____

_____

answer sheet

REASONING THROUGH LANGUAGE ARTS

150 Minutes • 49 Questions

Directions: The Reasoning Through Language Arts Test consists of passages of fiction and nonfiction reading material. Most questions are in multiple-choice format. Others are meant to prepare you for the electronically formatted questions that you will find on the test, such as drop-down, fill-in-the-blanks, and drag-and-drops. After you read a passage, answer the questions that follow it, referring back to the passage as needed. Answer all questions based on what is stated and implied in the passage. There is also an extended response question that requires you to read a paired passage that represents two views on a topic and write a well-organized essay supporting one of the view points. Record your answers on the Reasoning Through Language Arts section of the answer sheet provided.

QUESTIONS 1–6 REFER TO THE FOLLOWING PASSAGE.

He didn't want to go. He loathed the very thought of it. Every flinching nerve in him protested.

A masked ball—a masked
5 ball at a Cairo hotel! Grimacing through peep-holes, self-conscious advances, flirtations ending in giggles! Tourists as nuns, tourists as Turks, tourists as God-knows-
10 what, all preening and peacocking!

Unhappily he gazed upon the girl who was proposing this horror as a bright delight. She was a very engaging girl—that was the mis-
15 chief of it. She stood smiling there in the bright, Egyptian sunshine, gay confidence in her gray eyes. He hated to shatter that confidence.

And he had done little enough
20 for her during her stay in Cairo. One tea at the Gezireh Palace Hotel, one trip to the Sultan al Hassan Mosque, one excursion through the bazaars—not exactly
25 an orgy of entertainment for a girl from home!

He had evaded climbing the Pyramids and fled from the ostrich farm. He had withheld from
30 inviting her to the camp on the edge of the Libyan desert where he was excavating, although her party had shown unmistakable signs of a

willingness to be diverted from the
35 beaten path of its travel.

And he was not calling on her now. He had come to Cairo for supplies and she had encountered him by chance upon a corner of
40 the crowded Mograby [western section], and there promptly she had invited him to to-night's ball.

"But it's not my line, you know, Jinny," he was protesting. "I'm so
45 fearfully out of dancing—"

"More reason to come, Jack. You need a change from digging up ruins all the time—it must be frightfully lonely out there on
50 the desert. I can't think how you stand it."

Jack Ryder smiled. There was no mortal use in explaining to Jinny Jeffries that his life on the desert
55 was the only life in the world, that his ruins held more thrills than all the fevers of her tourist crowds, and that he would rather gaze upon the mummied effigy of any lady of
60 the dynasty of Amenhotep than upon the freshest and fairest of the damsels of the present day.

It would only tax Jinny's credulity and hurt her feelings. And
65 he liked Jinny—though not as he liked Queen Hatasu or the little nameless creature he had dug out of a king's ante-room.

Jinny was an interfering
70 modern. She was the incarnation
of impossible demands.

But of course there was no real
reason why he should not stop over
and go to the dance.

—from "The Fortieth Door" by
Mary Hastings Bradley

1. Which of the following lines from the
passage reveals Jack's profession?

(A) "he was excavating in the
Libyan desert"

(B) "he had come to Cairo for
supplies"

(C) "his life on the desert was the
only life in the world"

(D) "excursion through the bazaars"

2. Based on the passage, what word best
describes Jack's personality? In the
drop-down menu, select your answer.
On the online GED® test, you will
click on your answer. In this paper
version, please circle it.

Select   ▼

He is shy.

He is a loner.

He is outgoing.

He is adventurous.

3. How does Jack feel about attending
the ball?

(A) He hates parties and refuses
to go.

(B) He hates the idea, but he likes
Jinny and wants to please her.

(C) He doesn't like parties but he is
glad Jinny invited him anyway.

(D) He doesn't like to dance and
doesn't like Jinny, but he feels
obligated to be nice to her.

4. Jack's thoughts about Jinny reveal
that [   ]. Drag the
correct answer below into the space
provided to complete the sentence.
On the online GED® test, you will
click and drag your answer into the
provided space. In this paper version,
please circle it.

He thinks people are interfering.

He likes the dead mummies
better than he likes Jinny.

He is glad that he ran into Jinny
and gladly shows that her around
the city.

He likes Jinny and thinks that
it might not be so bad to be with
people after all.

5. What clues in the text illustrate that
Jack is well suited to his work?

(A) He likes to travel.

(B) He likes living in the desert.

(C) He is fascinated by the ruins
and what they hold.

(D) He lives in the desert area,
but also feels at home with
colleagues in Cairo.

6. How do Jack and Jinny know one
another?

(A) They met in the Cairo market.

(B) They both work as
archaeologists in the desert.

(C) They knew each other when
Jack lived in England.

(D) They were introduced by a
colleague at a tea in the hotel.

QUESTIONS 7–11 REFER TO THE FOLLOWING PASSAGE.

John Dewey and Education

John Dewey, an American educator and philosopher of education, was a prolific writer on the subject. He was particularly interested in the place of education in a democratic republic.

The place of public education within a democratic society has been widely discussed and debated through the years. Perhaps no one

5 has written more widely on the subject in the United States than John Dewey, sometimes called "the father of public education," whose theories of education have a

10 large social component, that is, an emphasis on education as a social act and the classroom or learning environment as a replica of society.

Dewey defined various aspects

15 or characteristics of education. First, it was a necessity of life inasmuch as living beings needed to maintain themselves through a process of renewal. Therefore,

20 just as humans needed sleep, food, water, and shelter for physiological renewal, they also needed education to renew their minds, assuring that their socialization

25 kept pace with physiological growth.

A second aspect of education was its social component, which was to be accomplished by providing the

30 young with an environment that would provide a nurturing atmosphere to encourage the growth of their as yet undeveloped social customs.

35 A third aspect of public education was the provision of direction to youngsters, who might otherwise be left in uncontrolled situations without the steadying

40 and organizing influences of school. Direction was not to be of an overt nature, but rather indirect through the selection of the school situations in which the youngster

45 participated.

Finally, Dewey saw public education as a catalyst for growth. Since the young came to school capable of growth, it was the role of

50 education to provide opportunities for that growth to occur. The successful school environment is one in which a desire for continued growth is created—a desire that

55 extends throughout one's life beyond the end of formal education. In Dewey's model, the role of education in a democratic society is not seen as a preparation for

60 some later stage in life, such as adulthood. Rather, education is seen as a process of growth that never ends, with human beings continuously expanding their

65 capacity for growth. Neither did Dewey's model see education as a means by which the past was recapitulated. Instead education was a continuous reconstruction of

70 experiences, grounded very much in the present environment.

Since Dewey's model places a heavy emphasis on the social component, the nature of the

75 larger society that supports the educational system is of paramount importance. The ideal larger society, according to Dewey, is one in which the interests of a

80 group are all shared by all of its members and in which interactions with other groups are free and full. According to Dewey, education in such a society should provide

85 members of the group a stake or interest in social relationships and the ability to negotiate change without compromising the order and stability of the society.

90 Thus, Dewey's basic concept of education in a democratic society is based on the notion that education contains a large social component

designed to provide direction and
95 assure children's development
through their participation in the
group to which they belong.

7. Choose the word that would best complete the sentence from the choices below and type it into the space provided. In the context of the passage, the best synonym for *recapitulated* is [   ]. On the online GED® test, you will type in your answer. In this paper version, please circle it.

   (A) surrendered

   (B) summarized

   (C) streamlined

   (D) digested

8. Based on the passage, which is the most reasonable inference about John Dewey's primary goal for public education?

   (A) teaching children how to behave

   (B) making the United States a strong military power

   (C) creating a strong and stable society

   (D) teaching children how to make friends

9. In the context of the passage, what does the word *catalyst* mean?

   (A) an agent of change

   (B) a substance that speeds a chemical reaction

   (C) the cause of a catastrophe

   (D) an agent of resistance

10. Which of the following is NOT one of the four aspects or characteristics of education as discussed in the passage?

    (A) socialization

    (B) mental renewal

    (C) organization and direction

    (D) preparation for adulthood

11. What, according to Dewey, is the primary characteristic of the ideal society?

    (A) one in which all citizens have adequate sleep, food, water, and shelter

    (B) one in which group interests are shared by all members and in which all members may interact with other groups freely

    (C) one in which human beings continuously expand their capacity for growth in an unending process

    (D) a democratic society wherein education is seen as a preparation for some later stage in life, such as adulthood

QUESTIONS 12–17 REFER TO THE FOLLOWING PASSAGE.

John Adams was an active participant in the movement toward independence, one of the writers of the Declaration of Independence, and after the Revolution, the country's first vice president and second president. During his time in Philadelphia meeting with other delegates to the Constitutional Convention, he and his wife Abigail continually wrote letters to one another. Their correspondence left a legacy of history and a glimpse of their relationship. The following is a letter John Adams wrote to Abigail just a few weeks after the Battle of Bunker Hill, the first battle of the Revolution.

Philadelphia, 7 July, 1775.

I have received your very agreeable favors of June 22 and 25. They contain more particulars than any
5 letters I had before received from anybody.

It is not at all surprising to me, that the wanton, cruel, and infamous conflagration of
10 Charlestown [the site of the

Battle of Bunker Hill], the place of your father's nativity, should afflict him. Let him know that I sincerely condole with him on that
15 melancholy event. It is a method of conducting war long since become disreputable among civilized nations. But every year brings us fresh evidence that we have
20 nothing to hope for from our loving mother country, but cruelties more abominable than those which are practiced by the savage Indians.

The account you give me of the
25 numbers slain on the side of our enemies is afflicting to humanity, although it is a glorious proof of the bravery of our worthy countrymen. Considering all the disadvantages
30 under which they fought, they really exhibited prodigies of valor. Your description of the distresses of the worthy inhabitants of Boston and the other seaport towns is
35 enough to melt a heart of stone. Our consolation must be this, my dear, that cities may be rebuilt, and a people reduced to poverty may acquire fresh property. But a
40 constitution of government, once changed from freedom, can never be restored. Liberty, once lost, is lost forever. When the people once surrender their share in
45 the legislature, and their right of defending the limitations upon the Government, and of resisting every encroachment upon them, they can never regain it.
50 The loss of Mr. Mather's library, which was a collection of books and manuscripts made by himself, his father, his grandfather, and great-grandfather, and was really very
55 curious and valuable, is irreparable. The family picture you draw is charming indeed. My dear Abby, Johnny, Charley, and Tommy, I long to see you, and to share with
60 your mamma the pleasures of your conversation. I feel myself much obliged to Mr. Bowdoin, Mr.

Wibird, and the two families you mention, for their civilities to you.
65 My compliments to them. Does Mr. Wibird preach against oppression and the other cardinal vices of the times? Tell him the clergy here of every denomination, not excepting
70 the Episcopalian, thunder and lighten every Sabbath. They pray for Boston and the Massachusetts. They thank God most explicitly and fervently for our remarkable
75 successes. They pray for the American army. They seem to feel as if they were among you.

You ask if every member feels for us? Every member says he
80 does, and most of them really do. But most of them feel more for themselves. In every society of men, in every club I ever yet saw, you find some who are timid,
85 their fears hurry them away upon every alarm; some who are selfish and avaricious, on whose callous hearts nothing but interest and money can make impression. There
90 are some persons in New York and Philadelphia to whom a ship is dearer than a city, and a few barrels of flour than a thousand lives—other men's lives, I mean.
95 You ask, Can they realize what we suffer? I answer, No. They can't. They don't. And, to excuse them as well as I can, I must confess, I should not be able to do it myself, if
100 I was not more acquainted with it by experience than they are.

I am grieved for Dr. Tufts's ill-health, but rejoiced exceedingly at his virtuous exertions in the cause
105 of his country. I am happy to hear that my brothers were at Grape Island, and behaved well. My love to them, and duty to my mother.

It gives me more pleasure than
110 I can express, to learn that you sustain with so much fortitude the shocks and terrors of the times. You are really brave, my dear. You are a heroine, and you have

115 reason to be. For the worst that can happen can do you no harm. A soul as pure, as benevolent, as virtuous and pious as yours, has nothing to fear, but everything to *120* hope and expect from the last of human evils. I am glad you have secured an asylum, though I hope you will not have occasion for it. ...

I am forever yours.

12. Which of the following quotes from the letter shows that Adams believed the Revolution was necessary for the colonists to get their freedom?

Select   ▼

"Liberty, once lost, is lost forever."

"For the worst that can happen can do you no harm."

"They seem to feel as if they were among you."

"a glorious proof of the bravery of our worthy countrymen"

On the online GED® test, you will click on your answer. In this paper version, please circle it.

13. Which words in the text confirm that this letter is one of many that John and Abigail wrote to one another while they were separated?

(A) They seem to feel as if they were among you.

(B) Our consolation must be this, my dear

(C) I long to see you.

(D) I am glad you have secured an asylum.

14. Abigail knows [   ], which John does not know. Drag the correct answer below into the space provided to complete the sentence.

On the online GED® test, you will click and drag your answer into the provided space. In this paper version, please circle it.

the number of British troops who were killed

about the disadvantages of the colonial army

the fight in Charlestown

where Abby and the children will take refuge if fighting breaks out nearby

15. What can you conclude about war from this letter?

(A) Wars are destructive.

(B) The Adams were patriotic people.

(C) People's lives are disrupted during war.

(D) People continue their normal lives during wartime.

16. When John says Abigail's description "is enough to melt a heart of stone," he means [   ]?

On the online GED® test, you will click and drag your answer into the provided space. In this paper version, please circle it.

Her description is tough.

Her description is endearing.

Her letters show she is clever with words.

Her letters are heartwarming.

17. What news has Abigail told John in previous letters?

(A) Dr. Tufts is sick.

(B) Abigail has moved the family to Weymouth.

(C) Mr. Mather acquired a collection of rare books.

(D) She and the children are praying for the American army.

QUESTIONS 18–22 REFER TO THE FOLLOWING PASSAGE.

Martin Luther King's Push for Civil Rights

The following speech was delivered on the steps of the Lincoln Memorial at the height of the 1960s civil rights movement by Dr. Martin Luther King, head of the Southern Christian Leadership Conference and the movement's most eloquent spokesperson.

We have...come to this hallowed spot to remind America of the fierce urgency of Now. This is no time to engage in the luxury of cooling
5　off or to take the tranquilizing drug of gradualism. Now is the time to make real the promises of democracy. Now is the time to rise from the dark and desolate valley
10　of segregation to the sunlit path of racial justice. Now is the time to lift our nation from the quicksands of racial injustice to the solid rock of brotherhood. Now is the time
15　to make justice a reality for all of God's children.

It would be fatal for the nation to overlook the urgency of the moment. This sweltering summer
20　of the Negro's legitimate discontent will not pass until there is an invigorating autumn of freedom and equality . . .Those who hope that the Negro needed to blow off steam
25　and will now be content will have a rude awakening if the nation returns to business as usual. And

there will be neither rest nor tranquility in America until the Negro
30　is granted his citizenship rights. The whirlwinds of revolt will continue to shake the foundations of our nation until the bright day of justice emerges.
35　But there is something that I must say to my people, who stand on the warm threshold which leads into the palace of justice: In the process of gaining
40　our rightful place, we must not be guilty of wrongful deeds. Let us not seek to satisfy our thirst for freedom by drinking from the cup of bitterness and hatred. We
45　must forever conduct our struggle on the high plane of dignity and discipline. We must not allow our creative protest to degenerate into physical violence. Again and
50　again, we must rise to the majestic heights of meeting physical force with soul force. The marvelous new militancy which has engulfed the Negro community must not lead
55　us to a distrust of all white people, for many of our white brothers, as evidenced by their presence here today, have come to realize that their destiny is tied up with our
60　destiny. And they have come to realize that their freedom is inextricably bound to our freedom. We cannot walk alone.

And as we walk, we must make
65　the pledge that we shall always march ahead. We cannot turn back. There are those who are asking the devotees of civil rights, "When will you be satisfied?" We can never
70　be satisfied as long as the Negro is the victim of the unspeakable horrors of police brutality . . .We cannot be satisfied as long as the Negro's basic mobility is from a
75　smaller ghetto to a larger one. We can never be satisfied as long as our children are stripped of their selfhood and robbed of their dignity by signs stating "For Whites Only."

80 We cannot be satisfied as long as
a Negro in Mississippi cannot vote
and a Negro in New York believes
he has nothing for which to vote.
No, no, we are not satisfied, and we
85 will not be satisfied until "justice
rolls down like waters and righ-
teousness like a mighty stream."

I am not unmindful that some
of you have come out of great trials
90 and tribulations. Some of you have
come fresh from narrow jail cells.
And some of you have come from
areas where your quest—quest for
freedom—left you battered by the
95 storms of persecution and staggered by the winds of police brutality. You have been the veterans
of creative suffering. Continue to
work with the faith that unearned
100 suffering is redemptive. Go back to
Mississippi, go back to Alabama,
go back to South Carolina, go
back to Louisiana, go back to the
slums and ghettos of our northern
105 cities, knowing that somehow this
situation can and will be changed.
Let us not wallow in the valley
of despair, I say to you today, my
friends.

18. In the context of the passage, what is
the definition of *mobility*?

(A) the ability to use vehicles for
transportation

(B) the ability to change
appearance, mood, or purpose

(C) the capability of being moved

(D) the ability to have the
opportunity for a shift in status
within the levels of a society

19. Which of the following is NOT among
the actions advocated by King in this
speech?

(A) use peaceful protests to achieve
goals

(B) continue to work within
communities and states to
achieve goals

(C) work only with other black
people

(D) to continue pushing for
immediate and dramatic change

20. When King states "[i]t would be fatal
for the nation to overlook the urgency
of the moment," for what or whom
would overlooking the urgency of the
moment be fatal?

(A) Martin Luther King, Jr.

(B) the Civil Rights Movement

(C) the Southern Christian
Leadership Conference

(D) the United States

21. King's main argument in the third
paragraph is [   ].
Type the correct answer choice from
below into the blank box to complete the sentence. On the online
GED® test, you will type in your
answer. In this paper version, please
circle it.

(A) that gradual change is not
adequate.

(B) that white people are part of
the Civil Rights Movement.

(C) that all protest must remain
peaceful.

(D) that now that summer is
over, autumn will bring
freedom and equality.

22. In the context of the passage, what
is the best definition for *hallowed*?
Choose the correct answer from the
drop-down menu. On the online GED®
test, you will click on your answer. In
this paper version, please circle it.

[Select   ▼]

An unfilled space or hole

Consecrated

Revered

Disreputable

QUESTIONS 23–28 REFER TO THE FOLLOWING PASSAGES.

Liberating Women

In 1848, a Woman's Rights Convention was held at Seneca Falls, New York. Sponsored by Lucretia Mott, Martha Wright, Elizabeth Cady Stanton, and Mary Ann McClintock, the convention featured the creation of a "Declaration of Sentiments," a document based on America's Declaration of Independence, in which men's unfair dominion over women was described. Crusader for the rights of African Americans and women, Sojourner Truth was born a slave on a Dutch estate around 1797 and named Isabella. The first edition of her biography was written by Olive Gilbert, a white friend of hers, and published in 1850.

Passage 1—Declaration of Sentiments

The history of mankind is a history of repeated injuries and usurpations on the part of man toward woman, having in direct object
5 the establishment of an absolute tyranny over her. To prove this, let facts be submitted to a candid world.

He has never permitted her to
10 exercise her inalienable right to the elective franchise.

He has compelled her to submit to laws, in the formation of which she had no voice. He has withheld
15 from her rights which are given to the most ignorant and degraded men—both natives and foreigners.

Having deprived her of this first right of a citizen, the elective
20 franchise, thereby leaving her without representation in the halls of legislation, he has oppressed her on all sides.

He has made her, if married, in
25 the eye of the law, civilly dead.

He has taken from her all right in property, even to the wages she earns.

He has made her, morally,
30 an irresponsible being, as she can commit many crimes with impunity, provided they be done in the presence of her husband. In the covenant of marriage, she
35 is compelled to promise obedience to her husband, he becoming, to all intents and purposes, her master—the law giving him power to deprive her of her liberty, and to
40 administer chastisement.

He has so framed the laws of divorce, as to what shall be the proper causes, and in the case of separation, to whom the guard-
45 ianship of the children shall be given, as to be wholly regardless of the happiness of women—the law, in all cases, going upon a false supposition of the supremacy of man,
50 and giving all power into his hands.

After depriving her of all rights as a married woman, if single, and the owner of property, he has taxed her to support a government
55 which recognizes her only when her property can be made profitable to it.

He has endeavored, in every way that he could, to destroy her
60 confidence in her own powers, to lessen her self-respect, and to make her willing to lead a dependent and abject life.

Passage 2—Sojourner Truth

After emancipation had been decreed by the State, some years before the time fixed for its consummation, Isabella's master told
5 her if she would do well, and be faithful, he would give her "free papers," one year before she was legally free by statute. In the year 1826, she had a badly diseased
10 hand, which greatly diminished her usefulness; but on the arrival of July 4, 1827, the time specified

for her receiving her "free papers," she claimed the fulfillment of
15 her master's promise; but he refused granting it, on account (as he alleged) of the loss he had sustained by her hand. She plead that she had worked all the time,
20 and done many things she was not wholly able to do, although she knew she had been less useful than formerly; but her master remained inflexible. Her very faithfulness
25 probably operated against her now, and he found it less easy than he thought to give up the profits of his faithful Bell, who had so long done him efficient service.

30   But Isabella inwardly determined that she would remain quietly with him only until she had spun his wool—about one hundred pounds—and then she would leave
35 him, taking the rest of the time to herself. "Ah!" she says, with emphasis that cannot be written, "the slaveholders are TERRIBLE for promising to give you this or
40 that, or such and such a privilege, if you will do thus and so; and when the time of fulfillment comes, and one claims the promise, they, forsooth, recollect nothing of the kind;
45 and you are, like as not, taunted with being a LIAR; or, at best, the slave is accused of not having performed *his* part or condition of the contract." "Oh!" said she, "I have
50 felt as if I could not live through the *operation sometimes.* Just think of us! *So* eager for our pleasures, and just foolish enough to keep feeding and feeding ourselves up with the
55 idea that we should get what had been thus fairly promised; and when we think it is almost in our hands, find ourselves flatly denied! Just think! how *could* we bear it?"

23. According to the first passage, under what circumstance does the government recognize women?

(A) in cases of divorce

(B) while voting

(C) when single and owning taxable property

(D) when employed and making a taxable income

24. In the context of this passage, what is the definition of *franchise*?

(A) the right to market goods or services

(B) a special privilege granted to an individual or group

(C) a constitutional or statutory right or privilege

(D) a person's freedom from a restriction

25. From whose point of view is the second passage written?

(A) Elizabeth Cady Stanton

(B) Olive Gilbert

(C) Isabella

(D) Mary Ann McClintock

26. Over approximately what period of time did the events in the second passage take place?

(A) fifty years

(B) a few decades

(C) a few years

(D) a few months

27. Which of the following is a likely reason the writers patterned the Declaration of Sentiments after the Declaration of Independence?

(A) to explain their own complaints against English rule

(B) to explain why they disapproved of Sojourner Truth's treatment at the hands of her master

(C) to demonstrate that women had similar complaints as did the Founding Fathers

(D) to demonstrate that women could write well

28. Drag the characteristics that fit the descriptions of Sojourner Truth or the sponsors of the Woman's Rights Convention, to the correct space in the Venn Diagram. If there is a common characteristic, drag it into the center of the diagram. On the online GED® test, you will click and drag your answers into the spaces provided. In this paper version, please draw a line to the correct space in the diagram.

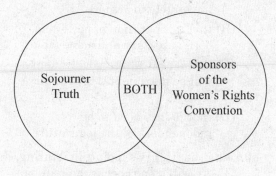

(A) Spent a life in slavery

(B) Legally able to vote after 1848

(C) Not treated as citizens of the United States

(D) Legally able to obtain a divorce

QUESTIONS 29–34 REFER TO THE FOLLOWING PASSAGES.

Debating the Constitution

The following two passages represent two views of the Constitution.

Passage 1

We are descended from a people whose Government was founded on liberty. Our glorious forefathers of Great-Britain, made liberty the
5 foundation of every thing. That country is become a great, mighty, and splendid nation; not because their Government is strong and energetic; but, Sir, because liberty
10 is its direct end and foundation. We drew the spirit of liberty from our British ancestors; by that spirit we have triumphed over every difficulty. But now, Sir, the American
15 spirit, assisted by the ropes and chains of consolidation, is about to convert this country to a powerful and mighty empire. If you make the citizens of this country agree
20 to become the subjects of one great consolidated empire of America, your Government will not have sufficient energy to keep them together.
25 Such a Government is incompatible with the genius of republicanism. There will be no checks, no real balances, in this Government. What can avail your specious
30 imaginary balances, your rope-dancing, chain-rattling, ridiculous ideal checks and contrivances? But, Sir, we are not feared by foreigners. we do not make nations tremble.
35 Would this, Sir, constitute happiness, or secure liberty? I trust, Sir, our political hemisphere will ever direct their operations to the security of those objects. Consider
40 our situation, Sir. Go to the poor man, ask him what he does; he will inform you, that he enjoys the fruits of his labour, under his own fig-tree, with his wife and children
45 around him, in peace and security. Go to every other member of the society, you will find the same tranquil ease and content; you will find no alarms or disturbances.
50 Why then tell us of dangers to terrify us into an adoption of this new Government? and yet who knows the dangers that this new system may produce; they are out
55 of the sight of the common people. They cannot foresee latent consequences. I dread the operation of it on the middling and lower class of people. It is for them I fear the
60 adoption of this system.

—Patrick Henry, The Virginia Ratifying Convention, June 5, 1788

Passage 2

In order to lay a due foundation for that separate and distinct exercise of the different powers of government, which to a certain
5 extent is admitted on all hands to be essential to the preservation of liberty, it is evident that each department should have a will of its own; and consequently should
10 be so constituted that the members of each should have as little agency as possible in the appointment of the members of the others. Were this principle rigorously adhered
15 to, it would require that all the appointments for the supreme executive, legislative, and judiciary magistracies should be drawn from the same fountain of authority, the
20 people, through channels having no communication whatever with one another. Perhaps such a plan of constructing the several departments would be less dif-
25 ficult in practice than it may in contemplation appear. Some difficulties, however, and some additional expense would attend the execution of it. Some deviations,
30 therefore, from the principle must be admitted. In the constitution of the judiciary department in particular, it might be inexpedient to insist rigorously on the
35 principle: first, because peculiar qualifications being essential in the members, the primary consideration ought to be to select that mode of choice which best secures
40 these qualifications; secondly, because the permanent tenure by which the appointments are held in that department, must soon destroy all sense of dependence on
45 the authority conferring them.

It is equally evident, that the members of each department should be as little dependent as possible on those of the others,
50 for the emoluments annexed to their offices. Were the executive magistrate, or the judges, not independent of the legislature in this particular, their independence
55 in every other would be merely nominal.

—James Madison,
The Federalist, No. 51

29. What is Madison's point in the second passage?

(A) that a separation of powers is impossible to achieve

(B) that a separation of powers is both necessary and achievable

(C) that a centralized government will be detrimental to ordinary citizens

(D) that judges need to be independent of the legislature

30. What is Henry's point in stating, "There will be no checks, no real balances, in this Government"?

(A) He thinks that the Federalists are lying.

(B) He does not believe in the principle of checks and balances.

(C) Since Great Britain does not have them, he thinks the United States does not need them.

(D) He thinks the government will lack the ability to enforce a separation of powers.

31. What is a possible synonym for *inexpedient* as it appears in the second passage? Choose the correct answer from the drop-down menu. On the online GED® test, you will click on your answer. In this paper version, please circle it.

Select ▼

Effective

Ineffective

Unbeneficial

Useful

32. Why is Madison arguing that the branches of government should be as separate as possible?

    (A) to prevent oversight of departments by other departments

    (B) to avoid having a government like Great Britain

    (C) so that the members of one branch have little influence over the members of the others

    (D) so that the citizens have more power

33. Henry's primary motivation for opposing a centralized government, according to the passage, is _____. Type the correct choice from below into the space provided to complete the sentence. On the online GED® test, you will type in your answer. In this paper version, please circle it.

    (A) he is concerned that a bureaucracy will take over the government.

    (B) he believes that other countries fear the United States.

    (C) he wants the United States to be an empire like Great Britain.

    (D) he fears that ordinary citizens will suffer under a centralized government.

34. Drag the statements into the provided Venn diagram underneath the politician who the statements support, according to the passage. If there is one that applies to both, place it in the center. On the online GED® test, you will click and drag your answers into the spaces provided. In this paper version, please draw a line to the correct space in the diagram.

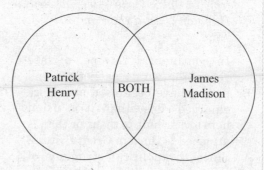

Patrick Henry   BOTH   James Madison

(A) limiting the power of the government is necessary to preserve liberty

(B) the government will corrupt the successes of the middle and lower class people

(C) it will be difficult for the government to maintain separation of powers

(D) the judiciary should be dependent on the legislature

QUESTIONS 35–36 REFER TO THE FOLLOWING PASSAGE.

Patriotism and Oratory

Frances Wright was a reformer, author, and orator; unusual occupations for a woman in the early nineteenth century. Born in Scotland, she became an American citizen in 1825. The following is from a speech she gave in New Harmony, Indiana, on July 4, 1828.

In continental Europe, of late years, the words patriotism and patriot have been used in a more enlarged sense than it is usual
5 here to attribute to them, or than is attached to them in Great Britain. Since the political struggles of France, Italy, Spain, and Greece, the word patriotism has been
10 employed, throughout continental Europe, to express a love of the public good; a preference for the interests of the many to those of the few; a desire for the emanci-
15 pation of the human race from the thrall of despotism, religious and civil: in short, patriotism there is used rather to express the interest felt in the human race in general
20 than that felt for any country, or inhabitants of a country, in particular. And patriot, in like manner, is employed to signify a lover of human liberty and human
25 improvement rather than a mere lover of the country in which he lives, or the tribe to which he belongs. Used in this sense, patriotism is a virtue, and a patriot
30 is a virtuous man. With such an interpretation, a patriot is a useful member of society capable of enlarging all minds and bettering all hearts with which he comes in
35 contact; a useful member of the human family, capable of establishing fundamental principles and of merging his own interests, those of his associates, and those
40 of his nation in the interests of the human race. Laurels and statues are vain things, and mischievous as they are childish; but could we imagine them of use, on such a
45 patriot alone could they be with any reason bestowed. . . .

If such a patriotism as we have last considered should seem likely to obtain in any country, it should
50 be certainly in this. In this, which is truly the home of all nations, and in the veins of whose citizens flows the blood of every people on the globe. Patriotism, in the
55 exclusive meaning, is surely not made for America. Mischievous every where, it were here both mischievous and absurd. The very origin of the people is opposed to it.
60 The institutions, in their principle, militate against it. This day we are celebrating protests against it. It is for Americans, more especially to nourish a nobler sentiment;
65 one more consistent with their origin, and more conducive to their future improvement. It is for them more especially to know why they love their country, not
70 because it is their country, but because it is the palladium of human liberty—the favoured scene of human improvement. It is for them more especially, to know why
75 they honour their institutions, and feel that they honour them because they are based on just principles. It is for them, more especially, to examine their institutions, because
80 they have the means of improving them; to examine their laws, because at will they can alter them.

35. Based on the passage, what is Wright's opinion on the reason for being patriotic as an American citizen?

    (A) Patriotism should be based in national pride.

    (B) Patriotism is a virtue, and a patriot is a virtuous man.

    (C) Patriotism is the love of country because of the principles on which it is founded, not on residency.

    (D) Patriotism is mischievous.

36. When Wright states that America "is truly the home of all nations," to what is she likely referring?

    (A) America is made up of immigrants from all over the world.

    (B) America has not been declared a country yet.

    (C) Every nation claims to own America.

    (D) People from all over the world like to visit America.

37. *The following passages represent two views of the value of arts education in society. Take 45 minutes to choose which of the two viewpoints you wish to support and use the paper provided to write a well-organized essay. Use reasons and examples to support your position.*

Debating the Importance of Arts Education

Passage 1

Allowing arts education to fall by the wayside will be detrimental for our students and their futures as a part of society. Teaching the arts to young students can change the way they learn and help them to develop life-long skills. Motor skills can be developed through arts and crafts participation: drawing with crayons, holding paintbrushes and cutting with scissors all help to develop dexterity—which is necessary for writing. Making art can also provide young students a simpler way to learn colors, shapes, and various actions, while also teaching them the importance of visual learning, an important aspect of interpreting and analyzing information. Although it seems obvious that learning the arts aids in creativity, it is sometimes misunderstood as to why this is so important if a student is going to pursue a degree not focused on one of these creative aspects. The arts, however, can teach students how to aptly express themselves and take risks, even encouraging students to seek alternative directions and other ways to conceptualize their thoughts. Furthermore, the arts give students a way to grasp their cultural surroundings. By teaching young students to understand artistic concepts—texture, shape, colors, etc.—a teacher can properly describe the characteristics of reality, and the student is more likely to accurately interpret these representations. Last but certainly not least, there are several studies that show a strong correlation between art and overall achievement. Americans for the Arts states that youth who participate in the arts for at least three hours a day, three days a week for a full year, are *four* times more likely to have their academic achievements recognized, to participate in a math or science fair, or even to win an award for writing an essay or poem than those students who do not participate in the arts. By teaching the arts, we can ensure that students will understand the place creative skills have in education, the workplace, and society.

Passage 2

With the increased dependency on technology and the never-faltering importance of math and sciences, focusing on the arts in schools is becoming less and less relevant. It is crucial to give our students an education that can best help them get into colleges upon graduating high school, and well-paying jobs upon graduating college. By adding more focus on art, we are taking away from other subjects that aid in college and job preparation. These days, many students do not graduate high school with any experience writing cover letters, formatting resumes, or overall real-world experience. If any subject should be added to our core curriculums, it should be job preparedness. Although the arts hone creativity and may help students inclined to work in fields where liberal arts are the main focus, they still need to know how to market themselves and know how to break into the job market. Most students who will end up in a creative field are born with these inclinations, finding themselves with an inherent attraction to these subjects. We should focus more on developing interview skills, salary negotiation, email etiquette and adapting in the workplace. These skills will make the biggest difference in the success of our students and ensure that they will be contributing members of our society.

QUESTIONS 38–49 REFER TO THE FOLLOWING DOCUMENT.

The following is a document you might find in the workplace.

Memorandum

(A)

To: All Staff Members
From: John Smith, CEO
Date: August 28, 2013
Subject: Workplace Etiquette

(B)

(1) Employees thrive in friendly focused environments, leading to the overall success of the company. (2) In order to be the best co-workers we can be, some workplace etiquette should be acknowledged.

(C)

(3) Your attire should be business-appropriate because we follow professional guidelines so men should wear slacks and button-down shirts with a tie (jacket not required) and women should wear slacks, skirts, or dresses (at least knee-length). (4) Women should avoid thin-strapped tops and maintain appropriate coverage. (5) We allow Business Casual attire on fridays: jeans are permitted. (6) However, the dress code is still *business* casual, not just casual. (7) Do not wear open-toed shoes, tennis shoes, and don't wear sandals at any time.

(D)

(8) Cell phones can be distracting during the day, so please keep it silenced. (9) If you need to make a personal call, please step into one of the break rooms and shut the door. (10) Minimize the time you spend making these calls or save them for your lunch hour.

(E)

(11) Remember that e-mails is still important conversations with your supervisors or co-workers, and it will not be taken lightly. (12) Try and match the tone of whomever you are e-mailing. (13) If they use your first name, its okay to use there's. (14) Respond to all e-mails, even if the response is as simple as a sentence saying it was received.

(F)

(15) We are an open office, meaning that we share communal spaces and have limited closed offices. (16) Although this is a positive environment for discussing project details, and makes it easier to get to know one another: it can sometimes lead to more distractions. (17) When you visit a co-worker's desk, weight for them to acknowledge you before diving in to your request. (18) If you are visiting an office, knock before entering. (19) We still want to promote an open office culture, so don't be afraid to visit others!

(G)

(20) Last but not least, the communal spaces—break room, copy room and

kitchen—are open to all employees. (21) Feel free to use office supplies, and help yourself to provided snacks in the cupboards, marked as shared food. (22) Feel free to use the refrigerator, coffee maker, and microwave. (23) Please clean up after yourself—we want a safe, clean, and welcoming environment for everyone.

(H)

(24) If you have any questions or concerns regarding this memo, please don't hesitate to email me at johnsmith@gmail.com re: Workplace Etiquette.

(I)

(25) Genuinely,
John Smith, CEO

38. Sentence 1: Employees thrive in friendly focused environments, leading to the overall success of the company.

Which of the following corrections should be made to sentence 1?

(A) Add a comma between *friendly* and *focused*.

(B) Remove the comma after *environments*.

(C) Add *nor* between *friendly* and *focused*.

(D) Change *environments* to *environment's*.

39. Which answers best describe proper etiquette in the workplace? Drag and drop the correct answers into the bubbles provided. On the online GED® test, you will click and drag the answers. For this paper version, please circle them.

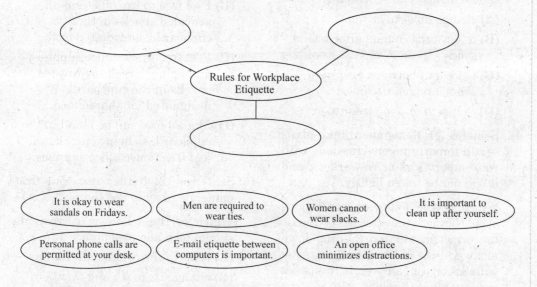

(A) It is okay to wear sandals on Fridays.

(B) Men are required to wear ties.

(C) Women cannot wear slacks.

(D) Personal phone calls are permitted at your desk.

(E) It is important to clean up after yourself.

(F) E-mail etiquette between co-workers is important.

(G) An open office minimizes distractions.

40. Sentence 8: Cell phones can be distracting during the day, so please keep it silenced.

Which of the following corrections should be made to sentence 8?

(A) Cell phones can be distracting during the day. Please keep it silenced.

(B) Cell phones can be distracting during the day, so please keep them silenced.

(C) Cell phones can be distracting during the day so please keep it silenced.

(D) Your cell phone is distracting during the day, so please keep them silenced.

41. Sentence 7: Do not wear open-toed shoes, tennis shoes, and don't wear sandals at any time.

Which of the following corrections should be made to sentence 7?

(A) change *don't* to *do not*

(B) remove the comma after *tennis shoes*

(C) place *and* between *open-toed shoes,* and *tennis shoes*

(D) change *and don't wear* to *or*

42. Sentence 11: Remember that e-mails is still important conversations with your supervisors or co-workers, and it will not be taken lightly.

Which of the following corrections should be made to sentence 11? Choose the correct answer from the drop-down menu. On the online GED® test, you will click on your answer. In this paper version, please circle it.

Select ▼

(A) replace *is* with *are* and *it* with *they*

(B) remove the comma after *co-workers*

(C) replace *is* with *are*

(D) change *e-mails* to *e-mail's*

43. Sentence 17: When you visit a co-worker's desk, weight for them to acknowledge you before diving in to your request.

Which of the following corrections should be made to sentence 17?

(A) change *weight* to *wait*

(B) change *in to* to *into*

(C) change *weight* to *wait,* and *in to* to *into*

(D) add a comma after *you*

44. Sentence 21: Feel free to use office supplies, and help yourself to provided snacks in the cupboards, marked as shared food.

Which of the following would be the best way to rewrite sentence 21?

(A) Feel free to use office supplies and help yourself to provided snacks in the cupboards marked as shared food.

(B) Feel free to use office supplies, provided snacks in the cupboards, and shared food.

(C) Feel free to use office supplies, and help yourself to provided snacks in the cupboards designated for shared food.

(D) Shared food can be found in the cupboard, so help yourself, and feel free to use office supplies.

45. Sentence 13: If they use your first name, its okay to use there's.

Which of the following corrections should be made to sentence 13?

(A) remove the comma after *name*

(B) change *its* to *it's* and *there's* to *theirs*

(C) change *there's* to *theirs*

(D) change *okay* to *ok*

46. Sentence 5: We allow Business Casual attire on fridays: jeans are permitted.

    Which of the following corrections should be made to sentence 5?

    (A) change *Business Casual* to *business casual*

    (B) change *fridays* to *friday's*

    (C) remove the colon after *fridays*

    (D) change *Business Casual* to *business casual* and *fridays* to *Fridays*

47. Sentence 12: Try ⬚ match the tone of whomever you are e-mailing.

    Complete the sentence with the correct word by typing it into the blank box. On the online GED® test, you will type in your answer. In this paper version, please circle it.

    (A) to

    (B) and

    (C) too

    (D) yet

48. Sentence 16: Although this is a positive environment for discussing project details, and makes it easier to get to know one another: it can sometimes lead to more distractions.

    Choose the sentence with the correct punctuation.

    (A) Although this is a positive environment for discussing project details, and makes it easier to get to know one another: it can sometimes lead to more distractions.

    (B) Although this is a positive environment for discussing project details and makes it easier to get to know one another, it can sometimes lead to more distractions.

    (C) Although this is a positive environment for discussing project details and makes

    it easier to get to know one another? It can sometimes lead to more distractions.

    (D) Although this is a positive environment for discussing project details, and makes it easier to get to know one another, it can sometimes lead to more distractions.

49. Sentence 3: Your attire should be business-appropriate because we follow professional guidelines so men should wear slacks and button-down shirts with a tie (jacket not required) and women should wear slacks, skirts, or dresses (at least knee length).

    Which of the following options is best?

    (A) Your attire should be business-appropriate because we follow professional guidelines so men should wear slacks and button-down shirts with a tie (jacket not required) and women should wear slacks, skirts, or dresses (at least knee length).

    (B) Your attire should be business-appropriate. We follow professional guidelines, so men should wear slacks and button-down shirts with a tie; (jacket not required), and women should wear slacks, skirts, or dresses (at least knee length).

    (C) Your attire should be business-appropriate. We follow professional guidelines: men should wear slacks and button-down shirts with a tie (jacket not required), and women should wear slacks, skirts, or dresses (at least knee length).

    (D) Your attire should be business-appropriate, because we follow professional guidelines, so men should wear slacks and button-down shirts with a tie (jacket not required), and women should wear slacks, skirts, or dresses (at least knee length).

MATHEMATICAL REASONING

90 Minutes • 37 Questions

General Directions: The Mathematical Reasoning Test consists of 37 questions intended to measure your general mathematics skills, including your ability to solve math problems. The test consists of 5 questions that you will not have access to a calculator to answer and 32 questions that you will have use of a calculator to solve.

Disclaimer: The Mathematical Reasoning Test will have calculator-allowed questions mixed with calculator-prohibited questions, with the calculator tool available to use when it is an option. However, for this test, the calculator-prohibited questions are grouped together as the first 5 questions.

To answer some questions you will need to apply one or more mathematics formulas. The formulas provided on the next page will help you to answer those questions. Some questions refer to charts, graphs, and figures. Unless otherwise noted, charts, graphs, and figures are drawn to scale.

Answering Alternative-format Questions

Most questions are multiple choice, but to answer some questions, you will be required to select from a drop-down menu, fill an answer in a blank, drag and drop correct answers, and select answers on a given graphic.

Mathematics Formula Sheet & Explanation

TESTING SERVICE®

The 2014 GED® Mathematical Reasoning test contains a formula sheet, which displays formulas relating to geometric measurement and certain algebra concepts. Formulas are provided to test-takers so that they may focus on *application*, rather than the *memorization*, of formulas.

Area of a:

parallelogram $A = bh$

trapezoid $A = \frac{1}{2}h(b_1 + b_2)$

Surface Area and Volume of a:

rectangular/right prism	$SA = ph + 2B$	$V = Bh$
cylinder	$SA = 2\pi rh + 2\pi r^2$	$V = \pi r^2 h$
pyramid	$SA = \frac{1}{2}ps + B$	$V = \frac{1}{3}Bh$
cone	$SA = \pi rs + \pi r^2$	$V = \frac{1}{3}\pi r^2 h$
sphere	$SA = 4\pi r^2$	$V = \frac{4}{3}\pi r^3$

(p = perimeter of base B; $\pi \approx 3.14$)

Algebra

slope of a line $m = \dfrac{y_2 - y_1}{x_2 - x_1}$

slope-intercept form
of the equation of a line $y = mx + b$

point-slope form of the
equation of a line $y - y_1 = m(x - x_1)$

standard form of a
quadratic equation $y = ax^2 + bx + c$

quadratic formula $x = \dfrac{-b \pm \sqrt{b^2 - 4ac}}{2a}$

Pythagorean Theorem $a^2 + b^2 = c^2$

simple interest $I = prt$

(I = interest, p = principal, r = rate, t = time)

1. There are 78 sophomores at a school. Each is required to take at least one year of either chemistry or physics, but they may take both. 15 are enrolled in both chemistry and physics, and 47 are enrolled only in chemistry. How many students are enrolled only in physics? On the online GED® test, you will type your answer in the box. For this paper test, please write it in.

   [   ]

2. Adding $4\frac{1}{2}$ to $3\frac{3}{4}$ and then subtracting $2\frac{2}{5}$ from the sum results in which value?

   (A) $\frac{57}{10}$

   (B) $\frac{231}{40}$

   (C) $\frac{117}{20}$

   (D) $\frac{23}{4}$

3. The perimeter of the hexagon below is 240 centimeters. What is the length of each side?

   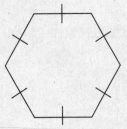

   (A) 40
   (B) 48
   (C) 80
   (D) 120

4. If $x = -1$, then what is the value of $x^{-2} + x^2$?

   (A) –2
   (B) –1
   (C) 0
   (D) 2

5. The average team score for the first 5 basketball games of the season is 45 points. The scores of the first 5 games are 54, 60, 28, 42, and

   | Select   ▼ |.

   31

   36

   41

   46

   On the online GED® test, you will click to select your answer. For this paper version, please circle it.

6. If two sides of a triangle are 6.5 and 8.5 inches long, which of the following CANNOT be the length of the third side?

   (A) 6.5 inches
   (B) 9.5 inches
   (C) 12 inches
   (D) 15 inches

7. What is the value of $|7-2| - |2-7|$?

   (A) –9
   (B) –5
   (C) 0
   (D) 10

8. A rectangular box with a surface area of 248 square inches is 4 inches high and 10 inches long. What is its width?

   (A) 6 inches
   (B) 10 inches
   (C) 40 inches
   (D) 60 inches

9. A farmer wants to construct a fence to create a square horse corral with an area of 10,000 square feet. Fence posts along each side will be 10 feet apart at their center.

   Including the four corner posts, how many posts are needed to construct the fence?

   (A) 36
   (B) 40
   (C) 44
   (D) 100

10. If $f(x) = x^4$, for what value of a does $f(a) = 1296$?

    (A) 4
    (B) 6
    (C) 648
    (D) 2592

11. A botanist observing the growth rate of a climbing vine records growth of 0.36 meters over one 24-day period. The vine's growth rate, per day, expressed in centimeters was

     Select ▼ .

    0.015 cm/day

    1.5 cm/day

    8.64 cm/day

    864 cm/day

    [1 meter = 100 centimeters]

    On the online GED® test, you will click to select your answer. For this paper version, please circle it.

12. The figure below shows two line segments connecting a circle's center to its circumference.

    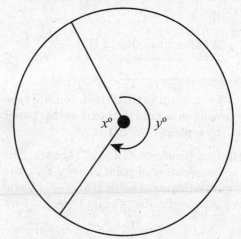

    What is the value of y in terms of x ?

    (A) $\dfrac{360}{x}$

    (B) $\dfrac{x}{180}$

    (C) $360 - x$

    (D) $\dfrac{x}{360}$

13. If $x^2 + 4x = 0$, how many values of x are possible?

    (A) none
    (B) one
    (C) two
    (D) infinitely many

14. If $x + y = a$, and if $x - y = b$, then which expression represents the value of x ?

    (A) $\dfrac{1}{2}(a + b)$

    (B) $a + b$

    (C) $a - b$

    (D) $\dfrac{1}{2}(a - b)$

15. In the number line shown below, the vertical marks are equally spaced.

What is the value of B?

```
┌─────────────────┐
│                 │
└─────────────────┘
```

On the online GED® test, you will type your answer in the box. For this paper test, please write it in.

16. Quadrilateral *ABCD* is a square. The coordinates of point *A* are (3, 2), the coordinates of point *B* are (–3, 2), and the coordinates of point *C* are (–3, –4).

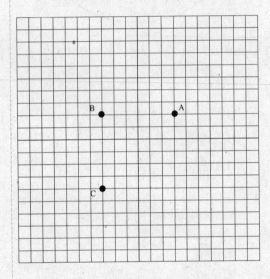

Click on the coordinate grid to show the location of point D. On the online GED® test, you click on the grid to indicate your answer. For this paper version, please mark the spot on the grid.

17. How many different ways can you add four positive, odd integers together for a sum of 10? The integers may be used more than once, and the sequence of the integers should not be considered.

(A) one

(B) two

(C) three

(D) four

18. The length of Cassie's family room is exactly half the length of her bedroom. Both rooms are rectangular, and the area of the two rooms is the same. If Cassie's family room has a length of *L* and a width of *W*, write an expression that represents the width of her bedroom.

On the online GED® test, you will type in your answer. For this paper version, please write it in.

```
┌─────────────────┐
│                 │
└─────────────────┘
```

19. Twice the sum of 3 and a number *N* is 1 less than 3 times the number *N*.

Which equation can you use to find the value of *N* ?

(A) $2(3 + N) - 1 = 3N$

(B) $6 - 2N = 3N - 1$

(C) $2(3 + N) = 1 - 3N$

(D) $6 + 2N = 3N - 1$

QUESTIONS 20 AND 21 REFER TO THE FOLLOWING GRAPH.

IMPORTS AND EXPORTS FOR
COUNTRY X AND COUNTRY Y, 2005–2010

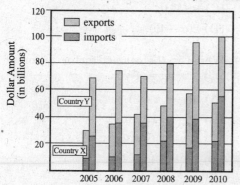

NOTE: For each year, the combined height of two bar segments shows total imports and exports of a country.

20. In which of the following years did Country Y's imports exceed Country X's imports by the smallest percentage?

(A) 2006

(B) 2007

(C) 2008

(D) 2010

21. Which best describes Country Y's overall import and export trend over the six-year period shown? On the online GED® test, you click to select your answers. For this paper version, please circle them.

The value of imports

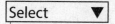

increased

declined

exhibited no clear trend

while the value of exports

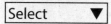

increased

declined

exhibited no clear trend

22. A group of travelers have assembled a tepee that has a circular base. As shown in the figure, the side of the tepee measures 17 meters from the ground to the tepee's peak, and the height of the tepee is 15 meters. What is the diameter of the tepee's circular base? On the online GED® test, you will type in your answer. For this paper version, please write it in.

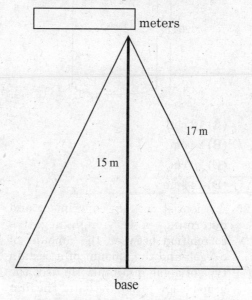

23. The expression

1, 2, 4, 5, 6, 10, 24

is equivalent to the expression $\frac{10^6 \cdot 10^4}{10^5}$. Drag and drop the correct numbers into the boxes to create the correct expression. Not all the boxes may be used to form the correct answer. On the online GED® test, you will drag and drop your answer in the boxes. For this paper test, please write them in.

24. A restaurant kitchen stores large cans of peas, as shown below. Each can has a volume of 2880π cm^3 and a height of 20 cm. A cook is trying to figure out how many cans of peas he can fit side by side on one shelf. What is the diameter of the can of peas?

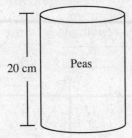

(A) 12 cm

(B) 24 cm

(C) 20 cm

(D) 144 cm

25. A scientist does an experiment and determines a very high negative correlation between the amount of oxygen and the amount of a certain type of algae in a tank. He uses the graph below to plot the data. The first data points he collected are already plotted. Use your mouse to click a possible last data point above the arrow on the y-axis that would show the high negative correlation determined by the scientist. On the online GED® test, you click on the grid to indicate your answer. For this paper version, please mark the spot on the graph.

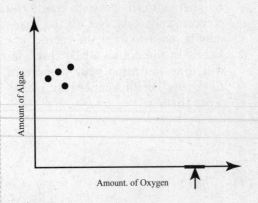

26. Which expression is equivalent to $-4(2a - b)$?

(A) $-8a + 4b$

(B) $-8a - 4b$

(C) $8a + 4b$

(D) $2(a - 4b)$

27. Which is the correct factorization of $2x^2 - x - 6$?

(A) $2(x^2 - x - 3)$

(B) $(x + 3)(x - 2)$

(C) $(2x - 3)(x - 2)$

(D) $(2x + 3)(x - 2)$

28. Herman is covering 20 square tiles with cloth. In order to calculate how much cloth he needs, he must square the length in centimeters, c, of each side of a tile and then add x extra centimeters to account for error. Which equation should Herman use to calculate how much total cloth he will need to cover the 20 tiles?

(A) $20c^2 + x$

(B) $20c^2 + 20x$

(C) $20 + c^2 \times x$

(D) $20c^2 + x^2$

29. Solve for x in terms of $2A(3x + 2B) = 12$.

(A) $12 - 4AB$

(B) $12 - 4AB - 6A$

(C) $\dfrac{12 - B}{2A}$

(D) $\dfrac{12 - 4AB}{6A}$

30. Click on a point on the number line below that satisfies the inequality $-2x - 3 > -1$. On the online GED® test, you click on the grid to indicate your answer. For this paper version, please mark the spot on the number line.

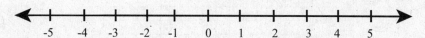

31. The cost to build sign posts in Everytown is a fee of $60 per hour for the labor plus $240 per sign post. Each sign post takes 1.5 hours to build. The retainer fee for the contractor who supplies the labor is $1200. Drag and drop the variables, numbers, and signs below to create an inequality that will determine how many sign posts, p, can be built in Everytown with a budget of $8000. Not all numbers may be used. On the online GED® test, you will drag and drop your answer in the boxes. For this paper test, please write them in.

Number choices: 60 90 240 300 330 1200 8000 1.5p 240p 330p

Signs: $+, -, \times, \div, \leq, \geq, <, >$

32. A computer company is trying to figure out what its sales in dollars will be for its new line of mini-computers. It has figured out that unit sales will follow the demand curve $45,000 - 160p$, where p is the selling price of the mini-computer. If this is how many computers it will sell, which equation will yield the total sales in dollars?

(A) $45,000 + 160p^2 = $ total sales

(B) $45,000 + 160p + p = $ total sales

(C) $45,000p - 160p^2 = $ total sales

(D) $160p^2 + p = $ total sales

33. Sal's Pizza has pizza parties for children's birthdays. Sal has determined that it's best to have 3 pizza pies for every group of 8 children at a party. Sal makes the graph below to quickly see how many pizzas he'll need for parties of different sizes. What is the slope of the line in Sal's graph?

(A) $\frac{8}{3}$

(B) $\frac{3}{8}$

(C) $\frac{1}{3}$

(D) $\frac{1}{8}$

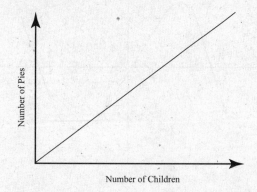

34. Which equation is graphed below?

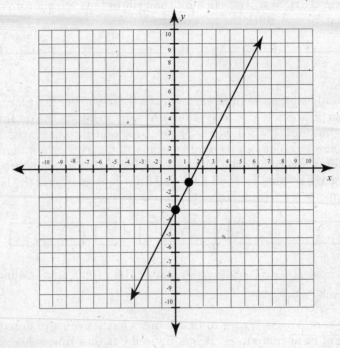

(A) $y = 2x - 3$

(B) $y = 2x + 3$

(C) $y = x - 3$

(D) $y = x$

35. Drag and drop numbers or variables to make the following statement true. The function graphed below is negative on the interval ⬚ $\leq x \leq$ ⬚. On the online GED® test, you will drag and drop your answers in the box. For this paper test, please write them in.

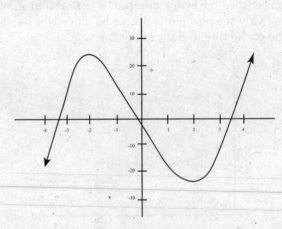

$-4, -2, -1, 0, 1, 2, 4, x$

36. What is the equation of a line passing through the points (−4, 5) and (2, 2)?

(A) $y = -\frac{1}{2}x - \frac{3}{2}$

(B) $y = -\frac{1}{2}x - 3$

(C) $y = \frac{1}{2}x + 3$

(D) $y = -\frac{1}{2}x + 3$

37. Two pools are being filled at a day camp. Pool A is being filled at a rate of 12 gallons per hour. Pool B's fill rate is graphed below. Which statement about the two rates is true?

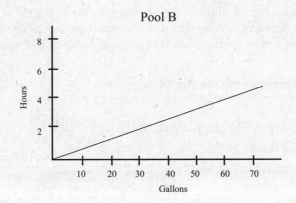

(A) Pool A's rate is equal to Pool B's rate.

(B) Pool B is filling at a rate that is 3 gallons per hour faster than Pool A's rate.

(C) Pool A is filling at a rate that is 3 gallons per hour faster than Pool B's rate.

(D) Pool A is filling at a rate that is half as fast as Pool B's rate.

SCIENCE

90 Minutes • 30 Questions

Directions: The Science Test consists of questions in several formats designed to measure your knowledge of general science concepts. The questions are based on brief passages of text and visual information (charts, graphs, diagrams, and other figures). Some questions are based on both text and visual information. Study the information provided, and answer the question(s) that follow, referring back to the information as needed.

You will have 90 minutes to answer all 30 questions. Record your answers on the answer sheet provided.

QUESTION 1 REFERS TO THE FOLLOWING INFORMATION.

If one side of a stemmed plant receives more sunlight than the other side, the growth hormone auxin, which stimulates vertical growth of the elongated stem, will concentrate on the shady side of the stem in order to stimulate more growth there.

1. What will be the result of this stimulation?

   The plant will

   (A) grow beyond its ability to nourish itself.

   (B) bend toward the light.

   (C) wither where auxin is absent.

   (D) bend toward the ground.

QUESTION 2 REFERS TO THE FOLLOWING DIAGRAM.

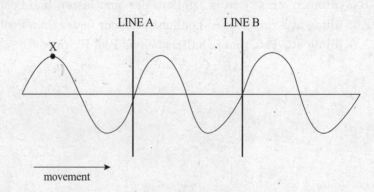

2. The wave crest shown as point X will reach line A in 3 seconds. In how many seconds will the same wave crest reach line B?

   (A) 7 seconds

   (B) 9 seconds

   (C) 10 seconds

   (D) 11 seconds

QUESTION 3 REFERS TO THE FOLLOWING INFORMATION.

When you cut yourself and begin to bleed, the damaged tissues immediately release a chemical that initiates a chain reaction. Tiny disk-shaped platelets in your blood build up to form a plug at the injury site, and proteins in the blood plasma reinforce the clot by forming fibrous strands at the site. If a sample of blood is carefully removed from the blood vessel without allowing it to come in contact with the damaged tissue, and then the sample is placed on a smooth plastic plate exposed to air, the blood will not clot. However, if a rough plastic plate or a rough glass plate is used instead, the blood will clot.

3. Which conclusion about the cause of blood clotting does this evidence support?

(A) Low blood pressure due to loss of blood causes blood to clot.

(B) Constriction of a blood vessel causes blood to clot.

(C) Accumulation of white blood cells causes blood to clot.

(D) A response from damaged tissue causes blood to clot.

QUESTION 4 IS BASED ON THE FOLLOWING INFORMATION.

The biosphere encompasses all life-sustaining regions of the Earth, its atmosphere, and its oceans. The following significant changes have been observed and documented during the last century.

- Wilderness areas have been deforested by the clear-cutting of trees to make wood products.

- Rivers and oceans have been polluted by fertilizer and sewage runoff.

- The protective ozone layer of the Earth's atmosphere has been depleted by the overuse of certain air pollutants.

- Livestock overgrazing has led to the desertification of grasslands, reducing agricultural output and available habitats for native plant and animal species.

4. How can all these findings be reconciled as having one common cause or characteristic?

(A) They are all caused by global climate change.

(B) They are all the result of human activity.

(C) They are all irreversible.

(D) They all affect the world's total food supply.

5. Sound travels four times as fast through water as through air, about 1490 meters/second as compared to about 330 meters/second. Which of the following would be most useful in confirming either one or the other of these two speeds?

(A) Record the altitude of a jet airplane passing far overhead.

(B) Observe a sprinter's reaction to a starter pistol fired near the starting line.

(C) From a submerged submarine, listen for sounds coming from the water's surface.

(D) Measure the speed of a race car as it passes by you.

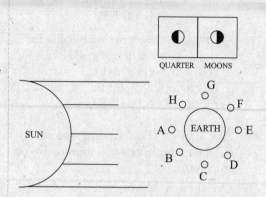

6. Referring to the illustration, at which moon positions would someone on Earth directly below the Moon see a quarter Moon in the sky? Images are not drawn to scale. Choose the accurate positions by clicking on the images of the Moon. More than one may be correct. On the online GED® test, you will click on the correct spot(s). For this paper version, please circle it/them.

7. How can a neutral atom have a negative ion? On the online GED® test, you will type your answer. In this paper version, please write it in the space provided.

_____

_____

_____

_____

_____

_____

R= DOMINANT GENE FORM (ALLELE)
r= RECESSIVE GENE FORM (ALLELE)

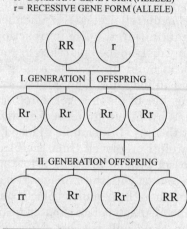

GENOTYPE	TRAIT FORM
RR	RED COLOR
Rr	RED COLOR
rr	WHITE COLOR

8. Select the correct number of total red offspring from the drop-down menu. On the online GED® test, you will click on your answer. In this paper version, please circle it.

Select ▼

1

2

3

4

5

6

7

8

9. Each genotype pair in the illustration represents a set of parents. Without any more information than what the diagram presents, which of the four sets of parents might possibly produce a white offspring? Click on all the genotype pairs that represent possible white offspring. They do not need to be in any particular order.

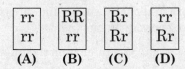

   (A)   (B)   (C)   (D)

QUESTION 10 REFERS TO THE FOLLOWING PASSAGE.

Plants consist of various types of cells that serve different functions. For example, epidermal cells, which form a plant's outer skin, often store food, while xylem cells, which are dead and hollow, transport water and nutrient salts to the other parts of the plant. Plant cells use structures called chloroplasts to make food for them by capturing the Sun's energy.

10. Why don't the cells that form the skin of an onion bulb contain chloroplasts?

   Onion bulbs

   (A) do not need water to survive.

   (B) receive their energy from the Sun.

   (C) grow underground.

   (D) have no roots.

QUESTION 11 REFERS TO THE FOLLOWING ILLUSTRATION.

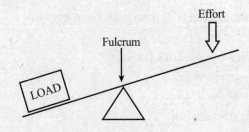

11. The simple machine shown here has a measurable mechanical advantage. A student wants to design an experiment to demonstrate and measure the mechanical advantage for this type of simple machine. Which of these tools should the student use as an example of the machine?

   (A) a crowbar

   (B) a wedge

   (C) a wheelbarrow

   (D) a nutcracker

12. Storks, which have long bills, are found mainly around waters where small fish swim just below the surface. What does this characteristic of storks show?

   (A) Some storks travel great distances to find food.

   (B) Long-billed storks do not mate with short-billed storks.

   (C) Storks developed long bills through evolution.

   (D) Storks do not prey on land-dwelling animals.

QUESTION 13 REFERS TO THE FOLLOWING DIAGRAM.

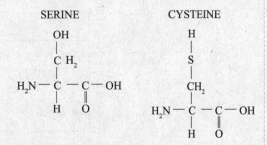

13. How does a serine molecule differ from a cysteine molecule?

   A serine molecule contains a different number of

   (A) oxygen atoms.

   (B) carbon atoms.

   (C) nitrogen atoms.

   (D) hydrogen atoms.

QUESTION 14 REFERS TO THE FOLLOWING INFORMATION.

The DNA of every human includes two sex chromosomes, which determine gender and the traits associated with gender. Female sex chromosomes are both of type X, while a male has one X chromosome and one Y chromosome.

14. How is the gender of human offspring determined?

   (A) solely by the male parent

   (B) solely by the female parent

   (C) equally by the male and female parents

   (D) predominantly by the male parent

QUESTION 15 REFERS TO THE FOLLOWING INFORMATION.

Earth's magnetic North Pole is shifting at an accelerating rate from its earliest known position in northern Canada toward Russia. Scientists theorize that at the planet's center is liquid magma rapidly circulating around an iron core and that the core and magma are constantly moving.

15. What can you infer from the information?

   (A) The magnetic South Pole is not shifting.

   (B) Earth's geographic poles are at different locations than the magnetic poles.

   (C) Compasses are of little or no use anymore.

   (D) Earth's magnetic core is moving toward the planet's surface.

QUESTION 16 REFERS TO THE FOLLOWING CHART.

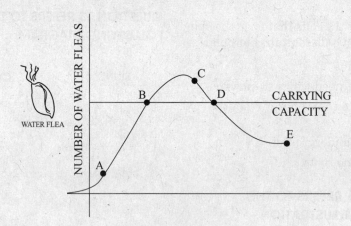

NOTE: When a population reaches carrying capacity, just enough resources are available to support the existing population.

16. Referring to the chart, what is occurring between points B and C?

   (A) The water flea population growth rate is slowing.

   (B) The water flea population's death rate is declining.

   (C) The average life span of a water flea is decreasing.

   (D) The total water flea population is declining.

QUESTIONS 17 AND 18 REFER TO THE FOLLOWING INFORMATION.

The Hertzsprung-Russell Diagram plots stars according to luminosity (brightness), surface temperature, and spectral class (color). NOTE: Absolute magnitude is a measure of luminosity (brightness) that uses an inverted scale.

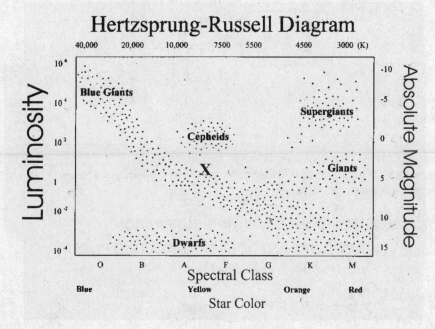

X = our solar system's Sun

17. Which statement does the Hertzsprung-Russell Diagram best support?

    (A) Red stars are hotter than blue stars.

    (B) Giants are among the coldest stars.

    (C) Dwarfs are more luminous than cepheids.

    (D) Orange stars are more luminous than red stars.

18. What conclusion can you draw from the Hertzsprung-Russell Diagram?

    (A) Our Sun is typical in terms of brightness and surface temperature.

    (B) Our Sun is old compared to most other stars.

    (C) The stars in the universe appear in broad bands and in clusters.

    (D) The number of stars in the universe is expanding.

QUESTION 19 REFERS TO THE FOLLOWING ILLUSTRATION.

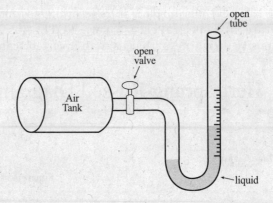

19. This simple instrument can be used to measure the [   ] of the air in the tank. On the online GED® test, you will type in your answer. In this paper version, please write it in.

QUESTION 20 REFERS TO THE FOLLOWING ILLUSTRATION.

DEVELOPMENT OF A FRUIT-BEARING PLANT

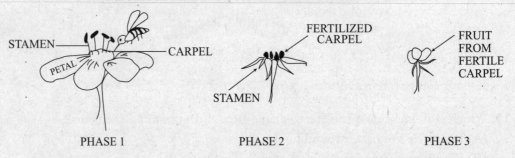

Phase 1: The flower attracts insects, which pollinate the carpel, resulting in fertilization. After fertilization occurs, the flower's petals wither.

Phase 2: A seed develops inside each carpel, an ovary wall encases each seed, and the ovary swells to form a pericap, while the flower's stamens wither.

Phase 3: The seed and pericap form a fruit, which attracts animals.

20. Among the following, which is probably responsible for spreading fruit-bearing plants from one location to another?

(A) rains that wash away the withered stamens

(B) insects that pollinate their flowers

(C) winds that scatter their petals

(D) animals that eat their ripe fruit

QUESTION 21 REFERS TO THE FOLLOWING ILLUSTRATION AND INFORMATION.

TYPES OF EPITHELIAL TISSUE

| SIMPLE CUBOIDAL | SIMPLE SQUAMOUS | SIMPLE COLUMNAR | PSEUDOSTRATIFIED CILIATED COLUMNAR | STRATIFIED SQUAMOUS |

★

The illustrations show five types of tightly packed epithelial tissues, which form the thin membranes lining most internal and external surfaces of an animal's body. Thinner tissues allow for the exchange of particles through the membrane, whereas thicker tissues serve largely as a barrier.

21. Which type of epithelial tissue lines a lung's air sacs, which must freely pass oxygen to blood vessels in exchange for carbon dioxide? Drag and drop the star onto the type of epithelial tissue that lines a lung's air sac. On the online GED® test, you will click and drag the star. In this paper version, please draw a line to your answer.

QUESTIONS 22 AND 23 REFER TO THE FOLLOWING INFORMATION.

In ecological communities, energy is transferred from producers (simple plant forms that obtain their energy through photosynthesis) up the food chain to primary, secondary, and tertiary consumers. Producers provide only about 1% of their energy, which they generate through photosynthesis, to primary consumers. On average, consumers pass along about 10% of the energy they obtain from the trophic level below theirs to the next level up.

22. About what percent of the energy that producers obtain through photosynthesis is passed up the food chain to secondary consumers? From the drop-down menu, choose the percentage that correctly answers this question. On the online GED® test, you will click on your answer. In this paper version, please circle it.

| Select ▼ |

    0.001 percent

    0.01 percent

    0.1 percent

    1.0 percent

23. Most ecological communities also include animal species that consume both plants and animals. They also include dentritivores (decomposers), which consume plants and animals that die without being eaten. Some dentritivores may also serve as prey for other animals. What would a diagram that accurately shows these relationships probably look like?

The diagram would be

(A) circular, or O-shaped.

(B) pyramid-shaped.

(C) separated into two or more chains.

(D) shaped like an inverted pyramid.

QUESTIONS 24 AND 25 REFER TO THE FOLLOWING ILLUSTRATION.

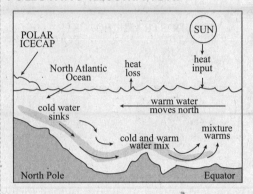

24. What overall idea does the diagram convey?

(A) The Atlantic Ocean's depth is greatest near the equator.

(B) Ocean water circulates between the equator and the North Atlantic Ocean.

(C) Warm ocean water rises, while colder ocean water sinks.

(D) Unusually warm air can disturb the normal currents of the Atlantic Ocean.

25. Which question does the diagram help answer?

(A) Which is greater: heat loss from the ocean or heat input from the Sun?

(B) Should scientists be concerned that the polar ice caps will melt away?

(C) How fast do ocean currents of the North Atlantic move?

(D) Which is denser—cold water or warm water?

26. During their evolution, frogs have gradually developed stronger shoulder girdles, longer hind legs, and shorter, more rigid spines. For what activity have frogs adapted?

(A) crushing their prey

(B) clinging to tree trunks

(C) moving quickly on land

(D) fending off predators

QUESTION 27 REFERS TO THE FOLLOWING GRAPH.

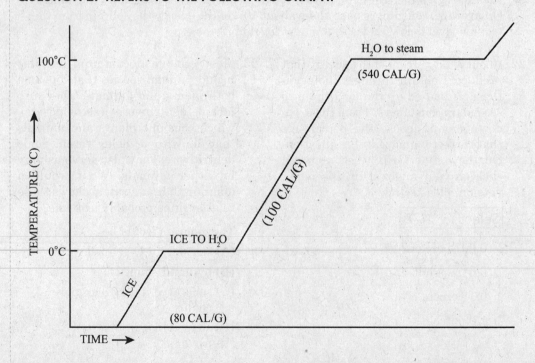

27. At a minimum, how much heat energy is required to change 1 gram of ice into steam? Fill in the box with the correct answer by typing in the provided space. On the online GED® test, you will type in your answer. In this paper version, please write it in.

```

```

28. Like light matter, dark matter attracts all other matter gravitationally, and so it sustains a gravitational field. As astronomers study a galaxy, they can infer the presence of dark matter if the galaxy's motion is different from that predicted by the mass of observable light matter alone. Therefore, the theoretical existence of dark matter is based on the application of an understanding of the force of ⎣_____⎦. On the online GED® test, you will type in your answer. In this paper version, please write it in.

QUESTION 29 IS BASED ON THE FOLLOWING ILLUSTRATION.

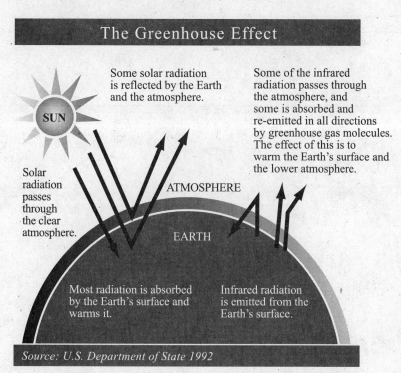

The Greenhouse Effect

Some solar radiation is reflected by the Earth and the atmosphere.

Some of the infrared radiation passes through the atmosphere, and some is absorbed and re-emitted in all directions by greenhouse gas molecules. The effect of this is to warm the Earth's surface and the lower atmosphere.

Solar radiation passes through the clear atmosphere.

ATMOSPHERE

EARTH

Most radiation is absorbed by the Earth's surface and warms it.

Infrared radiation is emitted from the Earth's surface.

Source: U.S. Department of State 1992

29. Which is an accurate statement about the greenhouse effect?

(A) Solar radiation is prevented from passing through the atmosphere.

(B) Much of the energy radiated from the Earth never leaves the atmosphere.

(C) Some radiation reaching the Earth is reflected off its surface.

(D) The Earth warms mainly due to atmospheric radiation.

QUESTION 30 REFERS TO THE FOLLOWING ILLUSTRATION.

FORMATION OF AN ATOLL

30. What does the sequence of illustrations show?

    (A) a rising sea level, which allows coral to grow in a volcanic island's lagoon

    (B) a lagoon forming when a volcanic lava flow erodes a coral reef

    (C) coral combining with volcanic ash to expand a volcanic island

    (D) a lagoon forming as coral builds up around an eroding volcanic island

SOCIAL STUDIES

70 Minutes • 34 Questions

Directions: The Social Studies Test consists of a series of questions involving general social studies concepts. The questions are based on brief passages of text and visual information (graphs, charts, maps, cartoons, and other figures). Some questions are based on both text and visual information. Study the information provided, and answer the question(s) that follow it, referring back to the information as needed. Most questions are in multiple-choice format. Others are meant to prepare you for the electronically formatted questions that you will find on the test, such as drop-down questions, hot spot maps, and fill-in-the-blanks. The extended response question requires you to write an essay in which you analyze certain documents. Record your answers on the Social Studies section of the answer sheet provided.

QUESTION 1 REFERS TO THE FOLLOWING INFORMATION.

In geography, *regions* are used to divide the world into units of study. All the common land and human characteristics define a region. For example, the British Isles is a region located in Western Europe. On the other hand, *place* is used to define specific points within a region and how humans interact with and perceive those points. Everything within a specific area makes up place, such as natural objects, artifacts, and culture. The British Isles consists of the Republic of Ireland, the United Kingdom, and the numerous islands around their coasts. Ireland is a predominantly Catholic country, while Great Britain is a predominantly Protestant country. Although considered part of the same region, the citizens of these two countries have come to develop cultural differences.

1. Which of the following statements identifies a similarity between the Irish and the British?

   (A) Irish and British people live in the same place.

   (B) The Irish and the British maintain some distinct cultural differences.

   (C) The British Isles is a region that only recently recognized the religions of both British and Irish citizens.

   (D) The Republic of Ireland and the United Kingdom reject their inclusion in the British Isles.

QUESTION 2 REFERS TO THE FOLLOWING INFORMATION.

The Native American nations of the Pacific Northwest lived primarily in what is now Oregon and Washington. They enjoyed access to abundant food sources, owing to their proximity to freshwater fishing and fertile farmland. Unlike their counterparts in the east, the Native Americans in this region built and lived primarily in longhouses. These structures were made of cedar trees. They recorded stories on elaborate totem poles. The nations of the Eastern Woodland Native Americans also lived in longhouses, as well as wigwams. Food sources primarily came from fruits, nuts, and berries; squash, corn, and beans; and meat from small animals.

2. Based on information in the passage, which statement correctly compares the Native Americans of the Eastern Woodlands to those of the Northwest Coast?

   (A) Native Americans of both the Eastern Woodlands and the Northwest farmed.

   (B) Only the Native Americans of the Northwest lived in longhouses.

   (C) The Eastern Woodlands Native Americans had a greater variety of totem poles than the those of the Northwest Coast.

   (D) The Native Americans of the Northwest Coast were more advanced than those of the Eastern Woodlands.

QUESTIONS 3 AND 4 ARE BASED ON THE FOLLOWING INFORMATION.

James Madison is sometimes known as the "father of the Constitution." He was a leading influence at the Constitutional Convention and wrote articles in support of the adoption of the Constitution. Here are some quotations from those articles:

"The accumulation of all powers—legislative, executive, and judiciary—in the same hands...is the very definition of tyranny."

—James Madison, *Federalist 47*

"In order to lay a due foundation for that separate and distinct exercise of the different powers of government...it is evident that each [branch of government] should have a will of its own..."

—James Madison, *Federalist 51*

3. Which statement best describes the argument Madison was making in both *Federalist* articles?

   (A) Instead of a president, executive power should be divided among several leaders.

   (B) The government's powers should be divided among Congress, the president, and the Supreme Court, and each of these institutions should operate independently.

   (C) A bill of rights should be added to the Constitution to prevent government from becoming tyrannical.

   (D) The president should carry out the will of Congress, which represents the people.

4. Based on the quotations from Madison, which one of the following values was most important to him?

   (A) the equality of all humans

   (B) democracy, or rule by the people

   (C) gaining power for himself

   (D) keeping the government from becoming oppressive

QUESTION 5 IS BASED ON THE FOLLOWING INFORMATION.

The origins of the Cold War are traceable to the period immediately following World War II. Although both the Soviet Union and the United States participated as part of the Allied Forces, the two countries grew distrustful of each other in the postwar period. Upon German surrender, the United States and the Soviet Union emerged as world superpowers. Following the war, the new superpowers, France, and England divided Germany into four militarized zones. As the midpoint of eastern and western Europe, the newly divided Germany represented a geographical and political threat to each superpower. The United States introduced the Marshall Plan in 1947. This provided economic aid to war-torn Europe, but, more importantly to the U.S., also reduced the influence of communist Soviet Union. As a result, West Germany was rebuilt and allied to the United States. East Germany, on the other hand, saw no benefit and therefore suffered because the Soviet Union refused to take advantage of the available assistance under the Marshall Plan.

5. Which of the following indicates a biased statement on the part of the author?

   (A) During World War II, the United States allied with the Soviet Union to defeat Germany.

   (B) Both the United States and the Soviet Union used the defeat of Germany as an opportunity to influence the development of political power throughout post-war Europe.

   (C) East Germany suffered because the Soviet Union refused to use the assistance available under the Marshall Plan.

   (D) As the midpoint of eastern and western Europe, the newly divided Germany represented a geographical and political threat to each superpower.

QUESTIONS 6 AND 7 ARE BASED ON THE FOLLOWING CARTOON AND PASSAGE.

This cartoon was drawn in 1874 during the Reconstruction, an era of rebuilding after the U.S. Civil War.

6. To what does the motto "worse than slavery" above the head of the freed slaves refer?

   (A) inhumane factory and farm labor conditions

   (B) denying the children of freed slaves an education

   (C) the Confederate South's cessation from the Union

   (D) the development of white reactionary groups

7. Which conclusion can best be drawn from this cartoon?

   (A) Newly freed slaves had a difficult time adjusting to being treated as equals.

   (B) Life for African Americans in the South improved as a result of the Civil War.

   (C) True freedom for the African American would be a long struggle.

   (D) The Ku Klux Klan was able and ready to help African Americans.

QUESTION 8 IS BASED ON THE FOLLOWING INFORMATION.

The founders of the United States government deliberately created a system in which no one person or group could assume a majority of power. After gaining independence from Great Britain, the framers of the Constitution paid close attention to the operations of the central government. The first three of seven Articles called for a separation of federal powers into three segments. The executive branch, administered by the President, enforces laws and holds veto power over bills. Congress presides over the legislative branch, which writes, debates, and passes bills into law. The nine justices of the U.S. Supreme Court oversee the judicial branch, interpreting law and intervening in conflicts among the branches of the government. The result is a system of checks and balances, although the executive branch should have more influence than the judicial and legislative branches. Each of the 50 states has a government modeled on the federal system, while cities and towns within each state have a local government.

8. Which statement expresses an opinion or a value judgment rather than a fact?

   (A) Each of the 50 states has a government modeled on the federal system, while cities and towns within each state have a local government.

   (B) The first three of seven Articles called for a separation of federal powers into three segments.

   (C) The founders of the United States government deliberately created a system in which no one person or group could assume a majority of power.

(D) The result is a system of checks and balances, although the executive branch should have more influence than the judicial and legislative branches.

QUESTION 9 IS BASED UPON THE FOLLOWING TWO PASSAGES.

By the beginning of the seventeenth century, New World exploration excited the imaginations of poets and adventurers alike. The reality of life in the new land, however, was quite different. Read the following two views of life in the Virginia colony, and then compose an essay in response to the prompt that follows.

You brave heroic minds
Worthy your country's name,
That honour still pursue;
Go and subdue!
Whilst loitering hinds
Lurk here at home with shame.

Britons, you stay too long:
Quickly aboard bestow you,
And with a merry gale
Swell your stretch'd sail
With vows as strong
As the winds that blow you.

Your course securely steer,
West and by south forth keep!
Rocks, lee-shores, nor shoals
When Eolus scowls
You need not fear;
So absolute the deep.

And cheerfully at sea
Success you still entice
To get the pearl and gold,
And ours to hold
Virginia,
Earth's only paradise.

Where nature hath in store
Fowl, venison, and fish,
And the fruitfull'st soil
Without your toil
Three harvests more,
All greater than your wish.

—Michael Drayton, from
"To the Virginia Voyage"

"A True Relation of Such Occurrences and Accidents of Noate as Hath Happened in Virginia . . ." (excerpts)

About the tenth of September there was about 46 of our men dead, at which time Captaine Wingefield having ordred the affaires in such sort that he was generally hated of all, in which respect with one consent he was deposed from his presidencie, and Captaine Ratcliffe according to his course was elected.

Our provision now being within twentie dayes spent, the Indians brought us great store both of Corne and bread ready made: and also there came such aboundance of Fowles into the Rivers, as greatly refreshed our weake estates, where uppon many of our weake men were presently able to goe abroad.

As yet we had no houses to cover us, our tents were rotten and our Cabbins worse than nought: our best commodities was Yron which we made into little chissels.

The president, and Captaine Martins sicknes, me to be Cape Marchant, and yet to spare no paines in making houses for the company, who notwithstanding our misery, little ceased their mallice, grudging and muttering.

As at this time were most of our chiefest men either sicke or discontented, the rest being in such dispaire, as they would rather starve and rot with idleness, then be persuaded to do any thing for their owne reliefe without con-straint: our victualles being now within eighteene dayes spent, and the Indians trade decreasing, I was sent to the mouth of the river to Kegquohtan an Indian Towne, to trade for Corne, and try the river for Fish, but our fishing we could not effect by reason of the stormy weather. The Indians thinking us neare famished, with carelesse kindnes, offered us little pieces of bread and small handfulls of beanes or wheat, for a hatchet or a piece of copper: In like maner I entertained their kindnes, and in like scorne offered them like com-modities, but the Children, or any that shewe extraordinary kundnes, I liberally confronted with free gifte such trifles as wel contented them.

—John Smith

9. These documents offer two distinct views of Virginia. The first is a highly idealized portrait of a kind of paradise, although a paradise never visited by the author who describes it. The second, a more starkly realistic piece, describes how one explorer tries to exist there. Beyond these obvious contrasts, how would you relate the con-cept of the explorer as presented by these two pieces? Note the qualities the first piece highlights to describe that role and then note how Smith extends, qualifies, or negates those qualities as they are tested in the actual experience of life in the colony.

_____

_____

_____

_____

_____

_____

_____

_____

_____

_____

QUESTIONS 10–12 REFER TO THE FOLLOWING GRAPH.

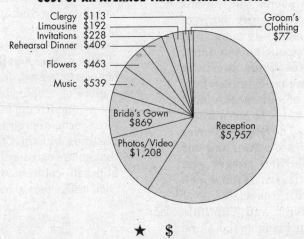

COST OF AN AVERAGE TRADITIONAL WEDDING

Clergy $113
Limousine $192
Invitations $228
Rehearsal Dinner $409
Flowers $463
Music $539
Bride's Gown $869
Photos/Video $1,208
Groom's Clothing $77
Reception $5,957

★ $

10. Drag the star next to the category in the graph that costs less than the limousine, but more than the groom's clothing. On the online GED® test, you will click and drag the star to your answer. For this paper version, please write it in.

11. Drag the dollar sign next to the category that would save the most money for a couple on a limited budget. On the online GED® test, you will click and drag the dollar sign to your answer. For this paper version, please write it in.

12. The average traditional wedding shown in the graph costs slightly more than
| Select ▼ | . | Select ▼ | of that amount is the cost of the reception.

$5000	Less than 10 percent
$8000	About 30 percent
$10,000	A little less than half
$13,000	About 60 percent

On the online GED® test, you will click to select your answers. For this paper version, please circle them.

QUESTION 13 IS BASED ON THE FOLLOWING INFORMATION.

A court of original jurisdiction has the authority to conduct the original trial of a case. This court is called the trial court. A court with appellate jurisdiction has the authority to hear an appeal of a case decided by a trial court. This court is called the appeals court. An appeals court does not conduct a new trial; instead it reviews the record of the trial and rules on whether or not the trial was conducted fairly and the law applied correctly.

U.S. FEDERAL COURT SYSTEM

Court	Original Jurisdiction	Appellate Jurisdiction
U.S. Supreme Court	Lawsuits between two state governments	Cases appealed from U.S. Court of Appeals and Cases appealed from state supreme courts
U.S. Courts of Appeals	None	Cases appealed from U.S. District Courts
U.S. District Courts	Cases involving federal law or the U.S. Constitution	None

13. What court would conduct the trial in a case in which the federal government charges a company with violating federal pollution regulations?

   (A) a state trial court in the state in which the violation occurred

   (B) the U.S. Supreme Court

   (C) a state supreme court

   (D) a U.S. District Court

14. Prior to the Pendleton Civil Service Reform Act of 1883, presidential and other federal government appointments were often made under an informal "spoils system," by which government jobs were given to loyal supporters rather than on the basis of merit. The Act mandated that jobs would henceforth be awarded on the basis of merit and prohibited the firing of any employee for political reasons.

   Which of the following resulted from the demise of the spoils system?

   (A) political lobbying

   (B) civilian jury duty

   (C) term limits for elected officials

   (D) civil service exams

QUESTIONS 15 AND 16 REFER TO THE FOLLOWING INFORMATION.

MILITARY CAMPAIGNS—U.S. REVOLUTIONARY WAR

Battle of Brandywine

On September 11, 1777, British General Sir William Howe sailed from New York City and landed near Elkton, Maryland in northern Chesapeake Bay. Howe engaged American General George Washington's army near Brandywine Creek. Howe sent the majority of his forces across the Brandywine and attacked Washington's rear flank.

Due to poor scouting, the Americans did not detect Howe's approaching forces until it was too late. Once discovered, they sent three divisions in an attempt to block Howe's advances.

Washington brought in General Nathaniel Greene to hold off Howe's forces long enough for the bulk of the American forces to retreat northeast, ultimately encamping at Valley Forge for the winter. The retreat of Washington's army resulted in Philadelphia being taken by the British on September 23. It remained under British control until June 1778.

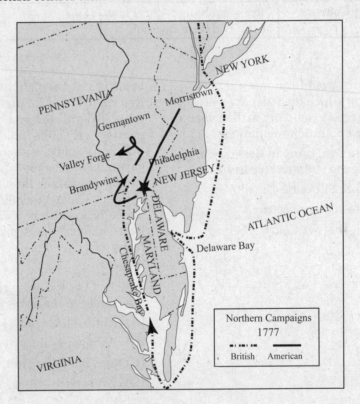

15. Identify where Washington's army retreated to from Howe's forces. On the online GED® test, you will click on the map to indicate your answer. For this paper version, please circle the spot.

16. Identify which city was left vulnerable by General Washington's retreat. On the online GED® test, you will click on the map to indicate your answer. For this paper version, please circle the spot.

QUESTIONS 17 AND 18 ARE BASED ON THE FOLLOWING INFORMATION.

President Franklin Roosevelt's New Deal (1933–1936) included a variety of programs that were introduced to relieve Americans from the economic fallout of the Great Depression.

1933	**Civilian Conservation Corps:** provides immediate work in reforestation, road construction, and national park development on government land to 250,000 men
	Securities Act of 1933: designed to provide oversight and regulation to stocks and bonds trading
	Banking Act of 1933: established the Federal Deposit Insurance Corporation (FDIC), which provided insurance to people with accounts in the case of bank failure
1934	**Farm Mortgage Refinancing Act:** provided farmers with assistance in mortgage refinance
	Securities Exchange Act: established to regulate the stock market and prevent corporate abuse of securities sales and reporting
	National Housing Act: introduced the Federal Housing Administration (FHA), which provides construction and renovation loans for homes
1935	**Social Security Act:** created to guarantee retirees a pension upon retirement at age 65

17. *Fiscal policy* refers to government trying to influence the economy through its taxation and spending policies. Which statement best describes the economic beliefs underlying the fiscal policy of the Roosevelt's administration?

   (A) Government should not try to fight a recession by creating government jobs; instead it should reduce regulation to encourage private enterprise to create jobs.

   (B) Government spending, especially to provide jobs for the unemployed, should be increased to stimulate the economy.

   (C) Government spending should be cut in order to balance the federal budget.

   (D) Since the government is taking in less money due to the recession, taxes should be raised to keep the government solvent.

18. Which New Deal program would most likely benefit an employed worker living in New York City who has saved some money in a bank account?

   (A) Federal Deposit Insurance Corporation

   (B) Civilian Conservation Corps

   (C) Farm Mortgage Refinancing Act

   (D) Social Security Act

QUESTIONS 19 AND 20 REFER TO THE FOLLOWING PASSAGE AND ILLUSTRATION.

The United States has seen steady, incremental monetary inflation going back to 1950. During a period of general monetary inflation, the price of goods and services increases (or "inflates") in terms of a specific currency (form of money), such as the U.S. dollar. At the same time, the value of that currency can decline relative to other currencies, depending on inflation rates in countries that use other currencies. The following illustration tells the story of the value of the U.S. dollar in selected years.

Purchasing Power of the Dollar

19. Referring to the illustration, which could be the base year, in which one dollar could buy one dollar's worth of goods?

(A) 2001

(B) 1976

(C) 1967

(D) 1983

20. During the first decade of this century, the Euro appreciated in value in relation to the U.S. dollar. How might a resident of a European country whose currency is the Euro be expected to respond to this relationship?

(A) by taking vacations in the United States instead of Europe

(B) by saving more money

(C) by investing in European real estate

(D) by exchanging their Euros for gold and silver

QUESTION 21 IS BASED ON THE FOLLOWING INFORMATION.

At the height of the Cold War struggle between the United States and the Soviet Union, President Kennedy stated in his inaugural address (January 20, 1961):

"In the long history of the world, only a few generations have been granted the role of defending freedom in its hour of maximum danger. I do not shrink from this responsibility—I welcome it. I do not believe that any of us would exchange places with any other people or any other generation. The energy, the faith, the devotion which we bring to this endeavor will light our country and all who serve it—and the glow from that fire can truly light the world. And so, my fellow Americans: ask not what your country can do for you—ask what you can do for your country."

21. What can we assume was President Kennedy's broad goal in making this speech?

    (A) encouraging people to accept higher taxes even if they don't get much in return

    (B) persuading Americans to join the Peace Corps

    (C) uniting Americans to support the struggle to contain the Soviet Union

    (D) getting more people to fight in the military

QUESTIONS 22 AND 23 ARE BASED UPON THE FOLLOWING PASSAGES.

Along with her husband Pierre, Marie Skłodowska Curie conducted pioneering research in the isolation of radioactive isotopes, resulting in the discovery of polonium and radium. The Curies and the physicist Henri Becquerel won the Nobel Prize for their discoveries in 1903. Marie Curie won a Nobel Prize for Chemistry in 1911.

"One of our joys was to go into our workroom at night; we then perceived on all sides the feebly luminous silhouettes of the bottles of capsules containing our products. It was really a lovely sight and one always new to us. The glowing tubes looked like faint, fairy lights."

—Marie Curie,
Autobiographical Notes

The Curies were happiest . . . immersed in their research. Pierre even strapped a glass with uranium salts to his right arm to observe the effects and found that they produced a burn, leaving a grey scar that would not heal even after six weeks; he also liked to carry around a small amount of uranium in his waistcoat pocket to illustrate its phosphorescent qualities to friends. Without knowing it, the Curies were inexorably poisoning themselves with massive doses of radioactivity.

—Philipp Blom, *The Vertigo Years: Europe, 1900–1914*

22. Which of the following best describes Marie Curie's attitude about her discovery?

    (A) fascination

    (B) delight

    (C) awe

    (D) trepidation

23. Which of the following best describes the main point that the author of the second passage wants to make about the Curies and their discoveries?

    (A) The Curies were egotistical intellectuals who loved to publicize the results of their work.

    (B) The Curies were dedicated scientists who recognized the potential impact of their discoveries.

    (C) The Curies were absorbed researchers who failed to recognize the potential harm of their discoveries.

    (D) The Curies were a profoundly romantic couple who bonded over their shared love of science.

QUESTIONS 24 AND 25 REFER TO THE FOLLOWING INFORMATION.

WORLD WAR I—CHRONOLOGY OF KEY DATES AND EVENTS

1914   **June:** Austrian Archduke Franz Ferdinand and his wife are assassinated by Serbian students.

July: Blaming the Serbian government for the assassination, Austria declares war on Serbia; Russia, joined by France, mobilizes to support Serbia.

August 1–4: Germany declares war on Russia and France and invades neutral Belgium. Britain demands that Germany withdraw from Belgium.

August 4: The Germans do not withdraw from Belgium, and the British declare war on Germany.

August 26–30: Russia marches on Prussia but is defeated by Germany at the Battle of Tennenberg.

August 13: Japan, through its formal alliance with Great Britain, declares war on Germany.

October 29: Turkey assists Germany in naval attack on Russia.

November 2: Russia declares war on Turkey.

November 5: Britain and France side with Russia to declare war on Turkey.

September–December: Germany initiates attacks on France and England (the attacks continue over the next two years).

1915   **May 25:** Italy enters the war on the side of Russia, Britain, and France.

1916   **February–November:** The Germans mount a continuing attack on France.

May 31–June 1: Germany and Britain engage in the war's only large-scale naval battle.

November 28: The Germans attack London for the first time, by air.

1917 **January–March:** In a German U-boat campaign, enemy and neutral ships, including some U.S. ships, are sunk on sight.

April 6: The United States declares war on Germany over the sinking of U.S. ships.

1918 **October:** The allies recover France and Belgium from German occupation.

October: The allies push Turkey back, forcing Turkey into an armistice treaty.

November: The allies push the Germans back beyond their critical line of defense.

November 9: Kaiser Wilhelm II of Germany abdicates his rule.

November 11: An Armistice is signed, bringing the war to an end.

24. Which of the following groups were allies in World War I?

   (A) Russia, Turkey, and Prussia
   (B) Russia, Britain, France, Italy, and the United States
   (C) Germany, Turkey, and Belgium
   (D) Japan, Germany, and Turkey

25. Based on the information in the timeline, what was the main reason that World War I ended up involving so many nations from so many parts of the globe?

   (A) Many nations entered the war because they were attacked.
   (B) Many nations entered the war because they were outraged over the assassination of Archduke Ferdinand and his wife.
   (C) Many nations entered the war because they were invaded.
   (D) Many nations entered the war in support of their allies.

QUESTION 26 IS BASED UPON THE FOLLOWING PASSAGE.

After the passage of the Stamp Act in 1765, a piece of English legislation that required American colonists to pay taxes on materials printed on special paper that bore the stamp of British manufacture, a series of secret societies sprang up in the colonies. The term "Sons of Liberty" became associated with these groups. Their members included artisans, merchants, and others concerned with what was perceived as the growing hostility of the British government towards the American colonies. While groups designating themselves as The Sons of Liberty were found in major American cities, they were not part of a larger, organized group. All groups shared a common motto "No taxation without representation."

26. A unifying ideology for the Sons of Liberty was the need for

   (A) grassroots organization.
   (B) publicity.
   (C) shared governance with Britain.
   (D) covert military strength.

27. The Vice President of the United States is given only one duty in the Constitution: to preside over the Senate. However, in practice, he seldom shows up to do this since this job is primarily a formality and doesn't give him any real power. His one responsibility in the Senate is to

[   ].

On the online GED® test, you will type in your answer. For this paper version, please write it in.

QUESTION 28 REFERS TO THE FOLLOWING CARTOON.

28. What idea was the artist who drew the cartoon trying to convey?

(A) The United States felt as though communism may spread problems in Western Europe if Congress did not offer assistance to Western European nations.

(B) The United States was in a race with the Soviet Union to help rebuild Western Europe.

(C) Communists felt as though the U.S. Congress was being reckless with its foreign policy.

(D) Western Europe needed assistance so badly that it would open its doors to democracy and communism as long as those nations received assistance.

As the population of the United States grew rapidly during the early nineteenth century, settlers began pushing further southeast to claim new land. Five nations—Cherokee, Creek, Choctaw, Chicasaw, and Seminole—lived in this region. Settlers pressured the U.S. government to aid in removing the Native Americans from this land. Initially, Indian migration was voluntary, with some nations agreeing to the terms of treaties that relocated them to new lands west of the Mississippi River. Other Indian nations remained, refusing to negotiate for land that they considered home. While the Cherokee appealed to the Supreme Court to maintain their territory, the Creeks and Seminoles resisted with force. Eventually, most Native Americans relocated to western territorial allotments. The Cherokee were the last to leave. In the winter of 1838, during what became known as the Trail of Tears, 4000 Cherokee people died of exposure, disease, and hunger. In the end, 46,000 Native Americans were relocated west. The result was 25 million acres of land comprising present-day Alabama, Florida, Georgia, Tennessee, Mississippi, Kentucky, and North Carolina available to settlers.

29. Of about 20,000 removed from their homes, 4000 died on the journey, which came to be known as the

☐ .

On the online GED® test, you will type in your answer. For this paper version, please write it in.

Jose and Taurabia Paivo emigrated from Portugal in 1933 and settled in Fall River, Massachusetts. Jose had been trained as a bookkeeper but was unable to find work. One day, as he stopped to rest and eat a sandwich his wife had packed for him, a stranger asked what he was eating. Jose explained that it was a cured fish that his wife had prepared according to an old family recipe. He tore off a piece and offered it to the stranger, who devoured it with relish. "You should sell this," the stranger remarked.

That night, Jose discussed the incident with his wife. They both mused that it would be fun and maybe profitable to open a restaurant, but they lacked the funds to start. Then Taurabia remembered that a small bodega up the street might possibly offer them space if they agreed to split the profits. As added incentive, Jose offered to help the owner maintain his books. Their delicacies caught on, and, within a few years, Jose and Taurabia had enough cash flow to rent a space of their own. As the 1930s turned into the 1940s, and the city's factories thrived with the need for wartime supplies like blankets, shoes, and uniforms, business expanded and Jose and Taurabia opened a second establishment. After the war, and their own children were old enough to help out, the Paivos opened still more restaurants, now in other cities and towns in New England.

But by the 1970s, things changed. Fast food chains began to lure business away, and economic conditions in many New England cities drove residents elsewhere, even as property taxes rose. One by one, the restaurants closed. By

1981, both of the senior Paivos had passed away, and their children closed the last eatery.

30. The success of the original business enterprise was due in large part to the Paivo's ability to

(A) barter.

(B) advertise.

(C) economize.

(D) wait.

31. A significant factor in the business's ultimate demise was

(A) property reassessment.

(B) unionization.

(C) poor management.

(D) inventory unavailability.

QUESTIONS 32 AND 33 REFER TO THE FOLLOWING INFORMATION.

The Constitution provides for changing times with a process for amendment, or change. Today, the Constitution includes 27 amendments. The first ten amendments, called the Bill of Rights, are outlined below.

BILL OF RIGHTS

First Amendment: Religious and political freedom

Second Amendment: The right to bear arms

Third Amendment: The right to refuse to house soldiers in peacetime

Fourth Amendment: Protection against unreasonable search and seizure

Fifth Amendment: The right of accused persons to due process of the law

Sixth Amendment: The right to a speedy and public trial

Seventh Amendment: The right to a jury trial in civil cases

Eighth Amendment: Protection against cruel and unusual punishment

Ninth Amendment: The rights of the people to powers that may not be spelled out in the Constitution

Tenth Amendment: The rights of the people and the states to powers not otherwise given to the federal government, states, or people

32. Which two amendments provide for changes over time in the circumstances and realities of American life?

(A) the First and Second Amendments

(B) the Fifth and Sixth Amendments

(C) the Third and Fourth Amendments

(D) the Ninth and Tenth Amendments

33. A family that was forced by the U.S. Army to provide housing and food for a group of soldiers could appeal to the courts based on which amendment to the Constitution?

(A) the Second Amendment

(B) the Third Amendment

(C) the Ninth Amendment

(D) the Tenth Amendment

QUESTION 34 IS BASED ON THE FOLLOWING INFORMATION.

Japan's unique culture is the result of centuries of influence, as well as its geographic characteristics. The closest point to it is in mainland Asia, 115 miles away. This geographic isolation resulted in diminished threats of foreign invasion. Peoples from various Asian countries migrated to Japan, chief among them Mongolians. During 250 B.C. to 300 A.D., the Yayoi, a matriarchal society, introduced rice cultivation, iron- and bronze-making, and weaving. During the third century, cultural shifts that are presumed to be the result of Korean influence introduced into Japanese culture advanced weaponry and the use of horses in combat. As Japan became an increasingly powerful nation, it became more open to Chinese cultural influence. The introduction of Confucianism signaled a significant shift in Japanese culture. By stressing adherence to hierarchical relationships and emphasizing education as a means to advance in government, Confucian values disrupted the hereditary Japanese nobility.

34. Which general statement about the study of history is supported by information in the previous passage?

(A) While historians sometimes disagree on the interpretation of history, they agree on the significance of particular events.

(B) Major changes in history often happen gradually and resist attempts to assign a specific date to them.

(C) History is the study of dates and events, which is more scientific than the less exact study of gradual or underlying changes.

(D) Historians tend to interpret history in the same way, although they disagree on the significance of particular events.

ANSWER KEY AND EXPLANATIONS

Reasoning Through Language Arts

1. (A)	18. (D)	35. (C)
2. he is a loner	19. (C)	36. (A)
3. (B)	20. (D)	37. See explanation below.
4. See explanation below.	21. (C)	38. (A)
5. (C)	22. revered	39. See explanation below.
6. (C)	23. (C)	
7. (B)	24. (C)	40. (B)
8. (C)	25. (B)	41. (D)
9. (A)	26. (C)	42. (A)
10. (D)	27. (C)	43. (C)
11. (B)	28. See explanation below.	44. (C)
12. See explanation below.	29. (B)	45. (B)
13. (D)	30. (D)	46. (D)
14. See explanation below.	31. ineffective	47. (A)
15. Valley Forge	32. (C)	48. (B)
16. Philadelphia	33. (D)	49. (C)
17. (A)	34. See explanation below.	

1. **The correct answer is (A).** An excavation tells the reader that he is digging in the desert, the work of archaeologists who look for clues about ancient peoples.

2. **The correct answer is he is a loner.** The description of Jack and his interactions with Jinny show that he prefers to be alone than with others. He even prefers the company of mummies to that of people.

3. **The correct answer is (B).** Jack is conflicted by the invitation. He hates the idea of any party, particularly a costume ball. On the other hand, he finds Jinny attractive (she's "a bright delight" and "very engaging") and therefore decides that he will go.

4. **The correct answer is he likes the dead mummies better than he likes Jinny.** Jack is comfortable away from crowds and people. He prefers to be with the ancient mummies than with others, including Jinny, even though he likes her.

5. **The correct answer is (C).** Jack prefers being in the presence of the ancient mummies than with "modern" people. Since the task of some archaeologists is to spend a lot of

time at such sites, digging for clues of the ancient past, his profession is a good fit.

6. **The correct answer is (C).** Jack runs into Jinny in the Cairo market, indicating that they knew one another before this encounter. Because Egypt was part of the British Empire, we can assume that "home" is in Great Britain.

7. **The correct answer is (B).** *Recapitulate* in this sentence means to sum up or restate. Dewey's vision for public education focused on present experiences.

8. **The correct answer is (C).** Much of the passage discusses the characteristics of a stable, strong, and/or ideal society, and how Dewey felt public education could best maintain such a society.

9. **The correct answer is (A).** In this context, a *catalyst* is something that causes a change in circumstances.

10. **The correct answer is (D).** The passage states that preparation for adulthood was not one of Dewey's goals.

11. **The correct answer is (B).** The passage says, "the ideal larger society, according to Dewey, is one in which the interests of a group are all shared by all of its members and in which interactions with other groups are free and full."

12. **The correct answer is "Liberty, once lost, is lost forever."** Adams explains that some things can be replaced, but that once the government takes away people's freedom, liberty can't be replaced.

13. **The correct answer is (D).** John responds to Abigail's news in a previous letter by commenting about her taking precaution in finding a secure place to stay should it become unsafe for her to stay in their home.

14. **The correct answer is the number of British troops who were killed.** John comments that Abigail has given him an account of the "numbers slain on the side of our enemies," implying that he had not known this detail.

15. **The correct answer is Valley Forge.** The map shows the American forces retreating and stopping at Valley Forge after retreating from Howe's forces.

16. **The correct answer is Philadelphia.** The map indicates the path of Washington's retreat, away from Philadelphia, which was left open to British attack. The city was under British occupation for nearly a year.

17. **The correct answer is (A).** We know that Abigail has told John of the doctor's illness because he says that he is upset at the news.

18. **The correct answer is (D).** In the context of this speech, King is referring to upward mobility, or the ability to rise to a higher social or economic position.

19. **The correct answer is (C).** King is advocating the opposite, that "[t]he marvelous new militancy which has engulfed the Negro community must not lead us to a distrust of all white people, for many of our white brothers, as evidenced by their presence here today, have come to realize that their destiny is tied up with our destiny."

20. **The correct answer is (D).** The second paragraph states that it "would be fatal for the nation to overlook the urgency of the moment." King is urging his listeners to continue working for civil rights and justice instead of just waiting for change to come.

21. **The correct answer is (C).** The main point of the third paragraph is that protests must remain peaceful. Uniting with white supporters is a secondary point.

22. The correct answer is revered. King was referring to the Lincoln Memorial as a revered spot, a deeply respected place.

23. The correct answer is (C). The passage states that the government recognizes women only when they are single and own taxable property.

24. The correct answer is (C). In this passage, the franchise refers specifically to the right to vote.

25. The correct answer is (B). Olive Gilbert is the author of the passage and offers her own opinion on events throughout.

26. The correct answer is (C). The latest date given in the passage shows that Sojourner Truth was thirty years old when she was meant to receive her "free papers," and the inclusion of the years 1826 and 1827 indicate that the events took place over the course of at least one year.

27. The correct answer is (C). The writers of the Declaration of Sentiments used the Declaration of Independence as a pattern to describe their dissatisfaction with their rights as citizens in comparison with those of men.

28. Answer (A) should be placed under Sojourner Truth, answers (B) and (D) should be placed under sponsors of the Woman's Rights Convention, and answer (C) should be placed in the center.

29. The correct answer is (B). Madison is arguing that the principle of separation of powers will be difficult to implement, but not as difficult as some people think.

30. The correct answer is (D). Henry says that the government will lack "sufficient energy" to keep the states united, and this argument applies to the checks and balances issue.

31. The correct answer is ineffective. While *inexpedient* can also mean something that is not beneficial, in this context it means ineffective.

32. The correct answer is (C). Madison is arguing for a separation of powers in order to prevent one branch or person having undue influence over others.

33. The correct answer is (D). Henry's primary concern is that ordinary citizens will suffer because the federal government will not work.

34. Answer (A) should be dragged into the center, as both support this idea. Answer (B) should be listed under Henry, and answers (C) and (D) should be listed under Madison.

35. The correct answer is (C). "It is for them more especially to know why they love their country, not because it is their country, but because it is the palladium of human liberty—the favoured scene of human improvement." Wright goes on to say that the citizens should love their country because they have control over its destiny.

36. The correct answer is (A). Francis Wright writes that American is made up of people in whose "veins . . . flows the blood of every people on the globe," meaning that it is a melting pot of nationalities.

37. Extended response. Answers will vary. You will find two sample essays on pages 103–105.

38. The correct answer is (A). Edit to ensure effective use of transitional words, conjunctive adverbs, and other words and phrases that support logic and clarity. *Friendly* and *focused* are words describing *environments*, while the sentence as is implies that *friendly* is modifying *focused* rather than *environments*.

39. **The correct answers are:** (B) Men are required to wear ties, (E) It is important to clean up after yourself, and (F) E-mail etiquette between co-workers is important.

40. **The correct answer is (B).** Edit to correct errors in pronoun usage, including pronoun–antecedent agreement, unclear pronoun references, and pronoun case. *Cell phones* is plural, so the pronoun should match in plurality: *them* should be used instead of *it*. Choice (A) does not change the pronoun reference and breaks up the sentence erroneously. Choice (C) makes the sentence a run-on, and choice (D) only switches the plurality of the antecedent and pronoun; it does not fix the sentence for pronoun–antecedent agreement.

41. **The correct answer is (D).** Edit to ensure parallelism and proper subordination and coordination. Choice (B) is incorrect, as removing a comma would create a run-on sentence. Adding *and* as in choice (C) would seem to correct the parallelism in the sentence, but if *do not wear* in the latter half of the sentence remains, it counteracts the parallelism created from adding *and*. Choice (D) is the only one that properly corrects the sentence without introducing additional errors.

42. **The correct answer is (A).** Edit to correct errors in straightforward subject-verb agreement. Choice (B) is incorrect, as removing the comma after *co-workers* would create a run-on sentence. Choice (C) only corrects one of the verbs, so the first half of the sentence is still incorrect. Choice (D) would introduce an additional error, breaking rules for possessives/plurals. Therefore, choice (A) is the only correct answer, properly fixing the subject/verb agreement in the sentence and making the verbs plural for the plural subject "e-mails".

43. **The correct answer is (C).** Edit to correct errors involving frequently confused words and homonyms. Choices (A) and (B) only fix half of the problem, while choice (C) fixes both. Choice (D) is erroneous.

44. **The correct answer is (C).** Edit to eliminate dangling or misplaced modifiers or illogical word order. Choice (A) creates a run-on. Choice (B) may not have errors, but it changes the intended meaning of the sentence. By changing *marked as* to *designated* in choice (C), it becomes clear that the *cupboards* are marked as shared food, not the individual food items: before, it was unclear as to what *marked* was modifying. Choice (D) makes the structure more confusing.

45. **The correct answer is (B).** Edit to correct errors involving frequently confused words and homonyms, including contractions. Choice (A) creates a run-on. Choice (B) changes both incorrect contractions. Choice (C) only fixes one incorrect contraction, and choice (D) does not fix either incorrect contraction.

46. **The correct answer is (D).** Edit to ensure correct use of capitalization. Choice (A) only fixes one of the capitalization problems. Choices (B) and (C) are erroneous, creating more problems, so choice (D) is the only correct choice. It fixes both instances of improper capitalization.

47. **The correct answer is (A).** Edit to eliminate nonstandard or informal usage. Choice (A) correctly uses *try to match* instead of *try and match*. Choice (B) uses the nonstandard and informal use of *try and* instead of *try to*. Choice (C) is the incorrect form of *to*. Choice (D) does not make sense.

48. **The correct answer is (B).** Edit to ensure correct use of punctuation (e.g., commas in a series or in appositives and other nonessential elements, end marks, and appropriate punctuation for clause separation). Choice (A) adds an unnecessary

comma after *details* and introduces a colon incorrectly. Choice (B) uses only one comma, making the sentence simple and clear without breaking it up awkwardly. Choice (C) ends with a question mark, making it interrogative, when it is a declarative sentence. Choice (D) changes *and makes it easier to get to know one another* into an independent clause, when it is a dependent clause that needs the pronoun *this* to function correctly.

49. **The correct answer is (C).** Edit to eliminate run-on sentences, fused sentences, or sentence fragments. Choice (A) is left as is and is a run-on lacking punctuation. Choice (B) introduces an incorrectly used semicolon. Choice (C) breaks up the sentences appropriately and does not use incorrect punctuation. Choice (D) uses an unnecessary number of commas, causing more breaks in the sentence, which makes it confusing.

Mathematical Reasoning

1. 16	16. (3, −4)	28. (B)
2. (C)	17. (C)	29. (D)
3. (A)	18. $\dfrac{W}{2}$	30. any point to the left of −1 on the number line
4. (D)		
5. 41	19. (D)	
6. (D)	20. (C)	31. $330p + 1200 \leq 8000$
7. (A)	21. increased; exhibited no clear trend	32. (C)
8. (A)	22. 16	33. (B)
9. (B)	23. 10^5	34. (A)
10. (B)		35. −2; 2
11. 1.5	24. (B)	36. (D)
12. (C)	25. close to the *y*-axis	37. (B)
13. (C)	26. (A)	
14. (A)	27. (D)	
15. 2.38		

1. **The correct answer is 16.** Let $C =$ the number of students enrolled in chemistry only. Let $P =$ the number of students in physics only. Let $B =$ the number of students in both chemistry and physics:

$C + P + B = 78$, so $47 + P + 15 = 78$.

$P = 16$

2. **The correct answer is (C).** Your first step is to convert mixed numbers to fractions:

$$\frac{9}{2} + \frac{15}{4} - \frac{12}{5}$$

The lowest common denominator is 20. Convert each fraction, then combine:

$$\frac{9}{2} + \frac{15}{4} - \frac{12}{5} = \frac{90 + 75 - 48}{20} = \frac{117}{20}$$

3. **The correct answer is (A).** The diagram shows that all sides of the hexagon are congruent. Therefore, $240 \div 6 = 40$.

4. **The correct answer is (D).** Any term raised to a negative power is the same as the reciprocal of the term—but raised to the *positive* power:

$$(-1)^{-2} + (-1)^2 = \frac{1}{(-1)^2} + 1 = \frac{1}{1} + 1 = 2$$

5. **The correct answer is 41.** If the average of the 5 games is 45, the sum of the 5 games must be equal to $45 \cdot 5 = 225$. Add the scores given: $54 + 60 + 28 + 42 = 184$ and then subtract this from 225: $225 - 184 = 41$.

6. **The correct answer is (D).** The sum of the lengths of any two sides of a triangle must be greater than the length of the third side. Thus, in the triangle at hand, the length of the longest side must be less than 15 inches.

7. **The correct answer is (A).**

$$|7 - 2| - |2 - 7| = |5| - |-5|$$
$$5 - 5 = 0$$

8. **The correct answer is (A).** To find the width of the rectangular box, you can use the equation $SA = 2(lh) + 2(lw) + 2(wh)$ or $248 = 2(4)(10) + 2(10)w + 2(w)(4)$. By isolating the variable, you find that $w = 6$.

9. **The correct answer is (B).** The corral is to be square, and so the length of any side equals $\sqrt{10,000} = 100$. Constructing one complete side, including both end posts, requires 11 posts (not 10) spaced 10 feet apart. Constructing two of the other three sides requires only 10 posts, while the fourth side requires only 9 posts since its end posts are already in place. The total number of posts needed is $11 + (2)(10) + 9 = 40$.

10. **The correct answer is (B).** $a^4 = 1296$. So $a = \sqrt[4]{1296} = 6$. (Apply the square-root operation twice.)

11. **The correct answer is 1.5.** In order to find the growth rate per day, first divide by 24 (the number of days):

0.36 meters $\div$ 24 = 0.015 meters

To convert to centimeters, shift the decimal point to the right by two places:

0.015 m = 1.5 cm

12. **The correct answer is (C).** The entire circle contains 360°, and so $y = 360 - x$.

13. **The correct answer is (C).** Factor out x on the left side of the equation: $x(x + 4) = 0$. There are two possible x-values, or roots: $x = 0$; $x = -4$.

14. **The correct answer is (A).** Add the two equations:

$$x + y = a$$
$$\underline{x - y = b}$$
$$2x = a + b$$
$$x = \frac{1}{2}(a + b)$$

15. **The correct answer is 2.38.** The region of the number line from 2.3 to 2.5 has been divided into 10 congruent regions. The distance from 2.3 to 2.5 is 0.2. Thus, the vertical marks are spaced at intervals of 0.02. Accordingly, B = 2.38.

16. **The correct answer is (3, –4).** When point A (3, 2), and point B (–3, 2) are connected, they form a horizontal line segment of length 6. Each side of the square must have a length of 6. The missing corner is 6 units below (3, 2), which puts it at (3, –4).

17. **The correct answer is (C).** Determine the answer systematically, beginning with the largest possible integer:

$7 + 1 + 1 + 1 = 10$

$5 + 3 + 1 + 1 = 10$

$3 + 3 + 3 + 1 = 10$

As you can see, there are three different ways.

18. **The correct answer is $\dfrac{W}{2}$.** The length of the bedroom (the longer room) is $2L$. Since the two areas both equal $L \times W$, the width of the bedroom must be $\dfrac{W}{2}$.

19. **The correct answer is (D).** Twice the sum of 3 and the number N is written as $2(3 + N)$, or $6 + 2N$. The phrase "1 less than 3 times the number N" is written as $3N - 1$.

20. **The correct answer is (C).** For each year, compare the heights of the two dark bars. The year 2008 was the only one among the four choices for which Country Y's imports (about \$39 billion) were less than twice Country X's imports (about \$21 billion).

21. **The correct answers are increased and exhibited no clear trend.** To answer this question, examine the right bar for each of the six years shown. The size of the dark portion (Country Y's imports) increases up to 2008 and then remains about the same from 2008 through 2009. It then increases again from 2009 to 2010. So the general trend over the six-year period was for the value of imports to increase. The size of the bar's light portion (Country Y's exports) decreases through 2007, then increases through 2009, and then decreases from 2009 to 2010. So there is no clear export trend for the six-year period as a whole.

22. **The correct answer is 16.** Assuming the teepee is symmetrical and level, it is an isosceles triangle. Any isosceles triangle can be split into two right angles, so we can use the Pythagorean theorem to find the unknown measurements.

Side A is 15 meters. $A^2 = 225$ meters. Side C is 17 meters. $C^2 = 289$ meters.

$$225 + B^2 = 289$$
$$B^2 = 289 - 225$$
$$B^2 = 64$$
$$B = 8$$

This is the radius, not the diameter, so we need to multiply it by 2.

The diameter is 16.

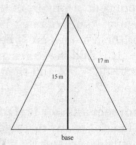

23. **The correct answer is $\dfrac{10^5}{1}$, or 10^5.** When multiplying the numbers in the numerator, add the exponents: $10^6 \cdot 10^4 = 10^{6+4} = 10^{10}$. Divide this by the denominator. When dividing, subtract the exponents: $10^{10} \div 10^5 = 10^5$.

24. **The correct answer is (B).** The volume of a cylinder is $\pi r^2 h$, where r is the radius and h is the height. The height is 20 cm and the volume is 2880 cm^3. Substitute these values into the formula for the volume to calculate the radius:

$$\pi r^2 20 = 2880\pi$$
$$r^2 \cdot 20 = 2880$$
$$r^2 = 144$$
$$r = 12$$

The radius is 12, so the diameter is 2 times the radius, or 24.

25. **The correct answer is anywhere very close to the *y*-axis.** A high negative correlation means that the data slants down to the right as shown below. The last data point would be very close to the horizontal *y*-axis above the arrow.

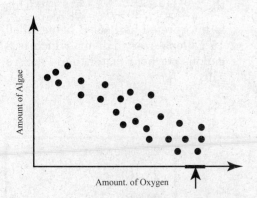

26. **The correct answer is (A).** Multiply −4 by each of the terms in parentheses: $-4 \times 2a = -8a$ and $-4 \times (-b) = 4b$. Add the two products: $-8a + 4b$.

27. **The correct answer is (D).** The product of the first terms of each factor must be $2x^2$ and the sign of the last term is negative, so the factors must be $2x$ and x and the operators must be different, which gives us: $(2x - \ )(x + \ )$ or $(2x + \ )(x - \ )$. The product of the second term in each factor is -6, so our choices are the factors of 6: 1, 2, 3, and 6. Try 1 and 6 first. Neither factor set works. Trying 2 and 3, we see that $(2x + 3)(x - 2)$ works.

28. **The correct answer is (B).** For each tile, Herman needs $c^2 + x$ centimeters of cloth. He needs this much cloth for each of 20 tiles, so he must multiply this expression by 20.

    $20(c^2 + x) = 20c^2 + 20x$

29. **The correct answer is (D).** Expand the expression on the left side of the equation by distributing $2A$: $(2A \times 3x) + (2A \times 2B) = 6Ax + 4AB = 12$. Isolate the x term by subtracting $4AB$ from both sides and then dividing both sides by $6A$.

30. **The correct answer is any point to the left of −1 on the number line.** Simplify the inequality by adding 3 to both sides: $-2x > 2$ and then dividing by −2:

    $$\frac{-2x}{-2} > \frac{2}{-2}$$

    $$x < -1$$

    (Remember to change the inequality sign when dividing by a negative.)

31. **The correct answer is $330p + 1200 \leq 8000$.** First calculate the cost for a single sign post. It is $240 plus $60 multiplied by 1.5: $240 + (60)(1.5) = 240 + 90 = 330$. Each sign post costs $330, so p sign posts cost $330p$. Add the retainer fee of $1,200: $330p + 1200$ to calculate the total cost of p sign posts. This number must be less than or equal to, $\leq$, 8000.

32. **The correct answer is (C).** The number of units sold is given as $45{,}000 − 160p$. Multiply this expression by the selling price of each unit, p:

    $(45{,}000 − 160p)(p) = 45{,}000p − 160p^2$ = total sales.

33. **The correct answer is (B).** The line Sal draws to represent the demand for pizza must go up, or rise, 3 units for every 8 unit increase in the number of children, which is the horizontal run on this graph. The slope of a line is the rise over the run, or $\frac{\text{rise}}{\text{run}} = \frac{3}{8}$.

34. **The correct answer is (A).** To figure out which line is graphed, find the *y*-intercept of the graph. In the point-slope format of the equation of a line, $y = mx + b$, the *y*-intercept is equal to the value of b, which in this case is −3.

35. **The correct answers are −2 and 2.** This is the graph of a positive cubic function. However, it is decreasing with a negative slope in the interval $-2 \leq x \leq 2$.

36. The correct answer is (D). First calculate the slope by finding the difference in the y-values divided by the difference in the x-values: $\dfrac{5-2}{-4-2} = \dfrac{3}{-6} = -\dfrac{1}{2}$. Insert a pair of x, y values and the slope into the point-slope form of a line: $2 = -\dfrac{1}{2}(2) + b$ to find the value of b: $2 = -1 + b$, $b = 3$. The equation is $y = -\dfrac{1}{2}x + 3$.

37. The correct answer is (B). To calculate the rate for Pool B, figure out the slope of the line in the graph. Take 2 points to calculate slope: $(0, 0)$ and $(30, 2)$. Find the difference in the y-values divided by the difference in the x-values: $\dfrac{2-0}{30-0} = \dfrac{2}{30} = \dfrac{1}{15}$. This is interpreted as Pool B being filled 15 gallons every 1 hour, which is 3 gallons per hour faster than Pool A's rate.

Science

1. (B)	11. (A)	22. 1 percent
2. (A)	12. (C)	23. (C)
3. (D)	13. (A)	24. (B)
4. (B)	14. (A)	25. (D)
5. (A)	15. (B)	26. (C)
6. positions G and C	16. (A)	27. 720 calories
7. by acquiring an electron	17. (B)	28. gravity
	18. (A)	29. (B)
8. 7	19. pressure	30. (D)
9. boxes A, C, D	20. (D)	
10. (C)	21. Simple Squamous	

1. The correct answer is (B). With added growth stimulation, the stem's shady side will grow vertically at a faster rate than the stem's sunny side. As a result, the stem will bend toward the light.

2. The correct answer is (A). The time it takes for crest X to reach line A is three-fourths the wave's period (the time it would take for crest X to reach the point of the next crest in the figure). Hence the wave's period is 4 seconds. Line B is located one full wavelength plus three fourths of a second wavelength to the right of point X. Multiply that distance by the wave's period:

$$1\dfrac{3}{4} \times 4 = 7 \text{ seconds}$$

3. The correct answer is (D). The chemical response from the damaged tissue initiates the chain of responses that results in a blood clot that minimizes blood loss.

4. The correct answer is (B). All four changes described in the passage are the result of human activity: clear-cutting forests, channeling fertilizer and sewage into rivers and oceans, overusing air pollutants, and allowing livestock to overgraze grasslands.

5. **The correct answer is (A).** If you know the altitude of the plane, along with the delay between the time the plane passes overhead and the time you hear the jet engines, you can determine the speed of sound by dividing the altitude by the time delay. Observing a sprinter's speed in reacting to a starter's pistol, choice (B) might be another way to measure the speed of sound. However, the pistol and sprinter might be too close to each other to create a measurable delay; what's more, the sprinter's reaction time will depend on other factors as well.

6. **Positions G and C are correct.** When the moon is at either position C or G, a person directly below the Moon would observe that half of the Moon's facing surface is lit by the Sun. Position A shows the new moon phase (none of the facing surface is lit). Position E shows the full Moon phase (unless a lunar eclipse is occurring). Positions B and H show crescent Moon phases (most of the facing surface is unlit). Positions D and F show autumn moon phases (most of the facing surface is lit).

7. **The correct answer is by acquiring an electron.** In the case of an atom whose outer shell is not complete, one or more electrons might acquire an electron from the outer shell of another atom. When this occurs, the acquiring atom becomes negatively charged (a negative ion), while the transferring atom becomes positively charged (a positive ion).

8. **The correct answer is 7.** Genotypes RR and Rr are expressed as red. All but one of the eight offspring shown in the diagram are red.

9. **The correct answer is boxes A, C, and D.** The diagram shows that pairing Rr with Rr, the choice provided in C, produces one rr (white) offspring. Although the diagram does not show either pairing provided in A or D, we cannot rule out the possibility that either or both of these pairings would produce a white offspring.

10. **The correct answer is (C).** Onion bulbs grow underground, where chloroplasts would serve no function. It is the onion's vertical shoot that traps the Sun's energy and makes food.

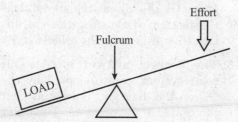

11. **The correct answer is (A).** By using a lever of the sort shown in the illustration, you can increase the output force (moving the load) applying the same amount of, or possibly less, input force (effort).

12. **The correct answer is (C).** The stork's long bill helps it survive by allowing it to pluck its prey from just below the water's surface. This feature is a classic evolutionary adaptation.

13. **The correct answer is (A).** Serine contains 3 oxygen atoms, while cysteine contains only 2.

14. **The correct answer is (A).** The gender of human offspring is determined solely by the male parent. The female can only donate an X chromosome, while the male can donate either a Y or X chromosome. Thus, it is the male that determines the gender of the offspring.

15. **The correct answer is (B).** Since the magnetic North Pole is moving from Canada toward Russia, it is in a different location from the geographic North Pole. And since the magnetic North Pole is shifting, the magnetic South Pole must be shifting as well.

16. **The correct answer is (A).** After exceeding carrying capacity, the still-growing population lacks enough re-

sources to support its current growth rate.

17. **The correct answer is (B).** The temperature scale is given across the top of the diagram. Temperatures *decrease* from left to right, so that stars with the lowest surface temperatures are plotted at the right end of the diagram. Giant stars are clustered near the diagram's right side, which means that they are among the coldest stars.

18. **The correct answer is (A).** Our solar system's Sun (denoted by the "X" on the diagram) is located near the center of the diagram. The other plotted points are distributed fairly equally above and below X, as well as to the left and to the right of X. This distribution tells you that the Sun is about average, or typical, in both its brightness (measured on the vertical scale) and its surface temperature (measured on the horizontal scale).

19. **The correct answer is pressure.** If the tube were open at both ends, the level of the liquid would be the same on both sides of the "U" in the tube, since the atmospheric air would be exerting equal pressure on both ends. But the higher level on the right side of the "U" indicates that the pressure from the air tank is greater than the atmospheric pressure. (The various level marks up and down the tube provide a quantitative measure of that pressure.)

20. **The correct answer is (D).** Choice (D) is the only one that makes sense. In Phase 3 of development, the ripened pericap (fruit) attracts animals, and they, of course, eat the fruit. The droppings of these animals spread the fruit's seeds, from which new plants of the same type grow.

21. **The correct answer is Simple Squamous.** An air sac within a lung functions by taking in oxygen, which it passes through its lining to blood vessels, which pass carbon dioxide back through the lining to be expelled into the air. To accomplish the exchange, the lining must be single layered, thin, and leaky (diffuse). The tissue shown as simple squamous best serves this purpose.

22. **The correct answer is 1 percent.** One percent (1%) of the producer's energy is passed along to primary consumers. Then, 10% of that 1%, or 0.1% of the producer's energy, is passed along to secondary consumers.

23. **The correct answer is (C).** The presence of dentritivores as well as animals that consume both plants and animals implies a complex, interconnected system resembling a web.

24. **The correct answer is (B).** Following the arrows in the illustration shows that cold water in the North Atlantic Ocean (near the North Pole) sinks and then travels south toward the equator, warming and mixing with warmer water along the way. Once warmer, that water rises to the surface and moves northward to where it started in the North Atlantic.

25. **The correct answer is (D).** The diagram indicates that cold water in the North Atlantic sinks. The diagram also shows warmer water near the equator rising to the surface. Together, these two pieces of information help show that cold water is denser than warm water.

26. **The correct answer is (C).** Longer hind legs enhance a frog's jumping ability, while a strong shoulder girdle and rigid spine help support the jump's landing. These abilities are useful only when moving about on land.

27. **The correct answer is 720 calories.** 80 calories represents what is needed to change the state from ice to water (the lower plateau); 100 calories are needed to raise the temperature from 0°C to 100°C, and an additional 540 calories are needed to change the

water into steam. The total amount of heat energy required is 720 calories.

28. **The correct answer is gravity.** Scientists infer the existence of dark matter from how gravity operates on light matter. Thus their understanding of dark matter is theoretical.

29. **The correct answer is (B).** The illustration indicates that some of the infrared radiation emitted from the Earth's surface is absorbed by gas molecules in the atmosphere, which then re-emit that radiation. Some of this radiation returns to the Earth's surface again, and so a portion of the energy radiated from the Earth never escapes the atmosphere.

30. **The correct answer is (D).** The volcano loses height as its material erodes from the top down. Eventually, the top of the volcano is at sea level, while coral has built up just above that level. The volcano's cavity fills with water, forming a lagoon. (Coral also accumulates in the lagoon.)

Social Studies

1. (B)	13. (D)	24. (B)
2. (A)	14. (D)	25. (D)
3. (B)	15. Valley Forge	26. (C)
4. (D)	16. Philadelphia	27. break tie votes
5. (B)	17. (B)	28. (A)
6. (D)	18. (A)	29. Trail of Tears
7. (C)	19. (C)	30. (A)
8. (D)	20. (A)	31. (A)
9. See explanation below.	21. (C)	32. (D)
10. clergy	22. (B)	33. (B)
11. reception	23. (C)	34. (B)
12. $10,000; about 60 percent		

1. **The correct answer is (B).** Although they live in the same region, the people of Great Britain generally subscribe to Protestantism, while the majority of Irish are Catholic. The other statements are untrue conclusions about the Irish and British experience of region and place.

2. **The correct answer is (A).** While Native Americans of the Northwest Coast relied heavily on fishing as their food source, both they and the Native Americans of the Eastern Woodlands farmed. Both the nations of the Eastern Woodlands and Pacific Northwest lived in longhouses, so choice (B) is wrong. Since the Pacific Northwest nations carved totem poles, choice (C) incorrect. From the information given, it's impossible to tell which group of Native Americans

was more advanced—a term that is very subjective and depends on how a person defines it—so choice (D) is incorrect.

3. **The correct answer is (B).** Madison argued that the government's powers should be divided among legislative, executive, and judicial branches of government and that each of these branches should "have a will of its own" or, in other words, be independent. He wanted to separate the branches, but not divide or separate leaders within those branches, choice (A). Since the two quotes do not mention a bill of rights, we don't know his position on a bill of rights, choice (C). The statement in choice (D) contradicts his belief that each branch of government should be independent and "have a will of its own."

4. **The correct answer is (D).** Madison's goal was to keep government from being oppressive, not to promote equality or democracy. Madison himself had slaves and supported limiting the right to vote to property owners, so neither equality, choice (A), nor democracy, choice (B), were values he held. Although Madison later became president, he's never been accused of trying to use the debate over the Constitution as a means of gaining power for himself, choice (C).

5. **The correct answer is (B).** The word "suffered" is a key word in indicating the author's bias.

6. **The correct answer is (D).** The cartoon illustrates the terrorizing of freed blacks by the Ku Klux Klan and other white reactionary groups.

7. **The correct answer is (C).** Nothing in the cartoon remotely suggests that freed slaves were being treated as equals, choice (A); or that their lives had improved, choice (B); or that the Klan helped them, choice (D). To the contrary, the cartoon suggests a continuing struggle for true equality.

8. **The correct answer is (D).** The use of the word "should" in the statement in choice (D) indicates it is not a fact, but rather a judgment or opinion. All the other answer choices are statements of facts broadly accepted as true.

9. As you review your essay, check for the following:

   - Do I have a clear thesis statement that responds exactly to what the prompt asks?

   - Is my essay well organized?

   - Have I analyzed the evidence carefully? Do I use evidence to support my ideas rather than just summarize what the documents are about?

   - Do I provide effective transitions between sections by noting how each section relates to the one before it (e.g., further clarification, contrast)?

   - Do I provide a thoughtful conclusion to my essay?

   You will find two sample essays on pages 105–107.

10. **The correct answer is clergy.** According to the graph, the clergy costs $113 which is between the cost of the limousine ($192) and the cost of the groom's clothing ($77).

11. **The correct answer is reception.** Since the reception is by far the greatest single expense, the greatest savings probably could be made there.

12. **The correct answer is $10,000; about 60 percent.** The wedding costs exactly $10,055, so an average wedding costs slightly more than $10,000. Also, if about $10,000 is the cost of the wedding, and the cost of the reception was just under $6000, then a little more than half, or about 60 percent, of the total cost was for the reception.

13. **The correct answer is (D).** The U.S. District Courts (of which there are 89 districts) have original jurisdiction

and conduct trials in cases involving federal laws and regulations. State supreme courts, choice (C), do not have original jurisdiction and cannot conduct trials. The Supreme Court, choice (B), has original jurisdiction only in special cases. State trial courts, choice (A), generally take cases involving state laws, not federal laws.

14. **The correct answer is (D).** Appointing based on "merit" means that a position is given to the person most qualified to perform it. One way to determine which applicants are best qualified for a job is by administering an appropriate exam. (In fact, civil service exams were established by the Pendleton Civil Service Reform Act.)

15. **The correct answer is Valley Forge.** The map shows the American forces retreating and stopping at Valley Forge after retreating from Howe's forces.

16. **The correct answer is Philadelphia.** The map indicates the path of Washington's retreat, away from Philadelphia, which was left open to British attack. The city was under British occupation for nearly a year.

17. **The correct answer is (B).** The belief underlying the New Deal was that government should create jobs to stimulate the economy. The New Deal brought more, not less, government regulation of business, choice (A). Stimulating the economy by creating jobs was deemed more important than balancing the budget, choice (C). Raising taxes would have hurt the economy and was not part of most New Deal programs, choice (D).

18. **The correct answer is (A).** Since the person has a bank account, the establishment of the FDIC would guarantee that his or her money in the bank would be safe. A resident of New York City would not be directly affected by the Farm Mortgage Re-

financing Act, choice (C). Since the person is actively employed, he or she would not be directly affected by the Civilian Conservation Corps, choice (B), or the Social Security Act, choice (D).

19. **The correct answer is (C).** As the passage notes, in terms of what a U.S. dollar can buy, its value has declined steadily since 1950. Although 1967 does not appear in the actual illustration, it is the only year listed among the choices that could be the base year used for comparison with the others.

20. **The correct answer is (A).** The growing buying power of the Euro compared to the U.S. dollar means that goods and services in the United States are relatively inexpensive to Europeans. It makes sense that they would take advantage of the weak U.S. dollar by spending their money here.

21. **The correct answer is (C).** President Kennedy was speaking in broad terms of the Cold War struggle against Soviet expansion. We can assume he wanted Americans to support this struggle in some way. Fighting in the military, choice (D), joining the Peace Corps, choice (B), and paying taxes, choice (A), might all be ways of supporting this struggle, but Kennedy wasn't just thinking of one of these things in particular, and the question specifically asks for the "broad" goal.

22. **The correct answer is (B).** The first passage records Marie's delight in observing "the lovely sight" of the glowing tubes that glowed "like faint fairy lights."

23. **The correct answer is (C).** In the course of the many hours in the laboratory, the Curies absorbed toxic amounts of radiation.

24. **The correct answer is (B).** In World War I, Russia, Britain, France, Italy,

and the United States were allied against Germany and Turkey.

25. **The correct answer is (D).** The timeline shows that most nations entered the war in support of their allies rather than each nation being attached, choice (A); or because of the assassination, choice (B); or by being invaded, choice (C).

26. **The correct answer is (C).** "No taxation without representation" was the motto of all Sons of Liberty groups, which shows a desire to have a say in the decisions of the British government.

27. **The correct answer is break tie votes.** The vice president does not vote in the Senate unless it is to break a tie vote.

28. **The correct answer is (A).** The United States wanted to help rebuild Western European nations so the United States, not the Soviets, would have influence over them. The cartoon conveys this idea. None of the other choices are as well supported by the cartoon.

29. **The correct answer is Trail of Tears.** The Cherokees viewed their forced migration with great bitterness and sorrow.

30. **The correct answer is (A).** Jose bartered with a store owner. He would offer help with the store's books in exchange for space.

31. **The correct answer is (A).** Rising property taxes forced the closure of many of the Paivo family's restaurants.

32. **The correct answer is (D).** The Ninth and Tenth Amendments give powers not otherwise described to the people and to the states.

33. **The correct answer is (B).** The Third Amendment protects citizens from having to house and feed troops during peacetime.

34. **The correct answer is (B).** This is an example of how many important developments in history happen gradually and can't easily be dated. Historians, who recognize their work is not scientific or exact, are generally more interested in gradual or underlying change than simple events and dates, so choice (C) is incorrect. There seldom is complete agreement among historians on either the meaning of specific events, choice (A), or general interpretations of history, choice (D).

Reasoning Through Language Arts Extended Response Sample Essays

High-Scoring Essay

Art should be defended from attacks on its importance in education. In educating our youth, the arts should continue to be taught for the important skills of dexterity and creativity. Many real-world problems require creative approaches to solving them and the arts teach students to think and act creatively. Indeed, reality is multi-faceted and the arts aid students in understanding and interpreting various representations of reality. Teaching students the arts is an important aspect of their education that should not be dismissed.

Teaching the arts encourages creativity in application to problem solving. Very few problems have one path to a solution; often many paths can lead to the correct solution. Encouraging students to think outside the box will help lead them to the correct answer. Individual students learn best in different ways and have skills that are stronger in one area than another. By encouraging different approaches to the same problem, students are more likely to be able to rely on their strengths rather than their weaknesses. Creativity allows students to apply different skills to the same problem.

The arts develop dexterity and motor-skills that are often overlooked in schools. Much teaching and learning is done with technology that requires little manual dexterity, but the arts require and teach fine motor skills. While it may be argued that technology encourages different motor skills rather than none at all, it is certain that the motor skills needed for the fine arts are finer than those required for a typist or for other devices. This craftsmanship can prepare students for vocations other than office-jobs and may have health benefits for being relaxing.

Finally, reality is multi-faceted and complex, and the arts teach students to think about complex issues in diverse ways. As the essay "The Importance of Art in Child Development" states, "A teacher can properly describe the characteristics of reality, and the student is more likely to accurately interpret these representations." In philosophy, this describing is especially important when encountering complex problems. In real life, too, for example in marketing, the ability to describe and interpret descriptions plays an important role, and the arts foster these skills.

It is no wonder, then, that according to the essay "The Importance of Art in Child Development," students who participated in the arts in school were more likely to have achievements in other fields such as science or literature. The arts are related to all fields in their usefulness and in the skills they teach.

EXPLANATION

This essay is high-scoring because it generates logical text-based arguments or explanations and cites relevant, specific, and sufficient evidence from source texts to support them. It contains ideas that are thoroughly and logically developed, with full elaboration of main ideas; contains purposeful, logical progression of ideas with details closely tied to their main points; establishes an effective organizational structure; applies transitional devices strategically and effectively; chooses words purposefully and carefully; applies advanced vocabulary; strategically applies awareness of audience and purpose of the task to enhance meaning throughout the response. It demonstrates competent and fluent application of conventions; demonstrates effectively varied sentence structure and an overall fluency that enhances clarity.

Specifically, the essay argues that the arts are still useful in education for their fostering of unique skills that are suitable to the real world and the abstract. It develops these ideas progressively with details closely tied to their main points (e.g., the motor skills acquired by the arts could be used in a variety of vocations); and it presents arguments against its case in order to respond to them (e.g., that technology encourages different motor skills). The essay contains advanced vocabulary.

Low-Scoring Essay

There are many reasons why we should continue to teach art in school. Art is not just beautiful it is also useful. Art teaches skills we would not otherwise learn. There are some things technology cannot impart. I think all students should be required to study the arts.

The arts are important to our cultural heritage. You have to know a lot about art history to enjoy a visit to the museum. The different styles and artists have evolved over the centuries. Studying art history can teach students an appreciation for the art their culture has produced. It can also teach students an appreciation for other cultures' arts.

Technology is more useful than art, but it does not provide the same lessons. Technology helps to get things done; art is more beautiful to admire. Technology helps prepare students for office work as in computer skills. Art on the other hand prepares the student for work at a museum. Both are important for society but one is more useful than the other.

There are concepts that can only be learned in an art class, such as color, shape, texture. These visual concepts can help people learn to interpret visual information in a variety of ways. Art history is also important to know for conversation, which can help getting a job.

When it comes to getting a job, that's one thing art history won't help you with. You might impress your employer if you know art in depth, but he or she will not hire you for that reason. It is much more important to have a well-written resume and cover letter. These are skills that you can learn in school instead of art. But that does not mean art should not be taught in school. Art should still be taught for its cultural value and beauty.

EXPLANATION

This essay does not attempt to create an argument; cites minimal to no evidence from source texts. The essay attempts to analyze the issue and assess the validity of the arguments in source texts, but demonstrates minimal or no understanding of the given arguments. It contains ideas that are insufficiently or illogically developed, with little elaboration on main ideas; contains an unclear progression of ideas; establishes no discernable organizational structure. The essay demonstrates minimal control of basic conventions; demonstrates consistently flawed sentence structure.

Specifically, this essay tries to develop the claim that "we should continue to teach art in school," but goes off in a variety of directions, not all of which are connected to the thesis, i.e. there is no discernible argument. The essay does not use the source texts, and does not analyze the given arguments. There is no organizational structure and no progression of ideas; if anything, the essay contradicts itself and forms a conclusion unrelated to the given arguments.

Social Studies Extended Response Sample Essays

High-Scoring Essay

In Michael Drayton's poem, explorers are idealized as the worthy representatives of the land, sent on a noble mission to subdue and harvest the fruits of the soil of Virginia. But in John Smith's account of actual life there, we find these men are despairing of their situation and struggling to maintain their livelihoods. While they are noble-minded, the facts of their situation in Captain Smith's account negate Drayton's idealized view of their mission.

In his poem, Drayton praises the explorers as "worthy of your country's name." They are doing a noble deed by going "to subdue" while Britons "lurk here at home with shame." Yet in Captain Smith's account, the explorers barely have cabins to reside in. Drayton's noble conceit of the Britons is extended, however, by Captain Smith's acknowledgment that the food they obtained from trading with the Indians went first to children or "any that show extraordinary kindness."

Drayton equates these men with "minds," but in Smith's account we hear of how they used up their rations or provisions in short time and were left almost without food. Drayton sees them "cheerfully at sea," but we know that when they arrived, many men were suffering to the point they "would rather starve and rot with idleness, then be persuaded to do anything for their own relief." Instead of being "worthy of their country's name," one of the first things we hear about from Captain Smith is how they needed to elect a new president of the mission after their current unpopular president was deposed.

Finally, Drayton sees these men as harvesters of the soil, but this image is negated by the fact that the explorers traded for their food with the Indians. The only commodity they had were iron chisels, which give an image of chipping away at something like a statue, rather than unveiling "Earth's only paradise" as Drayton imagines them as doing.

EXPLANATION

This is a high scoring essay because it meets the generates a text-based argument that demonstrates a clear understanding of the historical relationships among ideas, events, and figures as presented in the source texts and the contexts from which they are drawn i.e., Drayton's poem glorifying British explorers vs. John Smith's account of the problems they faced. The essay also cites relevant and specific evidence that an argument. It is well connected to both the prompt and the source texts. In addition it contains a sensible progression of ideas with understandable connections between details and main ideas (i.e., showing how Smith's account negates or extends Drayton's). It also contains ideas that are developed and generally logical. The essay demonstrates appropriate awareness of audience and the purpose of the task as well as adequate applications of conventions. The essay is written with largely correct sentence structure with variance from sentence to sentence and is fluent and clear.

Low-Scoring Essay

In Michael Drayton's poem, explorers are strong, happy souls who are destined to greatness in the new land. In Captain John Smith's history, the explorers are not strong or happy but weak and sick. Many of them have died. Michael Drayton's poem is idealistic while John Smith's account is realistic. John Smith talks about the Indians who lived in the new lands but Michael Drayton's piece does not mention them.

In Michael Drayton's poem the explorers are heroic and honorable, but in John Smith's account they are weak and sick. They can't go fishing because of the weather and they have to trade for food with the Indians who the poem never mentions. John Smith admits they ran out of food but Michael Drayton never thought about these necessities.

John Smith mentions that they elected a new president because the old one was unpopular, but Michael Drayton suggests that these men are "worthy of their country's name." Michael Drayton's imagery is of a ship sailing for the new land, but in John Smith's account they have already arrived. It is a problem to get food and shelter.

In conclusion Michael Drayton shows the explorers as happy sailors, but John Smith shows them living in misery. While Michael Drayton insists they are patriots, John Smith shows them to be full of "malice, grudging and muttering."

EXPLANATION

This essay is a low-scoring essay because it demonstrates minimal understanding of the relationship among ideas, events, and figures as presented in the source texts (i.e., does not move past the premise that "Drayton's poem is idealistic while John Smith's account is realistic."). It has some evidence from primary and source texts, but contains an unclear or no apparent progression of ideas. The ideas are also insufficiently developed or illogical (i.e., Drayton's poem is idealistic, Smith's account is realistic). It demonstrates minimal control of basic conventions and contains severe and frequent errors in mechanics and conventions.

ARE YOU READY TO TAKE THE GED® TEST?

Now that you have spent a great deal of time and effort studying for the GED® and taking this Practice Test, hopefully you are well-prepared to take the GED® test. But, it's best to make sure that you are completely ready. Check your scores from this Practice Test on the table below to see where you stand.

	All Set—Well-Prepared	Possibly Ready	Need More Preparation
Reasoning Through Language Arts	37–49	25–36	0–24
Mathematical Reasoning	26–34	17–25	0–16
Science	22–30	17–21	0–16
Social Studies	28–37	18–27	0–17

If your scores are in the "All Set—Well-Prepared" column, you are probably ready to take the actual GED® test, and you should apply to take the test soon. If some of your scores are in the "Possibly Ready" column, you should focus your study on those areas where you need to improve most. "Possibly Ready" means that you are probably ready enough to earn a GED® diploma, but it's not a bad idea to spend a little more time brushing up and improving your chances to pass the actual GED® test.

If any of your scores fell in the lowest category, take more time to review the pertinent chapters in this book—and in any high school text books, if necessary. Good luck!

PART III

REASONING THROUGH LANGUAGE ARTS

...ng Reading
...ehension

> ### ...ING THROUGH LANGUAGE ARTS
> ### ...COMPREHENSION IN A NUTSHELL
>
> ...s for the entire Reasoning Through Language
> ...5 minutes for the Extended Response as well as a
>
> ...ect 6 to 8 (the number can vary)
>
> ...400–900 words
>
> ...: 49 questions total for Reading Comprehension,
> ...d Writing (33 multiple choice, 5 drop down, 5 fill
> ...op, and 1 extended response)
>
> ...passage: Expect 6 to 8 (the number can vary)

...ING THROUGH LANGUAGE ARTS
...MPREHENSION

...uage Arts Test gauges your ability to understand, ..., and apply information contained in nonfiction as texts... ...sists of several reading passages, each one followed ... questions. Passages are drawn from a wide variety...

...gar...ess...f w...t s... as...ge you're dealing with, the questions will all cover ...basic reading skills. Here is the breakdown of the broad skill areas covered by the test questions. As indicated by the percentage numbers, some areas receive greater emphasis than others.

- **Comprehension (20 percent):** Understanding and recalling specific information from the passage

- **Analysis and Interpretation (30–35 percent):** Understanding what is suggested or implied in the passage and drawing reasonable inferences and conclusions from passage information

- **Evaluation and Synthesis (30–35 percent):** Understanding the passage's central idea and concern; inferring the author's intent or purpose; recognizing the purpose of and relationships among various parts of the passage; characterizing the passage as a whole

- **Application (15 percent):** Applying what is stated and implied in the passage to other contexts; applying the author's reasoning to other situations

During the test, expect several passages and 6 to 8 questions per passage—49 questions in total, which include the language conventions questions and extended response. Each passage will be 400 to 900 words in length (about one to two pages, on average). One feature common to all passages is that every fifth line of each passage will be numbered. Some questions might refer to portions of the passage by line number.

In the pages ahead, you'll learn how to read and understand the various types of fiction and nonfiction passages you'll encounter on the test. For each type, you'll read sample passages and attempt GED® test-style questions based on them. At the end of the lesson, you'll review some general strategies—ones that apply to every kind of reading passage.

UNDERSTANDING NONFICTION

A written work of **nonfiction** is one that involves real people and events, either past or present. Nonfiction can take a variety of different forms, from a brief article or diary entry to a book or even a multivolume work. On the GED® Reasoning Through Language Arts Test, you can expect at least four nonfiction reading passages involving informational text. Each passage will range from about 400–900 words in length. The passage may provide an entire work if it is brief, or it may be excerpted from a longer work. GED® test nonfiction passages reflect real-world experiences that are drawn from the following categories:

- Informational science passages that revolve around human health and living systems and energy and related systems;

- Informational social studies passages that are excerpts from or texts related to the theme "the Great American Conversation." These could include excerpts from historical documents, public speeches, Supreme Court decisions, and other primary or secondary documents that reflect concepts in America history, civics, and culture.

- Informational workplace passages are examples of documents from real-life situations. They could include work-related documents—e.g., e-mails, procedural documents, cover letters, and so forth—as well as community-related documents—e.g., letters to the editor or public postings.

All categories of GED® test informational nonfiction text will present a **main idea** or **central point.** You might find that the main idea is neatly expressed in either the opening or closing sentences. Or you might need to synthesize all of the information in the text to determine the main idea. The main idea will be broad enough to encompass the entire text without going beyond or off the topic.

Related to the text's main idea (central point) is its **central concern** or focus. To determine a text's central concern, ask yourself what issue, problem, events, or developments the text mainly addresses. The central concern will embrace the text's main idea and all supporting information, without departing from the topic at hand. In other words, a text's central concern is one that is neither too broad nor too narrow in focus.

Also related to the text's main idea is the author's **primary purpose** or **objective**, as revealed in the text. In the case of a purely informational text, the primary purpose might be to:

- Inform of facts
- Summarize and apply concepts
- Relate observations
- Provide explanations

Some texts express an opinion or point of view. In these cases, the author is clearly interested in accomplishing more than simply presenting facts. The author is also trying to convince or persuade the reader (or listener) in some way. In this case, the primary purpose might be to:

- Argue for or defend a certain position on an issue
- Advocate for a cause or a course of action
- Promote an ideology or a value system
- State problems and recommend solutions
- Forecast, predict, or warn of future events

After reading a passage for the first time, think about what the author wrote. Ask yourself what the overall topic is and why the author might have written the text. Formulate a sentence or two that expresses the main idea. You may even wish to jot it down in your test booklet.

Understanding the main idea, central concern, and primary purpose of a passage will help you handle many different types of test questions—not just ones that ask "What is the main idea of the passage?" or "What is the central concern of the text?" For example, understanding the "big picture" will help you apply the author's viewpoint to new situations as well as to determine what else the author would agree and disagree with.

In informational text the main ideas are facts, which are supported by **reasons and examples.** As you read the text, try to follow the author's line of reasoning, from main idea to the evidence used to support it.

You might find it helpful to jot down supporting points, so you can answer questions about them without reading the passage again. But don't try to jot down or remember every small detail from the passage. Instead, note where different kinds of details are located in the passage, so you can find them quickly if you need them for answering certain questions.

In some passages, it may help to pay attention to the author's **attitude** toward the subject being discussed. For example, in a letter to the editor, speech, or essay, the author's attitude may be highly critical or judgmental, or it may be supportive, admiring, or even praising. In the following sections, you'll learn more about all of these types of nonfiction, and you'll learn how best to read nonfiction in order to understand it in ways that will help you most on the GED® test. For each category, you'll also read a variety of sample passages and answer GED® test-style questions based on them.

Informational Science

The informational science passages you will see on the GED® test are related to either human health and living systems or energy and related systems. They may include diagrams or graphics, and some may tend to be academic in nature. Others will be geared toward a more general audience, but they will be relevant to living in the twenty-first century.

These passages, like other general nonfiction texts, have a purpose with a main idea and supporting details, along with other general features that you will be asked to analyze. Passages in this category are designed to inform the reader and are usually objective; that is, they relate facts in order to support a scientific concept or idea.

The following passage provides the reader with specific information. As you read, note the main ideas and how they are connected. If you come across an unfamiliar scientific term, don't focus on its specific meaning; instead, try to analyze its context and how it fits into the rest of the text. Then try to answer the accompanying questions.

QUESTIONS 1–3 REFER TO THE FOLLOWING PASSAGE.

Obesity and Cancer Risk

Obesity is a condition in which a person has an abnormally high and unhealthy proportion of body fat.

To measure obesity, researchers commonly use a scale known as the body mass index (BMI). BMI is calculated by dividing a person's weight (in kilograms)
5 by their height (in meters) squared. BMI provides a more accurate measure of obesity or being overweight than weight alone.

Guidelines established by the National Institutes of Health (NIH) place adults age 20 and older into the following categories based on their BMI:

BMI	BMI CATEGORIES
Below 18.5	Underweight
18.5 to 24.9	Normal
25.0 to 29.9	Overweight
30.0 and above	Obese

The National Heart Lung and Blood Institute provides a BMI calculator.
10   For children and adolescents (less than 20 years of age), overweight and obesity are based on the Centers for Disease Control and Prevention's (CDC) BMI-for-age growth charts:

BMI	BMI CATEGORIES
BMI-for-age at or above sex-specific 85th percentile, but less than 95th percentile	Overweight
BMI-for-age at or above sex-specific 95th percentile	Obese

Compared with people of normal weight, those who are overweight or obese are at greater risk for many diseases, including diabetes, high blood pressure,
15   cardiovascular diseases, stroke, and certain cancers.

How common is overweight or obesity?
    Results from the 2007–2008 National Health and Nutrition Examination Survey (NHANES) show that 68 percent of U.S. adults age 20 years and older are overweight or obese. In 1988–1994, by contrast, only 56 percent of adults
20   age 20 and older were overweight or obese.
    In addition, the percentage of children who are overweight or obese has also increased. Among children and teens ages 2 to 19, 17 percent are estimated to be obese, based on the 2007–2008 survey. In 1988–1994, that figure was only 10 percent.

25   **What is known about the relationship between obesity and cancer?**
    Obesity is associated with increased risks of the following cancer types, and possibly others as well: esophagus, pancreas, colon and rectum, breast (after menopause), endometrium (lining of the uterus), kidney, thyroid, and gallbladder.
    One study, using NCI Surveillance, Epidemiology, and End Results (SEER)
30   data, estimated that in 2007 in the United States, about 34,000 new cases of cancer in men (4 percent) and 50,500 in women (7 percent) were due to obesity. The percentage of cases attributed to obesity varied widely for different cancer types but was as high as 40 percent for some cancers, particularly endometrial cancer and esophageal adenocarcinoma.
35   A projection of the future health and economic burden of obesity in 2030 esti- mated that continuation of existing trends in obesity will lead to about 500,000 additional cases of cancer in the United States by 2030. This analysis also found that if every adult reduced their BMI by 1 percent, which would be equivalent to a weight loss of roughly 1 kg (or 2.2 lbs) for an adult of average weight, this
40   would prevent the increase in the number of cancer cases and actually result in the *avoidance* of about 100,000 new cases of cancer.
    Several possible mechanisms have been suggested to explain the association of obesity with increased risk of certain cancers:
    • Fat tissue produces excess amounts of estrogen, high levels of which have
45   been associated with the risk of breast, endometrial, and some other cancers.

- Obese people often have increased levels of insulin and insulin-like growth factor-1 (IGF-1) [A protein made by the body that stimulates the growth of many types of cells.] in their blood (a condition known as hyperinsulinemia or insulin resistance), which may promote the development of certain
50   tumors in their blood.
- Fat cells produce hormones, called adipokines, that may stimulate or inhibit cell growth. For example, leptin, which is more abundant in obese people, seems to promote cell proliferation, whereas adiponectin, which is less abundant in obese people, may have antiproliferative effects.
55 - Fat cells may also have direct and indirect effects on other tumor growth regulators, including mammalian target of rapamycin (mTOR) [A protein that helps control several cell functions, including cell division and survival.] and AMP-activated protein kinase. [A type of enzyme (a protein that speeds up chemical reactions in the body).]
60 - Obese people often have chronic low-level, or "subacute," inflammation, which has been associated with increased cancer risk.

Other possible mechanisms include altered immune responses, effects on the nuclear factor kappa beta system, and oxidative stress. [A condition in which antioxidant levels are lower than normal.]

—This article is from Cancer.gov: National Cancer Institute website,
Obesity and Cancer Risk, January 3, 2012

1. Which of the following statements represents a reasonable conclusion you could draw from the passage?

   (A) Obesity is a medical condition that requires treatment.

   (B) Obese people are more likely to get some form of cancer and other diseases.

   (C) Fat cells have a negative effect on the body.

   (D) Obesity causes many types of cancer.

Although statement (A) may be true, the passage doesn't talk about treating obesity; it discusses the correlation between obesity and cancer and other illnesses. The passage describes the role of fat tissue and fat cells, which may be implicated in some cancers but are not always negative—it depends on the quantity of these cells. Obesity is not a cause of cancer, but obesity has medical consequences that increase the odds of contracting cancer. **The correct answer is (B).**

2. According to the passage, which statement is true?

   (A) The incidence of obesity in the United States is increasing in both adults and children.

   (B) If you lose weight you will not get cancer.

   (C) Fat cells make people obese.

   (D) The risk of getting cancer is the same for people who are overweight and those who are obese.

The passage cites statistics that indicate how the incidence of obesity has grown over the last two decades. The cancer risk is higher for people with obesity, and while losing weight can reduce that risk, it cannot eliminate it. Obese people have more fat cells, and the passage talks about how fat cells behave to increase the likelihood of tumor formation, but fat cells in and of themselves don't make people obese. Cancer risk is lower for people who are of normal weight. The passage says both people who are overweight and people who are obese are at higher risk for many different diseases, but the link it discusses is that between obesity and cancer. **The correct answer is (A).**

3. A person who is in the 90th percentile for their age and sex has a BMI of

   (A) below 18.5.

   (B) between 18.5 and 24.9.

   (C) between 25.0 and 29.9.

   (D) 30.0 or higher.

Reading both charts, we can put the data together. *Overweight* and *obesity* are the two categories shown with BMIs. A person in the 90th percentile is in the overweight category, which would mean he or she has a BMI of between 25.0 and 29.9. **The correct answer is (C).**

The next passage is about space and what scientists are learning about our solar system from space probes. As you read the passage, think about what you already know about our solar system. Look at the picture that accompanies the passage and read the caption. What information can you infer from the picture alone, without even reading the passage?

QUESTIONS 4–7 REFER TO THE FOLLOWING PASSAGE.

Mystery of the Missing Waves on Titan

One of the most shocking discoveries of the past 10 years is how much the landscape of Saturn's moon Titan resembles Earth. Like our own blue planet, the surface of Titan is dotted with lakes and seas; it has river channels, islands, mud, rain clouds and maybe even rainbows. The giant moon is undeniably wet.

5   The "water" on Titan is not, however, H_2O. With a surface temperature dipping 290 degrees F below zero, Titan is far too cold for liquid water. Instead, researchers believe the fluid that sculpts Titan is an unknown mixture of methane, ethane, and other hard-to-freeze hydrocarbons.

   The idea that Titan is a wet world with its own alien waters is widely accepted
10 by planetary scientists. Nothing else can account for the observations: NASA's Cassini spacecraft has flown by Titan more than 90 times since 2004, pinging the Moon with radar and mapping its lakes and seas. ESA's Huygens probe parachuted to the surface of Titan in 2005, descending through humid clouds and actually landing in moist soil.

15   Yet something has been bothering Alex Hayes, a planetary scientist on the Cassini radar team at Cornell University.

If Titan is really so wet, he wonders, "Where are all the waves?"

Here on Earth, bodies of water are rarely still. Breezes blowing across the surface cause waves to ripple and break; raindrops striking sea surfaces also provide
20 some roughness. Yet on Titan, the lakes are eerily smooth, with no discernible wave action down to the millimeter scale, according to radar data from Cassini.

"We know there is wind on Titan," says Hayes. "The moon's magnificent sand dunes [prove] it."

Add to that the low gravity of Titan—only $\frac{1}{7}$th that of Earth—which offers
25 so little resistance to wave motion, and you have a real puzzle.

Researchers have toyed with several explanations. Perhaps the lakes are frozen. Hayes thinks that is unlikely, however, "because we see evidence of rainfall and surface temperatures well above the melting point of methane." Or maybe the lakes are covered with a tar-like substance that damps wave motion. "We can't
30 yet rule that out," he adds.

The answer might be found in the results of a study Hayes and colleagues published in the July 2013 online edition of the journal *Icarus*. Taking into account the gravity of Titan, the low viscosity of liquid hydrocarbons, the density of Titan's atmosphere, and other factors, they calculated how fast wind on Titan
35 would have to blow to stir up waves: A walking-pace breeze of only 1 to 2 mph should do the trick.

This suggests a third possibility: the winds just haven't been blowing hard enough. Since Cassini reached Saturn in 2004, Titan's northern hemisphere (where most of the lakes are located) has been locked in the grip of winter. Cold
40 heavy air barely stirs, and seldom reaches the threshold for wave-making.

But now the seasons are changing. In August 2009 the sun crossed Titan's equator heading north. Summer is coming, bringing light, heat and wind to Titan's lake country.

"According to [climate models], winds will pick up as we approach the solstice
45 in 2017 and should be strong enough for waves," he says.

If waves appear, Cassini should be able to detect them. Radar reflections from wavy lake surfaces can tell researchers a great deal. Wave dimensions, for instance, may reveal the viscosity of the underlying fluid and, thus, its chemical composition. Also, wave speeds would track the speed of the overlying winds,
50 providing an independent check of Titan climate models.

Hayes is excited about "bringing oceanography to another world. All we need now," he says, "are some rough seas."

This passage is the text of a slide show created by NASA scientist Dr. Tony Phillips. It is one of NASA's web-based science features.

—Science@NASA

4. How do scientists get their information about Titan?

  (A) by observing the changes in data and photos sent back from Cassini

  (B) by comparing it to the Earth

  (C) by using climate models

  (D) by measuring and comparing the temperatures to those on Earth

The article explains the role of the space probe, Cassini, to ping the moon with radar and map its lakes. These data are then used by scientists to form hypotheses about the data. Scientists may compare the data to Earth, but they do this after they have received data about Titan. It is not a direct comparison, and it is not one that is used to get information about Titan. Scientists do use climate models, and they use them with the data received from Cassini, but they don't use the climate models to get the information. The scientists use what they know about the Earth for comparison, but they don't get information about Titan from knowledge about the Earth. **The correct answer is (A).**

5. Why was the discovery of Titan's resemblance to Earth shocking to scientists?

   (A) They didn't think they would be able to see the surface closely enough to map it.

   (B) They didn't expect to find that the surface was wet.

   (C) They expected it to look like the Earth's moon.

   (D) They expected it to be completely frozen because of the extremely low temperatures.

The passage doesn't tell us what the expectations were before the probe started, but scientists were surprised when they saw photos that resembled the Earth's surface, which indicate the presence of liquid in order to give Titan its contours. The passage tells us that they were shocked by this discovery. **The correct answer is (B).**

6. What is the question about Titan that Alex Hayes is trying to figure out?

   (A) What is the composition of the surface?

   (B) Why are the lakes on Titan frozen?

   (C) Why aren't there waves in the bodies of liquid on Titan?

   (D) What is the density of the atmosphere of Titan?

The data received from the space probe tell scientists the composition of the surface, Titan's temperatures, and its density, along with other data. Hayes already knows about these data. His question is about the appearance of the surface of Titan's lakes. They are very smooth, unlike bodies of water on Earth, which have waves formed by wind and gravity. He asks why this may be and forms some hypotheses to help figure it out. **The correct answer is (C).**

7. Why do scientists think waves may appear on Titan after 2017?

   (A) because the seasons will change by then, and there should be more wind activity

   (B) because the cold air will stimulate wind activity

   (C) because scientists predict that the lakes will be frozen solid by then

   (D) because the methane will begin to melt as the moon completes its orbit

The article says that one of the reasons that there may be no waves is that everything may be frozen. They expect the temperatures to rise as the season changes, which will occur as Titan moves closer to the sun in its orbit. It is the warm air that scientists think will stimulate wind activity as the liquids on the surface begin to thaw. The methane is not frozen—the article says the temperatures are above the melting point of methane. **The correct answer is (A).**

The next passage represents one of the shorter informational science passages. The article is about a plant species and its uses. The italicized text indicates the Latin names for species. When you see terms like this in your reading, don't focus on them. Note how they are used, and, if they are used multiple times, you can refer back to the part of the passage in which they are located in order to clarify your understanding. Overall, however, you will not be expected to interpret such terms, and they are not important to the main ideas in the information provided.

QUESTIONS 8–10 REFER TO THE FOLLOWING PASSAGE.

Adam's Needle

The Catawba, Cherokee, Nanticoke, and other Native American tribes used *Yucca filamentosa* [Adam's needle] for a variety of purposes including food, medicine, cordage, and even soap. The roots, which contain saponin [a soapy lather substance in some plants], were prepared by boiling and pounding for use as soap. Roots
5   were beaten into a salve or poultice that would then be used to treat sprains or applied to sores on the skin. The roots were used to treat gonorrhea and rheumatism. Skin diseases were treated by rubbing the roots on the skin and by taking a decoction of the roots. The plant was used as a sedative to induce sleep. An infusion of the plant was used to treat diabetes. The flowers were eaten both
10   raw and cooked. The pounded roots were thrown into fishing waters to "intoxicate fish" allowing for easier catch. The green leaves are easily split into long strips that can be plied into cord. The leaves have long, very strong fibers, a type of sisal, which were twisted into strong thread used as cordage for binding and to construct baskets, fishing nets, fishing lines and clothing. The leaves of *Yucca*
15   *filamentosa* contain the strongest fibers native to North America. . . .

Yuccas are pollinated by small, white Yucca moths (*Tegeticula yucasella* and related species) with which they have a special plant-insect mutualism. At night, the fragrant flowers attract the female moth that feeds on the nectar. She then rolls pollen from the flowers into a ball that is three times the size of her head
20   and carries the pollen ball to the next flower. There, she first lays eggs inside the immature ovary and then deposits the pollen on the flower's stigma insuring that seeds will form to feed her progeny. Because the larvae mature before they are able to consume all of the seeds (60 to 80% of the seeds remain viable), the plants are able to reproduce as well.
25   Adam's needle is a native, evergreen, perennial shrub. The plants have long, thick underground stems and rarely have an aboveground stem. The grayish-green leaves appear from a rosette at or near the ground. The leaves are stiff and sword-shaped (30 to 76 cm long and 2.5 cm wide) with sharp, pointed tips and long, curly, filamentous threads at the margins. The bell-shaped flowers

30 (5 to 8 cm wide) are a creamy white to pale yellow or green with broadly ovate petals (4 to 5 cm). The flowers, which appear in late spring and summer, hang loosely in clusters from a large, central spike (1 to 4 m tall) that emerges from the rosette. The fruits are capsules that contain 120 to 150 small black seeds that are dispersed by wind.

—U.S. Department of Agriculture

8. The best subheading for the second paragraph is

   (A) Historical Use of Plants.

   (B) Reproduction.

   (C) Unusual Facts.

   (D) How Plants Thrive.

The first paragraph talks about ways that the Native Americans used Adam's needle. The second paragraph describes the specific pollination process used by this plant. There are no unusual facts given here, and the paragraph does not provide an overview of how plants thrive. **The correct answer is (B).**

9. The flowers in an Adam's needle

   (A) bloom in the fall.

   (B) have thick, long, above-ground stems.

   (C) have curly, filamentous threads.

   (D) bloom annually.

The third paragraph provides information about the characteristics of the plant. It does not bloom in the fall; rather, it blooms in the spring and summer, so it is an annual plant. Its stems are generally underground, not above-ground, and it is the leaves that are described as curly with filamentous threads. **The correct answer is (D).**

10. What conclusion could you draw about Native Americans from the information in the first paragraph?

   (A) They were vegetarians.

   (B) They knew how to identify plants that were edible and plants that were poisonous.

   (C) They learned how to use natural resources for multiple purposes.

   (D) They had a wide variety of food in their diet.

Although the paragraph says the Native Americans used Adam's needle for food, it does not say they did not also eat meat, and it does indicate that they ate fish. They knew that Adam's needle was edible, but there's no information given about poisonous plants. The passage does not discuss other aspects of the Native Americans' diets, so we don't know how much variety there was. The overall text shows ingenuity in using the Adam's needle for a wide variety of purposes, from food, to tools, to clothing, to medicines. **The correct answer is (C).**

The next passage documents some of the problems of lead in our environment. It contains a lot of details. One technique for reading such a passage includes reading the questions first to note what details are covered in the questions. Then pay extra attention to these parts of the passage.

QUESTIONS 11–14 REFER TO THE FOLLOWING PASSAGE.

Lead in the Environment

Lead is a naturally occurring element that can be harmful to humans when ingested or inhaled, particularly to children under the age of six. Lead poisoning can cause a number of adverse human health effects, but is particularly detrimental to the neurological development of children. . . .

5 For hundreds of years, lead has been mined, smelted, refined, and used in products (e.g., as an additive in paint, gasoline, leaded pipes, solder, crystal, and ceramics). Natural levels of lead in soil range between 50 parts per million (ppm) and 400 ppm. Mining, smelting, and refining activities have resulted in substantial increases in lead levels in the environment, especially near mining

10 and smelting sites. For example, near some types of industrial and municipal facilities, and adjacent to highways[1], soil lead concentrations have been reported to be more than 11,000 ppm[2].

Lead particles in the environment can attach to dust and be carried long distances in the air. Such lead-containing dust can be removed from the air by rain

15 and deposited on surface soil, where it may remain for many years. In addition, heavy rains may cause lead in surface soil to migrate into ground water and eventually into water systems. . . .

Lead poisoning can be a serious public health threat with no unique signs or symptoms. Early symptoms of lead exposure may include: persistent fatigue,

20 irritability, loss of appetite, stomach discomfort and/or constipation, reduced attention span, insomnia. Failure to treat lead poisoning in the early stages can cause long-term or permanent health damage, but because of the general nature of symptoms at early stages, lead poisoning is often not suspected.

In adults, lead poisoning can cause: poor muscle coordination, nerve damage

25 to the sense organs and nerves controlling the body, increased blood pressure, hearing and vision impairment, reproductive problems (e.g., decreased sperm count [in males]), retarded fetal development [in pregnant females] even at relatively low exposure levels.

In children, lead poisoning can cause: damage to the brain and nervous system,

30 behavioral problems, anemia, liver and kidney damage, hearing loss, hyperactivity, developmental delays, and, in extreme cases, death.

Although the effects of lead exposure are a potential concern for all humans, young children (less than seven years old) are most at risk[3]. This increased vulnerability results from a combination of the following factors:

35 • Children typically have higher intake rates (per unit body weight) for environmental media (such as soil, dust, food, water, air, and paint) than

adults, since they are more likely to play in dirt and put their hands and other objects in their mouths;

- Children tend to absorb a higher fraction of ingested lead from the gastro-
40   intestinal tract than adults;

- Children tend to be more susceptible than adults to the adverse neurological and developmental effects of lead; and

- Nutritional deficiencies of iron or calcium, which are common in children, may facilitate lead absorption and exacerbate the toxic effects of lead.

45   The national average blood lead levels in children have dropped over time as our understanding of lead risk has evolved, and as efforts are undertaken to reduce exposure to lead. While banning of lead paint and lead in gasoline were national efforts to stop childhood lead poisoning, contaminated sites require site-specific cleanups to reduce exposure to populations nearby.

50   The Centers for Disease Control (CDC) has identified that the current blood lead level of concern in children is 10 micrograms (µg) of lead per deciliter (dL) of blood (10 µg/dL); however, adverse effects may occur at lower levels than previously thought. In January of 2012, an advisory panel to the CDC recommended lowering the level that triggers intervention.

55   If you have concerns about possible lead exposure, contact your personal physician or county/state health department. Your doctor can conduct blood tests to determine lead concentrations in your blood. Blood tests are inexpensive and sometimes free; however, please consult your insurance provider to determine coverage of such tests. Lead in bone and teeth can be measured using x-ray
60   techniques, but this test is not used very often. In communities where houses are old and deteriorating, residents are encouraged to take advantage of available screening programs offered by local health departments and to have children living in the residence checked regularly for lead poisoning. Because the early symptoms of lead poisoning are similar to those of other illnesses, it is difficult
65   to diagnose lead poisoning without medical testing.

---

[1]Chaney et al., 1984; Shacklette et al., 1984
[2]National Research Council, 1980
[3]Reagan and Silbergeld, 1989

—From the U.S. EPA Office of Superfund Remediation and Technology Innovation. www.epa.gov/superfund

11. Why is lead considered a serious public health threat?

(A) Lead can poison people quickly before they know they have been exposed.

(B) Lead gets washed into the soil and then works its way into water systems, and people drink the contaminated water.

(C) Lead exposure causes many illnesses that others can catch, causing a wide-scale epidemic.

(D) Lead is dangerous because there's no way to diagnose it in your system.

A public health hazard is created when lead gets in waterways and the water supply, but it also can be inhaled, choice (B). Lead exposure does make people sick, but not with the kind of diseases that can be transmitted to other people, choice (C). There are tests to diagnose lead in the blood, choice (D). One danger of lead poisoning is that because of general symptoms at early stages, lead poisoning is often not suspected immediately. **The correct answer is (A).**

12. Why are children at greater risk when exposed to lead?

    (A) Children are more likely to have direct contact with soil that is lead contaminated.

    (B) Children can ingest lead, while adults can't.

    (C) Children are more likely to be anemic.

    (D) Children's immune systems are not as well developed as that of adults.

Anyone can ingest lead from many different sources, choice (B). Children are not more likely to be anemic, choice (C). Although children's immune systems are less developed than those of adults, that is not what puts them at higher risk, choice (D). Children are more likely to play in dirt and other sites of contamination, leading to an increased risk of exposure. **The correct answer is (A).**

13. Which of the following is true about the relationship between lead and the environment?

    (A) Because rain removes lead from the air, lead is only hazardous in dry climates.

    (B) Because lead is no longer an ingredient in gasoline or paint, it is no longer a big problem.

    (C) Because lead is a natural element, there is nothing people can do to prevent lead poisoning.

    (D) Because lead can get into the soil and the water supply, it remains a hazard for a long time.

Rain does remove lead from the air, but it then deposits it in the soil, where it can remain for years and can even contaminate the water supply, choice (A). Government regulation forced the removal of lead from paints and gasoline, but there are other sources, choice (B). It is true that lead is a natural element, but the toxic levels are present in man-made items, which is something that can be reduced or even eliminated, choice (C). Lead remains in older homes, commercial, and industrial structures, and it can stay in the soil and water; the damage can remain for a long time, choice (D). **The correct answer is (D).**

14. Lead poisoning in children can cause

(A) hyperactivity.

(B) cancer.

(C) diabetes.

(D) blindness.

According to the article, the health effects of lead exposure on children include brain and nervous system damage, behavioral problems, anemia, liver and kidney damage, hearing loss, hyperactivity, developmental delays, and, in extreme cases, death. **The correct answer is (A).**

Informational Social Studies

This section of the test will contain reading passages broadly related to American history and civics. Some will be excerpts from primary sources—original historical documents, the text of public speeches, or other such original writings. Primary sources are documents that were created at the time of the event; for example, a letter or an interview conducted at the time of an event. Others will be secondary sources—analyses and interpretations about the primary source; for example, a newspaper or magazine articles about a historical event. These sources may quote the primary source or others related to the event. Examples of secondary sources include biographies or journal articles about a primary source.

Author's Point of View

Personal accounts can tell us much about the history of a particular period. They can fill in details about events and provide a human perspective to the narrative. Primary sources like journals and memoirs, because of their personal natures, give the author's point of view about the events and the time in which the person was living. Combined with other sources, this can give us a more balanced record of actual events.

QUESTIONS 15–19 REFER TO THE FOLLOWING PASSAGE.

The following excerpt is from the memoir, The Narrative of Sojourner Truth. *Sojourner Truth was born into slavery in New York State before laws there abolished slavery in 1827. She escaped from her master and eventually became an active member of the abolition movement. As a former slave, Sojourner Truth had never learned to read or write; thus, her memoir was dictated to a friend. Truth's given name was* Isabella, *and she is referred to by that name in the passage.*

After emancipation had been decreed by the State, some years before the time fixed for its consummation, Isabella's master told her if she would do well, and be faithful, he would give her "free papers," one year before she was legally free by statute. In the year 1826, she had a badly diseased hand, which greatly

5 diminished her usefulness; but on the arrival of July 4, 1827, the time specified
for her receiving her "free papers," she claimed the fulfillment of her master's
promise; but he refused granting it, on account (as he alleged) of the loss he had
sustained by her hand. She plead that she had worked all the time, and done
many things she was not wholly able to do, although she knew she had been less
10 useful than formerly; but her master remained inflexible. Her very faithfulness
probably operated against her now, and he found it less easy than he thought to
give up the profits of his faithful Bell, who had so long done him efficient service.

But Isabella inwardly determined that she would remain quietly with him only
until she had spun his wool—about one hundred pounds—and then she would
15 leave him, taking the rest of the time to herself. "Ah!" she says, with emphasis
that cannot be written, "the slaveholders are TERRIBLE for promising to give
you this or that, or such and such a privilege, if you will do thus and so; and when
the time of fulfillment comes, and one claims the promise, they, forsooth, recollect
nothing of the kind; and you are, like as not, taunted with being a LIAR; or, at
20 best, the slave is accused of not having performed his part or condition of the
contract." "Oh!" said she, "I have felt as if I could not live through the operation
sometimes. Just think of us! so eager for our pleasures, and just foolish enough
to keep feeding and feeding ourselves up with the idea that we should get what
had been thus fairly promised; and when we think it is almost in our hands, find
25 ourselves flatly denied! Just think! how could we bear it?"

. . . The question in her mind, and one not easily solved, now was, "How can
I get away?" So, as was her usual custom, she "told God she was afraid to go
in the night, and in the day every body would see her." At length, the thought
came to her that she could leave just before the day dawned, and get out of the
30 neighborhood where she was known before the people were much astir. "Yes,"
said she, fervently, "that's a good thought! Thank you, God, for *that* thought!" So,
receiving it as coming direct from God, she acted upon it, and one fine morning, a
little before day-break, she might have been seen stepping stealthily away from
the rear of Master Dumont's house, her infant on one arm and her wardrobe on
35 the other; the bulk and weight of which, probably, she never found so convenient
as on the present occasion, a cotton handkerchief containing both her clothes
and her provisions.

As she gained the summit of a high hill, a considerable distance from her
master's, the sun offended her by coming forth in all his pristine splendor. She
40 thought it never was so light before; indeed, she thought it much too light. She
stopped to look about her, and ascertain if her pursuers were yet in sight. No one
appeared, and, for the first time, the question came up for settlement, "Where,
and to whom, shall I go?" In all her thoughts of getting away, she had not once
asked herself whither she should direct her steps. She sat down, fed her infant,
45 and again turning her thoughts to God, her only help, she prayed him to direct
her to some safe asylum.

15. What does the narrative of Isabella imply about slaveholders?

The slaveholders' cruelty toward their slaves was based on

(A) twisted emotions

(B) desire for profit

(C) fear of confrontation

(D) racism

The idea that slaveholders' cruelty was based on their desire for profit is implied in lines 7–8 ("the loss he had sustained by her hand") and in lines 11–12 ("to give up the profits of his faithful Bell . . ."). **The correct answer is (B).**

16. What is it about Truth's slaveholder that she mainly objects to?

(A) his harassment

(B) his brutality

(C) his unfairness

(D) his bigotry

In the passage, the author clearly depicts Isabella's slaveholder as unfair: he breaks his promises despite Isabella's faithfulness. On the other hand, nowhere in the passage does the author suggest that her slaveholder harassed or brutalized her, choices (A) and (B). And though he may have been a bigot or a hypocrite, choice (D), the passage does not indicate that Isabella noted that trait or objected to it. **The correct answer is (C).**

17. What did Truth believe about her master that made her plan her escape?

(A) She believed he was not trustworthy.

(B) She thought he would continue to punish her.

(C) She thought he was going to sell her to someone else.

(D) She believed he would grant her freedom but she didn't want to wait any longer.

Truth realized that her master had lied and broken his promises to let her go free, in spite of the law. The date of her freedom came and went, and her master found excuses to keep her. There is no indication that he planned to sell her to someone else or that he had caused her injury. He had broken his word, and she realized that she could not trust him. **The correct answer is (A).**

18. What can you infer about Truth's beliefs based on her plan for escape?

(A) The law would be enforced, and she would be free.

(B) The only way to get free was to go where she would not be recognized.

(C) She would be freed but would have to leave the state.

(D) She would be able to find safety with neighbors.

Truth's master did not free her after the law went into effect; he continued to hold her as an enslaved person, choice (A). The text doesn't say the law specified that freed slaves had to leave the state, choice (C). Truth's behavior indicates that she was afraid that people who knew her and her master would see her, and they would capture her and bring her back to him. Consequently, she did not feel safe taking refuge with her neighbors, choice (D). She hoped that once she was in a place where she was not known, she would be safe, because the law said she was free. **The correct answer is (B).**

19. Though *The Narrative of Sojourner Truth* is told in the third person by a narrator, what indications are there to show it's Truth's personal story?

(A) The narrator quotes Truth's words and thoughts about her experience.

(B) The narrator injects her own perspective that confirms Truth's experience.

(C) The narrator keeps the story in the third person to be objective.

(D) The narrator shows both her own and Truth's views, but only Truth's views are in the first person.

The narrator of *The Narrative of Sojourner Truth* uses the third person except where she includes direct quotes from Truth. The narrator does not inject her own perspective; she describes what Truth tells her and occasionally quotes Truth's own words. The narrator uses third person to tell the story from Truth's perspective, not to be objective. The narrator shows only Truth's views. **The correct answer is (A).**

Secondary Sources

A secondary source provides us with further information about historical events, eras, and cultures. A source of this type tells us about events after they have occurred and may or may not contain objective accounts. A secondary source can be an analysis, a summary, or an interpretation of a primary source. In some cases, it might describe or explain primary sources. For example, a textbook or an encyclopedia could be considered a secondary source.

The following passage is an example of a secondary source. Think about what primary sources the author might have used to obtain the information needed to write the text. When reading these kinds of texts, the same skills are needed.

QUESTIONS 20–23 REFER TO THE FOLLOWING PASSAGE.

The following passage, written by James H. Bruns, appeared in the January-March 1992 [vol 1, issue 1] issue of EnRoute, *the National Postal Museum's newsletter.*

Titanic's Mail

America's history is in the mail. This is no idle boast. From its beginnings, the post office helped make American history, and its growth parallels the history of the United States itself. This is true of major events, as well as many of the fascinating footnotes of our history . . .

5   This April marks the 80th anniversary of the loss of the R.M.S. *Titanic*, the world's most famous mail ship. (The abbreviation stood for "Royal Mail Ship.") On April 14, 1912, the ship went down with more than 1500 lives, including clerks of the Sea Post Service.

Aboard the *Titanic* was a Sea Post Office with a crew of five clerks. Two of
10   the clerks, Jago Smith and J. B. Williamson, were English. The others, John S. March, William L. Gwinn, and Oscar S. Woody, were Americans employed by the United States Post Office Department. On any ocean crossing, the receiving and sending countries would each assign clerks to the shipboard office. On the *Titanic*, the majority of the clerks were American because the ship was sailing
15   to America, and American clerks were used to sort mail coming into the States.

American sea post clerks basically earned about $1000 a year in 1912. They also ate their meals free with the passengers and were allotted an allowance for their board while awaiting the return of their ship.

For several hours before sailing, the *Titanic* clerks carried out the routine task
20   of checking all of the mail sacks and storing those that did not need to be opened during the voyage. As soon as the liner set sail on April 10, they would have begun making distributions, much like the crew of a railway mail train would do.

The postal crew aboard the *Titanic* worked well together, especially in those last hours of April 14. From available information, within minutes after the collision,
25   the mail storage room, which was located well below the ship's water line, began flooding, sending some of the mail sacks adrift. Frantically, the clerks brought as many sacks as possible up to the sorting room in preparation for moving the mailbags onto the deck for possible recovery by a rescue ship. According to the Postmaster General's 1912 *Annual Report:* "The last reports concerning their
30   actions show that they were engaged in this work . . . to the last moment."

The entire ship's cargo was lost, including 3423 sacks of mail. The mailbags contained over 7 million pieces of mail, including an estimated 1.6 [million] registered letters and packages. Within weeks of the sinking, postal officials began feeling the effects of the loss. About $150,000 in postal money orders had gone
35   to the bottom of the sea. These would have to somehow be processed. Four days after the sinking, Third Assistant Postmaster General James J. Britt advised local postmasters:

Among the millions of pieces of mail matter carried on the lost Titanic, there were doubtless thousands of dollars' worth of international money orders, together
40   with descriptive lists of such orders. It is assumed that many of the remitters of those orders will communicate with the payees in this country concerning them,

and that these payees, in turn, will take up the matter through their respective postmasters.

It is the earnest desire of the department that in all such cases postmasters
45 give careful attention to the inquiries made and promptly report the facts to the Third Assistant Postmaster General (Division of Money Orders), to the end that every effort may be made to insure early payments to the intended beneficiaries.

One of the first to be reimbursed for a lost money order was Miss Ethel Clarke, a maid who worked for President William Howard Taft's family. Her lost money
50 order was for seven pounds. Based upon an examination of available postal records, a replacement U.S. money order was issued to her from postal service headquarters for $35.

20. What can you infer about the author's attitude toward postal workers from the passage?

   (A) He thought postal workers should handle international mail only on a special mail ship.

   (B) He thought the postal workers were doing important work competently.

   (C) He thought the work of the postal workers was routine and boring.

   (D) He thought only Americans postal workers should handle American mail.

The author describes the tragedy of the *Titanic* in terms of the loss of one of its cargoes—that of the U.S. mail carried on the ship bound for the United States. The postal workers were free to eat their meals with the passengers, and the author gives no indication that he thinks they should be on a separate ship. The author explains that they were engaged in their normal work routines when the ship started to flood, not that their work was routine and boring. He describes how incoming international mail is handled by American postal clerks but does not state any objections to other nationalities. Overall, the author describes workers who were good at their jobs; jobs that he showed to have an impact on others. **The correct answer is (B).**

21. Which of the following details from the passage shows that the author's belief that the development of the United States Postal Service had a significant impact on the course of American history?

   (A) The author claims that he is not boasting when he says "history is in the mail."

   (B) People, including President Taft's maid, were given back their money for lost money orders.

   (C) The fact that the *Titanic* was carrying so much mail showed that Europeans wanted to communicate with Americans.

   (D) Millions of pieces of mail were lost, but the postal service was able to recoup some of the monetary claims.

The author says that his opening statement is not a "boast," showing that he believes that the growth and success of the postal service is tied to the growth and success of the nation, choice (A). People were able to file their claims and get money orders refunded, choices (B) and (D), but that detail is not related to the overall history of the event. New technology meant faster and larger ships that could deliver goods more quickly. The postal service was able to take advantage of the new service, but in this case, the technology was what contributed to the country's growth. **The correct answer is (A).**

---

22. What can you conclude about American life at the beginning of the twentieth century, based on the passage?

    (A) Mail service was quick and efficient if you had money to pay for it.

    (B) Many people wrote letters to friends and family.

    (C) Travel was dangerous, so most people stayed home.

    (D) The *Titanic* was carrying only wealthy passengers and crew.

We can infer that mail service was faster because of the advent of new technology that included large ships like the *Titanic*, which could carry millions of pieces of mail, making it easier and faster to send mail across the ocean. But nowhere does the author suggest that its cost was prohibitive, choice (A). The *Titanic* is only one of many ships that would have carried mail. The over 7 million pieces of mail that the author documents as having been lost indicates that large numbers of people were sending letters and packages to and from Europe. Some kinds of travel may have been dangerous by today's standards, but many people continued to travel, choice (C). The author doesn't talk about the passengers, except to say that the postal workers were allowed to have their meals with them. We may have an image of wealthy people aboard the ship from reading about it or seeing a film, but the passage alone does not give us this information. **The correct answer is (B).**

---

23. What primary sources would the author most likely have used to get the facts for this article?

    (A) a diary from a passenger

    (B) a survivor's story

    (C) a book about the building of the ship

    (D) the captain's log from the ship

A passenger's diary, choice (A), would be a primary source, but it would not supply the information provided in the article. Passengers would not have known how much mail was on board. A survivor could also be a primary source, choice (B), but not one who could have provided the kinds of details that are included in the passage. A book about building the ship is a primary source, but such a book would be focused on how the ship was built and would not have information about the ship's voyage, including the mail it was carrying and the people who died, choice (C). A captain's log would list passengers and cargo, so the author might have consulted this as a primary source. **The correct answer is (D).**

Interpreting Images and Words

Primary sources can also be photographs or other original material. Observing the details in an image can help to interpret what was going on when the photograph was taken. Look for details that give clues to the setting and note the expression(s) of the photo's subject(s) to give you clues about who they are. A written description with an image can often yield a lot of detailed information.

QUESTIONS 24–26 REFER TO THE FOLLOWING PHOTOGRAPH AND PASSAGE.

The following passage describes how this photograph, entitled "Migrant Madonna," came about. This information is a secondary source, and the photograph is a primary source.

Migrant Madonna

On a raw, soggy day in March 1936, Dorothea Lange was driving home to Berkeley after six weeks spent photographing migrant workers in California, New Mexico, and Arizona. Her staff position at the Resettlement Administration (RA), an agency set up to help tenant farmers during the Depression, was tenuous: since there
5 was no budget for a photographer, Lange had been hired as a clerk-stenographer, and she invoiced her film and travel expenses under "clerical supplies."

As Lange drove along the empty California highway that day, she noticed a sign that said Pea-Pickers Camp. Knowing that the pea crop had frozen, she debated for 20 miles before finally turning back. After pulling into the camp's
10 muddy lane, Lange approached a female migrant worker, requested and got permission to photograph her and shot just five exposures. Lange's field notes read in part: "I did not ask her name or her history. She told me her age, that she was 32. She said that they had been living on frozen vegetables from the surrounding fields and birds that the children killed. She had just sold the tires
15 from her car to buy food."

Back home, Lange developed the images and, clutching the still-wet prints, told the editor of the San Francisco *News* that migrant workers were slowly starving to death in Nipomo, California. The story the *News* ran about them featured

Lange's pictures; UPI picked it up, and within days the federal government sup-
20 plied the workers with 20,000 pounds of food. By that time, however, the woman
and her family, desperate to find work, had moved on . . .

—Excerpt from *Smithsonian* magazine, March 2002, by Rebecca Maksel

24. How is the text enhanced by the photograph?

(A) The text describes the woman's situation, but the photo communicates the harsh reality of it.

(B) The text describes her diet, but the photo shows that although the woman looks poor, she's not starving.

(C) The text gives information about the mother and family, but the photo shows what her three children look like.

(D) The text gives information about the photographer, but the photograph shows her talent with photography.

The photo reinforces the reality of the description in the text, choice (A). The family looks ragged, poor, and miserable, and the mother has a look of hopelessness; we can't tell from the photo whether the woman is starving or not, choice (B). The children can be seen, but they are hiding from the camera—whether out of fear or shyness, we don't know, but we can't see what they look like in the picture, choice (C). We can only glean a sense of the extent of their exhaustion. While the text does give us information about the photographer, and the photo is haunting, her talent does not inform the text, choice (D). **The correct answer is (A).**

25. How does the image combined with the text give us a better understanding of the Great Depression?

(A) The text fills in details about the period that the photo can't provide by itself.

(B) The text explains how the photograph started Lange's career.

(C) The words and the image together describe the family's situation.

(D) The photograph shows the effects of the Depression on real people described in the text.

The image shows us the victims of the Depression, and the text provides more details about the period; together, they give a broader picture, choice (A). How Lange's career started is irrelevant to understanding the Great Depression, choice (B). The words and image do describe the family's situation, but understanding the Great Depression goes beyond one family, which part of the text describes briefly, choice (C). The photo poignantly illustrates the effects of the Depression on real people; it is the additional text about other aspects of the Depression that creates a more complete picture of the era. **The correct answer is (A).**

26. What was the role of the Resettlement Administration (RA) during the Depression?

(A) to find work for farm laborers

(B) to document migrant workers

(C) to help tenant farmers

(D) to deport migrant workers

The text describes the Resettlement Administration as an "agency set up to help tenant farmers." Farm laborers could be included in the category of tenant farmers, but the agency's role was not to find work for them, choice (A). The mother in the photo was a migrant worker; that is, a farm worker who moves from place to place to find work. Lange's job was, on paper, as a clerk for the agency. She was not paid to document migrant workers, choice (B). The agency was not designed to deport anyone, choice (D). **The correct answer is (C).**

Finding Evidence

The next passage is a primary document that represents one of the most important Supreme Court cases in U.S. history, *Brown v. Board of Education*. The case was decided in 1954, a period when public schools across the country were mostly segregated, by law in the South and by practice in the North. The *Brown* case changed that and started a new era of civil rights. When you read the passage, notice the way details are used to support the main idea and the conclusion.

QUESTIONS 27–31 REFER TO THE FOLLOWING PASSAGE.

This is an excerpt from the Supreme Court opinion written by Chief Justice Earl Warren in the Brown v. Board of Education landmark case.

Segregation of white and Negro children in the public schools of a State solely on the basis of race, pursuant to state laws permitting or requiring such segregation, denies to Negro children the equal protection of the laws guaranteed by the Fourteenth Amendment—even though the physical facilities and other
5 "tangible" factors of white and Negro schools may be equal . . .

(a) The history of the Fourteenth Amendment is inconclusive as to its intended effect on public education.

(b) The question presented in these cases must be determined, not on the basis of conditions existing when the Fourteenth Amendment was adopted, but
10 in the light of the full development of public education and its present place in American life throughout the Nation.

(c) Where a State has undertaken to provide an opportunity for an education in its public schools, such an opportunity is a right which must be made available to all on equal terms.

15 (d) Segregation of children in public schools solely on the basis of race deprives children of the minority group of equal educational opportunities, even though the physical facilities and other "tangible" factors may be equal. . . .

In approaching this problem, we cannot turn the clock back to 1868 when the Amendment was adopted, or even to 1896 when *Plessy v. Ferguson* was written.
20 We must consider public education in the light of its full development and its present place in American life throughout the Nation. Only in this way can it be determined if segregation in public schools deprives these plaintiffs of the equal protection of the laws.

Today, education is perhaps the most important function of state and local
25 governments. Compulsory school attendance laws and the great expenditures for education both demonstrate our recognition of the importance of education to our democratic society. It is required in the performance of our most basic public responsibilities, even service in the armed forces. It is the very foundation of good citizenship. Today it is a principal instrument in awakening the child to cultural
30 values, in preparing him for later professional training, and in helping him to adjust normally to his environment. In these days, it is doubtful that any child may reasonably be expected to succeed in life if he is denied the opportunity of an education. Such an opportunity, where the state has undertaken to provide it, is a right which must be made available to all on equal terms.

35 We come then to the question presented: Does segregation of children in public schools solely on the basis of race, even though the physical facilities and other "tangible" factors may be equal, deprive the children of the minority group of equal educational opportunities? We believe that it does. . . .

To separate them from others of similar age and qualifications solely because
40 of their race generates a feeling of inferiority as to their status in the community that may affect their hearts and minds in a way unlikely ever to be undone. The effect of this separation on their educational opportunities was well stated by a finding in the Kansas case by a court which nevertheless felt compelled to rule against the Negro plaintiffs:

45 "Segregation of white and colored children in public schools has a detrimental effect upon the colored children. The impact is greater when it has the sanction of the law; for the policy of separating the races is usually interpreted as denoting the inferiority of the negro group. A sense of inferiority affects the motivation of a child to learn. Segregation with the sanction of law, therefore, has a tendency
50 to [retard] the educational and mental development of negro children and to deprive them of some of the benefits they would receive in a racial[ly] integrated school system."

Whatever may have been the extent of psychological knowledge at the time of *Plessy v. Ferguson,* this finding is amply supported by modern authority. Any
55 language in *Plessy v. Ferguson* contrary to this finding is rejected. . . .

We conclude that in the field of public education the doctrine of "separate but equal" has no place. Separate educational facilities are inherently unequal. Therefore, we hold that the plaintiffs and others similarly situated for whom the actions have been brought are, by reason of the segregation complained of, deprived
60 of the equal protection of the laws guaranteed by the Fourteenth Amendment. This disposition makes unnecessary any discussion whether such segregation also violates the Due Process Clause of the Fourteenth Amendment. . . .

27. What reason does Chief Justice Warren give to show that segregation in public schools creates unequal opportunities for learning?

(A) The Fourteenth Amendment bans segregation.

(B) Prior Supreme Court decisions show that segregation creates unequal schools.

(C) Separate is not equal.

(D) Education is naturally unequal.

Warren cites both the Fourteenth Amendment and prior Supreme Court decisions as legal support for making the decision, choices (A and B), but the reason he uses to illustrate why segregation can't be tolerated is that it deprives minority group children of equal educational opportunities. Although he states that education is important to a democratic society, he does not cite natural inequality as evidence for his argument, choice (D). **The correct answer is (C).**

28. According to Warren's decision, why is segregation a violation of the Fourteenth Amendment?

(A) because segregation has a negative effect on modern society

(B) because segregation prevented minorities from becoming U.S. citizens

(C) because segregation is a form of slavery and the Fourteenth Amendment ended slavery

(D) because segregation denies equal opportunity for an education

Segregation may have had a negative effect on society, but Warren's decision explains that the policy violates the equal protection clause of the Fourteenth Amendment, choice (A). The passage doesn't discuss the citizenship aspects of the Fourteenth Amendment, choice (B). Segregation is also not the same as slavery, choice (C). The first section of the Fourteenth Amendment guarantees all people in the United States equal opportunity for an education. Segregated minority groups are not equal to non-segregated groups, choice (D). **The correct answer is (D).**

29. According to Warren's decision, public education is a

(A) privilege.

(B) opportunity.

(C) right.

(D) responsibility.

Warren never refers to education as a privilege, choice (A). He says that minorities should not be denied equal opportunities in education, not that education is an opportunity, choice (B). Warren describes education as a right that must be made available to everyone equally, choice (C). He does not describe it as a responsibility, choice (D). **The correct answer is (C).**

30. At the time of the *Brown* decision, Warren believed that segregation in public schools had to change because

(A) we can't apply rules and ideas of the past to the way we live today.

(B) the Fourteenth Amendment can't always apply to modern times.

(C) public education is more important in modern society.

(D) state laws were outdated.

Warren explains that the prior *Plessy* decision and the time period when the Fourteenth Amendment was passed can't be used as the basis for current ideas and decisions, choice (B). He does not compare public education of the past to that of the time of the decision, choice (C). Warren says that states can't violate the rights of minority children by educating them in segregated schools by law because such laws, by design, deny minority children of equal protection and are therefore against the Fourteenth Amendment; he doesn't say the laws are outdated, choice (D). **The correct answer is (A).**

31. What is Warren's view of segregation in public schools?

(A) It is unjust and unfair, but since it is legal, the Court can't change it.

(B) Once examined, it can't be defended.

(C) It's an unfortunate offshoot of our past that can't be changed.

(D) It's acceptable as long as minority groups have schools that are equal to those of whites.

Warren argues that segregation can't be held constitutional because it violates the Fourteenth Amendment. Once is it declared unconstitutional, it is not legal, and laws will need to be taken off the books, choice (A). He examines the historical evidence that was used to maintain segregated schools and finds that the arguments don't hold up, choice (B). Warren talks about the negative effects of past segregation but does not conclude that they cannot change, choice (C). The past policy of "separate but equal" was shown not to be equal on any level and therefore could not continue, choice (D). **The correct answer is (B).**

Informational Workplace

The third type of nonfiction text on the test is what the test-makers call **workplace and community documents.** The text might be a statement of policy, guidelines or rules for workplace behavior, an excerpt from an employee handbook or training manual, a statement of employee benefits, a communication (e-mail, written memorandum, or letter), or even a legal document, such as an employment contract. Also, depending on the document type, the text might contain headings or numbered lists.

This category also includes what is referred to as "community" documents. These are communications such as letters to the editor of a local newspaper, complaint letters, and public notices. For example, a notice sent to people in the community about an upcoming event to be held in a municipal park or building would fall into this category.

All of these documents are drawn from real or simulated workplace and community documents. Applying reading skills to these types of documents is no different from other types of reading material. Your task is the same: to apply your comprehension, analysis, synthesis, and application skills to the text. As you read a workplace or community document, try to answer the following questions for yourself:

- Who is the intended *audience*? (A specific individual? All or only certain employees? A general community?)

- What is the overall *scope* of the document? (Does it address only specific policies, procedures, or problems? Or is it broader in scope?)

- What *goal* or *objective* of the institution is the document intended to further? (For example, the document's purpose might be to enhance workplace efficiency, thwart employee misconduct, increase profits or revenues, obtain funding, or attract new clients or customers.)

- What is the writer's *point of view*? (Does the document express an opinion about any specific issue, or does it simply provide information?)

- What is the overall *tone* of the document? (The overall tone might be objective; but if a document serves as a warning—to employees, for example—the tone might be somewhat sharp or even accusatory.)

Also, if the document has a title, ask yourself what it suggests about the document's audience, scope, and purpose.

If you encounter a statement of policy on the test, expect at least one question asking what the broad policy is. (A **policy** is a general principle or broad course of action adopted by an institution as a guide for conducting its affairs.)

To understand the policy, you may need to synthesize information from various parts of the document. Also, policy statements typically provide details explaining how the institution implements its policy. So expect test questions about those supporting details as well. A policy is typically implemented through specific rules, regulations, and guidelines. When reading a policy statement, try to:

- Distinguish between a general policy and a specific policy, which is a rule or guideline that supports a general policy.

- Distinguish between *rules*, which require or prohibit certain behavior, and *guidelines*, which are merely suggestions as to how to further a policy.

- Pay attention to any consequences (discipline or punishment) for violating a rule or regulation. If consequences are discussed, pay attention to whether they vary, depending on the specific violation.

A policy statement that provides rules and regulations may contain so-called "legalese," which refers to words and phrases used in legal documents. If you run across legalese, don't be surprised if one of the test questions focuses on it. Don't worry: you should be able to figure out what the legalese means from its context. In fact, this skill is exactly what you're being tested on.

The following excerpt could be part of a policy statement, an employee handbook or training manual, or even an employment agreement. All of these types of documents can contain statements of policy as well as specific rules, regulations, or guidelines.

QUESTIONS 32–34 REFER TO THE FOLLOWING DOCUMENT EXCERPT.

[The document begins with Section 1, and then continues with Section 2, as follows.]

Section 2

2.1. Metacorp has a no-tolerance policy with respect to employee pilfering. As used in this section, "pilfering" means the taking of any company property, regardless of its monetary value, for personal rather than company use, whether
5 temporarily or permanently.

2.2. Any employee who is determined to have pilfered company property will be subject to disciplinary action in accordance with the guidelines set forth herein concerning warnings and subsequent termination of employment, and with applicable state and federal laws.

10 2.3. If an employee submits a false report of a violation under this section, that employee will be subject to immediate disciplinary action, which may include termination of employment without warning. For purposes of this provision, a "false report" is any report that the reporting employee knew or should have known was untrue or inaccurate, either in whole or in part.

32. Why did the company include Section 2 in the document?

  (A) to catch employees suspected of pilfering

  (B) to discourage employees from pilfering

  (C) to encourage employees to report pilfering incidents

  (D) to attract employees who are trustworthy

The first sentence of paragraph 2.1 expresses the company's general policy that it will not tolerate pilfering, while the rules that follow warn employees of harsh consequences should they violate the policy. Clearly, the main purpose of the section is to discourage employees from pilfering. Choices (A) and (D) both provide advantages of having this type of policy, but neither expresses the *purpose* of the policy. Choice (C) is incorrect because paragraph 2.3 actually *discourages* the reporting of pilfering. **The correct answer is (B).**

> **33.** What would happen to a Metacorp employee who borrows a coffee carafe from work but forgets to return it?
>
> Under Section 2, the employee would probably
>
> **(A)** be required to replace the company's carafe with a new one
>
> **(B)** be fired by Metacorp because the company has a no-tolerance policy
>
> **(C)** not be subject to discipline, because the employee intended to return the item
>
> **(D)** receive a warning if this was the employee's first violation of Section 2

To answer this question, you need to distinguish between consequences for pilfering (Section 2.2) and those for falsely reporting pilfering (Section 2.3). The applicable section is 2.2, which mentions "warnings" as a pre-termination procedure. Assuming this was a first offense, the pilfering employee's only discipline would probably be a warning. **The correct answer is (D).**

> **34.** For which behavior would a Metacorp employee most likely be disciplined?
>
> **(A)** taking home a company desk that was just thrown away
>
> **(B)** reporting a pilfering incident that was never actually observed
>
> **(C)** using a company telephone to make long-distance, personal calls
>
> **(D)** driving a company vehicle to a business-related conference

To answer this question correctly, you need to understand the definition of "false report." Its definition, provided in paragraph 2.3, contains some legalese. Choice (B) describes what might be considered submitting a false report, depending on the circumstances. If the reporting employee had absolutely no reason to suspect a coworker of pilfering, then it is possible that the employee knew or *should have known* that the report was false *in whole or in part*. **The correct answer is (B).**

Another type of workplace or community document you might encounter is a communication such as an e-mail, memo, or letter. The communication might be to a particular person, or it might be to a group, or a response to another communication. It could even be a letter to the editor of a newspaper. In its ideas and its tone, this type of a communication is more likely than other workplace and community documents to be *subjective*—that is, to communicate a distinct point of view and attitude toward the topic at hand, and possibly toward the recipient of the communication as well.

Here are some suggestions for reading and understanding these more subjective communication documents:

- Try to identify its main idea, and note the details provided in support of that idea.

- Ask yourself: Why did the author compose this e-mail, memo, or letter? What was the author trying to accomplish by doing so?

- As with other workplace and community documents, look for policy statements, and distinguish between supporting rules and supporting guidelines.

- If the communication begins by identifying the sender, recipient, and/or the subject, pay attention to those lines. They can provide clues about the communication's topic and point of view.

QUESTIONS 35–37 REFER TO THE FOLLOWING MEMO.

From: Jason Renaldi <jason.renaldi@theberwyngroup.com>

To: All Berwyn Corporation employees

Subject: Employee dress code and lunchtime policy

Beginning on Wednesday, January 17, our company dress code requiring all men
5   and women to wear business suits will not apply on Wednesdays. All employees
will be permitted to dress casually each Wednesday, at their option. Jeans will
be considered appropriate attire, but T-shirts and/or shorts will be considered
inappropriate. Women may wear open-toed shoes, but men may not. Management
encourages you to enjoy the freedom of "casual Wednesdays" while still dressing
10   in good taste.

Also beginning on January 17, you may take up to one-and-a-half hours for lunch,
between 11:30 to 2:00. To make up the half-hour of work lost due to a longer
lunch, you must either arrive up to 30 minutes earlier to start your Wednesday
workday or leave 30 minutes later to end your workday. If you prefer a rela-
15   tively late Wednesday lunch, management has arranged for the mobile food
vendor Cuisine on Wheels to serve lunch in our parking lot from 12:45 to 1:45
every Wednesday—again, starting on January 17. For those of you leaving the
premises for Wednesday lunch, as always we encourage you to carpool and to
dine with your coworkers.

20   I'm confident that a more leisurely lunch and casual attire will leave us all that
much more excited about whatever challenges lie ahead during the rest of the
work week. As always, I welcome your continuing feedback on these and other
working conditions.

Jason Renaldi
Human Resources Director
Berwyn Corporation

35. Which is the most likely purpose of the e-mail?

   (A) to announce policies designed to improve employee morale

   (B) to inform workers of recent company developments

   (C) to introduce incentives for job performance

   (D) to defend the company's dress code and lunch-hour policy

The closing paragraph reveals the purpose of the new policies: to help workers face the second half of the work week with a positive outlook—in other words, to improve their morale. **The correct answer is (A).**

36. How is this memo structured to enable Berwyn employees to get the information?

   (A) The memo describes the changes in company policies in two detailed paragraphs.

   (B) The memo explains the consequences of not conforming to the dress code as part of the detail of the new dress code.

   (C) The memo's author made the memo short so that employees would be able to read it quickly.

   (D) The memo describes two new related policies so that employees understand their connection.

The main idea of the memo is to communicate updated and revised company policy. This is accomplished in two detailed paragraphs, one for each change, choice (A). The memo does not mention consequences for not following the dress code, choice (B). The memo is short but clear in its details and intent. The intent is to have employees conform to the new policies, so it is not to be skimmed over and read quickly, choice (C). The two changes are unrelated to each other, choice (D). **The correct answer is (A).**

37. What will be required of Berwyn Corporation employees in the future?

   On Wednesdays, employees of Berwyn Corporation must

   (A) eat lunch off the Berwyn premises.

   (B) carpool to lunch.

   (C) wear jeans to work.

   (D) work as long as on other work days.

The author implies that workers must compensate for a longer lunch by either starting the workday earlier or ending it later. All other details mentioned in the e-mail are guidelines, or suggestions, rather than rules or requirements. **The correct answer is (D).**

The following is a typical letter of complaint. Companies receive these kinds of letters regularly, and generally they respond to them. They are by nature subjective, since they refer to the unique experience of the customer who is making the complaint.

QUESTIONS 38–40 REFER TO THE FOLLOWING COMPLAINT LETTER.

October 20, 2014

Mr. Henry Jones, Manager
ABC Appliances
555 Main Street
Somewhereville, VA 55555

Dear Mr. Jones:

On September 15, I purchased from your store a GEM dishwasher (model GM249). I was told that it was as good—if not better than—the other name brands you sell. And it was considerably less expensive, so I was delighted with my purchase. I have attached a copy of my receipt for your information.

I am writing to you because
  • The dishwasher is very noisy.
  • The dishwasher sometimes stops before the timer has finished, making it impossible to get my dishes clean.

On October 1, I called your store and spoke to Cindy Smith, who said she didn't know the return policy. She stated that she would discuss the problem with you and would call me back. However, I received no return call from anyone in the company. I called again on October 8 and got your company voicemail, even though I called during business hours. I left a message but again have not received a call. On October 12, I called again and spoke to Ms. Smith, who apologized and said she would call back after discussing it with you. That was over a week ago, and I have still not heard from anyone.

It is now more than 30 days since my date of purchase, even though I informed your company of the problem well before that time period expired.

The dishwasher you sold me is poor quality, doesn't work properly, and is useless as is. Under consumer law, my contract is with the seller of the goods and, as such, I am writing to you to seek a full refund.* At this point, given my experience with your customer service, I do not wish to exchange it for another unit of the same brand or even another brand. Thus far, your company has been totally unresponsive to my inquiries and complaints. This is not the kind of customer service I expect.

I would appreciate your response within 10 working days. If you wish to discuss by phone, I am contactable by phone at 555-555-5555.

If you choose to continue to ignore my complaint, I will seek alternative options.

Yours sincerely,

Susan Smith

*"As a consumer, if you purchase faulty goods, the law entitles you to seek either a repair, replacement, or a refund. It is a matter for you to negotiate with the seller for your redress. However, if a repair is offered, then it should be permanent. If not, and if the same fault occurs again, then the buyer is entitled to seek another form of redress. If you cannot agree on the form of redress, your next step after a letter may be the Small Claims Procedure—see our website/booklets for full details."

38. What is the most likely action that Ms. Smith will take if she gets no response from Mr. Jones?

(A) She'll give up and drop it.

(B) She'll call a lawyer.

(C) She'll file a claim in small claims court.

(D) She'll call again and insist that she talk to Mr. Jones directly.

The tone of the letter is one of frustration and anger, so it is unlikely that Susan Smith will drop it completely, choice (A). She could call a lawyer, but in general, this would not be the outcome for a small item and a limited complaint, choice (B). The footnote refers to small claims court as an option, choice (C). Smith included the footnote in the letter, letting Jones know that she is aware of this option as a consumer. This implies that it might be her next step. An alternative option would not include calling again, as she has tried this multiple times with no desirable result, choice (D). **The correct answer is (C).**

39. What evidence does Smith provide to support her claim that she should get a refund?

(A) The timer doesn't work properly.

(B) She found a less expensive model elsewhere.

(C) No one has returned her calls.

(D) The dishwasher is still under warranty.

Smith documents the specific problems she has found with the dishwasher, one of which is the timer. Because it is not working properly, and consumer law gives her the right to seek redress, she wants her money back, choice (A). In spite of Smith's calls, no one ever called her back, but that's not the basis for her refund, choice (C). The letter doesn't mention what kind of warranty is on the appliance, choice (D). **The correct answer is (A).**

40. Why would Smith include in her letter the statement: "I was delighted with my purchase"?

(A) She wanted to tell them what a good shopper she is.

(B) She wanted to let them know that she did not start off being negative and disgruntled.

(C) She needed to give the manager information about her purchase.

(D) She didn't want to show her anger.

Smith starts her letter by giving the store proof of her purchase so they can look it up in their records, choice (C). Her feelings about her consumer skills, choice (A), are not part of that information, but they indicate good faith in her expectations for a positive experience with the store, choice (B). She does show her anger in the last part of the letter ("This is not the kind of customer service I expect."), choice (D), but she does not start off that way, choice (B). **The correct answer is (B).**

A letter to the editor is another form of communication that people may use to voice their complaints or concerns. These letters usually address a broader concern about the community rather than a very specific complaint directed at one person or company. These communications could even be in the form of a response to a political situation or an editorial position taken by the paper.

As you read the following letter to the editor, notice how the author argues his point of view. Ask yourself what facts he uses to support his position and note how he organizes his argument.

QUESTIONS 41–44 REFER TO THE FOLLOWING LETTER TO THE EDITOR.

Dear Editor,

This letter is in response to the recent letter in your publication disparaging bicycle drivers' use of roadways.

Different vehicle types have different advantages and disadvantages, and dif-
5 ferent people have different needs and preferences. Fortunately, our roadways and traffic laws allow accommodation of a diversity of vehicle types for transportation. If this were not the case, many people would be limited to vehicles they don't need, don't want, can't afford, or can't use.

An unfortunate reality of our roadway system is that all forms of traffic affect
10 all other forms of traffic. No road user is immune to traffic delays or innocent of creating them for others. Although the cause and nature of the delays generated by traffic may appear different from one vehicle type to the next, comparison of the total induced delays caused by different vehicle types fails to reveal any significant net difference long-term. Time and time again, our free society has
15 found that the advantages of allowing transportation via a diversity of vehicle types outweighs convenience-oriented arguments for prohibition of certain vehicle types on the surface streets that provide essential access to our local destinations. This is especially true for those vehicles that are the most affordable, are the most environmentally friendly, occupy the least space, do the least damage
20 to roadways, generate the least noise, and create the least danger for other innocent road users.

When issues of traffic-related inconvenience arise, the prudent response is to improve or supplement the transportation facility, not ban a segment of the population from travel. If some motorists feel that they are unreasonably delayed
25 by slow traffic, they can lobby for construction of extra road space for passing or promote a redundant system of expressways that slower travelers won't need to use. Many communities have elected to incorporate improved passing facilities into their roadways via construction of wide (14' or wider) outside travel lanes. In other locations, delays caused by slower traffic may be too small to warrant the
30 costs of roadway widening, and taxpayer money may be better spent in other ways.

Some motorists who wish to avoid the responsibilities and occasional inconveniences of motor vehicle travel have claimed that use of slow, open vehicles on roadways is unreasonably dangerous. However, analysis of safety data for bicycle transportation shows this to be untrue. Bicycle drivers who follow the

35 vehicular rules of the road when traveling on roadways enjoy a safety record similar to automobile users, safer than sidewalk cyclists, and much safer than motorcycle users. Our society's respect for the travel rights of vulnerable but lawfully operating road users is what keeps these bicyclists safe. Those impatient road users who treat bicycle drivers with disrespect and make inflammatory
40 statements intent on depriving other groups of their equal right to travel upon our public street system are the ones creating the real danger.

Often we hear claims from very vocal individuals that bicyclists are not taxed enough or regulated enough to deserve to use public streets. Advocates for bicyclists are willing to entertain these concerns when they are presented in a
45 constructive manner, but once a realistic discussion of the costs and benefits of various revenue collection and regulation schemes begins, the vocal complainants usually lose interest. It appears that these individuals are not really interested in ensuring that the system is fair or effective; rather, they are only interested in changes that will discourage bicycling. If these bicycling critics are primarily
50 interested in their own convenience as motorists, perhaps their efforts would be better spent lobbying for improved roadway facilities such as wide outside lanes. Bicycling critics may also point out that some bicycle operators create hazards for other road users by habitually violating the rules of the road. Lawfully operating bicycle drivers share this concern and advocate better education and enforcement
55 of the traffic laws we already have as they apply to all drivers of vehicles.

Sometimes members of the motoring public will express empathy for utilitarian bicyclists who don't use cars, but exhibit anger toward recreational cyclists who use popular roads at popular times. Some of these motorists suggest that the government place prohibitions on recreational bicycle travel. This concept is
60 fraught with problems. First, it is impossible to tell one's trip purpose simply from appearance, since many utilitarian cyclists use the same bicycles and clothing as recreational cyclists, and second, the government has never been granted an interest in the citizens' trip purpose for everyday travel on public streets. Do we wish to open a Pandora's box of civil liberty infringements where
65 our government can stop citizens for their appearance, demand to know their trip purpose, and arrest them for traveling for unapproved reasons? If recreational travel is subject to prohibition, does that mean that trips to sporting events and vacations may be prohibited to reduce traffic? May the government ban "sports cars," "sport utility vehicles," and "RVs" in order to spare the public from their
70 impact on roads? It seems far better to allow everyone to use our roadways, and to design and regulate them to make them as safe and efficient as possible for mixed traffic. That way we can continue to enjoy living in a free country, with equal opportunity for all.

Sincerely,

Your friendly neighborhood bicycle driver Tom

41. What is the author's purpose in addressing the critics of bicycle riders on the roadways?

   (A) to suggest ways to reduce congestion on the roads

   (B) to show that his critics are all wrong

   (C) to answer all of the critics in one letter

   (D) to make a stronger argument

The author cites the critics and provides evidence to show why each claim is not supportable. This makes a stronger argument, since there are fewer ways to punch holes in it, choice (D). The author does suggest some ways to reduce congestion, but these are given as part of his overall argument, choice (A). The author's argument does show the specific ways in which his critics are wrong, but the purpose of refuting their arguments is to make his own argument stronger, not merely to make critics wrong, choice (B). Although critics may not all be included, the author counters their arguments and not the critics themselves, choice (C). Putting it all in one letter or essay makes it easier to read and makes the argument more understandable, but it is not the author's purpose. **The correct answer is (D).**

42. What prompted the author's letter to the editor?

   (A) a proposal to tax bicycles on the road

   (B) a letter that was insulting to bicycles on the roadways

   (C) the increasing traffic congestion

   (D) road rage toward bicycle riders

The first sentence in the passage says that the letter is a response to an earlier letter that "disparages" bicycle riders on the road, choice (B). All of the other options are ideas that are mentioned as details in one of the counterarguments, but none is what the author says prompted his letter. **The correct answer is (B).**

43. Which phrase in the last paragraph is an example of figurative language that the author uses to help drive home his point?

   (A) "recreational cyclists who use popular roads at popular times"

   (B) "simply from appearance"

   (C) "a Pandora's box of civil liberty infringements"

   (D) "prohibitions on recreational bicycle travel"

Figurative language is language that is not literal; that is, it has meaning beyond the specific meaning of the words themselves. In the last paragraph the author gets more emphatic and uses hyperbole (exaggeration) to show how ridiculous the argument would be if one were to carry it to its logical conclusion. An example of such a phrase is "a Pandora's box of civil liberty infringements," in which he refers to a Greek myth in which a box that seems harmless turns out to contain the evils of the world. Referring to Pandora's box symbolizes opening the door to something that has unexpected and perhaps severe consequences. None of the other phrases are used figuratively. **The correct answer is (C).**

44. Which of the claims made by the author's critics does he think have some validity?

   (A) Bicycles on the roads should be taxed to discourage their use.

   (B) Bicycles on the road are a hazard to road safety.

   (C) Bicyclists do not follow the rules of the road.

   (D) Only bicyclists who use their bikes to get to work should be allowed on the roads.

The author addresses each critic with counterarguments. He shows that those who want to tax bicycle use are really only interested in reducing or even eliminating bicycles on the roads—these critics usually disappear when anyone actually tries to talk to them about such a policy, choice (A). To the claim that bicycles are dangerous to road safety, the author counters statistics that show that this is not true, so long as bicyclists are following road rules, choice (B). To the claim that bicyclists don't follow the rules of the road, he says that bicyclists who obey the rules share this concern. This statement implies that some (but not all) bicyclists do not follow the rules, choice (C). To the claim that bicycles for recreational use should not be allowed on the roads at certain times, the author provides several different statements that expose the lack of logic to this argument, choice (D). **The correct answer is (C).**

UNDERSTANDING FICTION

A work of **fiction** is one that is made up; in other words, it involves imaginary people and events. Works of fiction can take a variety of different forms, but the Reasoning Through Language Arts—Reading Comprehension test focuses on prose. You can expect one reading passage involving fiction, with approximately eight questions.

A passage may provide an entire work of fiction if the work is brief. Generally, however, passages are excerpted from longer works of fiction, whether novels or short stories.

In the following sections, you'll learn more about prose fiction, and you'll learn how best to read this type of fiction in order to understand it in ways that will help you most on the GED® test. You'll also read a variety of sample passages and answer GED® test-style questions based on them.

The Elements of Fiction

As was just noted, a fictional work is a work based on someone's imagination. In other words, the story, characters, and other elements of a fictional work are made up by the author. Even stories based on real people or real situations can be fiction. A work of fiction can be in the form of a short story, a novel, a poem, or a drama. The term

prose fiction is generally used in reference to short stories and novels, as opposed to plays or poems, and it is this type of fiction that will be used in the test. (The word *prose* refers to the ordinary form of writing or speaking.)

The **plot** in fiction is the story line—the story's events strung together in a particular sequence or order. A story's events can flow chronologically (in the order they occur in time) or they can be revealed out of order or sequence. Works of fiction usually begin with the first event and trace subsequent events chronologically. However, the author may choose a different sequence instead. For instance, the author may begin the story with the final event and then unravel the plot by going back to the first event in order to explain what led up to the event.

A story's **narrator** is the voice that tells the story—the storyteller. The narrator relates the story's events as he or she sees them unfold, from his/her *point of view*. Usually a story is told from either a first-person or a third-person point of view. A work written in **first person** is told from the narrator's own perspective. Throughout the story, the narrator speaks in terms of *I* or *me*, so the reader follows the story as seen through the narrator's eyes. When reading fiction that is written in first person, the reader is limited by the narrator's limited knowledge. The reader knows only what the narrator sees and thinks, and must interpret the actions and thoughts of the other characters through the narrator's eyes, responding to events and other characters through the narrator's subjective perspective. In contrast, a work of fiction written in **third person** is told from the perspective of a narrator who knows and reveals *everything* to the reader. From this point of view, the narrator does not speak in terms of *I* but rather in terms of *he*, *she*, and *they*. The third-person point of view allows the reader glimpses of all the characters' actions and feelings through an all-knowing, or omniscient, narrator.

The figures involved in the plot are known as **characters.** The main characters are those around whom the plot revolves. Minor characters are incidental characters who become involved in the plot to a lesser extent. A story's characters are revealed to the reader in several different ways. Usually, the narrator describes what the characters look like and tells the reader about their personalities, either directly or indirectly. Characters are also revealed by how they act and what they say. For instance, a character might behave in a consistently shy manner, or continually talk about herself, or use poor grammar in his or her speech. Finally, characters are understood by what the others in the story say or think about them. A character's spoken words to another character are referred to as **dialogue.**

The **tone** of a story is the attitude of the narrator or the author toward the subject or event. The reader's impression of the subject or event may be colored by how the narrator or author feels about it. The **mood** is an overall atmosphere the author creates by carefully selecting certain words and details. The **setting** of a story is the author's description of the time and place in which the story occurs. Not only does the setting make the story more real for the reader, it also helps to create the mood of the story. An event that occurs at midnight on a rainy night creates more of a mood of fear than the same event occurring on a sunny day.

Authors of fiction use a variety of **literary devices** to help convey ideas, emphasize certain points, incite the reader's imagination, and provide a more interesting and enjoyable reading experience. To help describe a story's setting or to describe how the story's characters experience certain events, fiction authors often employ **imagery**—the use of language to convey a sense experience (sight, sound, smell, taste, or touch). To help convey ideas and enhance interest, fiction authors often use **figurative language**—the use of language in ways that give words and phrases a meaning other than their common, or *literal*, meaning. A particular instance of figurative language is commonly referred to as a **figure of speech.**

Figurative language can be used to make an abstract idea concrete or to visualize an idea. Often a figure of speech will compare two seemingly different things to reveal their similarities. For instance, when someone says they are *on pins and needles* waiting for something to happen, that person is using a figure of speech. Obviously, the person is not literally on pins and needles. The expression, however, does convey the person's excitement about whatever might happen.

An author's use of figurative language might apply to larger elements of a story as well, perhaps even to the entire story. For example, an entire narrative might serve as a *metaphor* or as a *symbol*, by which the story's events are intended either to substitute for or represent some other story. Or a narrative might be intended as an *allegory,* which can either be understood literally or taken to mean something more, or deeper, as well.

Prose Fiction

Your GED® Reading Comprehension test will contain one prose fiction passage drawn from a short story or novel. The passage will be 400–900 words in length (one or two pages, more or less). Even a 900-word passage is a very manageable piece of text; you should have little difficulty reading 900 words and remembering the information within the passage.

The passage you will see on the test could reflect any number of characters, cultural settings, and historical references that could be from different time periods. A passage might contain only narrative, but could contain dialogue as well. A passage's style might be formal and heavy-handed, or it might be casual or even conversational. In short, expect anything. Keep in mind, though, that the GED® test will *not* test you on your knowledge of literature, literary traditions, or specific authors. To answer the test questions, all you'll need to know will be expressed or implied in the passages and in the questions themselves.

Regardless of when or by whom a work of prose fiction was written or what style of writing the author uses, the guidelines for reading and understanding prose fiction are essentially the same. As you read a passage of prose fiction, ask yourself the following questions that focus on the very same reading skills that the GED® test covers:

- **Who is the narrator?** Is the story told in the first person—from the narrator's perspective? Or is it told in the third person—from the perspective of an all-knowing observer outside the story itself?

- **What is the setting and mood of the passage?** Through the narrator or the characters, the reader might infer when and where certain events are taking place. Are they occurring during a particular era, decade, year, or season? During wartime, a time of prosperity and optimism, or a time of strife and despair? In a big city, in a rural village, or on a remote island? In a modest apartment, a large mansion, or a restaurant? What are the weather and other environmental conditions? Is the overall mood somber, joyous, upbeat, or tense? Understanding the setting and mood can help you interpret the passage's events and the characters' actions.

- **What is the author's main concern in the passage?** Think about the passage as a whole. Ask yourself what the author's intent is, as revealed through the narrator. Here are just a few examples of what an author might be trying to accomplish:

  - Describe a predicament or difficult situation

  - Explain implicit causes and their consequences by recounting a series of events

  - Reveal the relationship between characters through their conversation

  - Reveal a character through his or her thoughts, actions, and reactions

- **How does the narrator set the mood and tone for the story?** Look for specific words or phrases that paint a picture of the setting or create the mood for the overall story. Think about how these words influence the reader's perspective of the characters or point of view. Are there specific words that suggest a particular tone? Ask yourself how changing one or several of these words would alter your perception of what's taking place and/or the motives of the characters.

- **What does the passage reveal about the story's characters?** A character's specific actions, spoken words, and thoughts can reveal a lot about his or her personality, motives, attitudes, and mood. They can also reveal how the character sees and relates to the story's other characters. They can reveal, too, how the character might behave in other situations. Pay careful attention to these details.

- **What events might have led to or might follow the ones described in the passage?** More specifically, ask yourself questions such as the following:

  - How might the situation described in the passage have come about?

  - Are the characters behaving in a way that certain prior events might help explain?

  - Do the characters' thoughts and their dialogue suggest what they might do later in the story?

  - Given the circumstances, what would naturally and logically occur next in time?

- **Beyond their literal meaning, what do the passage's words and ideas imply or suggest?** As noted earlier, fiction authors use a variety of literary devices to convey ideas. These could include using figurative language; that is, words that suggest a non-literal meaning. Figurative language points beyond the generally understood meaning of words so that the words mean something else. The device creates a contrast to reality and helps establish an author's ideas. Often, figurative language enhances the emotional intensity and imaginative appeal of the work, and it does so with fewer words, since the larger meaning is embedded in the language itself. For example, some passages may use devices like some of the following to create a mood, set a tone, or otherwise embellish the story:

- *Irony:* a discrepancy between an actual situation and what one would normally expect under the circumstances. For example, dying of thirst while disabled within sight of a river could be considered ironic. Getting into a fender bender on the way to a driver's education class might also be thought of as ironic. Irony is a powerful tool because it allows the writer to convey an idea without asserting it directly. The irony of a situation is left to the reader to discover.

- *Paradox:* a situation that seems contradictory yet, in fact, is not. In fact, once understood, something paradoxical actually makes sense on a deeper level. For example, the expression *youth is wasted on the young* is a paradox. While the expression seems to be contradictory upon first glance, the deeper meaning is that many who are young do not appreciate the benefits of youth until they are no longer young. A paradox is different from an oxymoron in that paradoxes are larger concepts, whereas an oxymoron is made up of a two-word phrase; for instance, *thunderous silence* or *noble theft*.

- *Metaphor and simile*: techniques that both compare two unlike things. These literary devices are probably the most commonly used types of figures of speech. They are designed to heighten our senses and help the reader look at something in a new way. A simile makes a direct comparison by using the words *like* or *as*. A metaphor makes the comparison more indirectly without these words. We all use similes every day without thinking about it—for example, when we refer to *being tired as a dog* or *sleeping like a baby*. Common metaphors can be found in lyrics to music as well as in poetry; for example, *a sea of grief, a bridge over troubled water, the light of my life*, and so on. In each of these examples, the metaphor enriches the image conveyed through the language chosen.

- *Personification:* attributing human qualities to an animal, an object, or even a concept. Here are a few examples:

    The setting sun sang its lullaby.

    The barn gate jeered and complained to the sudden gust.

    Using personification lends special powers to inanimate objects, injecting them with qualities that emphasize a point.

- *Symbolism:* one thing used to represent something else that is more abstract. In prose, symbols give an expanded meaning to a specific aspect of the text. For example, a boy's white shirt may symbolize his innocence.

When reading a GED® test passage, look for use of the above-noted figures of speech. While you will not be tested on the definitions, you may be expected to understand and recognize their use. Ask yourself: What events might have led to or might follow the ones described in the passage?

Inferring context from the passage can help you interpret the passage's events and the characters' actions.

Rest assured that GED® test prose-fiction questions will not ask you to uncover obscure, hidden meanings behind the passage. Rather, the questions will focus on what we've just covered—the passage's main concern, setting, use of language to create mood and tone, sequence of events, and character development—all as stated or implied in the passage. It's important to read the passage carefully for what is implied as well as what is stated. As you read, try to develop an overview—a short who, what, where, when, why—so the passage has some context that will be assisted by the details given in the text.

In the following brief passage, imagery and figurative language are used effectively to establish setting, mood, and tone, all of which serve to make a point in a powerful way. Read the paragraph, and then answer the three questions that follow it.

QUESTIONS 1–3 REFER TO THE FOLLOWING PASSAGE.

Dark spruce forest frowned on either side the frozen waterway. The trees had been stripped by a recent wind of their white covering of frost, and they seemed to lean towards each other, black and ominous, in the fading light. A vast silence reigned over the land. The land itself was a desolation, lifeless, without movement, so
5 lone and cold that the spirit of it was not even that of sadness. There was a hint in it of laughter, but of a laughter more terrible than any sadness—a laughter that was mirthless as the smile of the Sphinx, a laughter cold as the frost and partaking of the grimness of infallibility. It was the masterful and incommunicable wisdom of eternity laughing at the futility of life and the effort of life. It
10 was the Wild, the savage, frozen-hearted Northland Wild.

— from *White Fang*, by Jack London

1. What does the setting described in this paragraph lead you to expect about the story?

   (A) It will be bleak and dark.

   (B) It will be all about nature.

   (C) It will contain some humor, or at least some moments of laughter.

   (D) It will contain a moral lesson.

London provides vivid details of the setting, which, all told, give a dark and bleak picture. The use of specific language (for example, *desolation*—solitude, loneliness, and isolation) and imagery (for example, the *frowned* forest, the *black and ominous* trees, the *desolate* and *lifeless* land that is *lone and cold*) all suggest a stark and bleak picture. Though nature is part of the description, a cold and lifeless nature is the expectation. The tone is definitely not humorous. The idea of laughter here is wicked and grim. Although the last line mentions wisdom, there is no hint of a moral to come. **The correct answer is (A).**

2. How does the author's use of the simile *a laughter that was mirthless as the smile of the Sphinx* contribute to painting a picture of the setting?

(A) He contrasts laughter with the cold landscape to show the human element in an otherwise stark environment.

(B) He uses the Sphinx, made out of stone, to remind us of the cold and hardened atmosphere.

(C) He uses the simile to show irony in the situation.

(D) He describes the smile of the Sphinx to show that there is laughter in nature.

The author is using figurative language here to convey an idea. Notice that he is using a simile to draw a comparison between two very different things: a land's laughter and a Sphinx's smile. (In fact, each of these two things is a figure of speech in itself, not to be read literally.) The fact that the Sphinx is made of stone and that the narrator describes the scene as cold and lonely both indicate that the smile of the Sphinx is one without warmth, further emphasizing the bleak environment. There is nothing ironic in the description. The laughter is a figure of speech—a hardened and lifeless form in contrast to a human voice. **The correct answer is (B).**

3. Which statement best captures the essential idea of the passage?

(A) The North is wild beyond compare.

(B) In the North, life is short and brutal.

(C) In the North, time defeats all life.

(D) Winter in the North can be deadly.

This deceptively difficult question essentially asks what the author's main point is in the passage. To answer it, you need to synthesize the passage's ideas and evaluate the passage as a whole. The narrator does refer to the "savage. . . Northland Wild"—choice (A), the futility of life—choice (B), and the "lifeless" land—choice (D). However, none of these observations captures the essence of the paragraph. The passage's main thrust is best expressed by the second-to-last sentence: "It was the masterful and incommunicable wisdom of eternity laughing at the futility of life and the effort of life" (lines 8–9). In other words, the passing of time ultimately defeats all life in the North. **The correct answer is (C).**

The next paragraph follows the paragraph from London's *White Fang* in the previous passage. On the GED® test, the two paragraphs would be shown as one passage. Together, they are about half the length of an average GED® test passage. Observe the contrast between the two paragraphs.

QUESTIONS 4–6 REFER TO THE FOLLOWING PASSAGE.

In advance of the dogs, on wide snowshoes, toiled a man. At the rear of the sled toiled a second man. On the sled, in the box, lay a third man whose toil was over—a man whom the Wild had conquered and beaten down until he would never move nor struggle again. It is not the way of the Wild to like movement.
5 Life is an offence to it, for life is movement; and the Wild aims always to destroy movement. It freezes the water to prevent it running to the sea; it drives the sap out of the trees till they are frozen to their mighty hearts; and most ferociously and terribly of all does the Wild harry and crush into submission man—man who is the most restless of life, ever in revolt against the dictum that all movement
10 must in the end come to the cessation of movement.

— from *White Fang*, by Jack London

4. How does this paragraph extend the ideas of the first paragraph?

   (A) It adds humans to the setting.

   (B) It contrasts the dogs with the humans.

   (C) It contradicts the first paragraph in showing that life can exist in this environment.

   (D) It fills in details by describing what the men were carrying.

The main point of this paragraph is as a continuation of the story. The paragraph drops men and their dogs into the harsh environment described in the prior paragraph, which serves as a backdrop. The dogs and the men are part of the description; they are not compared. There is no contradiction described here, although the text says that life (the dogs and men) is defiant, trying to overcome the brutality of the land. The description of what the men were carrying is a detail about the men. **The correct answer is (A).**

5. Which of the following statements correctly describes how the second paragraph advances the theme of the story thus far?

   (A) The brutal cold affects both the men and the dogs.

   (B) Men may try to conquer nature but don't always win.

   (C) Human ingenuity helps the men survive the cold and harsh environment.

   (D) In an environment of man against nature, the supplies will be very important to the men's survival.

This paragraph introduces the human element to the harsh environment and describes men who are trying to defy nature by surviving in the inhospitable Wild. The theme of man vs. nature starts to develop as the narrator describes not just how the cold affects the men and the dogs, choice (A), but their attempt to live and overcome the obstacles, choices (C) and (D). We see a hint of nature winning with the long and narrow oblong box—probably a coffin carrying someone who didn't survive, choice (B). **The correct answer is (B).**

6. Which figurative device is used throughout the paragraph?

(A) irony

(B) personification

(C) simile

(D) metaphor

Irony is when a discrepancy occurs between what is expected and what actually happens; this is not shown in this passage, choice (A). Similes and metaphors, choices (C) and (D), are both ways of comparing unlike things in a descriptive way, with the former using *like* or *as* and the later making a direct comparison. Throughout the passage *Wild* is capitalized and has human qualities attributed to it, for example saying that it "aims always to destroy movement." **The correct answer is (B).**

QUESTIONS 7–11 REFER TO THE FOLLOWING PASSAGE.

If ever a girl of the working class had led the sheltered life, it was Genevieve. In the midst of roughness and brutality, Genevieve had shunned all that was rough and brutal. She saw but what she chose to see, and she chose always to see the best, avoiding coarseness and uncouthness without effort, as a matter of
5 instinct. To begin with, she had been peculiarly unexposed. An only child, with an invalid mother upon whom she attended, she had not joined in the street games and frolics of the children of the neighborhood. Her father, a mild-tempered, narrow-chested, anaemic little clerk, domestic because of his inherent disability to mix with men, had done his full share toward giving the home an atmosphere
10 of sweetness and tenderness.

An orphan at twelve, Genevieve had gone straight from her father's funeral to live with the Silversteins in their rooms above the candy store; and here, sheltered by kindly aliens, she earned her keep and clothes by waiting on the shop. Being Gentile, she was especially necessary to the Silversteins, who would
15 not run the business themselves when the day of their Sabbath came round.

And here, in the uneventful little shop, six maturing years had slipped by. Her acquaintances were few. She had elected to have no girl chum for the reason that no satisfactory girl had appeared. Nor did she choose to walk with the young fellows of the neighbourhood, as was the custom of girls from their fifteenth year.
20 "That stuck-up doll-face," was the way the girls of the neighbourhood described her; and though she earned their enmity by her beauty and aloofness, she none the less commanded their respect. "Peaches and cream," she was called by the young men—though softly and amongst themselves, for they were afraid of arousing the ire of the other girls, while they stood in awe of Genevieve, in a
25 dimly religious way, as a something mysteriously beautiful and unapproachable.

— from *The Game*, by Jack London

7. Which of the following does NOT account for Genevieve's character?

   (A) the fact she was an only child

   (B) the neighborhood children

   (C) her mother's invalidity

   (D) her father's domestic nature

All choices except for choice (B) list factors that influenced Genevieve's character. The children in the neighborhood did not influence her because she had little contact with them. **The correct answer is (B).**

8. Which word best describes Genevieve?

   (A) anemic

   (B) predictable

   (C) timid

   (D) naive

Genevieve had clearly lived a sheltered life ("she had been peculiarly unexposed"). She intentionally avoided exposure to anything "rough and brutal" and to the "coarseness and uncouthness" of the real world. She preferred to keep to herself rather than joining in street games with other children. As a result, she was probably a bit innocent in the ways of the world, or *naive*. **The correct answer is (D).**

9. Which job would Genevieve's father probably be most suited for?

   (A) school teacher

   (B) business manager

   (C) car salesman

   (D) gentleman's butler

The father is described as "domestic because of his inherent disability to mix with men." What this probably means is that he lacked an ability to get along in the working world, where he would have to compete and deal with other men. Because he was accustomed to the domestic life, and in fact had provided a very nice home atmosphere, he would probably make an excellent gentleman's butler. **The correct answer is (D).**

10. What words in the passage could you use as clues to determine the meaning of the word *enmity* (line 21)?

    (A) Because she had no friends, Genevieve made enemies of her peers.

    (B) Genevieve didn't find the other girls suitable as friends, and they thought she was stuck-up.

    (C) The girls were jealous because Genevieve was beautiful.

    (D) Genevieve was afraid of being teased by the other girls and was afraid of their anger.

The passage states that Genevieve had no friends by her own choice. This made her peers brand her as *stuck-up*. The narrator describes her beauty, which the other girls resented. These factors show that the feelings between Genevieve and the other girls were mutual, as they were all full of ill will, which is the meaning of *enmity*. Choice (D) indicates Genevieve's feelings; choice (C) describes the girls' feelings toward Genevieve. Choice (A) suggests an incorrect definition of *enmity* (making enemies). Only choice (B) shows the mutual dislike that defines the word. **The correct answer is (B).**

11. What does Genevieve's rejection of brutality in the world imply about her nature?

    (A) that she is capable of ignoring what she doesn't like

    (B) that as a child she was brutalized by other children, causing her to be fearful

    (C) that she sees the world as a brutal place and became hardened to that reality

    (D) that her natural beauty can overcome brutality

Genevieve is shown to have had a hard life, especially compared to the other girls she sees during her regular days. But the narrator also describes her as someone who sees only what she chooses and is therefore unaware of the harsh realities that she doesn't want to see. She was not brutalized by other children, but instead by circumstances, although she opts not to see them and thus has not been hardened. Although she is described as beautiful, there is no indication that she is actually stuck-up. **The correct answer is (A).**

Unlike either of the previous passages, the next passage consists mainly of dialogue. (Its word length would be on the shorter side of a GED® test reading passage, although it might appear longer due to its many paragraph breaks.) As you read the passage, ask yourself who the narrator is and how the three characters are related to one another. Also pay close attention to what their behavior suggests about each of them individually and about their relationship with one another. To follow the events as they unfold in the passage, try to visualize the scene. As is typical of GED® test prose-fiction passages, the passage's concluding sentences leave you asking questions that are likely to be the focus of at least one or two *test* questions.

QUESTIONS 12–17 REFER TO THE FOLLOWING PASSAGE.

On the 24th of May, 1863, my uncle, Professor Liedenbrock, rushed into his little house, No. 19 Konigstrasse, one of the oldest streets in the oldest portion of the city of Hamburg. Martha must have concluded that she was very much behindhand, for the dinner had only just been put into the oven.

5   "Well, now," said I to myself, "if that most impatient of men is hungry, what a disturbance he will make!"

"Mr. Liedenbrock so soon!" cried poor Martha in great alarm, half opening the dining-room door.

"Yes, Martha; but very likely the dinner is not half cooked, for it is not two
10 yet. Saint Michael's clock has only just struck half-past one."

"Then why has the master come home so soon?"

"Perhaps he will tell us that himself."

"Here he is, Monsieur Axel; I will run and hide myself while you argue with him."

15   And Martha retreated in safety into her own dominions. I was left alone. But how was it possible for a man of my undecided turn of mind to argue successfully with so irascible a person as the Professor? With this persuasion I was hurrying away to my own little retreat upstairs, when the street door creaked upon its hinges; heavy feet made the whole flight of stairs to shake; and the master of
20 the house, passing rapidly through the dining room, threw himself in haste into his own sanctum.

But on his rapid way he had found time to fling his hazel stick into a corner, his rough broadbrim upon the table, and these few emphatic words at his nephew: "Axel, follow me!"

25   I had scarcely had time to move when the Professor was again shouting after me: "What! not come yet?" And I rushed into my redoubtable master's study.

Otto Liedenbrock had no mischief in him, I willingly allow that; but unless he very considerably changes as he grows older, at the end he will be a most original character.

— from *Journey to the Center of the Earth*, by Jules Verne

12. From whose point of view are the events in the passage described?

The events are described from the point of view of

(A) Martha

(B) Monsieur Axel

(C) an outside observer

(D) Otto Liedenbrock

The narration is in first person—from the point of view of Monsieur Axel, who is Professor Liedenbrock's nephew. The narrator's identity is not clear until Martha says "Here he is, Monsieur Axel; I will run and hide myself while you argue with him," after which the narrator comments, "I was left alone." **The correct answer is (B).**

13. Which description best characterizes the Professor, as he is revealed in the passage?

(A) absent-minded

(B) mischievous

(C) decisive

(D) demanding

In the passage the narrator (Axel) uses the words "impatient" (line 5) and "irascible" (line 17) to describe Professor Liedenbrock. (The word *irascible* means "disagreeable.") However, none of the four answer choices matches these two descriptive words. To answer the question, you must infer some other trait from the Professor's behavior, as seen through Axel's eyes. Notice that Martha is worried that she might be in trouble with the Professor because dinner was late. Notice also that the Professor shouts to his nephew, "Axel, follow me!" These portions of the narrative both strongly suggest that the Professor is a *demanding* person. **The correct answer is (D).**

14. What does the passage suggest about Martha?

(A) She is often late cooking dinner.

(B) She looks to Axel for support.

(C) She is afraid of losing her job.

(D) She is Otto Liedenbrock's niece.

When dinner is not ready for the Professor, Martha asks Axel to intercept the Professor while she hides in her quarters. Based on this narrative, we can infer that Martha looks to Axel to help her out in difficult situations. **The correct answer is (B).**

15. The narrator remarks that unless Otto Liedenbrock changes as he grows older, "at the end he will be a most original character" (lines 28–29).

The narrator's point about Otto Liedenbrock is that as he grows older,

(A) he will be known for his originality

(B) his students will no longer enjoy his teaching methods

(C) people will find him very difficult to be around

(D) he will begin imagining things due to old age

To interpret the meaning of the quoted words, look at their context. In the first part of the same sentence, Axel says, "Otto Liedenbrock had no mischief in him, I willingly allow that; but unless he changes. . . ." Axel seems to imply here that Liedenbrock might develop traits like mischievousness as he gets older, in which case other people may find him very difficult to put up with. **The correct answer is (C).**

> **16.** Based on his behavior, what can you conclude about why the Professor has come home early?
>
> **(A)** He is very hungry and wants to have his dinner right away.
>
> **(B)** He is angry at his nephew and wants to berate him immediately.
>
> **(C)** He isn't feeling well and needs to lie down and rest before dinner.
>
> **(D)** He has important news and wants to share it with Axel immediately.

We can see that the Professor is impatient and moves quickly, scattering his belongings about the house, illustrating that he is distracted. He doesn't demand food, so he has not come home early to eat. The Professor moves about with purpose. Though he appears to be in a rush, there is no indication that he is angry at anyone. He heads for his *own sanctum*—his study—so he has not come home to rest. He is in a hurry to speak to his nephew, since he impatiently calls him into his office. While we don't know the reason he is in such a hurry to speak to Axel, we can infer that it is so important that he has come home early, something he does not usually do. **The correct answer is (D).**

> **17.** Which of the following events is most likely to occur next?
>
> **(A)** The Professor will realize that dinner is late and will become angry.
>
> **(B)** The Professor will have a serious conversation with Axel.
>
> **(C)** Martha will apologize to the Professor for the half-cooked dinner.
>
> **(D)** Axel will sit down to eat with Martha but without the Professor.

Martha, who is probably the Professor's live-in cook, has hidden herself in her quarters. Meanwhile, the Professor has called his nephew Axel into his study. Since the Professor is nowhere near the dining area, he is not likely to suddenly realize that dinner is late, choice (A). Nothing in the passage indicates that Martha will be rushing to the Professor's study with an apology, choice (C). Martha is most likely the hired help and probably won't be eating with the Professor's family, choice (D). Only choice (B) provides a plausible continuation of the story. **The correct answer is (B).**

GENERAL TEST-TAKING STRATEGIES

Here are some general strategies for tackling the reading comprehension portion of the test. These points of advice generally apply to all types of passages and questions. Put these strategies to work on the practice tests in this book, and then review them again just before exam day.

Read the questions based on a passage before you read the passage itself.

Each reading comprehension passage will be followed by 6 to 8 questions that refer to it. Before you read the passage, read the question stems (the questions themselves, but not the answer choices). This task should only take you 20 seconds or so. Some of the questions will provide clues as to what you should look for and think about as you read.

Read each passage straight through before answering any questions based on it.

Read the passage from beginning to end. Focus mainly on the flow of ideas from one to another. Maintaining this mind-set will help you understand the passage's main ideas, as well as the author's overall concern and purpose in mentioning various details—all of which in turn will help you answer the questions.

Don't get bogged down in details as you read a passage.

Some GED® test reading passages will be loaded with details: examples, descriptions, dates, and so forth. If you try to absorb all of the details as you read, you'll not only lose sight of the ideas behind the details, you'll also lose reading speed. Don't get bogged down in the details, especially those you don't fully understand. Instead, gloss over them. Note where examples, lists, and other details are located. Then, if you're asked a question involving those details, you can quickly and easily locate them and read them more carefully.

Sum up a passage after you read it.

After reading an entire passage, take a few seconds to recap it. If the passage is nonfiction, ask yourself what the author's main point and major supporting points are. If the passage is from a fictional story, recap events in your mind. Remind yourself about the flow of the discussion or events, without thinking about all the details. Seeing the "big picture" may be enough to answer as many as half the questions.

If possible, formulate your own answer to a question before reading the answer choices.

For each question, try to formulate your own response to it, and *then* scan the choices for something resembling your home-grown answer. This technique will keep you from becoming confused and distracted by wrong-answer choices.

To answer a question that quotes the passage, expect to "read around" the quoted text.

A particular question might quote a word, line, or entire sentence from the passage. If so, be sure you understand the *context* of the quote before answering the question. Re-read the sentences preceding and following the quote. Chances are, you'll need to understand what precedes and follows the quote to recognize the best answer choice.

To avoid skipping around the passage, answer the questions in sequence.

The sequence of questions generally corresponds to where the passage addresses each one. For example, a question about the first paragraph will probably appear earlier than a question about the second paragraph. Answering the questions in sequence helps you "go with the flow" of ideas as the passage presents them. So avoid "shopping around" for easy questions, unless you're running out of time. Keep in mind, however, that some questions *might* appear out of sequence and that questions involving the entire passage can appear anywhere in the sequence.

Pace yourself properly.

Your time limit for answering all forty-nine questions in the entire Reasoning Through Language Arts test is 150 minutes. Try to answer ten questions about every 30 minutes, on average. If you're falling behind, try to pick up your pace. In any event, try to answer all questions with a few minutes to spare, so you can go back and reconsider any responses you were unsure about.

SUMMING IT UP

- In the Reasoning Through Language Arts Test, the reading comprehension questions gauge your ability to understand, interpret, evaluate, synthesize, and apply information contained in fiction as well as nonfiction texts. This portion of the test consists of several reading passages, each one followed by several multiple-choice questions.

- Reading comprehension passages are drawn from a wide variety of sources, including fiction; informational nonfiction that includes topics of interest related to science; social studies; and workplace and community documents.

- The broad reading skill areas tested in the reading comprehension portion of the test include comprehension, analysis and interpretation, evaluation and synthesis, and application.

- The entire Reasoning Through Language Arts Test lasts 150 minutes. You should expect six to eight passages with a total of 49 questions. Each passage of prose will be 400 to 900 words in length (about one to two pages).

Mastering Language Comprehension

OVERVIEW

- All about the Reasoning Through Language Arts Test—Language Comprehension
- Answering questions
- General test-taking strategies
- Summing it up

chapter 4

THE REASONING THROUGH LANGUAGE ARTS TEST—LANGUAGE COMPREHENSION—IN A NUTSHELL

Time allowed: 150 minutes for the entire Reasoning Through Language Arts Test, which includes 45 minutes for the Extended Response as well as a 10-minute break.

Number of passages: Expect 2 (the number can vary)

Length of each passage: 350–450 words

Total number of questions: 49 on the Reasoning Through Language Arts Test, which includes a reading component, language component, and extended response (question types include multiple choice, fill-in-the-blank, drag-and-drop, drop-down, and extended response)

Number of questions per passage: Expect 6 to 8 (the number can vary)

ALL ABOUT THE REASONING THROUGH LANGUAGE ARTS TEST—LANGUAGE COMPREHENSION

The newest edition of the GED® test language conventions portion of the test includes technology-enhanced questions such as drag-and-drop, hot-spot, drop-down, and fill-in-the-blank items. Drag-and-drop questions will require you to drag the "drag tokens" and place them on one or more correct "drop targets." Hot-spot items will be used so that you may select your answer by clicking or graphing a point on a designated sensor on graphs, maps, or diagrams. Drop-down questions will require you to choose the correct answer from a list of options in a drop-down menu. Fill-in-the-blank (FITB) questions will require you to write one or two words to complete a sentence.

Each passage for the language component of the test will be 350–450 words in length and will contain twelve to twenty-two sentences. Here is an example of a GED®

test-style workplace-related text. This one happens to come with a title, but some may not. This document illustrates certain features that all documents on the language component of the Reasoning Through Language Arts test share in common:

- Sentences are numbered in sequence.

- Paragraphs are lettered in sequence.

- Some (but not all) of the sentences are flawed in some way.

THANK YOU NOTE AFTER AN INTERVIEW

(A)

(1) Dear mr. Jones,

(2) I enjoy meeting you to discuss the position as the administrative assistant at Colton & Smith Co. (3) Thank you for taking time out of your busy schedule to meat with me--I appreciate your consideration for this position.

(B)

(4) After meeting with you, I am even more sure that I would not only be a good fit with Colton & smith Co. community but also in the assistant position. (5) My organizational and communication skills would compliment the necessary tasks for the job and my enthusiasm for learning align with the company mission.

(C)

(6) I look forward to hearing from you, once the final decision regarding the position is made. (7) Please feel free to contact me at any time if any further information was needed. (8) I can be reached at (123) 456-7890 or ksmith@email.com.

(9) Thank you again for your time and consideration,

(10) Sincerely,

Katherine

Regardless of what sort of text you're dealing with, the questions will all cover the same sorts of language convention issues. Below is the breakdown of the broad areas covered by the language component of the Reasoning Through Language Arts test. Note that the test questions cover only certain topics within each area, as listed here. Don't worry if you are unfamiliar with some of the terms here; this book's grammar review explains many common issues.

- **Grammar and usage**: Subject-verb agreement and pronoun reference/antecedents

- **Sentence structure**: Sentence fragments, fused sentences, and run-ons; parallelism; coordination and subordination; placement of modifiers

- **Writing mechanics**: Spelling (homonyms, contractions, and possessives only); capitalization of proper nouns; use of commas for punctuation, use of apostrophes with possessive nouns, frequently confused words

- **Effective writing**: Informal usage, transitional words, words that support logic and clarity

ANSWERING QUESTIONS

The language conventions questions on the Reasoning Through Language Arts Test are used mainly to test grammar, usage, mechanics, and sentence structure. Questions that focus on only one or two sentences from the document will restate those sentences. For example, look at a sentence correction question based on "Thank You Note After an Interview." In the online test, you would select from the drop-down menu the correct answer, and would then see your choice put into the sentence. For this print version, you see all 4 answer choices as if you had already clicked the select button.

In sentence 1, the writer is talking about an interview that already happened, so the verb chosen should be in the past tense. Choose *enjoyed* rather than present tense *enjoy*.

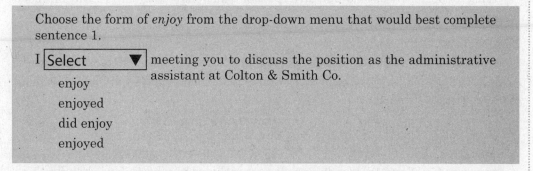

Choose the form of *enjoy* from the drop-down menu that would best complete sentence 1.

I | Select ▼ | meeting you to discuss the position as the administrative assistant at Colton & Smith Co.

enjoy
enjoyed
did enjoy
enjoyed

In the pages ahead, you'll take a closer look at types of questions that would appear on the language component of the Reasoning Through Language Arts Test. You'll also learn useful strategies and tips.

Below are some useful strategies and tips for handling questions you will see on the language component of the Reasoning Through Language Arts Test.

- Look out for answer choices that correct one error but create another. Remember that all parts of a sentence are interrelated. So when evaluating any answer choice, keep the entire sentence or passage in mind.

- Don't assume that an answer choice is the best one just because it proposes a change that would result in an effective and grammatically correct sentence. If an answer choice proposes a change, that change must be truly necessary in order to fix the sentence. Otherwise, look for a better answer choice.

- Resist the urge to "hyper-correct." In some questions you will have the option to leave the wording alone. Always consider this option. If you see it, be especially wary of the proposed changes in the other choices. Each and every one of them might either be unnecessary or create an error where there was none.

- Don't make your final selection until you've considered all four choices. More than one proposed revision might be better than the original version. Without examining all choices, you can't know for sure which is best.

- The sentences might be flawed in more than one way. An answer choice might fix one flaw but not another. Again, always consider all four choices before making your final selection.

- Be sure to consider the entire sentence. Keep in mind that all parts of a sentence are interrelated. By examining just one replaced part, or even that part along with what immediately precedes or follows it, you can easily overlook a problem. The same applies to each proposed revision as well.

- Remember your task is to identify "the best way to revise the sentence." What this means is that you should look not just for grammatical errors but also for other problems, such as awkwardness, misplaced modifiers, and problems in sentence sense or logic. Also, rule out any revision that distorts or alters the intended meaning of the sentence.

The following GED® test-style paragraph and sample questions illustrate question types you may see on the language component of the Reasoning Through Language Arts Test. The analysis that follows each question explains how to apply one or more of the strategies listed above.

(1) When starting a job, your boss will tell you the dress code they prefers. (2) Offices can be considered casual, considered formal, or a combination of the two. (3) You should make sure you know the dress code rules before going into work on you're first day. (4) Most dress codes are included in the employee handbook, can help you learn the rules.

Sentence 1: When starting a job, your boss will tell you the dress code they prefers.

Which correction should be made to sentence 1? Choose the correct answer from the options.

(A) change *boss* to *bosses*

(B) change *your* to *you're*

(C) change *they* to *he* or *she*

(D) change *prefers* to *prefer*

In sentence 1, the noun *boss* is singular, but the pronoun *they,* which refers to *boss* is plural. Here's the applicable rule of grammar: a pronoun must agree in number (either singular or plural) with the noun to which it refers (called the *antecedent*).

It might appear that choices (A), (C), or (D) correct the pronoun reference error in sentence 1. But does this mean that all three choices are correct? No. For example, trying out choice (D), if you read the sentence again using *prefer* and you'll "hear" the incorrect phrases "bosses will tell you...they prefers." Removing the "s" would correct the sentence, but the pronoun and noun agreement is still incorrect. By changing *they to "he or she,"* the antecedent agrees with the noun and allows you to leave "prefers" as is. **The correct answer is (C).**

> Sentence 2: Offices can be considered casual, considered formal, or a combination of the two.
>
> Which correction should be made to sentence 2? Choose the correct answer from the options.
>
> **(A)** change *considered* to *consider*
>
> **(B)** change *combination* to *combinations*
>
> **(C)** remove *the* after *of*
>
> **(D)** remove *considered* after *casual*

Notice that sentence 2 lists a series of three features. Here's the applicable rule of grammar: all items in a series should be grammatically parallel. Read sentence 2 with this rule in mind, and you'll notice what is called "faulty parallelism." The second feature (*considered formal*) is not parallel to the third feature (*a combination*). One starts with the verb *considered,* while the other one does not. One way to fix the problem is to insert the word *considered* immediately after *or.* However, this option is not listed among the four choices. Another way to fix the problem is to remove the word *considered* after *casual,* which is what choice (D) suggests. The result is a series of three parallel items: (1) *casual,* (2) *formal,* and (3) *a combination.* **The correct answer is (D).**

> Sentence 3: You should make sure you know the dress code rules before going into work on you're first day.
>
> Which correction should be made to sentence 3? Choose the correct answer from the options.
>
> **(A)** add a comma after *rules*
>
> **(B)** change *you're* to *your*
>
> **(C)** remove *make sure you*
>
> **(D)** add *of* before *dress code*

In sentence 3, the phrase *make sure you know* might not be as concise as the same phrase without the words *make sure you.* But the phrase is not grammatically incorrect, and its meaning is clear enough. So the change proposed in choice (C) is not necessary, and you should look for a better answer. The word *you're* is a contraction of the two-word phrase *you are.*

Read the sentence with *you are,* and you'll notice that the meaning of the sentence changes to "*before going into work on you are first day.*" This is clearly incorrect. As choice (B) suggests, *you're* should be replaced with *your.* **The correct answer is (B).**

> Sentence 4: Most dress codes are included in the employee handbook, can help you learn the rules.
>
> Which correction should be made to sentence 4? Choose the correct answer from the options.
>
> **(A)** change *are* to *have been*
>
> **(B)** change *included* to *includes*
>
> **(C)** change *are* after *codes* to *is*
>
> **(D)** add *and* after the comma

In sentence 4, the time frame for the action in the first clause is the present (*most... are included*). Choice (A) proposes to use the present-perfect tense (*have been included*). Here's the applicable rule of grammar: The present-perfect tense should be used to indicate action occurring in the past and ending at the present time. The present-perfect tense is not incorrect here, and it makes sense, especially since the second clause is framed in the same tense. However, the present tense works just as well, if not better. So the tense change that choice (A) proposes is unnecessary, and you should look for a better answer choice.

Read sentence 4 straight through. The clause after the comma sounds incomplete. Adding *and* after the comma transforms the second clause into an independent clause, connected to the original main clause by the word *and*. **The correct answer is (D).**

Here is the next part of the passage.

> (6) Whether your company <u>requires formal, or casual, attire</u>, choosing appropriate clothing is easy. (7) To avoid confusion if any rules are unclear, keep your shoulders covered, wear close-toed shoes, and always avoid jeans. (8) Also, try to choose neutral colors and solids, <u>because employees should not be distracted by your wardrobe in the workplace</u>.

> Sentence 6: Whether your company <u>requires formal, or casual, attire,</u> choosing appropriate clothing is easy.
>
> Which is the best way to write the underlined portion of sentence 6? If the original is the best way, select answer choice (A) from the options. Otherwise, choose the correct answer that best replaces the phrase in the sentence.
>
> **(A)** requires formal, or casual, attire,
>
> **(B)** requires formal or casual attire,
>
> **(C)** requires formal or casual attire:
>
> **(D)** require formal, or casual attire

In sentence 6, the object of the verb *requires* is *formal or casual*. Splitting this element with a comma makes for an awkward and confusing clause. The comma makes *or casual* an appositive phrase, implying that it can be removed without changing the meaning of the sentence. This is not true, because you need to know if your company requires formal or casual attire, so the comma should be removed. Choice (C) correctly removes the comma. However, it adds a colon at the end, making the sentence mechanically incorrect. By placing a colon after *attire*, it implies that the section of the sentence preceding the colon is an independent clause. This is untrue, and you can "hear" that it is incorrect by reading the section leading up to the colon, as if the second half is not there. **The correct choice is (B).**

> Sentence 7: To avoid confusion if any rules are unclear, keep your shoulders covered, wear close-toed shoes, and always avoid jeans.
>
> Which is the best way to rewrite sentence 7? If the original is the best way, select answer choice (B). Choose the correct answer from the drop down menu.
>
> **(A)** delete "To avoid confusion" and change *if* to *If*
>
> **(B)** leave the sentence the way it is
>
> **(C)** change "To avoid confusion" to "Avoided confusion"
>
> **(D)** change "To avoid confusion" to "To avoid being confused,"

You can quickly rule out choice (D) because it provides a very awkward-sounding phrase. Choice (C) introduces the past-tense verb form *avoided*. But does the past tense make sense in the context of the sentence as a whole? No. The sentence clearly intends to establish a present-to-future time frame. By mixing tenses, choice (C) confuses the time frame of the sentence's action.

To improve the sentence, you can eliminate "To avoid confusion" or "if any rules are unclear," since they say basically the same thing. **The correct answer is (A).**

> Sentence 8: Also, try to choose neutral colors and solids, <u>because employees should not be distracted by your wardrobe in the workplace.</u>
>
> Which is the best way to write the underlined portion of sentence 8? If the original is the best way, select choice (A). Choose the correct answer from the options.
>
> **(A)** because employees should not be distracted by your wardrobe in the workplace.
>
> **(B)** because they are less distracting.
>
> **(C)** since employees should not be distracted by your wardrobe in the workplace.
>
> **(D)** because your wardrobe should not distract employees.

As with the two previous examples (sentences 6 and 7), consider the four options in the context of the sentence as a whole.

The problem with the underlined part of sentence 8 is with the passive voice. If possible, it's preferable for a noun to be *doing* the action, not being the thing acted *upon*. Choices (A) and (C) say that the employees are being distracted *by* the wardrobe, instead of the noun performing the action. Choice (B) is incomplete and does not explain who might be distracted. Choice (D) removes the passive voice and states a fact as a result of the first clause. **The correct answer is (D).**

GENERAL TEST-TAKING STRATEGIES

Here are some general strategies for tackling the language component of the GED® Reasoning Through Language Arts Test. Most apply to all types of documents and questions. Put these strategies to work on the Practice Tests in this book, and then review them again just before exam day.

- **Read a document straight through before answering any questions based on it.** Read the document quickly from beginning to end. Don't bother to take notes, and don't pay too much attention to specific grammatical errors (you'll find plenty of them!). Instead, ask yourself the following questions:
  - Is the sequence of ideas logical and easy to understand?
  - Is the language and tone of the passage appropriate for the audience? For example, a business letter usually requires a formal tone and specific conventions.
  - Are there any places in the text in which the meaning is lost or obscured?

This strategy will help you to focus and to anticipate at least some of the questions. The documents are short (from 350 to 450 words), so up to a minute should be ample time for this task.

- **"Listen" to sentences for anything that doesn't sound right.** In answering questions about particular sentences, listen to them—as if you were reading aloud—for anything that sounds awkward, confusing, or just plain weird. If you hear something wrong, trust you ear and your instinct.

- **Apply the four basic principles for error-spotting in GED® test sentences.** If you're not sure what the problem with a particular sentence is, follow these four steps to uncover it:

  1 Find the verb, then its subject. Check for subject-verb agreement, including collective nouns and compound subjects.

  2 Examine all pronouns. Make sure each has a clear antecedent with which it agrees in person and number.

  3 Examine sentence structure. Make sure modifiers are attached to what they modify, parallel ideas are grammatically parallel, and comparisons are clear and logical.

  4 Listen for awkwardness or "gobbledygook" (anything that simply makes no sense).

- **Try to formulate an answer *before* reading the choices.** In tackling a replacement for part of a particular sentence, think about how you would write that part of the sentence. Do this before looking at any of the answer choices. Try rephrasing a faulty sentence part, figuring out what word or punctuation mark you'd eliminate, change, move, or add. You'll zero in on the correct choice more quickly this way, and you're less likely to become confused and tempted by wrong answer choices. Keep in mind that this strategy works for most, but not all, question types on the language component of the Reasoning Through Language Arts Test. Exceptions to the rule are noted in the grammar review, which follows this lesson.

- **Pace yourself properly.** The language portion of the Reasoning Through Language Arts Test consists of several distinct question sets, each set based on a different document. The number of questions per set can vary from 6 to 8. Plan to spend a bit more time on the longer question set than on the shorter one. Your time limit for answering all 49 questions in the entire Reasoning Through Language Arts Test is 150 minutes. Try to answer 10 questions about every 30 minutes, on average. If you're falling behind, try to pick up your pace.

SUMMING IT UP

- The language component of the Reasoning Through Language Arts Test is basically an *editing* test that is designed to measure your ability to review a document and spot grammatical errors and other writing problems that need to be corrected or revised. Expect approximately two documents altogether and 6 to 8 questions based on each document. Each document will be 350–450 words in length.

- The language component of the Reasoning Through Language Arts Test covers grammar and usage, sentence structure, and writing mechanics.

- All documents in the language component of the Reasoning Through Language Arts Test share the following things in common: the paragraphs are lettered in sequence, and some (but not all) of the sentences are flawed in some way.

- Be on the lookout for answer choices that fix one error but create another; and avoid correcting a sentence that doesn't need to be corrected.

- In addition to grammatical errors, look for other problems, such as awkwardness, misplaced modifiers, and problems in sentence sense or logic. Also, rule out any revision that distorts or alters the intended meaning of the sentence.

- Most sentence construction questions focus on sentence structure. However, some might cover usage and/or mechanics as well. Sentence construction questions vary in format; make sure you become familiar with these different types of questions, including the different styles of tech-enhanced items as outlined at the beginning of the book.

- Paragraph reconstruction questions ask you to recreate a paragraph by either *rearranging* the paragraph's sentences or *inserting* a new sentence, usually at the beginning of a paragraph.

Mastering Extended Response

OVERVIEW

- All about the Reasoning Through Language Arts Test—Extended Response
- How GED® test extended response essays are evaluated
- What's not tested
- How GED® test extended response essays are scored
- The extended response essay topic
- Writing your extended response essay: from brainstorm to final product
- Developing and connecting your paragraphs
- Writing style
- Sample extended response
- Suggestions for writing and evaluating your practice extended response essay
- General test-taking strategies
- Summing it up

THE REASONING THROUGH LANGUAGE ARTS TEST—EXTENDED RESPONSE IN A NUTSHELL

Time allowed: 150 minutes for the entire Reasoning Through Language Arts Test, which includes 45 minutes for the Extended Response as well as a 10-minute break.

Total number of questions: 1 essay based on two reading passages that offer opposing views

---

ALL ABOUT THE REASONING THROUGH LANGUAGE ARTS TEST—EXTENDED RESPONSE

The extended response component of the Reasoning Through Language Arts Test assesses your ability to communicate your ideas and thoughts in writing. You will be asked to present your opinion in response to a paired passage on a specific topic. You will not be given a choice of topics to write on, and you *must* write only about the topic provided.

Here are the basic rules and procedures for the extended response component of the Reasoning Through Language Arts Test:

- The allotted time to plan, write, and revise your extended response is 45 minutes. However, if you finish the first part of the Reasoning Through Language Arts Test early, you can start work on the extended response right away. Note that when you complete your extended response, you cannot go back to any earlier part of the Reasoning Through Language Arts Test.

- An erasable note board will be provided for jotting down notes, making an outline, and writing out a rough draft. The notes you make on the erasable note board will not be read or scored. If a new erasable note board is needed, a test-taker can trade in the old board for a fresh one. This takes the place of scratch paper and is more environmentally friendly and secure as the boards cannot be taken from the testing center.

- You must write your essay in the space provided on the computer screen. Passages will be broken up into tabbed pages for longer texts. Also, the question or prompt and instructions will be visible as you read the passage, through use of a split screen.

HOW GED® TEST EXTENDED RESPONSE ESSAYS ARE EVALUATED

The Extended Response essay will be evaluated on the basis of three rubrics, each one emphasizing a different aspect (trait) of the essay, as follows:

Rubric 1: Creation of arguments and use of evidence

Rubric 2: Development of ideas and organizational structure

Rubric 3: Clarity and command of standard English conventions

Each trait is worth up to 2 points, so responses will be scored on a 6-point scale. The final raw score on the ER item is then double-weighted so that it represents up to 12 raw score points on the overall RLA test.

\multicolumn{2}{l}{**RLA Extended Response Scoring Rubric**}	
Score	**Description**
\multicolumn{2}{l}{**Trait 1: Creation of Arguments and Use of Evidence**}	
2	• Generates **text-based argument(s)** and establishes **a purpose that is connected** to the prompt • Cites relevant and specific **evidence from source text(s)** to support argument (may include few irrelevant pieces of evidence or unsupported claims) • Analyzes the issue and/or evaluates the validity of the argumentation within the source text(s) (e.g., distinguishes between supported and unsupported claims, makes reasonable inferences about underlying premises or assumptions, identifies fallacious reasoning, evaluates the credibility of sources, etc.)
1	• Generates an **argument** and demonstrates some connection to the prompt • Cites some **evidence from source text(s)** to support argument (may include a mix of relevant and irrelevant citations or a mix of textual and non-textual references) • Partially **analyzes the issue** and/or **evaluates the validity of the argumentation** within the source text(s); may be simplistic, limited, or inaccurate
0	• May attempt to create an **argument** OR **lacks purpose or connection** to the prompt OR does neither • Cites minimal or no evidence from source text(s) (sections of text may be copied from source)

Non-scorable Responses (Score of 0/Condition Codes)
Response exclusively contains text copied from source text(s) or prompt; shows no evidence that test-taker has read the prompt or is off-topic; is incomprehensible; is not in English; has not been attempted (blank)

RLA Extended Response Scoring Rubric *(continued)*

Score	Description
Trait 2: Development of Ideas and Organizational Structure	
2	• Contains **ideas** that are well **developed** and generally logical; most ideas are **elaborated** upon • Contains a sensible **progression of ideas** with clear connections between details and main points • Establishes an **organizational structure** that conveys the message and purpose of the response; applies **transitional devices** appropriately • Establishes and maintains a formal style and appropriate tone that demonstrate awareness of the audience and purpose of the task • **Chooses specific words** to express ideas clearly
1	• Contains **ideas that are inconsistently developed** and/or may reflect simplistic or vague reasoning; **some ideas are elaborated** upon • Demonstrates **some evidence of a progression of ideas**, but details may be disjointed or lacking connection to main ideas • Establishes an **organizational structure that may inconsistently** group ideas or is partially effective at conveying the message of the task; **uses transitional devices inconsistently** • May **inconsistently** maintain a formal style and appropriate tone to demonstrate an **awareness of the audience** and **purpose of the task** • May occasionally **misuse words** and/or choose words that express ideas in vague terms
0	• Contains ideas that are **insufficiently or illogically developed**, with **minimal or no elaboration** on main ideas • Contains **unclear or no progression of ideas**; details may be absent or irrelevant to the main ideas • Establishes **ineffective or no discernible organizational structure**; does not apply transitional devices, or does so inappropriately • Uses an informal style and/or inappropriate tone that demonstrates **limited or no awareness of audience and purpose** • May **frequently misuse words**, overuse slang, or express ideas in a vague or repetitious manner
Non-scorable Responses (Score of 0/Condition Codes) Response exclusively contains text copied from source text(s) or prompt; shows no evidence that test-taker has read the prompt or is off-topic; is incomprehensible; is not in English; has not been attempted (blank)	

Score	Description
	**RLA Extended Response Scoring Rubric** (*continued*)

RLA Extended Response Scoring Rubric (*continued*)

Score	Description
	Trait 3: Clarity and Command of Standard English Conventions
2	• Demonstrates **largely correct sentence structure** and a **general fluency** that enhances clarity with specific regard to the following skills: 1) varied sentence structure within a paragraph or paragraphs 2) correct subordination, coordination, and parallelism 3) avoidance of wordiness and awkward sentence structures 4) usage of transitional words, conjunctive adverbs, and other words that support logic and clarify 5) avoidance of run-on sentences, fused sentences, or sentence fragments • Demonstrates **competent application of conventions** with specific regard to the following skills: 1) frequently confused words and homonyms, including contractions 2) subject-verb agreement 3) pronoun usage, including pronoun antecedent agreement, unclear pronoun references, and pronoun case 4) placement of modifiers and correct word order 5) capitalization (e.g., proper nouns, titles, and beginnings of sentences) 6) use of apostrophes with possessive nouns 7) use of punctuation (e.g., commas in a series or in appositives and other non-essential elements, end marks, and appropriate punctuation for clause separation) • **May contain some errors in mechanics and conventions**, but they do not interfere with comprehension; overall, standard usage is at a level appropriate for on-demand draft writing
1	• Demonstrates **inconsistent sentence structure**; may contain some repetitive, choppy, rambling, or awkward sentences that may detract from clarity; demonstrates inconsistent control over skills 1–5 as listed in the first bullet under Trait 3, Score Point 2 above • Demonstrates **inconsistent control of basic conventions** with specific regard to skills 1–7 as listed in the second bullet under Trait 3, Score Point 2 above • **May contain frequent errors in mechanics and conventions** that occasionally interfere with comprehension; standard usage is at a minimally acceptable level of appropriateness for on-demand draft writing
0	• Demonstrates **consistently flawed sentence structure** such that meaning may be obscured; demonstrates minimal control over skills 1–5 as listed in the first bullet under Trait 3, Score Point 2 above • Demonstrates **minimal control of basic conventions** with specific regard to skills 1–7 as listed in the second bullet under Trait 3, Score Point 2 above • Contains **severe and frequent errors in mechanics and conventions** that interfere with comprehension; overall, standard usage is at an unacceptable level for on-demand draft writing OR • **Response is insufficient** to demonstrate level of mastery over conventions and usage
	Non-scorable Responses (Score of 0/Condition Codes) Response exclusively contains text copied from source text(s) or prompt; shows no evidence that test-taker has read the prompt or is off-topic; is incomprehensible; is not in English; has not been attempted (blank)

Because test-takers will be given only 45 minutes to complete RLA Extended Response tasks, there is no expectation that a response should be completely free of conventions or usage errors to receive a score of 2.

Social Studies Extended Response Scoring Rubric

Score	Description
Trait 1: Creation of Arguments and Use of Evidence	
2	• Generates a **text-based argument** that demonstrates a clear understanding of the historical **relationships among ideas, events, and figures as presented in the source text(s)** and the contexts from which they are drawn. • Cites relevant the specific **evidence from primary and secondary source text(s)** that adequately supports an argument • Is well-connected to both the prompt and the source text(s)
1	• Demonstrates an **understanding of the relationships among ideas, events, and figures as presented in the source text(s)** • Cites some **evidence from primary and secondary source text(s)** in support of an argument (may include a mix of relevant and irrelevant textual references) • Is **connected to both the prompt and the source text(s)**
0	• Demonstrates minimal or no **understanding of the ideas, events, and figures presented in the source text(s)** or the contexts from which these texts are drawn • Cites minimal or no **evidence from the primary and secondary source text(s)**; may or may not demonstrate an attempt to create an argument • Lacks **connection either to the prompt or the source text(s)**
Non-scorable Responses (Score of 0/Condition Codes) Response exclusively contains text copied from source text(s) or prompt; shows no evidence that test-taker has read the prompt or is off-topic; is incomprehensible; is not in English; has not been attempted (blank)	

Score	Description
Social Studies Extended Response Scoring Rubric (*continued*)	
Trait 2: Development of Ideas and Organizational Structure	
1	• Contains a sensible **progression of ideas** with understandable connections between details and main ideas
	• Contains **ideas** that are **developed** and generally logical; multiple ideas are elaborated upon
	• Demonstrates appropriate **awareness of audience** and the **purpose of the task**
0	• Contains an unclear or no apparent **progression of ideas**
	• Contains **ideas** that are insufficiently **developed** or illogical; **just one idea is elaborated upon**
	• Demonstrates no **awareness of the task**

Non-scorable Responses (Score of 0/Condition Codes)
Response exclusively contains text copied from source text(s) or prompt; shows no evidence that test-taker has read the prompt or is off-topic; is incomprehensible; is not in English; has not been attempted (blank)

Social Studies Extended Response Scoring Rubric *(continued)*

Score	Description
Trait 3: Clarity and Command of Standard English Conventions	
1	• Demonstrates adequate applications of **conventions** with specific regard to the following skills: 1) frequently confused words and homonyms, including contractions 2) subject-verb agreement 3) pronoun usage, including pronoun antecedent agreement, unclear pronoun references, and pronoun case 4) placement of modifiers and correct word order 5) capitalization (e.g., proper nouns, titles, and beginnings of sentences) 6) use of apostrophes with possessive nouns 7) use of punctuation (e.g., commas in a series or in appositives and other non-essential elements, end marks, and appropriate punctuation for clause separation) • Demonstrates largely correct **sentence structure** with variance from sentence to sentence; is **generally fluent** and clear with regard to the following skills: 1) correct subordination, coordination, and parallelism 2) avoidance of wordiness and awkward sentence structures 3) usage of transitional words, conjunctive adverbs, and other words that support logic and clarity 4) avoidance of run-on sentences, fused sentences, or sentence fragments 5) standard usage at a level of formality appropriate for on-demand draft writing • May contain some errors in **mechanics and conventions**, but they do not interfere with understanding
0	• Demonstrates minimal control of basic **conventions** with specific regard to skills 1–5 as listed in the first bullet under Trait 3, Score Point 2 above • Demonstrates consistently flawed **sentence structure**, with minimal or no variance such that meaning may be obscured; demonstrates minimal control over skills 1–5 as listed in the second bullet under Trait 3, Score Point 2 above • Contains severe and frequent errors in **mechanics and conventions** that interfere with comprehension OR • **Response is insufficient** to demonstrate level of mastery over conventions and usage

Non-scorable Responses (Score of 0/Condition Codes)
Response exclusively contains text copied from source text(s) or prompt; shows no evidence that test-taker has read the prompt or is off-topic; is incomprehensible; is not in English; has not been attempted (blank)

Because test-takers will be given only 25 minutes to complete Social Studies Extended Response tasks, there is no expectation that a response should be completely free of conventions or usage errors to receive a score of 1.

Also, keep in mind that the automated scoring engine will evaluate your essay based on the *quality*, and not the quantity, of your writing, specifically taking into account how well you meet the items in the three rubrics. So a brief essay that is fully developed, well-organized, and well-written will, in all likelihood, earn a higher score than a much longer essay that is poorly developed, organized, and written.

Finally, notice that Rubric 3 covers the same knowledge areas as those covered by the language component of the Reasoning Through Language Arts Test. So knowing the rules and guidelines for grammar, usage, sentence structure, paragraph and document structure, and writing mechanics will serve double duty: it will help you edit GED® test documents *and* write your GED® test extended response essay.

WHAT'S NOT TESTED

In evaluating and scoring your essay, the GED® test automated scoring engine focuses only on the three rubrics previously described. Many test-takers will make the mistake of trying to write in an impressive manner, which will not be noticed by the automated scoring engine. Other test-takers will be too concerned about saying the "right thing" and not concerned enough about how they say it. To avoid these mistakes, here's what you need to keep in mind:

- **There is no "correct" answer.** First and foremost, remember that there is no "best" response or "correct" answer to any GED® test extended response question. What's important is how effectively you present and support your ideas. The essay is *expected* to be in paragraph form, and the following pages clearly state that you need at least one introductory paragraph, one body paragraph, and one summary paragraph. (A minimum of two body paragraphs is strongly suggested.)

- **Special knowledge about the topic at hand won't matter.** The extended response component of the Reasoning Through Language Arts Test is a *skills* test. So, you don't need any special knowledge of the topic presented in order to produce a high-scoring essay. Besides, the Writing Test topics are not technical in nature. So, though you'll need to know something about the subject, common everyday knowledge will be enough.

- **The extended response component of the Reasoning Through Language Arts Test is not a vocabulary exercise.** You won't score points from the automated scoring engine by using obscure or so-called "big" words. When it comes to vocabulary, all that matters is that the words you use make sense in context.

- **The extended response component of the Reasoning Through Language Arts Test is not a creative writing exercise.** Some test-takers will make the mistake of using an imaginative writing style or essay structure in order to receive a better score for originality. Simply put, this is a bad idea. The GED® test is not the place to experiment with imagery, to display wit or humor, or to show that you have "Hemingway potential." Focus on writing with strong organization and communication skills—not astounding creativity.

- **Occasional, minor mechanical errors will not hurt your score.** In evaluating your essay, the automated scoring engine will focus on how well you meet the criteria in the rubrics. The automated scoring engine will overlook the occasional punctuation error, awkward sentence, or even misspelled word.

HOW GED® TEST EXTENDED RESPONSE ESSAYS ARE SCORED

An automated scoring engine will use the three rubrics to score the Reasoning Through Language Arts Extended Response. These rubrics measure creation of arguments and use of evidence, development of ideas and organizational structure, and clarity and command of standard English conventions. This automated scoring engine uses algorithms to mimic the human scoring process. It has been programmed based on a computer evaluation of hundreds of responses that align to all possible scores on the rubrics. To ensure the accuracy of this engine, readers will manually score a sample of responses. Also, if the engine flags an essay as being unusual, it will be sent to a reader to be evaluated and scored.

THE EXTENDED RESPONSE ESSAY TOPIC

The topic for your GED® test extended response essay will be based on two passages offering opposing viewpoints on a subject. The text for these passages will not exceed 650 words. Your task will be to develop an argument that supports one side and defend it using text-based evidence. To complete the extended response, you will write a persuasive essay.

Persuasive Essays

A **persuasive** essay adopts a viewpoint or an opinion on an issue and then attempts to convince, or *persuade*, the reader to agree with that viewpoint or opinion. Below is a list of possible passage topics you might encounter in the prompt of the extended response.

1. A passage about the importance of teamwork paired with a passage about individual initiative
2. A passage about the benefits of high school students holding part-time jobs paired with a passage about why high school students should not hold part-time jobs
3. A passage about how colleges should focus on teaching real-world job skills paired with a passage on how colleges should focus on providing a general education
4. A passage about how innate talent is essential to individual success paired with a passage about how perseverance and effort is essential to individual success
5. A passage about how high school students should be required to wear uniforms combined with a passage about why uniforms do more harm than good

6 A passage about how digital books are better than printed books paired with a passage about how printed books are better than digital books

7 A passage about how cell phones, tablets, and other gadgets save us time paired with a passage about how these things rob us of time

WRITING YOUR EXTENDED RESPONSE ESSAY: FROM BRAINSTORM TO FINAL PRODUCT

Writing is probably something you do every day without giving it much thought. Whether you write letters, e-mails, or memos, you know that writing is simply putting your thoughts into written form. Some people get intimidated when they are required to write a formal essay that will be read and graded. You shouldn't be intimidated at all, though. For the GED® test, you just need to follow certain steps to ensure you've hit the marks on the rubric and will receive a good score from the automated scoring engine.

In writing their GED® test essay, many test-takers make the mistake of diving in head first. They immediately start typing in the designated box without planning their essays ahead of time. While a few test-takers may be able to compose a good essay this way, the vast majority won't. Essays written "on the fly" usually turn out poorly organized and written. Rather than expressing and developing a central idea in a clear, well-organized manner, these essays tend to lose focus and ramble, without a clear train of thought, and sometimes without a clear beginning or end.

Instead of simply jumping in and starting to type, you should spend some time up front thinking about what you should write and how you should organize your ideas. And you should save some time at the end to proofread your essay. Below is a 7-step plan to help you budget your time and produce a solid essay within your 45-minute time limit.

7-Step Plan for Writing a GED® Test Extended Response Essay

Plan your essay (5 minutes):

1 Brainstorm ideas and make notes.

2 Review your notes and decide on a central idea or viewpoint.

3 Decide the sequence in which you will present your main points. If you find outlines helpful, write your main points in outline format.

Write your essay (35 minutes):

4 Write a brief introductory paragraph.

5 Write the body paragraphs of your essay.

6 Write a brief summary or concluding paragraph.

Review your essay (5 minutes):

7 Proofread to find errors you can easily fix, and fix them.

The suggested time limits for each step are merely guidelines, not hard-and-fast rules. As you practice composing your own essays under timed conditions, start with these guidelines, and then adjust to a pace that works best for you personally.

In the following pages, you'll walk through each step in turn, applying the following GED® test-style prompt:

Extended Response Topic

Debating Hybrid Cars

The following passages represent two views of the value of hybrid cars, cars that are powered by gasoline or by electricity depending on whether they are in traffic or on the open road. Choose which of the two viewpoints you wish to support and write a well-organized essay, using reasons and examples to support your position.

Passage 1

Advocates of hybrids believe that the cars offer the best short-term solution to some long-term problems. By combining a regular gasoline-powered engine with an electric engine, hybrids cut down on gas consumption and decrease the pollution caused by gasoline engines. These cars help automakers meet government regulations for fuel efficiency and emissions controls—in some states, hybrid owners do not need an emission test for registration at all. Not only are the cars more gas efficient, but they are more efficient in the city: Hybrid cars can generate more electricity at lower speeds, also making them a good choice for heavy commuter traffic. This may put wear and tear on brakes for gas-powered cars, but hybrids use brakes that also regenerate electricity. This means that when a driver brakes, the mechanism that slows down the car creates energy that can be used or stored. Standard cars dispel this energy via friction in the brake linings, wasting the energy and wearing down the brakes. Most hybrids have warranties on their batteries that are good for up to 150,000 miles, and some hybrid models have been known to perform just as well at over 200,000 miles as they did when brand new. Automakers do not think that hybrids are the answer for the future, but these small cars provide a way for conservation-conscious consumers to do something for the environment. Automakers see another benefit to the development process for hybrids. The technology that has gone into creating and refining the dual-powered hybrid will help with the longer-term development of cars powered by hydrogen fuel cells.

Passage 2

Opponents of hybrids believe that automakers should be focusing on a longer-term solution. They believe that either hydrogen fuel cells or diesel fuel or both are better alternatives than hybrids. The cost of hybrids is higher than comparably sized gasoline-powered cars, forcing consumers who want "green" cars to pay anywhere from $2,500 to $4,000 more. Opponents say that the higher sticker price means lower demand and less likelihood of automobile companies making their development dollars back. Naysayers point to Europe as an example of lack of demand. Gasoline prices are much higher there than in the United States, but no mass movement from gasoline-powered cars to hybrids has occurred. Not all hybrids are equal, causing discrepancies about their accessibility for a large buyer's market. Some hybrids perform better than others in terms of gas mileage and electric efficiency, and some heating and air conditioning systems do not operate when the gasoline engine stops. Aside from temperature control issues, there are limited models with a third seat, making them unsuitable for large families. These large hybrids do not get very good gas mileage compared to other hybrids.

Step 1: Brainstorm Ideas and Make Notes

Your first step in developing an extended-response essay is to brainstorm ideas that are relevant to the topic. Be aware of how much room on the erasable board these notes take up since you only have one to use. To decide on which viewpoint you wish to support, and to come up with ideas for your essay, you can draw on any of the following:

- Your own experiences
- Books, articles, and other writings
- Stories people have told you
- Current events

As you think of ideas, don't try to filter out what you think might be unconvincing reasons or weak examples. Just let all your ideas flow onto your erasable note board, in no particular order. (You can sort through them during steps 2 and 3.) Here's what a test-taker's notes on the topic might look like after a few minutes of brainstorming:

Pros:

Save on gas money

Better for the environment

　　Less fuel used

　　Decrease in pollution

Last a long time (fewer repairs)

　　Brakes regenerate

　　Batteries last a long time

No smog tests

Good practice for developing hydrogen-powered cars

Cons:

Costs more to buy one

Hydrogen or diesel fuels are better than gas/electric combination

Companies lost money

Some don't have efficient air and heat while operating under electricity

Not big enough for large families

Notice that some notes are grouped together to reflect one train of thought. Other notes reflect assorted, random ideas. The notes aren't well organized, but that's okay. The point of brainstorming is just to generate a bunch of ideas—the raw material for your essay. Let your ideas flow freely, and you'll have plenty of material for your essay.

Step 2: Review Your Notes and Decide Which Side You Will Take for Your Argument

Decide on the basic view or opinion that you intend to support in your essay. Your notes from step 1 should help you decide. Review the ideas you jotted down, and then ask yourself for which viewpoint you can make a strong case.

Pick the three or four ideas from your notes that best support your view. These should be ideas that you think make sense and that you know enough about to write at least a few sentences on. Put a checkmark next to those ideas, to signify that these are the ones you're certain you want to use in your essay. If there aren't enough ideas, take one or two of the ideas you like and elaborate on them. Think of related ideas, add details or examples, and use these to fill out your list.

Step 3: Organize Your Ideas into an Outline

Next, decide on a sequence for the ideas. They should flow naturally and logically from one to another. Once you've decided on a sequence for your ideas, number them accordingly in your notes. At this point, you might want to create a separate outline, or you might be able to transform your notes from step 1 into an outline. Use the outline structure that works best for you; you may find numbers and bullet points easier and faster than the traditional hierarchy of roman numerals and letters.

For example, if you decide that you think hybrid cars offer the best short-term solution to some long-term problems, your outline might look something like this:

Pros:

(1) Save on gas money

(2) Better for the environment

    —Less fuel used

    —Decrease in pollution

(3) Last a long time (fewer repairs)

    —Brakes regenerate

    —Batteries last a long time

(2) No smog tests

(4) Good practice for developing hydrogen-powered cars

Cons:

(1) Costs more to buy one

(2) Hydrogen or diesel fuels are better than gas/electric combination

(4) Companies lost money

(3) Some don't have efficient air and heat while operating under electricity

(2) Not big enough for large families

As already mentioned, you might prefer to create a separate outline based on your notes. Doing so shouldn't take much time, and it will give you another chance to think about your ideas and how you should organize them into paragraphs. Here's what an outline based on this test-taker's initial notes might look like.

Hybrid cars are a helpful invention: the pros outweigh the cons.

(1) Money saved on gas will make up for the extra expense of buying the car.

(2) Even though they might not be the *most* efficient, they are the best on the market right now:

—Less fuel used, so no smog test needed

—Decrease in pollution

—By making hybrid cars we can learn about developing better models. Practice makes perfect.

—Ones with a third row big enough for a large family, don't get as good of gas mileage as other hybrids, but they still get better gas mileage than standard cars.

(3) Last a long time (fewer repairs)

—Brakes regenerate.

—Batteries last a long time

—Some don't have efficient air and heat while operating under electricity, so do your research in choosing between hybrids . . . in temperate areas this wouldn't be a problem.

(4) Companies may lose money up front, but will be pioneers for the technology, leading to profits in the long run.

Notice that the test-taker has combined a few points, jotted down the ideas in sequence, and filled out the notes a bit.

Following this outline, it appears that the test-taker plans to compose four body paragraphs, one for each numbered point. (The *body* of an essay includes all paragraphs except for an introductory and a concluding paragraph.) There is no "correct" or "best" number of body paragraphs for an extended-response essay. Three or four body paragraphs is a manageable number for a 45-minute essay. The prompt itself may help you decide on how many body paragraphs to include. But no matter which prompt you get, be sure to include *at least two* body paragraphs.

Step 4: Write a Brief Introductory Paragraph

Once you've spent about 5 minutes planning your essay, it's time to write it. You'll begin with a brief introductory paragraph. In your initial paragraph, try to accomplish the following:

- Show that you understand both sides of the argument.

- Show that you have a clear view of why you chose one side.

- Provide a glimpse of how you will support your ideas in your essay.

You can probably accomplish all three goals in two to three sentences. Don't go into details yet by listing specific reasons or examples that support your view. This is what your essay's body paragraphs are for. Also, don't begin your introductory paragraph by repeating the essay prompt word-for-word. Show from the very first sentence that you're thinking for yourself. Here's a good introductory paragraph for the provided essay topic:

> With the increasingly popular go-green movement and the controversy surrounding global warming, people are becoming more aware of their effect on the Earth. Purveyors of environmental awareness are worried about their "carbon footprints," the need to recycle, and the amount of pollution being released into the air. The environmentally aware who seek out both short-term and long-term solutions may find hybrid cars a good stepping-stone to a healthier world.

The opening paragraph is an important part of the essay, so take great care in writing it. To help ensure that it's as good as it can be, consider writing a rough draft of the paragraph on your erasable white board first.

Step 5: Write the Body Paragraphs of Your Essay

During step 5, your task is to get your supporting points out of your brain and off your erasable white board and into the space allotted for your extended response. Here's what you need to keep in mind as you write:

- Be sure the first sentence of each paragraph begins a distinct train of thought and clearly conveys the essence of the paragraph.

- Arrange your paragraphs so your essay flows logically and persuasively from one point to the next. Try to stick to your outline, but be flexible.

- Try to devote at least two, but no more than three or four sentences to each main point in your outline.

- Don't stray from the topic at hand, or even from the points you seek to make. Be sure to stay well focused on both.

Below are the body paragraphs of a response to the topic. These paragraphs are based on our notes from step 3, but there are a few differences.

Body paragraphs:

> One of the biggest arguments against standard cars is the depletion of fossil fuels—otherwise known as gasoline. By buying a hybrid car, less of this precious

fuel will be used and owners of hybrid cars can save money. Those opposed to hybrid cars may note that buying such vehicles is more expensive, but the money saved on gas will make up for the initial expense.

Because hybrids use less gas, there is a decrease in pollution. This is not only good for the environment, but it also means that some states do not require hybrid cars to go through an emissions test. This can save hybrid owners even more money: standard cars are required to go through emissions tests to be registered—some cars may need to be checked twice if they fail the first time.

Aside from smog tests, hybrid cars may not need brake or battery replacements as often as standard cars. Hybrid brakes are designed to be regenerative, meaning they use the energy created from braking rather than wasting it, which damages the brakes. In terms of batteries, most hybrid models are protected under extensive warranties—hybrid cars that were analyzed once they reached 200,000 miles reportedly performed as well as new models of the same brand, something standard cars cannot live up to.

Those opposed to hybrid cars argue that because hybrids are not accessible for all people—meaning that they are not designed for large families and are not affordable for those in certain financial situations—they are not the solution. Even though companies may lose money initially in creating the cars, these companies are pioneers for the technology: long-term financial goals may prove profitable as theories are tested and models are perfected.

Step 6: Write a Brief Summary or Concluding Paragraph

Make sure that your essay has a clear ending. Reserve time to wrap up your essay. Convey your main supporting ideas in a clear, concise, and forceful way. Two or three sentences should be enough for this purpose. If an especially insightful concluding point occurs to you, the final sentence of your essay is a good place for it.

Here's a brief but effective concluding paragraph for the response to the topic. Notice that this brief summary does not introduce any new reasons or examples. Instead, it simply provides a quick recap, which is all you need to accomplish with your final paragraph.

Overall, hybrid cars are more gas efficient, reduce the effect humans have on the environment, and can save drivers money if they are committed to the project's long-term efforts. Eventually, something better than a hybrid car may be released—but until then, these cars are strong contenders for a short-term solution that can teach creators about how to develop and perfect future models.

From beginning to end (including the introductory, body, and concluding paragraphs), the preceding sample essay runs just over 400 words in length. So it's not especially lengthy. Nor is it a literary masterpiece. Nevertheless, it expresses a clear viewpoint, supports a viewpoint with relevant reasons and examples, is well organized, and is written in a clear and effective manner. In short, it contains all the elements of a high-scoring GED® test extended response essay.

Step 7: Proofread to Find Errors You Can Easily Fix

Save the last few minutes to proofread your essay from start to finish for mechanical problems that you can quickly and easily fix, such as errors in spelling, punctuation, and word choice.

DEVELOPING AND CONNECTING YOUR PARAGRAPHS

An effective GED® test extended response essay will contain much more than just a series of general statements. Ideally, you will have only a few general statements, and the majority of your writing will be dedicated to creating purposeful, specific details that will support your premise.

Topic Sentences

Each body paragraph in your essay should help explain and support your extended response essay's central idea, of course. But each body paragraph should have its own central idea as well, which you should express in a **topic sentence.** The topic sentence of each paragraph should be a major point in support of the central idea. The paragraph's other sentences should all relate directly to the topic sentence, providing information that explains or supports the topic sentence's idea.

The sentences that make up a paragraph should be presented in a logical order. An essay that flows logically from one paragraph to another so that its ideas are easily understood is said to be *coherent.* Your body paragraphs should flow from and support your central idea, as well as flow logically from one to the next. As you introduce new ideas, use a consistent structure from one paragraph to the next. Repeating key words or phrases, or using variations of the same phrases, can be especially helpful. Here is an example:

First body paragraph:

One way that spending too much time on the Internet can be harmful . . . .

Second body paragraph:

A second problem with spending too much time on the Internet is . . . .

Third body paragraph:

A final problem with Internet overuse is . . . .

Try to develop your own arsenal of words and phrases that connect ideas together so they flow from one to another. Certain words and phrases move the extended response essay forward and imply the building of an idea or thought. Certain other words and phrases work to compare ideas or draw conclusions from the preceding thoughts. Following are several lists of words and phrases that writers often use as bridges between ideas.

Words and phrases that help connect ideas of *equal weight*:

first, second, . . .	finally	next
additionally	further	what's more
also	furthermore	
equally important	in addition	

Words and phrases that signal *comparison* and *contrast*:

although	conversely	to the contrary
but	however	whereas
by comparison	in contrast	while
by the same token	more importantly	
compared to	on the other hand	

Words and phrases used to *qualify* or point out an *exception* to an assertion of fact:

depending on	in some circumstances	sometimes
despite	in spite of	yet
infrequently	nevertheless	
in rare instances		

Words and phrases that signal *sequence* (chronological, logical, or rhetorical):

first, second, third, . . .	concurrently	previously
	consequently	simultaneously
after	finally	subsequently
beforehand	next	then

Words and phrases that signal the use of a supporting *example*:

as an illustration	in this case	take the case of
consider	in this situation	to demonstrate
for example	on this occasion	to illustrate
for instance	one possible scenario	
in another case		

Words and phrases that signal a *conclusion*:

accordingly	hence	therefore
as a result	it follows that	thus

Use these phrases for your concluding or *summary paragraph*:

all things considered	in essence	on balance
in a nutshell	in short	on the whole
in brief	in sum	summing up
in conclusion	in the final analysis	to recapitulate

It takes practice to develop a knack for writing paragraphs that use connecting words effectively. Be sure to complete all three Reasoning Through Language Arts extended responses on the practice tests provided.

WRITING STYLE

Your writing style refers to the words and phrases you choose to use and how you use them, how you structure your sentences, and the overall voice and tone you use in your writing. To ensure yourself a high score on your GED® test extended response essay, strive for writing that is

- appropriate in tone and "voice" for academic writing.

- clear and concise (easy to understand and direct rather than wordy or verbose).

- varied in sentence length and structure (to add interest and variety as well as to demonstrate maturity in writing style).

- correct and appropriate in word choice and usage.

All of this is easier said than done, of course. Don't worry if you're not a natural when it comes to writing the kind of prose that's appropriate for the GED® test. You *can* improve your writing for your exam, even if your time is short. Start by reading the suggestions and guidelines below. But, keep in mind: improvement in writing comes mainly with practice. So you'll also need to apply what you learn here to the Practice Tests in this book and to the supplementary writing prompts provided at the end of this lesson.

Overall Tone and Voice

In general, you should try to maintain a somewhat *formal* tone throughout your essay. An essay that comes across as casual or conversational—like a personal e-mail or blog entry—is probably a bit too informal for the GED® test. Here are some specific guidelines:

- The overall tone should be analytical, which means it should be a detailed explanation of your viewpoint. Don't overstate your view or opinion by using extreme or harsh language that appeals to emotions instead.

- When it comes to your main points, a very direct, even forceful, voice is perfectly acceptable. Just don't overdo it.

- It is perfectly acceptable, though optional, to refer to yourself from time to time in your essay. Just be consistent. For example, be sure not to mix phrases such as *I disagree with* or *In my view* with phrases such as *We cannot assume that*.

- Avoid puns, double-meanings, plays on words, and other forms of humor. Sarcasm is also entirely inappropriate for your GED® test extended response essay. The automated scoring engine will not realize that you're trying to be humorous, in which case your remark might be confusing.

Clear and Concise Writing

With enough words, anyone can make a point; but it requires skill and effort to make a point with concise phrases. Before you commit to any sentence you have in mind, ask yourself whether it seems a bit clumsy or too long, and whether you can express the same idea more concisely and clearly. You can use your erasable note board to write a rough draft of the sentence or sentences you're not sure how to write, or you can revise them as you type your essay.

Sentence Length and Variety

Sentences that vary in length make for a more interesting and persuasive essay. Your sentences should be varied in style and length. Abrupt, short sentences might be appropriate for making crucial points, but an entire paragraph written in short, choppy sentences is distracting and suggests a certain immaturity. Compare the following two passages:

Ineffective:

Some television shows have too much violence. This is not good for young children. They may learn to be violent themselves. They see too much fighting and shooting on television.

More effective:

The television shows that have too much violence may not be good for young children. The fighting and shooting on these shows may teach children to be violent themselves.

Effective Use of Language

To score high with your essay, you'll need to show that you can use the English language correctly and clearly. By all means, use a strong vocabulary, but don't resort to obscure, high-level vocabulary just to be impressive. Also avoid **colloquialisms** (slang and vernacular). Otherwise, instead of nailing your essay, it'll turn out lousy, and you'll be totally out of luck and end up on the skids, big time. (Did you catch the *four* colloquialisms in the preceding sentence?)

In evaluating your extended response GED® test essay, your **diction**—your choice of words as well as the manner in which a word is used—will be evaluated. When you commit an error in diction, you might be confusing one word with another because the two words look or sound similar. Or you might be using a word that isn't the best one to convey the idea you have in mind. Although it is impossible to provide an adequate diction review in these pages, here are some guidelines:

- If you're the least bit unsure about the meaning of a word you're thinking of using in your essay, don't use it. Why risk committing a diction error just to use a high-level vocabulary word?

- If a phrase sounds wrong to your ear, change it until it sounds correct to you.

- The fewer words you use, the less likely you'll commit an error in diction. So when in doubt, go with a relatively brief phrase that you still think conveys your point.

Persuasive Writing

As noted at the beginning of this lesson, the GED® Reasoning Through Language Arts Test extended response will prompt you to read two opposing viewpoints and select one to defend. In order for your essay to be effective, it must be persuasive. The best way to persuade the reader, of course, is to provide good ideas supported by sound reasons and relevant examples, all presented in a logical sequence. But you can also persuade the reader through your writing style. The art of persuasive writing (or speaking) is referred to as **rhetoric.** Effective rhetorical writing makes its points clearly and force-fully by placing appropriate emphasis on different ideas.

The main way to make a rhetorical point effectively is to use appropriate connecting words between ideas. In the first example that follows, notice that it is difficult to determine the writer's point because of a structure that gives both ideas equal weight. The second and third examples clarify the point by using appropriate connecting words (in italics), as well as by a few other revisions.

Equal weight on both ideas (ineffective):

We try to plan out every detail of our lives. We often change plans because of events we did not foresee.

Greater emphasis on one idea (effective):

It is futile to try planning out every detail of our lives, *since* we often end up changing our plans due to events we did not foresee.

Greater emphasis on the other idea (effective):

People often change their plans due to events they did not foresee. *Nevertheless*, most people continue trying, often in vain, to plan out every detail of their lives.

Another way to emphasize a point is by using an abrupt, short sentence. Good topic sentences for paragraphs are often written in this style. Just be sure that the sentences supporting that point are longer; otherwise, the emphasis will be lost. You should not have any trouble identifying the short, punchy topic sentence in either of the following two paragraphs.

Rhetorical emphasis on the last sentence:

While the richest people in our country find ways to add to their own wealth, thou-sands of people die on the streets in our nation each day, and thousands more go hungry or suffer from nearly intolerable living conditions. Millions have inadequate health insurance, and millions more have no health insurance at all. In short, we have an empathy crisis.

Rhetorical emphasis on the first sentence:

Corporations are not evil. The people who run them simply try to maximize profits for the corporation's owners. So when you hear complaints about a CEO cutting employee benefits or outsourcing jobs, remember that the CEO is only doing his job, which is what the company's owners want.

You can also use punctuation for rhetorical emphasis. To emphasize a particular idea, you can end a sentence with an exclamation mark instead of a period. Also, you can emphasize a particular word by italicizing it, as shown above. But use these two rhetorical devices *very* sparingly; one of each in your essay is plenty! (Notice the use of both devices in the preceding sentence.)

Sentences that pose questions can also provide rhetorical emphasis. Like short, abrupt sentences, **rhetorical questions** can help persuade the reader—or at least help to make your point. They can be quite effective. They also add interest and variety. Yet how many GED® test-takers think to incorporate them into their essays? (By the way, the previous question is a rhetorical question.) Just don't overdo it: one rhetorical question is plenty for one essay. And be sure to provide an answer to your question.

Finally, you can emphasize a point using rhetorical words and phrases such as *undeniably, absolutely, clearly, without a doubt, the fact is,* and *anyone would agree that.* By themselves, these words and phrases mean very little; to be truly effective, they must be backed up by sound ideas and convincing reasons and examples. But they can help add rhetorical flair to your essay. Just don't overuse them.

SAMPLE EXTENDED RESPONSE

A good way to review the principles of effective essay writing is to see how they are put into practice. First, take a look at a GED® test-style essay prompt that calls for a *persuasive* type of essay:

Sample Response:

With the increasingly popular go-green movement and the controversy surrounding global warming, people are becoming more aware of their effect on the Earth. Purveyors of environmental awareness are worried about their "carbon footprints," the need to recycle, and the amount of pollution being released into the air. The environmentally aware who seek out both short-term and long-term solutions may find hybrid cars a stepping-stone to a healthier world.

One of the biggest arguments against standard cars is the depletion of fossil fuels—otherwise known as gasoline. By buying a hybrid car, less of this precious fuel will be used and owners of hybrid cars can save money. Those opposed to hybrid cars may note that buying such vehicles are more expensive, but the money saved on gas will make up for the initial expense.

Because hybrids use less gas, there is a decrease in pollution. This is not only good for the environment, but it also means that some states do not require hybrid cars to go through an emissions test. This can save hybrid owners even more money: standard cars are required to go through emissions tests to be registered—some cars may need to be checked twice if they fail the first time.

Aside from smog tests, hybrid cars may not need brake or battery replacements as often as standard cars. Hybrid brakes are designed to be regenerative, meaning they use the energy created from braking rather than wasting it, which damages the breaks. In terms of batteries, most hybrid models are protected under extensive warranties—hybrid cars that were analyzed once they reached 200,000 miles reportedly performed as well as their brand new models, something standard cars cannot live up to.

Those who oppose hybrid cars argue that because hybrids are not accessible for all people—meaning that they are not designed for large families and are not affordable for those in certain financial situations—they are not the solution. Even though companies may lose money initially in creating the cars, these companies are pioneers for the technology: long-term financial goals may prove profitable as theories are tested and models are perfected.

Overall, hybrid cars are more gas efficient, reduce the effect humans have on the environment, and can save drivers money if they are committed to the project's long-term efforts. Eventually, something better than a hybrid car may be released—but until then, these cars are strong contenders for a short-term solution that can teach creators about how to develop and perfect future models.

Commentary on Essay 1

Evidence

This essay demonstrates a well-organized argument supported with multiple examples of source text. The writer covers various positions of the argument from information in the text—including environmental benefits, battery life, and financial benefits. The response is not limited to merely citing the first passage, which defends the same position. The writer uses information provided in the second passage to further strengthen his/ her argument, and provide factual and logical support.

Argument

This essay demonstrates a logical argument in favor of hybrid cars. The writer challenges the arguments against hybrid cars (e.g., the idea that they are not an effective solution because they are not available to the masses, which the writer dispels by arguing that hybrids are a short-term, not long-term solution) to further support his/her point.

Purpose

The introduction and topic sentence make it clear from the beginning what the writer's stance is going to be with regard to hybrid cars. Although the introductory paragraph could be shorter and still get the point across, the writer focuses on this topic alone and does not contradict his/her point by straying into the opposite side of the argument. The writer also makes sure to respond to the prompt, and does not get distracted, for instance, by the topic of global warming as a whole.

SUGGESTIONS FOR WRITING AND EVALUATING YOUR PRACTICE EXTENDED RESPONSE ESSAY

To improve your writing, there is no substitute for practice. Start by using the essay prompts in this book's Practice Tests.

Always practice under exam-like conditions. Limit your time to 45 minutes. Use an erasable note board for notes, outlines, and rough drafts of particular sentences as needed, but type your final draft on the computer. Experiment in allocating your time among your various tasks:

- Brainstorming (note-taking)
- Organizing your ideas (outlining)
- Writing rough drafts
- Writing the final draft
- Proofreading and fixing problems

Keep practicing until you've learned to allocate your time in a way that works best for you.

Be sure to evaluate each practice essay you write. Be critical. Try to identify your weaknesses so that you can focus on eliminating them. A good way to improve on weaknesses is to *rewrite* an entire practice essay. Spend no more than 25 minutes to write your revised version; focus mainly on correcting the most glaring problems with your earlier draft.

You may find it difficult to judge your own writing objectively, so consider asking a friend, family member, coworker, or teacher to read and evaluate your essays as well. You might be surprised how useful their feedback can be. In any case, use the following 3-point checklist to evaluate your practice essays. This list provides all of the elements of an effective, high-scoring GED® test essay.

1 Does the essay analyze the sources to make an effective argument? (Does it clearly convey your main argument, and does it cite evidence from the source texts to support them?)

2 Is the essay well-organized? (Are the ideas presented in a logical sequence, so they can be easily followed? Are transitions from one point to the next natural and logical? Does the essay show awareness of purpose in making its points? Does it demonstrate appropriate vocabulary? Does the essay have a clear ending, or did you appear to run out of time?)

3 Does your essay demonstrate fluency with the conventions of edited American English grammar, sentence structure, word choice, punctuation, and spelling?

Your GED® test essay will be scored based on how well it meets three rubrics. Each rubric is worth 4 points, for a total of 12 points. In evaluating your practice essay, look at the various points on the rubric. If your essay meets all of the characteristics in the 4-point cell, you would get 4 points on that rubric. If it meets all of the characteristics in the 3-point cell, you would get 3 points, and so on. To earn a high score of 12, your essay would have to match the description in the 4-point cell for each rubric.

GENERAL TEST-TAKING STRATEGIES

Here are some general strategies for writing GED® test extended response essays. Most reiterate key points of advice made earlier in this lesson. Apply these strategies to the Practice Tests and then review this list again just before exam day.

Organize your thoughts before you write.

Use your erasable note board to make notes and to construct an outline of your major points and supporting reasons and examples. Before you start typing your final essay, consider writing a rough draft of at least the introductory and first body paragraphs. Just be sure to leave enough time to write your final essay.

Express a clear view based on evidence supported by the passages.

The prompt will ask you to analyze the texts and cite them to support an argument. Whatever position you take, you must support it logically based on the information given in the texts. Remember: in writing your essay, there is no "correct" or "best" answer.

Develop each major point of your outline with reasons and/or examples.

Asserting your views and opinions without explaining or justifying them is not sufficient (or persuasive) and will not earn a high score. Develop your central idea and each major supporting point with sound reasons and relevant examples. In fact, the prompt will instruct you to do precisely that.

Stay well-focused on the topic at hand.

Don't digress from the specific topic that is presented. Your central idea must address the topic directly, and each body paragraph should relate directly to your central argument.

Appeal to reason, not emotion.

The GED® test essay is an *intellectual* exercise. It's perfectly appropriate to criticize particular behaviors or viewpoints. But do not use the essay as a forum to "preach" on the subject or make an emotional appeal. Avoid extremes in tone and attitude. In particular, do not provide even a hint of racial prejudice or jingoism (excessive patriotism).

Don't dwell on one point, but don't try to cover everything either.

Avoid harping on one particular supporting point, even if you think it's your strongest one. Instead, try to cover as many points from your outline as you have time for, devoting no more than one paragraph to each one. You might not have time to cover everything you want to, but that's okay. Stick to your outline, ration your time, and you'll do fine.

Keep it simple.

Don't make the GED® test essay task more difficult than it needs to be for you to attain a solid score. Keep your sentences clear and simple. Use a simple, straightforward structure for your essay. Avoid using "fancy" words just to be impressive.

Look organized and in control of the task.

Show that you know how to present your thoughts in an organized manner. Present your main points in a logical, easy-to-follow sequence, using logical paragraph breaks between major supporting points. Use a consistent voice and tone throughout your essay. Your introductory and concluding paragraphs are especially key to looking organized and in control. Be sure to include both, and make sure that both reveal your central idea.

It's quality, not quantity, that counts.

The only limitations on essay length are the time limit and the amount of space provided. You need to strive for high quality, not long length. Be sure to incorporate into your essay all the elements recommended in this lesson, and the length of your essay will take care of itself.

Don't lose sight of your primary objectives.

During the time you have to produce your essay, your three main objectives are to:

- Develop your argument using sound evidence and relevant examples from the texts provided.

- Present your ideas in a logical, well-organized manner.

- Express your ideas through simple, clear writing that is correct in grammar, diction, spelling, and punctuation.

Never lose sight of these three objectives. Accomplish them all, and you can be assured that you've produced a solid, high-scoring GED® test extended response essay.

SUMMING IT UP

- The Extended Response component of the Reasoning Through Language Arts Test assesses your ability to communicate your thoughts and ideas in writing. You will be asked to evaluate two documents that contain opposing viewpoints and present your opinion or explain why one or the other should be supported. You will not be given a choice of essays to write on, and you must write *only* about the ideas that are presented in the documents provided.

- You will have 45 minutes to plan, write, and revise your essay. Erasable note boards will be provided to jot down notes, but you must type your extended response essay in the space provided.

- There is no correct answer or best response, and there is no correct structure or number of paragraphs for a GED® test essay. The essay is **expected** to be in paragraph form, and the preceding pages clearly state that you need at least one introductory paragraph, one body paragraph, and one summary paragraph. (A minimum of two body paragraphs is strongly suggested.)

- An automated scoring engine will score your essay on a scale of 0–12 based on how well the essay meets the points on three rubrics each one emphasizing a different aspect of the essay, as follows:
  - Rubric 1: Creation of arguments and use of evidence
  - Rubric 2: Development of ideas and organizational structure
  - Rubric 3: Clarity and command of standard English conventions

- The essay prompt is designed for you to respond with a persuasive essay. A **persuasive** essay adopts a viewpoint or an opinion on an issue and then tries to convince, or persuade, the reader to agree with that viewpoint or opinion.

- When practicing essay writing—and during the real test—be sure to remember the following important steps: brainstorming (note-taking), organizing your ideas (outlining), writing the rough draft, writing the final draft, and proofreading and fixing problems.

Writing Review

OVERVIEW

- Sentence structure
- Usage
- Verb tense
- Writing mechanics
- Summing it up

SENTENCE STRUCTURE

Sentence structure refers to how a sentence's parts fit together as a whole. In this section, you'll learn to spot these problems and how to correct or revise GED® test sentences. It is also important to understand sentence structure when answering the extended response.

Structural Errors

A GED® test sentence might be structured in a way that results in one of the following grammatical errors:

- Sentence fragments

- Run-ons and comma splices

- Faulty parallelism involving series

- Faulty parallelism involving correlatives

Don't worry if some of the terms listed above are unfamiliar to you. You'll learn what they mean in the pages ahead.

Sentence Fragments

A complete sentence must include both a subject and a predicate. The **subject** of a sentence is the word or phrase that describes what the sentence is about. A complete subject is a noun or pronoun plus any of the words directly related to that noun or pronoun. The **predicate,** or complete verb, includes all the words that, together, say something about the subject. Look at this sentence:

Aaron tried to start his car but couldn't.

In this sentence, the word *Aaron* is the complete subject. The rest of the sentence, which says something about Aaron, is the predicate, or complete verb. The word *tried* is the verb that establishes the predicate.

chapter 6

An incomplete sentence is called a **sentence fragment.** On the GED® test, you probably won't have any trouble recognizing and fixing a short sentence fragment like the next one, which lacks a predicate. In the complete sentence, notice that the verb *are* establishes a predicate.

> **fragment (incorrect):** Expensive private colleges, which for most families are out of financial reach.

> **complete sentence (correct):** Expensive private colleges are out of financial reach for most families.

A longer fragment is more likely to escape your detection, especially if you're not paying close attention:

> **fragment (incorrect):** As most of the engineers and other experts have agreed, their responsibility for building safe bridges, as well as for maintaining them.

> **complete sentence (correct):** As most of the engineers and other experts have agreed, they are responsible not only for building safe bridges but for maintaining them as well.

In the complete sentence, the subject is *they,* and the predicate is the verb *are* and the words that follow that verb.

If you're not sure whether a sentence is complete, ask yourself two questions: What's the subject? Where's the verb that establishes a predicate?

Run-ons and Comma Splices

An **independent clause** is a sentence part that can stand alone as a complete sentence. There's nothing wrong with combining two such clauses into one sentence, as long as you connect them properly.

Connecting two independent clauses without using a punctuation mark or any words to make the connection results in a grammatical error called a **run-on** sentence. One way to correct the error is to split the sentence in two using a period. Another solution is to add a comma, followed by an appropriate connecting word:

> **run-on (incorrect):** Dan ran out of luck Mike continued to win.

> **correct:** Dan ran out of luck. Mike continued to win.

> **correct:** Dan ran out of luck, but Mike continued to win.

Connecting two independent clauses with only a comma results in an error known as a **comma splice.** One way to correct the error is to insert an appropriate connecting word after the comma:

> **comma splice (incorrect):** Dan ran out of luck, Mike continued to win.

> **correct:** Dan ran out of luck, though Mike continued to win.

It can be easy to overlook a longer run-on or comma splice unless you're reading carefully. Here's an example of a longer comma splice:

comma splice: The Aleutian Islands of Alaska include many islands near the populated mainland, the majority of them are uninhabited by humans.

In reading this sentence, it isn't until you reach the word *are* that the comma splice becomes apparent. One way to correct the error is to remove the word *are*. Another way to correct the error is to transform the second independent clause into a *dependent* clause by changing the word *them* to *which*.

Faulty Parallelism Involving Series

Sentence elements that are grammatically equal should be constructed similarly; otherwise, the result will be what is referred to as **faulty parallelism.** For instance, whenever you see a list, or series, of items in a sentence, look for inconsistent or mixed use of:

- Prepositions (such as *in, with*, or *on*)
- Gerunds (verbs with an *-ing* added to the end)
- Infinitives (plural verb preceded by *to*)
- Articles (such as *a* and *the*)

In the following sentence, the preposition *to* is not applied consistently to every item in the series:

faulty: Flight 82 travels first to Boise, then to Denver, then Salt Lake City.

(The word *to* precedes only the first two of the three cities in this list.)

parallel: Flight 82 travels first to Boise, then Denver, then Salt Lake City.

parallel: Flight 82 travels first to Boise, then to Denver, and then to Salt Lake City.

In the next sentence, the gerund *being* is not applied consistently:

faulty: Being understaffed, lack of funding, and being outpaced by competitors soon resulted in the fledgling company's going out of business.

(Only two of the three listed items begin with the gerund *being*.)

parallel: Understaffed, underfunded, and outpaced by competitors, the fledgling company soon went out of business.

parallel: As a result of understaffing, insufficient funding, and outpacing on the part of its competitors, the fledgling company soon went out of business.

In the next sentence, the article *the* is not applied consistently:

faulty: Among *the* mountains, *the* sea, and desert, we humans have yet to fully explore only the sea.

parallel: Among *the* mountains, sea, and desert, we humans have yet to fully explore only the sea.

parallel: Among *the* mountains, *the* sea, and *the* desert, we humans have yet to fully explore only the sea.

Faulty Parallelism Involving Correlatives

The preceding section described how a list of items in a series can suffer from faulty parallelism. A similar problem can occur in sentences that contain **correlatives**. Here are the most common ones:

either . . . or . . .

neither . . . nor . . .

both . . . and . . .

not only . . . but also . . .

When a correlative is used in a sentence, the element immediately following the first correlative term must be grammatically parallel to the element following the second term.

faulty: Students wishing to participate in the study group should *either* contact me by telephone *or* should e-mail me.

parallel: Students wishing to participate in the study group should *either* contact me by telephone *or* e-mail me.

faulty: Students wishing to participate in the study group *either* should contact me by telephone *or* e-mail.

parallel: Students wishing to participate in the study group should contact me by *either* telephone *or* e-mail.

Awkward and Confusing Sentence Structures

A GED® test sentence that is free of errors might nevertheless be structured in a way that makes the sentence's ideas confusing, vague, ambiguous, or even nonsensical. These sorts of structural problems include the following:

- Improper coordination or subordination

- Mixing of two structures together in one sentence

- Omission of a key word needed for sentence logic

- Improper placement of modifiers

- Dangling modifiers

- Improper splitting of a grammatical unit

- Stringing together too many subordinate clauses

Don't worry if some of the terms listed above are unfamiliar to you. You'll learn what they mean in the pages ahead.

Improper Coordination or Subordination

A GED® test sentence that is free of grammatical errors may nevertheless be structured in a way that overemphasizes certain ideas, so that the reader misses the sentence's main point. If a sentence conveys two equally important ideas, they should be separated as two distinct clauses of similar length—to suggest equal importance.

> **mixed and unbalanced:** Julie and Sandy, *who* are twins, are both volunteers.

> **separated but unbalanced:** Julie and Sandy were the first two volunteers for the fund-raising drive, *and* they are twins.

> **separated and balanced:** Julie and Sandy are twins, *and* they are both volunteers.

On the other hand, if a sentence involves only one main idea, that idea should receive greater emphasis, as a main clause, than the other ideas in the sentence.

> **balanced:** Julie and Sandy, *who* are twins, were the first two volunteers for the fund-raising drive.

In the preceding sentence, notice that the less important idea (that Julie and Sandy are twins) is contained in a brief, modifying clause that describes Julie and Sandy. This is an effective way to deemphasize an idea that is not the main idea of the sentence.

To suggest similarity in ideas, a **coordinating conjunctive** such as *and* should be used. To suggest dissimilarity, or contrast, in ideas, a **subordinating conjunctive** such as *but, though, although,* or *whereas* should be used.

> **similar ideas:** Julie and Sandy were identical twins, *and* they both liked to travel.

> **similar ideas:** Julie and Sandy were identical twins, *and* so were Tracy and Judy.

> **dissimilar ideas:** Julie and Sandy were identical twins, *but* they had completely different ambitions.

> **dissimilar ideas:** Julie and Sandy were identical twins, *whereas* Tracy and Judy were merely fraternal twins.

Mixing Sentence Structures

If two or more clauses in the same sentence express parallel ideas, they should be grammatically parallel to each other. Otherwise, the sentence may be awkward and confusing.

This problem often occurs when a sentence mixes the **active voice** with the **passive voice.** In a sentence expressed in the active voice, the subject *acts upon* an object. Conversely, in a sentence expressed in the passive voice, the subject *is acted upon by* an object. Here are two sets of examples:

> **mixed:** Although the house was built by Gary, Kevin built the garage.

> **parallel (passive):** Although the house was built by Gary, the garage was built by Kevin.

> **parallel (active):** Although Gary built the house, Kevin built the garage.

> **mixed:** All hardback books are to be sorted today, but wait until tomorrow to sort paperbacks.

> **parallel (passive):** All hardback books are to be sorted today, but paperbacks are not to be sorted until tomorrow.

parallel (active): Sort all hardback books today, but wait until tomorrow to sort paperbacks.

Sentence Logic

If a sentence excludes a necessary word, the omission can obscure or confuse the meaning of the sentence. The unintentional omission of "little" words—prepositions, pronouns, conjunctives, and especially the word *that*—can make a big difference.

omission: The newscaster announced the voting results were incorrect.

(What did the newscaster announce: the results or the fact that the results were incorrect?)

clearer: The newscaster announced *that* the voting results were incorrect.

Look out especially for an omission that results in an illogical comparison, as in the following sentences. It can easily slip past you if you're not paying close attention.

illogical: The color of the blouse is different from the skirt.

logical: The color of the blouse is different from *that* of the skirt.

illogical: China's population is greater than any country in the world.

(This sentence draws an illogical comparison between a population and a country and illogically suggests that China is not a country.)

logical: China's population is greater than *that of* any *other* country in the world.

In many cases, the word *that* is optional. For example, here's a sentence that makes sense either with or without it:

Some evolutionary theorists believe [that] humans began to walk in an upright posture mainly because they needed to reach tree branches to obtain food.

Improper Placement of Modifiers

A **modifier** is a word or phrase that describes, restricts, or qualifies another word or phrase. Modifying phrases are typically set off with commas, and many such phrases begin with a relative pronoun (*which, who, that, whose, whom*).

Modifiers should generally be placed as close as possible to the word(s) they modify. Positioning a modifier in the wrong place can result in a confusing or even nonsensical sentence.

misplaced: His death shocked the entire family, which occurred quite suddenly.

better: His death, which occurred quite suddenly, shocked the entire family.

misplaced: *Nearly dead,* the police finally found the victim.

better: The police finally found *the victim, who was nearly dead.*

unclear: Bill punched Carl while wearing a mouth protector.

clear: While wearing a mouth protector, Bill punched Carl.

Modifiers such as *almost, nearly, hardly, just,* and *only* should immediately precede the word(s) they modify, even if the sentence sounds correct with the parts separated. For example:

misplaced: Their 1-year-old child *almost* weighs *40 pounds.*

better: Their 1-year-old child weighs *almost 40 pounds.*

Note the position of *only* in the following sentences:

unclear: The assistant was *only* able to detect obvious errors.

clear: *Only the assistant* was able to detect obvious errors.

unclear: The assistant was able to *only* detect *obvious errors.*

clear: The assistant was able to detect *only obvious errors.*

The general rule about placing modifiers near the words they modify applies most of the time. In some cases, however, trying to place a modifier near the words it modifies actually confuses the meaning of the sentence, as with the modifier *without his glasses* in the following sentences.

unclear: Nathan can read the newspaper and shave *without his glasses.*

(It is unclear whether *without his glasses* refers only to *shave* or to both *shave* and *read the newspaper.*)

unclear: *Without his glasses,* Nathan can read the newspaper and can shave.

(This sentence implies that these are the only two tasks Nathan can perform without his glasses.)

clear: *Even without his glasses,* Nathan can read the newspaper and shave.

So don't apply the rule without checking to see whether the sentence as a whole makes sense.

Dangling Modifiers

A *dangling modifier* is a modifier that doesn't refer to any particular word(s) in the sentence. The only way to correct a dangling-modifier problem is to reconstruct the modifying phrase or the entire sentence.

dangling: *Set by an arsonist,* firefighters were unable to save the burning building.

(What was set by an arsonist?)

better: Firefighters were unable to save the burning building from *the fire set by an arsonist.*

dangling: *By imposing price restrictions on oil suppliers,* these suppliers will be forced to lower production costs.

(Who imposed the price restrictions?)

better: *If price restrictions are imposed on oil suppliers,* these suppliers will be forced to lower production costs.

Despite the rule against dangling modifiers, a dangling modifier may be acceptable if it is an **idiom,** which means it is considered correct because it has been in common use over a long period of time.

> **acceptable:** *Judging* from the number of violent crimes committed every year, our nation is doomed.

> (This sentence makes no reference to whomever is judging; but it is acceptable anyway.)

> **acceptable:** *Considering* that star's great distance from the Earth, its brightness is amazing.

> (This sentence makes no reference to whomever is considering; but it is acceptable anyway.)

Splitting a Grammatical Unit

Splitting clauses or phrases apart by inserting other words between them often results in an awkward and confusing sentence.

> **split:** The value of the dollar *is not,* relative to other currencies, *rising* universally.

> **better:** The value of the dollar *is not rising* universally relative to other currencies.

> **split:** The government's goal this year *is to provide* for its poorest residents *an economic safety net.*

> **split:** *The government's goal* is to provide an economic safety net *this year* for its poorest residents.

> **better:** The government's goal this year is to provide an economic safety net for its poorest residents.

Sentences should not split their infinitives. An **infinitive** is the plural form of an "action" verb, preceded by the word *to.* If *to* is separated from its corresponding verb, then you're dealing with a **split infinitive** and a sentence that is grammatically incorrect.

> **improper (split):** The executive was compelled *to,* by greed and ambition, *work* more and more hours each day.

> **correct:** The executive was compelled by greed and ambition *to work* more and more hours each day.

> **improper (split):** Meteorologists have been known *to* inaccurately *predict* snowstorms.

> **correct:** Meteorologists have been known *to predict* snowstorms inaccurately.

Strings of Subordinate Clauses

A *subordinate clause* is one that does not stand on its own as a complete sentence. Stringing together two or more subordinate clauses can result in an awkward and confusing sentence. If possible, these sentences should be restructured to simplify them.

> **awkward:** Barbara's academic major is history, *which* is a very popular course of study among liberal arts students, *with whom* political science is the most popular major.

better: Barbara's academic major is history, which is second only to political science as the most popular major among liberal arts students.

USAGE

The language component of the Reasoning Through Language Arts Test involves verb and pronoun *usage*—that is, whether these types of words are used correctly in sentences. The test covers only the following areas of usage:

- Subject-verb agreement
- Pronoun case, reference, and agreement

In this section you'll review the rules for these aspects of usage. It is also important to understand usage when answering the extended response.

Subject-Verb Agreement

A verb should always "agree" in number—either singular or plural—with its subject. A singular subject takes a singular verb, while a plural subject takes a plural verb:

incorrect (singular): The *parade were* spectacular.

correct (singular): The *parade was* spectacular.

incorrect (plural): The parades *was* spectacular.

correct (plural): The parades *were* spectacular.

In the preceding examples, it's easy to tell whether the subject is singular or plural. But in other cases, it's not so easy, as you'll learn in the following sections.

Interrupting Phrases

Don't be fooled by any words or phrases that might separate the verb from its subject. In each sentence below, the singular verb *is* agrees with its subject, the singular noun *parade:*

incorrect: The *parade* of cars *are* spectacular.

correct: The *parade* of cars *is* spectacular.

incorrect: The *parade* of cars and horses *are* spectacular.

correct: The *parade* of cars and horses *is* spectacular.

An intervening clause set off by commas can serve as an especially effective "smokescreen" for a subject-verb agreement error. Pay careful attention to what comes immediately before and after the intervening clause. Reading the sentence without the clause often reveals a subject-verb agreement error.

incorrect: John, as well as his sister, *were* absent from school yesterday.

correct: *John,* as well as his sister, *was* absent from school yesterday.

Pronoun Subjects

Determining whether a sentence's subject is singular or plural isn't always as simple as you might think. You can easily determine whether a personal pronoun such as *he*, *they*, and *its* is singular or plural. But other pronouns are not so easily identified as either singular or plural. Here are two lists, along with some sample sentences, to help you keep these pronouns straight in your mind:

SINGULAR PRONOUNS

anyone, anything, anybody
each
either, neither
every, everyone, everything, everybody

nobody, no one, nothing
what, whatever
who, whom, whoever, whomever

correct: *Every* possible cause *has* been investigated.

correct: *Each* one of the children here *speaks* fluent French.

correct: *Neither* of the pens *has* any ink remaining in it.

correct: *Whatever* he's doing *is* very effective.

correct: *Everything* she touches *turns* to gold.

Even when they refer to a compound subject joined by *and,* the pronouns listed above remain *singular*.

correct: *Each adult and child* here *speaks* fluent French.

correct: *Every* possible *cause and suspect was* investigated.

PLURAL PRONOUNS

both
few
many

others
several
some

correct: *Few* would *argue* with that line of reasoning.

correct: *Many claim* to have encountered alien beings.

correct: *Some thrive* on commotion, while *others need* quiet.

Compound and Other Types of Subjects

It's especially easy to overlook a subject-verb agreement problem in a sentence involving a compound subject (multiple subjects joined by connectors such as the word *and* or the word *or)*. If joined by *and,* a compound subject is usually plural (and takes a plural verb). But if joined by *or, either . . . or,* or *neither . . . nor,* compound subjects are usually singular.

plural: The chorus *and* the introduction *need* improvement.

singular: *Either* the chorus *or* the introduction *needs* improvement.

singular: *Neither* the chorus *nor* the introduction *needs* improvement.

In some cases, you can't tell whether a subject is singular or plural without looking at how it's used in the sentence. This is true of so-called *collective* nouns and nouns of *quantity*. These special situations might call for either a singular verb or a plural verb, depending on whether the noun is used in a singular or plural sense.

correct: Four years *is* too long to wait. (*four years* used in singular sense)

correct: Four years can *pass* by quickly. (*four years* used in plural sense)

Noun clauses are considered singular. A **noun clause** is one that starts with either a **gerund** (a noun ending in *-ing)* or an **infinitive** (a verb preceded by the word *to*). In each of the next two sentences, the italicized noun clause is accompanied by a singular verb (in bold):

correct: *Mastering several musical instruments* **requires** many years of practice.

correct: Among my least favorite chores **is** *to pick up after my husband.*

VERB TENSE

While verb tense is not specifically tested as part of the language component of the Reasoning Through Language Arts Test, it is expected that your extended writing sample will illustrate your command of proper use of verb tenses. The following sections will help you to review this aspect of grammar and incorporate the rules into your writing.

Verb **tense** refers to how a verb's form indicates the *time frame* (past, present, or future) of a sentence's action. In this section, you'll focus specifically on:

- Choosing a verb tense
- Verb forms used for each tense
- Improper shifting and mixing of tenses (including conditional perfect tenses)

The first two topics listed above provide a foundation for the third topic, which is the main verb-tense issue that the GED® test examines.

Verb Tenses and Verb Forms

There are six regular verb tenses in total. A sentence should use one of three *simple* tenses—either *present, past,* or *future*—to "simply" indicate one of the three time frames.

simple present: They *have* enough money to buy a car.

simple past: They *had* enough money to buy a car.

simple future: They *will have* enough money to buy a car.

simple present: I *am losing* my mind.

simple past: I *was losing* my mind.

simple future: I *will lose* my mind.

The present-perfect tense is used for actions that began in the past and continued up until the present:

present perfect: He *has eaten* enough food (but *has* continued to eat anyway).

present perfect: She *has been trying* to lose weight (for the past year).

The past-perfect tense is used for actions that began in the past and continued up until a more recent time in the past:

past perfect: He *had eaten* enough food (but *had* kept eating anyway).

past perfect: She *had been trying* to lose weight (until recently).

The future-perfect tense is used for actions beginning in the future and continuing up until a more distant point in the future:

future perfect: He *will have eaten* enough food (once he *has* finished eating dessert).

future perfect: By year's end, she *will have been trying* to lose weight (for nearly six months).

With many verbs, the same form is used for all tenses, except that *-ed* is added for the past tenses—as in *walk, walked*. However, other verbs take distinct forms for different tenses. Notice how forms of the following three verbs (in bold) vary, depending on the tense.

Tense	To Have	To Be	To See
present	has (have)	is (are)	see
past	had (had)	was (were)	saw
future	will have	will be	will see
present perfect	has had (have had)	has been (have been)	has seen (have seen)
past perfect	had had	had been	had seen
future perfect	will have had	will have been	will have seen

Determining the correct verb form for any tense is a matter of practice and experience with the English language. If a verb form "sounds" incorrect, your ear is probably telling you that it is. Test your ear by listening to the following incorrect sentences as you read them.

incorrect: We *be* too far along to quit now; we *have went* past the point of no return.

correct: We *are* too far along to quit now; we *have gone* past the point of no return.

incorrect: The pilot *seen* the mountain but *flied* too low to avoid a collision.

correct (present tense): The pilot *sees* the mountain but *is flying* too low to avoid a collision.

correct (past tense): The pilot *saw* the mountain but *flew* too low to avoid a collision.

correct (past-perfect tense): The pilot *had seen* the mountain but *had flown* too low to avoid a collision.

incorrect: After we *gone* to the training session, we *begun* to work on the job assignment.

correct (present tense): After we *go* to the training session, we *will begin* to work on the job assignment.

correct (past tense): After we *went* to the training session, we *began* to work on the job assignment.

correct (future-perfect tense): Even before we *go* to the training session, we *will have begun* to work on the job assignment.

If you have trouble hearing incorrect verb forms, consult an English usage book that contains lists of verbs and their conjugations (the word *conjugations* refers to verb forms for different tenses).

Shifting or Mixing Verb Tenses

A sentence should not needlessly *mix* tenses or *shift* tense from one time frame to another in a confusing manner.

incorrect: If it rains tomorrow, we cancel our plans.

correct: If it rains tomorrow, we will cancel our plans.

incorrect: When Bill arrived, Sal still did not begin to unload the truck.

correct: When Bill arrived, Sal still *had not begun* to unload the truck.

The problem with mixing and shifting tenses also applies to sentences like these:

incorrect: *To go* to war is *to have traveled* to hell.

correct: *To go* to war is *to go* to hell.

correct: *To have gone* to war is *to have traveled* to hell.

incorrect: *Seeing* the obstacle *would have allowed* him to alter his course.

correct: *Having seen* the obstacle *would have allowed* him to alter his course.

correct: *Seeing* the obstacle *would allow* him to alter his course.

Conditional Perfect Tense

To indicate that something would be completed at some point in time (past, present, or future) *if* a certain condition were met, a sentence should use the *conditional perfect tense*.

To employ the conditional perfect tense properly, a sentence will use words such as *would, should,* or *could,* as well as words such as *if, had,* or *were.* Here are three pairs of examples (all sentences are correct):

Should the college lower its tuition, I *would* probably enroll.

If the college *were* to lower its tuition, I *would* probably enroll.

Had he driven slower, he *would* have noticed the new building.

If he *had* driven slower, he *would* have noticed the new building.

They *could have* reached home in time for dinner *were* it not for the sudden storm.

Had it not rained suddenly, they *could have* reached home in time for dinner.

If a sentence mixes a regular verb tense (either simple or perfect) with the conditional perfect tense, then it is grammatically incorrect. For example, look at these incorrect versions of the preceding examples:

incorrect: If the college *lowers* its tuition, I *would* probably enroll.

(The first clause uses the present tense, but the second clause implies the conditional perfect tense.)

incorrect: *Had* he driven slower, he *will* notice the new building.

(The first clause implies the conditional perfect tense, but the second clause uses the future tense.)

incorrect: They *will have* reached home in time for dinner *were* it not for the sudden storm.

(The first clause uses the future-perfect tense, but the second clause implies the conditional perfect tense.)

Pronoun Case, Reference, and Agreement

Pronouns include **personal pronouns** and **relative pronouns.** Personal pronouns (words such as *they, me,* and *his*) refer to specific people, places, and things and indicate whether they are singular or plural. Relative pronouns (words such as *which* and *who*) are not specific in their reference.

Which personal or relative pronoun you should use in a sentence depends mainly on: (1) where the pronoun appears in the sentence, and (2) what noun, if any, the pronoun refers to.

Personal Pronoun Case

Personal pronouns take different forms, called *cases*, depending on how they're used in a sentence. You'll find all the various cases in the following table.

	Subjective case:	Possessive case:	Objective case:	Objective case—reflexive:
first-person singular	I	my, mine	me	myself
first-person plural	we	our, ours	us	ourselves
second-person singular	you	your, yours	you	yourself
second-person plural	you	your, yours	you	yourselves
third-person singular	he, she, it	his, hers, its	him, her, it	himself, herself, itself
third-person plural	they	their, theirs	them	themselves

You can generally trust your ear when it comes to detecting personal-pronoun errors. In some cases, however, your ear can betray you, so make sure you are "tuned in" to the following uses of pronouns.

> **incorrect:** Either him or Trevor *would be* the best spokesman for our group.

> **correct:** Either Trevor or *he would be* the best spokesperson for our group.

> **incorrect:** The best spokesperson for our group *would be* either him or Trevor.

> **correct:** The best spokesperson for our group *would be* either *he* or Trevor.

(Any form of the verb *to be* is followed by a subject pronoun, such as *he*.)

> **incorrect:** One can't help admiring *them* cooperating with one another.

> **correct:** One can't help admiring *their cooperating* with one another.

(The *possessive* form is used when the pronoun is part of a "noun clause," such as *their cooperating*.)

> **incorrect:** In striving to understand others, we also learn more about *us*.

> **correct:** In striving to understand others, *we* also learn more about *ourselves*.

(A *reflexive* pronoun is used to refer to the sentence's subject.)

Choice of Relative Pronoun

The English language includes only the following handful of *relative* pronouns: *which, who, that, whose, whichever, whoever,* and *whomever*. Don't worry about what the term "relative pronoun" means. Instead, just remember the following rules about when to use each one.

Use *which* to refer to things. Use either *who* or *that* to refer to people.

> **incorrect:** Amanda, *which* was the third performer, was the best of the group.
>
> **correct:** Amanda, *who* was the third performer, was the best of the group.
>
> **correct:** The first employee *that* fails to meet his or her sales quota will be fired.
>
> **correct:** The first employee *who* fails to meet his or her sales quota will be fired.

Whether you should use *which* or *that* depends on what the sentence is supposed to mean.

> **one meaning:** The third page, *which* had been earmarked, contained several typographical errors.
>
> **different meaning:** The third page *that* had been earmarked contained several typographical errors.

Notice that the first sentence above merely describes the third page as earmarked, while the second sentence also suggests that the page containing the errors was the third earmarked page. So the two sentences carry two different meanings.

Whether you should use *who* (*whoever*) or *whom* (*whomever*) depends on the grammatical function of the person (or people) being referred to. This is a tricky area of English grammar, and the GED® test-makers are reluctant to test on it. But you should be ready for it anyway, so here are two good examples.

> **incorrect:** It was the chairman *whom* initiated the bill.
>
> **correct:** It was the chairman *who* initiated the bill.

(When referring to the sentence's subject, the subjective pronoun *who* should be used.)

> **incorrect:** The team members from East High, *who* the judges were highly impressed with, won the debate.
>
> **correct:** The team members from East High, with *whom* the judges were highly impressed, won the debate.

(When referring to the sentence's object, the objective pronoun *whom* should be used.)

Agreement with Antecedent

An *antecedent* is simply the noun to which a pronoun refers. In GED® test sentences, make sure that pronouns agree in number (singular or plural) with their antecedents.

> **singular:** Studying other artists actually helps a young *painter* develop *his* or *her* own style.
>
> **plural:** Studying other artists actually helps young *painters* develop *their* own style.

Singular pronouns are generally used in referring to antecedents such as *each, either, neither,* and *one.*

> **correct:** *Neither* of the two countries imposes an income tax on *its* citizens.

> **correct:** *One* cannot be too kind to *oneself.*

If a pronoun and its antecedent are far apart, it can be especially easy to overlook an agreement problem, as in this example:

> **incorrect:** *Neither* a brilliant movie *script nor* a generous *budget* can garner critical acclaim without a good director to make the most of *them.*

In the above sentence, the antecedent of *them* (a plural pronoun) is *script* or *budget* (singular). One way to remedy the disagreement is to replace *them* with *it.* Since the antecedent and pronoun are so far apart, another solution is to replace the pronoun with its antecedent—for example, with *that script or budget.*

Ambiguous and Vague Pronoun References

Pronouns provide a handy, shorthand way of referring to identifiable nouns. But unless the identity of the pronoun's antecedent (the noun to which it refers) is clear, using a pronoun will leave the reader guessing what its intended antecedent is. In other words, *every pronoun in a sentence should have a clearly identifiable antecedent.*

Here's a sentence in which the pronoun could refer to either one of two nouns:

> **ambiguous:** Minutes before Kevin's meeting with Paul, *his* wife called with the bad news.

According to the sentence, whose wife called? Kevin's or Paul's? The answer is not clear. To correct this sort of ambiguous pronoun reference, either replace the pronoun with its antecedent or reconstruct the sentence to clarify the reference.

> **clear:** Minutes before Kevin's meeting with Paul, *Kevin's* wife called with the bad news.

> **clear:** *Kevin's* wife called with the bad news minutes before *his* meeting with Paul.

Another sort of ambiguous pronoun reference occurs when a sentence shifts from one pronoun to another in a way that leaves the reader confused. Here's an example:

> **ambiguous:** When *one* dives in without looking ahead, *you* never know what will happen.

In this sentence, *you* might refer either to the diver (*one*), to someone observing the diver, or to anyone in general. Here are two alternative ways of clearing up the ambiguity:

> **clear:** *One* never knows what will happen when *one* dives in without looking ahead.

> **clear:** When *you* dive in without looking ahead, *you* never know what will happen.

If a pronoun has no identifiable antecedent at all, the sentence should be reworked to eliminate the pronoun. Here's a sentence that makes this sort of vague pronoun reference, followed by a version that fixes the problem:

> **vague:** When the planets are out of alignment, *it* can be disastrous. (*It* does not refer to any noun.)

> **clear:** Disaster can occur when the planets are out of alignment.

WRITING MECHANICS

Part of the language component of the Reasoning Through Language Arts Test involves writing mechanics. The test covers only the following mechanics issues:

- Correct use of punctuation

- Use of the apostrophe for possessives and contractions

- Frequently confused words and homonyms (words that sound alike but are spelled differently)

- Capitalization (distinguishing between proper and common nouns), beginnings of sentences

In this section you'll review the rules for these aspects of writing mechanics, which are also important to keep in mind as you write your extended response essay.

Note that the GED® test does not test on any punctuation marks besides the comma and the apostrophe, and it does not test on the spelling of any words besides homonyms.

Proper and Improper Uses of Commas

A comma indicates a pause that should correspond to a pause in the logic of the sentence. The commas make it clear to the reader that the logic of the sentence is being (temporarily) interrupted. The GED® test tests four different uses (and misuses) of the comma.

- Overuse of the comma, resulting in the splitting of a grammatical unit

- Too few commas, resulting in a confusing sentence

- Commas in a series (a list of three or more items)

- Commas used in pairs to set appositives (parenthetical phrases) apart

Commas That Split a Grammatical Unit

Commas should not needlessly separate parts of the sentence that "want" to be together, such as the subject and verb:

> **incorrect:** Former Secretary of State Henry Kissinger, is the author of several books on the history of diplomacy.

In the above sentence, the verb *is* should not be separated by a comma from its subject *Henry Kissinger* (unless a parenthetical phrase intervenes between them—not the case here).

Similarly, no comma should come between the verb and a subject complement that may follow it:

> **incorrect:** The nineteenth-century explorers Lewis and Clark may be, two of America's most-admired historical figures.

In the same way, a preposition should not be separated from its object by a comma:

> **incorrect:** As the storm continued, pieces of driftwood as well as, large quantities of sand were blown up onto the front porch.

In the above sentence, the preposition *as well as* needs to remain connected to its object, the phrase *large quantities of sand*.

When commas are overused on the GED® test, it will usually be in sentences like these examples, where the commas jarringly separate parts of the sentence that seem to "want" to be together. These abuses are generally pretty easy to spot.

Commas for Sentence Sense

A tougher task is deciding whether a sentence uses too *few* commas, a problem that can easily confuse the reader. Here's the guideline: A sentence should use the minimum number of commas needed for a reader to understand the intended meaning of the sentence.

> **too few commas:** Chandra is learning Spanish although acquiring this new skill is not one of her job duties.

> **better:** Chandra is learning Spanish, although acquiring this new skill is not one of her job duties.

The first sentence above is a run-on sentence, which connects two or more independent clauses with a conjunction (such as *but, and,* or *although*) but no comma. Some run-on sentences, such as the previous example, can be fixed by inserting a comma immediately before the conjunction. Others, like the next example, are better split into two sentences:

> **too few commas:** Chandra is learning Spanish but acquiring this new skill is not one of her job duties and she should not be paid for the time she devotes to this activity.

> **better:** Chandra is learning Spanish, but acquiring this new skill is not one of her job duties. Therefore, she should not be paid for the time she devotes to this activity.

Commas in a Series

When three or more words, phrases, or clauses are presented in sequence, or series, they should be separated by commas sometimes called the serial comma. Here are examples of each:

commas separating a list of words: The Galapagos Islands boast some of the world's most unusual plants, birds, mammals, reptiles, and fish.

commas separating a list of phrases: We looked for the missing gloves under the sofa, in the closet, and behind the dresser, but we never found them.

commas separating a list of clauses: The plot of the movie was a familiar one: boy meets girl, boy loses girl, mutant from outer space devours both.

Notice two things about how these lists are crafted. First, you normally insert the word *and* before the final item in the series (*plants, birds, mammals, reptiles, and fish*). Second, the last comma (the one after *reptiles* in this example) is optional. It may be included or omitted according to taste. (The GED® test-makers have no special preference, and there's no "right" or "wrong" about it on the exam.) The other commas, however, are not optional; they must be used.

Commas for Setting Off Introductory Elements

Common introductory phrases such as *for example* and *first of all* should be followed by a comma; otherwise, the sentence won't make grammatical sense. For example, removing the comma from either of the next two sentences would confuse its meaning:

To begin with, the new ordinance does nothing to protect tenants.

However, we decided to drive west instead of east.

A longer introductory element, which is usually a dependent clause, can be more difficult to detect. Introductory, dependent clauses typically begin with words and phrases such as the following:

Although	Whenever	Regarding
Though	If	As for
Unless	With respect to	Since

Regardless of the specific word or phrase used to begin the introductory clause, a "pause" (comma) will probably be helpful, and may be needed, at the end of the clause in order for the reader to follow the flow of ideas in the sentence. Here are two examples:

Aside from the fact that his feet were blistered and swollen, there was no reason Jim should not have finished the race.

Without first setting up an account, you won't be able to purchase that item from the website.

Commas for Setting Off Appositives (Parenthetical Phrases)

An **appositive** is a phrase that names or describes a noun. Appositives should be set off by commas; otherwise, the sentence won't make grammatical sense. In the following example, the phrase *the great left-handed Dodger pitcher* is an appositive that describes Sandy Koufax. Notice that without *both* commas the sentence is rather confusing.

confusing: Sandy Koufax the great left-handed Dodger pitcher was the guest of honor at this year's sports club banquet.

still confusing: Sandy Koufax, the great left-handed Dodger pitcher was the guest of honor at this year's sports club banquet.

clear: Sandy Koufax, the great left-handed Dodger pitcher, was the guest of honor at this year's sports club banquet.

An appositive can be as brief as a few words. Or it can be quite lengthy, as in this example:

I was surprised to learn that Paula, my cousin Frank's former girlfriend and a well-known local artist, had decided to move to Santa Fe.

To determine the correct use of commas in sentences like the preceding ones, try this test: Read the sentence without the phrase. If it still makes grammatical sense and the meaning is basically the same, then the phrase is parenthetical and should be set off by commas. Both of the preceding examples pass the test:

Sandy Koufax ... was the guest of honor at this year's sports club banquet.

I was surprised to learn that Paula ... had decided to move to Santa Fe.

The Apostrophe (for Possessives and Contractions)

The apostrophe is used for two purposes: possessives and contractions. Both are frequently tested on the language component of the GED® Reasoning Through Language Arts Test and should be used correctly when writing your extended response essay. A **possessive** is used to indicate ownership or some other close connection between a noun or pronoun and what follows it. Form the possessive as follows:

- For a singular noun, add *'s* (apostrophe followed by the letter *s*):

    the company's employees

    the cat's meow

- For a plural noun ending in *s*, just add an apostrophe:

    the Jacksons' first home

    the wolves' pack leader

- For a plural noun that does not end in *s*, add *'s* (apostrophe followed by the letter *s*):

    the school alumni's favorite reunion spot

    the cattle's hooves

The possessive pronouns *his, hers, its, ours, yours,* and *theirs* contain no apostrophes.

Be especially careful about positioning the apostrophe in plural nouns such as the following three:

men's (not *mens'*)

women's (not *womens'*)

children's (not *childrens'*)

The other use of an apostrophe is in a **contraction,** which is a word made up of at least two words from which letters have been omitted for easier pronunciation.

The apostrophe is usually (but not always!) inserted in place of the letters omitted. If in doubt, mentally "expand" the contraction to determine which letters have been left out; this is often a useful guide to determine where the apostrophe belongs. For example:

> *We've* got to go. = *We have* got to go.
>
> She *won't* mind. = She *will not* mind.

The following is a list of common contractions, grouped according to the contraction's second word (in bold). Any of these contractions might be used on the GED® test to test you on word usage. Notice that some of these contractions are homonyms (they sound just like one or more other words).

not
can't = cannot (one word)
couldn't = could not
didn't = did not
hadn't = had not
hasn't = has not
haven't = have not
isn't = is not
wasn't = was not
weren't = were not
won't = will not
wouldn't = would not

have
I've = I have
they've = they have
we've = we have
who've = who have
could've = could have
would've = would have

had (would)
I'd = I had (I would)
she'd = she had (she would)
he'd = he had (he would)
they'd = they had (they would)
we'd = we had (we would)
where'd = where had (where did)
who'd = who had (who would)

is
it's = it is (do not confuse with *its*)
he's = he is
she's = she is
what's = what is
whatever's = whatever is
that's = that is
there's = there is
where's = where is
who's = who is (do not confuse with *whose*)

are
they're = they are (do not confuse with *their* and *there*)
we're = we are
you're = you are (do not confuse with *your*)

am
I'm = I am

will
I'll = I will
he'll = he will
she'll = she will
they'll = they will
it'll = it will

Homonyms (Words That Sound Alike)

A **homonym** is a word that sounds just like another word but is spelled differently. Here are two examples:

than

> Gary was taller *than* Joshua but shorter *than* Michael.

then

> First you should change your clothes, *then* you should eat dinner.

affect

> The blinking lights won't *affect* you if close your eyes.

effect

> The blinking lights had a slightly hypnotic *effect*.

On the language component of the GED® Reasoning Through Language Arts Test, expect several corrections that will test you on recognizing the misuse of homonyms. To prepare for these questions, study the following lists. They contain many of the homonyms you should know for the language component of the test. You should also keep them in mind when writing your extended response essay.

Contractions and Their Homonyms

Be sure not to confuse certain contractions with their homonyms. These tricky words appear frequently on the GED® test.

it's (it is)

> There no secret to scoring high; *it's* all a matter of practice.

its

> The groundhog saw *its* shadow, and so we can expect more cold weather ahead.

there's

> In case *there's* any doubt on your part, I've brought a letter of reference with me.

theirs

> Victory was once ours, but now it is *theirs*.

they're (they are)

> Once *they're* gone, we can finally have peace and quiet.

their

> The two employees set *their* differences aside and finished the project.

there

> In order to go *there* you'll need to take the ferry.

who's (who is)

Find out *who's* to blame for starting the fire.

whose

Find out *whose* car this is, and warn them that it might be towed.

Common Two-word Phrases and Their Homonyms

Be on the lookout for the following two-word phrases and their one-word homonym counterparts.

all ready

If the four of you are *all ready* to leave, then we can take the same bus.

already

Sherry has left *already*, so I need to find someone else to drive me home.

all together

Are we *all together*, then, in opposing the proposed law?

altogether

He counted six raccoons *altogether*, four gray and two red.

all ways

In *all ways*, the newly engaged couple seemed incompatible.

always

The problem with dessert is that it's *always* served last, when I'm already full.

any one

I'm sure *any one* of you can jump higher than I can.

anyone

Does *anyone* here know how to jumpstart a car?

every day

Tiffany runs 3 miles *every day* before work.

everyday

Gang violence is an *everyday* occurrence in this part of town.

every one

Each and *every one* of you must keep quiet, or else they'll hear us.

everyone

If *everyone* talks at once, we'll never accomplish anything.

there for

> I will always be *there for* you.

therefore

> I think, *therefore* I am.

Some Challenging Homonyms You Might Find on the GED® Test

You're probably familiar with most, if not all, of the following words. Nevertheless, it's remarkably easy to confuse any of these words with their respective homonyms. Be sure you know the difference in spelling and meaning between the words in each pair.

accept

> Please *accept* this gift as a token of my appreciation.

except

> Every staff member *except* Bruce attended the office party.

capital

> The nation's *capital* is Washington, D.C.

> Through its stock offering, the company was able to raise more *capital*.

capitol

> The dome of the *capitol* building shone brightly in the afternoon sun.

cast

> Jim was in a skiing accident, and his leg will be in a *cast* for two months.

> The fisherman *cast* his line toward the river, hoping to catch his dinner.

> The movie's *cast* included Daniel Day-Lewis and Penelope Cruz.

caste

> People born into a *caste* social system find it impossible to improve their standard of living.

complement

> The brick driveway is a perfect *complement* to the house's metal trim.

compliment

> She paid him a *compliment* by telling him that he had good fashion sense.

council

> The head of the community *council* made the final decision.

counsel

> A married couple wanting to divorce should seek separate legal *counsel*.

dual

Immigrants with *dual* citizenship can easily land a job in this country.

duel

The final tennis match turned out to be a long, drawn-out *duel*.

principal

Gwen's incompetence was the *principal* reason she was fired from her job.

The elementary school *principal* knew every student's name.

principle

My guiding *principle* is to treat others how I would like to be treated.

stationary

Riding a *stationary* bike is good exercise, but I prefer riding a real bike.

stationery

Since e-mail has become popular, few people buy *stationery* for writing letters.

Other Common GED® Test Homonyms

Here's a list of many of the other homonyms you might encounter on the language component of GED® Reasoning Through Language Arts Test. They're all common, everyday words, and so you probably know what they mean. Nevertheless, you can easily confuse any of these words with its homonym if you're not paying careful attention. Also be aware of these when writing your extended response essay.

aisle, isle	dear, deer	plain, plane
ate, eight	earn, urn	profit, prophet
bare, bear	for, fore, four	read, red
based, baste	know, no	right, write
beat, beet	ladder, latter	seas, sees, seize
blew, blue	lead, led	steal, steel
boar, bore	meat, meet	to, too, two
brake, break	might, mite	waist, waste
cell, sell	miner, minor	ware, wear
clause, claws	pair, pare, pear	weather, whether
coarse, course	peace, piece	would, wood

Capitalization of Proper Nouns

Of course, the first word in each new sentence is capitalized. But there are many instances where a word that falls somewhere within the sentence should be capitalized as well, and these are the words that the GED® test covers. Here's the general rule for capitalizing words:

> Capitalize all **proper nouns** and words derived from them, such as adjectives. Do not capitalize **common nouns.** A proper noun is the name of a specific person, place, or thing. All other nouns are common nouns.

This section covers the types of proper nouns you're most likely to encounter on the GED® test.

People

Any particular person's name is capitalized. Any title accompanying a person's name is also capitalized. Study and compare the italicized words in these sentences:

Send copies of the letter to *Mr. and Mrs. Stefanski* and to *Dr. Reed*.

While in the U.S. Army, *Corporal Yates* served directly under an ambitious *captain* who later became *General* Eisenhower and, eventually, *President* Eisenhower.

Peter Innis was *president* of the company the year that *Chairman Stanton* resigned as board *chairman*.

Titles for named relatives are capitalized. Otherwise, a word that identifies a family relationship is considered a common word. Study and compare the italicized words in these sentences:

We went to the art museum with *Father* and *Aunt Janice*.

Yesterday my *father* took my sister and me to the art museum. I think any *father* should take his child to an art museum at least once.

Institutions, Organizations, and Groups

Names of schools, businesses, and other organizations are capitalized. Specifically named offices, branches, and agencies are also capitalized. Study and compare the italicized words in these sentences:

Prior to Dr. Kingston's tenure as head of the *Office of Transportation*, he served as head of the *School of Architecture* at *Drysdale College*.

The chief financial officer of *Unicost Corporation* attended this state's most prestigious *university*, where she majored in *sociology*.

After graduating *Franklin High School*, he went to work for the U.S. *government*, at the *Bureau of Printing and Engraving*.

If you join the *U.S. Army,* the government will pay for your college tuition. Even so, I refuse to join an *army* that invades other countries.

Names that identify groups of people by nationality, ethnicity, religion, tribe, or other such category are capitalized.

> Sioux City, which is Iowa's capital city, is named for the *Sioux* tribe of *American Indians*.

> You'll find *Danes* to be most hospitable, although the *Danish* pastries alone are worth the trip.

Artistic and Other Creative Works

Titles of literary works (books, poems, short stories, treaties, etc.), as well as magazines, movies, songs, visual art works, and other similar works are capitalized.

> The new issue of *Time* includes an interesting article entitled "Movie Rags to Movie Riches."

> Apparently, *The Wizard of Oz* did not make a profit until a decade after the movie was released.

Depending on the type, a named artistic work is also italicized (or underlined) or enclosed in quotation marks. The GED® test does not cover these rules.

Specifically named artifacts (documents, treasures, etc.) are also capitalized.

> Every grade-school student in the United States learns to recite the *Pledge of Allegiance*. But very few students ever memorize the *Bill of Rights* or the *Gettysburg Address*.

> The *Dead Sea Scrolls* and the *Shroud of Turin* are subjects of great controversy among scholars.

Time Periods and Events

Days of the week, months of the year, and specific holidays are capitalized (even when preceded by the word *a*). But the words *week, month,* and *year* themselves are not.

> This year, *Thanksgiving* will fall on a *Thursday,* and *Christmas* will fall on a *Monday*. But next year they'll both fall on the last *Thursday* of the month.

> It rained every Sunday during the *month* of *April*.

Seasons of the year are not capitalized.

> I look forward to *autumn* and the brisk weather it will bring.

> The temperature has risen into the eighties nearly every day this *summer*.

Only specifically named historical events, periods, and eras are capitalized.

> The South's surrender to the North marked the end of the *Civil War*.

> The nation's bloody *civil war* claimed more than a half-million lives.

During the *Great Depression,* unemployment among working-age men reached 25 percent.

The current recession might turn out to be as bad as the *depression* of the 1930s.

Times of the day, such as *dawn, noon,* and *midnight,* and the word *o'clock* are common nouns (not capitalized).

Geographic Regions

Words involving compass direction (north, south, east, west, northeast, etc.) are capitalized when they refer to a specific geographical section or region (or, for example, when they are part of a street name).

The *Southeast* is more humid than the *Southwest.*

The *East* Coast of *North America* receives more annual rainfall than the continent's *West* Coast.

This restaurant is located on *South* Park Street.

But these words are not capitalized when used to merely indicate direction.

Hike up the *eastern* flank of the mountain, and you'll be treated to a spectacular view of the valley.

Turn *north* when you reach the stop sign, then look for City Hall on the *east* side of *West* 75th Street.

Specifically named municipalities (cities, townships, and counties), states, regions, and countries are capitalized. Otherwise, words such as *city, county,* and *state* are not capitalized. Study and compare the italicized words in these sentences:

When driving along *Thompson County's* main highway, expect to encounter numerous speed traps, especially within *Hilltown's city* limits.

Our entire *Scandinavian* excursion was a worthwhile experience. The fiords along the *Norway* coast were magnificent.

Streets, Landmarks, and Geographic Features

Only specifically named streets, roads, highways, freeways, and others are capitalized.

If you're driving south on *Skyline Parkway,* merge onto the *freeway,* and then look for the *Lake Street* exit.

We live near *Roosevelt Avenue,* which parallels *Park Lane.* You can take either *street* to get to our house.

Buildings and other landmarks, parks and monuments, mountains and valleys, and bodies of water (rivers, lakes, seas, and oceans) are capitalized. Study and compare the italicized words in these sentences:

No trip to Washington, D.C., is complete without a visit to the *Capitol* and the *Lincoln Memorial*. After seeing the *memorial,* be sure to take a stroll along the *Potomac River.*

The *Great Lakes* are the world's largest bodies of fresh water. Among the five *lakes, Lake Superior* is the largest.

As they approached Earth, the shuttle crew could clearly observe the *Great Wall of China* and even the *Three Gorges Dam.*

Celestial Bodies

Specifically named celestial bodies (planets, moons, stars, etc.) are also capitalized. Study and compare the italicized words in these sentences:

In a solar eclipse, *the moon* travels directly between *Earth* and *the sun.* During this type of eclipse the moon blocks out almost all *sunlight.*

Ganymede is the largest *moon* orbiting the planet *Jupiter.*

We could not dig any deeper because just beneath the *earth* we hit an impervious layer of hardpan.

SUMMING IT UP

- Sentence structure refers to how a sentence's parts fit together as a whole. Sentence structure questions account for a portion of the language component of the GED® Reasoning Through Language Arts Test.

- Among the kind of grammatical errors in structure, GED® test sentence structure questions might show sentence fragments, run-ons and comma splices, faulty parallelism involving series, or faulty parallelism involving correlatives.

- Part of the language component of the GED® Reasoning Through Language Arts Test involves verb and pronoun *usage*—that is, whether these types of words are used correctly in sentences. The test covers subject-verb agreement and pronoun case, reference, and agreement.

- The language component of the GED® Reasoning Through Language Arts Test involves writing mechanics. The test covers the following mechanics issues: use of punctuation, use of the apostrophe for possessives and contractions, homonyms (words that sound alike but are spelled differently), and capitalization (distinguishing between proper and common nouns).

- The GED® test does not test on any punctuation marks besides the comma and the apostrophe, and it does not test on the spelling of any words besides homonyms (a word that sounds just like another word but is spelled differently).

- In addition to being tested on the language component of the GED® Reasoning Through Language Arts Test, these skills are also important to know when writing the extended response essay.

PART IV
THE SOCIAL STUDIES TEST

Mastering the Social Studies Test

OVERVIEW

- All about the Social Studies Test
- What's tested
- Formats used for GED® Social Studies questions
- Subject areas for GED® Social Studies questions
- Source material for GED® Social Studies questions
- Question types based on the four skill areas
- Questions based on visual depictions
- General test-taking strategies
- Summing it up

THE SOCIAL STUDIES TEST— IN A NUTSHELL

Time allowed: 90 minutes

Total number of questions: 33 questions and one Extended Response

Format: Each question is based on a text passage and/or visual depiction

Length of text passages: Up to 150 words

Number of questions per passage or visual: Expect 1 to 5 (1 or 2 is most common)

ALL ABOUT THE SOCIAL STUDIES TEST

The broad academic field of **social studies** includes a wide variety of subjects, all involving human activity and relations. These subjects include history, civics and government, economics, sociology, anthropology, psychology, and geography (as well as some others). The GED® Social Studies Test is designed to measure a variety of abilities within the context of just four of these subject areas: history, political science (civics and government), economics, and geography.

The test consists of 34 multiple-choice questions. Here's the breakdown in terms of the subject areas that the test covers (percentages and numbers may vary slightly):

50% (17 questions)	Civics and Government
20% (7 questions)	U.S. history (or Canadian* history)
15% (5 questions)	Economics
15% (5 questions)	Geography

*Note that the version of the GED® test administered in the United States includes questions about U.S. history, while the Canadian version of the GED® test contains questions about Canadian history instead.

The test questions are *not* grouped by content area. Instead, questions from all areas listed above are mixed together.

WHAT'S TESTED

The GED® Social Studies Test is based upon content in the following areas: civics and government, history, economics, and geography. Responding to the questions in each of these areas will enable you to demonstrate the following set of skills:

- Comprehension (recalling and understanding)

- Analysis (drawing inferences and conclusions)

- Evaluation (synthesizing)

- Application (applying concepts and ideas to other situations)

Keep in mind that with prior knowledge of the content areas listed above, you can expect to handle the questions with greater ease and confidence. The review materials later in this part of the book are designed to help you in this respect.

FORMATS USED FOR GED® TEST SOCIAL STUDIES QUESTIONS

The GED® Social Studies Test utilizes an electronic format that provides for a variety of question formats. While the majority of your questions will be presented in a traditional multiple-choice format, others, such as drop-downs, hot-spots, drag-and-drops, and fill-in-the-blanks will allow you to provide a specific response in certain subject areas. Moreover, extended response questions will challenge you to analyze specific documents and synthesize your analyses in a coherent essay. Each multiple-choice question will list four choices. Most questions will be based on brief passages of text, which may vary in length from a few sentences to as many as 150 words (about one fourth of a page). A question involving a passage of text might refer to it either as a "passage" or as "information" or "text." The remaining questions will be based on maps, charts, cartoons, diagrams, and other visual depictions. Some (but not all) visual depictions will be accompanied by a brief passage of text. At times, you will be asked to analyze the text itself in terms of identifying fact and opinion, bias, and elements of propaganda. Finally, many of the questions will be presented in groups of two to five, all questions in a group based on the same passage and/or visual depiction.

Each test will contain two drop-down questions, three fill-in-the-blanks, three drag-and-drop questions, two hot-spot questions, and one extended response. Drop-down questions consist of passages with blanks that can be filled by selecting the correct answer from a drop-down menu. This text will simulate those questions by providing answer choices similar to that of a multiple-choice question. Comparably, fill-in-the-blanks will contain a blank space for you to provide the correct response.

Drag-and-drop and hot-spot questions are based on maps or charts. The former challenges you to supply the correct content, while the latter challenges you to locate a specific area on a map.

Finally, extended-response questions challenge you to apply your analytical and synthesizing skills to a grouping of primary and, possibly, secondary source documents. You will be challenged to respond to a prompt that requires you to analyze these documents and present your response in a coherent essay.

SUBJECT AREAS FOR GED® TEST SOCIAL STUDIES QUESTIONS

As outlined earlier, the subject areas you'll encounter on the Social Studies Test are limited to civics and government, history, economics, and geography. Though you can review each area in depth later in this part of the book, here's an initial survey of each one.

Civics and Government

Questions about **civics and government,** both of which are aspects of political science, account for about 50 percent of the test (17 questions). On the U.S. version of the GED® test, you might encounter questions dealing with any of the following aspects of civics and government:

- Types of modern and historical governments
- Principles that have contributed to the development of American constitutional democracy
- Structure and design of the United States government
- Individual rights and responsibilities
- Political parties, campaigns, and elections in American politics
- Contemporary public policy

On the U.S. version of the GED® test, many civics and government questions will be based on the concepts embodied in the following important documents:

- The U.S. Declaration of Independence
- The original (un-amended) U.S. Constitution
- Amendments to the U.S. Constitution
- The Federalist Papers
- Landmark U.S. Supreme Court decisions

A question involving one of these documents might quote the document, or it might paraphrase or summarize the document.

History

History can be defined as the record of past events or as the subject matter that makes up those records. On the GED® test, you'll review historical facts and records and glean information from them by applying reading-comprehension and analytical skills. Remember: the questions will not require you to recall random historical facts such as names, dates, or other trivial information, so you need only be able to work within a historical context to succeed in answering history questions. However, if you have a good background in history, particularly in U.S. (or Canadian) history, you will have an advantage when dealing with these questions.

History questions account for about 20 percent of the test—about 7 questions. Of these questions, expect 3 or 4 to involve U.S. history (or Canadian history if you are taking the test in Canada). If you're taking the U.S. version of the GED®, Test expect at least one question involving the following broad eras of U.S. history:

- European settlement and population of the Americas
- Key historical documents that have shaped American constitutional government
- Revolutionary and Early Republic Periods
- The Civil War and Reconstruction
- Civil Rights
- World Wars I and II
- The Cold War
- American foreign policy since 9/11

Economics

Economics questions, or those dealing with the study of how humans use resources to meet their material needs, will account for about 15 percent of the test (5 questions or so). Some questions deal with how economics relates to government policy or key events in history. Here are the broad aspects of economics you can expect these questions to involve:

- Key economic events that have shaped American government and policies

- Relationship between political and economic freedoms
- Fundamental economic concepts
- Macroeconomics and microeconomics
- Consumer economics
- Economic causes and impacts of wars
- Economic drivers of colonization and exploration
- Scientific and industrial revolutions

An economics question might be framed in a historical context (such as the Great Depression of the 1930s), or it might present a hypothetical scenario instead. Expect some economics questions to refer to tables, charts, and graphs. Finally, note that some economics questions might incorporate certain psychology concepts—especially those relating to advertising or consumer behavior.

Geography

Expect about 15 percent of the Social Studies questions (5 questions) to focus on **geography**, which is the study of Earth's physical features and the way humans adapt to those features through the development of cultures and communities. Among possible topics for a GED® test geography question are the following:

- Development of classical civilizations
- Relationships between the environment and societal development
- Borders between peoples and nations
- Human migration

On the GED® test, you'll probably encounter some geography questions based solely on textual information, while other questions will involve a visual depiction—a map, globe, graph, chart, or table—in addition to, or instead of, text.

SOURCE MATERIAL FOR GED® TEST SOCIAL STUDIES QUESTIONS

The source material for the GED® Social Studies Test includes primary as well as secondary sources. **Primary sources** are those that are original and contemporary to whatever event or development the source documents. Examples of primary sources include historical documents, laws, speeches, newspaper articles, political cartoons, and maps. **Secondary sources** are those that are based on primary sources or other secondary sources. A textbook is a good example of a secondary source.

A question may be from a textual source, a visual source, or a combination of textual and visual sources. Regardless of the source, remember that you will *not* need to recognize or identify any document or the source of any information. Rather, your task will be to understand, evaluate, analyze, or apply the source information you are given.

QUESTION TYPES BASED ON THE FOUR SKILL AREAS

To succeed on the GED® Social Studies Test, you will need to demonstrate proficiency in four critical-thinking skill areas: comprehension, analysis, evaluation, and application. You will use all four skills throughout the test. In the next few pages, you'll examine each skill more closely. Note that the GED® test-style example questions here are all based on passages of text, rather than on visuals. In the next section, you'll learn how to handle questions involving visuals.

Comprehension Questions

Comprehension questions require that you read and recall information contained in a passage. In most cases, they also require that you *understand* and *interpret*—in other words, grasp or comprehend—the ideas and concepts that the passage's words convey. Some comprehension questions will require you to understand the main idea of a passage—much like a main-idea question in the Reasoning Through Language Arts Test. To handle this sort of question, look for an answer choice that sums up the passage. Other comprehension questions focus instead on the passage's details.

Though the correct answer choice might restate a phrase from the passage word-for-word, more likely it will either paraphrase or provide an interpretation of passage information. In other words, comprehension questions typically focus on a passage's *ideas* rather than on exactly how those ideas are expressed. Incorrect answer choices will often contradict passage information or provide assertions that are unsupported by the passage or that do not respond to the specific question that is asked.

To understand how a comprehension question might require that you interpret—rather than merely recall—what you've read in a passage, study the following two examples.

QUESTION 1 REFERS TO THE FOLLOWING INFORMATION.

During the 1700s, Europeans reaped many benefits of the agricultural revolution. New methods of farming increased food production and variety on many farms. New foods added much-needed variety to the diets of many Europeans. Larger and more balanced diets bolstered the immune systems of many Europeans and helped them become stronger and healthier.

1. Which development occurred in eighteenth-century Europe?

(A) Over-farming left the soil unfertile for subsequent generations.

(B) Advances in farming technology enhanced the health of the population.

(C) Severe droughts resulted in famine throughout farming and other rural areas.

(D) Industrialization left Europe with relatively few farmers.

Notice that choice (B), which is the correct choice, does not simply repeat a particular part of the passage, word-for-word. Instead, it combines and paraphrases two closely related ideas: first, that new farming methods increased food variety, and, second, that greater food variety led to better health among many Europeans. The passage does not include the word "technology," nor does it refer to the "population." Nevertheless, choice (B) provides a good interpretation of these two closely related ideas from the passage. None of the other three statements is supported by the passage. **The correct answer is (B).**

QUESTION 2 REFERS TO THE FOLLOWING INFORMATION.

International trade occurs when goods manufactured in a country are sent elsewhere, or *exported*, for sale, while goods manufactured elsewhere are brought into the country, or *imported*, for sale in the country. Often, governments can raise money by imposing taxes (tariffs) on goods they import from other countries. Although tariffs are paid for by the manufacturers of the goods, the cost of the tax is usually built into the cost of the product itself, which means that the tax is passed on to the consumer. A manufacturer is often able to realize a profit by producing an excess of goods and then exporting the surplus. When the manufacturer can do this, often the cost of production is lowered on each unit produced, so the final selling price is reduced for the products sold in the country of production.

2. The lowest prices on manufactured goods are realized when a manufacturer can

 Select ▼

   (A) impose a tariff on imported goods

   (B) import materials it needs to make its products

   (C) pass along a tariff to consumers

   (D) export a surplus of goods

On the online GED® test, you will click on your answer. In this paper version, please circle it.

Choice (D) essentially provides the point of the final two sentences of the passage: by producing more units, a manufacturer often can reduce its per-unit cost and then pass the savings on to domestic consumers while charging more for surplus sales in foreign countries. Though the passage does not explicitly state that this is how the lowest price on manufactured goods is realized, you can interpret the information in this way.

Choice (A) contradicts the passage: it is a government, not a manufacturer, that imposes tariffs. Choice (B) is unsupported by the passage—whether a manufacturer can save money by importing materials depends on the cost of those materials. Choice (C) indicates an activity that manufacturers can do, according to the passage. But choice (C) is incorrect because passing along a tax is not how the lowest price is realized. So choice (C) does not answer the question. **The correct answer is (D).**

As the second of the above two examples illustrates, when handling comprehension questions involving lengthier passages, be sure to focus on the part of the passage that the question asks about. Some of the incorrect answer choices will probably involve other parts of the passage—parts that are not relevant to the question at hand.

Analysis Questions

Analysis questions go beyond understanding the information in a passage or visual. Analysis involves organizing the information; explaining how ideas, facts, or data connect together; identifying patterns; and recognizing inferences, conclusions, and meanings beyond what is stated. Some analysis questions may require you to *infer* historical or economic causes or effects. (To infer is to draw a reasonable conclusion based on certain information.) Other analysis questions might require you to point out similarities and differences between two events, eras, systems, or other phenomena. Still other analysis questions may require you to distinguish fact from opinion. These are just some of the many possibilities for analysis questions.

QUESTION 3 REFERS TO THE FOLLOWING INFORMATION.

Industrialized countries need uninterrupted supplies of oil in order for their economies to function. The Organization of Petroleum Exporting Countries (OPEC) has made major inroads in helping certain less-industrialized countries become more self-sustaining. Because these countries have a virtual monopoly on the export of oil, they have been able to raise oil prices substantially.

3. Why do some industrialized nations oppose OPEC?

(A) They don't want competition in the production of oil.

(B) Higher oil prices can raise the cost of running an economy.

(C) Some non-industrialized nations have little or no oil reserves.

(D) OPEC is not a member of the United Nations.

The passage does answer this question explicitly. To answer the question, you must infer an effect, or consequence, of what OPEC has achieved. Because oil is a valuable commodity in almost every area of an industrialized nation's economy, the cost of running such an economy would rise proportionately to the cost of oil, hurting the nation's economy (which is obviously a result that no nation would want for itself). **The correct answer is (B).**

QUESTION 4 REFERS TO THE FOLLOWING INFORMATION.

Communism is both a political and an economic system in which the major means of production and distribution of goods and products are shared in common by all the people. In its purest form, communism would mean even the sharing of all property. The term is generally used to describe the economic systems in Soviet Russia and China. *Socialism* is an economic system in which the majority of productive resources, both human-made and natural, are owned and controlled by the state or its agencies. Because production is divided among the population under socialism, production is assumed to be more equitable (fairer) and more efficient than under Western-style capitalism.

> **4.** What do Communism and Socialism have in common?
>
> **(A)** a preference for private ownership of resources
>
> **(B)** a preference for competition over cooperation
>
> **(C)** the fact that both are political as well as economic systems
>
> **(D)** the division of production among all the people

To answer this question, you must note the similarities and differences between the two systems.

Neither Communism nor Socialism promotes private ownership of resources, choice (A), nor does either promote competition in business, choice (B). Only Communism is considered both a political as well as an economic system, choice (C). Both systems, however, believe in the division of production among all the people, choice (D). How the division is made may differ, but both support the theory that division of production is good. **The correct answer is (D).**

QUESTION 5 REFERS TO THE FOLLOWING INFORMATION.

After the Great War, later referred to as World War I, the United States, Great Britain, and France joined forces and drew up terms for the defeated Germany. The terms, known as the Treaty of Versailles, reflected the allies' position that Germany was to blame for the war. Consequently, the treaty provided that Germany was forbidden to have a military air force and that the German army and navy were to be strictly limited in size. In addition, under the treaty, Germany was required to pay 132-billion gold marks in reparations to nations it had harmed during the war. Germany had no choice but to abide by all these terms.

> **5.** Which of the following is an opinion, rather than a fact, about the conclusion and immediate aftermath of World War I?
>
> **(A)** Germany had little or no say when it came to the terms of the treaty.
>
> **(B)** Germany's punishment was unfair since other nations had harmed Germany as well.
>
> **(C)** After the Great War, Germany was left without an air force to defend itself.
>
> **(D)** France was one of the nations that participated in the Great War.

Based on the passage information, choices (C) and (D) are clearly accurate, and so you can eliminate them. Choice (A) is not a fact provided in the passage. So does this mean that the statement in choice (A) is merely an opinion? No. The passage makes it clear that the treaty was drawn up by the countries that had opposed Germany, and that Germany "had no choice but to abide by" the terms of the treaty. So you can infer that Germany had little or no say in the treaty negotiations. In contrast, choice (B) is merely on opinion. Whether the treaty terms were fair may very well depend on one's perspective on the war. **The correct answer is (B).**

Evaluation Questions

Evaluation involves drawing on your comprehension and analytical skills in order to make an assessment, judgment, or critique or to draw a conclusion. An evaluation question might ask you to characterize an event, era, or system described or outlined in a passage. Or it might ask you to recognize a potential benefit or drawback of an economic or political policy, or with a particular statute (law). An evaluation question might present a point of view, along with numbered statements that either reflect or oppose that point of view. An evaluation might ask you to determine whether statements made in a passage are facts or opinions or whether the author of a passage seems to be a reliable expert or someone with biased opinions. Evaluation questions often involve quotations and historical documents.

In handling these questions, what's just as important as recognizing a fair assessment of the information is recognizing unfair assessments and judgments. Be on the lookout for wrong-answer choices that speculate too much—that jump to conclusions or judgments that are unreasonable based solely on the information provided.

QUESTION 6 REFERS TO THE FOLLOWING INFORMATION.

"The ostensible cause of the war was the issue of slavery. However, slavery was just one of many issues that drove a wedge between the two sides. One of the main points of contention between the two sides was the issue of states' rights. Another issue was the favoritism shown in Congress toward the North. The final straw, though, was the election of Abraham Lincoln, a candidate who did not receive a true mandate of the people based on the number of votes he received."

6. The war to which the quoted words referred was the U.S. Civil War. Which of the following is most likely true about the author of the quoted words?

The author

(A) sympathized with the South

(B) was opposed to slavery

(C) saw many causes of the war

(D) participated in the war

The question asks you to make an assessment or draw a conclusion about the author based on what he or she wrote. So you need to understand the quotation's specific points as well as the author's broader point. Because the author identifies several possible contributing factors leading to the Civil War, it is fair to conclude that the author, in fact, recognized that the war had many causes. Though some of the points that the author makes might be the same ones that a Southern sympathizer might have pointed out, it is unfair to conclude, based solely on the passage, that the author sympathized with the South, choice (A). **The correct answer is (C).**

QUESTION 7 REFERS TO THE FOLLOWING INFORMATION.

The Fourteenth Amendment to the U.S. Constitution provides in part: "... (C) No person shall be a Senator or Representative in Congress, or elector of President and Vice President, or hold any office, civil or military, under the United States, or under any State, who, having previously taken an oath, as a member of Congress, or as an officer of the United States, or as a member of any State legislature, or as an executive or judicial officer of any State, to support the Constitution of the United States, shall have engaged in insurrection or rebellion against the same, or given aid or comfort to the enemies thereof. But Congress may by a vote of two thirds of each House, remove such disability. . . ."

7. What is the intent of this portion of the Fourteenth Amendment?

(A) to encourage criminal prosecution of elected officials

(B) to ensure party loyalty at all levels of government

(C) to enhance the security of the nation and its states

(D) to encourage patriotic citizens to run for Congress

The question requires you to evaluate and characterize the quoted portion of the Fourteenth Amendment. The portion lists a number of government offices, and then forbids any person who poses a threat to the government from holding any of the listed public offices. Choice (C) provides a good characterization of what this provision was intended to accomplish. Notice that choices (A) and (D) go too far. The purpose of the quoted part of the Fourteenth Amendment is more limited than either choice (A) or choice (D) suggests. Choice (B) is incorrect because the provision is concerned with loyalty to the state and federal governments, not to any political party. **The correct answer is (C).**

Application Questions

Application questions require you to use information from a passage (or visual) in a way that is different from the way it is presented to you. In other words, your task is to apply the ideas to new situations and contexts. Use your understanding of the concept described in the passage, along with common sense, to identify the correct answer.

QUESTION 8 REFERS TO THE FOLLOWING INFORMATION.

During a period of economic recession, the nation's gross national product (GNP) is in decline, which means that the economy as a whole is producing fewer goods and providing fewer services than previously.

8. How is a small business LEAST likely to behave during an economic recession?

    (A) by putting its products on sale

    (B) by giving loyal employees a pay raise

    (C) by limiting the kinds of products it sells

    (D) by depleting its inventory of goods

This question requires you not only to understand the definition of a recession, but also to apply the concept to a situation not specifically described in the passage. When fewer goods and services are produced, everyone makes less money and, in turn, everyone has less money to spend. The behaviors described in choices (A), (C), and (D) make perfect sense in this situation. (Eliminate those choices.) **The correct answer is (B).**

QUESTION 9 REFERS TO THE FOLLOWING INFORMATION.

A *lobbyist* is a person who represents a group of people and whose job it is to work for the special interests of that group. A lobbyist will contact members of Congress in order to make sure that money is allocated for the group's work. The lobbyist will try to persuade them that the interests he or she represents are more worthy than others to receive a share of available financial resources.

9. Which activity would be most closely associated with lobbying?

    (A) explaining to a legislator why he or she should run for reelection

    (B) petitioning the city council to pass a law outlawing smoking in public places

    (C) convincing the boss to throw an office party that will improve worker morale

    (D) staging a labor-union strike in protest of unfairly low wages

Choice (C) is the only one that describes an interest held in common by a group of people (employees), and where someone representing the group attempts to obtain a benefit (a party) for the group from someone in a position to give it to them (the boss) by persuading that person of the benefits of doing so (improvement in worker morale). **The correct answer is (C).**

QUESTION 10 REFERS TO THE FOLLOWING INFORMATION.

On August 2, 1990, Iraqi president Saddam Hussein invaded Kuwait, an oil-rich neighboring state roughly the size of New Jersey and ignited a conflict that would, ultimately, lead to his downfall. Until that time, the United States had turned a blind eye to the repressive policies of Saddam's regime. National Security Directives advised "economic incentives," such as food supplies, to urge Iraq towards more humane policies. Following Iraq's invasion of Kuwait, the Bush administration denounced the "naked aggression" of Iraq's actions even as it feared an invasion of oil-rich Saudi Arabia. Economic sanctions were issued, but Saddam would not withdraw his forces from Kuwait. In November, the United States appealed to the United Nations Security Council for authorization for military intervention. In Resolution 678 the Security Council gave Iraq until January 15, 1991 to withdraw. Saddam Hussein promised that military invasion would result in the "mother of all battles," and critics at home warned of a long and bloody war. President Bush had claimed that an order by him for an American invasion to liberate Kuwait did not require Congressional approval, but he changed policy and asked Congress for authorization, which he received on January 12. The United States began an air war against Baghdad and Iraqi footholds in Kuwait. When Iraq responded by attacking Israel, the Bush administration provided Patriot missiles operated by American personnel. When Iraq set fire to Kuwaiti oil fields, American forces invaded Kuwait on February 23, an invasion that lasted for one hundred hours. Thousands of Iraqis were killed and tens of thousands surrendered or fled north. On February 27, President Bush declared that Kuwait had been liberated.

10. According to the author, President George H.W. Bush's decision to invade Kuwait

    (A) was done without Congressional approval.

    (B) reversed earlier American policy towards Iraq.

    (C) incurred widespread United Nations disapproval.

    (D) was ignored by Saddam Hussein.

In the earlier years of Bush's presidency, his administration had used economic incentives and diplomatic means to attempt to influence Iraqi policy. In a reversal of earlier policy, Bush ultimately decided to invade Kuwait, which was done with Congressional approval as well as UN support. Iraq responded to initial warnings by promising a bloody war and retaliated against American bombings with air strikes against Israel and incinerating Kuwaiti oil fields. **The correct answer is (B).**

QUESTIONS BASED ON VISUAL DEPICTIONS

Approximately 40 percent of the questions on the Social Studies Test are based on a visual depiction of some sort or on a brief passage of text accompanied by a visual depiction. The "visual" may be a chart, graph, or table; or it might be a political cartoon, photo, or other illustration; or it might be a map, diagram, or timeline.

Questions based on visuals are designed to gauge your ability to interpret the meaning of the visual (as well as the accompanying text, if any). Even if you do not recognize the visual or don't understand it initially, you can still figure out the best answer by looking for clues or for things you do recognize.

In the following pages, you examine the types of visuals appearing most frequently on the test. You'll see some examples of each type, and you'll learn how to handle them.

Editorial Cartoons

The kinds of cartoons on the GED® Social Studies Test are not the sort you'll find in the comics section of your newspaper. Instead, they're the type that appear in a newspaper's editorial section, which contains articles, essays, and cartoons expressing opinions about current events. These **editorial cartoons** are sometimes referred to as *political cartoons*, even though they often deal with a much wider range of issues—from political and economic to social and cultural.

Editorial cartoonists are not concerned with providing information. Instead, through their cartoons, they express their opinions and perspectives (their "slant") on current events and issues of the day. Their cartoons carry messages that are usually critical of prevailing ideas, well-established institutions, and influential individuals—especially political figures in the public eye at the moment. Editorial cartoonists often employ humor, sarcasm, and irony to convey their messages.

As for how these cartoonists convey their messages, their cartoons often show human-like characters, which the artist typically uses to depict a specific, well-known public figure—for example, a president or presidential candidate, a dictator or leader from another country, a high-ranking government official, or even an influential commentator from the media. The editorial cartoonist will usually portray the specific person as a **caricature,** which exaggerates the person's prominent physical features.

Of course, when a cartoon shows a caricature of a specific, well-known person, you know that the message of the cartoon has to do with that person. But editorial cartoonists often use human-like characters, animals, and even objects to represent, or *symbolize* something else, such as the following:

- A group of specific individuals—for example, the Supreme Court or a legislative body (such as the U.S. Senate)

- A geographically defined entity—for example, a particular state or nation, the North or the South (as during the U.S. Civil War), or the European Union

- An organization or alliance—for example, a political party, the United Nations, an oil cartel such as OPEC, political lobbyists, big business, or the so-called "tea baggers"

- An abstract idea, an ideology, or a cause—for example, free-market capitalism, white supremacy, religious fundamentalism, social welfare, environmentalism, the so-called "war on terror," or gun control

Here are just a few of the symbols often used in editorial cartoons:

- An eagle, to represent democracy or freedom

- A hammer-and-sickle, to represent Communism

- A donkey, to represent the Democratic political party

- An elephant, to represent the Republican political party

- A soldier, to represent one of the countries involved in a war

- A judge, to represent the concept of justice

- A beggar, to represent social welfare

- A pile of money, to represent greed or capitalism

Sometimes, specific individuals become so closely associated with an ideology, cause, or concept that a cartoonist will use a caricature of that person as a symbol—especially if the readership is sophisticated enough to understand the symbolism. For example:

- Lenin has come to represent Soviet-style Communism.

- Theodore Roosevelt has come to represent opposition to monopolies and big business.

- Adolf Hitler has come to represent persecution and is even seen as the embodiment of evil.

- Franklin D. Roosevelt has come to represent New Deal–style, or so-called "big" government.

- Richard Nixon has come to represent political scandal, secrecy, and dirty politics.

As you examine the characters and objects in an editorial cartoon, look for clues as to what they represent. The cartoonist may write a word or brief phrase directly on the characters (especially their clothing) as well as on other pictured objects to help the audience understand the symbolism. Look carefully for any such clues, as they typically appear in small print. Remember: if the cartoonist went to the trouble of writing words anywhere in the visual, those words will no doubt be useful in understanding the idea that the cartoonist was trying to convey.

Also pay close attention to how the characters appear and what they are doing or saying. A character might be drawn to appear noble and victorious or aggressive and evil; or a character might be drawn to appear defeated, injured, or victimized. Two characters may appear to be fighting or angry with each other, or they might appear friendly toward one another. Body postures, facial expressions, modes of dress, objects carried or held, and other visual clues can be useful in understanding a cartoon's message. In addition, spoken words—usually written in bubbles above the characters—are even more crucial to that message.

Finally, editorial cartoons sometimes come with **captions**—words appearing below the illustration. A caption might indicate what a character is saying, or it might provide a clue as to how to interpret or evaluate the cartoon. If the cartoon includes a caption, you can be certain that it is crucial in understanding the message of a cartoon.

QUESTION 11 REFERS TO THE FOLLOWING CARTOON.

WONDER HOW LONG THE HONEYMOON WILL LAST?

11. What idea is the artist who created the cartoon trying to convey?

Hitler and Stalin

(A) should be partners because they have a lot in common

(B) were on unfriendly terms before forming a partnership

(C) have formed an alliance that they hope to keep secret from their mutual enemies

(D) have formed a partnership whose prospects are uncertain

As with the previous question, your knowledge of twentieth-century history may be useful in interpreting the cartoon, yet it isn't needed to answer the question at hand. You may not have recognized Stalin in the cartoon. But notice the hammer-and-sickle symbol, together with the swastika, on the wedding cake. These symbols provide a clue as to the identity of both characters. In any event, the question provides this information.

In this question, the caption is crucial to understanding the message. Posing the question "Wonder how long the honeymoon will last?" suggests that a new marriage, though happy at first, might turn sour over time. The cartoon implies that the relationship is good at the onset, but the future of the relationship is uncertain, choice (D). Choice (A) is incorrect because the cartoon shows Hitler and Stalin already partners. Choices (B) and (C) may or may not provide accurate historical information, but since the cartoon provides no clue as to the past relationship between Hitler and Stalin, choice (B), or about whether their alliance was secret, choice (C), you can rule out both choices. Again: if a cartoon provides a caption, you can be sure that it is crucial to understanding the cartoonist's intended meaning. **The correct answer is (D).**

Maps

During the Social Studies Test, you'll encounter at least one or two geography and/ or history questions based on maps. Don't expect to find the kinds of maps you use in your everyday life to help you find your way across town or from one city to another. Instead, what you're likely to see are any of the following kinds of maps, depending on the sort of information the map is intended to provide:

Political map: This is the most familiar type of map to most people. It shows political boundaries of cities, states, and countries as well as capitals and other major cities. On the GED® Test, a map of this type might cover a multi-state region, an entire country, a multi-country region, or an entire continent (and possibly the seas and oceans around it).

Topographical map: This type of map shows the locations of natural features such as rivers, lakes, seas, mountain ranges, and deserts. It may also focus on the locations of natural resources such as minerals, timber (forests) and other forms of vegetation or crops, and even animal life. A topographical map may also provide elevations (altitude) at various locations.

Historical map: This type of map provides a timeline of key historical events according to where they took place. Historical maps often provide *callouts*, which list events and/or dates and point to the places on the map where the events occurred.

The three categories listed above are not mutually exclusive. For example, a map may provide political boundaries as well as geographical features. Historical maps typically show politically defined regions such as colonies, provinces, nations, territories, kingdoms, and even empires.

Regardless of which type of map a test question involves, you should start by reading the title of the map. The title will provide clues as to what information the map conveys. Next, locate the map key, or **legend** (if any). The legend is often located off to the side or at the bottom of the map. It will explain the symbols used on the map as well as any colors or shading used on the map. The legend may also contain a map **scale** that indicates distances on the map. Here's an example of a typical map legend:

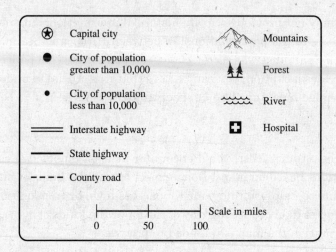

Since maps can be used to display any sort of geographically, anthropologically, or historically specific information, a myriad of specialized map types are possible. Remember, the new hot-spot or drag-and-drop interactive features allow you to pinpoint exactly where on a map a specific event occurred or specific information can be verified. The following two maps, each of which is accompanied by two GED® test-style questions, illustrate two such types.

QUESTIONS 12 AND 13 REFER TO THE FOLLOWING MAP.

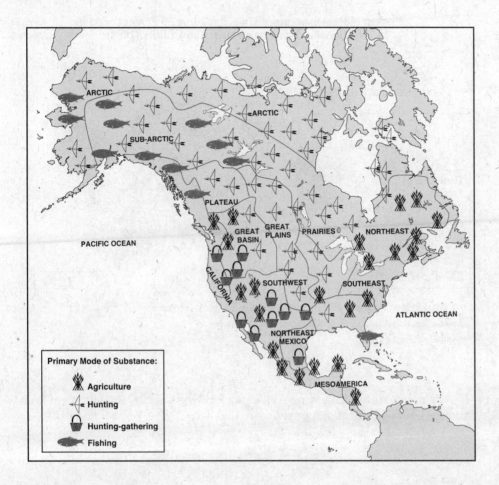

12. Click on the map to indicate in what region of North America the majority of Native Americans who fished for their sustenance were located? On the online GED® test, you will click to indicate your answer. For this paper version, write your answer on the map.

Referring to the map's legend, you can see that fishing, represented by the fish symbol, took place mainly in the northwestern part of the continent. An elementary knowledge of geography and directions is enough here to identify the northwestern part of North America. **The correct answer is the Northwest.**

13. [   ] were available to the early Native Americans of the Great Basin as a means of sustenance. On the online GED® test, you will type your answer in the box. For this paper test, please write it in.

To answer this question, you need to locate the Great Basin area on the map (in the map's left-central region). In that area you'll find the symbols for agriculture, hunting, and hunting-gathering. **The correct answer is hunting, gathering, and agriculture.**

QUESTIONS 14 AND 15 REFER TO THE FOLLOWING MAP.

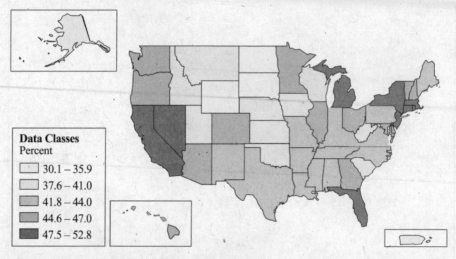

Percent of Renter-occupied Units Spending 30 Percent or More of Household Income on Rent and Utilities (2008)

Data Classes
Percent

- 30.1 – 35.9
- 37.6 – 41.0
- 41.8 – 44.0
- 44.6 – 47.0
- 47.5 – 52.8

United States: Estimate: 45.9 Percent, Margin of Error: +/-0.1 Percent

Source: U.S. Census Bureau, 2006-2008 American Community Survey

14. In how many states, including Alaska and Hawaii, is the percentage of households who rent their residence rather than own it 30.1 to 41.0 percent?

    (A) 11

    (B) 15

    (C) 46

    (D) not enough information is provided

This question illustrates the importance of reading the title of a map. According to this map's title, the map provides only the rent-to-income ratio in each state, which is entirely different from the renter-to-owner ratio. Not enough information is provided to answer this question. **The correct answer is (D).**

15. The map best supports which of the following conclusions?

    (A) On average, U.S. renters pay more for rent than for all other living expenses combined.

    (B) Arizona rental housing is less affordable than rental housing in most other states.

    (C) The average rent in Georgia is greater than in most other states.

    (D) States with the highest rent-to-income ratio have the highest home ownership rates.

This is a relatively difficult question. Focusing on choice (B), the rent-to-income ratio for Arizona residents is in the second-highest category (44.6–47.0 percent) among the five provided in the legend. Estimating the total number of states in the top two categories, you'll find that the total is far less than half of 51 (the total number of states, as well as Puerto Rico). Interpreting rent-to-income ratio as an indication of "affordability," Arizona is clearly less affordable than most states when it comes to rental housing, choice (B).

Now consider the other three choices. Since only the very highest rent-to-income ratio category exceeds 50 percent, and only by just a bit, it is safe to conclude that, on average, rent accounts for *less* (not more) than half of living expenses for U.S. renters, choice (A). The map and legend provide no information about actual rent amounts, choice (C), or about home ownership rates, choice (D). **The correct answer is (B).**

Graphical Data Displays

Several questions on the Social Studies Test will be based on data presented in graphical format. A question of this type might be based on a table, bar graph, line chart, picture graph, or circle graph (pie chart). These displays are usually used for test questions involving geography and economics. This book's Mathematics review explains how to read, interpret, and analyze data presented in each of these formats. Be sure to review those materials when preparing for the GED® Social Studies Test. Keep in mind, however, that on the Social Studies Test, the emphasis is not on number-crunching but, rather, on the following skills:

- Understanding what the graphical display is intended to show
- Reading and interpreting the data
- Understanding the significance of the data
- Drawing general conclusions from the data

Though you may need to perform simple arithmetic tasks, such as counting or adding, you won't need to calculate precise percents, ratios, or averages. (These skills are measured on the Mathematical Reasoning Test instead.) In addition to multiple-choice question, chart and graph items may ask you to use the interactive drag-and-drop feature.

The next two GED® test-style questions are based on the same picture graph and illustrate that the focus of data-display questions on the Social Studies Test is far more on understanding and interpreting graphs in a Social Studies context than on applying math.

QUESTIONS 16 AND 17 REFER TO THE FOLLOWING GRAPHS.

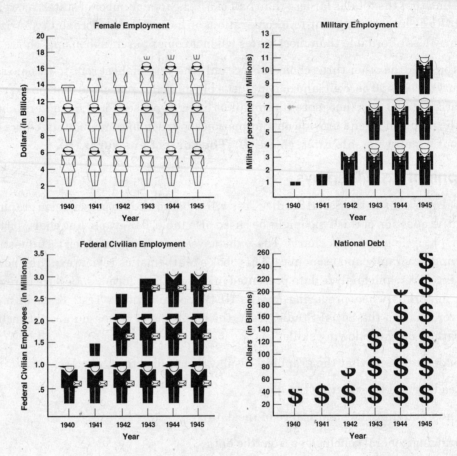

The Wartime Economic Boom, 1940-1945

16. What conclusion can you draw from the information presented in the charts?

From 1940 through 1945

(A) the employment rate among males was greater than among females

(B) all of the U.S. military personnel were males

(C) a rise in federal civilian employment contributed to increased government spending

(D) the greatest increase in employment was among females

Focusing on choice (C), the upper-right and lower-left charts show that military employment and federal civilian employment both rose over the course of the war. The lower-right chart shows that government *debt* rose over the course of the war. Together, the three charts strongly support the inference that the rise in federal civilian employment (as well as the rise in military employment) contributed to increased government spending. Though you cannot draw this conclusion with absolute certainty, the data strongly support it.

Now consider the other three choices. Notice that the upper-left chart expresses female employment in terms of *dollars* (in billions), not in terms of the number of females employed. So you cannot draw any conclusions about how many females were employed from 1940 through 1945. Eliminate choices (A) and (D). As for choice (B), although the symbols used in the upper-right chart look more like males than females, it is unfair to draw any conclusion about gender based solely on these symbols. (Keep this lesson in mind when analyzing picture graphs on the GED® test.) **The correct answer is (C).**

17. During how many of the years shown was the number of military employees more than double the number of federal civilian employees?

    (A) one

    (B) two

    (C) three

    (D) four

To answer this question you need to analyze and compare the lower-left and upper-right charts. (You can disregard the other two charts.) For each year, look at the height of the picture, then look to the left to see the employment number that the picture's height represents. Start with the year 1940. Notice that federal civilian employees (lower-left chart) and the number of military employees (upper-right chart) both numbered about 1.0 million. The second number is *not* more than twice the first number. Perform a similar analysis for each subsequent year (notice that approximating the numbers will suffice, and that very little math is involved):

1941: 2.0 million (military employment) is *not* more than twice 1.5 million (federal civilian employment).

1942: 3.5 million (military employment) is *not* more than twice 2.6 million (federal civilian employment).

1943: 8.0 million (military employment) is more than twice 3.0 million (federal civilian employment).

1944: 10.5 million (military employment) is more than twice 3.2 million (federal civilian employment).

1945: 12.0 million (military employment) is more than twice 3.3 million (federal civilian employment).

As you can see, during three of the six years, military employment was more than double federal civilian employment. **The correct answer is (C).**

EXTENDED RESPONSE (ER) ITEMS

Every Social Studies Test will have one extended-response prompt. This test item is a 25-minute task that requires you to analyze one or more source texts to produce a writing sample. These writing samples will be scored based upon

- the quality of your arguments and use of evidence

- the development of your ideas and your organizational structure

- the clarity with which you write and your command of standard English conventions

Writing samples will be graded on a 0- to 2-point scale for arguments and evidence, a 0- to 1-point scale for ideas and structure, and a 0- to 1-point scale for clarity and English conventions.

To help you to compose a successful extended response essay, consider the following

❶ **Analyze the prompt carefully.** Make certain that you understand exactly what the prompt is asking. Does it ask you to relate the documents to each other? Does it ask you to come to an understanding of how the documents represent a particular issue in a particular time period? Does it ask you to "read between the lines" to examine how the sources reveal the attitudes and beliefs that marked individual responses to larger historical events? Whatever the case, study the language of the prompt carefully and make certain that you understand what it requires of you as a reader, as well as what it requires of you as a writer.

❷ **Analyze the documents carefully.** For written documents, analyze them as you would any piece of literature. But in this case, use your knowledge of time periods or key historical characters to help you to discover meaning. What is the author's central idea? What details does he or she use to clarify that idea? Who is the intended audience for this piece of writing, and what is the piece's intended purpose? For visual documents, apply the same skills that you learned in previous sections about interpreting cartoons and other visuals. They, like written documents, usually have a central point or idea that is supported by key details relating to physical depiction of characters or other symbolic "props" meant to convey a point. Pay attention to these details as you would key details in a piece of writing.

❸ **Synthesize your analyses in a coherent thesis.** Use the details of the prompt as a kind of template with which to construct your thesis. Make certain that your thesis is specific in terms of proposing *how* the documents provide a glimpse into a character, time period, or both.

❹ **Outline and develop your essay.** With your thesis as a guide, develop a rough outline as to how you will use the evidence that you discovered in the documents. Make certain that your essay has distinct sections, and that those sections relate to each other in an effective way that develops your thesis. Try to provide "guide words" so that the reader can understand how you see documents relating to each other. Do the documents compare or contrast? If so, how?

⑤ **Review and proofread.** As time permits, review your essay and correct any errors, including those in spelling, grammar, or punctuation.

"As time permits" is key. Try and be organized and focused, and use your time judiciously.

Sample Extended Response Source Documents and Prompt

Study the following documents carefully. Then compose an essay in response to the prompt provided. Allow yourself 25 minutes to complete the task.

Abraham Lincoln, *Second Inaugural Address*

With malice toward none; with charity for all; with firmness in the right, as God gives us to see the right, let us strive on to finish the work we are in; to bind up the nation's wounds; to care for him who shall have borne the battle, and for his widow, and his orphan—to do all which may achieve and cherish a just, and a lasting peace, among ourselves, and with all nations.

Parole of Confederate General Robert E. Lee and Six of his Staff Officers

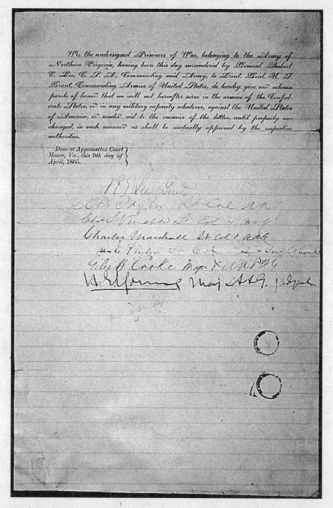

We, the undersigned Prisoners of War, belonging to the Army of Northern Virginia, having been this day surrendered by General Robert E. Lee, C. S. A., Commanding said Army, to Lieut. Genl. U. S. Grant, Commanding Armies of United States, do hereby give our solemn parole of honor that we will not hereafter serve in the armies of the Confederate States, or in any military capacity whatever, against the United States of America, or render aid to the enemies of the latter, until properly exchanged, in such manner as shall be mutually approved by the respective authorities.

Done at Appomattox Court House, Va., this 9th day of April, 1865.

Letter from Martha Cockrone to her husband, a Confederate prisoner of war May 25, 1865, after the Confederate surrender at Appomattox

May 25 1865

My Dear Husband

This will inform you that your letter of the 20 of April was received yesterday and it afforded me great pleasure to hear from you as I had not heard any thing from you since you left home. we are all tolerably well and hope you are likewise blessed. I want you to take the oath of allegiance and come home as soon as possible [three words crossed out] I have taken it Mrs. Southall the Dr and nearly every body in the neighborhood.

Every thing we had to eat was taken from us and we draw rations now from the Junction [?] by which means we make out tolerably well.

Tell Nick that his uncle Nick was captured at Mrs. Southalls and we have not heard from hims since Ira John & Robert are at home I saw brother John at the Jounction [?] a few days ago you must write to me as soon as you get this the children join in sending love to you I hope you will be at home very soon your devoted wife

Martha L[?] Cockrone

Enclosed you will find two dollars which is all have I don't suppose the Dr has any money he read your letter

[Written over the text up the center of the letter] No money enclosed when opened for examination [illegible signature]

Prompt: How do these documents provide insight into the ideals and lived realities of life in the Confederate South following the surrender of Robert E. Lee on April 9, 1865? Compare and contrast the experience of soldiers and civilians.

Suggested answer: A thorough analysis of these documents would relate the professed clemency articulated in Lincoln's desire for "malice toward none" with the desire for peace and order as evident in the document signed by Lee's officers, as well as the capitulation of Martha Cockrone and her neighbors. An analysis should include mention of the apparent fidelity to Lincoln's ideals in the trust of Lee's officers, as well as the rations provided for Mrs. Cockrone. However, a thorough analysis should also note that those dire conditions experienced by Mrs. Cockrone were due to the fact that "Every thing we had to eat was taken from us."

GENERAL TEST-TAKING STRATEGIES

Here are some general strategies for tackling the GED® Social Studies Test as a whole. These points of advice generally apply to all types of questions. Put these strategies to work on the Practice Tests in this book, and then review them again just before exam day.

First, read the question(s) based on a passage of text or visual depiction.

Before you look at a visual or read even a brief passage, read the question stem (the question itself, but not the answer choices). If the passage or visual comes with more than one question, read all the question stems first. This task should only take 10 to 15 seconds. The question(s) may provide clues as to what you should focus on and think about as you read the text or analyze the visual.

Read a passage of text straight through before answering any questions based on it.

If a question or group of questions refers to a passage of text, read the passage from beginning to end without interruption. Pay careful attention to how the ideas connect together. Think about what the overall message, or main idea, of the text is. Also think about whether the ideas lead naturally to any conclusion or inference. If they do, the chances are good that the question(s) will focus on this feature.

Use your noteboard as you read a longer passage.

Passages can run up to 150 words in length (about one fourth of a page)—long enough to merit taking notes while reading. Jotting down key words and phrases helps you think actively while reading, which will help you answer the questions about the passage.

When reading charts, graphs, maps, and timelines, don't get bogged down in every detail.

Some visual depictions will contain more information than you'll need to answer the question(s) based on them. In fact, one of the skills you're being tested on is your ability to sort through that information to determine what is relevant (and what is not relevant) to the question at hand. So don't waste time analyzing every detail in a visual. Instead, focus your attention on what the question asks about.

Read any title or caption accompanying a map, chart, graph, or cartoon.

Many times, the title or caption will give you a clue about the true meaning of the visual. You can then use this clue to help clarify the question and eliminate incorrect answers.

Apply common sense.

Many questions, especially about economics and geography, may be unfamiliar to you at first glance. However, remember that you use and make decisions concerning economics and geography every day. Use your real-life, practical economics and geography skills to help you on the test.

If possible, formulate your own answer to a question before reading the answer choices.

For each question, try to formulate your own response to it, and *then* scan the choices for something resembling your home-grown answer. This technique will keep you from becoming confused and distracted by wrong answer choices.

Pace yourself properly.

The 90-minute GED® Social Studies Test gives you 60 minutes to answer all the questions except the Extended Response. You will then have 25 minutes for the Extended Response. The questions in the first part of the test are not presented in any set order of difficulty. So after 30 minutes, you should have answered 16 or 17 questions. If you're falling behind, pick up the pace. In any event, try to answer all 34 questions with at least 5 minutes to spare, so you can go back and reconsider any responses you were unsure about. You will have only 25 minutes to read the source documents and question, formulate an answer, type your response, and made any edits you find.

SUMMING IT UP

- GED® Social Studies Test questions test your knowledge of important principles, concepts, events, and relationships.

- The Social Studies Test contains about 24 multiple-choice questions, 2 drop-down questions, 3 fill-in-the-blank, 2 drag-and-drop, and 2 hot spots. Most questions are based on brief passages of text, which vary in length from a few sentences to as many as 150 words (about a quarter of a page). A question involving a passage of text might refer to it either as a "passage" or as "information" or "text." Other questions are based on maps, charts, cartoons, diagrams, and other visual depictions. Some visual depictions are also accompanied by a brief passage of text. In addition, there will be one extended response question which will ask you to analyze certain documents and synthesize your findings in a coherent essay.

- The questions cover U.S. (or Canadian*) history, civics and government, economics, and geography. (*The Canadian version of the GED® test contains questions about Canadian history instead of U.S. history.)

- The GED® Social Studies Test requires you to demonstrate that you can comprehend the material, draw inferences and conclusions, evaluate the information, and apply concepts and ideas to other situations.

- The best way to do well on this test is to read the front section of a major newspaper every day, watch the news on TV, listen to serious discussions of current events on public radio, and think about current issues. It may also be helpful to go to your local library and look at the atlases, maps, and news magazines.

Social Studies Review

OVERVIEW

- History
- Civics and government
- The U.S. Government
- Canadian Government
- Economics
- Geography
- Historical documents on the GED® Social Studies Test
- Canadian History
- Summing it up

The GED® Social Studies Test is designed to measure critical-thinking skills rather than knowledge. Nevertheless, with some prior familiarity with the four content areas covered on the test (history, civics and government, economics, and geography) you can expect to handle the questions with greater ease and confidence. The review materials in this part of the book are designed to help you in this respect. Keep in mind that this review is intended only to highlight the four content areas listed above. It is by no means intended to be a comprehensive examination of these areas.

Review questions are provided throughout this Social Studies review. As you answer them, keep in mind that the passages of text on which they are based are longer than those on the actual GED® Social Studies Test. To assist readers preparing for the GED® test in Canada, sections focusing on Canadian history and government are included later in this review. Also later in the review are summaries of key U.S. historical documents covered on the Social Studies Test.

HISTORY

This history focuses mainly on U.S. history, although some of that history is presented in the context of the world affairs and relations between the United States and other nations. It begins with the European colonization of the Americas and includes questions about the Native American population that inhabited North America. It concludes with American foreign policy after 9/11.

European Settlement and Population of the New World

Beginning in the late fourteenth century, European explorers embarked on a series of expeditions of discovery and conquest. Their goals were to amass great wealth by conquering indigenous peoples, to bring fame to their monarchs and themselves for their daring exploits, and to bring Christianity to the regions that they explored and exploited. The first explorers were motivated by fabulous tales from the Orient brought back by Marco Polo and other Italian traders, and especially by the valuable products they brought with them, such as spices, silk, gold, and silver. Portugal's Prince Henry sought a sea route to India around Africa, so Portuguese traders could bypass the Italian middlemen who had monopolized the Oriental luxury trade. Under his direction, Portuguese explorers explored much of the African coast and established profitable trading posts in the Niger delta and farther south in Angola. Eventually, Portuguese explorers reached Southern India's trading cities. Within a mere fifty years, Portugal essentially controlled the Indian Ocean, with strategically located trading posts and naval military might.

While Portugal set its sights on dominating the Indian Ocean, Spain also began to explore and seek colonies. **Christopher Columbus,** an enterprising Italian merchant with sailing experience on Portuguese trade vessels in the Indian Ocean, attempted to voyage across the Atlantic to India and break the Portuguese trade monopoly. Columbus landed in the Bahamas, not in India, though he thought he had reached India.

By the end of the fifteenth century, Spain and Portugal dominated trade and territories in Asia and the Americas. Portugal controlled most of the Indian Ocean trade, as well as the spice plantations in Indonesia, while Spain controlled extensive parts of Central and South America. Fearing a war between the two rivals, the Pope helped negotiate the Treaty of Tordesillas, which essentially divided the world in half, with both countries receiving exclusive rights in their respective hemispheres. England, France, and the Netherlands refused to comply with the Treaty of Tordesillas and began to explore and establish their own colonies in the Americas.

France founded colonies in much of eastern North America, on a number of Caribbean islands, and in South America, primarily as trading posts for exporting products such as fish, sugar, and furs. Through the explorers Cartier and Champlain, France established a fur trading post in 1608 that would grow into the city of Quebec. Extending their reach, the French claimed a large territory in Canada and the Great Lakes region. Then "New France" grew west of the Great Lakes into Wisconsin and south to the Gulf of Mexico. In 1682, the entire Mississippi River watershed was claimed for France. Named Lousiane, it gave France control of the Mississippi Valley and the Great Plains in addition to its holdings in the Great Lakes and Canada.

> **1.** The European explorers of the fourteenth and fifteenth centuries were motivated by all of the following with the possible exception of
>
> | Select ▼ |
>
> **(A)** converting native peoples to their religion
>
> **(B)** acquiring new land for their countries
>
> **(C)** the possibility of personal fame
>
> **(D)** Papal proclamations to go forth and explore
>
> On the online GED® test, you will click to select your answer. For this paper version, please circle it.

European explorers were enlisted and supported in their explorations by their monarchs. They were not following any directives from the Pope. **The correct answer is (D).**

The New World

By 1700, the Portuguese, Spanish, French, and British had all established colonies in the New World. In 1607, Jamestown, Virginia, became the first permanent British settlement in the New World. Jamestown and other settlements and colonies were created as joint-stock companies. Joint-stock companies were business ventures in which a large number of people invested small amounts of money. This allowed the investors to avoid the risk of losing huge sums of money. A total of thirteen British colonies appeared on the eastern coast of North America over the next 125 years, each with its own identity. The British sponsored the colonies and the journeys of the colonists because the British hoped to make vast amounts of trade revenue from trade with the colonies. The colonists from England who sailed to the New World sought freedom of worship, a voice in their government, and a fresh start with land of their own. Some colonists, many of those in Georgia, for example, sought refuge from the law in the New World. By 1763, after an armed conflict with the French (known in the Americas as the French and Indian War and known in Europe as the Seven Years War), the British controlled a large portion of the North American continent. Unfortunately for those Native Americans who occupied the lands of North America before the arrival of the Europeans, colonization meant the end of many Native American cultures. Partly because of armed conflict and partly because of the introduction of European diseases into North America, the Europeans caused the death of many, many Native Americans.

Native Americans

Native Americans formed settlements in distinct regions around the continent. Each tribe or nation had a different culture, language, governing system, religion, and clothing, as well as their own types of dwellings and customs, such as feasts.

Northeast Woodland tribes lived in enormous longhouses, and hunted and grew corn, beans, and squash. On the opposite coast, tribes in the Northwest Coastal region built cedar houses, and hunted, fished, and gathered plants and clams. Native Americans living on the Great Plains lived in portable tipis, and harvested plants, hunted buffalo, and tamed horses. Tribes in the Southwest lived in multistory adobe houses, farmed crops, raised turkeys, and hunted. In the Southeast, tribes built homes with thatched roofs. They farmed, hunted, fished, and gathered berries and nuts.

> **2.** It was important for tipis to be easily moved to different locations so tribes could
>
> **(A)** fish in Northwest streams
>
> **(B)** raise turkeys across the Southwest
>
> **(C)** trade throughout the Northeast
>
> **(D)** hunt buffalo across the Great Plains

Tribes who lived on the Great Plains lived in tipis that could quickly be disassembled and relocated. These tribes had a nomadic lifestyle, following herds of buffalo that were their primary food source. **The correct answer is (D).**

> **3.** Regional variations affected all of the following aspects of Native American life, EXCEPT which one?
>
> Select ▼
>
> **(A)** style of housing
>
> **(B)** type of crops raised
>
> **(C)** trading with white settlers
>
> **(D)** species of animals hunted
>
> On the online GED® test, you will click to select your answer. For this paper version, please circle it.

Different types of housing, crops, and animal species characterized Native Americans in different regions; however, trade with settlers was not dependent upon location. **The correct answer is (C).**

The Struggle for American Independence

Between the time of their arrival in the New World and the years prior to the War for American Independence, the colonists developed their own ideas about the way the colonies should be governed. Consequently, many of the colonists disagreed with the way the British governed the colonies. Among these points of contention was the problem of taxation without representation. In other words, the colonists did not like the fact that they were being forced to pay increasing British taxes, but they were never allowed much, if any, say in the way the British governed the colonies. Many of the colonists also resented the presence of British troops throughout the colonies. These disagreements, among others, caused tension between the colonies and the British government and led to one of the most monumental events in history, the War for American Independence (also known as the American Revolution or Revolutionary War).

4. Why did the British sponsor expeditions and colonists in the New World?

(A) The British population explosion forced the British to seek relief from high population density by sending some of its population elsewhere.

(B) The British encouraged the expeditions and colonists so that the colonists could escape the widespread famine facing the British Isles.

(C) The British wanted to establish colonies and find new goods to bolster the British economy.

(D) The British government wanted to give the colonists an opportunity to experiment with new religions.

The British saw the economic benefits of establishing colonies and supporting exploring expeditions based on the examples of the Spanish and Portuguese. **The correct answer is (C).**

5. What was the colonists' main point of contention with the British government?

(A) taxation without being allowed a fair voice in the government of the colonies

(B) the brutality of the British soldiers against the Native Americans

(C) the high taxes on tea

(D) the slow communications between the British government and the colonies

The colonists thought it was unfair that they paid taxes to the British government yet had no say in the way they were governed by the British. **The correct answer is (A).**

Between 1765 and 1776, the British imposed a number of taxes on the colonies that the colonists viewed as unfair. Some of the items taxed by the British included sugar, playing cards, newspapers, and tea. In many cases, the colonists displayed their displeasure and anger by burning officials in effigy, tarring and feathering officials, and even throwing massive amounts of tea into harbors. In response, the British government tried to limit and control the trade of the American colonies. In further attempts to keep the colonies from straying too far from British rule, the British attempted to reduce the power of the American lawmaking assemblies. To even further discourage protest, the British legislature would pass special bills targeting specific troublesome colonists for imprisonment and to strip them of their wealth, which was then given to the Crown.

After much debate within the colonies, the colonial leaders, with the support of many of the colonists, decided to cut ties with Great Britain and declare the independence of the colonies from British rule. Some of the colonists, known as loyalists, however, did not want to break away from the mother country; they still felt a sense of duty and loyalty toward England. In 1776, the colonial leaders signed the **Declaration of Independence,** which officially declared that the colonies were no longer under British rule. The British refused to recognize the independence of the colonies. As a result, war broke out in the colonies between the American colonists and the British soldiers.

The colonists mustered an army made up of many militiamen, or citizen soldiers, but very few professional soldiers. The British, on the other hand, fielded an army of professionally trained soldiers along with a formidable navy. Although the revolutionary army was outnumbered and perhaps outclassed, they had a few advantages. The revolutionists had great leadership, they were fighting from a defensive position, and they passionately believed in the cause for which they fought. With the aid of the French, Dutch, and Spanish—all of whom were enemies of the British—the Americans won an improbable victory over the British and gained their independence. Interestingly, by the end of the war, the colonies were only a minor concern for the British as they were also in the midst of a global conflict, fighting against the nations of France, Holland, and Spain. Tired of war, American and British diplomats met in Paris and signed the **Treaty of Paris of 1783** in which Britain recognized the independence of the colonies. After the dust settled, the thirteen colonies stood loosely united as the United States of America.

6. From the Declaration of Independence: "The history of the present King of Great Britain is a history of repeated injuries and usurpations, all having in direct object the establishment of an absolute Tyranny over these States."

   All of the following are "injuries and usurpations" to which the Declaration of Independence refers, EXCEPT which one?

   (A) controlling trade

   (B) limiting lawmaking authority

   (C) imprisoning protesters

   (D) prohibiting public assembly

The British engaged in the activities described in choices (A) through (C). However, they did not prohibit public assembly. **The correct answer is (D).**

7. Which of the following conclusions can be drawn concerning the War for American Independence?

   (A) The Americans might not have won the war without the aid of foreign countries.

   (B) The British would have lost the colonies in America even if the French and Spanish had not declared war on the British.

   (C) Every colonist wanted independence from British rule.

   (D) Almost no colonists wanted independence from British rule.

If France, Spain, and Holland had not supplied money and supplies, and if these countries had not declared war on the British, the colonies might have lost the war and remained under British control. **The correct answer is (A).**

The Early U.S. Government

Over the next several years, the states worked hard to settle their differences and agree on a system of government that best suited all of the states. Since 1781, the colonies had operated under the **Articles of Confederation,** the first constitution of the United States. Under the Articles, the colonies were united as a loose union of states, the Congress held the majority of the political power, and there was no executive branch of the government. The entire national government was weak. In 1787, leaders from each of the states met at the Constitutional Convention and outlined a plan for a new government. Some argued for a weak central government that was unlike the British government, while others argued for a very strong central government. Eventually the states compromised. The resulting plan was the **U.S. Constitution.** Eventually, all of the states ratified, or approved, the Constitution, or plan of government; it became the official plan of government in 1789. In 1791, the United States adopted ten amendments, or changes, to the Constitution. These changes, known as the **Bill of Rights,** protected the rights of individuals.

About the same time, the nation's first political parties were forming as a result of disagreements over the proper political and financial policies for the new nation. The two parties that emerged were the **Federalists** and the **Republicans.** The Federalists, who were led by the wealthy and educated, sought a strong central government steered by the elite. The Republicans, on the other hand, believed in the ability of the common people to govern themselves. Republican leaders like James Madison and Thomas Jefferson wanted to limit the powers of the federal government and protect states' rights. The two parties also differed in the area of foreign policy. The Republicans supported the French Revolution while the Federalists thought that the French Revolution was a terrifying act against an established government. Disputes between the Federalists and the Republicans reached new heights in the election of 1800. The Republican candidate Thomas Jefferson was elected President. This election showed that the American people believed in the power of the people to determine the course the country would take. The Federalists never won another presidential election.

8. Those opposed to a strong central government in the early days of the United States were concerned most about which of the following?

   (A) the possibility of the government becoming oppressive the way that King George had been to the colonists

   (B) the possibility that no good candidates could be found to run such a government

   (C) the possibility that the states could not agree on a leader for such a government

   (D) the idea that the states had to be a part of a single nation instead of each forming its own country

Anti-Federalists did not want a government with the potential to oppress its constituents the way the king had done to the colonists. **The correct answer is (A).**

9. Disagreement over the correct path for the new government to take resulted in [Select ▼]

(A) the U.S. Civil War

(B) the creation of the first two American political parties

(C) the Bill of Rights

(D) the Articles of Confederation

On the online GED® test, you will click to select your answer. For this paper version, please circle it.

There were two predominant ideas about the direction that the new government should go. The politicians chose sides, and those two sides became the Federalists and the Republicans. **The correct answer is (B).**

U.S. Expansion and Growing Pains

One of the most important decisions Jefferson made as president was to expand westward. Jefferson acquired a huge amount of land known as the **Louisiana Purchase.** For a bargain price, Jefferson bought all the land between the Mississippi River in the east and the Rocky Mountains in the west, from the Gulf of Mexico in the south to the Canadian border in the north. For only $15 million, the United States doubled the size of its territory. Eventually, the United States would create fourteen more states in the land of the Louisiana Purchase. The growing size of the United States helped earn international respect. The westward expansion of the United States was a difficult task. Settlers faced uncharted land, harsh climates, and Native Americans who did not welcome those who might drive them out of their homeland. Nevertheless, the Americans pressed onward and gradually adapted to life on the frontiers.

As the new nation continued to grow and become more self-sufficient, it struggled with policies concerning international trade. The United States passed legislation that hurt trade between the United States and Great Britain and France. The British took exception to this and responded with animosity. The British navy made it a common practice to stop American ships on the open seas, claiming that it was searching for deserters, those who had illegally left the British navy. Often the British captured Americans on these ships and forced them into the British navy. They also confiscated American ships and goods. These actions, along with reports of British aid to hostile Native Americans, moved Congress to declare war on the British. Known as the **War of 1812,** this conflict did not settle any of the issues that started it, but the United States emerged victorious. The war brought the nation together and earned the United States respect in the eyes of many European countries. The period of time that followed the war was marked by further expansion, with the addition of Florida, and an increased American role in international diplomacy and politics. President Monroe issued the **Monroe Doctrine** and declared that the United States would not allow any further European colonization or expansion in the Western Hemisphere. As the United States earned a reputation as an up-and-coming nation, it was able to increase its trade with other nations. This helped stimulate the country's economy and that of each of the states. The northern states concentrated on manufacturing and production while the southern states focused on agriculture, or farming. The northern states, most of whose population was urban (in cities), became a society centered on industry and big business. The southern states, most of whose population was rural (in the countryside), became a society centered on plantations and the production of crops such as cotton and sugar. Large plantations grew throughout the South and became the economic backbone of the southern economy. Although all the states maintained loyalty to the nation, the two regions were often very competitive. The two sections of the country competed for political power within the Congress and for the presidency. As a result of this competition, along with other major issues such as slavery, tensions between the North and the South grew.

In the West, the United States continued to expand by annexing Texas and Oregon. The **annexation** of these two regions stirred great emotion. Adding Texas to the Union meant the addition of a slave territory. This possibility angered many in the North until the situation with Oregon developed. If the United States added Oregon, a non-slave territory, it could add Texas, a slave territory, and maintain equilibrium between the slave states and non-slave states. By 1846, both territories were added to the United States. However, Mexico went to war with the United States over Texas. Eventually, the United States negotiated a treaty with Mexico that added California, New Mexico, and part of Arizona to U.S. holdings in exchange for $15 million. The issue of **slavery** moved front and center again as both the North and the South argued over whether or not the new territories should allow slavery. In an attempt to divert or delay major problems between the North and the South, politicians passed legislation such as the **Compromise of 1850,** which made sure the number of free states and slave states remained equal as new states were added to the nation. After 1850, some of the new territory prohibited slavery, while other territories permitted the settlement of slave owners and non-slave owners alike. The United States then passed fugitive slave laws that required runaway slaves to be returned to their owners. Then the Supreme Court issued the **Dred Scott decision,** which opened all new territories to slavery. The South felt that the North was trying to abolish slavery, an act the southern states saw as a violation of their state rights.

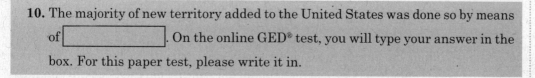

10. The majority of new territory added to the United States was done so by means of [   ]. On the online GED® test, you will type your answer in the box. For this paper test, please write it in.

Although some U.S. territory came after war, most land was purchased from other countries. The Louisiana Purchase is a good example of such a purchase. **The correct answer is purchases.**

11. Which of the following was perhaps the MOST controversial issue surrounding new territories that were added to the United States?

Whether the new territory would

(A) be Federalist or Republican

(B) be industrial or agricultural

(C) be hostile or friendly to Native Americans

(D) allow slavery or prohibit slavery

Slave states wanted all the new territory to be open to slavery, while non-slave states wanted slavery prohibited in the new territories. **The correct answer is (D).**

The U.S. Civil War and Reconstruction

In the presidential **election of 1860,** the issue of slavery came to a head. The southern Democrats split into two factions, or groups, and put forth two different candidates, each with different, yet pro-slavery, beliefs. The Republicans nominated Abraham Lincoln, a candidate who did not support the idea of slavery in the new territories. A fourth party put forth yet another candidate. With American votes scattered among the four candidates, Lincoln won the controversial election with less than 40 percent of the popular vote. After Lincoln won, South Carolina seceded, or withdrew, from the Union. Shortly thereafter, ten more southern states followed South Carolina and created the **Confederate States of America.**

Lincoln made it clear that he had no intention of allowing any state to secede from the Union. He called up troops from the remaining loyal states and went to war to preserve the Union. In 1861, the South was at a disadvantage in the **Civil War** because it lacked the manufacturing power and transportation that the North had. In addition, most of the fighting was done in the South. After four years of bloody fighting, in what was often known as the War Between the States, the South surrendered. Slavery ended, and the United States survived. Although America suffered heavy casualties in both the North and the South, the war resolved two important issues. First, the authority of the federal government took precedence over the states. Second, slavery was abolished throughout the United States.

Lincoln, thankful that the Union was still intact, intended to allow the southern states back into the Union with relatively easy terms. However, he was assassinated before he could put his plan into action. After Lincoln's death, a vindictive Congress initiated a period known as Reconstruction, during which time the South lived under very oppressive conditions. The Union had been saved, but the South harbored great resentment against the North for the harsh treatment it endured after the war. Many Southerners were especially resentful of having to allow African Americans to vote and hold public office. These feelings endured in the southern states for several generations after the war.

12. Which of the following statements is true?

(A) The South seceded from the Union because Southerners feared Reconstruction.

(B) The South seceded from the Union because of the issue of slavery.

(C) The South seceded from the Union because of the issue of slavery, its concern about states' rights, and other issues.

(D) The South seceded from the Union because the North threatened to take all political power away from the South.

The issues of slavery, states' rights, the threat of new free territories upsetting the equilibrium, and other issues all played a part in the South's secession. **The correct answer is (C).**

13. President Lincoln decided to go to war with the South in order to

 .

(A) end slavery

(B) punish the South for having slaves

(C) confiscate its wealth

(D) preserve the Union

On the online GED® test, you will click to select your answer. For this paper version, please circle it.

Lincoln refused to allow the nation to be dissolved over any issue, so he sent troops into the South to preserve the Union. **The correct answer is (D).**

Reconstruction

After the Civil War ended, the United States entered a Reconstruction period from 1865 through 1877. The North and South were still divided. During this period, the Southern states that had composed the defeated Confederacy were incorporated into the Union in an attempt to rebuild the South. The Southern states, attempting to rebuild after the devastation caused by the war, viewed Reconstruction as an unreasonable penalty.

The driving force behind Reconstruction were the nearly four million slaves who had been freed following the Civil War. President Abraham Lincoln had recommended that the South's African American slaves be given the right to vote; however, he was assassinated before his plans were put into action. Lincoln's successor, President Andrew Johnson, vetoed the Civil Rights Act of 1866, which Congress had enacted, although his veto was overridden. The Southern states enacted laws called "black codes" that restricted freed blacks' activities, enraging Northerners.

During the period of Reconstruction, Congress passed a Reconstruction Act in 1867 that temporarily divided 10 Confederate states into 5 military districts. The act required that these states ratify the 14th Amendment to the U.S. Constitution, which stated that all people born in the United States are citizens granted equal protection under the law, including the right to vote, regardless of race. The Southern states were readmitted to the Union by 1870, although Reconstruction didn't come to an end until 1877 when Rutherford B. Hayes became president.

14. Reconstruction can be summed up in which of the following statements?

    (A) Southern states that had seceded during the Civil War were reorganized under Congress and later restored to the Union.

    (B) Freed slaves in the South were given equal opportunities for employment throughout the region.

    (C) The Northern states did not recognize the rights of former slaves from the South.

    (D) President Lincoln rejected the Civil Rights Act of 1866.

The former Confederacy, composed of 11 Southern states that seceded from the United States, was readmitted into the Union during the Reconstruction period. **The correct answer is (A).**

15. What does the 14th Amendment define?

    (A) how many terms the president is allowed to serve

    (B) which branch of the government can collect income tax

    (C) what it means to be a U.S. citizen

    (D) at what age people are allowed to vote

The 14th Amendment defines what it means to be a citizen of the United States and protects the rights of African Americans to citizenship. **The correct answer is (C).**

World Wars I and II

The beginning of the twentieth century saw more reform in many areas of life in the United States. Trusts, or combinations of companies that reduced competition, came under government scrutiny. Conditions in factories drew much attention, and the government responded by cleaning up unsanitary conditions. This made working conditions better for the factory and food-packing plant workers and made the products safer for consumers. The government set aside many acres of land for national parks and wildlife preserves. The United States also began construction of the **Panama Canal** to join the Atlantic and Pacific Oceans; this would allow ships to pass through the canal instead of rounding the entire South American continent.

During the early twentieth century, the United States devoted much time and energy to international diplomacy. The American policy of "Speak softly and carry a big stick" meant that the United States let its policies and intentions be known through diplomacy, and it backed that up with military action when needed. When World War I, or the Great War, as it was known then, erupted in Europe, the United States faced a dilemma. President Wilson wanted to maintain **neutrality** in the war. However, after German **submarines** sank the *Lusitania*, a British passenger ship that carried 128 U.S. passengers, the United States entered the war on the side of the Triple Entente (Great Britain, France, and Russia). The United States tipped the scales in favor of the Triple Entente, and U.S. troops returned home victorious. At the conclusion of World War I, the United States led a failed attempt to establish the **League of Nations** as an international peacekeeping organization; the U.S. Congress refused to allow the United States to join, so the League proved ineffective.

In the years following the war, the United States enjoyed a period of terrific prosperity. Business and industry grew and expanded. Individuals invested heavily and spent large sums of money on things like sporting events, parties, movies, nightclubs, and other forms of entertainment. Politically, the United States implemented many new tariffs on imports to protect U.S. interests at home. The government began regulating public utilities and the rates they charged both businesses and consumers. The government used a Constitutional amendment to ban the production and sale of alcoholic beverages; this period was known as **Prohibition.** Another Constitutional amendment gave women the right to vote for the first time in the United States. Millions of immigrants flocked to the United States from war-torn Europe seeking new financial opportunities.

During this era of prosperity, many individuals purchased stocks by putting up a small percentage of the stock purchase price and borrowing the rest of the purchase price from a stockbroker. This was a very risky investment strategy. Stock prices continued to rise and investors continued to borrow money to buy stocks. Then in 1929, the Stock Market crashed, and banks failed in the United States and in Europe. In other words, panicked investors began selling off their high-priced stocks at a feverish pace. The feeling of panic struck not only the United States but also the rest of the world. By 1932, many banks had failed, factories closed, workers found themselves unemployed, and mortgages were foreclosed. Facing record unemployment and economic hardships, Americans elected **Franklin D. Roosevelt** as president in 1932. He instituted reforms and economic recovery programs in his **New Deal.** Roosevelt's New Deal programs included relief for businesses and individuals through new government agencies that put people to work doing public works projects. These measures, along with the onset of World War II, eventually led the United States out of the Great Depression.

On December 7, 1941, the Japanese attacked the U.S. military base at Pearl Harbor in Hawaii. Almost immediately, the United States entered **World War II** on the side of the Allies (Great Britain and the Union of Soviet Socialist Republics, or USSR) against the Axis Powers (Germany, Italy, and Japan). The massive war effort stimulated the economy and created millions of jobs for Americans. In 1945, after four years of fierce fighting against the Axis Powers in Europe and in the Pacific, the United States dropped two **atomic bombs** on Japan. Shortly thereafter the war ended, and the United States stood victorious alongside the other Allied Powers. The United States emerged from World War II not just as a legitimate world power but as a superpower. After the war, with the influence and leadership of the United States, world leaders divided Germany into different zones of influence, established the United Nations, and launched efforts to help rebuild war-torn nations. The United States joined the International Court of Justice, launched the National Security Council, and established the CIA, or Central Intelligence Agency.

In the years that followed World War II, the United States found itself in an ideological disagreement with the **Soviet Union** and the Eastern Bloc, or eastern European nations under the influence of communism in the Soviet Union. The United States committed itself to stop the spread of communist ideas and eventually became the enemy of the Soviet Union and its allies. For years, the United States remained deadlocked in a Cold War, or a war of rhetoric and ill will, with the Soviet Union. The fear of nuclear holocaust and communism marked the next forty-five years.

American troops did not stay home long after they returned from World War II. Only five years after World War II, American troops were deployed to South Korea to fight against the communist threat posed by the North Koreans in an undeclared war (**Korean War**) that ended with no real winner. Then, in the 1960s, the United States deployed more troops to **Vietnam** in another controversial, undeclared war. The American troops were eventually brought home, and Vietnam fell to the communists. Each time the troops returned home from fighting in Vietnam, they had a difficult time readjusting to civilian life. The troops were not received as heroes the way World War II and Korea troops were, and many of the soldiers faced emotional problems as a result of their experiences abroad.

16. Why was the League of Nation formed after World War I?

It was formed to

(A) promote trade among nations

(B) prevent another world war

(C) pressure Germany into surrendering to the allied forces

(D) prevent the spread of Communism

At the close of World War I, U.S. President Wilson insisted that all countries signing the Treaty of Versailles agree to form the League of Nations for the purpose of keeping world peace through deterrence, so that another world war would not happen again. (The U.S. Congress, which under the Constitution must ratify all treaties that a U.S. President enters, refused to agree to U.S. membership in the League.) **The correct answer is (B).**

17. The Great Depression followed an era of which of the following?

(A) careful financial planning by individuals but not by businesses

(B) widespread corruption with the savings and loan corporations

(C) carefree lifestyles, risky investing, and poor financial management on the part of brokers

(D) world war

It was an era of carefree lifestyles, risky investing, and poor financial management. Investors speculated wildly, and brokers unwisely issued credit to individuals who wanted to purchase large amounts of stocks. **The correct answer is (C).**

Civil Rights

The 1950s were a tumultuous decade in the United States as many Americans reacted to the struggle for civil rights. In 1954, the Supreme Court desegregated schools in the landmark decision *Brown* v. *Board of Education of Topeka*. The civil rights movement built on that momentum. As people like Rosa Parks and Martin Luther King, Jr. led the **civil rights movement** in a dignified and peaceful manner, groups like the Ku Klux Klan promoted violence against African Americans and those who fought for the rights of African Americans, and individuals like Arkansas Governor Faubus inhibited progress toward equal rights for American citizens. In 1957, Congress created the Civil Rights Commission, which investigated civil rights violations. As a result of the Commission's investigations, the government appointed officials to safeguard the voting rights of African Americans.

The Cold War

The 1960s saw heightened tensions between the United States and the Soviet Union reach a boiling point during the **Cuban Missile Crisis.** The two world powers moved dangerously close to nuclear war as President Kennedy forced the Soviets to remove missiles from Cuba. Then, in 1963, to the horror of the nation, President Kennedy was assassinated. The rest of the decade was marked by domestic problems concerning the deployment of troops to Vietnam to fight communism. Many Americans disagreed with American involvement there, and they took to the streets in protest. The civil rights situation improved during the 1960s with the passage of the 24th Amendment, which eliminated the poll tax, and the **Voting Rights Act of 1965,** which aided African Americans in the voting process. The 1960s ended with a cultural phenomenon known as Woodstock, a massive free concert in New York, where thousands of young Americans spent days reveling in drugs, sex, and rock and roll to forget about the problems that faced the nation.

Many Americans grew wary of the government as corrupt officials and oil shortages marked the 1970s. **President Nixon** resigned following a scandal in which several people were arrested for breaking into the Democratic National Headquarters. Nixon and his advisers knew about the break-in and about illegal wiretaps. In 1973, Vice President Spiro Agnew was indicted for tax evasion and bribery, further damaging citizens' trust in the government. The tension between the United States and the USSR declined in the 1970s in what became known as détente. Economically, the end of the 1970s brought further recession, an unfavorable balance of trade, high unemployment, and a very high rate of inflation.

In the 1980s, conservative Republican leadership under **President Ronald Reagan** pushed for less government and more military spending. The economy recovered, but the government's deficit spending caused national debt to spiral. U.S. relations with the Soviets grew tense again as the United States unveiled its "Star Wars" program, a missile defense system. At the end of the decade, U.S. and Soviet leaders agreed to reduce and end existing stockpiles of weapons.

During the 1990s, the United States enjoyed the end of the Cold War and celebrated the collapse of the Soviet Union. However, the 1990s also saw the liberal use of U.S. military power in many places around the world, including Panama, Iraq, Bosnia, and Somalia. Eventually, the government cut military spending, along with some social programs, in an attempt to reduce the national debt. **President Bill Clinton**'s administration was marked by scandals as the millennium drew to a close.

American Foreign Policy Since 9/11

The new millennium brought with it a presidential election unlike any that the United States had ever seen. By a very controversial margin of just a very few votes, **George W. Bush** defeated Al Gore. Less than a year later came the terrorist attacks on the Pentagon, the World Trade Center, and in Pennsylvania. In the immediate aftermath of the "9/11" event, the United States sent forces to Afghanistan to flush out Osama Bin Laden and his terrorist group. Shortly thereafter, the Bush administration convinced the U.S. Congress that in order to prevent further terrorist attacks on U.S. soil and to stem the development of nuclear weapons by dictator enemies, the United States should invade Iraq and topple Saddam Hussein's regime. In April 2003, the United States invaded Iraq, and in December of that year Hussein was finally captured.

The U.S. occupation of Iraq grew controversial over the next few years. Widely publicized abuse of Iraqi prisoners captured by U.S. forces and generous "no-bid" contracts given to U.S. companies loyal to the Bush administration brought the occupation under increasing scrutiny and criticism. In the meantime, Osama bin Laden, the apparent mastermind of the 9/11 terrorist attacks, remained at large, and loose networks of terrorist organizations were proliferating throughout the Middle East, especially in Afghanistan. In November 2008, Barack Obama was elected President, and by the close of the decade, the United States had begun to take affirmative steps to extricate the country from Iraq and return to a policy of diplomacy rather than unilateral military action against would-be enemy states—while at the same time increasing U.S. presence in Afghanistan for the purpose of defeating terrorist organizations that pose a threat to U.S. security.

On the economic front, the first decade of the new millennium saw federal economic policies that were decidedly favorable to big business. The Federal Reserve Bank lowered interest rates to historically low levels in order to bring the nation out of the recession that followed the "dot-com" era collapse and the events of September 2001. Low interest rates encouraged spending and borrowing, which stimulated economic growth. Nevertheless, real economic growth remained stagnant throughout the decade. The only growth occurred in the health-care, financial, and real-estate sectors. At the same time, true production declined. Traditional manufacturing jobs continued to move overseas, leaving middle-class Americans worse off economically at the end of the decade than when it began.

At the same time, federally chartered banks were permitted to engage for the first time in high-risk, high-return leveraged investing: A combination of lax lending standards for home loans (mortgages), upon which many of the banks' investments hinged, and low interest rates created a debt "bubble" in which consumers and large businesses alike would ultimately be unable to repay their debts. By the end of 2008, the U.S. economy was on the verge of collapse—a collapse that was prevented only by a massive infusion of credit from the federal government to save the large commercial banks. As the decade came to a close, a home-foreclosure crisis and an escalating unemployment rate had left **President Barack Obama**'s administration little choice but to engage in a massive spending, or stimulus, campaign to create new jobs, bolster the manufacturing sector, help struggling homeowners, and reign in the imprudent investments and lending practices of previous years.

18. The 24th Amendment, which was ratified in 1964, outlawed the use of a tax as a precondition to voting in any federal election. Given the historical context in which the 24th Amendment became law, whose rights were advocates of the amendment most concerned with protecting?

    (A) tax evaders

    (B) unwed mothers

    (C) convicted felons

    (D) African Americans

It was during the 1960s that the struggle for civil rights on the part of African Americans came to a head, led by individuals such as Martin Luther King, Jr. Poll taxes levied by certain Southern states had the effect of disenfranchising poor people, and in the South, that meant that a disproportionate number of African Americans were effectively denied the right to vote. **The correct answer is (D).**

19. What was responsible for the collapse of the Soviet Union in the late 1980s and early 1990s?

    (A) civil war among its states

    (B) overthrow of the central government by an Eastern European alliance

    (C) the Soviet leaders' decision that a democratic government would work better

    (D) economic and military burdens that weakened the Soviet Union internally

By the mid-1980s, the centralized, or command, economy of the Soviet Union was becoming too burdensome and expensive to manage. At the same time, the Soviets were draining their resources fighting a losing war in Afghanistan. Ultimately, the Soviet Union collapsed under the weight of these burdens it had put on itself. **The correct answer is (D).**

CIVICS AND GOVERNMENT

Simply put, political science is the study of government, the methods of governing, and those who lead governments. As long as people have been organized into states, people have needed a government to maintain order. The form of government each society has used throughout history has depended on a number of factors, including the size of the state and the traditions of the state. Many of the forms of government used throughout history, though, have been determined, directly affected, or influenced by the means the leader used to assume the leadership of a government. Although there are many different types of government, there are a few basic political systems in which all governments may be classified.

Types of Modern and Historical Governments

One very old political system is **democracy.** Democracy means "rule by the people." In a democracy, the people make decisions in matters of government. Democracy dates back to ancient Greece and has changed only slightly since its birth so many years ago. There are two types of democracies that exist: a true democracy and a representative democracy. In a **true democracy,** also called a direct democracy or pure democracy, the people make all the decisions. A true democracy is only possible within a small geographic area, such as a small country or a small town, because a large area makes the exchange of information slow and inefficient. In a **representative democracy,** the people elect representatives to make decisions for them. A republic is a representative democracy. The United States is a good example of a representative democracy.

Another very old political system, even older than democracy, is a **monarchy.** Monarchy means "rule by monarch," which can be either a king or queen. In a monarchy, the right to rule is hereditary, meaning that the right is passed down through a king's or queen's family from generation to generation. There are a few types of monarchies that exist. An **absolute monarchy** is one in which the monarch controls every aspect of life within his or her kingdom. The absolute monarch controls every facet of economics, politics, diplomacy, and, often, religion and culture. Louis XIV of France was the epitome of an absolute monarch. A **constitutional monarchy,** such as Great Britain, is a monarchical government in which the power of the monarch is limited by a constitution or written laws.

Dictatorship is a third form of government. The ruler of a dictatorship, a dictator, has complete rule over his state. Often the dictator assumes control of the state after a military takeover of a government and then maintains control through military force. A dictator usually rules strictly and controls most aspects of the government, often to the point of being oppressive. Cuba under Fidel Castro and Iraq under Saddam Hussein are good examples of dictatorships.

A fourth political system is an **oligarchy.** Oligarchy means "rule by a few." The "few" is often a group of people who lead in the style of a dictator. This group is not a group that is elected. Rather, the group usually takes control in much the same way as a dictator, after a military takeover. Also like a dictator, an oligarchy maintains control with the military. If the group takes control after a revolution, the group is referred to as a junta. Ancient Sparta, a very militaristic society, maintained an oligarchy.

A form of government rarely seen anymore is an **aristocracy.** An aristocracy, ruled by aristocrats, is a system in which the best suited to rule have the power to rule. The best suited to rule, according to the aristocrats, are those who are of privileged birth and who are well educated. Usually aristocrats have great wealth and vast amounts of land.

20. The most efficient form of government in a time of crisis would most likely be which of the following?

(A) dictatorship

(B) oligarchy

(C) democracy

(D) aristocracy

Because one person with total control of a government can make decisions much more quickly than any other kind of government, a dictatorship is the most efficient, especially in a time of war or other emergency. **The correct answer is (A).**

21. Which of the following political systems allows citizens the most opportunities to participate in the political process?

(A) dictatorship

(B) oligarchy

(C) democracy

(D) aristocracy

Democracy is the correct answer because this political system is built on the idea that the people should control the government. **The correct answer is (C).**

THE U.S. GOVERNMENT

The U.S. government can be classified as a **republic,** an indirect democracy. The men who created the foundations of the U.S. government believed the government should be carefully laid out in a written plan, or constitution. According to the U.S. Constitution, the U.S. government is a **federal government.** In other words, the power and authority of the government is divided between the national government, state governments, and local governments. Each level of government has certain authority and responsibilities. Also, according to the Constitution, each level of government is split into three branches, each with separate duties. The three branches include the legislative branch, the executive branch, and the judicial branch. This is known as **separation of powers.** The founders of the United States deliberately divided all the power between the different levels and the different branches of government so that no one person or part of the government could assume too much power. In addition, the founders made sure that each branch of government had the authority to limit the power of the other two branches. This, too, was a preventive measure against any one branch becoming too powerful.

The Three Branches of Government

As you have already learned, the U.S. Constitution divides the government into three branches, each with its own responsibilities and duties. The **legislative branch** makes the laws, the **executive branch** enforces the laws, and the **judicial branch** interprets the laws. Let's examine each of the three branches more closely.

The Legislative Branch

According to Article I of the Constitution, the power to make laws belongs to the legislative branch of government. The word legislative means "law making," so the legislative branch of government is the one that makes laws. The legislature, or the law-making body, is the U.S. Congress. The U.S. Congress is known as a bicameral legislature. In other words, the Congress has two parts, or houses. These are the House of Representatives and the Senate. Although their powers are practically the same, the House of Representatives, sometimes referred to as the House, is the lower house, while the Senate is the upper house of the legislature. The legislators, or lawmakers, in the **House of Representatives** total 435. The representatives represent each of the fifty states, and the number of representatives from each state is based on that state's population. Each state is guaranteed at least one representative regardless of population. Each representative is elected from a district within his or her home state. Representatives serve two-year terms of office, and all of the representatives are elected in their states every two years. In order to run for the office of U.S. Congressional Representative, a person must meet three criteria or qualifications. The candidate must

- be at least 25 years old.
- have been a U.S. citizen for at least seven years.
- live in the state he or she intends to represent.

There are no limits on the number of terms that a representative may serve.

The **Senate** is slightly different from the House of Representatives. There are 100 senators in the Senate, 2 from every state regardless of how large or small a state's population. Senators serve six-year terms, and one third of the senators are elected every two years. In order to be a U.S. Senator, a candidate must meet some stricter requirements than those for a candidate for the House. A candidate for the U.S. Senate must

- be at least 30 years old.
- have been a citizen of the United States for at least nine years.
- be a resident of the state he or she intends to represent.

Currently, there is no limit on the number of terms a senator may serve.

As you just learned, the legislative branch of government makes laws. Let's look at exactly how the legislature creates a law. First, a legislator must present an idea for a potential law in the form of a **bill.** After the legislator—senator or representative—writes the bill, the bill goes to either the clerk of the House or the clerk of the Senate, where the bill receives a name and a number. From here, the bill travels to a committee. A committee is a small group of members of Congress who specialize in a particular area of legislation. For example, the Armed Service Committee deals specifically with legislation concerning the U.S. armed forces. If the committee does not like the bill, it may "pigeonhole" it or "table" it by setting it aside and not dealing with it again. If this happens, the bill is said to have died in committee. If the committee likes the bill, it sends the bill to the House and Senate where the members of Congress debate the bill, make any changes they feel are necessary, and then vote on the bill. If either house votes against the bill, or defeats the bill, the bill dies. If majorities of both houses approve the bill, the bill goes before the entire Congress for a vote. If a majority of Congress approves the bill, it goes before the President for his approval. The President may sign the bill and make it law, or he can veto, or kill, the bill. However, another majority vote in Congress can override the veto and make the bill law. This process may seem slow and inefficient, but this slow process prevents the government from making any hasty decisions.

The Constitution grants Congress a number of powers that are clearly defined in the text of the Constitution. These powers are known as enumerated powers, expressed powers, or delegated powers. Some of these powers include the authority to tax and collect taxes from the American people, coin or print money, declare war on another country, borrow money, and maintain a proper national defense with an army and a navy. Some powers of Congress are limited to only one house or the other. For example, only the House can impeach, or bring formal charges against, the president, but only the Senate can hold a trial for the president. In addition, only the Senate can approve treaties with other countries. The Constitution granted Congress other unnamed powers through the elastic clause. The elastic clause allows Congress some amount of flexibility to deal with new issues that the founders could not foresee.

22. Which of the following may indicate that the Senate is the upper house of the U.S. legislature?

   (A) Senators must have graduate degrees.

   (B) Candidates must be lawyers before they can be elected to the Senate.

   (C) Requirements for senatorial candidates are a little stricter than requirements for those seeking a seat in the House.

   (D) There are fewer senators than there are representatives.

The fact that senatorial candidates must meet more demanding qualifications indicates that the founders of the United States wanted senators to be more qualified than representatives. This indicates that the Senate must have been held in higher regard at one point in history. **The correct answer is (C).**

23. Which of the following is a reason why California may have more influence than Alaska in the House of Representatives?

 (A) California covers a larger geographical region than Alaska.

 (B) California is located within the continental United States and Alaska is not.

 (C) Alaska has not been a part of the United States as long as California.

 (D) California has a larger population than Alaska.

Seats in the House are appropriated to states according to population. If a state has more representatives than another state, it likely also has more influence than that state. **The correct answer is (D).**

The Executive Branch

Article II of the Constitution lays forth the powers of the executive branch of government. It is the responsibility of the executive branch to see that the laws of the land are carried out, or enforced. The head of the executive branch is the President. Underneath the President are the Vice President and all the departments and agencies necessary to make sure that the country's laws are enforced and administered properly.

According to Article II, a candidate for president must meet only three qualifications or requirements. The presidential candidate must be

- a native-born (not naturalized) citizen.
- at least 35 years of age.
- a resident of the United States for at least fourteen years.

Presidential elections are held every four years. Although the American people cast their votes for the President (and Vice President), the Electoral College actually elects the President. The Electoral College consists of electors from each state who cast their votes for presidential candidates one month after the popular election. Originally, no law set a limit on the number of terms, although George Washington suggested that no president serve more than two terms so as not to build and maintain too much power. The Twenty-second Amendment, ratified in 1951, set the term limit at two terms.

The President serves in three major roles during his term in office. First, the President serves as the **Chief Executive.** As the Chief Executive, the President is responsible for making sure that all the laws of the land are carried out properly. Obviously, one person cannot carry out all the laws. Therefore, the President must appoint officials to head executive agencies and departments to carry out and enforce the laws. The heads of the executive departments are members of the President's cabinet. Cabinet members are among the President's closest advisers, and they offer advice to the President about issues within their departments. Also, as Chief Executive, the President can issue executive orders. An executive order is a directive or command that has the weight of law but does not require approval of either the Congress or the Supreme Court. Most often, executive orders are issued during times of war, crisis, or emergency. Second, the President serves as the **Chief Diplomat.** As the Chief Diplomat, the President has the responsibility of appointing ambassadors, meeting and greeting foreign dignitaries, and making treaties. The Senate must approve any appointments or treaties, though. The third major role of the President is that of **Commander in Chief** of the military. Although the President cannot declare war, the President can deploy troops to foreign lands or activate troops here in the United States to help in times of emergency. Additionally, during war the President is the highest commander of all the U.S. armed forces.

In addition to these major responsibilities, the President also plays many smaller roles. As the legislative leader, the President often introduces legislation into Congress, influences the direction of legislation, and vetoes, or rejects, proposed legislation. As the party leader, the President promotes his political party, appoints leadership positions within the party, and endorses party candidates who are seeking election. As the judicial leader, the President appoints justices to the Supreme Court and other federal courts. Furthermore, the President may grant a pardon to someone convicted of a crime. Finally, as Chief of State, the President serves as a symbol of the American people. For example, the President may visit another country on behalf of the United States or issue a public statement on behalf of the United States.

The immediate assistant to the President is the **Vice President.** The Vice President is the only other member of the executive branch mentioned in Article II of the Constitution. If for some reason the President dies, leaves office, or becomes unable to carry out the Presidential duties, the Vice President becomes the new President. In 1947, Congress decided to lay out a plan for exactly who is next in line for the Presidency in the case of some emergency. After the Vice President, the Speaker of the House is next in line, followed by the President Pro Tempore of the Senate, the Secretary of State, Secretary of the Treasury, Secretary of Defense, the Attorney General, and the other cabinet members.

As you learned earlier, the President's closest advisers are the members of his **cabinet.** The cabinet members are the heads of the executive departments. Some of the departments include the following: Department of State, which carries out the nation's foreign policy; Department of the Treasury, which collects taxes and prints money; Department of Defense, which controls the U.S. armed forces; Department of Justice, which heads national law enforcement; and Department of Education, which guides and provides funding for the nation's schools. In all, there are currently fifteen cabinet positions. The cabinet members receive appointments from the President. Then, the cabinet members choose other worthy candidates to fill positions within the executive departments that they oversee.

The last part of the executive branch is the collection of agencies known as the executive agencies. Within each Executive Department, many smaller agencies exist. Some of these agencies include the Central Intelligence Agency (CIA), the National Aeronautics and Space Administration (NASA), and the Environmental Protection Agency (EPA). Some of these agencies, including the Federal Reserve System and the National Labor Relations Board, are called regulatory commissions. Some agencies, such as the U.S. Postal Service, are government corporations.

24. Powers of the President include all EXCEPT which of the following?

   (A) the power to introduce legislation

   (B) the power to veto legislation

   (C) the power to send troops into a country

   (D) the power to declare war

Only Congress can declare war on another country. **The correct answer is (D).**

25. Which of the following would be the responsibility of a cabinet member?

   (A) overriding an executive order

   (B) heading a department within the executive branch of government

   (C) declaring war

   (D) approving or rejecting a presidential appointment

Each member of the cabinet heads one of the executive departments within the executive branch. **The correct answer is (B).**

The Judicial Branch

The third branch of the U.S. government, outlined in Article III of the Constitution, is the judicial branch. The Constitution establishes the **Supreme Court** as the head of the judicial branch. The Supreme Court's main responsibility is to hear cases appealed from lower courts. However, the Supreme Court's other responsibility is to determine the constitutionality of the laws and actions of other branches of government and lower courts. This is the power of judicial review. The Supreme Court has 8 justices, or judges, who are appointed by the President, and a Chief Justice, also appointed by the President. Although the President can appoint anyone to be a Supreme Court justice, the Senate has the power to reject a President's nomination. The justices maintain their seats on the Supreme Court for life.

The Supreme Court has the authority to hear, or has jurisdiction over, both criminal and civil cases that have been appealed to the high court. Criminal cases are those dealing with crimes, while civil cases are those that deal with disputes between two or more parties. The Supreme Court has original jurisdiction over cases in which a foreign diplomat is involved or in which a state is involved. In other words, these two kinds of cases may originate with the Supreme Court instead of only being appealed to the Supreme Court. The Supreme Court is the highest court in the United States, but the lowest federal courts in the United States are known as Federal District courts. The District courts are the courts in which federal trials and lawsuits begin, or originate. Federal District courts hear both criminal and civil cases. If one of the parties involved in a case at the district-court level believes that an error occurred during the trial, the case can be appealed to a Federal Court of Appeals. If one of the parties involved in the appealed case still believes that the case needs to be heard by a higher court, the party can appeal the case to the Supreme Court. Federal Appeals Courts and the Supreme Court can decide to hear a case or dismiss a case and leave it as is.

> **26.** Which of the following is true of the Supreme Court?
>
> The Supreme Court
>
> **(A)** hears only civil cases
>
> **(B)** hears only criminal cases
>
> **(C)** is the highest court in the United States
>
> **(D)** can be overruled by a presidential veto

Once a case has been decided by the Supreme Court, there are no more courts to which the case may be appealed. **The correct answer is (C).**

> **27.** What is the main responsibility of the Supreme Court?
>
> **(A)** to hear and decide appealed cases
>
> **(B)** to hear and decide cases between foreign countries
>
> **(C)** to represent the United States in international court
>
> **(D)** to declare presidential acts unconstitutional

The Supreme Court's greatest responsibility is to hear and decide cases that have been appealed from the lower courts. **The correct answer is (A).**

Checks and Balances

As you learned earlier, the writers of the Constitution divided the U.S. government into three branches—the legislative, executive, and judicial—so that no one part of the government would develop too much power. The writers of the Constitution also included in the plan of government another system of safeguards against one branch dominating any other branch. This is known as the **system of checks and balances.** Each branch of government has the ability to check the power of the other two branches and that helps balance the powers of the branches.

Let's look at a few examples of some of the checks each branch has on the others. The executive branch can check the power of the legislative branch by vetoing legislation and can check the power of the judicial branch by appointing judges. The legislative branch can check the power of the executive branch by overriding vetoes, by rejecting presidential appointments or nominations, and by impeaching the President. The legislative branch can check the power of the judicial branch by impeaching judges and by rejecting judicial appointments. The judicial branch can check the power of the executive branch by declaring acts of the President unconstitutional. The judicial branch can check the power of the legislative branch by declaring laws unconstitutional. This system may seem like it could cause inefficiency in the government, but it helps maintain a healthy balance of power among the three branches.

The U.S. Federal System

When the thirteen colonies first came together under the Articles of Confederation, they still governed themselves. Once they permanently united as the United States of America, the states retained many rights to continue governing themselves. The government of the country became the shared responsibility of the national government and the state governments. Things such as marriage laws, educational standards, and election laws were left to the discretion of the states. In addition, some powers were set aside even for local governments. This division of government on different levels is known as **federalism.**

State and Local Governments

The powers set aside specifically for the states are known as reserved powers and are provided for in the **Tenth Amendment.** To avoid any conflict between state and federal law, the writers of the Constitution made sure to include in Article VI a provision that states that the Constitution and the laws created by Congress take priority over any state or local laws. This clause in Article VI is known as the Supremacy Clause.

The United States requires that each state have a republican form of government. In other words, each state must operate as a republic. There are no other requirements for state governments than that. Most states, however, used the U.S. Constitution as the model for their state constitutions. Therefore, most state governments are very similar to that of the U.S. government, even though they do not have to be. All states have a governor who serves as the head of the executive branch in his or her state. All states, with the exception of Nebraska, have two legislative houses in their legislative branch. Each state has its own court system, although there are many variations of court system structures.

The Constitution requires that the state governments and the federal government work together. For example, a state law enforcement agency may work with a federal law enforcement agency on a special case. The Constitution also facilitates cooperation among states. The "full faith and credit clause" of the Constitution requires that states accept each other's legal decisions and documents. It is the "full faith and credit clause" that makes one state recognize the marriage licenses or drivers licenses from another state. States also cooperate through the process of extradition. Extradition is when a state sends a suspected criminal back to the state in which the suspect is accused of committing a crime.

Although state governments tend to be very similar to the federal government, local governments vary greatly. Some local governments are headed by a mayor, or a chief executive officer, elected by the people of the city or town. In these municipalities, a city council often aids the mayor in the administration of the local government. In other municipalities, a council is elected, and then a city manager is hired to handle the business operations. Still other municipalities are run by elected commissioners; each commissioner is responsible for a certain area of operation, such as water or public safety.

28. Which of the following did the writers of the Constitution provide in their plan of government to ensure that no branch of government grew too powerful?

(A) government monitors who watch for corruption

(B) Supreme Court elections

(C) three separate divisions of government, each with different responsibilities

(D) two houses in the legislature

With the political power divided three ways, no part of the government has the ability to dominate politically. **The correct answer is (C).**

29. According to the Constitution, state governments must do which of the following?

(A) establish a pure democracy

(B) establish a republican form of government

(C) establish a federal system at the state level

(D) require municipalities to have a republican form of government

The only requirement a state government must meet according to the Constitution is that it have a republican form of government. **The correct answer is (B).**

Political Parties, Campaigns, and Elections in American Politics

Since the earliest days of the United States, Americans have had differing opinions on the way the country should be governed. These differences in opinions in the formative years of the nation led to the development of the first two political parties, the Federalists and the Republicans. A political party is a group of people who hold similar values and have similar ideas about the proper leadership of the government. Often people form or join political parties based on beliefs about how weak or strong the central government should be, how much or how little the government should tax or spend, or how federal money is spent. Both political parties and members of political parties can be classified based on their ideas about government. On the one hand, liberals, who are often referred to as being on the left, generally advocate political change and social progress. Conservatives, on the other hand, generally advocate very slow change, if any, to the existing political and social order. Conservatives are often referred to as being on the right. Those individuals who fall somewhere in between liberal and conservative are often referred to as moderates.

The basic goal of a political party is to influence public policy in a way that is in line with its ideology. To do so, the parties try to get their candidates elected to public office. The political parties also have another important function in the U.S. political system. In addition to influencing the policies of the government, political parties further strengthen the system of checks and balances. The parties keep a close eye on the actions of the other parties in power and help ensure that there is no abuse within the system. Furthermore, political parties give citizens a sense of belonging in the political arena and give citizens a voice in all levels of politics.

As you just learned, political parties want their candidates elected to office. In order to elect a candidate, the political party and the candidate must go through a long process. In many elections, candidates must first win a preliminary election called a primary. Each party holds a primary election in which voters choose a candidate to represent their party in the main election. For example, in a Republican primary, Republican voters choose from a list of potential Republican candidates. The winner of the Republican primary will run against candidates from other parties in the main election. Some primary elections, known as open primaries, are open to all voters. Closed primaries are primary elections in which voters must declare a party and choose from that party's candidates. One of the ways candidates get elected is by promoting their platforms. A platform is a list of beliefs, values, or ideas that a particular candidate or political party holds as their own. Voters usually use candidates' platforms to evaluate and choose the candidate they want to be in office.

Individuals who are not content with simply participating in a political party often form or join pressure groups. Pressure groups are those with a particular agenda or list of needs and wants. These pressure groups work diligently to persuade legislators in the lawmaking process. This active persuasion of legislators is known as lobbying. Lobbyists often try to meet with legislators to sway the legislators one way or the other during the lawmaking process. For example, an environmental lobbyist would try to persuade legislators to pass legislation that seeks to improve the environment.

30. People may join a political party for any of the following reasons EXCEPT which one?

(A) to voice an opinion collectively instead of individually

(B) to discover ideas of governing different from their own

(C) to promote a particular candidate in an election

(D) to vote in a closed primary

People do not join political parties to find new and different ideas. **The correct answer is (B).**

31. Which of the following would most likely hire a lobbyist to persuade legislators to pass a new law?

(A) the Boy Scouts of America

(B) a church in Georgia

(C) a tobacco company in North Carolina

(D) a single parent on welfare

A tobacco company would want certain laws passed or certain laws changed, and they could afford to hire lobbyists to try to accomplish that goal. **The correct answer is (C).**

CANADIAN GOVERNMENT

The Canadian Constitution establishes the responsibilities of the federal government, or a government in which responsibilities are divided between national, provincial, and municipal governments. In addition to those duties enumerated, or named, in the Constitution, the federal government also controls all issues not specifically charged to the provincial or territorial governments. Like the government of the United States, powers are divided among three separate branches of government.

Governor General

As a constitutional monarchy, Canada is governed by a monarch whose powers are defined by the Constitution. The monarch, or Head of State, is Queen Elizabeth II. The Queen, on the advice of Canada's Prime Minister, appoints a Governor General. The Governor General is traditionally appointed to a five-year term. The Governor General then fulfills all of the duties of the Head of State on behalf of the Queen.

The duties of the Governor General include executing orders-in-council and other state documents, appointing all superior court judges, and giving "royal assent" to bills passed by the House of Commons and the Senate before they can become law. The Governor General also summons, prorogues (ends a session), and dissolves Parliament.

Prime Minister

The Prime Minister is the leader of the party with the most seats in the House of Commons. In addition to controlling the House of Commons, the Prime Minister advises the Queen on her appointment of the Governor General and thus enjoys quite a bit of power. The Prime Minister also oversees the Cabinet. Members of the Cabinet include the heads of the Ministries, the Prime Minister's Office, and the Privy Council Office. Canada has eighteen Ministries that cover all areas of government. Some of the Ministries are Finance, Canadian Heritage, Health, Justice, and Veteran Affairs. The Prime Minister's Office handles issues related to the Prime Minister's role as Party Leader. For example, the Prime Minister's Office handles public relations and decides which matters need the Prime Minister's attention and which do not. The Privy Council Office has a number of responsibilities that range from advising the Prime Minister on national security matters to working as a liaison between the Prime Minister and the Cabinet.

Parliament

Canada has a bicameral legislature, or a legislature with two houses. The two houses include the House of Commons and the Senate. The House of Commons, also called the Green Chamber, is made up of 301 members who are elected in general elections at least every five years. The number of members is based on population. At any given time, several different political parties may be represented in the House of Commons. However, the party with a majority of seats in the House of Commons is asked to form the government of Canada. If no party holds a majority, then the parties are asked to form a partnership to form a minority government.

The Senate, or Red Chamber, was created to protect regional, provincial, and minority interests. Unlike the House of Commons, senators are appointed by the Governor General on the basis of "equal representation" and are not elected based on population. There are 105 seats in the senate. To be appointed as a Senator, one must be at least 30 years old, be a Canadian citizen by birth or naturalization, have a net estate worth at least $4000, own property in the province for which they are appointed worth $4000, and be a resident of the province he or she is appointed to represent.

The Judiciary

The Supreme Court consists of a Chief Justice and 8 justices. Each is appointed and holds office until the age of 75. A justice may be removed from office for incapacity or misconduct by the Governor General (on address of the Senate and House of Commons). The Supreme Court issues judgments and advises on questions concerning constitutional interpretation, the constitutionality of legislation, and the powers of Parliament and the Provinces. Another important branch of the Judiciary is the Tax Court. Created in 1983, the Tax Court is the first level of appeals for taxpayers.

Below the Supreme Court and the Tax Court is the Federal Court. A superior court of record with both civil and criminal jurisdiction, the Federal Court of Canada is divided into the Federal Court of Appeal and the Federal Court, Trial Division. The trial division hears lawsuits and applications to review government actions. The Court of Appeal hears appeals from the Trial Division and supervises the decisions of government tribunals. Appeals from the Court of Appeal are made to the Supreme Court.

The Provincial and Territorial Government

Each of the ten provinces and the three territories has its own capital in which its government is centered. Each province is headed by a Lieutenant Governor, and a Commissioner heads each territory. Generally speaking, provinces and territories differ in a few ways. All land in a province is controlled by the province itself while land in a territory is controlled by the federal government. Also, provinces are included in the Constitutional amendment process while territories are not. The governments of both provinces and territories are responsible for the education and welfare of their inhabitants, the administration of justice, and the protection of natural resources within the boundaries.

The Municipal Government

Below the provincial and territorial governments are the municipal governments. Within each province and territory there exist many municipalities in the form of regions, counties, and districts called "Upper Tier" municipalities. "Lower Tier" municipalities are cities and townships. The provincial and territorial governments have the power to create and modify the municipal, or local, governments. Also, the provincial and territorial governments have the power to assign certain responsibilities to the townships. These may include things such as animal control, water and sewage management, and economic development.

32. Which of the following statements concerning the Canadian federal government is true?

(A) The Canadian government has loose ties with Great Britain, most notably its association with the Sovereign.

(B) The Judiciary clearly has more power than the other two branches of Canadian government.

(C) Because of the structure of the Canadian government, it would be relatively easy for one person or one party to abuse powers and take control of the government.

(D) The municipal governments have nearly the same amount of authority as the provincial and territorial governments.

The Sovereign is still the highest position in the order of precedence in Canada, so it would be correct to state that the Canadian government has loose ties with Great Britain, most notably its association with the Sovereign. **The correct answer is (A).**

33. Which of the following government positions indicates the importance of political parties in the Canadian government?

(A) Mayor

(B) Governor General

(C) Queen

(D) Prime Minister

The Prime Minister is the leader of the party that has the most seats in the House of Commons. **The correct answer is (D).**

ECONOMICS

Macroeconomics and Microeconomics

The study of economics is the study of the way society uses limited resources to meet its material needs. To be more specific, economics deals with the production, distribution, and consumption of goods. The field of economics can generally be divided into two major areas: microeconomics and macroeconomics. Microeconomics, also known as price theory, examines how supply, demand, and competition cause differences in prices, profits, wages, and other aspects of economics. In the area of microeconomics, economists assume that proprietors or entrepreneurs seek to make the most profit possible and that consumers spend their money to seek the most value possible. Macroeconomics looks at the larger picture of economics and examines such things as employment and national income. Macroeconomics developed after the publication of a book called *The General Theory of Employment, Interest, and Money* in 1935 by a British economist named John Maynard Keynes.

Although economics has been a vital part of the life of every state in history, the academic field of economics did not take on a life of its own until a brilliant Scottish moral philosopher, Adam Smith, wrote *Inquiry into the Nature and Causes of the Wealth of Nations* in 1776. Smith's landmark work is still used today by economists and students of economics. Paramount to Smith's economic theory was the idea of the "invisible hand." Smith believed that the government should be directly involved in the economy as little as possible. He argued that if consumers were left alone to act in their own interests and on their own behalf, a natural force, an invisible hand, so to speak, would point the national economy in a direction that would benefit the greatest number of people. As a result, Smith was a critic of the economic policy of mercantilism. Mercantilism, a popular government practice during the time, was a system in which all national economic policy was directed by the goal of national self-sufficiency. In other words, a mercantilist nation sought to make its economy better by becoming less and less reliant on other nations' goods. Mercantilist nations sought to stockpile gold and silver, to keep wages as low as possible, and to keep the population growing. Smith disagreed with this policy of government manipulation of the economy.

A group of French economists, known as physiocrats, reacted to the mercantilists by advocating free trade and a laissez-faire approach to the economy. *Laissez faire* is a term that means the government takes a "hands off" approach to economic policy. Free trade means that the government allows both imports and exports to come and go freely. The physiocrats believed in a single tax to raise money for the state instead of the manipulation of the economy; Smith agreed with their ideas.

Other notable economists include Thomas Malthus, David Ricardo, and John Stuart Mill. Although these economists had some philosophical differences, they all basically agreed on some major principles. They all believed in a free market economy, the right to own private property, and the ability of competition to drive an economy. Another economist was Karl Marx. Marx took a different approach to economic theory, though. Marx, a socialist, believed that those who owned the means of production historically had exploited the working class. Therefore, Marx advocated the elimination of private property and the collective ownership of both property and industry. Marx outlined his economic theories in the historic Communist Manifesto, co-authored by Frederick Engels.

Basic Economic Concepts

Factors of Production

When economists talk about production within an economic system, they must consider the three factors of production. These factors are natural resources, capital, and labor. Usually the factors of production cannot fully meet the demands of the consumers, or people who use the goods produced. **Natural resources** are the raw materials necessary for the production of goods. For example, trees are necessary for the production of houses, paper, and wooden furniture.

Capital can be any equipment, factories, or property necessary for the conversion of raw materials into finished goods. This type of capital is referred to as fixed capital.

Capital can also refer to money that is invested to support the production of goods. This type of capital, called circulating capital, can be wages paid to laborers or raw materials used in production. Any capital that can be sold for cash is considered liquid capital, while capital that cannot be easily converted to cash is known as frozen capital.

In economics, the term **labor** is used to describe the work it takes to convert raw materials into goods and services. Labor may refer to the people who actually do the work processing the raw materials and producing the goods. Laborers may be factory assembly line workers, truck drivers, sales agents, or other people involved in the production and distribution of goods. Labor may even refer to people in a service industry, such as doctors or teachers that provide services for others.

When considering productivity, economists also consider the **law of diminishing returns.** The factors of production, when used together in the correct proportions, will produce an end result sufficient for a society. However, according to the law of diminishing returns, at a certain point, any additional resources (raw materials, labor, or capital) fail to produce any additional product. In fact, according to the law, at a certain point, additional resources may even result in less production than before the additional resources were added.

34. The natural resources required to build a log home include which of the following?

    (A) trees, land, and construction workers

    (B) land and construction workers

    (C) trees

    (D) trees and land

The answer choice "trees" is correct because land is considered capital and construction workers are considered laborers. **The correct answer is (C).**

35. The law of diminishing returns could be applied to which of the following situations?

    (A) salaries of factory workers are raised

    (B) new raw materials are supplied to a factory to produce a brand-new product

    (C) the number of assembly line workers in an efficient factory is cut in half to reduce company spending

    (D) the number of assembly line workers in an efficient factory is doubled while the amount of raw materials remains the same

With twice as many workers in an already efficient factory, the workers will probably get in each other's way and reduce efficiency and production. **The correct answer is (D).**

Supply and Demand

The primary force and one of the basic principles of economics is that of **supply and demand.** Supply can be defined as all the goods available regardless of price. Demand can be defined as the desire of the consumers to purchase goods. Producers supply goods with the hope that consumers will demand goods. Producers must set prices on the goods high enough that they still make a profit after paying for all the costs of production. Consumers seek to pay the lowest price possible for goods. Producers must set the amount of production based on the demand for goods. The price and the availability of goods determine the demand. These factors working together make up the principle of supply and demand.

If a given item, a car for example, has a high profit yield, a great number of producers will be interested in production of the good. The producers of the cars will compete for a share of the market. If the market is flooded with cars, or if there are too many cars on the market, and the supply of cars is greater than the demand, buyers either cannot or will not buy all of the supply of cars. If this happens, there will be a surplus that will then cause car prices to fall. This may increase the demand for the cars. If an item, such as a car, has a price that is low enough to make consumers want the item, it will be in demand. If the price of the car falls too much, there may be such a demand that producers cannot supply the item fast enough to meet the demand. If the demand exceeds the supply, the prices will rise.

SUPPLY CURVE FOR CARS

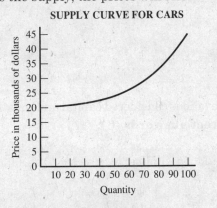

DEMAND CURVE FOR CARS

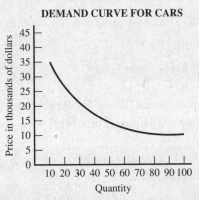

To make a market stable, producers must exactly determine the amount of goods that consumers will demand and the price that the consumers will pay for those goods. When this point is reached, it is called **equilibrium.** On the following chart, the point of equilibrium is the point at which the two curves intersect. When the price for goods rises above equilibrium, there is a decreased demand and, therefore, more goods than consumers want. This creates a surplus. If the opposite happens, that is, if the price falls below equilibrium, the demand increases, and there is a shortage. These are the laws of supply and demand.

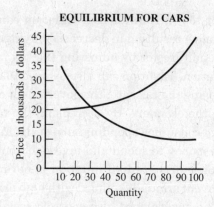

EQUILIBRIUM FOR CARS

It should be noted that the laws of supply and demand are only valid in an economic system in which the markets are relatively undisturbed by the government. Because supply and demand depend on market conditions, an economy in which the government controls the market would not follow the laws of supply and demand. For example, during times of war in the United States or at any given time in the former USSR, the markets were somewhat manipulated by the government. That invalidated the mechanisms of supply and demand in those places.

36. What conclusion can be drawn from the principles of supply and demand?

(A) The lower the profit an item generates, the more producers will be interested in producing that item.

(B) The higher the price of an item, the higher the demand will be for that item.

(C) The more consumers demand an item, the lower the prices will go.

(D) The more consumers demand an item, the higher the prices will go.

If there is a high demand among consumers for an item, the producer can charge a higher price, and consumers will still buy the item. **The correct answer is (D).**

37. Market stability will occur when which of the following occurs?

(A) prices rise above the point of equilibrium

(B) producers produce the amount of goods that consumers want at the price that consumers want to pay

(C) a surplus is created

(D) a shortage is created

Stability occurs when producers produce the amount of goods the consumers want at a price that consumers feel is fair. **The correct answer is (B).**

Government and Economic Policy

The United States has a free market economy, yet the government still plays a vital role in steering the economy. Through the use of taxation, the government can create revenue for its own use or to control inflation. Inflation can be defined as a rise in prices or a devaluing of money, resulting in decreased buying power for consumers. By reducing government expenditures or by adjusting the tax rate, the government can help control or correct inflation. Taxation can also be used to increase or decrease consumer spending. By increasing the tax rate, the government can discourage consumer spending thereby slowing the economy. By decreasing the tax rate, the government can stimulate or encourage consumer spending, investing, and business transactions because people have more money to spend and invest. It should be noted that not all inflation is bad, though. Slow and gradual inflation is normal and even good for an economy. Inflation of 10 percent annually coupled with high price increases would cause concern for economists. The government also controls social programs like welfare, unemployment benefits, Medicare, and Social Security. The government manages the funds used to operate these programs and distributes the funds to citizens who need assistance. All of these practices are part of the government monetary policy known as the fiscal policy. The practice of increasing taxation or restricting public spending is called the contractionary fiscal policy. The practice of reducing taxation and stimulating public spending is known as the expansionary fiscal policy.

Money, Monetary Policy, and Financial Institutions

The use of money is the method of exchange employed in economic systems in lieu of bartering. Whatever currency an economic system uses is its money. The money supply of a nation is mostly coins and paper money, or bills, along with deposits made to banks. The use of money in an economic system is controlled through monetary policy. In the United States, the Federal Reserve Board controls the monetary policy. The Federal Reserve Board directs the monetary policy by regulating the money and credit available for use in the country. It does this by setting the reserve ratio and setting the discount rate. The reserve ratio is the amount of money that lending institutions can lend and the amount of money they must hold in reserve. By setting the reserve ratio, the Federal Reserve Board controls the supply of money that is available for banks and savings and loan associations to lend to consumers. The Federal Reserve Board tightens the supply of money by raising the reserve ratio. On the other hand, the Federal Reserve Board loosens the supply of money by dropping the reserve ratio. The discount rate is the interest rate that the Federal Reserve Board charges to member banks to borrow money. Banks then charge consumers a higher interest rate on loans than they pay to the Federal Reserve. The more money that banks want to borrow, the more it costs to borrow the money. The hike in the cost discourages banks from borrowing more and reduces bank demand for extra reserve money. The Federal Reserve Board also sets the margin requirement that determines the amount of cash a purchaser must pay up front when buying stocks; this helps deter speculation, as in the kind that led to the Great Depression.

Labor Relations

As you learned earlier, when speaking within the realm of economics, labor refers to the people who actually do the work and produce goods, or the people who provide services for others. All dealings between labor and management over labor issues are called labor relations. Many years ago, laborers constantly fought for better wages and working conditions, often with little or no success. One reason for the lack of success during pre-industrial America was because employers dealt directly with individual employees. As industrialization took over, though, employers faced many employees instead of just a few individuals. Government regulations eventually set limits on the number of hours workers had to work and the minimum wages workers could receive. These regulations helped curb dangerous working conditions. Labor, however, remained largely unorganized.

In the 1930s, the Wagner Act allowed laborers to organize and negotiate with management concerning disputes. The labor organizations became known as unions, and these negotiations became known as **collective bargaining.** Collective bargaining occurs when leaders of the labor unions meet with employers and management to negotiate wages, hours, conditions, benefits, or other issues. Collective bargaining is often successful. Many times independent arbitrators handle the negotiations between the two sides. However, when collective bargaining does not work, laborers may go on strike. When workers strike, or stop working, the government may intervene and end the strike, or the government may help facilitate successful negotiations. The threat of a strike is most successful during negotiations when the unemployment rate is relatively low. If there are plenty of unemployed workers who are willing to replace the strikers, the strike loses its effectiveness.

38. Government can control aspects of the economy by controlling which of the following?

(A) unemployment

(B) checking and savings accounts

(C) salary caps

(D) taxation

Taxation is the correct choice because a higher tax rate slows the economy, while a lower tax rate stimulates the economy. **The correct answer is (D).**

39. The Federal Reserve Board is vital to the economy because of its policies concerning which of the following?

(A) labor disputes

(B) Social Security

(C) interest rates

(D) minting of new coins and bills

The Federal Reserve Board's policies on the reserve ratio and discount rate directly affect the nation's interest rates. **The correct answer is (C).**

Consumer Economics

Historically, people around the world used the barter system to exchange goods and services in return for other goods and services that they needed. However, problems arose with bartering. Each trader needed to have goods or services that the other trader desired. Trading could be difficult and time-consuming. It could also be unfair, as when colonists adopted the Native American custom of trading with wampum. These small beads made from shells were easy for the colonists to produce, and they made so many that wampum declined in purchasing value.

Money facilitates a fair exchange for goods and services. It also has the advantage of being portable and accepted around the world by exchanging a unit of currency of one country for a unit of another country. Today, consumers use currency, coins, checks, and credit and debit cards to pay for goods and services. The trend to use "plastic," or debit or credit cards as a form of payment instead of cash or checks, has lead to spiraling consumer debt and bankruptcy. The barter system is making a comeback in our nearly cashless society, but consumers still need to learn to make wise financial decisions.

Goods that are shipped out of a country to another country are known as **exports;** goods brought into a country from another country are called **imports.** To maintain a healthy economy, the goal of a country is to export more goods than it imports. Economists call this occurrence a favorable balance of trade. In order to protect domestic goods, countries often add a special tax, called a **tariff**, to imports so that domestic goods are more competitively priced. If the tariffs are too high, the country whose imports are being taxed will retaliate with tariffs of their own on imported goods.. Another way that countries protect their interests is through the use of import quotas. Import quotas limit the number of particular foreign goods that may enter a country. Quotas are often very successful in reversing trade imbalances. On occasion, government health or safety standards prevent foreign goods from entering the domestic market. Government support of domestic industries provides additional advantages for those industries and puts foreign competitors at a disadvantage. It is very important that governments carefully manage their overseas trade; many workers in each country depend on producing goods for overseas trade.

40. Which of the following might occur as a result of relying too heavily on "plastic"?

(A) the price of goods would be inflated

(B) the foreign exchange system would collapse

(C) the country would go bankrupt

(D) the consumer would be tempted to purchase without thinking

The lure of debit and credit cards causes people to buy goods and services without consideration of paying back their debts. **The correct answer is (D).**

> **41.** Why did Native Americans have a disadvantage when colonists started trading with wampum?
>
> **(A)** The shells to make wampum became difficult to locate.
>
> **(B)** Colonists made countless beads, so they diminished in worth.
>
> **(C)** Native Americans preferred to trade with currency instead.
>
> **(D)** The beads couldn't be used to purchase food.

After colonists produced a plentiful supply of wampum, the purchasing value of these beads declined. **The correct answer is (B).**

The Role of Economics in Social and Historical Events

Throughout history, economics has played a role in exploration and colonization of new territories. During the Age of Exploration, a period that began in the early 15th century and lasted until the 17th century, European explorers sailed from their homes in the Old World—Portugal, Spain, Great Britain, France, and Holland. Rulers of these nations financed the explorers' journeys, paying for ships, supplies, and crews. All of them anticipated wealth resulting from their investment. The European economy relied on gold and silver, yet these highly valued metals were a rare resource.

Along with precious metals, European explorers were searching for a new route to the Far East where the profitable spice trade flourished. Nutmeg, for example, was worth more than a comparable amount of gold. Prior to the Age of Discovery, Venice had been the trade port for spices harvested in the east and shipped to Europe. This city became wealthy by charging exorbitant tariffs on spices. Explorers, lead by the Portuguese, circumnavigated Africa and sailed to India, where they accessed spices without the additional high tariffs levied by the middlemen along the overland trade routes. Other explorers from different countries followed, and conflict broke out in a struggle for control of the spice trade.

At the same time, explorers such as Christopher Columbus explored new regions that Europeans would later colonize. Investors in 16th-century Europe set up chartered companies to encourage overseas trade and exploration in new territories such as Africa, Asia, the Caribbean, India, and North America. The company would gain a trading monopoly in that region; the colonists would then establish settlements on the coast to facilitate trade.

Economics also is the motivation behind countless wars, as power over new territories leads to control of valuable commodities, such as minerals. Although victory can lead to increased wealth and trade, wars can be also costly and disrupt trade. Supplies become scarce, with shortages causing food to be rationed and prices to skyrocket as living standards tumble. The consequences of war can be measured in economic terms. Military spending can spur economic growth or, at the other end of the spectrum, it can result in a devastated economy. After World War I, for example, Germany suffered a draining defeat, which it attempted to recover from by printing enormous amounts of money. This tactic backfired and led to extreme inflation and increasing unemployment.

The poor economic state launched Hitler into a powerful position with his promise of economic growth.

Wars can also lead to scientific and industrial innovations. New technologies developed by the military can lead to positive economic consequences when ordinary citizens use an invention commercially. To cite a modern example, the GPS navigation device was developed by the military and today has become a popular consumer product.

GEOGRAPHY

Geography is more than states and capitals or latitude and longitude. Geography is the study of the Earth's physical features and the way people have adapted to these physical features. Geography is concerned not only with physical geographic features but also with cultural geographic features. Physical geographic features include things such as land, water, mountains, and plains. Cultural geographic features include things such as human architecture or man-made changes to the Earth's physical features. The study of geography can also include how early civilizations developed within their environments, as well as the ways in which societies continue to develop in relation to their environments, including when environmental conditions require that peoples migrate elsewhere. The science of geography can be divided into two branches: systematic and regional. Systematic geography deals with individual elements of the Earth's physical and cultural features. Regional geography, on the other hand, deals with the physical and cultural features within a particular region, or area, of the Earth's surface.

Systematic geography includes a number of different fields within the realm of physical geography. Part of physical geography is cartography, or mapmaking. Another important part of physical geography is oceanography, or the study of the Earth's oceans; climatology examines the Earth's weather patterns; and geomorphology looks at the way the surface of the Earth has changed. Other areas of physical geography include biogeography, or the study of the distribution of plants and animals, and soil geography, or the study of the distribution of soil and soil conservation. Systematic geography also includes a number of fields within the realm of cultural geography, or the study of how human social and cultural life affects geography. Economic geography, for example, examines how business and industry have affected the geographic environment. Political geography looks at nations, states, cities, and other man-made areas and examines how geography influences these political units; political geography often involves some political science, too. Military geography is the study of how the geography of a particular area may affect military operations. Military geography is especially important today in light of the events in the Middle East.

Development of Classical Civilizations

Beginnings and Early Civilizations

It is generally believed that at the start of the most recent Ice Age, which lasted from about 20,000 years ago until about 12,000 years ago, the world's entire human population numbered less than 1 million. Their existence revolved around hunting and gathering rather than growing plants or raising animals for food. Hunter-gatherer families belonged to larger groups of tribes. Though the cold temperatures of the Ice Age killed off some tribes, others moved toward the equator, seeking warmer temperatures. Yet, at the end of the Ice Age humans were finding life even more difficult. As temperatures and sea levels rose, Earth's plant and animal life dwindled. To survive, humans learned to control the development of various plant and animal species. By cultivating small plots of land through what is called *horticulture*, human families could accumulate surplus food, and by breeding animals according to traits they found desirable, they could cultivate a predictable source of meat and other animal products.

Around 4500 BCE, *agriculture* began making rapid inroads in five areas worldwide. These five areas are sometimes called cultural hearths because of their role in establishing both culture and civilization in their regions of the world. Four of these areas came into existence in river valleys. One area was Egypt, in which the Nile River became a garden country quite early. The second region was Mesopotamia, located in the Tigris and Euphrates river valley. The third area was the Indus River valley in India, and the fourth area was in China. The fifth region was Mesoamerica, or what is now southern Mexico and Central America. This area followed a substantially different pattern from the other four. It had no vast river systems in which to build elaborate agricultural systems. Here, agriculture grew out of horticulture, as the gardens needed to sustain the local populations that became larger and larger.

Known as the ancient Near East, the areas of Egypt and Mesopotamia are considered to be the cradle of Western civilization. The people of the Near East were the first to practice intensive year-round agriculture. They produced the first writing system, invented the potter's wheel and then the vehicular and mill wheels, and created the first centralized governments, law codes, and empires. The people of the Near East also introduced social stratification, slavery, and organized warfare, and they laid the foundation for the fields of astronomy and mathematics.

Between 5000 BCE and 500 BCE, the Near East was home to successive waves of cultures, borrowing from and cooperating with one another for resources, ideas, and culture as well as competing with one another militarily for land and prestige. The Near East is where the first cities appeared. Near the confluence of the Tigris and Euphrates Rivers, several city-states competed for land, power, and prestige while fending off barbarians. These city-states became the ancient Greece of the region, providing written language, architecture, religion, and cultural norms to the societies that followed. Babylon, located not far from modern-day Baghdad, was the first city-state to assemble a true kingdom around itself in Mesopotamia. The Babylonians used the waterways for communication and to control their wide empire that spread across the river valleys.

In the area of Greece, from around 3000 to 1100 BCE, the Minoan civilization inhabited the Aegean island of Crete, and, from around 1600 to 1100 BCE, the Mycenaean culture dominated the mainland. Mycenaean civilization began with the arrival of many tribes, which by around 1600 BCE had established themselves as political units. The Mycenaeans quite possibly lived under Minoan dominance until around 1400 BCE, when they conquered Crete. Sometime around 1100 BCE, the Dorian tribe from the north invaded and destroyed the Mycenaean civilization. Greece was subsequently thrown into a Dark Age, from which it took several centuries to recover. It was during the Dark Ages that the city-state began to develop.

Around the Nile River, even by 6000 BCE, advanced agricultural practices had developed, as did large-scale building construction. By about 3000 BCE, Egypt had become united as a kingdom under a single monarch, ushering in a thousand-year period of great order and stability. Protected from outside forces by impassible desert, and immune to change because of the orderly, predictable nature of life, Egypt thrived and advanced in all aspects of culture—from religion and art to language, customs, and overall quality of life. It was during this time that the Egyptian dynasties erected the pyramids as monuments to their god-kings. By around 1500 BCE, Egypt had risen to become an international power, solidifying its power on a regional scale.

Classical Traditions, Empires, and Religions

The classical civilizations (roughly the first millennium BCE) differed from earlier civilizations in that their basic need for water and food was met. Freed from a preoccupation with mere survival, civilizations of this period could devote more attention to the arts, architecture, religion, and philosophy and to developing systems of law and government that divided decision-making power. They could also turn their attention outward—toward overseas trade and toward expanding their territories by military force. Still, classical civilizations in many ways developed in terms of the pphysical environment that surrounded them.

The Rise of Rome

By the beginning of the ninth century BCE, the seven hills that rose from the marshy land along the Tiber River's eastern shore were occupied by people in village communities who kept farms in the low-lying areas and retreated to their hilltops for defense. Once the seven villages united, they constructed a wall around their territory and began charging a toll for the use of a ford (and later the bridge) across the marshy lowland. This toll was to prove an early source of Rome's wealth. The city of Rome itself was founded sometime between 850 and 700 BCE. It remained a minor town for a hundred years or so, until the Etruscans—a confederation of towns to the north—took over the city relatively peacefully around 640 BCE. A series of kings governed the town for more than a century thereafter. In 509 BCE, the Romans expelled their king and established a Republic that ruled Rome for the next four centuries. The Republic was in essence a broad oligarchy, with the city's aristocrats dominating politics, economics, and social life. The Romans developed effective military and foreign policies, which enabled them to conquer Italy, and then, between 394 and 290 BCE, to engage in three wars with another early superpower, Carthage, for control of the western Mediterranean Sea.

The Emergence of Classical Greece from Its Dark Ages

Little is known with certainty about ancient Greece during its Dark Age, since the Dorian tribes, who had destroyed and replaced the Mycenaean civilization, had no written language. They were a warring people, who devoted themselves instead to developing tools for battle. (They replaced bronze with the lighter material iron for weaponry and armor, thereby ushering in the Iron Age.) During the Dark Age, the region was a collection of warring city-states called *poleis* (singular: *polis*). Two of the more important poleis were Athens and Sparta, which spoke different dialects of Greek and had different cultural bases and histories. Ultimately, these differences expressed themselves in distinct forms of government. (Athens is credited with creating democracy: equal rule by all citizens.)

Despite their warring ways and the mountains that separated them, the various independent poleis of ancient Greece developed commonalities in culture, language, religion, and government. It was during this time period that Greeks began to identify themselves and each other as *Hellenes*. In spite of their rivalries, they became culturally united. Contributing to this sense of loose unity were the Olympic Games, which began in 776 BCE and featured athletes from the various poleis who competed against one another as a religious ritual. Eventually, around 600 BCE, Greece's Dark Age came to an end, and what followed was an explosive surge of Greek culture.

Classical Greek culture held a distinct set of ideals concerning beauty, life, and the world in general. During the classical era, Greek playwrights and poets came to express the harsh realities of the human condition through various gods and goddesses. The Greek ideals found physical expression in architecture and art that emphasized simplicity and realism. Greek scholars established a study of history emphasizing a communal identity among humankind. And philosophers laid the groundwork for modern ideas of government, law, and justice, which emphasized reason, intellectual inquiry, and the pursuit of wisdom over superstition and religion.

While flourishing culturally, the Greek poleis lost interest in maintaining a strong and unified military. The Greek independent city-states and loose confederations were no match against Philip of Macedon or his son Alexander the Great. They also were inferior against the rising power of Rome, which, under its generals, would eventually come to conquer Greece. But the Romans would come to adapt the classical Greek culture, keeping it alive.

The Decline and Fall of Egypt

Drought, famine, and the rise of an aristocracy helped bring about the end of the Old Kingdom of dynastic rule in Egypt and usher in a period of new prosperity, in which nobles and ordinary citizens began to share in Egypt's wealth. The appearance of foreign invaders, the Hyksos, also changed and renewed Egyptian culture. The resurgence of Egyptian power after the pharaohs of the Sixteenth Dynasty drove out the Hyksos and led to Egyptian imperialism and major building programs that proclaimed the might of the pharaohs and the gods who watched over them.

However, new ideas in religion and political changes in the wider world tended to limit Egyptian power in unexpected ways. Successive waves of invasion made Egypt a land of outward-looking leadership and inward-looking commoners, and it widened the divide between governors and those governed. Egypt became the breadbasket of two successive empires, but the very nature of its wealth—in agriculture and critical products—made it a tempting target to Persian and Islamized Arab alike. At the same time, lacking in other material resources it needed (particularly iron and straight timber), Egypt had no choice but to import these items, thereby depleting its wealth and losing control of the Africa-Asia trade routes. Regular conflicts with other states sapped Egypt's military resources. Eventually, in the 6th century BCE, Egypt fell to the Second Babylonian Empire. The Persians added Egypt to their empire in the fifth century BCE, Alexander the Great conquered Egypt in the third century BCE, and then Julius Caesar and Octavian Augustus Caesar annexed Egypt for the Roman Empire in the first century BCE Egypt would not achieve independence from outside forces until the seventh century CE.

42. The origins of the Roman Empire can be traced to [   ]. On the online GED® test, you will type your answer. For this paper version, please write it in.

Rome's village communities could keep farms in the low-lying areas along the Tiber River's eastern shore while retreating to their hilltops for defense. Moreover, once they united and constructed a bridge across the marshy lowland, they began to amass wealth by charging a toll for accessing the mountains from the river. **The correct answer is the distinctive geography of the city of Rome.**

43. A student of classical Greek literature would most likely read

[Select   ▼]

(A) a poem about the fall of the Roman Empire

(B) a battle tale written by a Dorian warrior

(C) a philosophical essay about the meaning of life

(D) a ballad once sung by traveling troubadours throughout Europe

On the online GED® test, you will click to select your answer.
For this paper version, please circle it.

Classical Greek literature includes philosophical works by Plato, Socrates, Aristotle, and their contemporaries about life's larger questions. **The correct answer is (C).**

Classical civilizations that had lasting influence over vast populations developed around the world.

Africa: The Cradle of Civilization

Africa is often referred to as the cradle of civilization, giving rise to ancient Egypt. Nomads settled along the banks of the Nile River, which flooded annually and left rich silt behind. The rise and fall of the river caused the land to cycle from fertile to barren. This was mirrored in the Egyptians' belief in death and rebirth. They preserved the dead through mummification, and buried the bodies along with "grave goods," such as food, tools, and weapons to assist the journey into the afterlife. Egyptian pharaohs were entombed in enormous triangular stone tombs, such as the pyramids of Giza, which are the oldest of the Seven Wonders of the Ancient World.

Ancient Egyptians formed an advanced society with culture and customs. They created decorative art, including pottery painted with hieroglyphics, an ancient form of writing using symbols and pictures. They also used metal tools and sculpted in stone. And they built ships, performed surgeries, and developed plows to harvest wheat and barley.

China: A Trio of Dynasties

In ancient China, three dynasties—the Zhou, Qin, and Han—ruled for centuries. Members of these dynasties were ranked in a hierarchy, from kings to nobles to commoners to slaves. The ancient Chinese settled along the Huang He, the second longest river in the country, which is known as the cradle of Chinese civilization.

Ancient Chinese created decorative art such as pottery, and invented silk and wheels. They also created calendars and religions such as Confucianism, which emphasizes self-control and social and political order. And they excelled in technology, inventing the compass, paper, gunpowder, and mechanical clocks.

India: Two Major Religions

Classical India encompassed two major religions. Hinduism, one of the oldest religions in the world, is characterized by a belief in reincarnation. Buddhism, a world religion based on the teachings of a prince called Buddha, encourages a state of enlightenment by rejecting worldly desires. Artists created Buddhist shrines called *stupas*. Ancient Indians also made important discoveries, such as the mathematical concept of zero, the world's first university, and furnaces to make steel products.

Latin and South America: Three Ancient Cultures

Three vital ancient cultures flourished in Latin and South America: the Mayan, Aztec, and Incan. Each of these civilizations had distinct societies and achievements.

The Maya built pyramids and temples, used a system of hieroglyphic writing, and developed accurate calendars. Similarly, the Aztecs excelled in math and science, especially astronomy. Their sophisticated calendar stone contains pictorial symbols for twelve months and 365 days of the year. They also used healing herbal remedies gathered from Central American plants. Along the same lines, the Inca gained fame for their agricultural engineering feats. They constructed tiers of terraces up mountainsides to grow corn, potatoes, and other crops.

44. Which of the following did NOT characterize ancient Latin and South American cultures?

(A) precise calendars

(B) silk fabrics

(C) herbal medicines

(D) terrace cultivation

The ancient Chinese culture was renowned for developing silk fabrics. Luxurious silks were reserved for royalty. **The correct answer is (B).**

45. Ancient Egyptians reinforced their belief in death and rebirth by all of the following, with the possible exception of

| Select ▼ |

(A) practicing cannibalism

(B) entombing in pyramids

(C) preserving through mummification

(D) burying objects with the dead

On the online GED® test, you will click to select your answer. For this paper version, please circle it.

The Egyptians believed in an afterlife following death; therefore, they treated the deceased with dignity to ensure eternal life. They did not practice cannibalism. **The correct answer is (A).**

Environment and Societal Development

Societal Development

The Fertile Crescent is known as the cradle of civilization because the earliest known cultures originated there. Located in the modern-day Middle East, this crescent-shaped area of land was a lush, fertile slice in an arid region. Here, the Tigris and Euphrates rivers converged, and this source of water irrigated the land to help crops grow. This ancient region, known as Mesopotamia, was the site of an advanced society with cultural and social organization.

The first civilization in Mesopotamia was Sumer, where its residents, the Sumerians, rose to power and prosperity around 3000 BC. A dozen city-states had separate walled cities and villages until one king united them following a great flood. Sumerians were prolific inventors. They invented new technologies, such as the sundial, potter's wheel, and wheeled carts and wagons. They built reservoirs to store water, and canals to carry it to farmland. They also created cuneiform, the earliest writing system, in which wedge-shaped characters were made on clay tablets. In addition, this advanced civilization created the first codes of law. Sumer faced frequent invasions from neighboring communities. It fell into decline around 1760 BC, when it was absorbed into Babylonia.

Other civilizations, including Babylonia, took over the Fertile Crescent. Its most famous leader was Hammurabi, who established a code of laws dealing with various aspects of Babylonian culture. He wrote numerous laws about water rights, which were crucial in a region that depended upon irrigation agriculture.

As in ancient Mesopotamia, the world's topography continues to influence regional borders, with many borders delineated by natural features such as deserts, rivers, and mountains. For example, the Rio Grande forms part of the border between Mexico and the United States.

Human Migration

Humans often move from one country to another in response to environmental issues. People have been forced to migrate from their home territories due to sudden or gradual changes in their environment. Desertification, droughts, earthquakes, floods, global warming, and rising sea levels can trigger migration. All of these issues can have a detrimental effect on food production and can lead to water shortages.

About 12,000 years ago, scientists speculate that humans migrated from Asia to North America by passing over the Bering Strait on a temporary land bridge. According to archeologists, the most likely reason that these early Native Americans left the continent of Asia to walk far into a new land was due to climate change. Temperatures rising or plummeting would affect human survival. The migrating hunter-gatherers may have tracked herds of hoofed creatures from Siberia into Alaska, ensuring that their food supply would continue.

Food was also the motivating factor behind the Irish emigration of the 1840s. In 1845, a destructive fungus raged throughout Ireland, destroying the potato crop that formed the backbone of the Irish diet, and, therefore, economy. More than a million people perished from starvation during the Irish potato famine. Approximately two million Irish immigrated to new countries, with one-quarter of that number settling in the United States.

46. Ancient Sumerians were renowned for all of the following inventions EXCEPT which one?

(A) classical guitar

(B) written language

(C) reservoirs

(D) wheeled vehicles

On the online GED® test, you will click to select your answer. For this paper version, please circle it.

Cuneiform, reservoirs, and wheeled carts and wagons all were Sumerian inventions; however, they did not invent the guitar. **The correct answer is (A).**

47. Mass migration might be caused by all of the following factors EXCEPT which one?

| Select   ▼ |

(A) food shortages

(B) desertification

(C) rising sea levels

(D) safe drinking water

On the online GED® test, you will click to select your answer. For this paper version, please circle it.

Shortages of food, desertification, and rising sea levels due to climate changes could cause millions of people to migrate. However, safe drinking water is not a cause, although an unsafe water supply would lead to mass migration. **The correct answer is (D).**

HISTORICAL DOCUMENTS ON THE GED® SOCIAL STUDIES TEST

The Social Studies Test will contain excerpts from at least one of the following key historical documents relating to the American constitutional form of government: the Declaration of Independence, the U.S. Constitution, the Federalist Papers, or landmark Supreme Court cases. To help you become more familiar with each of these documents, we will examine them closely here. Before you take the Social Studies Test, take time to read some of each of these documents just to familiarize yourself with the language and the style of each one.

The Declaration of Independence

On July 4, 1776, the members of the Philadelphia Congress adopted a motion that "The united colonies are, and of right ought to be, free and independent states..." Thomas Jefferson led a committee appointed to write a statement declaring the thirteen colonies officially free of British reign. The resulting document was the Declaration of Independence. Jefferson's task was not an easy one, however. He needed to clarify the colonies' purpose in fighting Britain. He succeeded, and by doing so, he appealed to other colonies to declare their independence and encouraged other nations to support the colonies against Britain.

Jefferson begins the Declaration of Independence by asserting that all people have rights to which they are entitled by nature. He states that governments are established to protect those rights, and when a government fails to do so, people should abolish it and create a new government that will protect their rights.

The Declaration of Independence then takes on a more personal tone, stating that the King of Great Britain, George III, has misused his power in a number of specific ways. Basically, half of the Declaration is devoted to listing the ways in which King George abused his power. Pointing out that their previous attempts to compel the king to respect human rights had failed, Jefferson asserts that logically the Americans did the only thing they could do to preserve the rights of all people—they declared independence from Great Britain. The Declaration, a moving document, had the desired effect and enticed great support for the war against Britain.

The U.S. Constitution

The Preamble

"We, the People of the United States, in Order to form a more perfect Union, establish Justice, insure domestic Tranquility, provide for the common defense, promote the general Welfare, and secure the Blessings of Liberty to ourselves and our Posterity, do ordain and establish this Constitution for the United States of America."

A preamble is a statement of purpose. The Preamble to the Constitution paraphrases the purpose of the Constitution. It answers the question of why the Constitution was created.

Articles of the Constitution

The Articles of the Constitution outline the plan for the government under which we currently live. As discussed earlier, three branches of government, the executive, legislative, and judicial, divide the power and keep any one part of the government from dominating another. Each branch keeps a check on the others, thus the terms "separation of powers" and "checks and balances." To balance the power of the three branches of government, each has a "check" to limit the powers of the other two. For example, although Congress may pass a bill, the president has the power to veto it. Congress may, however, override a presidential veto by a two-thirds majority vote. Finally, the Supreme Court may declare a law unconstitutional. These powers are named, or enumerated, in Articles I, II, and III of the Constitution. Let's look more closely at each of these Articles.

ARTICLE I. LEGISLATIVE BRANCH

The legislative branch is outlined in Article I of the Constitution. The U.S. legislature, called Congress, is made up of two houses—the House of Representatives and the Senate. Both houses are made up of representatives elected from the states. The House representation is based on state population, while the Senate consists of two senators from each state. The representatives are elected to two-year terms, while the senators are elected to six-year terms. The legislative branch "creates" the law under which we are governed.

ARTICLE II. EXECUTIVE BRANCH

Article II of the Constitution details the executive branch of government. The executive branch consists of the president, vice president, and various agencies and departments that administer and enforce the laws.

The president serves a four-year term and cannot serve more than two terms. The president and the vice president are elected by a vote of the people. However, there is a process known as the Electoral College, through which the results of the popular election must be certified. A president can, although it is rare, receive a majority of the popular vote and still lose the election because of the Electoral College vote. The executive branch "enforces" the laws under which we live.

ARTICLE III. JUDICIAL BRANCH

Article III of the Constitution provides that the "judicial power belongs to the federal courts." It is in this Article that the Supreme Court and inferior, or lower level, courts are created. As you've already learned, the Supreme Court "checks" the other two branches of government by declaring certain laws unconstitutional. The Supreme Court has the power to rule on cases involving a state and a citizen of another state, disputes between states, between citizens of different states, between a state and its citizens, or between a foreign state and U.S. citizens. It also may consider conflicts arising at sea or regarding patents and copyrights. Most of the time, the Supreme Court hears "appeals" of decisions made by "inferior" courts. However, the Court does have "original" jurisdiction, or the right to hear an original case and not an appealed case, in some instances. These include cases involving ambassadors or other public ministers, consuls, and those cases in which a state is a party.

Although originally created with a Chief Justice and five associate judges, the Supreme Court is now composed of nine justices, each appointed for life by the president with approval from the Senate. The Court acts by issuing decisions that explain why the Court makes particular rulings. The judiciary "interprets" the law.

ARTICLE IV. RELATIONS OF THE STATES TO ONE ANOTHER

The goal of this article is to promote respect between the states, also known as "full faith and credit." It requires that the citizens of different states be treated similarly. It also requires states to honor the legal decisions and legal documents of other states.

ARTICLE V. THE PROCESS OF AMENDMENT

This article explains the manner in which the Constitution may be amended or changed.

ARTICLE VI. GENERAL PROVISIONS

Article VI notes that the United States took on debts of the Confederacy, confirms that the Constitution, federal laws, and treaties "are the supreme law of the land," and requires federal and state officers to take an oath to support the Constitution.

ARTICLE VII. RATIFICATION OF THE CONSTITUTION

The authors of the Constitution wrote this article with an eye toward putting the Constitution into action. Article VII provides that the Constitution becomes effective when ratified by the conventions of nine states.

The Amendments

In the years following the ratification, or approval, of the Constitution, many leaders wanted to make sure that the rights of individuals were protected. The Constitution did not specifically list those protected rights, so the states' leaders decided to add amendments, or changes and additions, to the Constitution. The first ten amendments are known collectively as the Bill of Rights. The other amendments were added periodically as the need arose throughout the course of American history. Let's look at each one of those amendments.

THE BILL OF RIGHTS

The first ten amendments to the Constitution are known as the Bill of Rights. Many states ratified the Constitution only because they believed it would be amended to include the rights outlined in the Bill of Rights.

First Amendment—Religious and Political Freedom: The First Amendment prevents Congress from interfering with the freedom of religion, speech, and the press. It also incorporates the right to assemble and to petition the government.

Second Amendment—Right to Bear Arms: This amendment gives citizens a limited right to arm themselves, or keep weapons. There is some debate over whether this right is intended to be the right of the states or the right of individuals.

Third Amendment—Quartering of Troops: The purpose of the Third Amendment was to stop soldiers from taking over homes for their own use without the consent of the owner. The amendment provides that such "quartering," or "room and board," may occur "in a manner to be prescribed by law."

Fourth Amendment—Searches and Seizures: The Fourth Amendment forbids "unreasonable searches" and the issuance of warrants without "probable cause," or good reason.

Fifth Amendment—Right to Life, Liberty, and Property: The Fifth Amendment guarantees a citizen's rights while on trial as well as the rights to life, liberty, and property. When someone refuses to testify at trial and "takes the Fifth," they are said to be invoking their rights as established in the Fifth Amendment. It is also called a right against self-incrimination. The Fifth Amendment also provides that an individual must not be held for committing a crime without being "indicted." In addition, the Fifth Amendment protects against "double jeopardy," or the risk of being tried twice for the same offense. The Fifth Amendment also ensures individuals' "due process" rights, or the right to be moved through the criminal justice system in a proper fashion.

Sixth Amendment—Protection in Criminal Trials: Citizens are guaranteed a right to a speedy trial, an impartial jury, and the right to an attorney in the Sixth Amendment. The accused also has a right to "confront witnesses" against him or her at trial.

Seventh Amendment—Suits at Common Law: If there is a dispute over something valued at $20 or more, then the Seventh Amendment provides that citizens have a right to a jury trial in federal court. However, this type of case is not normally heard in federal court now.

Eighth Amendment—Bail and Punishment: The Eighth Amendment prohibits fines and punishments that, in essence, "don't fit the crime." It is said to be "cruel and unusual" to sentence someone unfairly, and the Eighth Amendment prohibits this.

Ninth Amendment—Considering Rights Not Enumerated: Fearing that the enumeration of certain rights would lead to the exclusion, or omission, of other rights, the authors of the Bill of Rights included the Ninth Amendment that establishes that citizens are not limited to the rights specifically listed in the Constitution.

Tenth Amendment—Powers Reserved to States and to People: Similar to the rationale behind the Ninth Amendment, the Tenth Amendment was created to reassure the states that they would retain power in those areas not specifically granted to the Federal Government.

THE OTHER AMENDMENTS

Eleventh Amendment—Suits Against a State: The Eleventh Amendment clarifies the original jurisdiction of the Supreme Court concerning a suit brought against a state by a citizen of another state.

Twelfth Amendment—Election of the President and Vice President: The Twelfth Amendment explains how the Electoral College chooses the president and vice president. It also states that the two should work together, and that the vice president should become president if the president can no longer stay in office.

Thirteenth Amendment—Slavery Prohibited: Slavery was abolished in the United States by the addition of the Thirteenth Amendment.

Fourteenth Amendment—Civil Rights for Ex-Slaves and Others: The Fourteenth Amendment ensures that all citizens of all states enjoy rights on the state level as well as the federal level. It has also been interpreted as providing for "due process" at the state level.

Fifteenth Amendment—Suffrage for Blacks: This amendment prohibits the use of race as a requirement or disqualification for voting.

Sixteenth Amendment—Income Taxes: The Sixteenth Amendment authorizes the collection of income taxes.

Seventeenth Amendment—Direct Election of Senators: Prior to the Seventeenth Amendment, senators were selected by the legislatures of the various states. Since its passage, they are elected by the vote of the citizens.

Eighteenth Amendment—National Prohibition: This amendment prohibited the sale or manufacture of alcohol in the United States. It was later repealed by the Twenty-First Amendment.

Nineteenth Amendment—Woman Suffrage: Just as the Fifteenth Amendment prohibits the use of race as criteria for voting, the Nineteenth Amendment prohibits the use of gender as a requirement or disqualification for voting.

Twentieth Amendment—Presidential and Congressional Terms: The Twentieth Amendment sets new start dates for congressional terms and also addresses what to do if a president dies before he is sworn into office.

Twenty-First Amendment—Prohibition Repealed: The Twenty-First Amendment repealed the Eighteenth Amendment, which had prohibited the sale or manufacture of alcohol in the United States.

Twenty-Second Amendment—Anti-Third Term Amendment: This amendment limits a president to two 4-year terms in office. There is an exception for a vice president who takes over because the president is unable to continue. In that case, the limit is a total of ten years as president.

Twenty-Third Amendment—District of Columbia Vote: This amendment gave Washington, D.C., representation in the Electoral College.

Twenty-Fourth Amendment—Poll Tax: The Twenty-Fourth Amendment prohibits charging a tax for placing a vote in a federal election.

Twenty-Fifth Amendment—Presidential Succession and Disability: This amendment states the order of succession should the president be unable to continue holding office.

Twenty-Sixth Amendment—Lowering Voting Age: Citizens who were 18 years old could vote after the passage of this amendment.

Twenty-Seventh Amendment—Congressional Pay Increases: The Twenty-Seventh Amendment requires that any law that increases the pay of legislators may not take effect until after the next election.

The Federalist Papers

The Federalist Papers are a collection of eighty-five essays written by John Jay, James Madison, and Alexander Hamilton. They are considered one of the most important contributions made to American political thought. The papers were intended to influence states, particularly New York, to adopt the Constitution.

The delegates who signed the Constitution stipulated that it would take effect only after approval by ratifying conventions in nine of thirteen states. Because New York and Virginia were big and powerful, a vote against ratification from either of them would have been disastrous. The New York governor, George Clinton, clearly was opposed to the Constitution.

Hoping to persuade the New York convention to ratify the Constitution, Jay, Madison, and Hamilton wrote a series of letters defending the Constitution to New York papers under the pseudonym Publius. These letters are known collectively as The Federalist Papers. Clinton Rossitor said, "The message of The Federalist reads: no happiness without liberty, no liberty without self-government, no self-government without constitutionalism, no constitutionalism without morality—and none of these great goods without stability and order."

Landmark Supreme Court Cases

The Supreme Court has issued many cases of historical significance that have directly affected our rights as individuals. Let's look at a summary of some of those "landmark" cases that definitely changed rights in America.

Marbury v. Madison—1803

Prior to his death, President John Adams attempted to fill a number of judicial vacancies. Some of the commissions were not delivered to the appointees prior to Adams's death. One of the appointees who did not receive his commission, William Marbury, sued Secretary of State James Madison to get his commission as Justice of the Peace.

This issue came before the Court on its "original jurisdiction" (i.e., it was not on appeal from an inferior court), and it placed the Court in a difficult position. If the Court were to issue a writ of mandamus, or order, forcing Madison to turn over the commission, and he refused, the power of the Court would be weakened. On the other hand, to refuse to issue the writ of mandamus could be perceived as weakness or fear of the executive branch.

Ultimately, the Court's decision declared that Madison should have delivered the commission to Marbury but held that it did not have the power to issue a writ of mandamus. The Court declared that such power exceeded the Court's authority as granted in Article III of the Constitution. The writ of mandamus authority had been given to the Court by the Judiciary Act of 1789, a congressional act. Thus, the Court held an act of Congress unconstitutional. Ironically, by declaring that it did not have the power to order Madison to turn over the commission, the Court effectively strengthened its power over the other two branches of government.

This case exemplifies the Court's power as the "last word" on the meaning of the Constitution. It established the judicial branch as an equal power in the three branches of government. The power to declare acts of Congress unconstitutional is one that the Court has used sparingly over the years. The legislature is, however, always aware that the Court could declare a law unconstitutional.

Dred Scott v. Sandford—1857

Dred Scott was a black slave who lived on free (non-slavery) land with his owner for several years. He tried, unsuccessfully, to sue in state court for his freedom. He then filed suit in federal court. The basis of his claim to establish his freedom was that he had lived on free soil for more than five years in an area of the country where the Missouri Compromise of 1820 forbade slavery.

The Supreme Court ruled that Scott was a slave and not a citizen and therefore did not have the right to sue in federal court. The right to file suit is a right limited to citizens in Article III of the Constitution. A majority of the Court held that, because a slave was the private property of his master, the Missouri Compromise unconstitutionally took the slave owner's property without due process of law. Thus, a slave could be taken into any territory and held there. The reason? The Fifth Amendment clearly forbids Congress from depriving people of their property without due process. To allow Scott his freedom would be to deprive his owner of his "property." The Court found the Missouri Compromise unconstitutional, and Dred Scott remained a slave.

Plessy v. Ferguson—1896

Homer Adolph Plessy was a resident of Louisiana and a citizen of the United States. He was of partial African descent. He paid for a first-class ticket on the East Louisiana Railway, a passenger train that ran through Louisiana. When he boarded the train, Plessy found a seat in a car that was filled with white people and was designated for white passengers. The train conductor informed Plessy that he would have to find a seat in a car not designated for white people or he would be forced to leave the train. Plessy refused and was arrested.

Plessy was found guilty of violating a state statute that required passenger trains to provide "separate, but equal" accommodations for white and black people. The statute also imposed criminal punishment on those passengers who refused to comply. Plessy brought suit challenging the Louisiana statute as an unconstitutional violation of his due process rights under the Fourteenth Amendment. The Supreme Court held that the statute requiring "separate but equal" facilities was constitutional, rationalizing that separate facilities for blacks and whites satisfied the Fourteenth Amendment as long as they were equal. In other words, the Court found that segregation does not in itself constitute unlawful discrimination.

Brown v. Board of Education of Topeka, Kansas—1954

Linda Brown, a black third-grade student, walked a mile every day to get to her "black" school, even though a school designated for white children was much closer to her home. Linda's father tried to enroll her in the "white" school, but the school refused to accept Linda as a student. The Browns got help from the National Association for the Advancement of Colored People (NAACP) and sued the school board. The Supreme Court, hearing the case on appeal, ordered oral arguments in the case twice before reaching a decision. The question before the court: "Does segregation of children in public schools solely on the basis of race, even though the physical facilities and other 'tangible' factors may be equal, deprive the children of the minority group of equal educational opportunities?"

Thus, the question of "separate but equal" was once again before the court. The Court's decision in *Plessy* v. *Ferguson,* a finding that separate facilities are not unconstitutional as long as they are equal, seemed to hold the answer in this case as well. However, fifty-eight years had passed, and this time, the Court's ruling was quite different. Significantly, the opinion of the Court was unanimous. The decision: "We conclude that in the field of public education, the doctrine of 'separate but equal' has no place. Separate educational facilities are inherently unequal."

The *Brown* decision did not abolish segregation in any areas other than public schools, but it was a start toward integrating the races in many areas of life. The Court did not overrule *Plessy* v. *Ferguson,* because it limited the decision in Brown to public schools. The ruling did, however, have a significant impact on the segregation of the races in many public facilities. Slowly, integration began. We can only imagine how different integration might have been if the Court's decision in *Plessy* over 100 years ago had held separate facilities to be "inherently unequal."

Miranda v. Arizona—1966

Ernesto Miranda was arrested for raping an 18-year-old girl. The police arrived at Miranda's home at night and asked him to go with them to the police station. Miranda, claiming he did not realize he had a choice, went with the police. After 2 hours of interrogation, Miranda confessed to the crime.

On appeal to the Supreme Court, Miranda argued that he would not have confessed to the crime if he had been advised of his right to remain silent and to have an attorney. In a 5-4 decision, the Court determined that a suspect must be warned prior to custodial interrogation of his right to remain silent, that any statement he does make may be used against him, and that he has a right to an attorney. Specifically, the Court stated: "He must be warned prior to any questioning that he has the right to remain silent, that anything he says can be used against him in a court of law, that he has the right to the presence of an attorney, and that if he cannot afford an attorney one will be appointed for him prior to any questioning if he so desires." Thus, the infamous "Miranda" warnings were created.

Roe v. Wade—1973

Roe was a single, pregnant woman who brought suit to challenge the constitutionality of the Texas laws that made getting an abortion or performing an abortion illegal. The laws did except those abortions performed on medical advice to save the mother's life.

The Court held that the law violated the due process clause of the Fourteenth Amendment, which protects the right to privacy against state action. This right, the Court found, includes a woman's qualified right to terminate her pregnancy. The Court acknowledged that the state has a legitimate interest in protecting both the pregnant woman's health and the potentiality of human life, and placed those rights on a scale that tips further to the state's interests as the pregnancy progresses.

During the first trimester, the Court stated, the decision should be left to the attending physician. After that, the state could regulate the abortion procedure in ways "reasonably related" to the mother's health. Subsequent to "viability," or the ability of the child to live outside of the womb, the Court held that the state could regulate abortion and even prohibit it except where necessary to save the life of the mother. Many abortion cases have followed *Roe,* but this was the first to hold that a woman's right to privacy outweighs the state's interest in protecting her health and the unborn child.

Nixon v. United States—1974

During the presidential election of 1972, burglars broke into the Democratic National Committee's headquarters in Watergate. A federal grand jury indicted the Attorney General and others, alleging conspiracy and obstruction of justice. The grand jury named President Richard Nixon as a co-conspirator.

Investigations revealed that Nixon taped many conversations that took place in the oval office. The tapes were subpoenaed, and Nixon released edited transcripts but refused to release anything more, claiming "executive privilege." Executive privilege protects the president from being compelled by the judicial branch to turn over confidential executive branch material.

The question before the Court: Does the president have the right under executive privilege to refuse to surrender material to federal court? In a unanimous (8-0, Justice Rehnquist did not participate) decision, the Court held that Nixon had to turn over the tapes. The Court stated: "[N]either the doctrine of Separation of Powers, nor the need for confidentiality of high-level communications, without more, can sustain an absolute, unqualified Presidential privilege of immunity from judicial process under all circumstances. The President's need of complete candor and objectivity from advisors calls for great deference from the courts. However, when the privilege depends solely on the broad, undifferentiated claim of public interest in the confidentiality of such conversations, a confrontation with other values arises. Absent a claim of need to protect military, diplomatic, or sensitive national security secrets, we find it difficult to accept the argument that even the very important interest in confidentiality of Presidential communications is significantly diminished by production of such material for in camera inspection with all the protection that a district court will be obliged to provide." With this decision, the Court limited the president's use of "executive privilege" to the need to protect military secrets, diplomatic secrets, or national security. The rationale is based on the idea that the courts will protect the information and treat it as confidential.

Hustler Magazine, Inc. v. Falwell—1988

Reverend Jerry Falwell filed suit against *Hustler* magazine because the magazine published a cartoon that portrayed Falwell as engaging in an incestuous relationship with his mother in an outhouse.

The Supreme Court held that, in order to protect the free flow of ideas and opinions, the First and Fourteenth Amendments prohibit public figures and public officials from recovering for "intentional infliction of emotional distress" when the speech that causes the distress could not reasonably be taken as implying the truth. In essence, because the cartoon was obviously a joke, and because Falwell was a "public figure," *Hustler* had the right to print the cartoon under the First Amendment to the Constitution. If an individual places himself in a position to be known by the public, then he takes on the risk of being the topic of jokes.

Boy Scouts of America v. Dale—2000

The Boy Scouts revoked Dale's position as assistant scoutmaster in a New Jersey troop after learning that he was homosexual. Dale sued, claiming violation of a state statute prohibiting discrimination on the basis of sexual orientation. The Supreme Court held that the Boy Scouts could not be required to include Dale in its organization. The Court stated that to require mandatory inclusion of unwanted individuals into the organization would violate the Boy Scouts' First Amendment right of "expressive association." Forced membership, the Court found, is unconstitutional if it affects the group's ability to advocate its collective viewpoints. Because the Boy Scouts believed that a homosexual lifestyle conflicted with its philosophies, the inclusion of Dale would have hindered the Boy Scouts' ability to teach its views. Thus, to protect the Boy Scouts' First Amendment rights, it could not be forced to include Dale in its membership.

CANADIAN HISTORY

The Earliest Canadians

The earliest inhabitants of Canada most likely traveled from Asia to North America across a land bridge that spanned the Bering Strait. The nomadic hunters probably followed large game into North America at least 10,000 years ago. Once in North America, they scattered across the continent and formed their own communities, each with its own distinct language. A new wave of nomads probably migrated to North America about 4,000 years ago. The earliest concentrations of Canadians were located along the Pacific Coast and in what is now Ontario. Over the centuries, the inhabitants of Canada developed a number of languages and cultures unique to Canada, including the Algonquian and the Athapaskan language groups. These groups, and others, interacted only with each other until AD 985.

The Arrival of Europeans

In approximately 985, the first Europeans, the Vikings, landed on, explored, and settled Greenland. They also explored the northeastern coast of Canada. About fifteen years later, the famous Viking Leif Ericson sailed from Greenland to a place he called Vinland, which was probably modern-day Newfoundland. Although exploration and trade continued along the northeast coast of Canada, the Viking colonies did not last long, and by the early fifteenth century, Europeans no longer maintained contact with North America.

Toward the end of the fifteenth century, European explorers began exploring North America's eastern coast again. John Cabot unsuccessfully searched the coast for the Northwest Passage, a sea route that Europeans believed would lead to the wealthy Asian trade empires. In the sixteenth century, France sponsored Jacques Cartier to continue the search for the Northwest Passage. Cartier was also unsuccessful in locating a sea route to Asia and was later unsuccessful at establishing a colony in North America.

Later attempts at colonization also met with little success. However, the Europeans discovered the vast wealth of fish and whales available to commercial fishermen off the coast of Labrador, in the Gulf of St. Lawrence, and in the Grand Banks. Fishermen from Spain, France, England, and Portugal took advantage of the bountiful catch found here. Eventually, the English explorer Sir Humphrey Gilbert claimed Newfoundland for England. After the Spanish and Portuguese left the area, the English settled the northern part of Newfoundland and the French settled the southern part. These settlers entered into a trade relationship with the natives. The bulk of the trading was done with furs, especially beaver furs. The European demand for beaver products, particularly hats, launched an industry in Canada that remained a vital part of its economy for many years to follow.

The indigenous, or native, peoples of Canada traded with the European settlers and formed many alliances with the Europeans. Because of the large amount of Canadian territory and the relatively small number of Europeans in Canada, few conflicts emerged between Europeans and the indigenous nations they encountered in Canada. The Europeans made some attempts to Christianize the natives, but they found little success. The greatest negative effect of the trade relationship was the transmission of European diseases to the indigenous people of Canada. Diseases in epidemic proportions spread quickly and decimated vast numbers of natives wherever the Europeans went. The indigenous population of Canada continued to decline even into the twentieth century.

1. Which of the following is most likely true of the first inhabitants of Canada?

    (A) The first inhabitants of Canada were probably civilized.

    (B) The first inhabitants of Canada were probably of Asian descent.

    (C) The first inhabitants of Canada settled in permanent shelters as soon as they arrived in Canada.

    (D) The first Canadians were indigenous to North America.

The first people in Canada likely crossed the land bridge between Asia and modern-day Alaska. **The correct answer is (B).**

2. Which of the following best describes the relationship between the Europeans who explored North America and the natives of Canada?

    (A) The two groups were involved in nearly incessant warfare.

    (B) The two groups formed a military alliance.

    (C) The two groups had a relationship based on trade.

    (D) The two groups freely exchanged information about cultures and farming techniques.

The Europeans and the natives exchanged many goods and generally maintained a good relationship. **The correct answer is (C).**

Early Canadian Colonies

As France began to see the huge dividends paid by the fur trade in Canada (which was known as New France), it officially claimed and began defending the area. England, a perennial enemy of France, disputed the claim. France realized that new, permanent settlements needed to be built if the claim to New France was going to be legitimate. Therefore, France used the fur trade to finance the construction of new forts and settlements. France settled at Quebec, an inland site well protected from foreign aggression. France then employed an economic policy known as mercantilism. Under mercantilism, a trade company was given control over New France. In exchange, the company agreed to ship all exports to France and to purchase all of its raw materials and supplies from France. The French also created strong alliances with the Huron and the Algonquin, two local nations of indigenous peoples. With the help of these two peoples, the French colony grew and prospered. The French also created many maps of the area, and in the 1630s and 1640s, they established colonies at Trois-Rivières and Montreal. The colonies remained dependent upon the fur trade and their relationship with the natives. This presented a problem in the mid-1600s, though, when the French aided the Huron in a losing effort against the Iroquois. The devastation of the Huron nearly cost France the colonies.

Conflict with the British

In the second half of the seventeenth century, the French increased their defenses and population in New France. Also during the late seventeenth century, the French sponsored significant exploration of North America, both westward across Canada and southward along the Mississippi River in the Louisiana territory. The English re-entered the picture during this same time period when the Hudson Bay Company, an English trade company, began competing with the French for the fur trade. The French responded by building more forts in French territory and along the frontier.

In the 1680s, the French found themselves in conflict with the British in several parts of the world, including North America. In King William's War during the 1690s, the French and British troops in North America exchanged guerrilla raids and attacks for nearly a decade before signing a treaty that returned North America to the way it was before the war. In 1702, Queen Anne's War erupted between the two powers and later ended with France giving up some of its territory. The next half-century or so was a period of high tensions but no war. France continued to expand its fur trade and its relationship with the indigenous peoples in and around New France.

However, in 1754, the French and Indian War broke out between the French and the British. Many natives fought on both sides of the conflict. The French held their ground well against the British, who greatly outnumbered the French. However, at the war's end in 1763, France ceded its territory to Great Britain. Quebec, Nova Scotia, Newfoundland, and Rupert's Land were now under British control. Great Britain immediately sought to ease tensions between the British and the natives in Canada by signing treaties with them.

> **3.** The French and the English competed most for which of the following in Canada?
>
> **(A)** the fur trade
>
> **(B)** Indian alliances
>
> **(C)** the western territories
>
> **(D)** access to the Mississippi River

Both nations wanted control of the lucrative fur trade, which brought about fierce competition between the two rivals. **The correct answer is (A).**

4. Which of the following is true about the situation after the end of the French and Indian War?

(A) No indigenous peoples had become involved in the conflict between France and Great Britain.

(B) The French territories remained unchanged from the beginning of the war.

(C) The French added to their territories much land formerly under British rule.

(D) France lost much land to Britain.

Rupert's Island, Quebec, Nova Scotia, and Newfoundland all went to Great Britain after the war. **The correct answer is (D).**

Early British Rule

At first, Britain hoped to institute British customs and British-style government in its new territory. However, that plan did not work because of the resistance of the Canadian people, most of whom were originally French. With the Quebec Act of 1774, Great Britain allowed French law, French customs, and even Catholicism to continue in Canada. This went a long way toward reconciliation between the French Canadians and the British government. The Quebec Act also returned some land to Quebec and saved Montreal's fur trade, the backbone of its economy. The Canadian colonies grew, but they remained only loosely linked to each other.

With relative peace and security in Canada, the bulk of British forces left Canada. This opened the door for trouble with the thirteen British colonies to the South. In 1775 and 1776, the British colonies along the Atlantic coast (now known as the United States) decided to break away from British control. During the time the colonies fought the British, they also invaded Quebec and Montreal. The British eventually drove the Americans out of Canada, but they failed to prevent the colonies from winning their independence. During and after the war, many loyalists—those Americans still loyal to Great Britain—fled the colonies and sought refuge in Canada. The British government rewarded these refugees for their loyalty by granting them land and other financial benefits.

The loyalists who settled in Canada expected they would be living in a British land, but what they found was an unfamiliar and uncomfortable French-style society. By 1791, these loyalists had voiced their displeasure with the situation on many occasions. The British government responded by dividing Quebec into two separate colonies called Upper Canada and Lower Canada. Each colony received a new constitution. The predominantly French Lower Canada retained its French culture and laws while the mostly British Upper Canada received new English laws that favored both the English nobility and the Protestant religion.

When the United States declared war on Great Britain in 1812, the United States thought it might be able to take advantage of the perceived vulnerability of Canada.

U.S. troops invaded Upper Canada but were soundly defeated by British forces and natives allied with the British. This act of aggression created an anti-American sentiment throughout much of Canada, particularly in Upper Canada.

5. For which of the following reasons might the Canadian people have been resistant to British rule?

   (A) Most of the people in Canada liked the government that they had already established there.

   (B) Most of the people in Canada did not like people who spoke English.

   (C) Most Canadians at the time were of French descent, and the French and British generally have never gotten along very well.

   (D) The British refused to allow French customs and traditions to be practiced in Canada.

The French and British had a long history of disputes. **The correct answer is (C).**

6. What steps did the British take to give aid to refugees from the thirteen colonies during the War for American Independence?

   (A) The government gave them safe passage back to Great Britain.

   (B) The government granted them tracts of land in Canada.

   (C) The government refused to give them any aid and encouraged them to return to America.

   (D) The government took land and wealth away from the natives and gave it to the refugees.

The British government wanted to reward the loyalists for their loyalty to Great Britain. **The correct answer is (B).**

Westward Expansion and Immigration

In the late eighteenth and early nineteenth centuries, two companies battled for control of the fur trade and sparked westward expansion in Canada. The Hudson Bay Company had been granted a monopoly on the fur trade, but a company founded by French-Canadian fur traders defied the monopoly. The North West Company explored, mapped, and tapped the natural resources of Canada all the way to the Pacific Coast. Both companies struggled for influence throughout the western territories. Friction between the two companies often resulted in outbreaks of violence in frontier towns. Finally, in 1821, the two companies merged and the Hudson Bay Company assumed control of the Canadian fur trade. However, by the end of the nineteenth century, the timber industry replaced the fur trade as the leading industry in Canada.

During the nineteenth century, millions of Europeans migrated to North America to seek new opportunities. Perhaps 1 to 2 million of these people, most from England, Ireland, and Scotland, migrated to Canadian territories. They were willing to take the risk of moving to the frontier because of the promise of free farmland. Upper Canada grew faster than any other part of the Canadian territory. Relatively few immigrants, on the other hand, moved to the far north or the far west. Not until the gold rush in the second half of the nineteenth century did a significant number of settlers move to the Pacific region. As the immigration continued, the native peoples of British North America gradually became the minority of the population.

7. Which of the following statements could be made concerning the competition between the two trade companies in Canada?

(A) The competition between the two companies nearly caused a civil war.

(B) The indigenous people were caught in the middle of the war between the two trade companies.

(C) The two trade companies encouraged good, healthy competition in the marketplace.

(D) The competition between the two companies ultimately led to the mapping and exploration of some of the western parts of Canada.

In order to find more resources and stay competitive with the Hudson Bay Company, the North West Company moved westward, exploring and mapping as it went. **The correct answer is (D).**

8. Which of the following was the primary reason for the massive immigration to Canada during the early 1800s?

(A) The government offered land grants to anyone who wanted to settle on the frontier.

(B) World War in Europe drove millions from their homes.

(C) The prospects of finding a job in the factories of Canada prompted many Europeans to immigrate.

(D) The gold rush made many people seek their fortunes.

Immigrants to Canada received large tracts of land on which they could settle and build homes. **The correct answer is (A).**

Radicals, Reformers, the Act of Union, and Confederation

Because most of the non-indigenous inhabitants of Canada during the early 1800s were hardworking farmers and fishermen, the traditional British aristocratic system of government did not please many of the Canadians. In the early 1800s, two groups called for a change in the government. The moderate group of people who sought change was known as reformers. The reformers liked the British system of government, but they wanted a parliamentary system with an elected legislature instead of one that was appointed. The radicals, the more liberal of the two groups, sought publicly elected officials within a republic modeled after the governments of France and the United States. Many in Canada, especially in Lower Canada, pointed to Britain as the root of many of the social, political, and economic problems that Canada faced. These feelings erupted in an armed rebellion in 1837 that eventually ended in victory for the British. The political climate in Lower and Upper Canada convinced Great Britain that something needed to be done in order to maintain peace.

In 1841, the British passed the Act of Union, which created the province of Canada. This province had two sections, Canada East and Canada West (formerly Lower Canada and Upper Canada, respectively). The act gave Canada West the same representation as the larger Canada East, and it made English the official language. Eventually, the government, which the Act of Union created, was dissolved. The Canadian provinces won the right to local self-government, and Britain retained the right to manage foreign affairs, defense, and the appointment of provincial governors.

During this time, a two-party system emerged in Canadian politics. Also during this time, industry began to grow in Canada. Trade restrictions and tariffs were eased, and North American trade flourished. Railroads were built across Canada to carry both passengers and cargo. Telegraph lines connected many parts of Canada and North America. Shipbuilding reached an all-time high in British North America. For some parts of Canada, this period was a golden age.

During the 1850s, talk of unifying the Canadian provinces was a topic of great debate. In the 1860s, when the Southern states of the United States tried to secede from the United States, talk of Canadian unification intensified. Canada, Nova Scotia, New Brunswick, Prince Edward Island, and Newfoundland met to discuss unification, or Confederation, as it came to be known. The legislative leaders approved the Seventy-two Resolutions, which was a draft of a constitution.

Under the Confederation, the governmental responsibilities would be split between a national government and provincial governments. The Confederation was not a move toward independence, though. Leaders wanted to maintain ties with Britain to prevent aggression from the United States. After ratification of the Seventy-two Resolutions, the Dominion of Canada was created in 1867. The new Canada had four provinces: Quebec, Ontario, New Brunswick, and Nova Scotia. Ottawa was chosen as the national capital. Great Britain did not repeal the Confederation, so in 1871, the last British troops left Canada.

The new nation moved immediately to expand westward. In 1869, Canada added the Northwest Territories, land that Canada purchased from the Hudson Bay Company. In 1871, British Columbia joined Canada, followed by Prince Edward Island two years later. Canada later added the Arctic Archipelago, Newfoundland, and Labrador. Two other important steps taken by the new Canada were the creation of the Royal Mounted Police and the beginning of the transcontinental railroad.

9. One of the major concerns about the Act of Union was which of the following?

   (A) It did not preserve the heritage and culture of Quebec.

   (B) It gave two areas the same vote even though the populations of the two areas were not the same.

   (C) It allowed for no more than two parties in the Canadian political system.

   (D) It united all of Canada under a new government and not under the British monarch.

Upper and Lower Canada received equal representation, but the populations of the two were not equal, thus making the representation unfair. **The correct answer is (B).**

10. Which of the following statements best defines *confederation*?

    (A) Confederation meant that Canada would no longer have ties with Britain.

    (B) Confederation meant that Britain and Canada would become united as one nation under God.

    (C) Confederation meant that the Canadian provinces would be loosely united but still under the monarch.

    (D) Confederation meant that some of the Canadian provinces would secede from the British Empire the way the Southern states did in the United States.

Confederation meant that the provinces would be united, but they would remain under the control of the British monarch. **The correct answer is (C).**

Industrialization and Immigration

The late 1800s proved to be a time of industrial growth for many parts of Canada. Many cities located along the railroad benefited by having their goods shipped by rail. The main areas of industrial growth were in Montreal and Ontario. The populations in those two cities grew as people flocked to the cities in search of work. Many people made the transition from rural workers to urban wage laborers. This brought with it organized labor in the form of unions. The Atlantic cities, however, suffered during this time because their wooden ships were becoming obsolete due to the new steel ships. The government also implemented tariffs during this time to help boost the Canadian economy. Another economic boost to the Canadian economy was the discovery of gold in the Yukon Territory just before the turn of the century. People rushed by the thousands to the Yukon Territory to seek their fortunes. Further economic boosts came with the development of Canada's natural mineral and hydroelectric resources in central Canada.

As the economy boomed in Canada at the turn of the twentieth century, immigrants flocked to Canada. Many of these immigrants moved to Canada from Britain and the United States. However, for the first time, many immigrants moved to Canada from other European nations, particularly from Eastern Europe. The Canadian government granted many tracts of land in the far west to the immigrants, and the immigrants began to develop the frontier. Many Canadians distrusted the immigrants who did not come from Britain, though. This fear and distrust caused backlash against the immigrants several times in the late 1800s and the early 1900s.

Canada, the British Empire, and Problems in Quebec

In the 1890s, a new Prime Minister adopted the popular Conservative political view that Canada should stand by the British Empire no matter what, even in matters of imperialism, or expansion into other lands. This policy was popular with most of the Canadians of British descent, but many of the French-speaking Canadians strongly opposed the policy. When Great Britain entered the Boer War in South Africa, many Canadians were ready to fight alongside the British. However, the French-speaking population opposed the popular policy because they were not willing to fight in Britain's wars on other continents. Furthermore, the French-speaking Canadians, most of whom were in Quebec, believed that the rest of Canada did not respect them, which caused a deep rift between Quebec and the other provinces.

The Canadian government felt pressure from both French and British Canadians over the extent to which Canada should help the British Empire. In 1910, Britain expected Canada to contribute to its navy. Instead of contributing, Canada built a small fleet of its own to sail alongside the British navy. Popular opinion turned to outrage again when Canada ratified a treaty with the United States that reduced tariffs and duties, a treaty that U.S. officials saw as a step toward the annexation of Canada. The people of Canada expressed their displeasure, which led to the Conservative Party winning the election of 1911.

In 1914, the British declared war on Germany. This meant that all British holdings, including Canada, were at war, too. Canada responded quickly to Britain's call and sent tens of thousand of Canadians to help with the war effort. The war had a huge impact on Canada. The government imposed Canada's first income tax in 1917. Also, women replaced men in the factories and subsequently earned the right to vote. Another result of the war was the increased tension between Quebec and the rest of Canada. One of the biggest points of contention was the conscription, or draft, that began in 1918. This draft practically split the country because it proved to Quebec that English-speaking Canada would ignore French-speaking Canada in matters of national importance.

After the war, Canadians felt a deeper sense of nationalism than they ever had before, due mostly to the large number of Canadian casualties in the war. Canada began to act as an independent, sovereign nation during treaty negotiations. In 1926, the British government acknowledged Canada's equality with Great Britain. Then, in 1931, Canada was declared a sovereign state; however, it remained under the British monarch.

11. Which of the following was a result of industrialization in Canada?

(A) People moved from urban areas to rural areas in search of jobs.

(B) People moved from rural areas to urban areas in search of jobs.

(C) Railroads were built after Canada completed all of its factories.

(D) Millions of people lost their jobs because machines replaced humans at work.

People moved from the country into cities to find work in factories. **The correct answer is (B).**

12. Which of the following was a major concern of Quebec during the late eighteenth and early nineteenth centuries?

(A) Quebec feared that the United States would annex its territory.

(B) Quebec feared that the rest of Canada did not respect its heritage and culture and, therefore, did not respect Quebec in important matters.

(C) Quebec feared that French would be outlawed within its own borders.

(D) Quebec feared that all its inhabitants would be drafted for World War I.

English-speaking Canada often ignored the needs and wants of French-speaking Quebec. **The correct answer is (B).**

The Twentieth Century After World War I

Canada faced many problems after the First World War. Returning soldiers had a difficult time returning to a normal life in Canada. The economy did not boom during the 1920s in Canada as it did in the United States. Industry had difficulty making the transition from wartime production to peacetime production. Unemployment was high, and labor unrest loomed large, especially in the Atlantic regions. To make matters worse, Canada felt the effects of the Great Depression immediately. Many of Canada's trade partners closed their doors to Canadian goods, and foreign investors no longer had money to invest in Canada.

Even though the economic decline slowed in the 1930s, the economy did not fully recover until World War II. Canada was initially hesitant to become involved in the war, but the government felt it had no other choice. As the war progressed, the government put the issue of conscription to a vote by the people. All of Canada, with the exception of Quebec, favored the draft. Canada launched a major war effort, and the economy bounced back and did well during the war years.

After the war, the Canadian government moved more and more toward governmental control of the economic and financial aspects of the country. Government spending increased to compensate for the lack of business investments in Canada. A number of major social programs, including medical insurance and health care, were launched in the twenty years after the war. The economy boomed because Canada suddenly found itself with a seemingly endless number of markets for Canadian goods in Europe. Both industry and the population increased greatly after the soldiers returned from the war. Also after the war, Canada joined the North Atlantic Treaty Organization (NATO) and played an increased role in international politics.

Problems in Quebec refused to go away, even after World War II. Many in Quebec wanted to break away from English-speaking Canada. Quebec wanted self-government and reduced Canadian control over affairs within Quebec. The situation in Quebec came to a head in the early 1970s when terrorism, kidnappings, and mass arrests occurred as a result of the Quebec dispute. Other provinces and indigenous peoples followed the lead of Quebec and demanded more provincial control and less national control over provincial affairs.

In 1982, Canada cut its final formal legislative ties with Britain by earning the right to amend its constitution. In 1987, the subject of Quebec came up again. Quebec asked for special legislation that would protect its special culture and heritage. The accord, however, did not survive. Again in 1992, Canada had an opportunity to recognize Quebec as a "distinct society," yet, that, too, failed to succeed. Throughout the 1990s, Quebec talked of secession, but the highest court in the land declared secession unconstitutional.

Indigenous peoples did reap one reward in the late 1990s as a new province, Nunavut, was added. In addition, Canada established a Healing Fund to help apologize to the indigenous peoples for the many years of injustice. Even today, the subjects of indigenous peoples' rights and an independent Quebec are at the forefront of Canadian issues.

13. Which of the following can be said of Canada after World War I?

    (A) Canada strengthened its ties to Great Britain.

    (B) Canada moved to cut all ties with Great Britain.

    (C) Canada cut some of the last ties with Great Britain.

    (D) Canada had the strongest military in the Western Hemisphere.

Although Canada did cut some ties, it remained under the British monarch after World War I and remains so even today. **The correct answer is (C).**

14. Which of the following is true of Canada immediately after World War II?

    (A) The Canadian economy declined tremendously because of the Canadian war efforts.

    (B) The Canadian economy boomed because of an increase in foreign markets for Canadian goods.

    (C) Canada's role in international politics dwindled until Canada no longer had any input in the international political arena.

    (D) Canada's population doubled because of Eastern European immigration.

Following World War II, Canada shipped many of its goods to the war-torn countries of Europe. **The correct answer is (B).**

SUMMING IT UP

- The GED® Social Studies Test is designed to measure critical-thinking skills rather than knowledge. However, reviewing the four content areas covered on the test—history, civics and government, economics, and geography—will help you handle the questions with greater ease and confidence.

- The history review focuses mainly on U.S. history, although some of that history is presented in the context of the world affairs and relations between the United States and other nations.

- The Social Studies Test will contain an excerpt from at least one of the following historical documents: the Declaration of Independence, the U.S. Constitution, the Federalist Papers, or landmark Supreme Court cases. Before you take the Social Studies Test, read through parts (if not all) of each of these documents to familiarize yourself with their language and style.

- A review of Canadian government, civics, and history is also provided here for those students preparing to take the GED® test in Canada.

PART V

THE SCIENCE TEST

Mastering the
Science Test

chapter 9

OVERVIEW

- All about the science test
- What's tested—and what's *not* tested
- Formats used for GED® science questions
- Subject areas for GED® science questions
- Question types based on the four skill areas
- Application questions
- Questions based on visual depictions
- General test-taking strategies
- Summing it up

THE SCIENCE TEST—IN A NUTSHELL

Total time allowed: 90 minutes

Total number of questions: 30 questions: 20 multiple-choice questions with four answer choices per question and 10 questions that involve manipulating presentations with the computer cursor and supplying short answers in various ways.

Format: Each question is based on a text passage and/or visual depiction

Length of text passages: Up to 250 words (but most are 2 to 4 sentences)

Number of questions per passage or visual: 1 to 4 (1 or 2 is most common)

ALL ABOUT THE SCIENCE TEST

The broad academic field of science includes a wide variety of subjects, all involving the **natural sciences** (as opposed to the social sciences, which are covered on the Social Studies Test). These subjects include life science (biology), earth science (geology and oceanography), space science (astronomy), and physical science (chemistry and physics). The GED® Science Test is designed to measure a variety of abilities within the context of all of these subject areas. The test consists of 30 questions. Here's the breakdown in terms of the subject areas that the test covers (percentages and numbers may vary slightly):

45% (13 or 14 questions)	Life science (biology)
20% (6 questions)	Earth science and astronomy
35% (10 or 11 questions)	Physical science (chemistry and physics)

The test questions are *not* grouped by content area. Instead, questions from all areas listed above are mixed together.

WHAT'S TESTED—AND WHAT'S *NOT* TESTED

The most important point to keep in mind about the GED® Science Test is that it is *not* primarily a knowledge test. Regardless of content area—life science, earth or space science, or physical science—all but the most basic information you'll need to answer a question will be provided. That said, the test assumes, or presupposes, a certain level of common knowledge about the physical world around us. For example:

- That all animals require food, which they convert to energy, in order to grow and survive
- That gravity works to keep us grounded, and that Earth has an atmosphere of air, which becomes thinner with altitude
- That the Moon revolves around the Earth, which revolves around the Sun in 365 days
- That water freezes (or melts) and vaporizes (boils) at different temperatures
- That pushing an object up a steep incline requires more total force than pushing it across flat ground

But beyond these sorts of everyday facts, which most people know from observation and experience, no specific knowledge of science is required to perform well on the test. (In this respect, the GED® Science Test is a lot like the GED® Social Studies and Reasoning Through Language Arts Tests.) Rather than demonstrating subject knowledge, your primary task during the Science Test will be to apply the following skills:

- Comprehension (recalling and understanding)
- Analysis (drawing inferences and conclusions)
- Evaluation (synthesizing)
- Application (applying concepts and ideas to other situations)

Though the Science Test is designed to measure skills rather than knowledge, keep in mind that with some prior knowledge of the subject areas covered on the test, you can expect to handle the questions with greater ease and confidence.

FORMATS USED FOR GED® TEST SCIENCE QUESTIONS

The GED® Science Test consists of 20 multiple-choice questions and 10 questions in other formats. Each multiple-choice question lists four choices. The other formats involve manipulating presentations with the computer cursor and supplying short answers in various ways. Most questions are based on brief passages of text, which vary in length from a few sentences to as many as 250 words (about one third of a page). A question involving a passage of text might refer to it either as a "passage" or as "information" or "text." The remaining questions will be based on graphs, charts, tables, diagrams, illustrations, and other visual depictions. Some visual depictions will be accompanied by a brief passage of text. Finally, some of the questions will be presented in groups of two to four (two is most common); all questions in a group are based on the same passage and/or visual depiction.

The formats other than multiple choice will include two each of the following:

- **Hot Spot:** Click on a value on a number scale to indicate a numerical answer to a question.

- **Drag and Drop:** Use the cursor to move objects, words, or numbers across the screen to positions that answer the question.

- **Short Answer:** Type a brief written statement from the length of a phrase to a few short sentences.

- **Fill in the Blank:** Type words or numbers in one or more blank spaces to correctly complete a statement.

- **Drop Down:** Like fill in the blank, except that the choices for the blanks are selected from items on drop down menus.

SUBJECT AREAS FOR GED® TEST SCIENCE QUESTIONS

As outlined earlier, the subject areas you'll encounter on the Science Test include life science (biology), earth and space science, and physical science (chemistry and physics). Here you can take a brief survey of each area.

Don't be intimidated by the scope of any one of these subject areas, or by the technical terminology and complex concepts they often involve. Rest assured: The GED® covers only the most basic concepts taught in basic high school science classes. And, as noted earlier, all technical definitions and other information you'll need to answer the questions will be provided. Remember: the GED® Science Test is not a trivia or science knowledge quiz; rather, its main purpose is to measure your reading and critical-thinking skills within the context of science subject matter.

Life Science (Biology)

Biology can be defined as the scientific study of living organisms, including plants and animals. Biology is a broad and deep field, which is why a greater portion of GED® science questions involves biology than any of the other fields. One way to break down this vast field of study is into its three major branches:

Zoology: the scientific study of *animals*, including their structural characteristics, physiology (vital functions for growth, sustenance, and development), reproduction, and pathology (diseases)

Botany: the scientific study of *plants*, including their structural characteristics, physiology (vital functions for growth, sustenance, and development), reproduction, and pathology (diseases)

Ecology: the scientific study of how plants and animals interact with their environment

Another way to break down the field of biology is by scale:

Cellular biology involves the cell as the basic structural unit of living matter

Molecular biology involves the structure and actions of proteins and nucleic enzymes as well as heredity and how organisms process the energy needed to sustain life

Organism biology explores the individual forms of life (for example, an oak tree or a human being)

Population biology studies the organism as a member of a community and as part of an environment, or ecosystem

Biology questions account for approximately 45 percent of the Science Test—about 13 or 14 questions. Among these questions, there is no set number from each branch listed above, although you can expect a fairly even distribution.

Earth and Space Science

Earth science is the study of origins, composition, and physical features of the Earth. Like life science (biology), earth science can be broken down into various branches:

Geology: the scientific study of the Earth's rocks, minerals, land forms, and the processes that have directed them since the Earth's origins

Oceanography: the scientific study of the oceans' physical characteristics and composition, the movement of their waters, and the topography of ocean floors; oceanography also includes the study of ocean life (in this respect, oceanography and biology overlap)

Meteorology: the scientific study of the Earth's atmosphere and of atmospheric conditions (weather and climate)

Mineralogy: a branch of geology that involves the study of minerals—their composition and properties, as well as where they are found and their extraction

Space science refers to the following two related fields:

Astronomy: the scientific study of the universe and of the size, composition, motion, and evolution of celestial bodies (stars, planets, galaxies, and nebula)

Astrophysics: a branch of astronomy that deals with the physical and chemical processes that occur in the universe and in interstellar space, including the structure, evolution, and interactions of stars and systems of stars

On the GED®, questions about earth and space science account for about 20 percent of the test (6 questions). Expect to encounter more questions dealing with earth science than with space science, although there is no fixed proportion.

Physical Science (Chemistry and Physics)

Physical Science includes the fields of chemistry and physics. **Chemistry** is the scientific study of the composition, properties, and interactions (or reactions) of elements and compounds (combinations of elements) and of the changes that elements and compounds undergo.

Physics is the scientific study of matter, energy, space, and time—and how they are interrelated. Physics is closely related to all other fields of science, since its laws are universal. The living systems of biology are made of matter particles that follow the laws of physics. Chemistry explores how atoms, small units of matter, interact to form molecules according to the laws of physics. And, to a great extent, the study of geology and astronomy deals with the physics of the Earth and celestial bodies, respectively.

Chemistry and physics questions account for about 35 percent of the test (10 or 11 questions). Expect about the same number of questions from each of these two fields.

QUESTION TYPES BASED ON THE FOUR SKILL AREAS

To succeed on the GED® Science Test, you will need to demonstrate proficiency in four critical-thinking skill areas: comprehension, application, analysis, and evaluation. You will use all four skills throughout the test. In the next few pages, you'll examine each skill more closely. Note that the GED®-style example questions here are all based on passages of text, rather than on visual depictions. In the next section, you'll learn how to handle questions involving visuals.

Comprehension Questions

Comprehension questions require that you read and recall information contained in a passage. The material to be comprehended may include science text, data, illustrations, or symbols. And in most cases, they also require that you *understand* and *interpret* that information—in other words, to grasp or comprehend—the ideas and concepts that the passage's words convey. Some comprehension questions will require you to understand the main idea of a passage, much like a main-idea question in the reading comprehension portion of the Reasoning Through Language Arts Test. To handle this sort of question, look for an answer choice that sums up the passage. However, most comprehension questions on the Science Test focus instead on the passage's details.

Comprehension questions usually involve passages of text that are longer than average—at least four or five sentences and sometimes more than one paragraph. You may discover that you need to read the passage more than once to answer these questions. That's perfectly okay, since the total time allowed for taking the test, 90 minutes, should provide enough time for you to read the passages more than once.

Though the correct answer choice might restate a phrase from the passage word-for-word, more likely it will either paraphrase or provide an interpretation of passage information. In other words, comprehension questions typically focus on a passage's *ideas* rather than on exactly how those ideas are expressed. Incorrect answer choices will often contradict passage information or provide assertions that are unsupported by the passage or that do not respond to the specific question that is asked.

Don't make comprehension questions more difficult than the test-makers intend them to be. These questions are not meant to trick you, to test your ability to find underlying, "hidden" meanings within the language of the text, or to find out which test-takers already possess in-depth knowledge of the complexities of the science topic at hand. To understand how comprehension questions require merely that you understand and interpret what you've read in a passage, study the following two example questions. Both questions are based on a brief passage involving physics.

QUESTIONS 1 AND 2 REFER TO THE FOLLOWING INFORMATION.

Light travels in waves consisting of vibrating electric and magnetic fields. Stronger vibrations cause an increase in brightness. The frequencies of the waves can also be different. Blue light, for example, has a higher frequency than red light, and the distance between its vibrations, or its wavelength, is shorter than the wavelength of red light. Black is the absence of light, and white light is the mixture of all colors. When white light passes through a prism, it is split into a band of colors called the spectrum.

1. Which statement is best supported by the information?

(A) Short waves have a stronger magnetic field than longer waves do.

(B) Light waves vibrate more strongly and at a higher frequency than sound waves do.

(C) White light, which lacks any color, has no measurable wavelength or wave frequency.

(D) Short waves have higher frequencies than longer waves do.

This question focuses on the idea that frequencies among different colors of light waves vary. To illustrate this idea, the passage points out that a blue light wave has a higher frequency and a shorter length than a red wave does. Choice (D) provides a more general way of making this point. In other words, it captures the idea conveyed in the third and fourth sentences.

Let's briefly examine the other three answer choices. The passage makes no connection between magnetism and wave frequency, choice (A), and it never mentions sound waves, choice (B). As for choice (C), it contradicts the passage, which tells us that white light is a mixture of all colors—not that it lacks color. Besides, the passage does not state, nor does it suggest, that the frequency or length of a white light wave cannot be measured. **The correct answer is (D).**

> **2.** Which of the following explains why a rainbow occurs when drops of water act as a prism?
>
> **(A)** A rainbow is made up of white light.
>
> **(B)** There are a number of frequencies involved.
>
> **(C)** White light from the sun is dispersed through the drops.
>
> **(D)** The electric and magnetic fields have strong vibrations.

Answering this question requires that you read and understand the last sentence of the passage. Don't let the fact that the question involves a rainbow, which is not mentioned in the passage, confuse you. The question simply requires that you interpret a rainbow as one way to see the color spectrum—the band of colors mentioned in the paragraph's last sentence. The drops of water act as a prism when the white light from the sun is dispersed through the water; the drops split the light into bands of color. Of course, to answer this question you need to know what a rainbow looks like. But this is just the sort of common, everyday knowledge that the GED® Science Test presumes you have. Choice (C) appears to provide a good explanation.

Let's examine the four other answer choices. Choice (A) is incorrect because we all know that a rainbow shows many colors. Choice (B) provides an accurate statement in that different color bands of the spectrum have different frequencies. But choice (B) does not explain why this occurs—in other words, it does not respond to the question. Choice (D) is incorrect because the passage makes no connection between a magnetic field (mentioned only in the first sentence) and a prism. **The correct answer is (C).**

The preceding two questions demonstrate the sort of wrong-answer choices to look for in comprehension questions. Be on the lookout for any answer choice that contradicts the passage information, goes off the passage's topic, or provides true information that nevertheless does not answer the specific question asked.

Analysis Questions

Analysis questions go beyond understanding the information in a passage or visual. Analysis involves organizing the information; explaining how ideas, facts, or data connect together; identifying patterns; and drawing inferences and conclusions from the information given. Many analysis questions will require you to *infer* cause or effect in terms of a biological, chemical, or physical process. (To infer is to draw a reasonable conclusion based on certain information.) Other analysis questions will require you to point out similarities and differences between two or more types of organisms, processes, or other scientific phenomena. You might also be asked to identify sources of error in an investigation or cite evidence to support a scientific claim. These are just some of many possibilities for analysis questions.

The next question is based on a passage involving botany (a branch of biology). To analyze the question, you need to first understand different facts and then connect those facts together in order to draw a logical conclusion from them.

QUESTION 3 REFERS TO THE FOLLOWING INFORMATION.

All of the Earth's energy is produced through photosynthesis, which is the process by which green plants, algae, and some bacteria take light from the sun and convert it to chemical energy. Only organisms that contain chlorophyll can undergo photosynthesis. Chlorophyll is the pigment that makes plants green. The process of photosynthesis usually occurs in the leaves of plants.

3. What can you conclude from the information?

   (A) If a plant does not have leaves, it cannot produce energy.

   (B) If a plant is not green, it cannot produce energy.

   (C) On cloudy days, photosynthesis does not occur.

   (D) Photosynthesis does not occur in the winter.

The paragraph does not answer this question explicitly. To answer the question, you must draw an inference, or conclusion, from the information provided. According to the paragraph, only organisms with chlorophyll can undergo photosynthesis—the process by which plants produce energy—and it is chlorophyll that gives plants their green color. Thus, you can conclude that only green plants produce energy. Stated differently, this process cannot occur in anything other than a green plant, choice (B).

Compared to choice (B), the other answer choices provide unreasonable, poorly supported conclusions based on the information provided. Choice (A) goes too far, by assuming that chlorophyll exists only in the *leaves* of plants. But the paragraph does not say this is so, and our everyday observations suggest otherwise. For example, most of us have observed the green color in pine needles, which are not leaves. In order for choice (C) or choice (D) to be correct, you must assume that absolutely no light is available for photosynthesis on cloudy days, choice (C), or during the winter, choice (D). These are not reasonable assumptions, as they violate common sense as well as our everyday experience. **The correct answer is (B).**

The next question is based on a passage involving astronomy. To analyze the question, you first need to understand and organize various facts about two different things. Then you need to analyze the differences between those two things.

QUESTION 4 IS BASED ON THE FOLLOWING INFORMATION.

Like Earth, Mercury—the smallest planet—revolves around the Sun. It takes nearly 88 days to make one revolution around the Sun. Earth takes 365 days to complete one revolution around the Sun. Earth completes one revolution on its own axis in 24 hours, or one day. Mercury, on the other hand, takes 58.5 Earth days to slowly make one turn on its axis.

> **4.** Based on the information, which is an accurate distinction between Mercury and Earth?
>
> **(A)** Any spot on Mercury's equator is sunlit longer than any spot on Earth's equator.
>
> **(B)** Earth passes Mercury as they both revolve around the Sun.
>
> **(C)** Mercury's orbit around the Sun is circular, whereas Earth's orbit is elliptical.
>
> **(D)** Mercury orbits the Sun at a slower speed than Earth does.

Any spot on the surface of Mercury's equator is exposed to the Sun for longer periods of time because it takes Mercury 58.5 Earth days to make one turn on its axis. (A spot on Mercury's equator faces the Sun for approximately 29 hours at a time, whereas on Earth the maximum is approximately 12 hours.) So answer choice (A) is a good answer.

Let's examine the other three choices. Choice (B) contradicts the information in the passage. Choice (C) is completely unsupported by the passage, which tells us nothing about the shape of either orbit. Choice (D) is more difficult to assess than the others. We know from the paragraph that Mercury orbits the Sun in fewer days than Earth does. But does this mean that Mercury is moving at a faster or slower speed than Earth? We don't know, at least not from the information provided. The answer depends not only on the time of one orbit around the Sun but also on the distance traveled during one such orbit. The passage does not give enough information to compare the speed of the two planets. **The correct answer is (A).**

The preceding questions demonstrate the sort of answer choices to be wary of when handling analysis questions:

- A choice that contradicts the passage information
- A choice that relies on crucial facts that the passage does not provide
- A choice that violates common sense or simple logic
- A choice that is inconsistent with your everyday observations and experiences

Synthesis and Evaluation Questions

Synthesis and evaluation questions involve drawing general assessments and conclusions from specific information. To "synthesize" science information is to understand what various pieces of information mean when you consider them all together, as a whole. In the context of the Science Test, a synthesis question might ask you to characterize a phenomena, process, or system described in a passage. An evaluation question might ask you to recognize a potential benefit or drawback with a new science technology, or with the way that technology is applied. Or it might ask you to recognize a flaw in a scientific claim or hypothesis, possibly related to a certain experiment, or to assess the features of an experimental design. Other possible synthesis questions might require reasoning from data to evidence, making a prediction based on data, evaluating a theory, or reconciling multiple findings.

In handling these questions, what's just as important as recognizing a reasonable assessment or conclusion is recognizing unfair assessments and conclusions. Be on the lookout for wrong-answer choices that speculate too much—answer choices that jump to conclusions that are unwarranted based solely on the information provided.

Here is a synthesis question based on a passage involving mineralogy, one of the earth sciences.

QUESTION 5 REFERS TO THE FOLLOWING INFORMATION.

There are three types of rocks on the Earth's surface: igneous, metamorphic, and sedimentary. Igneous rocks have been formed by the cooling of molten magma where temperatures are extremely high. Metamorphic rocks have been formed by the compression of older rocks. They are formed below the surface of the Earth where both the temperature and pressure are high. Sedimentary rocks are formed by weathering or the remains of living organisms. These are formed on the surface of the Earth under low pressures.

5. Based on the information, which of the following is most probably true about the three types of rock?

The three types of rocks

(A) can be found only on Earth

(B) look very much the same

(C) are found in different places

(D) are all approximately the same age

This question doesn't focus on just one part of the passage. To answer it, you instead need to read and understand all the details, and then synthesize them to form a broader perspective. The passage tells us that some rocks are formed below the surface of the Earth, that some come from volcanoes, and that some are the result of weathering or the remains of living organisms that have been found in different locations. Because the three types of rocks are all formed differently under different conditions, they cannot all be found in the same location. Choice (C) is a good answer.

Let's examine the other answer choices. The passage mentions nothing about whether these types of rocks are found on other celestial bodies, choice (A); about what the three types look like, choice (B); or their relative ages, choice (D). **The correct answer is (C).**

Next, look at an evaluation question based on a passage involving meteorology, another one of the earth sciences.

QUESTION 6 REFERS TO THE FOLLOWING INFORMATION.

Water moves through a natural cycle of evaporation, cloud formation, rainfall, collection, and evaporation. In this cycle, water is self-purifying. Thus, smoke from industrial sites that is brought to earth by rainfall is not a problem because the water purifies itself of the pollutants.

6. Which of the following, if true, would weaken the claim that water purifies itself through the cycle described above?

(A) The polluters creating the industrial smoke are unwilling to reduce the amount of their pollution.

(B) When the pollutants enter the clouds, much of them stay there.

(C) Many of the pollutants evaporate with ground water into the air.

(D) Water vapor containing industrial pollutants can travel great distances through the air.

This question asks you to assess, or critique, the assertion made in the brief passage. Your task is to recognize additional evidence that would weaken the conclusion that the smoke is not a problem because the water purifies itself. The passage describes a self-purifying cycle. But if smoke from industrial sites is brought back to the Earth by rainfall and then evaporates with the water, it will return to the clouds where it becomes part of the cycle. In this event, the water would not purify itself properly. So choice (C) provides information that, if true, would weaken the conclusion in the passage.

Let's examine the other answer choices. Choice (A) is incorrect because the fact the industrial pollution carries on does nothing to disprove the claim that water rids itself of that pollution. The statement in choice (B), if true, would actually make the purification cycle easier, since the pollutants would not cycle around with the water. Choice (D) is incorrect because the distance that the pollutants travel before falling to the Earth in rain has nothing to do with the process of evaporation—water can evaporate anywhere. **The correct answer is (C).**

APPLICATION QUESTIONS

Application questions require you to use information in a passage (or visual) in a way that is different from the way it is presented to you. For example, a question might ask about the effect of a particular biological or chemical process or a law of physics under specific conditions. Or, a question might ask you to identify an example or a practical use of a concept, principle, or process. You might also be asked to apply sampling techniques, models, theories, formulas, or statistical analysis to solve a problem or make a prediction. These are just some of the possibilities. Use your understanding of the information in the passage, along with your everyday experience and common sense, to identify the correct answer.

Here are two application questions involving physics.

QUESTION 7 REFERS TO THE FOLLOWING INFORMATION.

A fluid can exert a buoyant force, helping an object to float, but it can also exert a compressing force because of the weight of the fluid above it. The suit of a deep-sea diver resembles a rigid suit of armor that is water-tight and can maintain an internal pressure of 1 atmosphere.

7. Why do deep-sea divers wear water-tight rigid suits?

   (A) They protect a diver from high levels of surrounding external pressure.

   (B) They make a diver more buoyant in the water.

   (C) They allow a diver to defy gravity.

   (D) They keep a diver from drowning in case there is a leak in his suit.

The information to be taken from the passage and applied is that pressure increases with depth. It is logical that this is dangerous to a diver. The only protection against external pressure would be a rigid, water-tight enclosure. Noting the similarity to the design of submarines is helpful. The explanation provided by choice (A) makes sense.

Let's examine the other three answer choices. The suit might make the diver more buoyant, choice (B), which means that it would help the diver to float. But deep-sea divers want to go deep into the water rather than float, and so it makes no sense that a diving suit would be used mainly for buoyancy. You can eliminate choice (C) for essentially the same reason. Choice (D) asserts essentially the same reason: the air in the suit can be used for breathing. But this function has nothing to do with external water pressure, which the passage indicates is the reason for the design of this type of suit. **The correct answer is (A).**

QUESTION 8 REFERS TO THE FOLLOWING INFORMATION.

Newton's First Law: An object will remain in motion or in a state of rest unless something influences it and changes its course. (This property is referred to as inertia.)

Newton's Second Law: The change of motion is proportional to the force of change. (The greater the applied force, the greater the change in motion.)

Newton's Third Law: For every action (or applied force) there is an equal and opposite reaction.

8. Which is an example of Newton's Second Law?

   (A) two shopping carts colliding in a grocery store

   (B) the whiplash you would experience in a car by suddenly applying the brake

   (C) a car coming to a stop at a stop sign

   (D) allowing air to escape from a balloon

The force applied by the brakes causes a change in the motion of the car, so choice (C) seems an apt illustration of Newton's Second Law.

Let's examine the other answer choices. Choice (A) is an example of the first law, while choices (B) and (D) are examples of the third law. **The correct answer is (C).**

QUESTIONS BASED ON VISUAL DEPICTIONS

The GED® Science Test is more visually oriented than any of the other tests in the GED® battery. Nearly half of the questions on the Science Test will be based on a visual depiction of some sort. Some of these questions will also be accompanied by a brief passage of text. The "visual" might be a chart, graph, or table displaying quantitative information (data); it might be a flow chart showing a biological or chemical system or process; it might be a diagram or table that organizes information into classes, categories, or characteristics; it might provide a sequence of illustrations showing multiple steps, phases, or stages in a biological, geological, or chemical process, or it may be a drawing, photo, or even a cartoon showing science as it applies to our everyday lives.

Questions based on visuals are designed to gauge your ability to understand what these visuals depict and what they mean, to analyze the information they contain, and to apply them to real-world situations. Even if you do not recognize a visual or don't understand it initially, you can still figure out the best answer to the question at hand by looking for clues in the visual, the accompanying text (if any), and the question itself.

In the following pages, you'll examine some of the types of visuals appearing frequently on the test. You'll see some examples of each type and learn how to handle them.

Illustrations That Include Arrow Symbols

The arrow symbol is used extensively in the Science Test. Arrows are used in physics questions to show the direction of physical flow or travel, as from a light or sound source, and to show the direction of pressure or other force on an object. Arrows are used in astronomy questions to show direction of travel, rotation, and orbit. Arrows are used in earth science and biology questions to indicate flow and circulation in oceans, the atmosphere, organ systems, and ecosystems. Arrows are even used in chemistry questions to indicate chemical reactions.

Pay careful attention to any arrows in an illustration, as you can be sure that they will be crucial to answer the question at hand. Note whether an arrow is pointing:

- Upward (against gravity) or downward (pulled by gravity)

- Toward or away from an object (possibly suggesting the direction of a force)

- In a straight line versus a bent line (which might suggest *reflection, deflection,* or *refraction*)

- Through an opening versus a membrane or wall (which might suggest *permeability*)

- In a one-way circular pattern (possibly suggesting *rotation* or a continuous *cycle*)

- In each of two opposite directions (possibly suggesting an *exchange* of energy, gases, liquids, etc.)

- In a single, continuous line versus a line that splits in different directions (which might suggest a *dispersion* pattern for light or sound waves, or the dispersion of atoms or molecules)

QUESTIONS 9 AND 10 REFER TO THE FOLLOWING ILLUSTRATION AND BRIEF PASSAGE OF TEXT.

The following diagram illustrates three types of levers. All three are dependent on the effort (E), load (L), and fulcrum (F). Any lever in which the load and effort balance each other is said to be in equilibrium.

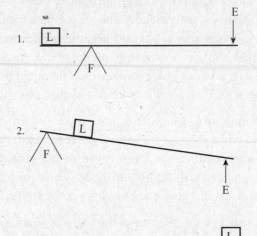

9. Which general principle do all three illustrations help demonstrate?

(A) The function of a fulcrum is to balance effort and load.

(B) Effort and load are equal physical forces.

(C) A load is pulled down toward the Earth by effort and gravity.

(D) Effort and load are opposing physical forces.

To answer this question, you need to compare the pictures and note their similarities and differences. In all three pictures, the fulcrum provides a fixed point of rotation for the plank and the load. Apply your common sense and everyday experience to visualize what is happening in each picture. Pictures 2 and 3 show the effort pushing *up* to counteract the weight of the load. Picture 1 shows a *downward* effort that serves to push the load *up*, as in a seesaw. So in all three pictures, the effort and load are opposing physical forces. Choice (D) is a good answer, but let's examine the other three answer choices. Only in Picture 1 does the fulcrum balance the effort and the load, and so choice (A) is an incorrect general principle. None of the three pictures assumes that the effort and load are equal in force, and so choice (B) provides an unfair generalization. Choice (C) is only partially correct. It is true that the gravity works to push the load downward; however, all three pictures show the effort working to lift the load upward. **The correct answer is (D).**

10. Which of the following provides one example of each of the three types of levers shown in the three pictures, in the order they are shown?

(A) pliers; diving board; crane

(B) hammer; wedge; seesaw

(C) crowbar; wheelbarrow; baseball bat

(D) saw; forklift; bottle opener

To answer this question, you need to interpret what is happening in each of the three pictures by applying your sense of how physical forces operate in the real world. Notice that Picture 1 shows a seesaw type of lever: you apply downward effort at one end of the rigid object, and move the load on the other side of the fulcrum upward. A crowbar works in the same way. Picture 2 resembles a wheelbarrow, where the fulcrum is the wheel. Lifting from the far right, where the handles are located, reduces the effort needed to lift the load up from the ground. Focusing on Picture 3, imagine yourself applying effort near the pivoting fulcrum thereby magnifying the speed with which the other end of the rigid object moves in the same direction as your effort. You are imagining how tools such as a hammer and a baseball bat work. As your grip on the hammer or bat moves farther up toward the load (the nail or ball), the magnifying effect of your effort diminishes. **The correct answer is (C).**

Graphical Data Displays

Several questions on the Science Test are based on data presented in graphical format. A question of this type might be based on a table, bar graph, line chart, or circle graph (pie chart). These displays may be used for any of the subject areas covered by the test.

This book's Mathematics lesson explains how to read, interpret, and analyze data presented in each of these formats. Be sure to review those materials when preparing for the GED® Science Test. Keep in mind, however, that on the Science Test the emphasis is not on number-crunching but rather on the following skills:

- Understanding what the graphical display is intended to show

- Reading and interpreting the data

- Understanding the significance of the data

- Drawing general conclusions from the data

- Applying the ideas conveyed by the display to specific scenarios

Though you may need to perform simple arithmetic tasks such as counting or adding, you won't need to calculate precise percents, ratios, or averages. (These skills are measured on the Mathematical Reasoning Test instead.)

The next two GED®-style questions both illustrate that the focus of data-display questions on the Science Test is far more on understanding and interpreting scientific data than on performing math on the data.

QUESTION 11 REFERS TO THE FOLLOWING ILLUSTRATION.

(STARFIELD)

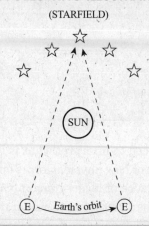

11. The diagram shows the arrangement of several celestial objects. Which INCORRECT perception of such objects does this diagram illustrate?

(A) The Moon grows larger and smaller over the course of a month.

(B) The stars move across the night sky during the course of the year.

(C) Earth's orbit is perfectly circular.

(D) The sun does not give off light at night.

The figure shows the Earth moving through an arc of its orbit. As it circles the sun, the positions of the stars appear at different places in the night sky as if they were orbiting Earth. The illusion is caused by the sensation that the earth under feet is fixed in place. **The correct answer is (C).**

QUESTION 12 REFERS TO THE FOLLOWING INFORMATION AND CHART.

Cell metabolism, the creation of energy by the processing of glucose and other sugars at the cellular level, can be accomplished either (A) in the presence of oxygen, through the process of aerobic respiration, or (B) without oxygen, through the process of anaerobic respiration.

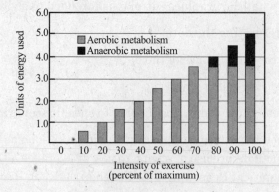

12. What can you infer from the information presented above?

(A) Intense exercise uses more anaerobically metabolized energy than light exercise.

(B) Most of the energy you spend is through some form of exercise.

(C) The longer you exercise, the more fuel you metabolize anaerobically.

(D) Intense exercise requires less oxygen than moderate exercise.

This question requires application of the information displayed in the graph to everyday physical activity. Only choice (A) has the possibility of reaching high intensity. Some of the others use a large total amount of energy, but none of them have the possibility of reaching high intensity. **The correct answer is (A).**

Illustrations That Show Spatial Relationships

Some questions on the Science Test focus on how the physical world around us (as well as inside us) arranges itself spatially. Showing where different distinct objects or other masses are located in relation to one another is usually best accomplished with a visual depiction, which might show, for example:

- Locations and distances involving celestial bodies

- Layers of the Earth's atmosphere

- Stratification (layering) of rocks, minerals, and sediments that form the Earth

- Configurations of chemical compounds, in which molecules link together in specific ways

- Separation of gases, liquids, or solids, either naturally or in a laboratory experiment

- Layers of cells and tissues in a plant or animal

The possibilities listed above are just some of many. The next GED®-style question involves the earth sciences as well as physics. As with most questions based on both textual and visual information, you'll need both to help you answer the question.

QUESTION 13 REFERS TO THE FOLLOWING DIAGRAM AND INFORMATION.

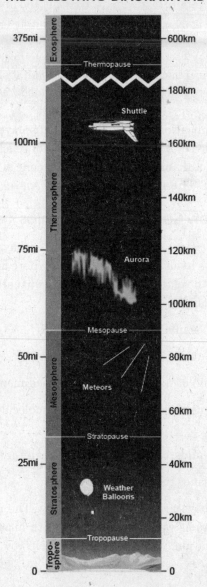

National Oceanic and Atmospheric Administration

Temperature levels fall from ground level to the top of the troposphere, but then they rise with altitude in the stratosphere.

13. Which of the following statements, assuming it is true, would best account for the rise in temperature?

   (A) The troposphere blocks the Sun's rays.

   (B) The surface of the Earth is warming gradually.

   (C) Air is thinner at higher altitudes than at lower ones.

   (D) Gases in the upper stratosphere trap radiant heat from Earth.

One knows from experience that temperature falls with altitude. Pictures of snowcapped mountains in the tropics confirm this. There must be something different about the gases in the stratosphere to reverse this trend, as choice (D) suggests. So choice (D) is a good answer.

Let's examine the other answer choices. Choice (C) does not respond to the question because it does not explain why temperature trend would reverse at upper altitudes. Choice (A) is incorrect because the troposphere is below the stratosphere (as the figure shows) and hence cannot interfere with the amount of sunlight reaching the stratosphere. Choice (B) is incorrect because global warming makes sense as a *result* rather than a cause of the atmosphere's trapping heat. **The correct answer is (D).**

The next GED®-style question involves astronomy and is based solely on visual information. Don't be concerned that it contains very few words to help you interpret it. Rest assured: all you'll need to answer the question, aside from your common sense and everyday experience, is provided in the picture.

QUESTION 14 REFERS TO THE FOLLOWING ILLUSTRATION.

Solar Eclipse

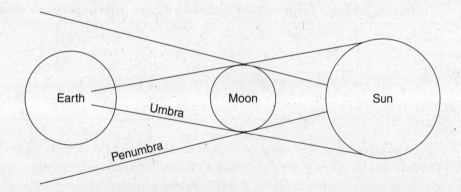

14. Referring to the illustration, what is true during a solar eclipse?

  (A) The Moon appears brightest from within the boundaries of the penumbra.

  (B) The side of the Moon not seen from Earth is cast in darkness.

  (C) Sunlight is dimmest within the field referred to as the umbra.

  (D) The shadow cast by the Earth hides the Moon from our view.

If you are unfamiliar with solar eclipses, use your everyday experience to figure out what is happening in the illustration. You know that when any object is lit from one direction, it casts a shadow in the opposite direction. Use this common knowledge along with the illustration to figure out what happens during a solar eclipse. The Moon is positioned between the Earth and Sun, thereby casting a shadow on the Earth. It makes sense that the area at the center of the shadow (identified in the illustration as the umbra) will be darkest, while the shadow around its periphery (the penumbra) will be somewhat lighter. Choice (C) is a good answer.

Let's examine the other answer choices. Choice (A) contradicts what the illustration shows: the Moon is casting a shadow within the boundaries of the field labeled as the penumbra. Choice (B) contradicts what the illustration shows: the side of the Moon facing away from the Earth is bathed in direct sunlight. Choice (D) is incorrect because the illustration shows the Moon's shadow cast on the Earth, not the other way around. **The correct answer is (C).**

In the preceding example, did you notice that the illustration was accompanied by a title? Remember: some (but not all) illustrations on the Science Test will come with a title or descriptive caption that may help you understand and interpret the illustration.

Math and the GED® Science Test

As noted earlier, though some Science Test questions will involve numbers, you won't be asked to calculate precise ratios, percents, or averages or to do any number-crunching to speak of. Those skills are measured by the Mathematical Reasoning Test. For example, consider the following table, which involves nine celestial bodies within our solar system:

	Mercury	Venus	Earth	Mars	Jupiter	Saturn	Uranus	Neptune	Pluto
Years to revolve around Sun	0.24	0.62	1	1.88	11.86	29.46	84	164.79	247.7
Radius (Earth = 1)	0.38	0.45	1	0.53	11.2	9.42	4.01	3.88	(0.06)

A Mathematical Reasoning Test question based on the data in this table might ask you to calculate a ratio of one radius to another, or it might ask you to calculate a time difference (measured perhaps in Earth days) between one planet's year and another planet's year. But the Science Test would not pose these sorts of questions. Instead, a Science Test question might ask you how many of the celestial bodies other than Earth have a greater radius than that of Earth—or a longer year than Earth's year. Or the question might ask you what kinds of conclusions you can, or cannot, draw from the data. (For instance, the table provides no information about rotation, distance between planets, or distance from the Sun.)

But this does not mean that math plays absolutely no part on the Science Test. For at least a few questions, expect to perform some arithmetic such as counting or adding numbers. For example, a chemistry question might ask for the total mass of a chemical compound, in which case you would add up the atomic masses of the elements that make up the compound, accounting for the number of molecules per element. (Don't worry: the question will provide all the information you need.)

A physics question might ask you to apply the definition of a unit of measurement to a specific situation. Here's a GED®-style example involving *hertz*, which is the unit of measurement used for sound-wave frequency. As you can see, all the information about sound waves you need to answer the question is provided.

QUESTION 15 REFERS TO THE FOLLOWING INFORMATION.

The frequency of a sound wave is measured in units referred to as the *hertz*. One hertz is equal to one wave per second, and 1 kilohertz is equal to 1000 hertz. If you tune your radio dial to 89.0, that number would signify the frequency of the radio station, in kilohertz.

15. What is the frequency of radio waves received at 98.6 on the radio dial?

    (A) 9800 waves per second

    (B) 98,600 waves per second

    (C) 98.6 hertz

    (D) 98,600 hertz

If the radio dial is tuned to 98.6, this would mean that the waves are traveling at 98,600 waves per second because 1 kilohertz is equal to 1000 waves per second: $1000 \times 98.6 = 98,600$. **The correct answer is (B).**

Or, a Science Test question might ask you to apply one of the simple formulas that expresses the basic laws of physics. Here are just some of those formulas:

$$v = \frac{d}{t}$$ 　　　velocity = distance ÷ time

$$a = \frac{9.80 \text{ m}}{s^2}$$ 　　acceleration during freefall = 9.80 m / (number of seconds)²

$$F = m \cdot a$$ 　　　force = mass × acceleration

$$w = F \cdot d$$ 　　　work = force × displacement

$$v = l \cdot f$$ 　　　velocity = wavelength × frequency

$$P = \frac{W}{t}$$ 　　　Power = work ÷ time

Don't worry: you won't need to memorize any formulas for the test. If a question requires you to apply a formula, it will provide that formula, along with the numbers you need to answer the question.

QUESTION 16 REFERS TO THE FOLLOWING INFORMATION.

In an electrical circuit, the amount of voltage is equal to the electric current (measured in amperes) multiplied by total resistance, measured in ohms (Ω). A certain battery generates 8 volts of electricity, which is sent through a wire circuit to a small electric motor. Three resistors, each of which provides 6 ohms (Ω) of resistance, have been placed in the circuit.

16. An object of mass m is at rest until a force, F, acts on it for a period of 10 seconds. Which expression shows the average velocity of the object during those 10 seconds?

(A) $5F$

(B) $10Fm$

(C) $\dfrac{5F}{m}$

(D) $\dfrac{10F}{m}$

$F = ma$, so $a = \dfrac{F}{m}$. $v = at$, and $t = 10$, so final $v = 10a = \dfrac{10F}{m}$. Because acceleration is constant, average $v = $ final $\dfrac{v}{2} = \left(\dfrac{1}{2}\right)\dfrac{10F}{m} = \dfrac{5F}{m}$. **The correct answer is (C).**

GENERAL TEST-TAKING STRATEGIES

Here are some general strategies for tackling the Science Test. Put these strategies to work on the Practice Tests in this book, and then review them again just before exam day.

First read the question(s) based on a passage of text or visual depiction.

Before you look at a visual or read even a brief passage, read the question stem (the question itself, but not the answer choices). If the passage or visual comes with more than one question, read all the question stems first. This task should only take 10 seconds or so. The question(s) may provide clues as to what you should focus on and think about as you read the text or analyze the visual.

Read a passage of text straight through before answering any questions based on it.

If a question or group of questions refers to a passage of text, read the passage from beginning to end without interruption. Pay careful attention to definitions. If more than one term is defined, pay special attention to any differences between the two concepts, processes, or features defined. Think about whether the information in the passage leads logically to a particular conclusion or inference. If it does, the chances are good that you'll be asked about this feature.

Take notes when reading longer passages.

You will be given an erasable note board before you start the test. Use it to jot down key words and phrases and other notes. It will help you find information in the passage you need as you answer the question(s).

When examining visuals that provide quantitative information, don't get bogged down in the data.

A Science Test question may refer to a table, chart, or graph that presents quantitative information. The visual may very well contain more data than you'll need to answer the question(s) based on it. In fact, one of the skills you're being tested on is your ability to sort through that data to determine what is relevant (and what is not relevant) to the question at hand. So don't waste time analyzing every piece of data in a visual. Instead, focus your attention on what the question asks about.

Mine diagrams and illustrations for helpful clues for answering the questions.

Many visuals will include arrows showing cause-and-effect, sequence of events in a process, or direction of motion, energy, or force. Pay special attention to these arrows, as they are often crucial to analyzing the question at hand. Also pay attention to labels used for various objects shown in an illustration. Finally, some visual depictions will come with a descriptive title or caption, which you should use to help you interpret the visual, understand the question, and eliminate incorrect answers.

Make realistic assumptions when interpreting illustrations.

Some questions will involve illustrations depicting aspects of the physical world, but in a simplified manner. Make commonsense assumptions when interpreting these figures. For example, you can assume that lines that appear straight are intended to depict straight lines, that the natural forces of gravity, motion, and energy operate normally, and so forth. In other words, don't try to outsmart the test-makers by splitting hairs; you'll only defeat yourself.

Apply your common sense and real-world experience—up to a limit.

Many questions on the Science Test—whether they involve physics, earth sciences, ecology, biology, chemistry, and even astronomy—deal with phenomena that most of us have observed or experienced in our own lives. Use your life experiences, along with your common sense, to help you answer these questions. But don't use your outside knowledge as a *substitute* for reading and trying to understand the text and/or the visual depiction provided. Rather, use that knowledge to safeguard against selecting answer choices that are contrary to common sense and real-life experience—in other words, that simply don't make sense.

Take care when handling questions stated in the negative.

Some questions may be stated in the negative rather than the affirmative. These questions are likely to use capitalized words in phrases such as "NOT accurate," "EXCEPT which one," or "LEAST likely." These questions are not intended to trick you, but they can be confusing. Take great care not to turn these questions around in your head when answering them.

Pace yourself properly.

You're allowed 90 minutes to answer all 30 questions. GED® Science Test questions are not presented in any set order of difficulty. So after 30 minutes you should have answered at least 12 questions (more than a third of all 30 questions), and after 60 minutes you should have answered at least 24 questions (more than two thirds of all 30 questions). If you're falling behind, pick up the pace. In any event, try to answer all 30 questions with at least 5 minutes to spare, so you can go back and reconsider any responses you were unsure about.

SUMMING IT UP

- The GED® Science Test consists of twenty multiple-choice questions and ten questions in other formats. The subject areas covered include life science (biology), earth science and astronomy, and physical science (chemistry and physics).

- GED® Science Test questions require that you read passages and comprehend or analyze the material presented in the passages, along with the charts, diagrams, graphs, illustrations, tables, and other visual depictions.

- The GED® Science Test is more visually oriented than any of the other tests in the GED® battery. Pay careful attention to any arrows in an illustration; you can be sure that they will be crucial as you answer the question at hand.

- Synthesis and evaluation questions involve drawing general assessments and conclusions from specific information. You will need to be able to recognize unfair assessments and conclusions—wrong-answer choices that jump to conclusions that are unwarranted given the information provided.

- You won't need to memorize any formulas for the GED® Science Test. If a question requires you to apply a formula, it will provide that formula, along with the numbers you need to answer the question.

- Some GED® Science Test questions will involve numbers, but you won't be asked to calculate precise ratios, percents, or averages, or to do any serious number-crunching.

- Many questions on the Science Test deal with phenomena that you have observed or experienced in your everyday life. Use your experiences, along with your common sense, to help you answer these questions.

Science Review

OVERVIEW

- What you'll find in this review
- Science and the scientific method
- Life science: biology
- Earth and space science
- Chemistry
- Physics
- Summing it up

WHAT YOU'LL FIND IN THIS REVIEW

The GED® Science Test is designed primarily to measure critical-thinking skills rather than knowledge. Nevertheless, with some prior familiarity with the three content areas covered on the test (life sciences, earth and space science, and physical science) you can expect to handle the questions with greater ease and confidence. The review materials in this part of the book are designed to help you in this respect. Keep in mind that this review is intended only to highlight the content areas listed above. It is by no means intended to be a comprehensive examination of these areas.

Review questions are provided throughout this review. As you answer them, keep in mind that the sections of text on which they are based are longer than selections of text on the actual GED® Science Test.

SCIENCE AND THE SCIENTIFIC METHOD

Since the dawn of humankind, people have searched for explanations as to why the physical world around them is the way it is. Early explanations were most often based on religious and superstitious ideas. **Science** attempts to provide explanations for natural phenomena through investigation—more specifically, through observation and experimentation, as well as through theoretical explanation.

In order to sort out unreasonable explanations from plausible ones, scientists apply logic and common sense by means of a process called the **scientific method.** This method involves four fundamental steps:

1. **Observation:** During this first step, the scientist carefully observes a particular natural phenomenon, either directly (by using the five senses) or with the aid of any number of tools, such as telescopes, microscopes, temperature and pressure gauges, and other recording and measuring devices.

chapter 10

2 **Hypothesis:** During this second step, the scientist thinks about the set of facts obtained through observation, and he or she formulates a statement (the *hypothesis*) or series of statements that appear to logically explain the set of facts in a unified way. A good hypothesis is a simple statement intended to apply to a general set of circumstances.

3 **Experiment:** During the third step, the scientist designs and conducts experiments to determine whether the hypothesis is acceptable or whether it should be rejected or modified—in other words, to test the hypothesis.

4 **Conclusion:** During the fourth step, the scientist analyzes the results of the experiment(s) conducted during the third step. The results might support the hypothesis, or they might suggest that the hypothesis should be rejected or modified.

The proper conclusion (the final step described above) depends on whether the experimental results are consistent with the hypothesis. If the hypothesis is rejected or needs to be modified to fit the experimental results, new experiments are then designed and conducted to test a modified or new hypothesis in light of the experimental results. It is through a continuous cycle of new observations, new hypotheses, and further experimentation that scientists arrive at the best answers to their questions about the natural world.

Most people, including non-scientists, apply the scientific method in their everyday lives, often without realizing it. For example, assume that you are experiencing a stinging sensation in your stomach (an *observation*). You would probably want to know its cause so that you can remedy the problem. You might *hypothesize* that drinking coffee is the cause. In order to test your hypothesis, you might *experiment* by discontinuing coffee consumption for a period of days and monitoring the results. You would then reach a *conclusion* based on the results.

Reliable scientific conclusions depend on properly designed and conducted experiments. In the preceding experiment, for example, suppose you had discontinued coffee *and* alcohol consumption and observed that your stomach discomfort disappeared after a week. You could not reliably conclude that it was the coffee—rather than the alcohol or a combination of coffee and alcohol—that caused your stomach discomfort. A good test of your hypothesis would require that all possible factors other than coffee consumption remain unchanged, or constant, during the experiment. Researchers refer to such factors as **controls,** and they refer to factors that are changed to test the hypothesis as **variables.**

QUESTION 1 REFERS TO THE FOLLOWING INFORMATION.

A researcher combines equal amounts of three different clear liquids—X, Y, and Z—in a beaker, and she observes that the mixture turns blue in color. The researcher hypothesizes that liquid X turns blue when combined with any other liquid.

1. Which is the best way to test the hypothesis?

    (A) Repeat the experiment, but change the proportions of the three liquids.

    (B) Combine liquid X with a liquid other than Y or Z.

    (C) Perform the same experiment again.

    (D) Heat liquid X by itself, and observe its color response.

Liquid X is the control, and the other liquids are the variables. Change the variable to test the hypothesis. **The correct answer is (B).**

LIFE SCIENCE: BIOLOGY

Biology is the scientific study of living organisms, including plants and animals. This field consists of three major branches: *zoology* (the study of animals), *botany* (the study of plants), and *ecology* (the study of how plants and animals interact with each other and their environment).

Cell Theory

The **cell** is the basic unit of structure and function for most living things. Cells arise from pre-existing cells by independent self-reproduction. All living organisms are composed of one or more cells. Cells vary in size, shape, and function. A bacterial cell, for instance, is invisible to the naked eye. Bacteria only become visible when they appear as colonies of millions of cells. At the other extreme, a single muscle cell can reach 9 inches in length (about a million times larger than a bacterial cell). It is estimated that the human body is composed of some 100 trillion cells.

Cell Structure

Cells are the basis of life, heredity, structure, and function of every organism. Each cell contains a variety of different structures called **organelles** ("little organs"). The **nucleus** of a cell is one of the most important organelles. The nucleus is the control center for all cellular activity. Within the *nucleoplasm* of a nucleus are long, thin fibers called *chromatin* on which are found *genes,* which contain all the genetic information for each cell. (This topic is examined in greater detail later in this review.)

Every cell has a **membrane** that encloses the cell and is selectively permeable to what enters and exits the cell. Inside the membrane, organelles are embedded in a gelatinous substance called **cytoplasm,** which fills the cell. The cytoplasm is the cell's manufacturing area and contains small *vacuoles,* which are storage areas; *mitochondria,* which release energy for cell operations; and *ribosomes,* which combine amino acids into proteins.

Cells are classified as **prokaryotic** (before a nucleus) and **eukaryotic** (possessing a true nucleus). Prokaryotic cells lack a nuclear membrane and membrane-bound organelles. They are unicellular, mainly microscopic organisms, such as bacteria and cyanobacteria. It is estimated that prokaryotes appeared some 3.5 billion years ago, and many scientists hypothesize that prokaryotic organisms evolved into eukaryotic cells. Eukaryotes include all cells in animals and plants, as well as in *protists,* unicellular organisms that can be plant-like or animal-like in unique ways. Eukaryote cells are characterized by a true nucleus that is bound by a membrane and membrane-bounded subcellular organelles. Eukaryotes can be unicellular, as in the case of the amoeba, or multicellular, as seen in humans. Eukaryotic cells possess many organelles to carry out cellular processes such as energy production, waste disposal, cellular transport, and product production.

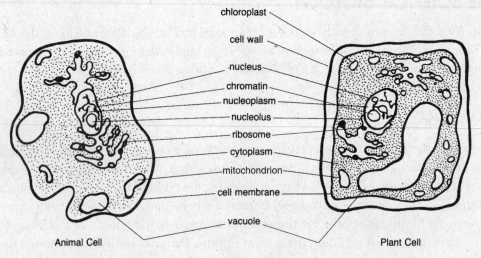

Animal Cell   Plant Cell

Although all eukaryotic cells are similar in structure, plant cells differ from animal cells in three important respects:

- Plant cells have a firm outer boundary called the *cell wall*. This wall supports and protects the plant cell.

- Vacuoles (storage areas) in the plant cell are much larger than those in the animal cell.

- Within the cytoplasm, many plant cells contain small green structures called *chloroplasts*. These chloroplasts contain *chlorophyll*, which enables the plant cell to make food.

CELL MEMBRANE AND TRANSPORT

As noted earlier, cell membranes control the movement of materials into and out of the cell. The cell membrane is semi-permeable and allows only certain materials to enter and leave the cell. A cell membrane is a fluid-like sheet that is embedded with proteins and carbohydrate chains. This sheet creates an effective barrier against lipids (fats), while the sheet's proteins and carbohydrates act as receptors or identifiers for the movement of molecules from external sources.

While many factors are necessary for cell survival, **cellular transport**—the movement of particles into and out of the cell—is one of the most important. Cellular transport can be either passive or active. Movement by **passive transport** is accomplished through **diffusion,** by which particles move from an area of high concentration to an area of lower concentration until equilibrium is reached. Water is the largest component of the cell protoplasm. The diffusion of water through a semi-permeable membrane is known more specifically as **osmosis.** Diffusion is a "passive" form of transport because it requires no energy. In contrast, **active transport** is used when a cell needs to move a substance from an area of lower concentration to an area of higher concentration; to do this, a cell must use energy.

CELLULAR FUNCTIONS—METABOLISM AND ENERGY PATHWAYS

All cells require a constant source of energy. Gathering, storing, and using this energy is referred to as a cell's **metabolism.** We consume nutrients to provide our bodies with the building blocks necessary to synthesize new materials needed by our cells. Unlike plants and some microscopic organisms, humans and other animals can't simply absorb energy through our skin. Instead, animal cells have to break food down in order to release the energy stored in the food.

Both plant and animal cells rely on metabolic pathways to convert substances into forms of energy that can be used by each cell. These conversions are controlled through **enzymes,** which are proteins that act as a biological catalyst. What this means is that enzymes speed up the rate of a reaction by lowering the amount of activation energy needed. Without enzymes it would take weeks, even months, for foods to break down completely.

Enzymes are also necessary in order for the vital cellular reactions of *photosynthesis* and *cellular respiration* to occur.

Cells are the first level of the hierarchy of levels of organization in an organism. These levels are cells, which make up tissues, which make up organs, which make up organisms. Cells that make up tissues are specialized to perform a specific function. For example, muscle cells can release large amounts of energy needed to contract a muscle. Muscles made of such cells are part of the musculoskeletal system.

ENERGY FOR LIFE FUNCTIONS

Photosynthesis is the food-manufacturing process by which green plants convert carbon dioxide (CO_2) from the air and water (H_2O) from the soil into glucose ($C_6H_{12}O_6$), which is a simple sugar, and oxygen (O_2). The sugars that the plant produces through photosynthesis can be used to make other compounds needed for the plant to sustain itself and grow. The green pigment in plants, called **chlorophyll,** captures the Sun's light energy, which fuels this manufacturing process. Oxygen is a byproduct of this reaction and is released into the atmosphere or used in cellular respiration (see below). Here's the chemical equation for photosynthesis:

$$6\,CO_2 + 6\,H_2O \rightarrow C_6H_{12}O_6 + 6\,O_2$$

Note that one molecule of glucose (sugar) combined with six molecules of oxygen to form six molecules of carbon dioxide and six molecules of water. The energy produced by this reaction is used by the cell.

Cellular respiration is used to free chemical energy from molecules of glucose for biological work. There are many types of respiration, but the most familiar is *aerobic* respiration, which converts carbohydrates (glucose) into carbon dioxide, water, and high-energy molecules of **ATP,** which is the source of energy for many metabolic processes. Here's the chemical equation for aerobic respiration:

$$C_6H_{12}O_6 + 6\ O_2 \rightarrow 6\ CO_2 + 6\ H_2O + ATP$$

Respiration begins in the cytoplasm of the cell in a process known as **glycolysis** (sugar-breaking). The products of glycolysis then move to the mitochondria, where they are converted into energy-rich ATP molecules. Catabolic reactions such as respiration produce energy by the breakdown of larger molecules.

Cellular respiration occurs outside aerobic conditions as well. **Fermentation** and other forms of anaerobic respiration occur daily in fungi, bacteria, and even in the human body. While much of the inputs and outputs of cellular respiration are present in anaerobic respiration, the lack of oxygen is critical to the process.

The most well-known form of fermentation takes place through use of the common fungus yeast (*Saccharomyces*). In this form of cellular respiration, glucose is broken down through catabolic reactions to provide energy for the fungus. However, the byproduct of this form of respiration is not water, but *ethanol*—drinking alcohol. The formula for this reaction looks like this:

$$C_6H_{12}O_6 \rightarrow 2\ C_2H_5OH + 2\ CO_2 + 2ATP$$

Yeasts and other fermenters convert sugars like glucose to ethanol and carbon dioxide (note the lack of water as a byproduct). This process is utilized in the food and alcohol industries.

Our bodies can also ferment sugar when oxygen is lacking, albeit for short periods of time. When normal cellular respiration occurs in an oxygen-depleted environment, the breakdown of glucose stops at a three-carbon sugar—*pyruvate*. Pyruvate is converted to a carboxylic acid—*lactic acid*. The formula for this reaction looks like this:

$$C_6H_{12}O_6 \rightarrow 2C_3H_6O_3 + 2ATP$$

Lactic acid genesis can only last for a short time period in animals, as the need for oxygen is essential to life. However, the process can be sustained for brief intervals. This process actually occurs any time a person exercises beyond their conditioning level. As the body is stressed for oxygen, the lactic acid buildup increases. This buildup causes muscle soreness, and the effects of the lack of oxygen can be felt for days later. As conditioning increases, it takes longer for the body to start the fermentation process.

Another important form of anaerobic respiration is **methanogenesis**. As the name suggests, this is a process that creates methane. There are a number of bacteria species that can convert organic molecules into methane. Two examples of methanogenesis are carbon dioxide conversion and acetic acid conversion:

$$CO_2 + 4H_2 \rightarrow CH_4 + 2H_2O$$

$$CH_3COOH \rightarrow CH_4 + CO_2$$

Unlike other forms of cellular respiration, bacteria responsible for methanogenesis—*methanogens*—do not begin their respiration with sugars, but with products of other organismal cellular respiration. These bacteria often live in symbiotic relationships with other animals within the animals' digestive tracts. For example, methanogens can live within cows and aid in the digestion of cellulose—the sugar that makes up plant cell walls. This relationship can produce up to 250 liters (about 66 gallons) of methane a day.

QUESTIONS 2 AND 3 REFER TO THE FOLLOWING DIAGRAM AND INFORMATION.

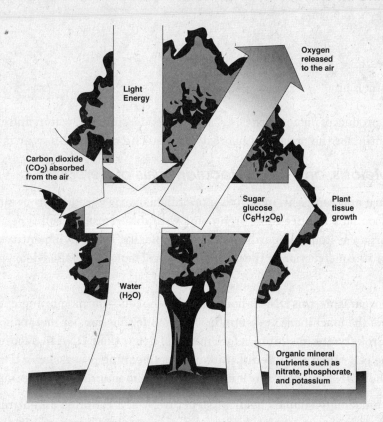

The oxygen produced by photosynthesis is necessary for cellular respiration, and the carbon dioxide produced by respiration is necessary for photosynthesis. In short, photosynthesis and cellular respiration are the Yin and Yang of energy: they are two complementary parts of a cycle of energy that is necessary for life to exist.

2. Which of the following exhibits passive cellular transport in a plant?

(A) The plant's chloroplasts absorb light energy from the Sun.

(B) The plant's leaves emit oxygen into the air as a waste product.

(C) The plant's roots absorb water from nearby soil.

(D) The plant's stem delivers ATP molecules to the plant's leaves.

Passive transport involves a natural diffusion process, by which water moves from an area of higher concentration to one of lower concentration until equilibrium is reached. When you water a plant, the roots absorb it through osmosis, a form of diffusion, as needed to deliver that water to drier parts of the plant. **The correct answer is (C).**

3. Which is NOT required in order for a plant to carry out photosynthesis?

(A) carbon dioxide

(B) glucose

(C) water

(D) chlorophyll

Glucose is a product of photosynthesis. Carbon dioxide, sunlight, water, and chlorophyll are all essential for the process of photosynthesis. **The correct answer is (B).**

Mitosis, Meiosis, and the Molecular Basis of Heredity

The structure and composition of living organisms varies greatly, from single-celled bacteria to complex multicellular organisms with differentiated cell types and interconnected organ systems. Regardless of the complexity, every living entity contains a blueprint for its construction in the form of a chain of molecules called deoxyribonucleic acid (**DNA**).

In all living organisms, this DNA is housed inside the cell—the membrane-enclosed unit that contains the machinery and supplies for the life functions or metabolic processes of the cell. Prokaryotes (meaning before nucleus) house their DNA in a loosely defined region of the cell called a **nucleoid.** Eukaryotes (meaning possessing a true nucleus) sequester their DNA inside a **nucleus**—a separate, membrane-bound compartment.

DNA is an amazingly simple chemical structure, yet it contains an entire library of information on how to make, maintain, and reproduce an organism; it also keeps a record of clues to the organism's evolutionary history. The entire sequence of DNA in an organism is called its **genome.** The genetic blueprint so carefully preserved in a genome is stored in the DNA's linear sequence of molecules, referred to as **bases.** A DNA chain is constructed with four different bases: *adenine* (A), *guanine* (G), *cytosine* (C), and *thymine* (T). Two strands of *nucleotides* lain side by side are connected by chemical pairings of complementary (matching) bases: adenine (A) pairs with thymine (T), and guanine (G) pairs with cytosine (C). The bonds between these molecules impose a twisting force (torsion) on the structure and cause it to wind slightly, much like a spiral staircase. This creates the familiar *double helix* shape of a DNA molecule.

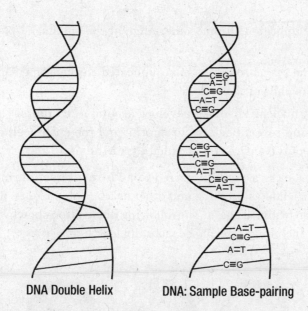

DNA Double Helix   DNA: Sample Base-pairing

Duplication of a cell's DNA is required both for cellular replication—to replenish dying cells—and for reproduction. In unicellular organisms, these two processes are the same. DNA is duplicated before the cell divides to produce two separate organisms, each with the original amount of DNA. This asexual method of reproduction is known as **binary fission.**

In multicellular organisms, a similar process called **mitosis** is used to replenish lost cells. However, reproduction is more complex and begins with specialized cells called **gametes** (eggs and sperm in animals), each of which provide only half of the DNA contained in other cells.

MITOSIS

All cells must have a mechanism for perpetuation, growth, maintenance, and repair. If you've ever had a bad haircut or painful sunburn, in time your hair grew back and your skin peeled to reveal new skin. You can thank cellular division for this.

This process begins first with nuclear division—before the remainder of the cell divides. In cells of eukaryotic (multicellular) organisms, the nucleus normally carries two sets of genetic information. In this case the cell is said to be **diploid.** If a cell carries only one set of genetic information, it is said to be **haploid.** To begin cell division, unorganized DNA exits the nucleus in the strand-like form called *chromatin*. Once a cell is ready to divide, this chromatin coils and condenses into structures called **chromosomes,** which carry units of inheritance called *genes*. A chromosome in a non-dividing cell exists in a duplicated state where two copies—sister *chromatids*—are attached together at a central point. A nonreproductive human cell contains 46 chromosomes altogether—23 pairs of chromatids.

The process of mitosis consists of four sequential stages:

❶ **Prophase:** The nuclear envelope dissolves; chromatin organizes into chromosomes; a fibrous spindle forms to connect opposite ends of the cell.

2 Metaphase: Duplicated chromosomes align at the equatorial plane of cell, along the spindles.

3 Anaphase: The two chromatids of a duplicated chromosome separate and move toward opposite ends of the cell.

4 Telophase: A nuclear envelope develops around a "daughter" cell; the chromosomes uncoil and revert back to chromatin; and the entire cell divides into two. (This division of the entire cell is called **cytokinesis.**)

Between cell divisions is a period referred to as **interphase,** during which the cell increases in volume, makes proteins and other crucial components, and replicates its DNA in preparation to divide again. The following illustration shows what the different phases of mitosis, including interphase, actually look like.

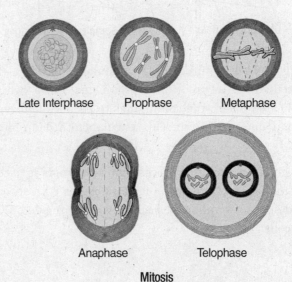

Late Interphase   Prophase   Metaphase

Anaphase   Telophase

Mitosis

Animal cell division is similar to plant cell division, but there are a few differences. In animal cells, cytokinesis results in a *cleavage furrow* (shown below), which divides the cytoplasm. In plant cells, a *cell plate* forms in the center and progresses to the cell membrane. The result is a cell wall separating the two cells.

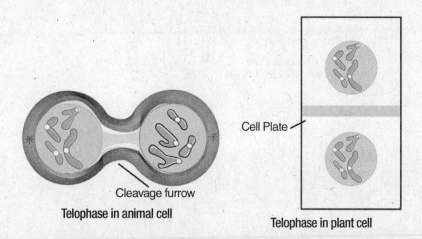

Cell Plate

Cleavage furrow

Telophase in animal cell

Telophase in plant cell

In animal cells, after mitosis is complete, a cell has replicated the same genetic information initially donated by the egg and sperm cells. Except for random mutations, all of an organism's cells produced by mitosis have the same genes. The earliest cells created by mitosis are referred to as **stem cells.** Cells then differentiate into specialized cells by activating certain genes while repressing others. For example, muscle cells produce contractile proteins while thyroid cells produce hormones that control metabolism. Each of these types of cells has a specific function, but it cannot perform the function of the other. The differentiating process is crucial—it explains why hair cells replace hair cells while skin cells replace skin cells.

MEIOSIS

The process of cell division known as **meiosis** occurs only in specialized reproductive cells of eukaryotic (multicellular) plants and animals. In animals, organs called **gonads** produce these reproductive cells, which are called **gametes.** In humans, the testes produce sperm and the ovaries produce ova (eggs).

Human *non*-reproductive cells contain 23 pairs of chromosomes, as noted earlier. Of these 23 pairs, 22 are non-sex-related, or *autosomal,* while the 23rd pair is exclusively responsible for determining sex (male or female) and sex-related traits. A reproductive cell (sperm or ovum), however, does not carry a duplicate of any of the 23 chromosomes. Instead, it contains a total of only 22 *single* chromosomes and one *single* sex chromosome—23 chromosomes altogether. (The genetic complement is later restored once an egg is fertilized by a sperm cell.)

Meiosis, like mitosis, is a multiphase process. However, meiosis involves two divisions—*meiosis I* and *meiosis II*—rather than just one, and the *four* resulting daughter cells are each genetically different from the parent cell. This important distinction ultimately explains why you are uniquely different from each of your two parents.

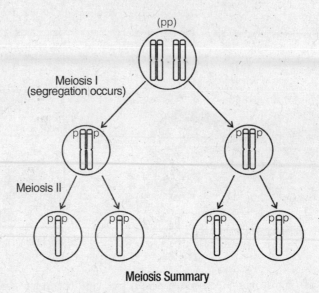

Meiosis Summary

The first step in meiosis I is **Interphase,** during which DNA is replicated in preparation for division. The chromatin organizes into chromosomes—each of 46 chromosomes consisting of two identical chromatids (diploids), just as in cells about to undergo mitosis. Then comes **Prophase I,** during which the nuclear envelope dissolves and *homologous* chromosomes (which have genes for the same trait) pair up and exchange genetic material in a process called "crossing over." This process does not occur during mitosis. Next comes **Metaphase I,** during which the chromosomes line up as a unit along an equatorial line.

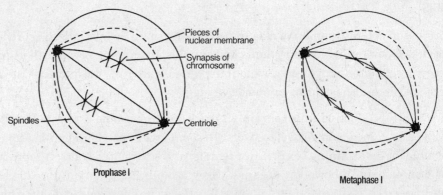

In the next phase, **Anaphase I,** each chromosome pair separates, its two sister chromatids moving toward opposite poles of the cell. Thus, 23 chromosomes end up at one end of the cell, and 23 end up at the other end. During the final phase, **Telophase I,** a nuclear envelope re-forms around each new daughter nucleus, and the cell itself divides. Each of the two daughter cells has one set of 23 chromosomes. However, every chromosome still consists of two chromatids at this point. In other words, each of the two daughter cells is diploid.

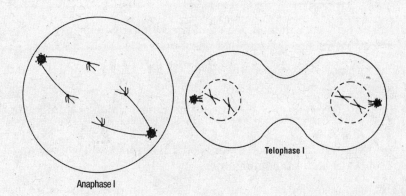

Immediately after meiosis I, the two daughter cells undergo the second meiotic division (Meiosis II). This second division is similar to mitosis. Chromatids from each of the 23 chromosomes separate and move to opposite poles, and then each of the two daughter cells divides. The 23 chromatids in each of the four new cells form the chromosomes of those cells. At this point each daughter cell is haploid.

The four new cells become gametes (reproductive cells), each with 23 chromosomes that vary genetically from the original parent cell. In a human female, just one of these new reproductive cells can become a functional gamete (an egg). In the human male, however, all four new cells become viable sperm cells. The union of the egg and one of the sperm restores the full complement of 46 chromosomes in the fertilized human cell, or *zygote*.

  4. In what respect is reproduction in unicellular organisms different from reproduction in multicellular organisms?

  (A) Unicellular organisms reproduce simply by replacing dying cells.

  (B) Unicellular organisms divide before their DNA is duplicated.

  (C) Unicellular organisms depend on egg fertilization for reproduction.

  (D) Unicellular organisms duplicate their DNA before they divide into separate organisms.

Before dividing into two separate organisms, a unicellular organism duplicates its DNA. In contrast, multicellular organisms do not simply duplicate their DNA but rather combine one half and another half of DNA from two different gametes, such as a sperm cell and an egg cell. **The correct answer is (D).**

5. In terms of cell reproduction, which of the following helps explain the genetic differences between a child and its parents?

(A) Chromosomes' pairs exchange genes before the first meiotic cell division occurs.

(B) Reproductive cells create new chromosomes, which are unique to the child.

(C) After the initial meiotic cell division, all chromosomes break apart and reconfigure in a random manner.

(D) During the second meiotic division, each pair of chromosomes fuses together to become one.

In meiosis, the "crossing over" process that occurs just before the first meiotic cell division results in an exchange of genes between each of the 23 pairs of chromosomes. It is this exchange that all but ensures that daughter cells will differ genetically from their "mother" cell. **The correct answer is (A).**

Genetic Inheritance

Genetics is the study of the principles of heredity and the variation of inherited traits among related organisms. These principles, upon which the field of modern genetics is based, were established in the nineteenth century by Austrian monk Gregor Mendel. In 1866, Mendel performed a number of simple but ingenious breeding experiments with garden pea plants and observed consistent, predictable patterns in terms of what traits are passed down from generation to generation. Mendel understood that some sort of hereditary factor was involved.

Mendelian Inheritance

We now know that the traits (or **phenotypes**) Mendel discovered are controlled by **genes.** Genes exist as heritable units on a **chromosome.** A chromosome may possess thousands of genes. Since each human is a product of the combination of both maternal and paternal chromosomes—23 from the egg and 23 from the sperm—we carry genes from both parents. Genes determine our physical and mental development and dictate all of our individual characteristics or traits, everything from eye and hair color to blood type to the ability to roll your tongue. Genes come in alternative forms called **alleles.** We receive one allele from each parent. These alleles determine how each specific phenotype (such as eye color) is expressed. For example, the gene governing eye color can take the form of an allele for brown eyes or an allele for blue eyes.

Mendel proposed that a gene can be either a **dominant** allele for a certain trait or a **recessive** allele for that trait. The distinction between them is key to understanding heredity. Dominant alleles are *expressed*, which means they are actually shown as a trait. What's more, dominant alleles can "mask" the expression of recessive alleles. Recessive alleles can only be expressed when they are in the **homozygous** state, which means that alleles from both parents are the same. (A **heterozygous** state exists when the alleles are different.)

These principles, set forth by Mendel based on his observations of pea plants, are referred to today as Mendel's Laws of Inheritance:

The Law of Segregation: Each allele possessed by a parent will be passed into separate gametes (for example, egg and sperm cells in animals) during meiosis.

The Law of Independent Assortment: In each gamete, alleles of one gene separate independently of all other genes, allowing for new combinations of alleles through recombination.

The Law of Dominance: Each gene has two alleles, one inherited from each parent. Alleles are either **dominant** or **recessive** in their expression; dominant alleles "mask" the expression of recessive alleles.

Statistical Predictions of Individual Inheritance

Based on the patterns of inheritance that Mendel observed, it is possible to make predictions about the probability of a particular allele being passed on to an offspring and to make predictions about the phenotypic expression of an allele in the next generation.

All the genes that dictate the expression of a person's phenotypes are referred to collectively as the person's **genotype.** When certain genotypes of the parents are known for a specific trait, a simple diagram called a **Punnett square** can be used to predict the probability that the trait will be expressed in their offspring. Consider, for example, a genetic *cross* between the genes of two parents involving a single trait: the ability to roll the sides of one's tongue to form a "U" shape. We will designate **R** as the dominant allele, representing tongue-rolling ability, and **r** as the recessive allele representing a lack of tongue-rolling ability. Assume, for example, that the genotype of one parent is **RR** and the genotype of the other parent is **rr.** To construct a Punnett square for a cross such as this, the genes for one parent are placed along the side of the square and the genes for the other parent are placed along the top:

(Parents) **RR × rr**

The Punnett square for this cross:

All the resulting offspring of this cross are heterozygous dominant (Rr)—this is their genotype. As a result, all offspring will be tongue rollers—this is the expression of their phenotype. Now, members of this first generation can be crossed to assess the probability that their offspring will be tongue-rollers:

(Parents)   **Rr × Rr**

The Punnett square for this cross:

	R	**r**
R	**RR**	**Rr**
r	**Rr**	**rr**

Notice in this cross that three of the four squares are dominant—either RR or Rr. This means that there is a 75 percent probability that any member of this generation will be a tongue-roller. This is a phenotypic probability, of course, since it involves the actual expression of the trait.

You can also determine genotypic probabilities by examining the square:

- Homozygous dominant (RR)—25 percent probability

- Heterozygous dominant (Rr)—50 percent probability

- Homozygous recessive (rr)—25 percent probability

In genetics, phenotypic and genotypic probabilities are often expressed as ratios. Referring to the preceding Punnett square, the phenotypic ratio for tongue-rolling is 3:1, while the genotypic ratio for tongue-rolling is 1:2:1.

A Punnett square can also be used for crosses involving two traits that are independent of each other. The possible combinations are greater, yet the method is the same. Consider, for example, the texture and color of pea plants. Suppose that a yellow wrinkled pea will be crossed with a green smooth pea. The yellow color (Y) is dominant to green (y), and the smooth texture (S) is dominant to wrinkled (s). A cross between a purebred green, smooth pea plant and a yellow, wrinkled pea plant yields the following results:

(Parents)   **SSYY × ssyy**

The Punnett square for this cross:

	SY	**SY**	**SY**	**SY**
sy	SsYy	SsYy	SsYy	SsYy
sy	SsYy	SsYy	SsYy	SsYy
sy	SsYy	SsYy	SsYy	SsYy
sy	SsYy	SsYy	SsYy	SsYy

All the offspring from this cross will be green and smooth (these are their phenotypes). Genotypically, they will all be heterozygous dominant for both traits (Ss and Yy). If we cross two heterozygous peas to one another, though, the offspring will not all look alike. In the following cross, notice all the different genotypes produced:

SsYy × SsYy

	SY	Sy	sY	sy
SY	SSYY	SSYy	SsYY	SsYy
Sy	SSYy	SSyy	SsYy	Ssyy
sY	SsYY	SsYy	ssYY	ssYy
sy	SsYy	Ssyy	ssYy	ssyy

Tallying up each different phenotype, you will find four different specific types, in a 9:3:3:1 ratio:

- 9 squares show dominance for both traits (SYYY, SSYy, SsYY, or SsYy)

- 3 squares show dominance for one trait and recessive for the other (SSyy or Ssyy)

- 3 other squares show dominance for one trait and recessive for the other (ssYY or ssYy)

- 1 square shows recessive for both traits (ssyy)

As several generations pass, it is important to note which individuals carry or have a specific trait. This can help develop an understanding of the trait as well as enable scientists to estimate the chance that a trait will be passed on. When a map of several generations is created, we call this a *pedigree*. A pedigree is a chart that shows direct and extended family members and highlights who has a specific trait. In medicine, genetic counselors use pedigrees to help expecting parents understand the probability that a child may have a specific trait. By looking at family histories, the counselor can advise the parents on these inheritable traits.

The diagram below is an example of a pedigree. To understand the way a pedigree works, it is important to understand the symbols used: squares represent males, circles represent females, blank shapes indicate a lack of the trait, while shaded shapes indicates having a trait; some pedigrees will also have half-shaded shapes indicating people who are carriers for the trait. The lines in a pedigree are also significant. Lines directly connecting a male and a female indicate that these two individuals had children together, while shapes that are all connected via vertical lines to a common horizontal line indicates that these individuals are siblings. These siblings are listed from left (oldest) to the right (youngest).

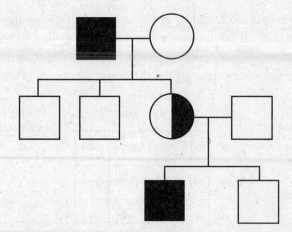

6. Assume that two parents are both heterozygous for a certain physical trait, which can either be present or absent in its expression. What is the expected genotypic ratio among their offspring?

    (A) 1:1

    (B) 2:1

    (C) 1:2:1

    (D) 3:1

Since both parents are heterozygous, the cross would be Tt × Tt (where T = dominant and t = recessive). Constructing a Punnett square would reveal the following: **TT** (one possibility), **Tt** (two possibilities), and **tt** (one possibility). The ratio is 1:2:1. **The correct answer is (C).**

7. When neither of two different alleles governing the same trait is dominant over the other, what could be the result (each choice considered individually)?
    I. Both alleles will be distinctly expressed.
    II. The alleles will be expressed as a hybrid.
    III. A genetic mutation will express itself in a unique way.
    IV. Neither allele will be expressed.

    (A) I and II only

    (B) II and III only

    (C) III and IV only

    (D) I, II, III, and IV

The alleles might be co-dominant, in which case both will be distinctly expressed, as noted in statement A. Or they might be incomplete dominance, in which case a mix or hybrid will result, as noted in statement B. **The correct answer is (A).**

Deviations from Classic Mendelian Patterns

Since Mendel's discoveries, other patterns of gene expression have been identified that deviate from the "classic" Mendelian dominant/recessive patterns. Noteworthy among these are the following:

Co-dominance: In this deviation, neither of the two different alleles governing the same trait is dominant over the other, and *both* are expressed. For example, three alleles—A, B, and O—determine human blood type. The A and B alleles are co-dominant, and the O allele is recessive. Individuals with the AB genotype are phenotypically distinct (type AB blood) from individuals with the AA or AO (type A), BB or BO (type B), and OO (type O) genotype.

Incomplete dominance: In this deviation, neither of the two different alleles governing the same trait is dominant over the other, and the heterozygote is an intermediate between the two homozygous phenotypes—for example, a mix or hybrid of two colors. A snapdragon homozygous for a red allele (RR) has a red flower, and one that is homozygous for a white allele (WW) has a white flower. But a heterozygous (RW) cross results in a *pink* flower.

Sex linkage: One of our 23 pairs of chromosomes determines our sex—either male (**X**) or female (**Y**). The combination XX results in a female, while XY results in a male. These sex chromosomes carry the genes that govern the development of sex organs as well as secondary sex characteristics—body shape, body hair, and so forth. The X chromosome is much larger than the Y chromosome. As a result, a variety of recessive alleles on an X chromosome have no dominant alleles on the Y chromosome to mask them. This explains why only males experience color blindness or male pattern baldness: these alleles are recessive but will always be expressed because they cannot be masked by dominant *non*-color-blindness or *non*-balding alleles from the female.

Mutations: In this deviation, something goes awry during genetic replication. During mitosis, the genes of a cell do not replicate properly, causing a change in the genetic code of the new cell. This effect can be fatal to the cell or fatal to the organism. If this mutation continues to replicate, it may do nothing to the organism or cell, or it may create a new gene within the organism or cell. There are several different types of genetic mutation that can occur. Three common ones are **deletion, insertion,** and **base substitution.** As the name suggests, in *deletion mutations,* the mutated part of the DNA is deleted from the sequence. When *insertion mutations* occur, a portion of genetic material is added. Meanwhile, in *base substitution mutations,* the nucleotide bases—C, G, T, or A—are switched around.

Environmental Altering of Traits: There are two different forms of this deviation: one in which climatic events affect the gene, and one in which an agent in the environment—often a chemical—causes some form of mutation. An example of the first deviation can be seen in the arctic fox. During winter periods, when the temperatures can be well below freezing, the coat of the fox is all white, allowing the fox to blend into its environment. However, as summer—and warmer weather—approaches, the change in temperature alters the coat color genes, and the fox's hair takes on a reddish-brown color.

A *mutagen*—an agent that causes a mutation—can cause great, and even fatal, harm to the individual. Radiation (even as common as solar radiation) and the common solvent benzene are two such agents. While one is naturally occurring and the other not (or at least not as readily available), both attack the genetic code and can lead to alterations to the code.

Chromosomal Crossover: In this deviation, portions of two non-sister chromosomes are swapped. This event happens almost exclusively during Prophase I of meiosis. A non-sister chromosome is a homologous chromosome that is not part of the other chromosome. For example, portions of the first 21st chromosomes may switch with part of the second 21st chromosome. This can create new traits that are not present, even in a carrier form, in either parent.

Epigenetics: *Epigenetics* literally means "outside of genetics" and is a form of gene expression where traits are expressed differently from the parent cell, but the DNA sequence stays the same. In this deviation, a biochemical reaction within the DNA causes slight changes to the DNA; this may be the addition of a methyl group or a change in a protein. Regardless of the alteration, the DNA base pairs are not altered. This leaves an identical set of DNA sequence with a completely different trait expressed. An epigenetic change is hereditable and reversible.

Transmission of Disease and Pathogens

Bacteria and Viruses

Beginning in this section, this review enlarges the scale on which it examines biological life from the molecular level to that of the individual organism. At this level, a good starting point is with two of the smallest such forms—bacteria and viruses. **Bacteria,** also known as *microbes* or *germs*, are microscopic organisms that reproduce primarily asexually. Most other organisms, including humans, are covered inside and out with what is referred to as a normal *flora* of bacterial populations. **Viruses** differ from bacteria in their simplified body structure and composition, their mode of replication, and in their dependence on a living host cell for replication.

TYPES OF BACTERIA

Bacteria are neither animals nor plants—they occupy their own pigeonhole in the modern classification system for biological life. (The system is outlined later in this review.) Bacteria can be either **autotrophic** (they synthesize food by converting light to chemical energy) or **heterotrophic** (they require other organisms to serve as a food source). They can also be divided into three main groups based on characteristics such as shape, motility (ability to move about on their own), metabolism, and mode of reproduction:

- **Eubacteria** (true bacteria) come in three shapes: coccus (spherical), bacillus (rod-shaped), and spirillum (spiral-shaped). One example of eubacteria is *Escherichia coli*, or *E. coli*, a bacterium that grows in small numbers as a part of the natural flora of human skin, intestinal tract, and genital tract. Under a compromised immune system, however, overgrowth of this bacterium can result in illness or even death.

- **Cyanobacteria** perform photosynthesis to convert light energy into chemical energy for food. The green gooey stuff you sometimes see in standing pools of water (also known as pond-scum) is an example of cyanobacteria.

- **Archaeobacteria** is a recently discovered group of bacteria. These microbes are typically found in extreme environments, such as on glaciers and in underwater volcanic vents.

Bacteria have simple structures. Since they are prokaryotes, they lack a membrane-bound nucleus and membrane-bound organelles. The following diagram shows the basic body plan for a typical bacterium. A bacterium cell contains strands of DNA, a plasma membrane, a cell wall, and a capsule. This simple structure allows for the rapid division of the bacterium, usually by way of binary fission—a form of asexual reproduction.

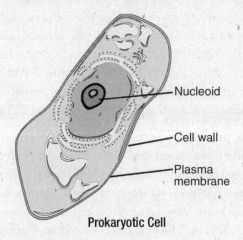

Nucleoid

Cell wall

Plasma membrane

Prokaryotic Cell

Bacteria that are parasitic are called **pathogens,** meaning that they are disease-causing. Pathogenic bacteria invade healthy tissues. Their metabolic processes release enzymes that destroy the normal physiology of this tissue. Human diseases caused by pathogenic bacteria include leprosy, syphilis, gonorrhea, tuberculosis, strep throat, and Lyme disease—to list just a few. Through their bacterial metabolism, other pathogens produce toxins that are poisonous to humans. Botulism, for example, is caused by a toxin that infects food and liquids. When ingested, it can cause illness and even death.

To combat pathogens, scientists have developed a host of different kinds of **antibiotics** that disrupt bacterial metabolism. An antibiotic works by weakening and rupturing the cell wall of a bacterium, thereby killing the cell. But bacteria often develop immunity to a particular antibiotic, especially when the antibiotic is overused. As bacteria divide rapidly, they can develop into new and more virulent strains. For example, antibiotics such as penicillin are now ineffective against more resistant strains of some bacteria.

Researchers are continually developing new and stronger antibiotics to combat the ability of bacteria to develop immunity to existing antibiotics.

VIRUSES

Viruses cannot reproduce on their own accord or perform basic cellular tasks such as protein synthesis, and so most scientists do not consider them to be independent living organisms. A **virus** is simply a strand of genetic material, either DNA or RNA, encapsulated in an outer protein shell. Viruses act as intracellular parasites in all types of organisms. They can only reproduce inside a living cell. Once inside the host cell, viruses take over the replication machinery of the host cell. They transfer their genome into the cell of the host organism, integrate their DNA sequence into the host DNA, and let the host cell replicate, transcribe, and translate the virus's genes. Viral genomes contain genes for directing the replication and packaging of complete copies of the virus, so that eventually the host cell bursts open and releases new viruses to infect other cells.

The living host upon which viruses absolutely depend for replication can be of plant, bacterial, or animal origin. Viruses are host-specific in that they invade only one type of cell, which provides necessary *receptor sites* for the virus to attach itself. For example, the virus that causes polio attaches to neurons, the virus responsible for mumps attaches to salivary glands, and the virus that causes chicken pox attaches to skin cells. Though they are the smallest infectious agents known to humans, what they lack in size they more than make up for in destructive power. They are responsible for a wide variety of devastating human diseases, such as HIV/AIDS, hepatitis B, and herpes.

To treat viral infections, prevention is the key. Early investigations into the spread of disease, in particular smallpox, prompted the development of **vaccines**. In 1796, Dr. Edward Jenner discovered that milkmaids who contracted cowpox from cows showed a natural immunity against the more virulent smallpox. From this discovery, a new form of disease prevention was born. Vaccines are developed by using nonpathogenic strains of viruses or killed viral strains. The vaccine is introduced into an organism, and then the organism's immune system produces antibodies to fight the inactive virus. Later, if the organism encounters these particles again, it has already developed a defense, or immunity, to them.

Through genetic engineering in recent decades, scientists have devised ways for organisms other than the infected one to independently produce inactive components of a virus. For example, plants such as bananas can be engineered to become "edible vaccines" by splicing genes from a bacterium or virus with a bacterium that naturally occurs in the soil in which the banana plant grows. The bacterium in the soil then infects the growing plant, transferring the foreign gene along with it. Scientists hope that in this way, large quantities of vaccines can be produced inexpensively and distributed to areas of the world that lack conventional health care. Through this and other innovative approaches, researchers hope to eventually win the ongoing battle against these unseen and potentially deadly invaders.

8. Bacteria reproduce at a higher rate than any other organism. What allows bacteria to replicate so rapidly?

    (A) Their cell structure is very simple.

    (B) They feed on host organisms without providing any benefit in return.

    (C) Vaccines are generally ineffective in killing bacteria.

    (D) They can reproduce in nearly any environment, no matter how hostile.

The simple cell structure of bacteria is the key to their ability to replicate so rapidly. **The correct answer is (A).**

9. How does a vaccine work to prevent a viral infection?

    It works by

    (A) boosting the immune system with viral-fighting vitamins

    (B) introducing a bacterium that encounters and kills the virus

    (C) stimulating the production of antibodies to fight the virus

    (D) strengthening cell walls so that the virus cannot enter the cells

A vaccine introduces an inactive strain of the virus. The body's immune system then produces antibodies to fight the inactive virus. If the body is later exposed to a pathogenic strain of the virus, the appropriate antibodies are already there to fight it off. **The correct answer is (C).**

Species Relationships

Symbiosis

Bacteria provide an ideal illustration of **symbiosis** in action. Two different types of organisms are said to have a *symbiotic* relationship when there is an ongoing, close association between them. A symbiotic relationship can be either **mutualistic** or **parasitic.** In a mutualistic relationship, each organism obtains a benefit from its association with the other. In a parasitic relationship, one organism obtains a benefit while the other organism is harmed by the relationship. (In a third type of symbiosis, called *commensalism,* one organism benefits while the other is neither benefited nor harmed.)

Bacteria maintain mutualistic relationships with many different species of plants. For example, the roots of bean plants form a mutualistic relationship with bacteria that are capable of converting atmospheric nitrogen into a usable form, which not only benefits the plant, but also the soil surrounding the plants. This process is known as **nitrogen fixation.**

Bacteria maintain mutualistic relationships with animals as well—including humans. For example, the digestive system in humans relies on intestinal bacteria to aid in digestion and to produce antibiotics that prevent the growth of pathogenic bacteria. Another example involves herbivores such as cows, which lack the enzyme needed to digest cellulose and thus depend on certain bacterial microbes to convert their food into simple sugars.

Bacteria are not the only species to form symbiotic relationships. For example, lichens are formed by a mutualistic symbiosis between fungus and algae. The two grow and live together in lichen form in some of the most hostile terrestrial environments on the planet. Their symbiotic relationship enables them to anchor on rocks and trees, provide nutrients, and survive the harsh climate. Ant species also form a number of mutualistic relationships. Some species of ants raise and care for aphids so that the ants may feed on the dew that aphids produce. Remoras and sharks share a mutualistic symbiotic relationship as well. Remoras attach themselves to the bottom of a shark and eat bits of food that the shark misses or that get caught on the shark. Meanwhile, the shark is cleaned by the remoras.

Parasitic relationships are classified into three types (although some classify up to five): endoparasites, ectoparasites, and brood parasites. Endoparasites live inside of their hosts. Examples, of these include the tapeworm, pinworm, trypanosoma (the protozoan responsible for malaria), and even flies, such as the botfly. Some parasites like the tapeworm and pinworm harm the host only slightly while they feed. Others, like trypanosoma, will eventually kill their hosts as they reproduce within the body. Some, like the botfly, only spend their larval stage within vertebrates where they grow and eat. Once mature, the botfly flies off and lives like other flies. Ectoparasites live outside of the body. For example, the tick bites and burrows its head into the skin of its host, drawing blood to feed. Others examples include fleas, mites, mosquitoes, and lice.

Brood parasites are animals that leave their eggs to be raised by other closely related organisms. Given the opportunity, the cowbird will push the eggs out of a host bird's nest and lay her own eggs before the host returns. If the host does not notice the switch, it will raise the parasite's young as its own. Cuckoo birds as well as cuckoo wasps have a similar method of raising their young.

The last type of symbiosis is known as commensalism. In a commensalistic relationship, one member of the relationship benefits, while the other is unaffected. For example, barnacles are sedentary crustaceans that, as adults, attach to objects for life. Barnacles attach to numerous animals, including whales and clams, without affecting the host. Another example is the relationship between clownfish and anemones. The clownfish, which is immune to the anemone's sting, finds safety and shelter from predators within the anemone's tentacles. Meanwhile, the anemone is not affected by the clownfish.

It should be noted that some scientists do not consider the latter two types of symbiosis, parasitism and commensalism, to be actual forms of symbiosis. These scientists cite mutualism as the only form of symbiosis because the prefix *sym-* means *together* or *united*. Since parasitism and commensalism only benefit one member of the relationship, these species are not together or united.

Predator-Prey

Predator and prey interactions occur at all trophic levels throughout a food web. For example, a mouse in a grassland habitat may be the prey of a snake that is in turn preyed on by a hawk. That same mouse also preys upon insects, worms, and larvae. In a simple predator-prey relationship, such as that of the hare and the lynx, the interdependence of their populations can be seen. If the rabbit population is low, there is not enough food for the lynx and its population will stay relatively low. If the population of rabbits increases, the lynx population will also soon increase. Increased lynx population will then be followed by a decrease in hare population, and the cycle will repeat.

The changes in the population of a single species can result in the alteration of a number of other species' populations by a process known as **trophic cascade**. This effect was apparent when the gray wolf was reintroduced into Yellowstone National Park. When the wolf, an **apex predator**, went extinct in that region, the entire food web was altered. The gray wolves' primary prey population, the elk, increased rapidly in number. This affected the growth of many trees, such as the cottonwood, and the populations of other herbivores such as beavers. A lesser predator, the coyote, also increased its population. Shortly after the reintroduction of the wolf in 1995, the elk population returned to its former level. Populations of cottonwoods, beavers, and coyotes also returned to their old levels.

However, the balance of a healthy ecosystem can be disrupted a number of ways. Two general ways that can affect an ecosystem's stability are climatic/structural and organismal events. In the latter, species are added or removed, thus disrupting the food chain. For example, invasive species are species that are not native to a particular ecosystem. They may be very similar to another species in the ecosystem, but since they are not native to this ecosystem, they often do not have the stresses that a native species has. For example, the vining plant kudzu was introduced in the south years ago as an erosion prevention plant. It grows rapidly and is adapted to warm, humid climates. However, since it is not native to the area, there are no, or few, organisms that feed on the kudzu. Because of this lack of stress on the plant, it has grown and smothered other plants and trees out of existence with little mechanism, outside of human interaction, to slow its growth. Kudzu now runs rampant in the south, and its range is growing. Other examples of invasive species include zebra mussels, flying carp, snakehead fish, and Chinese mantises.

Climatic and structural changes can also disrupt an ecosystem. These events can include flooding, desertification, and habitat destruction. In climatic events like flooding and desertification, the *biogeoclimate*—the climate involving the soil and biotic community—of the region is altered and can no longer support the ecology that was once present. Flooding kills plants and many animals via drowning, while desertification, marked by arid climate conditions and a loss of soil fertility, does the same via dehydration. Structural changes like deforestation and habitat destruction in general destroy an ecosystem that may have taken several hundred to several thousand years to establish. This requires the ecosystem to change or start over.

Common Ancestry and Cladograms

Besides interspecies and intraspecies competition like predation and finding mates, animal populations are also affected by disease. Some diseases kill only a few species every year. For example, chronic wasting disease, CWD, is an infectious protein disease (prion) that affects cervids like elk, whitetail deer, and mule deer. The disease is always fatal and turns a normally healthy animal into a slowly starving animal. There is no known cure and no known method of transmission. While this disease is always fatal, it does little to the overall population. Meanwhile, some diseases, such as Dutch elm disease, have had detrimental effects on the elm population since it was introduced in America in the late 1920s. Once the disease, a form of fungus spread by the elm beetle, infected the first native American elm tree, it spread rapidly. Since its introduction, nearly 40 million elm trees in North America have died from the disease, devastating the natural elm stock.

Attempts to categorize or classify all life forms date back to ancient times. Our current classification system is based on the one developed by Carolus Linnaeus, who in the 1700s made a major step in bringing order to the natural world. He laid the foundation for modern **taxonomy,** our system of classification and nomenclature (naming). Linnaeus used Latin to name organisms, so that everyone involved in the field of science could use a universal language for the names of organisms. He then created a system of *binomial nomenclature*, which uses a two-part name that illustrates the special characteristics of each organism. The binomial later evolved into the *genus* and *species* of modern taxonomic classification (see below).

Our modern classification scheme starts with five major groups, called **kingdoms.** This is the largest grouping category. As classification continues, it becomes increasingly specific. The seven main hierarchical levels in this classification system are as follows (note that in plants the term *division* is used instead of *phylum*):

<u>Modern Taxonomy</u>

Kingdom
Phylum
Class
Order
Family
Genus
Species

The following is a brief overview of the five kingdoms: Prokaryotae (also called Monera), Protista, Mycetae, Plantae (plants), and Animalia (animals).

Kingdom Prokaryotae (Monera)

Prokaryotae (also called Monera) are simple, single-celled, microscopic organisms and are the most primitive and ancient of all life forms. They lack a distinct cell nucleus, and their DNA is not organized into chromosomes. Prokaryotae play a variety of roles in the biological world:

- Some are pathogenic (disease-causing).

- Some serve to break down gaseous nitrogen into inorganic compounds that are biologically usable (through a process called **nitrogen fixation**).

- Some serve to decompose organic matter, so that it can enrich the soil and nourish plant life.

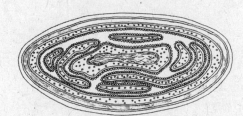

Typical Prokaryotic Cell

Members of this Kingdom Prokaryotae include **bacteria** and **cyanobacteria** (a special form of bacteria). There are more than 4,800 known kinds of bacteria. Most need oxygen to live, but other bacteria do not. Within the latter group, some can withstand small amounts of oxygen, while others find oxygen poisonous and will die if subjected to large amounts. (Bacteria are examined in more detail elsewhere in this review.)

Cyanobacteria are a special type of bacteria that are autotrophic and photosynthetic, which means that they manufacture their own food by harnessing the Sun's light and absorbing inorganic substances such as carbon dioxide and ammonia. The most common cyanobacteria are blue-green algae (though they belong to a different kingdom than other types of algae). If a body of water contains appropriate and abundant nutrients, a growth explosion of blue-green algae can occur, creating a "floating carpet," or algal bloom. Much—perhaps even most—of the Earth's oxygen is attributable to the photosynthetic activity of these great masses of Cyanobacteria, which come in nearly 8,000 known species.

Kingdom Protista

Many members of this kingdom are single-celled and move about freely as individual organisms. Others, however, form colonies with other organisms of their type. The latter are *eukaryotic* cells—they have a distinct nucleus as well as other structures found in more advanced cells.

PROTOZOA

Protozoa are distinguished from other protists in their locomotive ability and by how they obtain food. Two common protozoa are the amoeba and the paramecium. An **amoeba** is a formless cell that uses *pseudopods* to move and to obtain food by simply engulfing it. A **paramecium** moves about by using hairlike *cilia*, which is also used by the paramecium to direct a current of water containing food into the organism's gullet (like a mouth and stomach all in one).

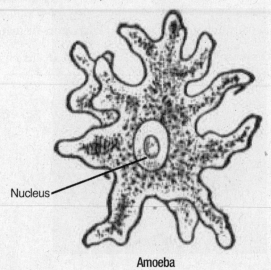

Nucleus

Amoeba

Some protozoa are pathogenic. Different types of protozoa are responsible for serious diseases such as amoebic dysentery, malaria, and African sleeping sickness (a debilitating, wasting disease).

ALGAE (PLANT-LIKE AUTOTROPHS)

Algae are classified in the Kingdom Protista, but algae are quite different from amoebas and paramecia. Algae are *autotrophic*—they contain chloroplasts with pigment for photosynthesis—and include green, brown, red, and golden algae, as well as diatoms, euglena, and dinoflagellates. Most seaweed is a collection of algal cells. Due to seaweed's high nutritional value, it accounts for a major portion of the human diet in many parts of the world, especially near the coasts in Asia.

- *Diatoms* are widely used commercially for the reflective and abrasive nature of their shells. Paints used for marking highway lanes often contain *diatomaceous* earth, and many types of toothpaste contain diatom shells because of their abrasive quality.

- *Euglena* are perhaps the most curious of the various forms of algae. Euglena are normally *autotrophic*—they contain chloroplasts with pigment for photosynthesis. However, under low light or the absence of light, they can switch to a *heterotrophic* mode, meaning they can obtain their energy by consuming other organisms. They move by flagella, which is more characteristic of protozoa.

- *Dinoflagellates* are one of the main components of plankton. Some species can undergo explosive population growth, creating seas of red or brown referred to as "red tide" and producing great amounts of neurotoxins that kill both marine and human life.

SLIME MOLDS (FUNGUS-LIKE HETEROTROPHS)

You may have seen **slime molds** when camping or hiking. These amoeba-like cells dwell in dark, warm, moist areas—on damp soil or in decaying plant matter such as rotting leaves and logs—and move about, often in slug-like colonies, when food becomes scarce. During a portion of its lifecycle, one type of slime mold develops into a multicellular structure that produces and releases spores. In this form, a slime mold resembles a fungus, which is discussed next.

Kingdom Mycetae

The common name for any member of the Kingdom Mycetae is **fungus.** These are mainly non-motile, non-photosynthetic heterotrophic organisms. What this means is that they have no independent means of mobility, and they obtain the energy they need by consuming other organisms. Most fungi, including molds and mushrooms, are multicellular. However, this kingdom does include a few unicellular types as well, such as yeast. Fungi survive and spread by producing and releasing spores, which are made sexually or asexually. When released, the spores are carried by wind or water and can travel hundreds of miles from their point of origin.

Fungi can be either *saprophytic* or *symbiotic*. Saprophytes absorb nutrients from dead organisms. Symbiotic fungi are either parasitic (causing, for example, athlete's foot and ringworm) or mutualistic. Lichens are a form of mutualistic fungus; they afford protection to algae and cyanobacteria in exchange for the food energy that algae and cyanobacteria provide.

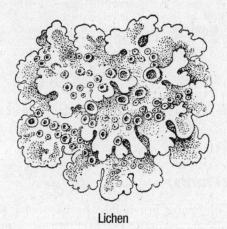

Lichen

A variety of commercial foods—mushrooms, blue cheese, beer, and soy sauce, to name a few—are fungi products.

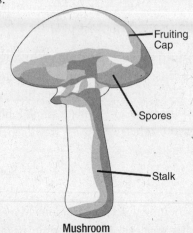

Mushroom

10. Which of the following is the most specific category in the modern taxonomic classification system?

    (A) class

    (B) family

    (C) phylum

    (D) order

Of the five categories listed, the most specific is *family*. **The correct answer is (B).**

11. What do all protists share in common?

    (A) They are a food source for humans living near the ocean.

    (B) They must consume organic matter to survive.

    (C) They can reproduce either asexually or sexually.

    (D) They dwell in water or in watery tissues of organisms.

Protozoa and algae are water dwellers, and slime molds dwell in the moist tissues of rotting leaves or logs. Choices (A), (B), and (C) each describe some, but not all, protists. **The correct answer is (D).**

Kingdom Plantae (Plants)

Organisms in the three kingdoms previously discussed are very simple compared to the organisms in Kingdom Plantae (plants). All plants are multicellular, and they all are autotrophic, which means that they generate their own food. Nearly all plants do so by using their photosynthetic pigment **chlorophyll** found in organelles called **chloroplasts.**

NONVASCULAR PLANTS AND VASCULAR PLANTS

Plants have adapted to live in practically every type of environment. They evolved in form, activity, and function over millions of years. The multitude of plants within this kingdom is staggering. But they all fall into two major groups of plants: nonvascular and vascular. By far, the simpler of the two forms is **nonvascular** (division *Bryophyta*). Nonvascular plants have no true roots, stems, or leaves. Lacking these structures, they are limited in two ways. First, they cannot grow very high—only a few inches in height, on average. Second, they can dwell only in a consistently moist environment. Nonvascular plants include mosses, liverworts, and hornworts. Among these forms, only mosses contain specialized tissues for transporting water or other nutrients from one part of the plant to another, and only to a limited extent.

A **vascular** plant is one that contains specialized tissues for carrying water, dissolved nutrients, and food from one part of the plant to another. Vascular plants represent the vast majority of plants. Their complex vascular tissues show that they have successfully adapted to living on land. They are mainly diploid throughout their lifecycle, which means that they reproduce sexually—one pair of chromosomes from each parent are inherited by offspring.

Vascular plants generally have roots, stems, and leaves. **Roots** anchor a plant into soil, from which the plant draws water and nutrients through osmosis. Humans eat a variety of roots, including carrots and radishes, to name just a few. **Stems** support leaves and transport raw materials from roots to leaves and synthesized food from leaves to roots and other parts of the plant. Humans eat the stems of a variety of plants, including celery, sugar cane, and several others.

Leaves are the major photosynthetic portion of a plant. Their *chlorophyll*—the pigment that gives plants their green appearance—receives sunlight, while the underside of the leaf takes in carbon dioxide through tiny openings called **stomata.** The plant then combines the carbon dioxide with water to produce energy in the form of glucose. As a waste product of the process, oxygen is then released through the leaf's pores. (The process by which a leaf exchanges gases in this way is called **transpiration.**)

The major parts of a typical leaf are as follows:

- *Epidermis:* Outer layer of stomata and hair cells, as well as a waxy cuticle that prevents water loss

- *Guard cells:* Epidermal cells that change shape according to water amounts in leaf; create tiny openings called stomata, which close or open to control the rate of water loss and gas exchange

- *Palisade layer:* Contains chloroplasts, arranged vertically for maximum photosynthesis

- *Spongy layer:* Loosely arranged chloroplasts that allow for water, oxygen, and carbon dioxide circulation

- *Vascular bundles:* Xylem and phloem tissues in bundles

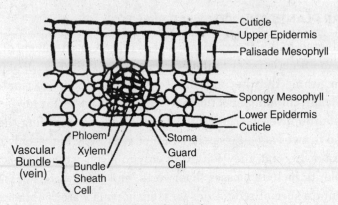

Cross section of a typical leaf

Vascular bundles of xylem and phloem are present in most other parts of a vascular plant as well. A plant's **xylem** consists of hollow cells that form tubes for carrying water from soil into roots and for transporting water to above-ground portions of the plant. A plant's **phloem** consists of thickened sieve-like cells that transport organic molecules produced in one part of the plant to storage regions in another part (for example, the sugars produced by photosynthesis in the leaf move to the root for storage).

SEEDLESS AND SEED-BEARING VASCULAR PLANTS

Some vascular plants are seedless. These plants propagate by producing and disseminating spores. Examples include club mosses, horsetails, and ferns. Other vascular plants are seed-producing. A **seed** is actually a reproductive organ—a specialized structure that contains an embryo enclosed in an outer, protective seed coat. Under the right conditions and with water, the seed can germinate and grow into an adult plant.

Seed-producing vascular plants include gymnosperms and angiosperms. Literally translated as "naked seed," **gymnosperms** produce seeds on the surfaces of woody, leaf-like structures called cones. The pine tree is one well-known example of a gymnosperm. Gymnosperm cones are reproductive structures: male cones produce pollen, and female cones produce ovules on the same tree. During the process of pollination, pollen is transferred by wind, insects, or rain from a male cone to the eggs of the female cone.

Angiosperms produce fruits, which attract animals that eat the fruit and then disperse its seeds. This group of plants is considered the highest order of evolution in the plant kingdom. Unlike gymnosperms, angiosperms produce coated seeds that are enclosed by tissues of an ovary, which is part of the plant's flower. The ovary and other tissues develop into the mature structure that is the fruit. When you eat a piece of fruit, you are actually consuming a plant's mature ovary.

There are 300,000 varieties of plants that produce flowers, fruits, and seeds. All flowering plants are considered angiosperms. The two major categories of angiosperms are **monocots** and **dicots.** The distinction between the two involves a structure called a **cotyledon.** The cotyledon contains the embryo and stores nutrients for germination of the embryo. A monocot's seed contains only one cotyledon. Examples include orchids as well as grasses such as rye, corn, wheat, and rice. A dicot's seed contains two cotyledons.

Dicots account for the majority of angiosperms—about 180,000 varieties—including most herbaceous (non-woody) plants, flowering shrubs, and trees. Examples of dicots include legumes (beans), apples, and oak trees.

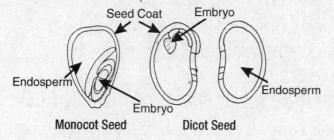

Monocot Seed   **Dicot Seed**

Flowers are the specialized reproductive organs for flowering plants. They contain both the male and female portions of the plant, as shown and described in the following diagram:

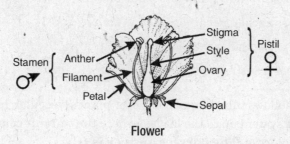

Flower

- **Petals:** The floral portions of the plant, usually ornate to attract pollinators

- **Pistil:** The female reproductive parts (stigma, style, ovary)
  - *Stigma*—the portion on which pollen lands
  - *Style*—the slender tube-like portion between the stigma and ovary
  - *Ovary*—contains the egg and site of fertilization; the ovary matures into the fruit with seeds

- **Stamen:** The male reproductive parts (anther, filament)
  - *Anther*—produces pollen
  - *Filament*—the stalk on which the anther sits

- **Sepals:** The protective portion of the unopened flower

In an angiosperm, pollination occurs when pollen is transferred from the anther to the stigma. Some angiosperms can self-pollinate, while others rely on insects, birds, or wind to carry pollen from the anther of one plant to the stigma of another.

12. All of the following characteristics clearly distinguish vascular plants from nonvascular plants EXCEPT for which one?

Vascular plants can

(A) grow in a vertical direction

(B) obtain water and nutrients from beneath the earth

(C) manufacture their own food

(D) survive for a time without moisture in their immediate environment

All plants, vascular and nonvascular alike, can manufacture their own food. **The correct answer is (C).**

13. Which statement about a typical vascular plant is LEAST accurate?

(A) The roots store water and other nutrients.

(B) The leaves exchange carbon dioxide for oxygen.

(C) The xylem regulates the plant's water intake.

(D) The xylem transports glucose from leaves to roots.

The xylem is the hollow, tube-like portion of a plant's vascular bundle that carries water from the root system up to the leaves, where the water is combined with carbon dioxide to produce glucose. **The correct answer is (C).**

Kingdom Animalia (Animals)

Animals have adapted to live in practically every environment on Earth. From habitat to size and from form to color, animals show amazing variety. There are at least 4 million known species of animals. But all are multicellular; and all are heterotrophic, meaning they must obtain food by consuming other organisms. All members of the animal kingdom share the following characteristics:

- They are *motile*, which means they can move from place to place during all stages of their life; they can also move one part of their body in respect to the other parts.

- They are not photosynthetic (they do not produce their own energy but rather obtain that energy by consuming other organisms).

- They reproduce sexually (although some may reproduce asexually as well).

- They consist of multiple cells (they are *multicellular*), many of which organize into tissues and then into complex organ systems.

Within the animal kingdom are different phyla (the next level down in the taxonomic classification system). Following are the main features and representative members of each phylum. Note that the phyla listed here begin with the more basic forms and advance to more complex forms. The phylum *chordata*, the last one listed here, is examined in greater detail than the others.

PHYLUM PORIFERA (SPONGES)

- **Features:** Stationary (sessile) organisms as adult; contain pores for circulation of water and food

- **Members:** Marine and freshwater sponges

PHYLUM CNIDARIA (CNIDARIANS)

- **Features:** Secrete a hard, surrounding covering for protection; have a two-form lifecycle (a stationary, or sessile, *polyp* produces a free-floating *medusae*); radial symmetry (body forms symmetrical around a center); stinging tentacles surround a mouth used for both ingesting food and eliminating waste.

- **Representative members:** Hydra, jellyfish, corals, sea anemone

PHYLUM PLATYHELMINTHES (FLATWORMS)

- **Features:** Free-living, nonsegmented carnivores with a sac-type digestive system

- **Representative members:** Planarian, tapeworm, fluke (tapeworms are segmented parasites that live in the digestive tract of vertebrates and have no digestive system; flukes are both external and internal parasites with flattened bodies that live off of fluids from their host)

PHYLUM ASCHELMINTHES (ROUNDWORMS)

- **Features:** Cylindrical bodies and a complete digestive tract; not segmented; can be free-living or parasitic; especially useful for recycling in soil habitats

- **Representative members:** Nematode, pinworm

PHYLUM ANNELIDA (SEGMENTED WORMS)

- **Features:** Occupy marine environments (exception: earthworms); segmented bodies; can be parasitic (example: blood-sucking leech); have developed organ systems, including circulatory, muscular, digestive, and nervous system.

- **Representative members:** Earthworm, leech, polychaetes

PHYLUM ARTHROPODA (ARTHROPODS)

- **Features:** Some possess a head, thorax, and abdomen (insects, spiders); have appendages such as jointed legs, antennae, mouthparts, and wings; have external exoskeleton armor; metamorphose from egg, larva, and pupa to adult; most are terrestrial, but some are marine dwellers (Class *Crustacea*)

- **Members:** Class *Insecta* (insects), Class *Arachnida* (spiders), Class *Diploda* (millipedes), Class *Chilopoda* (centipedes), Class *Crustacea* (crustaceans)

PHYLUM MOLLUSCA (MOLLUSKS)

- **Features:** Soft bodies (some are protected by shells); some have a ventral, muscular foot (example: bivalves, in which two shells are hinged together); have well-developed circulatory and nervous systems

- **Representative Members:** Bivalves (clam, mussel), squid, snail, octopus

PHYLUM ECHINODERMATA (ECHINODERMS)

- **Features:** Marine dwelling; possess tubular feet and a water-circulating system; lattice-like internal skeleton and usually a hard, spiny outer covering; adults exhibit radial body symmetry (a five-pointed body form)

- **Representative members:** Starfish, sand dollar, sea cucumber, sea urchin

PHYLUM CHORDATA VERTEBRATA (VERTEBRATES)

This is the most advanced phylum in terms of evolutionary development. Three evolutionary developments make the *chordata* phylum so advanced:

- A *notochord*—a flexible rod that provides structural support

- A *dorsal nerve chord* on the back or upper surface, which in some animals differentiates into a brain and spinal cord

- One or more *pharyngeal gill slits* for carbon dioxide/oxygen exchange (in higher animals, these slits can appear as passages leading from the nose and mouth to the esophagus)

The phylum *chordata* includes several different classes—the taxonomic system's next level down—as listed and briefly described below. Animals in the first four classes are *cold-blooded,* which means that their internal body temperature varies directly with external temperature. Animals in the remaining two classes are *warm-blooded,* meaning they normally maintain a constant internal body temperature. (Note that only two of several classes of fish are listed here.)

- **Class Chondrichthyes (cartilaginous fish)**
  - **Features:** Cold-blooded; cartilage skeleton and fins
  - **Members:** Sharks and rays

- **Class Osteichthyes (bony fish)**
  - **Features:** Cold-blooded; bony skeleton, fins, and scales; use gills to process oxygen from water; mainly external fertilization
  - **Members:** trout, bass, carp

- **Class Amphibia (amphibians)**
  - ○ **Features:** Cold-blooded; moist skin with no scales; external fertilization; undergo *metamorphosis* (dramatic change from fishlike form to four-legged, air-breathing terrestrial form) during development after birth or hatching; three-chambered heart
  - ○ **Members:** Frog, salamander, toad
- **Class Reptilia (reptiles)**
  - ○ **Features:** Cold-blooded; body covering of scales and horns; internal egg fertilization
  - ○ **Members:** Snake, turtle, crocodile, lizard
- **Class Aves (birds)**
  - ○ **Features:** Warm-blooded; wings and forelimbs; hard bill that covers the jaw; covering of feathers; internal fertilization; eggs enclosed in calcium-enriched shell; four-chambered heart
  - ○ **Members:** Chicken, crow, eagle
- **Class Mammalia (mammals)**
  - ○ **Features:** Warm-blooded; hair covers body, feed young with mammary glands; internal fertilization; four-chambered heart
  - ○ **Members:**
    - *Monotremes* (primitive egg-laying)—duck-bill platypus
    - *Marsupials* (mother carries young in body pouch)—kangaroo
    - *Rodents* (incisor teeth that grow continually)—rat, squirrel, mouse
    - *Cetaceans* (marine; forelimbs modified to flippers)—dolphin, porpoise, whale
    - *Carnivores* (meat-eaters)—dog, wolf, cat
    - *Primates* (large brain; stand erect; ability to grasp and hold objects)—human, ape, monkey, lemur

14. Animals belonging to which of the following phyla have body forms that exhibit radial symmetry?
    - I. cniderians
    - II. roundworms
    - III. arthropods
    - IV. echinoderms

    (A) I and II only

    (B) I and IV only

    (C) II and III only

    (D) II, III, and IV only

All cniderians and echinoderms have body forms that exhibit radial symmetry. In this shape, the body extends symmetrically outward from a central mouth or other opening. **The correct answer is (B).**

15. Which *chordata* class could be characterized as a "hybrid," exhibiting a combination of characteristics from two other such classes?

    (A) cartilaginous fish

    (B) amphibians

    (C) reptiles

    (D) birds

Amphibians undergo a metamorphosis after birth or hatching, beginning as water-breathing, fishlike animals and then transforming into terrestrial, air-breathing animals with four legs. In this respect, they are a hybrid of fish and reptiles, both of which are also cold-blooded. **The correct answer is (B).**

To better understand the relationship of one class of animals to another, scientists use a method of mapping known as a *cladogram*. A cladogram essentially creates an evolutionary family tree. The base of a cladogram depicts a common ancestor of the animals represented. As the cladogram moves up, branches shoot out, representing groups of animals that branched away from the common ancestor; these branches start from the earliest or least evolved organisms and move upward toward the most evolved organism. Cladograms can be very general, covering an entire animal kingdom, or very specific, covering only a single genus. Most cladograms are based on physiological differences, such as scales, feathers, and mammary glands. However, with the increase in genetic mapping, cladograms based on genetic relationships are also sometimes used. The cladogram below shows the ancestry of humans.

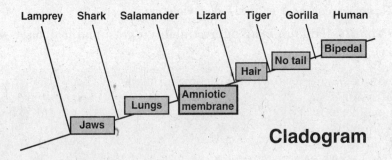

Natural Selection and Adaptation

Evolution is the process by which species of plants and animals arise from earlier life forms and undergo change over time. Our understanding of evolution is rooted largely in the theories of nineteenth-century scientist Charles Darwin. Based on his observations of different traits among certain animal species, Darwin theorized that species evolve as a result of **natural selection**—a process by which the strongest, or "fittest," among offspring survive to reproduce, passing on to the next generation the particular traits that helped them survive. When a species's environment changes, those members that have inherited traits that help them survive the change are more likely to survive. These survival traits are called **adaptations**. Darwin's theory has been verified by studies of the fossil record and by DNA studies. **Artificial selection** refers to human manipulation of traits in a species by selective breeding. This is done most often to produce desired traits in crop, livestock, and pet species. Over many, many generations, genetic traits that help a species adapt to its environment become increasingly common among individuals, while less useful traits wither.

Darwin's theories of evolution and natural selection have since been refined to accommodate the theories of punctuated equilibrium, sexual selection, and genetic drift.

- **Punctuated equilibrium:** Darwin proposed that species evolution is a gradual, nearly constant process. Recent investigations involving fossil evidence suggest, however, that evolution occurs in spurts (*punctuations*), between which are long time periods of stability (*equilibrium*) when no change in the species occurs. Environmental events such as sudden and dramatic climate changes, which we know have occurred many times both globally and regionally throughout our planet's history, lend support to this idea: it is when a species confronts a sudden environmental change that it is forced to adapt to that change by evolving.

- **Sexual selection:** This type of selection occurs when individuals in a population compete not for resources and survival, but rather for mates. For example, males with characteristics such as aggressiveness, great size, or strength or colorful feathers might be more successful in attracting mates, and thus their genetic traits will ultimately survive over many generations.

- **Genetic drift:** Studying isolated and relatively small populations, researchers have shown that certain genetic traits sometimes survive or wither over time by random chance. Like rolling genetic dice and getting the same trait many times in a row, against the statistical odds, a species can evolve in an aimless, or drifting, manner that has nothing to do with survival of the fittest.

Given that populations continually evolve, at what point does a population evolve into a new species? The generally accepted definition of the biological species concept is a population of organisms that is reproductively isolated from all other populations. This definition is generally accepted for vertebrate species, although other legitimate alternative definitions exist that take into account the diversity of reproductive biology (sexual, asexual, budding, etc.), and natural histories and life cycles.

Speciation occurs in three stages:

1. **A population becomes isolated.** Speciation begins when a group of individuals separates into an isolated population that no longer exchanges individuals with the parent population. Physical or geographical barriers to migration can occur from changes in the environment, such as a new stream resulting from a storm, creating allopatric (living separately) species. Isolation can also be due to a change in a trait, such as behavior or coloration that prevents individuals from interbreeding with dissimilar individuals in the population, even if they are living together in the same geographical area.

2 **The isolated population evolves independently.** Once isolated, individuals will naturally accumulate random mutations, but they will also be subjected to a different set of selective pressures and/or evolutionary processes from that of the original population, and thus evolve differently from the parent population.

3 **Reproductive isolating mechanisms evolve.** Eventually the separated populations will evolve to a point where they can no longer interbreed because of reproductive isolating mechanisms. These are grouped into two categories: *Pre-zygotic mechanisms* prevent reproduction, and include physical mechanisms that prevent successful copulation or fertilization; behavioral mechanisms that prevent successful solicitation of a mate; or temporal mechanisms in which mating seasons or fertility patterns are no longer synchronized. *Post-zygotic mechanisms* result in offspring with gene combinations that are fatal, cause sterility, or otherwise prevent reproduction.

---

16. Which of the following is LEAST likely to contribute to the development of a new species?

(A) volcanic activity that reforms a region's landscape

(B) a shift in a population's sexual selection criteria

(C) an adaptive response to the appearance of a new predator

(D) a local climate change that alters a population's breeding season

---

Choice (C) simply describes natural selection, whereby the traits of a species' fittest and most adaptable individuals are the ones that are passed on to subsequent generations. In itself, natural selection does not cause speciation. **The correct answer is (C).**

Energy Flows in Ecosystems

Ecology is the scientific study of the interactions among organisms and between communities of organisms and the environment. All of these interactions determine where organisms are found, in what numbers they are found, and why they are found where they are. In this section, we will briefly explore the main concepts in this field of study.

The Biosphere

The term **biosphere** refers to the entire part of the Earth that supports life. The biosphere consists of the surface of the Earth, of course, but it also encompasses the lithosphere (the rocky crust of the Earth), atmosphere (the air we breath, which consists mainly of nitrogen and oxygen), and the hydrosphere (all of the water on Earth). This section examines the part of the biosphere appearing on the Earth's surface. The lithosphere, atmosphere, and hydrosphere are examined in the Earth Science review.

Environments, Ecosystems, and Biomes

Ecologists define an **environment** as any external factor that can influence an organism during its lifetime. These environmental influences can be divided into two categories:

- *Biotic factors:* living things that affect an organism
- *Abiotic factors:* nonliving things, such as water, air, geology, and the Sun, that can affect an organism

Biotic and abiotic factors are interrelated. For example, plants rely on many abiotic factors, including rainfall and temperature, for proper growth. If either should change dramatically in a particular region, plant growth will decline, which in turn will reduce food sources and habitats for animals.

The term **ecosystem** refers to an entire community of organisms, their physical environment, and how the interactions among that community and between the community and that environment.

Flow of Energy and Matter in Ecosystems

Ecosystems are structured according to each organism's main source of food. **Producers** are *autotrophic*—they manufacture their own food from inorganic substances. Autotrophs include green plants and photosynthetic bacteria, both of which use solar energy to convert nutrients into glucose. (Autotrophs include other types of bacteria as well.) **Consumers** are *heterotrophic,* which means that they rely on other organisms as their food source. There are three sub-types of consumers:

- **Primary consumers** (herbivores), which feed directly on producers
- **Secondary consumers** (carnivores), which feed only on primary consumers
- **Tertiary consumers** (carnivores), which feed on secondary consumers

Decomposers are heterotrophic but feed on waste or dead material: dead plants of all kinds, fecal waste, and dead animals; they recycle raw materials to the ecosystem. A simple feeding pathway among organisms in an ecosystem can be shown in a **food chain.** Here is an example of a simple food chain:

Humans (secondary consumer) → fish (primary consumer) → plankton (producer)

Food chains represent a transfer of energy from one organism to another. All organisms need a source of food to survive, so all organisms participate in food chains. Energy (food) moves through a series of levels—from producer to herbivore to carnivore. These levels are called **trophic levels** (the word *trophic* means "feeding"). The following diagram shows the hierarchy of the feeding levels:

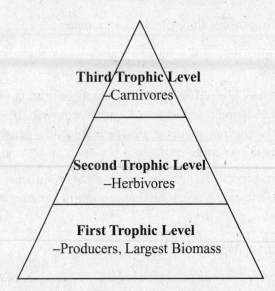

Producers account for the main portion of the **biomass**—the total amount of food available for consumption in the ecosystem. On average, producers pass only about 1 percent of their biomass to primary consumers, which in turn pass about 10 percent of their biomass to secondary consumers. At each higher level, again, about 10 percent of biomass is passed up to the next trophic level. The great majority of biomass is not consumed but rather is converted to energy used for growth and survival.

Of course, humans don't only eat fish, herbivore populations don't only eat one kind of plant, and carnivore populations don't consume only one type of herbivore. Thus the simple food chain is an oversimplification for most ecosystems. A more complete model is a **food web,** which links many food chains together into a matrix that represents complex feeding relationships.

Energy is not recycled, but matter is. This cycling is usually studied in terms of the paths of several chemical elements found in organic compounds. For example producers take in carbon as carbon dioxide and convert it into glucose. Consumers extract energy from glucose and release carbon back into the atmosphere as carbon dioxide, where it is once again available to producers. Carbon also takes long, complicated side trips, as when it is converted to fossil fuel over millions of years, but it never disappears. Other elements, such as nitrogen and oxygen, also have complex cycles. These are explained in greater detail in the pages on earth science.

As mentioned above, energy relationships among trophic levels can almost never be described completely by simple, one-to-one linear food chains. To see the complete picture, we must construct a food web that combines the energy exchanges among all producers, consumers, and decomposers. In the food web shown here, the arrows show the direction of energy transfer.

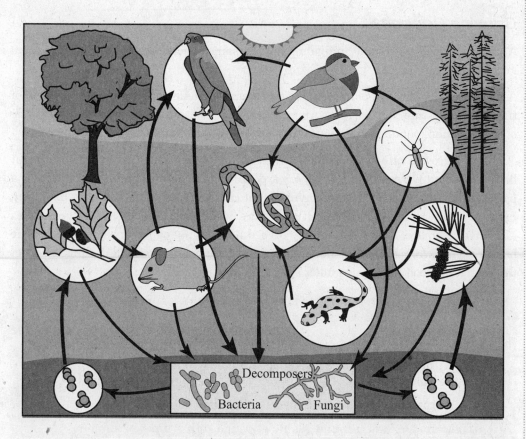

Pick any member of the food web and think about what would happen if that species were removed or if their population changed. Take the mouse, for example. A decrease in mouse population will mean a decrease in snake population but also a decrease in lizard population because snakes will have to prey more heavily on them. This will lead to an increase in insect population, and so forth. If you continue with this line of reasoning, you will see that changing the population of any one species in an ecosystem affects the populations of all other species.

Habitats and Niches

Feeding relationships dominate the structure of an ecosystem. However, an ecosystem isn't just one giant free-for-all characterized by severe interspecies competition for food. Each population of animals occupies a particular **habitat**—a particular locale such as a forest community or an arid, grassy plain in which a species is best suited to live according to its biological adaptations. Different species can even become "specialists" within their habitats by occupying a **niche.** A niche refers to all specific biotic and abiotic elements an organism incorporates for its survival, such as feeding location, food source, feeding schedule, source of shelter, and nesting location. For example, many birds may occupy a forest habitat, but some eat seeds and others eat worms and insects; some birds eat high up in a tree and others closer to the ground. In other words, various types of birds in the same habitat occupy different niches.

Carrying Capacity

A **population** is a group of individuals of the same species occupying the same geographical region.

A population's growth depends largely on its male-female ratio and on the portion of the population that is at or below reproductive age. With too few individuals capable of reproduction, population growth will slow or even decline.

Just as the growth rate of any population is limited, so is its size. A given environment has only so many resources to support a population. The maximum population of a particular organism that a given environment can support is referred to as **carrying capacity.** The most significant limiting factors in carrying capacity are food resources and physical space. A population may exceed its carrying capacity temporarily if the birth rate is extremely great, though eventually the population will decline to reflect the scarcity of food resources and/or space.

17. Which of the following best helps to explain why feeding structures in most ecosystems are better described as food "webs" rather than food "chains"?

    (A) Many different types of plants can exist in the same community.

    (B) Without a sufficient food source, animals will move to another community.

    (C) If animal life disappears, then so does plant life.

    (D) Many animals consume plants as well as other types of animals.

The simple model of linear food "chain" does not account for the fact that the same animal might be a primary consumer (plant-eater) in one chain *and* a secondary consumer (meat-eater) in other chain. A "web" in which various chains are interconnected better represents a community's complete feeding structure. **The correct answer is (D).**

18. A colony of termites feeds off the wood frame of an old house for several years, but then the colony disappears. Assuming that the termites were not exterminated by humans, what most likely happened?

    Eventually, the termite population

    (A) exceeded its life span

    (B) was consumed by secondary consumers

    (C) exhausted all of its available biomass

    (D) exceeded its carrying capacity

The termites' environment (the house's wood frame) contained a limited amount of food resources to support the growing termite population. Once this *carrying capacity* was exceeded, in all likelihood the termites died off. **The correct answer is (D).**

Body Systems

The body's organ systems work together in many other ways. The best way to understand these connections is to examine each of the organ systems, in turn. This section briefly describes the structure, components, and functions of the body's various organ systems, as well as how they function together with one or more of the other systems.

The Integumentary System

The integumentary system includes skin, sweat glands, oil glands, hair, and nails. It is the largest organ in the body. Our skin is a barrier between our bodies and the external environment. It prevents water loss, mechanical and chemical damage, and microbial invasion. Skin is composed of two distinct regions: the **epidermis** and the **dermis.** These two regions are further divided into several functional layers. The third region just beneath the skin is the **hypodermis.** It is not considered a part of the skin, but it serves a protective function similar to skin.

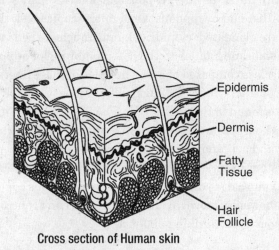

Epidermis

Dermis

Fatty
Tissue

Hair
Follicle

Cross section of Human skin

The Skeletal System

The skeletal system supports the body and acts as a lever system for the muscles, creating movement at joints. This system contains **bones,** of course, which provide for movement and support. But bones also serve as a mineral depository. What's more, the marrow at the center of our bones is where our new blood cells are formed. The 206 bones in the normal human body can be divided into two major groups: the *axial* skeleton (80 bones that run the axis of the skeleton) and the *appendicular* skeleton (126 bones that include the limbs and the pectoral and pelvic girdles).

Bones articulate, or meet, with one another at joints. **Cartilage** lines the joints to prevent bones from rubbing against each other. Depending on the type of movement at a joint, the cartilage can provide either a smooth articulating surface or a strong adhesion between bones. To help stabilize movable joints, such joints utilize a band-like type of connective tissue known as a **ligament.** Finally, **tendons** attach muscles to bone at joints.

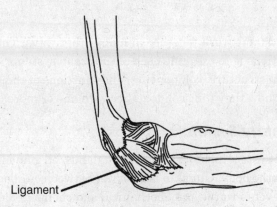

Ligament

The Muscular System

The more than 600 muscles in the human body come in three types: skeletal, cardiac, and smooth. **Skeletal muscles** are responsible for the body's movement and are attached to bone at either end by tendons. On a microscopic level, the fibers that make up skeletal muscles are elongated, cylindrical, multinucleate cells that are encased by a **sarcolemma:** a membrane similar to the cell membrane of other cells containing a single nucleus. A muscle is composed of many bundles of these fibers working together. Each time a muscle contracts and shortens itself, it moves the body part it is attached to. **Cardiac muscle** is found in the walls of the heart. This muscle allows for the strong pumping action of the heart's ventricles. **Smooth muscle** is found in the walls of hollow organs, such as the stomach and intestines. Cardiac and smooth muscles coordinate with the nervous system in an entirely different way than skeletal muscles do. The movement of skeletal muscle is voluntary—you have conscious control over it. Cardiac and smooth muscles, however, move involuntarily—you can't control them consciously. They work without your even thinking about it.

The Nervous System

The nervous system, along with the endocrine system (you will read about this next), is responsible for coordinating all of the physiological processes in the body. The nervous system responds rapidly to external stimuli and to messages from the brain. It regulates a myriad of actions from breathing and digestion to the blink of an eye and the beating of the heart.

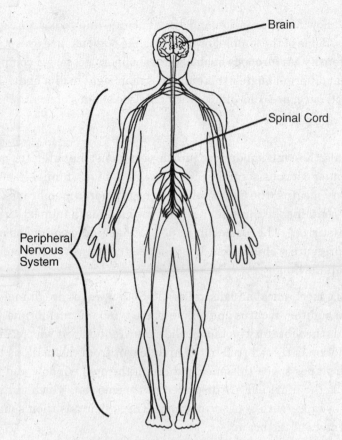

Peripheral Nervous System

The **peripheral nervous system** extends away from the spine and into the limbs. It carries impulses from sensory neurons to the **central nervous system,** which consists of the brain and spinal cord. The brain processes incoming sensory information and translates it into instructions. It then sends those instructions to the appropriate organs of the body, so the body can respond to the initial sensory information. The **neuron** is the functional unit of nervous tissue that is used by the central and peripheral nervous systems.

Taste, vision, hearing, balance, and smell are integral parts of the nervous system. They allow us to interact with and interpret external stimuli as well as monitor internal changes of a chemical or physical nature. Different animals utilize these senses to different degrees. Also, some nonhuman animals possess senses that humans lack altogether. For instance, some species of birds detect the magnetic field of the Earth; honeybees see ultraviolet light; and rattlesnakes sense infrared radiation from objects at a distance.

THE EYE

Visual perception in humans is like a camera lens. Light enters through an adjustable lens that, like film, focuses the image on a receptor called the **retina.** Within the retina are specialized photoreceptors called **rods** and **cones** that detect different properties of light. Cones allow for color vision and visual acuity, and rods are responsive in low light conditions. Some of the simpler organisms, like euglena, use eyespots that merely detect light intensity. Arthropods such as grasshoppers possess a compound eye that lets light enter at different angles; this enhances their sight in dim light. Other animals, such as deer and mice, are colorblind—they only see shades of gray.

THE EAR

In higher animals, the ear is subdivided into three regions: the outer, the middle, and the inner ear. The outer ear consists of the pinna (a cartilaginous, funnel-like structure), the external auditory meatus (the ear canal), and the tympanic membrane (the eardrum). The middle ear contains the three ear ossicles: the malleus (hammer), the incus (anvil), and the stapes (stirrup). The Eustachian tube in the middle ear opens into the throat and allows for pressure stabilization. The inner ear contains the receptors for hearing, balance, and equilibrium.

Hearing is both a mechanical and neural event. Sound waves are funneled into the ear via the external auditory meatus and arrive at the tympanic membrane. The tympanic membrane sends the vibratory motion at the same frequency it was received to the ear ossicles. The motion is transferred to the middle ear, from the malleus to the incus to the stapes. The stapes sends this energy through the oval window and into the inner ear. The fluids in the inner ear are displaced by this motion, which in turn stimulates hair cells that synapse with sensory neurons. These neurons then send messages to the auditory centers of the brain.

The Endocrine System

The **endocrine system** is composed of specialized organs called **glands,** which secrete chemical messengers called hormones. These hormones are carried throughout the body by the circulatory system, but they have only site-specific responses and can only attach to recognized receptor molecules of certain cells. The response time of hormones varies according to the outcome that is needed. For instance, epinephrine and norepinephrine (released from the adrenal medulla gland) can cause a rapid behavioral response known as the "flight or fight" response. This causes the heart rate, blood pressure, and breathing rate to increase as well as directing blood to skeletal muscle. The following table lists each major gland, the major hormones it releases, and its function.

Major Endocrine Glands and Functions

Endocrine Gland	Hormones Released	Functions
*Pituitary (both anterior and posterior)	1. Growth hormone 2. Anti-diuretic hormone	1. Regulator of muscle, bone, and connective tissue growth 2. Increases re-uptake of water into blood from renal tubules; increases blood pressure
Thyroid	1. Thyroxin 2. Calcitonin	1. Regulates cellular metabolism 2. Decreases calcium ions in blood
Parathyroid	Parathyroid hormone	Increases calcium ions in blood
Pancreas	1. Insulin 2. Glucagon	1. Lowers blood-sugar levels; increases rate of metabolism of stored sugar 2. Increases blood-sugar levels by converting glycogen to glucose; synthesizes glucose; and releases glucose to blood from liver cells
Adrenal glands	1. Corticosteroid 2. Epinephrine	1. Decreases sodium ion excretion; influences cellular metabolism and provides resistance stressors; contributes to secondary sexual characteristics during puberty 2. Increases blood-sugar levels, heart rate, blood pressure, and respiratory rate; shunts blood to skeletal muscle; mobilizes the sympathetic nervous system for short-term stressors or emergencies
Testes	Testosterone	Starts the maturation of male reproductive organs, secondary sexual characteristics at puberty, and sex drive
Ovaries	1. Estrogen 2. Progesterone	1. Initiates maturation of female reproductive organs and secondary sexual characteristics at puberty 2. Promotes breast development and menstrual cycle

*The pituitary gland has an effect on all of the major glands. The few listed in this table do not represent the total number of hormones released from the pituitary.

19. Which of the following is the best analogy to the nervous system?

   (A) a motor

   (B) a radio broadcast

   (C) a computer

   (D) a bee hive

A computer receives input, which is transmitted to a central processor, which then provides instructions as to the proper response to that input. The nervous system functions in a similar way. **The correct answer is (C).**

The Cardiovascular System

Many multicellular organisms, such as humans, consist of trillions of cells that need a rapid and efficient way to meet their physiological needs. During cellular metabolism, cells take in nutrients, create waste, and store, make, and use molecules—all of which need to be transported to other parts of the body. The cardiovascular system provides transportation by using several integrated parts. The heart pumps blood into **arteries,** which distribute the blood to the organs. Blood is pumped into successively smaller arteries until it enters thin-walled vessels called **capillaries.** Blood is diffused through capillary beds so material can be exchanged between the blood and organ tissues. Blood then percolates through the capillary beds and into **veins,** which gradually merge with larger veins until the blood returns to the heart.

CARDIAC PHYSIOLOGY

The right side of the heart, the **right ventricle,** pumps blood to the lungs, which are near the heart. The larger **left ventricle** sends blood to the **aorta,** the main artery that delivers blood to the rest of the body. The left ventricle must contract with greater force, and this force creates a higher pressure in the arteries. Each contraction of the heart is reflected in the heartbeat. (When you take your pulse, you are actually measuring your heartbeat rate.)

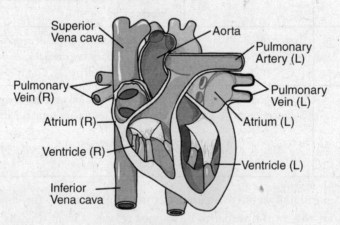

Heart and Associated Vessels

Blood pressure is measured through the heartbeat. There are two phases to a heartbeat. The first is referred to as **systolic pressure** and is the result of the strong contraction of the ventricles as blood is pumped into the aorta. The second phase is **diastolic pressure,** which is the result of ventricular relaxation.

BLOOD

The largest component of blood is a fluid matrix called **plasma.** Blood plasma, which is mostly water, transports a host of materials, including wastes, nutrients, hormones, electrolytes, and proteins, cells, and heat from one body region to another. Most notably, within the plasma are erythrocytes (red blood cells), leukocytes (white blood cells), and thrombocytes (platelets), each of which performs a unique function:

- **Red blood cells** consist mainly of **hemoglobin,** which are the molecules that transport oxygen throughout the bloodstream.

- **White blood cells** serve as a defense mechanism against disease, tumors, parasites, toxins, and bacteria; they move from blood to tissues, and they produce antibodies for long-term protection.

- **Platelets** are tiny disk-shaped cells that seal small ruptures in blood vessels and assist in blood clotting.

Human blood is categorized by four types—A, B, AB, and O—according to which type of antigens are present on the surface of a person's red blood cells. (Letters A and B represent different types of antigens.) An **antigen** is a substance that stimulates the production of an **antibody** when introduced into the body. Antibodies circulating throughout a person's bloodstream normally recognize the antigens in that same person's blood and do not react with them. However, if one type of blood is transfused with another type of blood, antibodies in the new blood can react with the foreign antigens by binding to them, resulting in clumping of the blood. Thus, a safe **blood transfusion** requires that the antigens of the donor's blood match those of the donee's blood:

- Blood type O contains no antigens and thus can safely be used for any blood transfusions, regardless of the blood type of the person receiving the transfusion. On the other hand, individuals with blood type O can receive transfusions only from donors with type O blood.

- Blood type AB contains both antigens A and B and thus can safely be transfused with any other blood type but cannot be donated for transfusions with any other blood type.

- Blood types A and B can be donated for transfusion with blood type AB.

Human blood that contains a special antigen known as the **Rh factor** is considered *Rh positive*, while blood that lacks this antigen is considered *Rh negative*. If given a blood transfusion from an Rh-positive donor, a person who is Rh-negative can produce antibodies that destroy red blood cells. The fetus of an Rh-negative mother can nevertheless be Rh positive, in which case the mother's blood will produce these antibodies, thus threatening the life of the fetus. Under this circumstance, a transfusion of blood from an Rh-positive donor can save the life of the fetus.

The Respiratory System

The cyclic exchange of respiratory gases within an organism is known as **respiration.** Most vertebrates use lungs for gas exchange, although animals such as frogs use both a lung and moist skin to exchange gases.

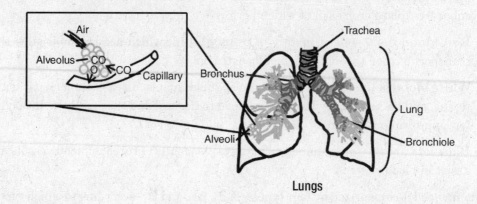

Lungs

Mammals have the most complex respiratory systems of all animals, with successively smaller branching tubes that open into vascularized sacs. Oxygen enters the lungs through the **bronchi**—two large tubes that branch off the trachea—which phase into smaller **bronchioles,** which then terminate in **alveolar sacs.** These sacs are covered with capillaries to facilitate gas exchange across the thin walls of the **alveoli.**

The Digestive System

Cells need a constant supply of nutrients for energy and as building blocks to assemble macromolecules. The **digestive system** allocates and processes these nutrients. The human digestive system, in all its complex functions, is nothing more than a long muscular tube extending from the mouth to the anus. Along this pathway are several modified pouches and segments to perform specific tasks, including nutrient intake, mechanical and chemical processes of digestion, nutrient uptake, and the elimination of undigested material.

When food reaches the stomach, both mechanical and chemical functions go to work on it. The muscles in the walls of the stomach churn, mixing the food with gastric juice and **pepsin,** which digests proteins. The majority of chemical digestion and nutrient absorption occurs in the **small intestine.** To assist with this process, the **pancreas** delivers several **enzymes:** *trypsin,* which breaks large polypeptides into amino acids; *amylase,* which changes polysaccharides to simpler forms; and *lipase,* which breaks fat down into glycerol and fatty acids. The **liver** assists by producing **bile,** which physically emulsifies fats to improve digestion. Virtually all nutrient absorption occurs in the small intestine, where the nutrients pass through the walls into the blood vessels. The nutrient-laden blood is taken to the liver and then to the body tissue.

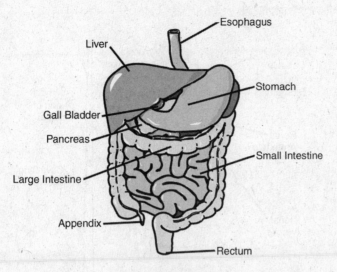

Digestive System

Not all food is digested, of course. Some moves into the **large intestine** to be processed. Any water and available minerals from the food are absorbed into the blood vessels of the walls of the large intestine and are returned to circulation. Bacterial action produces vitamin K, which is also absorbed into blood vessels and returned to circulation. The remainder of bacteria and undigested food form the main component of feces, which are passed as waste from the body.

The Renal System

Cellular metabolism of every organism produces fluid waste products, such as urea and nitrogenous wastes, which need to be separated from useful products, such as water, and then disposed of. Simple organisms perform this task by diffusing waste directly into their surrounding environment. More complex organisms, on the other hand, use a tube system, or **renal system,** to excrete fluid wastes.

Vertebrates have one of the most complex renal systems of all organisms. It centers around the **kidney,** which is responsible for several functions:

- Blood filtration (the kidneys separate the filtrate from cellular components within blood)

- Monitoring of waste concentrations in blood

- Reabsorption from filtrate

- Return of reusable components back to blood

- Secretion for eventual removal of filtrate

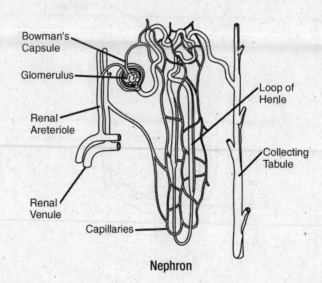

Bowman's Capsule

Glomerulus

Renal Areteriole

Renal Venule

Capillaries

Loop of Henle

Collecting Tabule

Nephron

Each kidney is composed of more than 2 million specialized units called **nephrons,** which play a large role in maintaining homeostasis by retaining useful substances and getting rid of waste products. Any usable molecules, including water, are reabsorbed and returned to circulation. Whatever is still left after this reabsorption process is waste, which is moved through the ureter to the bladder, where it waits to be passed from the body.

The Reproductive System

The primary goal of the reproductive system is the continuation of a species. There are many forms of reproduction, yet the degree of an organism's complexity is a good indicator of how it reproduces. **Asexual reproduction** does not require any of the complex structures used by eukaryotic cells. **Binary fission** is a type of asexual reproduction that is used by prokaryotic cells like bacteria. These cells merely replicate a simple loop of DNA and then undergo cytokinesis. **Fragmentation,** as seen in phylum *Porifera* (sponges), is another asexual form of reproduction. In this form, a piece of the body breaks away and matures into a larger form.

Vertebrates reproduce sexually by producing **gametes** (eggs and sperm) through their reproductive organs, called **gonads.** Females produce ova, or eggs, within their main reproductive structures, the ovaries. A hormone released by the pituitary gland stimulates egg production. An embryo develops from the initial **zygote,** a fertilized egg. If fertilization does not occur, the egg and its newly created uterine lining are sloughed off the walls of the uterus and moved out of the body. Males manufacture sperm within their major reproductive organ, the **testes.** The hormone **testosterone** signals and maintains sperm production. As with the female reproductive system, a pituitary hormone stimulates the production of sperm cells.

20. Which of the following is responsible for oxygen transport throughout the body?

   (A) nephrons in the kidneys

   (B) capillaries and veins

   (C) alveolar sacs in the lungs

   (D) hemoglobin in red blood cells

Red blood cells consist mainly of hemoglobin molecules, which are responsible for transporting oxygen throughout the body through the bloodstream. Choice (B) is incorrect because veins return oxygen-depleted blood back to the lungs. **The correct answer is (D).**

21. Where does most nutrient absorption occur in the body?

   (A) the small intestine

   (B) the stomach

   (C) the liver

   (D) the large intestine

It is through the lining in the long, serpentine small intestine that the nutrients from the food we eat are absorbed into the bloodstream and transported to cells throughout the body. **The correct answer is (A).**

Homeostasis

The body is a remarkable complex of various organ systems that function together in unison—like the components of a properly calibrated and well-oiled machine. For example, the organ systems naturally work together to ensure that the body's internal conditions remain stable and, if conditions deviate from their normal ranges, to return them to normal. Appropriate organ responses to internal changes help ensure steady body temperature, blood pressure, and the chemical composition of body fluids. The body's tendency to maintain the stability of these and other internal conditions is referred to as **homeostasis.**

There are many homeostatic mechanisms within the body, including temperature and water regulation. When the body gets overheated, sweat glands are activated and the body releases water. As air moves over the water that is being released through pores, the water evaporates, cooling the body. Conversely, when the body is too cold, the muscles will begin to contract involuntarily, causing the body to shiver. These small muscle contractions create heat via movement. By either sweating or shivering, the body will attempt to stay within the homeostatic range until it can no longer do so or until environmental conditions change.

Another homeostatic mechanism is water regulation, which is done primarily in the kidneys. Inside the kidneys are millions of specialized cells called nephrons. Nephrons filter the blood for excess water and nutrients and then flush this excess out in the form of urine. Depending on the ratio of nutrients to water in the blood, the nephrons will regulate the amount of each it removes from the blood. When the body is slightly dehydrated, the urine is more concentrated, and when the body has plenty of water, the urine is less concentrated. This is an attempt at maintaining proper water levels throughout the body.

22. Which of the following helps provide for homeostasis in the human body?

   (A) cardiac muscles, which pump more blood to skeletal muscles when you sense danger

   (B) retinal cones, which allow you to see the difference between red and green traffic lights

   (C) sweat glands, which help cool your body on a hot summer day

   (D) inner ear receptors, which help you keep your balance during a tennis match

Through the process of homeostasis, your body seeks to maintain optimal states, including an optimal internal body temperature. When your body heats up too much, the integumentary system goes to work to secrete sweat, which helps reduce body temperature. **The correct answer is (C).**

In order to carry out basic functions and maintain homeostasis, the body must have fuel. This fuel comes in the form of food. But not all foods are the same nutritionally. Foods are divided into three basic categories: *carbohydrates, proteins,* and *fats*. Comparatively, fats have more than twice the calories per gram (9 calories per gram) than either carbohydrates or proteins (4 calories per gram each). To put this into perspective, the United States Department of Agriculture (USDA) recommends a daily intake of approximately 2600 calories for the average man and approximately 1800 calories for the average woman. Rarely does a person eat a food that is fully a carbohydrate, protein, or fat. Because foods can have a mixture of these basic groups, the USDA breaks all food into six categories: grains; vegetables; fruits; milk/dairy; oils; and meat and beans (proteins). Each group is labeled with recommended serving amounts for a balanced daily diet. These servings amounts are: 6 oz. of grains; 5.5 ounces of meats and beans; 2 cups of fruit; 2.5 cups of vegetables; 3 cups of dairy; and a sparing amount of oils. A diet based on these portions would provide a person with approximately 2000 calories. The food pyramid shown here illustrates the relative amounts of the various food groups.

By eating a variety of foods within these guidelines, a person is also more apt to ingest essential vitamins and minerals. Vitamins are divided into two groups: water soluble and water insoluble. Water-soluble vitamins include Vitamin C and the B vitamins. Vitamin C is found in citrus fruits such as oranges, among other foods. While no food has all eight B-complex vitamins, they are found in a variety of foods, ranging from leafy greens to meats and beans to potatoes. Water-insoluble vitamins include A, D, E, and K, and are found in a variety of foods as well, ranging from leafy greens to meats and grains.

Minerals are also divided into two groups: **macronutrients** and **micronutrients**. This division is not based on the size of the mineral itself but on the amount needed in order for the body to function properly. *Macronutrients*, of which the body may require up to 1 to 2 grams daily, include sodium, potassium, calcium, and chloride. In contrast, the body may only require a few micrograms per day of *micronutrients*, also known as *trace minerals*. These include chromium, copper, iron, and zinc. By eating a variety of food, the body is able to ingest all the vitamins and nutrients it needs to operate at optimal levels.

EARTH AND SPACE SCIENCE

The study of our planet and outer space encompasses several fields of science. Geology deals with the composition of the Earth and past and present events (both interior and exterior) that have shaped it. Oceanography involves physics, biology, chemistry, and geology as they pertain to ocean-related processes. Meteorology is the study of the Earth's atmosphere, weather, and climate. Astronomy is the study of the universe and the objects in it, including stars, planets, nebula (dust particles), and so forth.

The Earth's History

Among physicists, the prevailing theory today about the formation of the Earth is that our solar system was born out of a rotating cloud of dust and gas, a *nebula,* that flattened into a disk, rotated, and then contracted under the influence of gravity. This theory would explain how the planets' orbits came to lie in nearly the same plane as they move around the Sun. Scientists think it took more than 1 billion years for gravity to cause the Earth to settle and contract. Once this occurred, a sorting process called **differentiation** took place in which materials making up the forming proto-planets were sorted by densities. Materials with heavier densities sank to become the core material, and the lighter materials rose to the surface. The outer surface cooled and became the crust.

Earth's History

Based on radiometric evidence, the Earth is estimated to be 4.5 billion years old. Earth's history has been divided into eras. You may be familiar with some of these eras. Here are the four major geologic eras of Earth's history:

Precambrian: Approximately 4 billion years ago; no life on land; life flourished in the ocean, first with bacteria, then sponges, corals, jellyfish, and worms

Paleozoic: From 545 to 245 million years ago; defined by the advent, evolution, and extinction of many life forms; life began moving from water to land as land emerged and formed; the first plants and amphibians emerged

Mesozoic: From 245 to 66 million years ago; spans the Triassic, Jurassic, and Cretaceous periods; each period has unique characteristics, but one unifying element is the presence of dinosaurs, which first appeared in the Triassic period but experienced mass extinction by the end of the Cretaceous period

Cenozoic: From 66 million years ago to the present; characterized by extensive evolution and natural selection; many distinct species began to form; hominids (a branch of animals that includes modern humans) first began to develop

Radiocarbon Dating

Much of what we know about past life forms and eras has been gathered from fossil evidence. **Fossils** represent the remains of living things preserved in layers of ancient rock, or *strata*. Fossils can be petrified when deposited minerals replace the original organism; petrified wood is one example. Other fossils are created when impressions form through compression, leaving a carbonaceous film of an organism. Sometimes an entire plant or organism is preserved, such as when a piece of amber (petrified tree sap) traps an insect. When strata are exposed, as they are on the walls of the Grand Canyon, fossils can be put in chronological order. This is based on the law of **superposition**, which is simply that the deeper the layer, the older it is.

Fossils provide proof that different life forms have existed at different times throughout Earth's history. Geologists can use the mineral and biological samples in various strata to determine the age of rock layers through a method referred to as **absolute dating** or **radiocarbon dating.** In general terms, this dating method involves the element carbon, which is found in all biological life. Carbon 12, the normal form of the element, contains 6 protons and 6 neutrons. However, the isotope carbon 14 contains 8 neutrons and hence is unstable. It decays radioactively into other elements at a certain rate. The time required for 50 percent of a pure sample of a radioactive isotope, such as carbon 14, to decay is referred to as the isotope's **half-life.** Through radiocarbon dating, the amount of a particular radioactive isotope in a sample can be measured and used to determine the age of the sample.

Composition of the Earth

The Earth consists of several layers. The Earth's **lithosphere,** or outer shell, is made of the crust and upper mantle. The **crust** is the outermost, thinnest layer, and shows the greatest degree of variation; the average thickness of the crust is 3 to 25 miles. It is composed of rocks enriched with silicon, potassium, and sodium. The oceanic crust is denser than the continental crust.

The **mantle** is a middle layer that extends halfway to the Earth's center at a depth of 1,800 miles. It is composed of silicate enriched with magnesium and iron and is slightly denser than the crust. Due to high temperatures and pressure, the rocks in the mantle tend to be fluid.

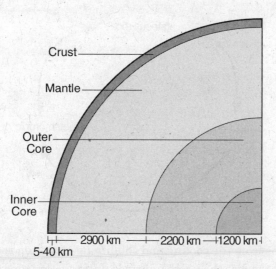

The **core,** which is the innermost layer, consists of an outer and an inner core. The **outer core** is mainly molten and consists of nickel, iron, and sulfur. It is 1400 miles thick. The **inner core** is solid and is composed of iron and nickel. The core is much denser than either the mantle or the crust.

23. Which of the following is a possible objective of radiocarbon dating?

(A) to determine the composition of layers deep beneath the Earth's surface

(B) to compare the length of one geologic era to another

(C) to determine the age of extinct species of animals

(D) to determine the age of the Earth

Fossils are remains of living organisms and contain carbon that decays over time. By determining the extent of the decay through radiocarbon dating, it is possible to calculate how long ago the organism lived. **The correct answer is (C).**

24. Which of the following statements about the Earth's composition is true?

(A) The outer crust is uniform in its thickness.

(B) The Earth's core is a fiery, gaseous ball.

(C) Deeper layers are colder because they receive less warmth from the Sun.

(D) Deeper layers are denser than layers nearer the surface.

The Earth's core is denser than the mantle (the middle layer), which is denser than the crust. **The correct answer is (D).**

Rocks, Soil, and Changes to the Land

Rocks are composed of combinations of different minerals. As described next, there are three basic categories of rock: igneous, sedimentary, and metamorphic. As the Earth undergoes gradual changes, each type of rock is constantly, but slowly, transformed into one of the other types in a continuous process called the **rock cycle.**

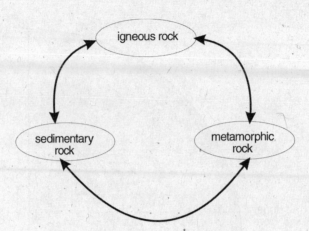

Igneous rock forms from the cooling and solidifying of molten rock, or magma, which becomes lava once it reaches the Earth's surface. *Intrusive* igneous rock, such as granite, forms from magma cooling slowly below the Earth's surface. This allows for a larger crystal size. *Extrusive* igneous rock forms when magma cools quickly on the Earth's surface, resulting in a finer texture. Volcanic rock in the form of basalt is an example of extrusive igneous rock.

Sedimentary rock appears as small rock fragments formed from the deposition of sediment due to erosion or weathering, or by chemical processes. These small fragments can be carried into bodies of water (by wind or rain), where they sink to the bottom and deposit in layers. Sedimentary rock can be classified further into the following three types:

- *Clastic* rocks are formed by bits of previously existing rock. The pieces can be small and sand-like or larger pebbles. Sandstone is one example of clastic rock.

- *Organic* rocks are formed from previously living life forms.

- *Chemical* rocks are formed from dissolved minerals left from evaporated water. Limestone and chalk are examples of chemical rocks.

Metamorphic rock, like the other types, forms from preexisting rock. The unique feature of metamorphic rock is that it is formed when rocks are subjected to high temperatures and pressure, which chemically change the original rock into a new material. Marble is one example of a metamorphic rock.

Weathering

Weathering encompasses a variety of mechanical and chemical events that slowly disintegrate and decompose rocks. **Mechanical events** such as the freezing and thawing of water within the cracks of rocks can cause the rocks to expand and crack. Rocks can be mechanically worn away by the movement of wind as well. Fine sand particles act as an abrasive and wear rock away over time. Water that flows continuously over rocks can also result in mechanical weathering. Rock particles scrape against each other in the flow of water in a lake or river, smoothing one another.

Rocks can also weather as a result of **chemical events** that act to dissolve rocks. One example of such an event involves **acid rain,** which occurs when human-made pollutants in the atmosphere combine with rainwater and become acidic. The acid compounds that are formed, including sulfuric acid, can be strong enough to weather rocks.

Soil

Soil is created from weathered rocks. There are two main types of soil. **Residual soil** is found on top of the rock from which it formed. **Transported soil** has moved from its rock of origin, so it may not resemble the underlying rock. Another type of soil, **humus,** is created from dead organisms such as animals—especially worms, insects, bacteria, and fungi—and decayed plant matter. This form of soil is very important for plant growth. So soil is actually a mixture of weathered rock and organic material, and hence varies depending on the type of rock from which it formed and the organisms in the soil.

Forces of Erosion and Deposition

Erosion is a major force that is responsible for the gradually changing landscape of the Earth. Erosion occurs when rocks and soil are moved from one place and are ultimately deposited in another place. Erosion can be caused by a variety of forces, including water, wind, gravity, and glaciers.

WATER

Running water produced as run-off by rain flows downhill, carrying particles with it as it moves. When the water moves onto land, it can erode the land and create gullies. Arid regions that do not have much vegetation to hold down the soil (by roots) or to absorb the water experience even more erosion. The gullies can become deep enough to form streams that cause further erosion by the abrasion of moving sediments against rocks. Rapidly moving water can carry a huge amount of sediment, and over time it can completely change a landscape. Hillsides that lack any vegetation show the most pronounced effects of water erosion. The Grand Canyon was formed over the course of many millennia in this way.

The term **alluvium** refers to the silt, clay, sand, gravel, and other sedimentary material deposited by flowing water. Alluvium can be deposited in riverbeds or at the mouths of rivers to form *deltas*. It can also be spread out across a plain in a fan-shaped way that is referred to as an **alluvial fan.**

WIND

Wind carries sediments many miles, and the abrasive effects of the sediments can create new sediments.

GRAVITY

The force of gravity is a constant on Earth—and it plays a role in erosion. Just as we are pulled by gravity, so, too, are land masses. Gravity pulls on rocks and soil, sending them down slopes in an action called **mass wasting.** Rapid mass wasting occurs in the forms of landslides and mudslides. Landslides result when earthquakes loosen soil or when rain water pushes rocks down a slope.

GLACIERS

The size of glaciers makes it easy to understand how they can cause erosion. Glaciers are like huge rivers of ice moving slowly across a landscape and pushing large rocks on a layer of ice and mud. This results in heavy glacial abrasion. Glaciers also leave large boulders or foreign particles from different regions behind as they melt and move. An example of glacial abrasion is Yosemite Valley in California.

25. Which would NOT be considered a cause of rock weathering?

(A) compression at high temperatures

(B) the freezing of water in cracks between rocks

(C) fine windblown sand particles

(D) rapidly flowing water, as in a river

The force of compression does not aid in the disintegration of rocks. To the contrary, at high temperatures compression forms metamorphic rocks such as marble. All choices other than choice (A) are causes of rock weathering. **The correct answer is (A).**

26. How was the Grand Canyon formed?

(A) by soil erosion

(B) by the natural rock cycle

(C) by glacial abrasion

(D) by water erosion

The Grand Canyon was formed by the continuous downhill water flow that carried away rock sediments, resulting in gullies that grew deeper and deeper over time. **The correct answer is (D).**

Global Change—Plate Tectonics and Land Forms

Approximately 225 million years ago, all of the continents were joined together as one major continent called Pangea. This land mass eventually broke up into several smaller land masses that drifted apart until they became today's seven continents. On a map or globe, they look as though they could fit together, like pieces of a jigsaw puzzle. This and other evidence gave birth to the **continental drift theory.** Scientists are convinced that the continents are continuing to shift, driven by the interactions between tectonic plates. According to **plate tectonics theory,** the thin crust of the Earth (both the bottom of the oceans and the continents) floats on the surface of the semi-solid mantle. The crust is separated into plates, separated by cracks called faults, somewhat like pieces of egg shell on a cracked egg. There are about seven major plates and two dozen minor plates that make up the Earth's crust. This theory explains earthquakes, volcanic action, how mountain ranges are formed, and the locations of the continents.

As noted earlier, the Earth's lithosphere, or outer shell, is made of the crust and upper mantle. Within the upper mantle, differences in temperature cause currents to form. Magma heated by the core rises toward the crust, while magma close to the crust cools off and sinks. The result of this cycle is the formation of **convection currents,** which move the plates, pulling apart or compressing the plates. The consequences of this phenomenon can be dramatic and devastating where plates meet at **faults.** There are four basic types of movement that can occur between adjacent plates:

- Convection currents can move magma to the surface, **splitting** apart the surface and creating a gap that is filled with solidified molten material. Mid-ocean ridges were created in this manner. These are **divergent faults**.

- Plates can gradually slide past one another in a process called **shearing.** This movement can cause earthquakes. The San Andres Fault in California is a prime example of shearing. These are **strike faults**.

- One plate (the more dense of the two) slides under the plate that is less dense in a process called **subduction.** As the plate that is sliding under is forced down through the crust, it melts, and periodically it will erupt to the surface. Mount Saint Helens, a volcano that erupted in 1980 in Washington State, was induced when one plate off the Pacific Coast slid under the continental plate.

- Two plates can **collide** with one another at faults. This may produce earthquakes, but its more gradual effect is the formation of mountains. The compression forces cause the plates to lift up and form mountains. The Himalaya Mountains in Central Asia provide the Earth's most conspicuous demonstration of plate collision. These are **convergent faults**.

Let's look closer at how the forces of plate tectonics transform the Earth's surface.

Mountains

Folded mountains develop by the slow compression of sedimentary and/or volcanic rock layers. This process results in mountains that are wavelike—they look like a carpet that has been pushed together. Examples of this type of mountain range include the Appalachians, Alps, and Northern Rockies. **Fault mountains** develop when tensile force is exerted along a crack in the crust. Over time, a mountain is formed, with one side bounded by a normal fault of a medium to high angle. The spreading of the crust segments by tensile force causes cracking, and the crust is lifted up. An example of this sort of mountain formation is the Sierra-Nevada range in California.

Volcanoes

Volcanoes are formed by igneous activity—the cooling and hardening of magma—below the lithosphere. When the hot magma beneath the lithosphere is under great pressure and high temperatures, it erupts to the surface and forms a volcano. When the magma reaches the surface of the lithosphere, it is called lava. Not all volcanic activity is the same. Some eruptions are violent, while others are calm. Most major volcanic eruptions, as well as major earthquakes, occur in three major zones of the world where most of the Earth's plates meet.

Earthquakes

Pressures built up within the Earth can also result in **earthquakes.** When the crust shifts and moves, vibrations of varying degree—earthquakes—are created. As noted earlier, tectonic plates move along boundaries, or faults. Plates can push together, pull apart, or slide along each other. These movements reduce the tension and compression forces created by convection currents within the upper mantle. The released tension is the earthquake.

The strength of earthquakes is measured and compared based on the amplitude of the waves they create, called **seismic waves.** These waves are divided into three types:

- **Primary waves** (P, or longitudinal, waves) are compressed waves that travel very fast, especially through denser materials of a solid, liquid, or gaseous nature. The damage they cause is moderate.

- **Secondary waves** (S, or transverse, waves) are side-to-side waves that travel at speeds slower than P waves. S waves only travel through solids and cause more damage than P waves. We know that the Earth's outer core is molten because these waves are lost in seismograph analysis.

- **Surface waves** (L, or Love and Rayleigh, waves) cause a shifting and shaking in the Earth's crust, both up and down and side to side. L waves are the slowest waves, but they cause the most extensive damage.

An earthquake or volcanic eruption occurring on the ocean floor can cause massive waves called **tsunamis.**

27. Plate tectonics theory explains all of the following phenomena EXCEPT

    (A) the direction of ocean currents.

    (B) earthquake activity.

    (C) volcanic eruptions.

    (D) the formation of mountain ranges.

Ocean currents have nothing to do with plate tectonics. On the other hand, the shifting of the plates that make up the Earth's crust are what causes the earth to quake, volcanoes to erupt, mountain ranges to form, and continents to move. **The correct answer is (A).**

28. Which force is at work both in earthquakes and volcanic eruptions?

    (A) subduction

    (B) gravity

    (C) pressure

    (D) shearing

Convection currents are created when magma nearer the core heats up and rises while magma closer to the crust cools and sinks. These currents create compression (pressure), as well as tension (pulling) on the plates, resulting in earthquakes. When magma beneath the lithosphere becomes hot enough, sufficient pressure to cause a volcanic eruption can build up. **The correct answer is (C).**

Natural Resources

A **natural resource** is anything we obtain from the natural environment to meet our basic needs of food, energy, clothing, and shelter. Renewable resources, such as air and water, are replenished in the environment through natural cycles. Many natural resources are finite or nonrenewable—when the supply is depleted, they are gone forever. Nonrenewable resources include copper, iron, oil, coal, and natural gas.

Renewable Energy

Renewable energy sources can be replenished in a short period of time. The five types of renewable sources used most often are biomass, solar, hydropower (water), wind, and geothermal.

Biomass: Biomass is organic material that has stored sunlight in the form of chemical energy. It includes wood, straw, and manure.

Solar: Solar energy is the sun's solar radiation that reaches the Earth. It can be converted directly or indirectly into other forms of energy, such as heat and electricity.

Hydropower: Hydropower is created when moving water, such as a river or a waterfall, is directed, harnessed, or channeled. Water flows through a pipe and then turns the blades in a turbine to spin a generator that produces electricity.

Wind: Humans have used the wind as an energy source for thousands of years. For example, sails capture wind to propel boats, and wind turbines use wind to generate electricity.

Geothermal: When steam and hot water have been naturally trapped in the Earth's crust, engineers drill into the crust and allow the heat to escape, either as steam or very hot water. The steam then turns a turbine that generates electricity. This is known as geothermal energy.

Nonrenewable Energy

Nonrenewable energy sources are extracted from the earth as liquids, gases, and solids. Oil, coal, and natural gas are called **fossil fuels** because they are created from the carbon in the buried remains of plants and animals that lived millions of years ago.

Oil: Oil is formed from the remains of marine animals and plants that have been covered by layers of mud. Heat and pressure from these layers turn the remains into crude oil. After the oil is removed from the ground, it is sent to a refinery, where the different parts of the crude oil are separated into usable products ranging from motor gasoline and propane to ink, bubble gum, and dishwashing liquid.

Coal: Coal beds are found near the ground's surface. Power plants burn coal to make steam; the steam then turns turbines to generate electricity. Separated ingredients of coal (such as methanol and ethylene) are used to make plastics, tar, and fertilizers. Coal also plays an integral role in the steel-making process.

Natural Gas: Like oil and coal, natural gas is formed when plant and animal remains decay and are covered by mud and soil. Pressure and heat change this organic material to natural gas. The main ingredient in natural gas is methane. It is used to heat homes and is an essential material for products such as paints, fertilizer, and antifreeze.

Uranium ore is the source of fuel for nuclear reactors that is mined and converted to a fuel. Uranium is not a fossil fuel. **Nuclear power** plants produce energy through the fission or splitting of uranium atoms, which creates heat. That heat boils water to make the steam that turns a turbine-generator. The part of the plant where the heat is produced is called the reactor core.

The distinction between renewable and nonrenewable resources is explained in the energy section of physical science. For renewable resources, it is also important to note the difference between sustainable and unsustainable use. If a renewable resource is being used faster than it is being renewed, it is being used unsustainably. In some places on Earth, water, wood, and soil are being used unsustainably.

29. Which of the following is involved in the process of converting renewable as well as nonrenewable natural resources to energy?

    (A) steam

    (B) carbon

    (C) wind

    (D) fossils

Geothermal energy is produced when steam (a renewable resource) is released from the Earth's crust; energy is produced from coal (a nonrenewable resource) by burning the coal to make steam; and energy is produced by nuclear fission when the heat from fission boils water to make steam. In all three processes, steam is used to drive turbines that generate electric power. **The correct answer is (A).**

Oceanography

Oceans cover just over 70 percent of the Earth's surface and account for about 97 percent of the planet's total water. Globally, the composition of ocean water includes a variety of ions, including chloride, sodium, sulfate, magnesium, calcium, potassium, and bicarbonate. The average salinity (salt concentration) of ocean water worldwide is 3.5 percent.

Oceans produce **currents** that have predictable patterns worldwide (see map below). These currents, which develop from global wind patterns and water-temperature differences, help determine temperatures within the oceans as well as in the atmosphere.

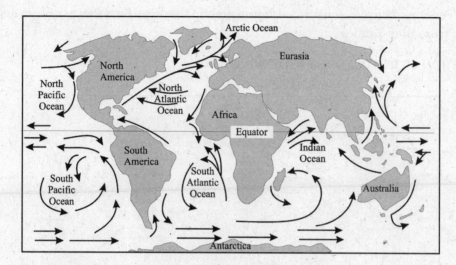

Continental margins are areas where the continents meet the oceans. Continental margins are made of continental shelves, which are submerged extensions of the continental crust beneath the oceans. The **continental shelf** projects outward from the coast at a depth of about 100 meters (325 feet). It is thought that the continental shelf may have been dry land at one time when oceans were smaller than their present sizes. The continental shelf gives way to the **continental slope,** which drops steeply to the ocean's bottom. The continental shelf then becomes the **abyssal plain** of the deep ocean floor. The abyssal plain is about 4000–5000 meters below sea level. This depth does not make it habitable for most forms of sea life. In fact, the abyssal plain is like a barren desert. Most sea life and vegetation are clustered closer to shallow shore waters where sunlight is more abundant.

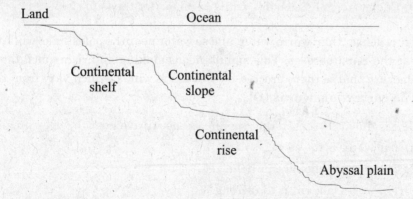

Notable topographical features of sea floor include the following:

- **Seamounts:** Submarine volcanic peaks that, above sea level, form islands (Hawaii is an example of a seamount)

- **Mid-ocean ridges:** Long linear walls that can rise about 1.5 miles above the surrounding ocean floor and are formed by pronounced seismic and volcanic activity (when the ocean floor spreads apart and new ocean crust is created)

- **Trenches:** Narrow, steep-sided depressions in the ocean floor that can reach depths of more than 7 miles

QUESTION 30 REFERS TO THE FOLLOWING MAP.

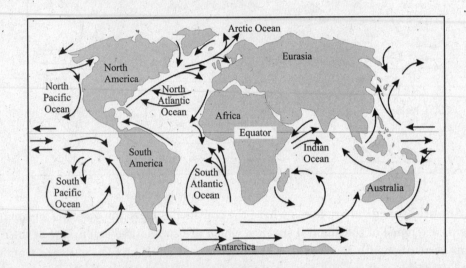

30. Which of the following helps explain the ocean-current patterns shown on the above map?

(A) Rainfall is heaviest near the Equator and lightest near the poles.

(B) Global winds generally blow from north to south.

(C) The narrow ocean straits between some continents increase current speed.

(D) Cold water tends to sink, while warm water tends to rise.

Cold water is denser than warm water, and so water near the poles sinks while warmer water near the Equator rises. This simultaneous sinking and rising facilitates a circulation pattern that is then directed by prevailing winds, which vary from region to region. **The correct answer is (D).**

31. What is the main reason that sea life cannot thrive near the deep ocean floor?

(A) The water is too cold.

(B) There is not enough sunlight.

(C) The ocean current is too strong.

(D) The pressure of overhead water is too great.

The ocean depths receive practically no sunlight. Green plants need sunlight to produce their own food through photosynthesis, and animal life in the sea relies on those plants for food. Thus, life cannot thrive near deep ocean floors. **The correct answer is (B).**

Meteorology

Meteorology is the scientific study of the Earth's atmosphere and atmospheric conditions, especially as they relate to weather and climate. The Earth's atmosphere not only sustains life, but it also acts as a shield that filters out harmful radiation and small meteors. The atmosphere is dominated by two major gases, nitrogen at 78 percent and oxygen at 21 percent.

Earth's Atmosphere

There are four layers to the Earth's atmosphere: the troposphere, stratosphere, mesosphere, and thermosphere (see the following figure). Generally speaking, both air pressure and temperature drop as altitude (distance from the Earth's surface) increases. However, at certain altitudes, temperatures increase instead, as discussed next.

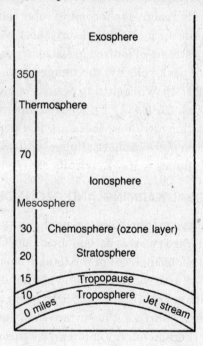

THE TROPOSPHERE

The **troposphere** is the lowest layer and accounts for about 80 percent of the Earth's atmosphere by weight. From ground level, it extends to an altitude that varies from 4 to 10 kilometers. The troposphere is the main layer of atmospheric circulation. The lowest portion of the troposphere (the "jet stream" in the figure) is where most of Earth's weather occurs.

THE STRATOSPHERE

The **stratosphere** is above the troposphere. Though air temperature generally drops with altitude, in the stratosphere it remains constant and actually increases up to the mesosphere. The reason for the increase is that greenhouse gases at this level trap heat radiating from Earth's surface (discussed in more detail under "Greenhouse Gases, Global Warming, and Ozone Depletion").

THE MESOSPHERE

The **mesosphere** lies above the stratosphere and is the layer where meteors first start to burn upon entering the atmosphere. The boundary between the mesosphere and stratosphere marks the outer limit of the high ozone concentration, and so it is at this boundary where temperature once again begins to drop as altitude increases.

THE IONOSPHERE (OR THERMOSPHERE)

Above the mesosphere, at about 62 miles, are the **ionosphere** and **thermosphere.** These two terms are often used interchangeably to describe the same layer. The air at this level is thin and highly reactive to incoming solar radiation. Within this layer, temperatures rise again as the air molecules absorb short-wave radiation produced by **solar wind.** Solar wind is a stream of ionized gases blown from the Sun at supersonic velocities. During periods of peak velocity, the temperature in the thermosphere can reach as high as 1225°C (2237°F), while during periods of low solar wind activity temperatures can fall to as low as 225°C (437°F). These temperature fluctuations are due to the thin nature of air at this altitude—there are few molecules present to absorb and distribute heat. (The term *therm*osphere alludes to this layer's high temperatures, while the term *ion*osphere alludes to its electrically charged nature.)

GREENHOUSE GASES, GLOBAL WARMING, AND OZONE DEPLETION

In addition to nitrogen and oxygen, Earth's atmosphere contains trace amounts of other gases as well. One of these trace gases is carbon dioxide (CO_2). What this gas lacks in abundance—it is only about 0.035 percent of the total atmosphere—it makes up for in impact. Carbon dioxide, along with water vapor and methane, make up what are known as **greenhouse gases,** which are also naturally occurring in Earth's atmosphere. When sunlight is absorbed by Earth's surface, the surface heats up and emits infrared rays (heat waves). Much of this thermal energy cannot pass through the greenhouse gases and warms the atmosphere. In other words, the effect happens because the atmosphere is transparent to visible light rays but not to infrared rays. The resulting global warmth, called the **greenhouse effect,** plays a vital role in maintaining Earth's hospitable climate and its fragile ecosystems. In fact, without these gases, the Earth would be quite a bit colder, rendering it an ice-cold planet unsuitable for many forms of life.

Since the early twentieth century, and especially in recent decades, polluting emissions from cars, factories, and homes have increased the amount of carbon dioxide in the atmosphere. Because carbon dioxide traps heat, scientists believe that there is a direct cause-and-effect relationship between increased carbon dioxide and increased temperatures around the world. This phenomenon is called **global warming** or, by the more general term, **climate change**. Current trends indicate that the atmospheric temperatures are on the rise. At the same time that humans have been producing more and more greenhouse gases through industrialization, they have been stripping the world's forests. Trees and other plants absorb CO_2 during photosynthesis, and then emit the oxygen we breathe as a waste product. But fewer forests means more carbon dioxide accumulation in the atmosphere, which contributes further to global warming.

Along with global warming is another human-induced atmospheric problem referred to as **ozone depletion.** The Earth's ozone layer acts as a natural filter in the stratosphere, protecting life on Earth from overexposure to the Sun's harmful ultraviolet radiation. However, the stratosphere's ozone layer has become compromised by human use of harmful chemicals, especially a group of chemicals called **chlorofluorocarbons (CFCs),** which are used in refrigerants, foam, solvents, and propellants. The overuse of CFCs has actually caused "holes" to appear in the ozone layer. The problem has recently reached an alarming level, and most of the world's developed nations have agreed by treaty to drastically limit their use and production of CFCs.

32. What accounts for increasing temperatures in the thermosphere?

(A) friction from incoming meteors

(B) variations in air pressure

(C) exposure to short-wave solar radiation

(D) a high concentration of ozone

As the atmosphere's outermost layer, the thermosphere absorbs the Sun's short-wave radiation (solar wind), which can increase temperatures dramatically there. **The correct answer is (C).**

33. Which is an accurate statement about greenhouse gases?

(A) They protect us from the Sun's harmful radiation.

(B) They are toxic to most humans and therefore pose a threat to our species.

(C) They keep the Earth warm enough to sustain life.

(D) They are harmful to many plants that humans depend on for food.

Greenhouse gases trap some of the Sun's radiation after it reflects off the Earth's surface, thereby helping to keep the Earth warm enough to sustain life as we know it. **The correct answer is (C).**

Weather and Climate

Although the Sun hits the Earth everywhere, solar energy is strongest at the equator, where light rays are received most directly, and weakest at the poles, where the Sun's light waves hit the surface at a slant. The air in the Earth's atmosphere circulates, which has the effect of making temperatures less extreme. It is this circulation that initiates what we call **weather**—the many atmospheric conditions at any one place in a given time frame.

ATMOSPHERIC (AIR) PRESSURE

The Earth's atmosphere has a mass of 5 thousand million tons. Most of this is in the troposphere, within 18 kilometers (11 miles) of the planet's surface. Gravity maintains this mass in an envelope surrounding the Earth. The mass of the atmosphere applies pressure, called **atmospheric pressure.** The greater the air density, the greater the atmospheric pressure. Pressure decreases with altitude because density decreases. Temperature and humidity affect air pressure as well. Colder temperatures produce denser air and greater air pressure; warm air has a lower density and pressure than dry air.

AIR MASSES

Air masses are large bodies of air distinguished by their temperature, pressure, and humidity. Air masses develop due to local conditions in their place of origin. For instance, if an air mass develops over the tropics, it is going to be warm. If an air mass develops over the poles, it will be cold.

When two air masses of different characteristics collide and mix, fluctuating weather conditions result. This meeting of two air masses is called a **front.** A **cold front** develops when cold, dry air pushes under warmer, moister air, forcing the warmer air up. A **warm front** develops when warm, moist air pushes over colder, dryer air. In either case, the warm air, being lighter than cold air, rises and cools, then condenses along the boundary, resulting in precipitation such as rain or snow. Thunderstorms are often associated with cold fronts. Other front types include a **stationary front** (when air masses move parallel to one another without mixing) and the **occluded front** (when a fast-moving cold front overtakes a warm front).

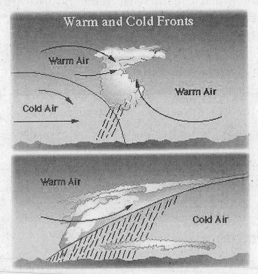

Warm and Cold Fronts

HUMIDITY

Humidity increases when the Sun's energy warms up a body of water, and then the water evaporates into the air as vapor. At any given temperature, the air can hold only a limited amount of moisture. If the saturation point is surpassed, water vapor condenses and returns back to the Earth as precipitation (rain or snow).

Relative humidity refers to the ratio between the amount of water vapor in the air and the maximum amount of water vapor the air can hold without condensing, at a given temperature. The ratio is expressed as a percentage. As relative humidity reaches 100 percent, precipitation is likely because the air cannot hold any additional water vapor. Warm air can hold more water vapor than cold air, which explains why humidity is usually associated with warm temperatures, especially near large bodies of water.

The temperature at which water vapor condenses and turns to liquid is called **dew point.** At dew point, large droplets of water may appear on surfaces as **dew,** while smaller droplets may remain suspended in the air as **fog.** As just suggested, humid air, which is usually warm, has a higher dew point than dry air. This explains why dew and fog tend to form when the air temperature is relatively cold.

CLOUD FORMATION

Clouds form when warm air rises and then cools below the dew point, forming fine water droplets or ice particles suspended in the atmosphere. Clouds almost always form along weather fronts, where cold and warm air masses collide. **Cumulus clouds,** which appear puffy, are the type most often associated with the unstable weather conditions of weather fronts. By observing the movement of cumulus clouds, it is possible to assess the movement of fronts. (The word suffix –*nimbus* signifies a certain type of storm cloud. For instance, *cumulonimbus* clouds are cumulous clouds that are likely to produce violent thunderstorms.)

Of course, there are other types of clouds as well. The two most common types are **cirrus** and **stratus.** Cirrus clouds are wispy and are composed mainly of ice crystals. Stratus clouds are relatively flat and occur in moist, stable air; these clouds are composed of water droplets.

WIND

Wind is created when air moves from an area of high atmospheric pressure to one of lower atmospheric pressure. Large-scale wind patterns on Earth are mainly the result of uneven heating of the Earth's surface by the Sun. More solar radiation is received near the equator than at the poles. As the warm air at the equator rises, it creates a zone of low pressure that draws air up toward it. After the warm air rises, it moves toward the poles, cooling along the way until it is dense enough to descend, about midway between the equator and the two poles. From there, some of the air continues toward the poles, where it meets colder, dry air flowing away from the poles toward the equator. In this way, a continuous cycle of air currents is created between the poles and the equator.

Of course, global wind patterns are actually a bit more complex than just described. The Earth's rotation is the most significant additional factor in these patterns. When the winds descending near the Tropic of Cancer and Tropic of Capricorn reach the Earth's surface, they are deflected east by the Earth's rotation, creating **prevailing westerly** winds, which move from west to east. (In meteorology, wind direction is indicated by the directional source of the wind, not the direction that the wind is moving.) Conversely, winds that are returning from the poles to the equator are deflected west. These **prevailing easterlies** generally blow from about 30° north of the equator to 30° south of the equator. Broad-scale wind patterns are determined to a lesser extent by other factors as well—including ocean currents, the arrangement of continents and oceans, and topography.

CLIMATE

Climate refers to a region's general weather conditions, such as temperature, winds, and rainfall. A region's climate is affected mainly by **latitude** (distance from the equator). In general, regions located at or near the equator experience continuous warming and high rainfall and are virtually seasonless. Regions farther above and below the equator become more seasonal, with warm-to-hot summers and cool-to-cold winters. Near the poles, winters become increasingly longer.

Latitude is not the only determining factor in a region's climate. Broad-scale wind patterns play a significant role as well, as do temperature differences between land and sea. Warm ocean currents affect the climate of regions near the ocean. In general, coastal regions experience more moderate temperatures than inland regions. The relatively warm water near these regions warms the air above the water, which in turn raises temperatures of the air above the nearby land.

A region's topography also plays a role in determining its climate. Elevation is especially significant. It is not uncommon to see snow-capped mountains in regions near the equator. The higher the elevation, the more likely a region is subjected to thin air, which does not hold heat well.

Cycles of Matter

The Water Cycle

The process that begins when the Sun's energy warms a body of water to the point of evaporation and ends when the vapor condenses and returns to Earth is referred to as the **water cycle.** Water moves to the atmosphere by evaporation in the form of water vapor. If the air is warmer, it rises through the atmosphere, where it is cooled. Condensation occurs when this cooled air becomes saturated and the water vapor condenses into water droplets or ice particles, which then return to the Earth's surface as precipitation.

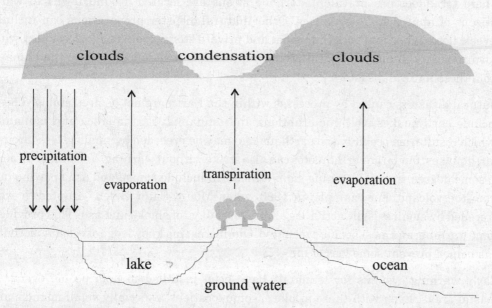

Alongside this component of the water cycle is a second component involving plants. Ground water is absorbed by plant roots, which make use of the nutrients contained in the water. Then, through the process of **transpiration,** the plant gives off vapor containing water as well as waste products. The water vapor rises, cools, and condenses, resulting in precipitation that returns the water to Earth, and the cycle repeats.

Other Cycles

In addition to water, several important elements are cycled. Carbon and oxygen are cycled continuously by the processes of photosynthesis and respiration. These cycles also include several long side trips that can take millions of years. Dead plants and animals can sink to the ocean floor where these elements spend long periods as oil, coal, or sedimentary rocks.

Natural Hazards

Many natural disasters originate in Earth's atmosphere, including hurricanes, tornadoes, floods, and blizzards. Natural disasters such as these can cause widespread injury and fatalities among humans and can cause enough property damage to affect the national economy. Tornadoes, floods, and hurricanes generally happen in the late spring and summer months when temperatures are increasing and snow packs are melting. There is a designated hurricane season, from late June to until October, during which hurricanes typically occur.

To mitigate the damage and loss of lives, governments have implemented safety regulations and evacuation plans. For example, Florida, which is prone to hurricanes, has special building codes for roofs and framing. These include hurricane straps for roof trusses, special plate anchors and straps for corner beams, and increased nails in shingles. The state has also established well-defined evacuation routes to help move large numbers of people from areas such as Miami to inland areas. In the Midwest, where tornadoes are prevalent, tornado sirens are located around towns to warn citizens of approaching tornadoes. Other natural-disaster preparations can include levees, flood gates, and both municipal and private storm shelters. This, coupled with advancements in meteorological predication models, has helped reduce the damage from these natural disasters.

Natural disasters caused by processes within the Earth are not as predictable. These include earthquakes, volcanic eruptions and tsunamis. Earthquakes and tsunamis (which result from ocean-based earthquakes) may be preceded by smaller, less intense earthquakes, but large earthquakes can also strike without warning. Volcanic eruption, to some degree, give off warning signs which can include smoke and ash spewing out from the volcano. For example, in 1980, when Mount Saint Helens erupted, it was preceded by small seismic activities and several days of smoke and ash. This provided some warning, and most people evacuated. Our increasing knowledge of volcanic activity has helped prevent some loss of life.

Early warning systems for tsunamis have been installed to help people evacuate coastal areas. Even with these in place, some locations, especially small islands, are not completely safe. In recent history, the 2004 tsunami in Indonesia and the 2011 tsunami in Japan brought widespread devastation resulting in the deaths of thousands of people. To reduce property damage, governments have altered building codes to help structures withstand earthquakes. These design changes generally make a building less rigid, allowing it to sway and move with seismic shocks. Preventative measures, such as building codes and warning systems combined with individual preparedness (storing emergency supplies and learning evacuation routes) have made people better able to cope with natural disasters.

34. Warm, moist air is generally associated with which of the following?

　　(A) low air pressure

　　(B) easterly winds

　　(C) cirrus clouds

　　(D) a stationary front

Warm air is less dense than colder air, and moist air is less dense than dry air. Air density is related directly to air pressure: the higher the density, the heavier the air and the more downward pressure it exerts. **The correct answer is (A).**

---

35. Which of the following does NOT contribute to the Earth's broad-scale wind patterns?

   (A) air temperatures

   (B) the presence or absence of clouds

   (C) atmospheric pressure

   (D) the Earth's rotation on its axis

The presence or absence of clouds, choice (B), is partly the result rather than the cause of wind patterns. Each of the other answer choices provides a contributing factor in the Earth's broad-scale wind patterns. **The correct answer is (B).**

Astronomy

Astronomy is the scientific study of the universe and of the size, composition, motion, and evolution of celestial bodies: stars, planets, galaxies, and nebula (fine gas and dust particles). **Astrophysics,** a branch of astronomy, deals with the physical and chemical processes that occur in the universe and in interstellar space, including the structure, evolution, and interactions of stars and systems of stars.

The Universe

Current theories propose that the universe began about 14.4 billion years ago in an event called the **Big Bang**. Scientists have arrived at this age by extrapolating backward from background radiation thought to be left over from that event. The universe began as an infinitely small point and has been expanding rapidly outward ever since. Astrophysicists believe that this continued expansion is propelled by what they call **dark energy**. This is energy that is undetectable but must be there because, if it were not, the gravitational pull of all the mass in the universe would cause it to shrink instead of expand.

Earth's Orbit, Rotation, and Tilt

Earth exhibits two kinds of movement: **rotation** and **revolution.** Rotation is the spinning action of Earth on its **axis,** an imaginary line extending from pole to pole through the Earth's center. The Earth rotates once every 24-hour period. This produces daily cycles of daylight and night. Day and night exist because only half the planet can face the Sun at any one time. **Revolution** is the movement of Earth around the Sun. It takes Earth about 365 days to complete one revolution around the Sun at a distance of 93 million miles. This orbit is in an oval, or *elliptical,* pattern. Planets closer to the Sun take less time to orbit the Sun than planets farther away. For example, Mercury's complete orbit takes only eighty-eight "Earth days," whereas Jupiter's complete orbit takes about twelve "Earth years." The Sun's gravitational pull keeps the planets within their orbital paths.

Term	Definition	Diagram
rotation	the spinning of a body on its axis, like a top	axis
revolution	the movement of a body around another body	Earth Sun

The seasonal variations experienced between the equator and each of the two poles are mainly due to rotational **tilt** of the Earth. The Earth's axis is not perpendicular to the elliptical plane that defines its orbit around the Sun. The Earth's axis is inclined at a tilt of about 23° from perpendicular. This tilt causes some parts of Earth to receive more sunlight and other parts to receive less, accounting for the different seasons.

The Moon

Except for Mercury and Venus, all of the planets in our solar system have satellites, or **moons.** Earth's moon (referred to simply as "the Moon") is about 238,000 miles from Earth and orbits Earth once every twenty-eight days in a slightly elliptical orbit. The Moon's rate of rotation as it orbits Earth is such that from Earth we see only the same half of the Moon. The so-called "dark side" of the Moon always faces away from Earth.

The Moon does not emit its own light; rather, it reflects light from the Sun. As the Moon orbits the Earth, it appears to cycle through a series of **phases** as the Sun lights it at different angles in relation to the Earth's position. On nights when we do not see any of the sunlit portion of the Moon, the side of the Moon facing the planet is completely dark. This is called a **new Moon.** As the Moon continues its 28-day orbit of Earth, more and more of it becomes visible to us. When half of the Moon's circular face is visible, it is known as a **quarter Moon.** When the entire circular face of the Moon is visible, it is known as a **full Moon.** During the second half of each month, we see less and less of the Moon's face until, at the end of a 28-day cycle, the sunlit portion of the Moon is entirely out of our view, and the cycle renews with the new Moon.

The gravity on the Moon is about one-sixth that of Earth. It is the gravitational attraction of the Moon and, to a lesser extent, the Sun that causes **tides** here on Earth. The highest high tides occur when the Moon and Sun are in the same direction from Earth, so that their gravitational pulls reinforce each other. The lowest high tides occur when the Moon and Sun are at right angles in relation to the Earth, so that their gravitational forces counteract each other.

Solar and Lunar Eclipses

The Sun and Moon appear to be approximately the same size in our sky. This is because the Sun is about 400 times wider than the Moon *and* about 400 times farther than the Moon from Earth. When the Moon is positioned directly between the Sun and the Earth, the Moon blocks our view of the Sun. This infrequent alignment of the Sun, Moon, and

Earth is referred to as a **solar eclipse.** During this type of eclipse, the Moon casts a shadow on the Earth. At the center of the shadow, where the Sun is entirely hidden from view, the shadow is darkest. (This area is referred to as the **umbra.**) Farther away from the shadow's center, where only part of the Sun is hidden from view, the shadow is lighter, (This area is referred to as the **penumbra.**) A solar eclipse is the only event during which stars are clearly visible in the daytime sky. Since the Moon and the Earth both travel in elliptical orbits, the Moon is closer to the Earth during some solar eclipses than during others. The duration of a solar eclipse is longer when the Moon is closer to the Earth. The maximum duration of a total solar eclipse is between 7 and 8 minutes. A **lunar eclipse** occurs when the Earth is positioned directly between the Sun and the Moon so that the Earth's shadow is cast upon the Moon.

The Solar System

Our **solar system** includes all celestial bodies that orbit around the Sun. The planets in our solar system can be divided into two categories based on physical characteristics. The **terrestrial planets** include Mercury, Venus, Earth, and Mars. They are composed of the same basic rock materials—hence the name "terrestrial." The **Jovian** (Jupiter-like) planets are Jupiter, Saturn, Uranus, and Neptune. They are made mostly of gases such as hydrogen, helium, and methane. Due to its position on the edge of our solar system, its small size, and what scientists now know about its composition, Pluto is no longer considered a planet.

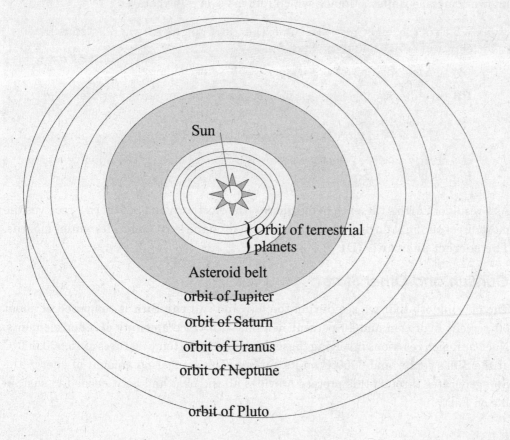

Mainly due to differences in size and distance from the Sun, the two type of planets—terrestrial and Jovian—differ in their basic characteristics. Because the terrestrial planets are much smaller than the Jovian planets, they have weaker gravitational fields, which account for their lighter atmospheres. Terrestrial planets have high densities and consist mainly of a solid mineral crust with metals, along with some gases and ice. The Jovian planets are characterized by lower densities because they consist mainly of gaseous emission and varying degrees of ice.

Between Mars and Jupiter is a great **asteroid belt,** as shown in the preceding illustration. The largest of these rocky, irregularly shaped bodies is about 620 miles in diameter. The total number of asteroids in this belt may be as high as a million, but their total mass is believed to be less than 3 percent of the Moon's mass. It is generally thought that during the formation of our solar system, a plethora of smaller planets were drawn outward by Jupiter's gravitational pull. Through frequent collisions with one another, they fragmented into smaller bodies and then established their own belt of orbit about the Sun, just inside Jupiter's orbit.

Comets are yet another type of object that orbits the Sun. They are small compared to planets and moons and are composed of ice and other materials. Comets travel in very elongated, elliptical orbits, with one end close to the Sun and the other far beyond the orbits of the planets. As they near the Sun, they begin to glow and exhibit a long, cone-shaped tail. Comets return after a predictable span of time. One of the most well-known comets is Halley's Comet, which returns every 76 years.

36. Which of the following is a result of the tilt of Earth's axis in relation to Earth's elliptical orbit around the Sun?

(A) the ebb and flow of tides along ocean and sea shores

(B) the difference in temperatures between equatorial regions and polar regions

(C) differences in total glacial accumulations between the two polar ice caps

(D) clearly seasonal weather patterns midway between the Equator and each pole

As a result of Earth's tilt, each hemisphere—the Northern and Southern—receives the most direct sunlight during its summer months and the least during its winter months. **The correct answer is (D).**

Our Sun and Other Stars

The glowing orb that we see during the day and call **the Sun** is composed of about 90 percent hydrogen and 10 percent helium, with trace amounts of other elements. Nuclear fusion reactions involving these elements create temperatures of 15,000,000°C at the Sun's center and 6000°C on its surface. The staggering amount of energy the Sun generates through this process provides all the heat and light needed to sustain life on Earth.

The Sun is about 93 million miles away, and its mass is about 330,000 times that of the Earth. Compared to other stars, the Sun is actually medium-sized. It appears so much larger to us only because it is so much closer than any other star. The next closest star is light-years away. (One light-year is defined as the distance light travels in one Earth year.)

CHARACTERISTICS AND LIFE CYCLES OF STARS

Scientists are now able to measure and analyze stars to distinguish among star types according to various characteristics. Following is one version of the **Hertzsprung-Russell (H-R) diagram** (named for its creators). The H-R diagram organizes and presents key characteristics of stars in graphical form. The diagram plots stars according to luminosity (brightness), surface temperature, and spectral class (color). Absolute magnitude and luminosity measure the same phenomenon, except that absolute magnitude is measured on an inverted scale. (Notice that the numbers at the right side decrease as you move up the scale.) The temperature scale is given across the top of the diagram. Notice that temperatures *decrease* from left to right, so that stars with the highest surface temperatures are plotted at the *left* end of the diagram.

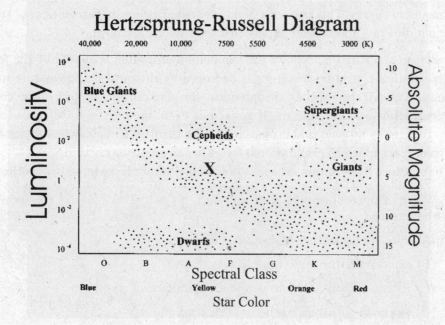

The Hertzsprung-Russell diagram shows most stars plotted in a large cluster that sweeps from the diagram's upper left to its lower right. This swath of stars is referred to as the **main sequence.** This swath suggests that brighter stars are generally hotter and, conversely, that darker stars are cooler. The Sun—marked by an X on the diagram—is classified as a yellow main-sequence star. Notice that the Sun is a fairly average star in terms of its temperature and brightness. Relative to the main sequence, stars classified as **Giants** and **Supergiants** are relatively bright in comparison to their temperature. Conversely, stars classified as **Dwarfs** are relatively dark in comparison to their temperature.

The life of a star is sustained by the thermonuclear reactions in its core. The energy produced by these reactions prevents gravitational collapse of the core onto its own center. Referring to the H-R diagram, main-sequence stars are believed to be in the middle phase of their development, when a star's nuclear reactions are stable and its fluctuations in temperature and luminosity are minor.

As a star increases in age, the nuclear fuel of its core runs low and eventually exhausts itself. At this point, it is thought, the star moves off the main sequence and may become either a white dwarf, a giant, or a supergiant—depending on the star's mass:

- Low-mass stars (lower right in the main sequence) continue to burn until all fuel is used and then collapse into white dwarfs.

- Medium-mass stars (middle of the main sequence) temporarily expand into red giants as their gravitational energy is converted to heat. Once the red giant has exhausted its remaining energy, it will also shrink into a white dwarf. In some cases, the gas released as a red giant collapses and creates a glowing sphere of gas called a planetary nebula.

- High-mass stars (upper left in the main sequence) collapse, releasing a tremendous amount of energy. This creates a rapid expansion as the star becomes a supergiant, and it dies in a spectacular explosion known as a supernova.

The collapse of a star that follows the exhaustion of its fuel is caused by the force of gravity. In an active star, this force is balanced by the outward force of its nuclear fusion reactions. If the star has enough mass, the electron clouds of its atoms collapse until its matter is solid neutrons. If a star has even *more* mass, it collapses further, but there is really no conceivable place to go. The result is a black hole. A black hole is an area of space in which gravitational forces are so great that nothing can escape, not even light. Since light cannot escape, a black hole cannot be seen, only hypothesized.

37. Which of the following is NOT an effect of the weather storms that occur on the Sun's surface?

    (A) telecommunications disruptions on Earth

    (B) explosive hydrogen eruptions

    (C) reactions between hydrogen and helium nuclei

    (D) ionization of atoms in the Earth's atmosphere

Choice (C) describes nuclear fusion, which is the process by which the Sun's energy is produced. In other words, nuclear fusion is the cause rather than an effect of the Sun's weather storms. **The correct answer is (C).**

QUESTION 38 REFERS TO THE FOLLOWING DIAGRAM.

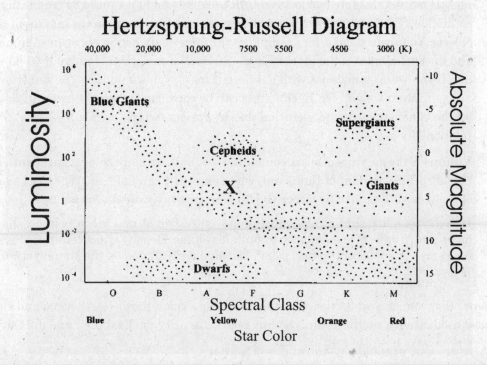

38. According to the Hertzsprung-Russell diagram above, how can main-sequence stars be characterized?

Main-sequence stars

(A) are similar to one another in temperature

(B) are relatively bright compared to their age

(C) are medium-sized for their age

(D) are stable in temperature and luminosity

Main-sequence stars are believed to be in the middle phase of their development, when a star's nuclear reactions are stable and its fluctuations in temperature and luminosity are minor. **The correct answer is (D).**

Physical Science

Properties and Physical States of Matter

Matter describes anything that occupies space and has mass (defined below). It is found in everything, but not all matter is the same. For instance, compare the matter found in concrete to the matter in a cheese steak. Both are considered matter, yet each has properties that make it uniquely different. There are four basic properties that are shared by all matter (although these are physics concepts, they are essential in chemistry as well):

- **Mass** is a measure of the amount of matter in an object. In everyday language, mass is "stuff." Mass gives objects **weight** because weight is caused by gravitational attraction. The force of gravity is the force of attraction between the masses of two objects. Your own weight, for example, is the force of attraction between your mass and the entire mass of the planet Earth. Your mass is constant, but your weight is not. If you were on a planet with a different mass, you would have the same mass but a different weight. On Earth, mass can be converted to weight by multiplying by the constant g, the acceleration due to gravity, which equals 9.80 m/s². The relationship is $w = gm$.

- **Volume** is the measure of space something occupies. An empty glass can potentially hold a specific amount of fluid, and, when empty, it can hold air. When the space of the glass is occupied by either the fluid or air, it represents the volume.

- **Density** is a measure of how much mass is contained in a given volume and is measured in units of mass divided by units of volume. Density is most often expressed in grams per cubic centimeter, g/cm³. Density is calculated by the simple formula:
  $$D = \frac{\text{mass}}{\text{volume}}$$

Some other common properties of matter are: shape, color, hardness, thermal and electrical conductivity, melting point, boiling point, viscosity, malleability, and ductility.

There are four possible physical states of matter:

- **Gas:** Matter in the gaseous state relies on its container for both shape and volume. (Example: steam)

- **Liquid:** Matter in the liquid state takes on the shape of whatever container it is put in. However, a liquid has a definite volume that does not depend on the container it is put in. (Example: water)

- **Solid:** Matter in the solid state has a definite shape and volume regardless of the container. (Example: ice)

- **Plasma:** A unique state of matter that only appears to be solid. In reality, it is an ionized gas. (To *ionize* an atom or collection of atoms is to give it an electrical charge either by adding or removing one or more electrons.)

The states of gas, liquid, and solid can be better understood by considering the states of motion of the particles (atoms and molecules) that make up materials. In the solid state, particles are close together and vibrate back and forth but cannot change position. This explains why solids cannot take the shape of its container.

In a liquid, particles are still close together but can change position, which explains why liquids take the shape of their container.

In a gas, particles are much farther apart, can change position, and move much faster. Gas particles are not close enough to be attracted to one another, which explains why gases take up as much space as they are given.

Matter can change both physically and chemically. A physical change is a change in a substance's shape, size, or state. No chemical reaction is involved with a **physical**

change. The particles that make up the substance remain essentially the same. So a diamond that is pulverized into diamond powder or a potato that gets mashed are both examples of a physical change. In each instance, the diamond and potato take on a different appearance, but they are still made of the same particles.

A **chemical change** is a bit different. When matter experiences a chemical change, it actually changes into a new substance with different properties from its former self. For example, when you crack an egg shell, the egg comes out translucent and fluid. However, when you scramble the egg in a pan and start cooking it, the egg turns yellow and becomes solid. It has changed chemically and cannot return to its former composition.

---

39. Which of the following illustrate chemical rather than physical changes to matter?
  I. a car chassis rusting from overexposure to water
  II. butter melting in a pan
  III. gasoline burning and becoming vapor
  IV. water vapor condensing and turning to rain

(A) I and II only

(B) I and III only

(C) II and IV only

(D) II, III, and IV

Melted butter can be cooled to return it to its former solid state. Rain water can be boiled to return it to its former gaseous state (water vapor.) On the other hand, water reacts chemically with the iron in a car chassis to disintegrate it, and, as gasoline burns, it becomes oxygen and carbon dioxide, which cannot be recombined to form gasoline. **The correct answer is (B).**

---

40. Assume that you poured two liquids—one green and one yellow—in a glass. Then, no matter how much you stir the mixture, the green liquid settles to the bottom, and the yellow liquid rises to the top. What can you reliably conclude from this observation?

(A) The two liquids are incapable of reacting chemically with each other.

(B) The green liquid is denser than the yellow liquid.

(C) The green liquid has more weight than the yellow liquid.

(D) The green liquid contains solid matter, whereas the yellow liquid does not.

Denser substances sink in relation to substances that are less dense. Choice (A) is incorrect because although the two liquids clearly did not undergo a chemical change, they might do so at some other temperature or pressure. Choice (C) is incorrect because we do not know how much liquid of either type was poured into the glass. **The correct answer is (B).**

CHEMISTRY

Chemistry is the study of the composition, interactions, properties, and structure of matter and the changes that matter undergoes. It involves looking at ways to take substances apart and put the parts together again in new ways. For example, scientists are able to create substances as varied as metal alloys, paint, plastics, medicine, and perfumes by manipulating elements and compounds.

The Universe of the Atom

All matter is made up of atoms. The **atom** is the smallest particle of matter that cannot be broken into smaller parts by chemical processes. (The word atom is derived from the Greek *atomos,* meaning "not cuttable.") Though theories about atoms date back to ideas proposed by ancient Greek philosophers, it would be another 2,000 years before researchers would develop a provable atomic theory. In the eighteenth century, building upon the work of his contemporaries, John Dalton proposed that the essential difference between atoms is their mass. Dalton proposed the Law of Conservation of Mass and constructed the first table of relative atomic weights and postulated the Law of Multiple Proportions. During the nineteenth century, Russian scientist Dmitri Mendeleev correctly ordered atoms by mass. In the early twentieth century, Ernest Rutherford discovered the "empty" nature of atoms, meaning that the mass of an atom concentrated at a positively charged central core, which he named the *nucleus.* And in 1913, Danish scientist Niels Bohr proposed that energy levels of an atom were like the orbits of planets—a proposal that led to the "solar system" model of the atom. While some of these scientists' proposals and theories have since been disproved, by providing the fundamentals upon which their successors could build, they were invaluable in advancing modern atomic theory.

Atomic Structure

All matter is made up of atoms, and all atoms are made up of subatomic particles: **electrons, protons,** and **neutrons.** While all three particles have mass, there are three major differences:

- Electrons have a negative charge (–).

- Protons have a positive charge (+).

- Neutrons have no charge.

- Protons and neutrons have about the same mass.

- The mass of an electron is only about $\frac{1}{2000}$ that of a proton or neutron.

Electrons and protons can repel and attract each other without physically touching. Opposite charges attract (electron to proton), and like charges repel (proton to proton or electron to electron).

Each atom has a specific arrangement for its subatomic particles. The nucleus of an atom, or central core, contains protons and neutrons. The electrons occupy several energy levels around the nucleus. In the past, scientists thought these energy levels orbited the nucleus like the planets orbit the sun. Today, the location of an electron in an atom is described as a "cloud," based on calculated probabilities of an electron being at various locations. The denser parts of the cloud are the places the electron is most likely to be found. It is experimentally and mathematically impossible to determine the exact speed and the exact position of an electron at a given point in time. This problem is called *Heisenberg's uncertainty principle.* The uncertainty arises from the fact that we can't tell how something really behaves because the act of observing it changes its behavior.

Electron Configuration

The term **electron configuration** refers to the distribution of electrons among available levels of an atom. Electrons reside in energy levels called **atomic orbitals.** The number and location of electrons in any atom determine how atoms of that element react chemically with other atoms. Different types of atoms vary in their number of energy levels. The outermost energy level is also called the **valence shell.** An atom will seek to complete its outer valence by reacting to or bonding with other atoms:

- The first energy level (level 1) is completed when it holds 2 electrons.

- The second energy level (level 2) is completed when it holds 8 electrons.

- The third energy level (level 3) is completed when it holds 18 electrons.

The next figure shows electron configurations for four types of atoms that have relatively simple structures (the inner circle represents the nucleus, where protons and neutrons reside):

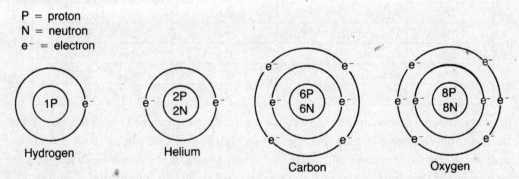

Notice that hydrogen and helium atoms have only one energy level, whereas carbon and oxygen have two energy levels. Also notice that of the four types of atoms, only helium has a completed valence shell. The other three types—hydrogen, carbon, and oxygen— will seek to complete their outer valances by reacting to or bonding with other atoms.

Protons, Neutrons, Atomic Mass, and Isotopes

The number of protons in an atom defines the atom as a specific **element.** For example, the nucleus of a carbon atom *always* contains six protons, and this number of protons is exclusive and unique to carbon. The number of protons can be used as an identifying marker for an element. This marker is referred to as an element's **atomic number.** The following table ranks the first twenty-two elements by their atomic number—that is, by the number of protons. For each element, the table also shows the element's symbol and electron distribution among orbitals.

ATOMIC NUMBER	ELEMENT	SYMBOL	ELECTRON DISTRIBUTION
1	Hydrogen	H	1
2	Helium	He	2
3	Lithium	Li	2 – 1
4	Beryllium	Be	2 – 2
5	Boron	B	2 – 3
6	Carbon	C	2 – 4
7	Nitrogen	N	2 – 5
8	Oxygen	O	2 – 6
9	Fluorine	F	2 – 7
10	Neon	Ne	2 – 8
11	Sodium	Na	2 – 8 – 1
12	Magnesium	Mg	2 – 8 – 2
13	Aluminum	Al	2 – 8 – 3
14	Silicon	Si	2 – 8 – 4
15	Phosphorus	P	2 – 8 – 5
16	Sulfur	S	2 – 8 – 6
17	Chlorine	Cl	2 – 8 – 7
18	Argon	Ar	2 – 8 – 8
19	Potassium	K	2 – 8 – 8 – 1
20	Calcium	Ca	2 – 8 – 8 – 2
21	Scandium	Sc	2 – 8 – 9 – 2
22	Titanium	Ti	2 – 8 – 10 – 2

All neutral atoms of an element have the same number of protons (which are positively charged) and electrons (which are negatively charged). However, they do not necessarily have the same number of neutrons. When atoms of the same element differ in the number of neutrons in the nuclei, they are said to be isotopes of that element. For example, here are three isotopes of the element hydrogen:

Hydrogen's neutral form (*Hydrogen*): 1 proton, no neutrons

One hydrogen isotope (*Deuterium*): 1 proton, 1 neutron

Another hydrogen isotope (*Tritium*): 1 proton, 2 neutrons

Neutrons have no charge, but they have the same mass as protons. The **atomic mass,** or **mass number,** of an atom is the number of protons plus the number of neutrons (the unit of measurement is called the *Dalton*). For example, hydrogen has an atomic mass of 1, whereas deuterium and tritium have atomic masses of 2 and 3, respectively.

41. If atom X has an atomic mass of 19, which of the following is a possible combination of particles within that atom?

(A) 19 electrons, 19 protons, and 8 neutrons

(B) 9 electrons, 9 protons, and 18 neutrons

(C) 10 electrons, 9 protons, and 9 neutrons

(D) 9 electrons, 9 protons, and 10 neutrons

The atomic mass is the sum of the number of protons and neutrons. Only in choice (D) do those two numbers total 19. **The correct answer is (D).**

42. What is the distinguishing feature of each different element?

(A) the number of protons it contains

(B) the number of neutrons it contains

(C) the number of atoms it contains

(D) the total number of protons and neutrons it contains

The number of protons is what distinguishes each element from all the others. **The correct answer is (A).**

Elements and Compounds

An **element** is a substance that cannot be broken down into simpler substances by chemical processes. Atoms (or ions) of different elements join by chemical bonds in certain proportions to form a **compound.**

Elements

More than 115 different elements are currently known; 92 of these elements are known to occur in nature. Elements include such substances as hydrogen, carbon, potassium, and lead. Each element has been assigned a one-letter or two-letter symbol. Most of these symbols include the first letter of the element's name, though some do not. For example, the symbol for carbon is **C,** and the symbol for iron is **Fe.** Each element is composed of atoms having the same **atomic number,** which means that each atom contains the same number of protons as all other atoms of that element. Atoms of each element also share the same electron configurations.

The modern **Periodic Table of Elements** ranks all of the elements according to the atomic number and organizes them into *families* based on similar chemical and physical properties. Each horizontal row in the Periodic Table is called a *period*. Moving from left to right in a row, the elements in a period transition from metals to nonmetals, and atomic numbers and mass increase. The elements in each column are together called a *group*. Groups contain elements that have the same number of electrons in their outermost energy level (valence shell).

The following figure shows a left-hand and a right-hand portion of the Periodic Table. Notice that hydrogen (H), lithium (Li), sodium (Na), and potassium (K) are in the far left column (group) because they each have just one outer-valence electron. Also notice that the gases in the right-hand group have completed outer valances. These gases are called **noble gases** and are completely inert, meaning that they seldom react or bond with other types of atoms. This is because atoms of these elements have a complete valence shell, which is a very stable configuration. Finally, notice that each element has its own "calling card" on the Periodic Table, showing its symbol, electron distribution, atomic weight, and atomic number.

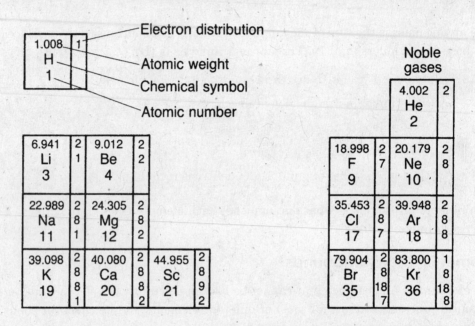

Elements fall into three categories: metals, nonmetals, and metalloids.

- **Metals** conduct electricity, are malleable, and can be drawn into wires or flattened into sheets. Metals can also be polished for shine and have high melting points (although mercury turns liquid at room temperature). Elements such as copper, silver, and iron are just a few examples of metals.

- **Nonmetals** are unsuitable for conducting electricity, and they are non-shiny. Also, some solid nonmetals are not very malleable and can shatter on impact. Finally, nonmetals have lower melting points than metals. (Nonmetals occupy the upper right-hand corner of the periodic table.)

- **Metalloids** are elements such as silicon and boron that have properties that are similar to both metals and nonmetals.

Compounds and Bonds

There are two major types of "friendships" that atoms like to form: **ionic bonds** and **covalent bonds.** In this section, you'll learn what each term means, and you'll learn the laws related to these relationships.

IONS: FORMATION AND COMPOUNDS

Electrical forces of attraction hold matter together. As noted earlier, however, an element's atoms are electrically neutral. So how can different atoms attract each other if they are neutral? Though atoms can't attract, combinations of atoms can transfer electrons or share electrons to form **compounds.** When atoms reorganize their electrons in this way, they are "reacting" to other atoms and are no longer called "atoms." At this point, they become **ions.** An ion is an atom with a charge, either positive or negative. The neutral state is altered because the atom has either gained or lost one or more electrons. In the nomenclature of chemistry, an ion with a positive charge keeps the same name as the atoms from which it was made, while a negatively charged ion is renamed to end with *-ide.*

Now is the time to clarify some terms: Atoms, ions, and molecules are types of *particles.* Elements and compounds are types of *materials.*

Ions of opposite charges attract one another strongly. When they get together, they form **ionic compounds.** Consider table salt, for example. Normally, the parent elements, sodium (Na) and chlorine (Cl), can't be brought together. However, certain changes in their electron configurations can take place, creating the ionic compound NaCl, which we know as table salt.

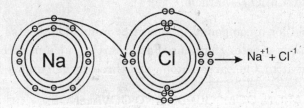

Formation of Ions

As the previous illustration shows, the single electron in the outermost energy level in the sodium ion (Na) is transferred to the outer valance of the chlorine ion (Cl). The outer valance of the chloride ion gains an electron from the sodium ion. This forms a stable ionic bond with an *octet* formation (four pairs of two electrons in the outer valance). Atoms and ions whose outer valance contains eight electrons enjoy more stability than those that lack eight electrons at this level.

Because like charges repel, all the new sodium ions move away from one another. The same is true for all the chloride ions. But the chloride and sodium ions attract each other, thereby becoming a stable compound we know as sodium chloride, or table salt. The net force of attraction between the oppositely charged ions is called the **ionic bond.**

REDOX REACTIONS AND IONIC COMPOUNDS

The simple reaction that drives the formation of ionic compounds is a **redox reaction.** This reaction draws its name from two important chemical events that occur during electron transfer:

- *Reduction:* The gaining of electrons
- *Oxidation:* The losing of electrons

In a redox reaction, one substance is the **oxidizer**—it causes the oxidation of the other substance by accepting electrons from it. The other substance is the **reducer**—it reduces a substance by giving it electrons. In table salt, sodium is the reducer because it gives electrons to the chlorine atom, which makes the chloride ion. Chlorine is the oxidizer; by accepting electrons from sodium, it oxidizes sodium atoms to ions. The oxidizing agent is the one that is always reduced. Look at another example:

$$^2Mg \quad + \quad O_2 \quad \rightarrow \quad ^2MgO$$

electron configuration electron configuration Magnesium Oxide

2 8 ② 2 ⑥

In this example, magnesium (Mg) is the reducing agent. It reduces oxygen and loses two electrons, becoming Mg^{2+}, magnesium ion. Oxygen is the oxidizing agent. It oxidizes magnesium and gains two electrons, becoming O^{2-}, oxide ion. Here are some additional examples of ionic compounds:

Sodium fluoride (NaF)—prevents cavities

Silver chloride (AgCl)—photographic film

Magnesium sulfate ($MgSO_4$)—laxative

Calcium carbonate ($CaCO_3$)—antacid

NOTE: In the symbol for a compound, a subscript number indicates the number of atoms if that number is greater than one. For example, calcium carbonate ($CaCO_3$) contains one calcium atom, one carbon atom, and three oxygen atoms.

MOLECULES: FORMATION, COMPOUNDS, AND COVALENCE

There are some nonmetals whose atoms cannot become ions by the transfer of electrons (as described in the previous section). So some other form of bonding must occur. Compounds that are composed only of nonmetals consist of **molecules** instead of ions. Molecules are small particles of neutral charge, consist of at least two atoms, and have enough electrons to make the system neutral (no net charge). A compound consisting of molecules is called a **molecular compound.**

Note, however, that some elements exist with two atoms to each molecule—in other words, they react with themselves. These are called **diatomic molecules** and contain atoms of only one element. Notable examples include the following (the right-hand column shows how the molecule is illustrated):

Cl_2	Cl—Cl
O_2	O=O
N_2	N≡N
I_2	I—I
Br_2	Br—Br
F_2	F—F
H_2	H—H

Covalent bonds are formed by the sharing pairs of electrons between atoms. One outer-valance electron from each atom can be shared between their atomic nuclei. The following diagrams show two ways covalent bonds can be depicted in the phosphorous trichloride (PCl_3) molecule:

$$:\overset{..}{\underset{..}{Cl}}:\overset{..}{P}:\overset{..}{\underset{..}{Cl}}: \qquad :\overset{..}{\underset{..}{Cl}}-\overset{..}{P}-\overset{..}{\underset{..}{Cl}}:$$
$$:\overset{..}{\underset{..}{Cl}}: \qquad\qquad\qquad :\overset{..}{\underset{..}{Cl}}:$$

The left-hand diagram shows an electron-dot configuration where only outer electrons are shown. The right-hand diagram shows the bond-line structure. If you count the shared pair for each atom in the PCl_3 molecule, you notice that each has eight electrons in the outermost energy level (the outer valance). Atoms whose outer valance contains eight electrons are most stable.

In the list of diatomic molecule formulas, the double lines between the oxygen atoms indicate that they are sharing two pairs of electrons, which is called a *double bond*. Likewise, the three lines in the nitrogen formula indicate three pairs of electrons being shared to form a *triple bond*. Atoms of nonmetal elements differ in their ability to share electrons. Oxygen can form two bonds, nitrogen can form three bonds, and carbon can form four bonds. The term **valence** refers to the number of valence shell electrons an atom of an element can share to form bonds in a way that will complete the valence shell. In most cases, the outer shell holds eight electrons, and so this is called the **octet rule**. The exception is hydrogen, which as two electrons in the valence shell, and so it has a valence of 1 because it completes its shell by sharing its one electron. Here are four different element families and the valence number of each:

Carbon family: $8 - 4 = 4$ valence

Nitrogen family: $8 - 5 = 3$ valence

Oxygen family: $8 - 6 = 2$ valence

Halogen family: $8 - 7 = 1$ valence

BALANCING CHEMICAL EQUATIONS

Chemical reactions obey the law of conservation of mass. This means that not only does the mass of reactants equal the mass of the products, but that the number of atoms of each element involved is the same on both sides of the equation for a reaction. Consider the reaction of sodium metal (Na) with chlorine gas (Cl_2), $Na + Cl_2 \rightarrow NaCl$.

This equation is not balanced because there are two Cl atoms on the left and only one on the right. This is fixed by adding coefficients, that is, the numbers before the symbols that indicate the number of atoms of that element.

$$2Na + Cl_2 \rightarrow 2NaCl$$

To check whether an equation is balanced, count the numbers of atoms of each element on both sides of the equation. Consider a more complicated example:

$$2Al(OH)3 + 3H_2SO_4 \rightarrow Al_2(SO_4)_3 + 6H_2O$$

The subscript after a parenthesis means that everything inside the parentheses is multiplied by that number. Now count the atoms of each element:

Al: $_2$ left = $_2$ right

O: 6 + 1$_2$ left = 1$_2$ + 6 right

H: 6 + 6 left = 1$_2$ right

S: 3 left = 3 right

LIMITING REACTANT

What if the reactants are not present in the ratio indicated by the equation? Charcoal, which is mostly carbon (C), reacts with oxygen (O_2) in the air according to the simple equation: $C + O_2 \rightarrow CO_2$. The amount of carbon dioxide (CO_2) produced depends only on the carbon available because the amount of oxygen is practically unlimited. Carbon is the limiting reactant.

If we know the mass of each reactant, we can calculate which is the limiting one and how much product will be produced. In such calculations, masses are converted to moles (mol). A mole is the atomic or molecular mass expressed in grams. What is true for atom ratios is true for mole ratios. Look back to the equation for the sodium-chlorine reaction. Suppose 23 g of Na reacted with 71 g of Cl_2. The atomic mass of Na is 23 g/mol and the molecular mass of Cl_2 is 71 g/mol. This means that we have 1 mol of Na and 1 mol of Cl_2. The balanced equation shows that each mole of Cl_2 requires 2 moles of Na, but we only have one. Therefore, Na is the limiting reactant, and there will be Cl_2 left over. Furthermore, there will be only 1 mole of NaCl produced, which is equal to 58.5 g.

43. What is the difference between an atom and an ion?

   (A) An atom is positively charged, but an ion is negatively charged.

   (B) An atom is neutral, but an ion has an electrical charge.

   (C) An atom has an electrical charge, but an ion does not.

   (D) An atom is negatively charged, but an ion is positively charged.

An atom has the same number of protons as electrons, and so it has no net charge (it is neutral). When an atom gains or loses an electron to a different atom, it becomes an ion—with either a positive or negative charge. **The correct answer is (B).**

44. Which of the following best explains why carbon atoms form covalent bonds with atoms of many other elements?

    (A) Carbon is the only element that has enough electrons to bond with more than four other atoms.

    (B) Carbon's valence of 4 leads to several possible ways to complete its outer shell.

    (C) Carbon is present in every kind of living organism on Earth.

    (D) A carbon atom contains the same number of protons as outer-shell electrons.

Carbon has a valence of 4, which means it will seek to add four additional electrons for its outer shell. Several combinations are possible—for example: 4, 3 + 1, 2 + 2, or 1 + 1 + 1 + 1. Thus atoms with a valence of 1, 2, 3, or 4 are all candidates for covalent bonding with carbon. **The correct answer is (B).**

Mixtures, Solutions, and Solubility

A **solution** is a uniform mixture of two or more substances that are mixed at the molecular level. Salt water is a good example of a solution. This solution consists of NaCl (table salt) and water. The salt seems to disappear into the water, but it is still there. You could physically separate them by evaporating the water, leaving the salt behind.

Solutions are **homogeneous mixtures**. Materials, such as soil, that are not uniformly mixed are called **heterogeneous mixtures.**

Solubility

The **solute** of a solution is the substance that dissolves. A solute can be a liquid, a gas, or a solid. The **solvent** is the medium in which the solute dissolves. In chemistry, water is referred to as the "universal solvent," which means that the properties of water give it the ability to dissolve many substances. In the case of salt water, salt is the solute that dissolves in water, the solvent.

Soluble refers to the ability of a solute to dissolve in a solvent under certain conditions, such as a given temperature or pressure. If additional solute can be dissolved in a volume of solvent, then the solution has not yet reached **saturation**. The maximum amount of solute that dissolves in a given volume of solvent is called its **solubility**. Solubility is usually measured in moles (of solute) per liter (of solvent) and also in grams of solute per hundred grams of solvent. In saturated solutions, a point has been reached in which no more solute can be dissolved in the solvent.

In some cases, creating a solution can result in a net temperature change. For example, calcium chloride releases heat upon dissolving. On the other hand, ammonium nitrate decreases in temperature, becoming cooler upon dissolving. Chemical processes that release heat (increase temperature) are referred to as **exothermic reactions,** and those that absorb heat (decrease temperature) are referred to as **endothermic reactions.**

This is the chemistry behind the hot and cold packs that are used to ease swelling tissue and soothe pulled muscles.

In both cases, a certain amount of energy, called the **activation energy**, must be added to get the reaction started. In the case of an exothermic reaction, after it has gotten over the "hump," the reaction produces its own activation energy. This explains why a match is needed to light a candle but can be taken away after the wick begins to burn. If you subtract the energy of the products from the energy of the reactants, the difference is the energy released by an exothermic reaction. For an endothermic reaction, the result will be a negative number equal to the energy absorbed.

Temperature and pressure can affect solubility—the amount of the solute that can be dissolved in a given amount of solvent. For most solid solutes, an increase in temperature will lead to an increase in solubility. For gases, the effect of temperature is opposite: gases become less soluble at higher temperatures. This is why carbonated drinks are served with ice to keep them cool longer; the cooler temperature decreases the formation of carbon dioxide bubbles. Changes in pressure have a very small effect on the solubility of a liquid or a solid, but for gases an increase in pressure increases solubility.

Increasing the temperature not only increases solubility, it also increases the rate at which a solute dissolves. Stirring and increased surface area also increase the rate of dissolving but do not change the solubility.

45. A powdery substance is added to pure hot water and seems to disappear. The mixture remains clear but now has a distinct odor. What conclusion can be drawn from this observation?

(A) The water has not yet reached boiling point.

(B) The water is not beyond full saturation with the powder.

(C) Any additional powder will settle to the bottom of the water.

(D) The mixture has absorbed heat and is now cooler.

The fact that the powder disappears, leaving clear water, strongly suggests that it has dissolved in the water. Thus, the mixture is a solution (not a colloid or suspension) that has not surpassed its saturation point at the current water temperature. **The correct answer is (B).**

PHYSICS

Physics is the scientific study of matter, energy, space, and time—and how they are interrelated. Physics is closely related to all other fields of science, since its laws are universal. The living systems of biology are made of matter particles that follow the laws of physics. Chemistry explores how atoms, small units of matter, interact to form molecules according to the laws of physics. And the study of geology and astronomy deal to a great extent with the physics of the Earth and of celestial bodies.

Motion: Velocity, Mass, and Momentum

Our universe is filled with objects in motion. **Motion** is described in terms of speed, velocity, and acceleration. **Speed** refers to rate of motion and can be either instantaneous—as recorded by the speedometer of a car, for instance—or an average rate over a period of time. Speed can be expressed in many ways—for example, as kilometers per hour (km/h) or centimeters per second (cm/sec). **Velocity** refers to speed *in a given direction:* for example, 50 miles per hour *east.* Velocity can change if either speed or direction changes. So a body in motion along a curved path is undergoing a continuous change in velocity, whether or not the speed is changing. **Acceleration** is the rate at which velocity changes. Acceleration is determined by dividing the change in velocity by the change in time:

$$a = \frac{V_2 - V_1}{T}$$

An increase in velocity over a period of time is referred to as **positive acceleration,** while a decrease in velocity over time is referred to as **negative acceleration.** Referring to the preceding formula, if the initial velocity (V_1) is greater than the subsequent velocity (V_2), then the acceleration over time T is negative. Since acceleration is expressed in terms of velocity, any change in direction is also a change in acceleration. A body in motion along a curved path is undergoing a continuous change in acceleration, whether or not the speed is changing.

Mass and Momentum

The term **mass** is not the same as weight. Mass refers to the amount of matter contained in a particular object or body. Weight is the force of attraction between the mass of the planet Earth and an object near its surface. The mass of an object is constant; its weight changes if the force of gravity changes.

Momentum is defined as mass multiplied by velocity (*mass × velocity*) and remains constant unless an outside force—such as friction—acts upon it. In other words, to change the momentum of an object, a force is required. For example, in a vacuum (a "closed system"), a 10-pound object moving in a straight path at 50 meters per second has the same momentum as a 25-pound object moving in the same straight direction path at a speed of 20 meters per second.

Momentum is conserved during collisions, according to the equation

$$m_{A1}v_{A1} + m_{B1}v_{B1} = m_{A2}v_{A2} + m_{B2}v_{B2},$$

where m and v are the masses and velocities of objects A and B before (1) and after (2) a collision. Suppose a 60-kg roller skater rolling along at $6\frac{m}{s}$ overtakes a 50-kg skater traveling $4\frac{m}{s}$. They clasp hands and continue to roll along together. What is their final velocity? Since $v_{A2} = v_{B2}$, the equation can be rearranged and solved for v_2, the final velocity.

$$v_2 = \frac{(m_{A1}v_{A1} + m_{B1}v_{B1})}{(m_{A2} + m_{B2})}$$

$$v_2 = \frac{(60 \cdot 6 + 50 \cdot 4)}{(60 + 50)} = 5.1 \frac{m}{s}$$

Objects in motion under the influence of gravity are in **free-fall.** Objects released from rest, thrown upward, or thrown downward, are in free-fall once released. All objects in a near-vacuum, regardless of their mass, accelerate at the same rate of 9.8 m/sec^2. This is a constant on or near Earth's surface. It is called acceleration due to gravity and given the symbol g. It is the proportionality constant used to convert mass, m, to weight, w: $w = mg$.

Energy and Work

There are two major types of energy. **Potential energy** is energy that results from the position or condition of an object rather than from its motion. In general, potential energy is stored energy and includes chemical and nuclear energy. A coiled spring, a charged battery, or a weight held above the ground are all examples of this potential energy. In contrast, **kinetic energy** refers to the energy an object (or wave) possesses due to its motion. The amount of the kinetic energy depends on the object's velocity and mass—or, in the case of waves, the wave's velocity, frequency, and amplitude. Thermal energy is basically kinetic energy because it is the energy of motion of atoms and molecules.

SOURCES OF ENERGY

Most sources of energy can be traced back to the Sun. Plants convert solar energy to chemical energy and store it in the form of carbohydrates. In the short term, this energy can be used as food energy, biomass energy, and firewood. In the very long term, plants are converted to fossil fuels: coal, oil, and natural gas. The Sun also drives the winds that power wind turbines, and the Sun powers the water cycle that fills hydroelectric dams with water. Photo-voltaic cells capture solar energy directly. Only geothermal and nuclear energy do not come in some way from the Sun.

Fossil fuels are nonrenewable and are the source of pollution problems. Fuel for nuclear power is also nonrenewable but the reserves are much greater than those of fossil fuels. There are concerns about the safety of nuclear power and about what to do with the radioactive waste products. Wind, geothermal, solar, hydroelectric, and biomass are all renewable. Availability and cost are sometimes problems with renewable sources. The amount of energy that can be derived from given mass of fuel (energy density) varies widely.

WORK

In physics, the word **work** refers to the transfer of energy from one object to another. Potential energy can be transferred to kinetic energy. In most instances, work is performed in order to move the other object over a distance. To accomplish work, the application of **force** is required. Pushing a lawn mower across the lawn, lifting a bucket of water, and pulling open a refrigerator door are all examples of work. In each case, you transfer your potential energy to another object by applying force upon it. Of course, applying a force upon an object does not always result in work done on that object. For example, pushing on a stationary wall results in no work because the wall doesn't move.

Work is equal to the amount of force multiplied by the distance over which it is applied:

$$\text{Work} = \text{Force} \times \text{Distance}$$

Work and energy are generally measured in a unit called the *joule* (j), although other units are used as well, depending on the forms of energy involved—for example, light, heat, chemical, mechanical, or electrical.

Power (P) is the rate at which work is done and is measured in joules per second (J/s). 1 J/s = 1 watt (W). Since Work = Force × Distance, P = fd/t. If a 600-N man climbs a 3-m flight of stairs in 6 s, he generates 300 W of power. P = (600)(3)/6. If the same man runs up the stairs in 3 s, he generates twice as much power, but does the same amount of work.

46. Which is most likely to occur if a loose bundle of feathers and a golf ball, each having a mass of 1 kilogram, are thrown straight up with equal but slight force from the Moon's surface?

   (A) The golf ball will fall to the Moon's surface before the feathers.

   (B) The feathers will fall to the Moon's surface before the golf ball.

   (C) Neither object will return to the Moon's surface.

   (D) They will fall to the Moon's surface at the same time.

The two objects have the same mass and velocity, and so they have the same constant momentum. Without atmospheric air friction to alter the momentum of either one, both will maintain the same velocity regardless of their form or shape. Eventually, however, both will fall to the Moon's surface—and at the same time—but only because of the Moon's gravitational pull. **The correct answer is (D).**

QUESTION 47 REFERS TO THE FOLLOWING GRAPH.

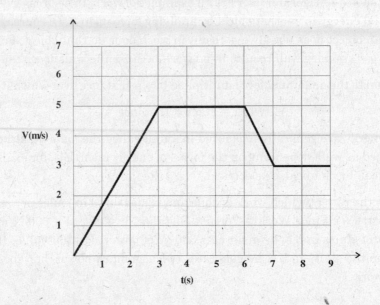

47. The graph shows a track athlete running a race along a straight track. Velocity as a function of time is shown for the first 9 seconds of the race. What is occurring from 3 to 6 seconds into the race?

(A) negative acceleration

(B) positive acceleration

(C) constant velocity

(D) a change in direction

Up to second 3, the runner is accelerating (velocity is increasing). From second 3 through second 5, velocity is constant at 5 meters per second. During second 6, negative acceleration is occurring, and during seconds 7 through 9, velocity is once again constant. **The correct answer is (C).**

Inertia, Force, and the Laws of Motion

Force refers to any of a variety of factors that cause an object to change speed or direction. It can be a push or pull that starts, stops, or changes the direction in which an object may be traveling. You apply force when you lift a can of soda to your mouth or when you slam a door shut. Motion or a change in direction only occurs when there is a non-zero *net* force. For example, if 2 people are pulling on opposite sides of a rope, both applying equal force, no motion occurs because the net force is zero (0). The most ubiquitous force in nature is gravity; in order to stand, a person must continually apply an opposing force to counteract gravity.

Sir Isaac Newton, a seventeenth-century English physicist, proposed three fundamental laws concerning the relationship between force, motion, mass, and inertia. These laws provided the foundation for classical mechanics and are referred to as **Newton's Three Laws of Motion:**

1. Newton's First Law of Motion, also known as the **Law of Inertia**, states that objects at rest and objects in uniform motion will remain at rest or in motion at a constant velocity unless acted on by an external force such as gravity, friction, or other resistance. The greater the inertia, the greater the force required to start, stop, or change the object's direction of motion. An object of great mass has more inertia than an object of lower mass.

2. Newton's Second Law of Motion states that the net force acting on an object is equal to its mass times its acceleration, or $F = m \times a$. This law is also called the **Law of Force.** The unit of force is known as a *Newton*. In this formula, m is the mass of the object, measured in kilograms, and a is the acceleration in meters per second per second m/s^2. Thus, a force of 1 newton (N) = 1 kg m/s^2.

3. Newton's Third Law of Motion states that for every action there is an equal and opposite reaction. In other words, when one object exerts a force on a second object, the second object exerts an equal force on the first in an opposing direction. This law is also called the **Law of Action and Reaction.** For example, when you hit a tennis ball with a racket, the racket exerts a forward force on the ball while the ball exerts an equal backward force on the racket. Another way to look at the third law is to understand that a force never appears out of nowhere, acting alone. Rather, forces always occur in pairs.

As explained in the discussion of properties, mass is not the same as weight. The mass of an object is constant, but weight changes if the force of gravity changes. The pull of gravity on mass (m) gives an object its weight (w), according to the equation $w = mg$, where g is acceleration due to gravity, equal to 9.80 m/s^2 at Earth's surface.

The force of gravity is the force of attraction between the masses of two objects. If the masses of objects A and B are m_A and m_B, that are separated by a distance, d, then the force of gravitational attraction between the objects is given by:

$$F = \frac{G(m_A m_B)}{d^2}$$

where G is a universal constant equal to 6.67×10^{-11} Nm^2/kg^2. This is Newton's law of universal gravitation. The squared distance in the denominator shows that gravitational force decreases very rapidly with distance. For example, if the Moon were twice as far away from Earth, the gravitational attraction between these two bodies would only be ¼ as great.

48. What force must a baseball bat exert on a baseball of a mass 0.2 kg to give it an acceleration of 8500 m/sec² ?

(A) 42.5 newtons

(B) 170 newtons

(C) 425 newtons

(D) 1700 newtons

Apply the equation $F = m \times a$:

$F = 0.2 \times 8500 = 1700$ Newtons. **The correct answer is (D).**

49. Which of the following demonstrate(s) Newton's First Law of Motion?
   I. the thrust of a rocket engine during liftoff
   II. the exertion of a weightlifter pressing a barbell overhead
   III. the lean of a motorcyclist in the direction of a turn
   IV. the effort needed to stop yourself after stepping off a moving bus

(A) II only

(B) IV only

(C) I and IV only

(D) III and IV only

A moving motorcycle and a moving bus passenger both have inertia—they tend to remain in motion in the same direction and at the same velocity. Force is required to change a motorcycle's direction or to stop forward movement after jumping off a moving bus. Statement A demonstrates Newton's Third Law, and statement B demonstrates Newton's Second Law. **The correct answer is (D).**

Heat and Thermodynamics

Heat refers to the energy that flows from a body of higher temperature to one of lower temperature. The physical tendency is for energy to continue to flow in this direction until **thermal equilibrium** is reached—in other words, until the temperatures of the two systems are equal. For example, if you mixed two glasses of water of unequal temperatures together, the warmer portion becomes cooler until the entire mixture is equal in temperature. Heat is energy that is transferred. The energy itself is correctly called **thermal energy**.

An object has thermal energy because of the motion of its atoms and molecules. The faster they move the more thermal energy the object has. Thermal energy, then, is really a form of kinetic energy. The thermal energy of an object is equal to the total kinetic energy of its particles. The temperature of an object is a measure of the average kinetic energy of its molecules. The standard unit of heat is the *calorie,* defined as the amount of heat required to increase the temperature of 1 gram of water by 1° Celsius. (Another type of calorie, the food calorie, is defined as 1000 calories.) The preferred unit of measurement for thermal energy in most science applications is the joule (J): one calorie equals 4.186 J.

Transfer of Heat

The scientific study of heat transfer is called **thermodynamics.** Among the four laws of thermodynamics, the first two are the most fundamental. The first law states that the amount of energy added to a system is equal to the sum of its increase in heat energy and the work done to the system. The second law states that heat energy cannot be transferred from a body at a lower temperature to a body at a higher temperature without additional energy.

Heat can be transferred in three ways:

- **Conduction** is the transfer of heat through a solid material. In conduction, kinetic energy is transferred from faster molecules to slower molecules by direct contact. But the positions of the molecules change very little, if any, so the solid material (the conductor) maintains its structure. Conduction explains how the handle of a cooking pan or the portion of a teaspoon sticking out of a hot cup of tea heats up, even though the handle or spoon is not in direct contact with the heat source. Different solid materials vary greatly in their ability to conduct heat. Poor conductors absorb more heat than they transfer and hence make good heat insulators.

- **Convection** refers to the transfer of heat through a fluid (either a liquid or gas). The liquid or gas near the heat source heats up, and then expands outward from the source, resulting in currents. The heated (less dense) liquid or gas rises, and cooler (denser) liquid or gas moves inward toward the heat source, where it is then heated. It is this circulatory process that is at work in convection ovens and many ocean currents.

- **Radiation** is the transfer of heat by electromagnetic waves. The molecules of a substance receiving these waves of energy absorb that energy, thereby increasing their own kinetic energy and thus the temperature of the substance. Radiant energy is widely used in everyday life. For example, microwaves provide the energy for heating food in a microwave oven, and ultraviolet waves provide the energy that can tan and burn your skin.

Substances often undergo changes of state—solid to liquid (or vice versa) or liquid to gas (or vice versa). During the time that a change of state occurs, a substance either absorbs or releases heat while the temperature actually remains constant. This type of heat is called **latent heat.** The latent heat absorbed by the air when water condenses is what is behind the power of thunderstorms and hurricanes. A cold drink with ice cubes stays at 0°C until all the ice is melted. This is because of the latent heat of melting. The ice absorbs heat from the surroundings to free the water molecules from their rigid arrangement in the solid state.

50. Which of the following statements is NOT accurate?

(A) Heat can flow only from a body of higher temperature to one of lower temperature.

(B) Heat energy is produced by the vibrations of molecules.

(C) Kinetic energy in a solid substance is transferred from faster molecules to slower molecules by direct contact.

(D) Thermal equilibrium occurs when the temperature under a shade tree drops as the surrounding air becomes warmer.

The statements in choices (A), (B), and (C) are accurate statements. The statement in choice (D), however, contradicts the first law of thermodynamics. **The correct answer is (D).**

51. A steel spoon and a silver spoon are put into a cup of hot coffee at the same time. The silver spoon rapidly approaches the temperature of the coffee, while the steel spoon increases in temperature only slightly. What explains the difference?

(A) The steel spoon has a lower specific heat.

(B) The silver spoon has a lower specific heat.

(C) The steel spoon retains more latent heat than the silver spoon.

(D) The silver spoon retains more latent heat than the steel spoon.

The steel spoon has a lower thermal capacity, as measured by specific heat. **The correct answer is (B).**

Waves

The concept of a **wave** is one of the most important in physics. A wave can be an oscillation or vibration that creates a disturbance in a medium, such as water or air, as in the case of sound waves. Or a wave can be a series of quantitative values moving through space, as in the case of electromagnetic waves.

Scientists measure waves in various ways, and these measurements are used to identify such phenomena as the visibility and color of light, the pitch and loudness of a sound, and the strength of an electromagnetic wave. These measurements are based on the various features of any wave, as shown in the next diagram.

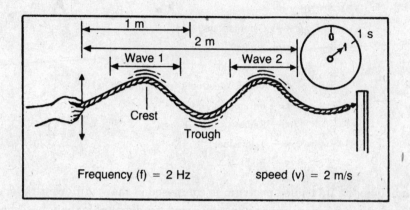

As you can see in this diagram, the **crest** of a wave is its top, and the **trough** of the wave is its bottom. A wave's **amplitude** is *half* the vertical distance from peak to trough and is used to measure the strength, or magnitude, of a wave. The **wavelength** is the distance between consecutive troughs or consecutive crests. Referring to the diagram, assume that the wavelength is 1 meter. Visualize the waves moving from left to right at 2 meters per second, which is the wave's velocity. The number of crests passing a certain point per unit time (a "cycle") is the **frequency** of a wave. At a given wave velocity, the shorter the wavelength the higher the frequency. Each of the following two equations expresses a wave's frequency:

$$\text{frequency} = \frac{\text{velocity}}{\text{wavelength}}$$

$$\text{frequency} = \frac{\text{wave cycles}}{\text{unit of time}}$$

Wavelength is generally measured in meters, while frequency is measured in *hertz*. (1 hertz = 1 cycle per second.) Electromagnetic waves vary in wavelength and frequency, but in a vacuum they all travel at the speed of light, which is 3×10^8 m/sec. Note that the rope only moves up and down, not right or left. This illustrates the fact that all waves transfer energy, but waves never transfer matter. This is even true of waves, such as ocean waves, that appear to be moving toward the shore.

Light Waves

Light travels in waves. The variations of colors we see are a result of different frequency ranges of light. The light spectrum ranges from long radio waves to short gamma rays. Humans can see color only within a particular range called the **visible spectrum.** The visible spectrum for humans ranges from low-frequency red waves to high-frequency violet waves.

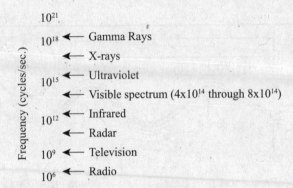

As shown above, the invisible spectrum is composed of many different rays, each one marked by a distinct frequency range. Infrared rays are detectable though as heat; X-rays travel through matter and are used to view structures beneath the skin; ultraviolet rays from the sun can damage skin; and gamma rays—the shortest rays—originate from radioactive substances. Gamma rays and x-rays are the most dangerous because their high frequency gives them high energy, which makes them more penetrating.

Light normally moves along a straight line called a **ray**. When a ray of light hits a surface such as a mirror, the light is reflected back. The light ray moving toward the mirror is the **incident ray**. The ray of light bouncing back is the **reflected ray**. As the next figure shows, the angle of the incident ray and the angle of the reflected ray are equal.

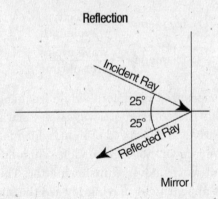

Sound Waves

Sound waves are created by vibrations from a source such as vocal chords or speaker cones. Unlike light waves, sound waves require a medium such as air, water, or an elastic solid through which to travel. The vibrations at the sound's source push the air or other medium away from the source, resulting in variations in pressure, density, and even temperature. It is these variations that our ears perceive as distinct sounds.

Like other types of waves, sound waves vary in frequency. High-frequency sound waves are higher in pitch than lower-frequency waves. The frequency of a sound wave is measured in hertz (1 hertz (Hz) = one cycle per second). The normal range for human hearing is between 20 and 20,000 hertz. Dogs can typically hear frequencies of 50,000 Hz. Ultrasound technology uses a very high frequency of 106 Hz. Sound waves also vary in amplitude. The greater the amplitude of the wave, the "louder" the sound, as measured in *decibels*. Look back to the diagram of the rope for a graphic illustration of amplitude.

52. Ultraviolet waves and X-rays differ from each other in which respect?

(A) wavelength

(B) amplitude

(C) velocity

(D) angle of reflection

The key distinction among various kinds of waves in the light spectrum involves their frequencies, which depend on wavelength. They all travel at the same speed, and so the longer the wavelength the lower the frequency. **The correct answer is (A).**

53. A certain AM radio station broadcasts at a frequency of 550 kHz. What does this mean in terms of the radio wave that carries the station's broadcast?

(A) The wavelength is 0.55 meters.

(B) The wavelength is 0.55 millimeters.

(C) The wave is received by radios at a rate of 550 cycles per second.

(D) The wave is received by radios at a rate of 550,000 cycles per second.

One kilohertz = 1000 hertz. (550 × 1000 = 550,000) So the wave frequency is 550,000 cycles per second. **The correct answer is (D).**

Simple Machines

The mechanical devices that allow us to perform everyday tasks are called machines. Everyday devices such as door knobs, zippers, and scissors are all based on certain basic mechanical principles. Most mechanical devices are composed of variations on the six **simple machines** described next. These machines provide a **mechanical advantage,** which means that by using them properly, the force required to move an object over a given distance is reduced. (In other words, they make work easier.) Be clear that machines do not reduce the amount of work; they just change the amount of force and the time needed to do work.

The Lever

A **lever** consists of a rod or pole that rests on an object at a fixed point called a **fulcrum.** The object to be lifted is referred to as the **load** and may be placed at various positions with respect to the fulcrum. There are three types of levers based on fulcrum placement, as illustrated and described here:

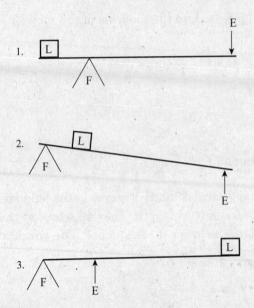

1. **First-class levers** have a fulcrum that is positioned centrally, between the load (what is being lifted) and the **force** (the exertion applied to do the lifting). Examples of this class of lever include a seesaw, scissors, pliers, and a crowbar.

2. **Second-class levers** have a fulcrum at one end, the force at other end, and the load in the middle. A wheelbarrow is a good example of this type of lever.

3. **Third-class levers** have a fulcrum and force at one end and the load at the other. Examples of this type of lever include a baseball bat, an axe, and the hammer.

The mechanical advantage, MA, of a lever can be calculated in two ways:

The load force divided by the effort force: $MA = L \div E$

The effort-fulcrum distance divided by the load-fulcrum distance: $EF \div LF$

The Pulley

A **pulley** alters the direction in which a force moves a load so the load moves upward as the force is applied downward. The basic pulley consists of a single wheel over which a belt, chain, or rope is run to change the direction of the pull on the load.

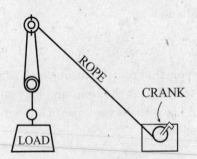

As shown above, a pulley system that consists of two or more wheels further reduces the force needed to lift a load by distributing the work over a longer length of belt, rope, or chain. The total amount of work that must be done to lift the load a given distance is the same as with a single-wheel pulley. However, the work is distributed over a greater distance, and so less force (exertion) is required. Mechanical advantage of a pulley system is simply the number of ropes attached to the load. The mechanical advantage (MA) is also the length of rope you must pull in divided by the distance the load rises.

The Incline Plane, the Screw, and the Wedge

An **incline plane** (shown below) is simply a ramp. Heavy objects can be moved to a higher position more easily by pushing or pulling them up a ramp rather than lifting them vertically. The more gradual the incline, the less force is required to move the load but the more distance the load must be moved to reach the top. In any case, the total work required is the same. A sloping driveway and a staircase are two examples of inclined planes.

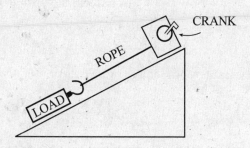

A **screw** is an incline plane in a spiral rather than a straight-path configuration. Drilling into a piece of wood at the gradual angle of the screw's threads requires less force (exertion) than hammering a nail straight down into the wood. A **wedge** is another specialized incline plane, actually two inclined planes back-to-back. When you use a wedge, you apply force to the plane to move it under the load, thereby lifting the load up onto the plane (the wedge). Examples of a wedge include a letter opener and an axe. Mechanical advantage of an inclined plane equals the length of the ramp surface divided by the height the load is raised.

The Wheel and Axle

The mechanical advantage of a **wheel-and-axle** machine is provided by the large diameter of the wheel compared to that of the axle. The wheel's circular path is greater, but less force is required to rotate it than to rotate the smaller axle. Examples of a simple wheel-and-axle machine include a door knob, bicycle pedals, a steering wheel, and a screwdriver. The cranks shown in the preceding diagrams are also wheel-and-axle machines. The mechanical advantage of a wheel-and-axle equals the radius of the wheel divided by the radius of the axle.

The wheel-and-axle can also be seen as a type of lever. Now the six types of simple machines can be reduced to just three basic types: lever, pulley, and inclined plane.

54. How might you enhance the mechanical advantage of a first-class lever?

(A) Move the fulcrum closer to the load to be lifted.

(B) Increase the load and decrease the force.

(C) Move the fulcrum closer to where the force is to be applied.

(D) Shorten the bar that rests on the fulcrum.

Moving the fulcrum closer to the load (and farther from where the force is applied) increases the leverage—less force is required to lift the load. **The correct answer is (A).**

55. What do a double-wheel pulley, an incline plane, a screw, a wedge, and a wheel-and-axle device share in common?

Each type of machine provides a mechanical advantage by

(A) applying force more directly on an object to be moved

(B) distributing the same work over a greater distance

(C) reducing resistance of an object by circular motion instead of straight-line motion

(D) decreasing the distance over which an object must be moved

Each type of machine reduces the force required to move an object by distributing the total work over a greater distance. **The correct answer is (B).**

SUMMING IT UP

- The GED® Science Test measures critical-thinking skills rather than knowledge. However, a review of the three content areas—life sciences, earth and space science, and physical science—will help you to handle the test questions with greater ease and confidence.

- Science attempts to provide explanations for natural phenomena through investigation. In order to sort out unreasonable explanations from plausible ones, scientists apply logic and common sense by means of the scientific method, which involves four fundamental steps: observation, hypothesis, experiment, and conclusion.

- Biology is the scientific study of living organisms, including plants and animals, and consists of three major branches: zoology, botany, and ecology. This review began by examining biological life at the cellular and molecular level; then, biological organisms were examined in terms of organ systems and as individuals. The review concluded by examining individual organisms as members of a community and as part of an ecosystem.

- Geology deals with the composition of the Earth and past and present events (both interior and exterior) that have shaped it. Oceanography involves physics, biology, chemistry, and geology as they pertain to ocean-related processes. Meteorology is the study of the Earth's atmosphere, weather, and climate. Astronomy is the study of the universe and the objects in it.

- Chemistry is the study of the composition, interactions, properties, and structure of matter and the changes that matter undergoes. It involves looking at ways to take substances apart and put the parts together again in new ways.

- Physics is the scientific study of matter, energy, space, and time—and how they are interrelated. Physics is closely related to all other fields of science, since its laws are universal. The living systems of biology are made of matter particles that follow the laws of physics. Chemistry explores how atoms, small units of matter, interact to form molecules according to the laws of physics. The study of geology and astronomy deal to a great extent with the physics of the Earth and of celestial bodies.

PART VI
THE MATHEMATICAL REASONING TEST

Mastering the Mathematical Reasoning Test

chapter 11

OVERVIEW

- All about the Mathematical Reasoning Test
- Format and features of the Mathematical Reasoning Test
- Measurements and the Mathematical Reasoning Test
- Using the Texas Instrument TI-30XS Calculator
- Alternate format questions
- Strategies for solving math problems
- Analyzing graphical data (graphs, charts, and tables)
- Rounding, simplifying, and checking your calculations
- General test-taking strategies
- Summing it up

THE MATHEMATICAL REASONING TEST—
IN A NUTSHELL

Time allowed: 90 minutes

Total number of questions: 37

ALL ABOUT THE MATHEMATICAL REASONING TEST

The GED® Mathematical Reasoning Test is based on Common Core State Standards for Mathematics and Principles and Standards for School Mathematics. The test is designed to measure a variety of skills, including:

- Understanding and applying mathematical concepts and formulas

- Quantitative reasoning and problem solving

- Translating verbal language into mathematical terms

- Manipulating and evaluating arithmetic and algebraic expressions

- Analyzing and interpreting graphical data (charts, graphs, tables)

To measure these skills, content will focus on:

- Quantitative problem solving (approximately 45%)

  ○ Demonstrating fluency with operations using rational numbers

  ○ Using rational numbers to formulate solutions to problems set within real-world contexts

- Solving problems with rational numbers that involve proportionality
- Engaging with geometric figures in a variety of graphic presentations
- Engaging with descriptive statistics in a variety of graphic presentations
- Using formulas or decomposition to calculate perimeter, area, surface area, and volume of figures

- Algebraic problem solving (approximately 55%)
  - Writing linear mathematical expressions and equations that correspond to given situations
  - Evaluating the expressions for specific values of the variable
  - Solving linear equations, inequalities, and systems of linear equations and finding the equation of a line with varying criteria
  - Interpreting the slope of a line as rate of change or unit rate
  - Understanding and applying the concept of a function
  - Using function notation
  - Translating a variety of representations of a function, including tables and equations
  - Solving quadratic equations
  - Interpreting key features of both linear and nonlinear functions
    These two subject areas cover a variety of topics that you will be questioned on, including:
    - Basic operations with numbers
    - Integers, divisibility, factoring, and multiples
    - Number signs, absolute value, the real number line, and ordering
    - Decimals, place value, and scientific notation
    - Percents and fractions
    - Exponents (powers) and roots
    - Ratio and proportion
    - Undefined numerical expressions
    - Measures of central tendency (mean, median, mode, and range)
    - Frequency distribution
    - Probability
    - Setting up and evaluating algebraic expressions
    - Linear equations and equation systems
    - Algebra word problems
    - Algebraic inequalities
    - Factorable quadratic expressions
    - Functional relationships, including series and patterns
    - Parallel lines, transversals, and perpendicular lines

- ○ Properties of triangles, quadrilaterals, and other polygons
- ○ Properties of circles (area, circumference, interior degree measures)
- ○ The Pythagorean theorem
- ○ Right triangle trigonometry
- ○ Three-dimensional figures (rectangular solids, right cylinders, square pyramids, cones)
- ○ Coordinate geometry
- ○ Systems of measurement for length, area, volume, weight, and mass

Keep in mind that many of questions will involve more than one of the areas listed above. For example, solving a geometry problem might also require algebra.

FORMAT AND FEATURES OF THE MATHEMATICAL REASONING TEST

The GED® Mathematical Reasoning Test actually consists of 37 questions, and you will have 90 minutes to answer them. The test content is broken up into two categories: 45% of the exam focuses on quantitative problem solving, while the other 55% is made up of algebraic problem solving.

Five of the questions you have to answer without the help of a calculator. For 32 questions, you are permitted to use an online calculator. The calculator you will use is the TI-30XS Multiview Scientific calculator. (You'll examine that calculator's functions a few pages ahead.) You will also be provided with an on-screen formula sheet for the entirety of the test, as well as a symbol tool, which will allow you to enter mathematical symbols for fill-in-the-blank problems.

A large portion of the questions on the Mathematical Reasoning Test are multiple-choice questions with four choices. The remaining questions will require you to provide your own answer using one of four alternative formats: hot spots, fill-in-the blank, drop-down, and drag-and-drop. These question types are used for a variety of subject skills and will be addressed later in the math chapters.

Here are some additional features of the Mathematical Reasoning Test:

- Many of the questions are presented in "real-world" settings involving practical, everyday situations.

- Expect at least a third of the questions to refer to charts, graphs, tables, and geometry figures. These figures are drawn to scale unless otherwise noted.

As with every other part of the GED® test, you will be provided with an erasable note board to jot down notes and make calculations. You will also be able to access the same list of formulas on-screen as the one that appears before each of the Mathematical Reasoning practice tests in this book. You may or may not need all of these formulas during the test.

Finally, during each part of the Mathematical Reasoning Test, easier questions generally appear before more challenging questions. This is only a general rule; you may find some earlier questions to be more difficult for you than some of the subsequent questions.

MEASUREMENTS AND THE MATHEMATICAL REASONING TEST

During the Mathematical Reasoning Test, you will be solving problems involving measurement of currency (money), time, length, weight, volume, and possibly mass. Some of these questions will require you to convert one unit of measurement to another. You will be expected to know the most commonly used conversion rates—the ones that people in the United States use in their everyday lives and that are listed next.

NOTE: An asterisk (*) signifies that the test question might provide the conversion rate.

Currency (money) conversions:

100 cents = 1 dollar

10 dimes = 1 dollar

20 nickels = 1 dollar

4 quarters = 1 dollar

Time conversions:

60 seconds (sec.) = 1 minute (min.)

60 minutes = 1 hour (hr.)

24 hours = 1 day

7 days = 1 week (wk.)

12 months (mo.) = 1 year (yr.)

365 days = 1 year

Length conversions:

12 inches (in.) = 1 foot (ft.)

3 feet = 1 yard (yd.)

Weight conversions:

16 ounces (oz.) = 1 pound (lb.)

* 2000 pounds = 1 ton (T)

Liquid measure conversions:

* 8 ounces (oz.) = 1 cup

* 2 cups = 1 pint (pt.)

* 2 pints = 1 quart (qt.)

* 4 quarts = 1 gallon (gal.)

Answering a test question may require you to convert numbers from one *system* of measurement to another—especially to and from the metric system. You will not be expected to know these sorts of conversion rates. The question at hand will provide the rate you should use.

USING THE TEXAS INSTRUMENT TI-30XS CALCULATOR

During the GED® Mathematical Reasoning Test, a calculator will be allowed for all but 5 questions. The use of a calculator is not *required*, though in order to avoid careless computational mistakes, it is suggested you use a calculator for all but simple calculations.

For the online GED® test, you will be provided with an on-screen, multi-view, scientific calculator. The easy-to-use qualities of the Texas Instrument TI-30XS calculator has made it a standard mathematics tool used in middle and high school math courses. You will not be permitted to bring and use your own calculator during the test. It is highly recommended that you become familiar with the TI-30XS before your testing date.

You are permitted to use the calculator for 32 of the 37 questions. When you come across a question in which you need your calculator, click the "Calculator" button in the top left-hand corner of the screen. The on-screen TI-30XS will appear as a pop-up for use in your calculations for that question. You can move the pop-up by clicking and dragging the window with your mouse. To close the calculator window, click the X in the top right-hand corner of the pop-up window. The "Calculator" button will not be activated during the 5 questions you need to answer without the help of a calculator.

When the calculator appears, it will be on and ready for use in the standard settings. To enter numbers or operations symbols, use your mouse to click on the keys. Click the enter key to view the answer to your calculation, which is located in the bottom right-hand corner of the calculator window.

Basic Operations

To add or subtract numbers, enter the numbers and the + or − keys.

To multiply or divide, use the × or ÷ keys.

To use parentheses in your calculation, click the keys indicating parentheses in the order you see the problem written.

To enter a negative number, click the (−) key located to the right of the enter key.

To find the square of a number, click the x^2 key located to the right of the 7 key.

Using the 2nd Key

Looking at the TI-30XS, you will see yellow symbols, letters, and functions around the larger, white or black keys. If you wish to use these functions, you must first click the yellow 2nd button in the upper left-hand corner of the calculator, and then the key that the function is located above. The two functions that involve this sequence that you are most likely to use are *percent* and *square root*.

The percent symbol (%) is located above the left parenthesis button. To show a number as a percent, click the number, then click the 2nd key, and then the left parenthesis key.

The square root function is located above the x^2 key. To find the square root of a number, enter the number, then click the 2nd key, and then the x^2 key.

Clearing the Memory

In order to perform a new calculation, you'll need to clear the calculator of the previous one. To do this, press the clear key, located above the division key and below the arrow pad. Clicking this key will clear the calculator's memory of all previous calculations.

ALTERNATE FORMAT QUESTIONS

The newest edition of the GED® test includes technology-enhanced questions such as drag-and-drop, hot-spot, drop-down, and fill-in-the-blank items. Drag-and-drop questions will require you to drag the "drag tokens" and place them on one or more correct "drop targets." Hot-spot items will be used so that you may select your answer by clicking or graphing a point on a designated sensor on graphs, maps, or diagrams. Drop-down questions will require you to choose the correct answer from a list of options in a drop-down menu. Fill-in-the-blank (FITB) questions will require you to write a word or phrase in a box in order to complete a sentence.

STRATEGIES FOR SOLVING MATH PROBLEMS

About 50 percent of the questions on the Mathematical Reasoning Test will involve problem solving—in other words, working to a solution expressed as either a number or an expression containing variables (such as x and y). In this section, you'll learn specific strategies for solving problems. Most of these strategies apply only to multiple-choice questions, which account for 80 percent of all questions on the test.

The examples you'll see here run the gamut in terms of the concepts covered. If you don't fully understand a certain concept illustrated here, you can come back and review it later.

Scan the Answer Choices for Clues

Scan the answer choices to see what all or most of them have in common—such as radical signs, exponents, factorable expressions, or fractions. Then try to formulate a solution that looks like the answer choices.

EXAMPLE 1 (EASIER):

If $a \neq 0$ or 2, then the expression $\dfrac{\frac{1}{a}}{2-a}$ is equivalent to which of the following?

(A) $\dfrac{1}{2a - a^2}$

(B) $\dfrac{2}{a - 2}$

(C) $\dfrac{1}{a^2}$

(D) $\dfrac{2}{2a - 1}$

Notice what all the answer choices have in common: Each one is a fraction in which the denominator contains the variable a, but the numerator doesn't. And, there are no fractions in either the numerator or the denominator. That's a clue that your job is to manipulate the expression given in the question so that the result includes these features. Multiplying the numerator fraction by the reciprocal of the denominator will give you a result that has these features:

$$\frac{\frac{1}{a}}{2-a} = \frac{1}{a} \times \frac{1}{2-a} = \frac{1}{2a - a^2}$$

The correct answer is (A).

EXAMPLE 2 (MORE CHALLENGING):

A team of archeologists and engineers plan to build a pyramid using ancient construction materials and methods. As shown below, the base of the pyramid is to be square, and each of the four angles at the apex of the pyramid is to measure 90°.

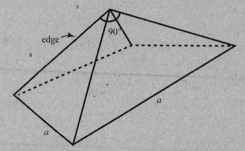

If the pyramid's base measures a meters on each side, which of the following represents the length of any of the four edges that extend from the pyramid's base to its apex?

(A) $\frac{a}{3}\sqrt{2}$

(B) $\frac{a}{2}\sqrt{2}$

(C) $\frac{3}{4}a$

(D) $\frac{12}{13}a$

Notice that $\sqrt{2}$ appears in two of the four expressions listed among the answer choices. With sufficient knowledge of the Pythagorean theorem, you will recognize this value as the hypotenuse of a certain right-triangle shape. With this clue in mind, bisect any triangular face of the pyramid into two smaller right triangles, as shown below.

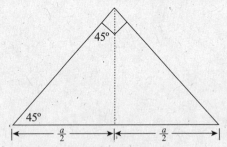

The length of each leg of a smaller triangle is $\frac{a}{2}$. From the Pythagorean theorem, you know that the length of the hypotenuse of any 90°-45°-45° triangle is the product of $\sqrt{2}$ and the length of either leg. So, in this case, the hypotenuse, or "edge" of the pyramid, measures $\frac{a}{2}\sqrt{2}$ meters. **The correct answer is (B).**

Don't Be Lured by Obvious Answer Choices

Expect to be tempted by wrong-answer choices that are the result of common errors in reasoning, in calculations, and in setting up and solving equations. Never assume that your solution is correct just because you see it among the answer choices.

EXAMPLE 3 (EASIER):

What is the value of $(8 + 8)^2 - (7 + 7)^2$?

    (A) 30

    (B) 60

    (C) 256

    (D) 452

Each wrong answer choice is the result of a common error:

If you make the mistake of distributing the power to each term in parentheses, you might select choice (A): $8^2 + 8^2 - 7^2 - 7^2 = 64 + 64 - 49 - 49 = 30$.

If you make the mistake of distributing the subtraction sign to both "7"s before squaring, you might select choice (C): $(8 + 8)^2 - (7 - 7)^2 = 16^2 - 0 = 256$.

If you make the mistake of adding instead of subtracting, you might select choice (D): $(8 + 8)^2 + (7 + 7)^2 = 16^2 + 14^2 = 256 + 196 = 452$.

Here is the correct calculation: $16^2 - 14^2 = 256 - 196 = 60$, choice (B).

The correct answer is (B).

EXAMPLE 4 (MORE CHALLENGING):

The average of six numbers is 19. When one of those numbers is taken away, the average of the remaining five numbers is 21. What number was taken away?

    (A) 2

    (B) 6.5

    (C) 9

    (D) 20

In this example, two of the wrong answer choices are especially enticing. Choice (A) would be the correct answer to the question: "What is the difference between 19 and 21?" But this question asks something entirely different. Choice (D) is the other too-obvious choice. 20 is simply $19 + 21$ divided by 2. If this solution strikes you as too simple, you've got good instincts. You can solve this problem quickly by simply comparing the two *sums*. Before the sixth number is taken away, the sum of the numbers is 114 (6×19). After taking away the sixth number, the sum of the remaining numbers is 105 (5×21). The difference between the two sums is 9, which must be the value of the number taken away. **The correct answer is (C).**

Size Up the Question to Narrow Your Choices

If a multiple-choice question asks for a number value, you can probably narrow down the answer choices by estimating the size and type of number you're looking for. When handling word problems, use your common sense and real-world experience to formulate "ballpark" estimates.

Also, keep in mind that if the answer choices are all numbers, they'll be listed in order—from least in value to greatest in value. This feature can help you zero-in on viable choices.

EXAMPLE 5 (EASIER):

Stephanie deposited $1000 in an account that earns 5% **compound** interest. If she made no additional deposits, what was Stephanie's account balance after two years?

(A) $1050

(B) $1100

(C) $1102.50

(D) $1152.25

If you understand that compound interest is an *annual* rate that applies interest not only to the principal balance, but also to any previous interest earned, and if you know that 5% of $1000 is $50, then you can narrow your choices. The account earned $50 in interest the first year, but *slightly more* than $50 the second year because it earned interest on the first year's interest. So the correct answer must be a bit greater than $1100. You can eliminate choices (A) and (B). All that's left is to perform the calculation:

$$5\% \text{ of } \$1050 = 0.05 \times \$1050 = \$52.50.$$

Add this amount of interest to the $50 earned during the first year:

$$\$1000 \text{ (initial deposit)} + \$50 \text{ (year 1 interest)} + \$52.50 \text{ (year 2 interest)} = \$1102.50.$$

The correct answer is (C).

EXAMPLE 6 (MORE CHALLENGING):

A container holds 10 liters of a solution that is 20% acid. If 6 liters of pure acid are added to the container, what percent of the resulting mixture is acid?

(A) 20

(B) $33\frac{1}{3}$

(C) 40

(D) 50

Common sense should tell you that when you add more acid to the solution, the percent of the solution that is acid will increase. So you're looking for an answer that is a percent greater than 20. Only choices (B), (C), or (D) fit the bill. If you need to guess at this point, your odds are one in three of answering the question correctly. Here's how to solve the problem:

The original amount of acid is (10)(20%) = 2 liters. After adding 6 liters of pure acid, the amount of acid increases to 8 liters, while the amount of total solution increases from 10 to 16 liters. The new solution is $\frac{8}{16}$, or 50%, acid, choice (D). **The correct answer is (D).**

Know When to Plug In Numbers for Variables

If the answer choices contain variables such as x and y, the question might be a good candidate for the "plug-in" strategy. Pick simple numbers (so the math is easy), and substitute them for the variables. You'll need your pencil and scratch paper for this strategy.

EXAMPLE 7 (EASIER):

If one dollar can buy m pieces of paper, how many dollars are needed to buy p reams of paper? [1 ream = 500 pieces of paper]

(A) $\dfrac{500}{p+m}$

(B) $\dfrac{m}{500p}$

(C) $\dfrac{500p}{m}$

(D) $\dfrac{p}{500m}$

You can solve this problem conventionally or by using the plug-in strategy.

The conventional way: The question is essentially asking: "1 is to m as what is to p?" Set up a proportion (equate two ratios, or fractions). Then convert either pieces of paper to reams (divide m by 500) or reams to pieces (multiply p by 500). The second conversion method is used below. Cross-multiply to solve for x:

$$\frac{1}{m} = \frac{x}{500p}$$
$$mx = 500p$$
$$x = \frac{500p}{m}$$

The plug-in strategy: Pick easy-to-use values for m and p. Let's try $m = 500$ and $p = 1$. At $1 for 500 sheets, it obviously takes exactly $1 to buy one ream of paper. Start plugging these values into each of the five expressions in turn. The correct choice will provide a value of 1. Choice (A) doesn't work, and neither does choice (B). But choice (C) works:

$$\frac{500p}{m} = \frac{500(1)}{500} = 1$$

There's no need to test choice (D). **The correct answer is (C).**

EXAMPLE 8 (MORE CHALLENGING):

If a train travels $r + 2$ miles in h hours, which of the following represents the number of miles the train travels in 1 hour and 30 minutes?

(A) $\dfrac{3r + 6}{2h}$

(B) $\dfrac{3r}{h + 2}$

(C) $\dfrac{r + 2}{h + 3}$

(D) $\dfrac{r}{h + 6}$

This is an algebraic word problem involving rate of motion (speed). As in the previous problem, you can solve this problem either conventionally or by using the plug-in strategy.

The conventional way: Notice that all of the answer choices contain fractions. This is a clue that you should try to create a fraction as you solve the problem. Given that the train travels $r + 2$ miles in h hours, you can express its rate in miles per hour as $\dfrac{r + 2}{h}$. In $\dfrac{3}{2}$ hours, the train would travel $\left(\dfrac{3}{2}\right)\left(\dfrac{r + 2}{h}\right) = \dfrac{3r + 6}{2h}$ miles.

The plug-in strategy: Pick easy-to-use values for r and h. Let's try $r = 8$ and $h = 1$. Given these values, the train travels 10 miles $(8 + 2)$ in 1 hour. So obviously, in $1\frac{1}{2}$ hours the train will travel 15 miles. Start plugging these r and h values into the answer choices. For this question, you won't need to go any further than choice (A):

$$\dfrac{3r + 6}{2h} = \dfrac{3(8) + 6}{2(1)} = \dfrac{30}{2}, \text{ or } 15$$

The correct answer is (A).

The plug-in strategy can be very useful when you don't know how to set up the algebraic expression or equation that the problem requires. But keep in mind that this strategy can be time-consuming if the correct answer is far down in the list of choices. So use it only if you don't know how to set up the correct algebraic expression or equation.

Know When—and When Not—to Work Backward

If a multiple-choice question asks for a number value, and if you draw a blank as far as how to set up and solve the problem, don't panic. You might be able to work backward by testing the answer choices, each one in turn.

On the GED® Mathematical Reasoning Test, numerical answer choices are always listed in order of value, from least to greatest. So when working backward from the answer choices, the best place to start is with choice (C), which provides a value close to the middle. If choice (C) provides a number that is too great, then the correct answer must be either choice (A) or choice (B). Conversely, if choice (C) provides a number that is too small, then the correct answer must be choice (D).

EXAMPLE 9 (EASIER):

A ball is dropped from 192 inches above level ground. After the second bounce, it rises to a height of 48 inches. If the height to which the ball rises after each bounce is always the same fraction of the height reached on its previous bounce, what is this fraction?

(A) $\frac{1}{8}$

(B) $\frac{1}{4}$

(C) $\frac{1}{3}$

(D) $\frac{1}{2}$

The fastest route to a solution is to plug in an answer. Try choice (C), and see what happens. If the ball bounces up $\frac{1}{3}$ as high as it started, as choice (C) provides, then after the first bounce it will rise up $\frac{1}{3}$ as high as 192 inches, or 64 inches. After a second bounce, it will rise $\frac{1}{3}$ as high, or about 21 inches. But, the problem states that the ball rises to 48 inches after the second bounce. So, choice (C) cannot be the correct answer. We can see that the ball must be bouncing higher than one third of the way; that eliminates choices (A) and (B) and leaves you with only one possible answer. Try plugging in choice (D), and you'll see that it works: $\frac{1}{2}$ of 192 is 96, and $\frac{1}{2}$ of 96 is 48.

The correct answer is (D).

In the previous example, although it would be possible to develop a formula to answer the question, doing so would be senseless, considering how quickly and easily you can work backward from the answer choices.

Working backward from numerical answer choices works well when the numbers are easy, and when few calculations are required, as in the preceding question. In other cases, applying algebra might be a better way.

EXAMPLE 10 (MORE CHALLENGING):

How many pounds of nuts selling for 70 cents per pound must be mixed with 30 pounds of nuts selling at 90 cents per pound to make a mixture that sells for 85 cents per pound?

(A) 8.5

(B) 10

(C) 15

(D) 16.5

Is the easier route to the solution to test the answer choices? Let's see. First of all, calculate the total cost of 30 pounds of nuts at 90 cents per pound: $30 \times 0.90 = \$27$. Now, start with choice (C). 15 pounds of nuts at 70 cents per pound costs $10.50. The total cost of this mixture is $37.50, and the total weight is 45 pounds. Now you'll need to perform some long division. The average cost of the mixture turns out to be between 83 and 84 cents—too low for the 85 cent average given in the question. So you can at least eliminate choice (C).

You should realize by now that testing the answer choices might not be the most efficient way to tackle this question. Besides, there are ample opportunities for calculation errors. Instead, try solving this problem algebraically by writing and solving a system of equations. Here's how to do it. The cost (in cents) of the nuts selling for 70 cents per pound can be expressed as $70x$, letting x equal the number that you're asked to determine. You then add this cost to the cost of the more expensive nuts ($30 \times 90 = 2700$) to obtain the total cost of the mixture, which you can express as $85(x + 30)$. You can state this algebraically and solve for x as follows:

$$70x + 2700 = 85(x + 30)$$
$$70x + 2700 = 85x + 2550$$
$$150 = 15x$$
$$10 = x$$

At 70 cents per pound, 10 pounds of nuts must be added in order to make a mixture that sells for 85 cents per pound. **The correct answer is (B).**

Look for the Simplest Route to the Answer

For many GED® test math questions, there's a long way and a short way to get to the correct answer. When it looks like you're facing a long series of calculations or a complex system of equations, always ask yourself if there's an easier, more intuitive way of answering the question.

EXAMPLE 11 (EASIER):

Type your answer in the box. You may use numbers and/or a decimal point (.) in your answer.

What is the value of $\dfrac{150}{450} \times \dfrac{750}{300} \times \dfrac{450}{1500}$? [   ]

Whether or not you use a calculator for this question, multiplying and dividing these large numbers is needlessly time-consuming. What's more, the more calculations you make, the more likely you'll commit a computation error. Look carefully at the numbers involved. Notice that you can factor all of these numbers across fractions. After factoring, the three fractions that remain can be easily combined. Here's one possibility:

$$\frac{150}{450} \times \frac{750}{300} \times \frac{450}{1500} = \frac{1}{1} \times \frac{1}{2} \times \frac{1}{2} = \frac{1}{4}$$

The correct answer is 1/4 or .25. To receive credit for a correct answer, you would enter either **1/4** or **.25** in the blank box.

EXAMPLE 12 (MORE CHALLENGING):

What is the difference between the sum of all positive **even** integers less than 32 and the sum of all positive **odd** integers less than 32?

(A) 0

(B) 1

(C) 15

(D) 16

To answer this question, should you add up two long series of numbers on your scratch paper or with the calculator? No. In this case, it is a waste of time, and you risk committing calculation errors along the way. A smart test-taker will notice a pattern and use it as a shortcut. Compare the initial terms of each sequence:

even integers: 2, 4, 6, . . . , 30

odd integers: 1, 3, 5, . . . , 29, 31

Notice that for each successive term the odd integer is one less than the corresponding even integer. There are a total of 15 corresponding integers, so the difference between the sums of all these corresponding integers is 15. But the odd-integer sequence includes one additional integer: 31. So the difference is $31 - 15 = 16$. **The correct answer is (D).**

Keep in mind: GED® test math questions are not designed to gauge your ability to make lengthy, repetitive calculations on your scratch paper or with the calculator. Combining three or four numbers using basic operations will probably be the limit of what is expected of you. So again, if you're facing a long series of computations, especially with large numbers, look for a quicker, easier way to answer the question.

Solve Problems by Starting with What You Know

It's easy to get lost in a complex math problem requiring several steps to solve. If you're at a loss as to how to begin, start with the information you know. Then ask yourself what you can deduce from that information. This approach will very likely lead you, step-by-step, to the solution.

EXAMPLE 13 (EASIER):

Type the answer in the box. You may use numbers and/or a decimal point (.) in your answer.

Cassie can assemble 4 computers in one hour, and Hillary can assemble 12 computers in one hour. Working at the same time, Cassie, Hillary, and a third worker, Jodie, can assemble 192 computers during an 8-hour shift. How many computers can Jodie assemble in one hour? [   ]

Two of the numbers are given as an hourly rate of work, and the other number is given as a rate of work per 8-hour shift. A good place to start is to convert one rate to the other. Let's try converting the total per-shift work rate to an hourly rate: $192 \div 8 = 24$. So you know that Hillary, Jodie, and Cassie can assemble 24 computers in an hour. Now ask yourself what else you know. You know that Cassie's hourly rate of work is 4 and that Hillary's hourly rate of work is 12. Now ask yourself what you deduce from this information. If you subtract those two numbers from 24, you'll find Jodie's hour rate of work, which is the answer to the question:

$$24 - 4 - 12 = 8$$

The correct answer is 8. To receive credit for a correct answer, you would enter **8** in the blank box.

EXAMPLE 14 (MORE CHALLENGING):

In a group of 20 singers and 40 dancers, 20 percent of the singers are under 25 years in age, and 40 percent of the entire group are under 25 years in age. What portion of the dancers is under 25 years in age?

(A) 20 percent

(B) 24 percent

(C) 40 percent

(D) 50 percent

To answer this question, you need to know the total number of dancers as well as the *number* of dancers under 25 years in age. The question provides the first number: 40. To find the second number, start with what the question provides, and figure out what else you know. Keep going, and eventually you'll arrive at your destination. Of the whole group of 60, 24 are under 25 years in age (40% of 60 is 24). 20 percent of the 20 singers, or 4 singers, are under 25 years in age. Hence, the remaining 20 people under 25 must be dancers. That's the second number you needed to answer the question. 20 is 50% of 40. **The correct answer is (D).**

Search Geometry Figures for Clues

Some GED® test geometry questions will be accompanied by figures. They are there for a reason: the pieces of information a figure provides can lead you, step-by-step, to the answer.

EXAMPLE 15 (EASIER):

This is how you will see the question worded on the online GED® Test. For this print version mark the grid to show the correct coordinates.

$\overline{PQ}$ has a midpoint M. $\overline{PM}$ is congruent to $\overline{MQ}$. Click on the grid to show the correct (x, y) coordinates of point M.

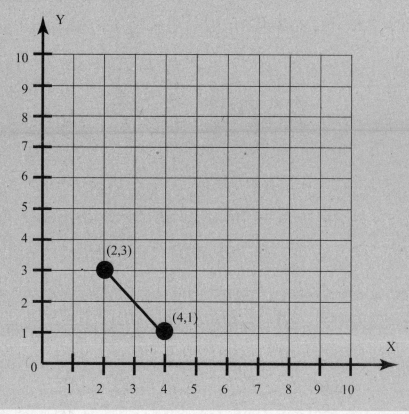

To answer the question, you need to examine the specific coordinates provided in the figure. Given that $\overline{PM}$ is congruent, or equal in length, to $\overline{MQ}$, the x-coordinate of point M is half the horizontal distance from 2 to 4 (P to Q), at 3. Similarly, the y-coordinate of point M is half the vertical distance from 3 to 1 (P to Q), at 2. The (x, y) coordinates of point M are (3, 2). **The correct answer is (3, 2).**

EXAMPLE 16 (MORE CHALLENGING):

Type the answer in the box.

Point O lies at the center of the circle shown in the figure.

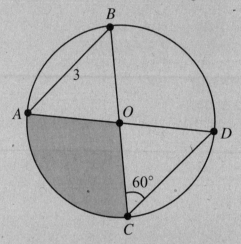

What is the area of the circle's shaded region, expressed in square units?

[   ] π

This question asks for the area of a portion of the circle defined by a central angle. To answer the question, you'll need to determine the area of the entire circle as well as what portion (fraction or percent) of that area is shaded. Search the figure for a piece of information that might provide a starting point. If you look at the 60° angle in the figure, you should recognize that both triangles are equilateral (all angles are 60°) and, extended out to their arcs, form two segments, each $\frac{1}{6}$ the size of the entire circle. What's left are the two largest segments, each of which is twice the size of a small segment. So the shaded area must account for $\frac{1}{3}$ the circle's area.

Now you've reduced the problem to the simple mechanics of calculating the circle's area, then dividing it by 3. In an equilateral triangle, all sides are congruent. Examining the figure once again, notice length 3, which is also the circle's radius (the distance from its center to its circumference). The area of any circle is πr^2, where r is the circle's radius. Thus, the area of the circle is 9π. The shaded portion accounts for $\frac{1}{3}$ the circle's area, or 3π. **The correct answer is 3.**

As the preceding examples show, GED® test geometry figures are intended to provide information helpful in solving the problem. But they're not intended to *provide* the answer through visual measurement. Make sure you solve the problem by working with the numbers and variables provided, not simply by looking at the figure's proportions.

Sketch Your Own Geometry Figure

A geometry problem that doesn't provide a figure might be more easily solved if it had one. Use your scratch paper and draw one for yourself. It will be easier than trying to visualize it in your mind.

EXAMPLE 17 (EASIER):

Line A is perpendicular to line B, and the intersection of line B and line C forms a 35° angle. Which statement about the relationship between line A and line C is correct?

(A) Line A is perpendicular to line C.

(B) The intersection of line A and line C forms a 35° angle.

(C) The intersection of line A and line C forms a 125° angle.

(D) The intersection of line A and line C forms a 145° angle.

It's difficult to visualize all the lines and angles in your head in order to answer this question. So first draw perpendicular lines A and B. Then draw line C through line A at an acute angle of approximately 35° (a rough approximation will suffice), and mark that angle measure. You can now see a *right* triangle with interior angles 90°, 35°, and 55°. (The interior angles of any triangle total 180° in measure.)

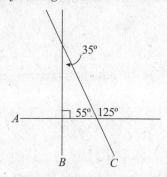

Since 55° is not among the answer choices, you need to determine the measure of either adjacent angle, which is *supplementary* to the 55° angle. (This means that the two angles combine to form a straight, 180° line.) Either of the two exterior angles adjacent to the 55° angle must measure 125° (180° − 55°). **The correct answer is (C).**

EXAMPLE 18 (MORE CHALLENGING):

On the xy-coordinate plane, points $R(7, -3)$ and $S(7, 7)$ are the endpoints of the longest possible chord of a certain circle. What is the area of the circle?

(A) 7π

(B) 16π

(C) 20π

(D) 25π

There are lots of "7"s in this question, which might throw you off track without at least a rough picture. To keep your thinking straight, scratch out your own rough xy-grid and plot the two points. You'll see that R is located directly below S, so chord $\overline{RS}$ is vertical.

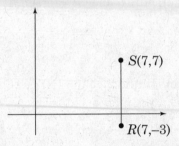

Accordingly, the length of $\overline{RS}$ is simply the vertical distance from -3 to 7, which is 10. By definition, the longest possible chord of a circle is equal in length to the circle's diameter. In this case, the circle's diameter is 10, and thus its radius is 5. The circle's area is $\pi(r)^2 = 25\pi$. **The correct answer is (D).**

ANALYZING GRAPHICAL DATA (GRAPHS, CHARTS, AND TABLES)

GED® test data-analysis questions are most often based on the following types of data displays:

- Bar graphs
- Line charts
- Picture graphs
- Circle graphs (pie charts)
- Tables

GED® test data-analysis questions are designed to gauge your ability to read, compare, and interpret charts, graphs, and tables, as well as to calculate numbers such as percentages, ratios, fractions, and averages based on data presented in a graphical format. Here are some features of GED® test data-analysis questions you should know about:

- **The number of displays per question and questions per display can vary.** The questions usually come in sets of 2–3, each question in a set referring to the same graphical data. Some questions or sets may involve just *one* chart, graph, or table; other questions or sets may involve *two or more* charts, graphs, or tables.

- **Important additional information may be provided.** Any additional information that you might need to know to interpret the graphical display will be indicated above, below, or to the side of it. Be sure to read this information!

- **Some questions might ask for an approximation.** This is because the test-makers are trying to gauge your ability to interpret graphical data, not your ability to crunch numbers to the "nth" decimal place.

- **Answering a question often involves multiple steps.** Though an easier question might simply involve locating a certain number value on a chart or graph, most questions ask you to perform one or more calculations as well. Also, you may need to refer to more than one graph or chart in order to answer a question, which will involve additional steps.

- **Bar graphs and line charts are drawn to scale.** That's because visual *estimation* is part of what's required to analyze a bar graph or line chart's graphical data. But they aren't drawn to test your eyesight. Instead, they're designed for a comfortable margin for error in visual acuity. Just don't round up or down too far.

- **For picture graphs, pie charts, and tables, visual scale is not important.** You'll interpret these displays based strictly on the numbers provided.

Bar Graphs

A **bar graph** looks like what the name implies: it consists of a series of vertical or horizontal bars representing number values. The higher (or longer) the bar, the greater the number value.

A bar graph includes a **vertical axis** and a **horizontal axis.** Each scale shows a different measure or other variable. Examine the following graph. The vertical scale indicates a number expressed in *thousands*. The numbers on this vertical scale range from 0 to 22,000. The horizontal scale indicates ages ranging from 25 to 65+ (which means 65 and older). Notice that the ages are given in five-year intervals; ages falling between these intervals are not represented.

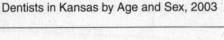

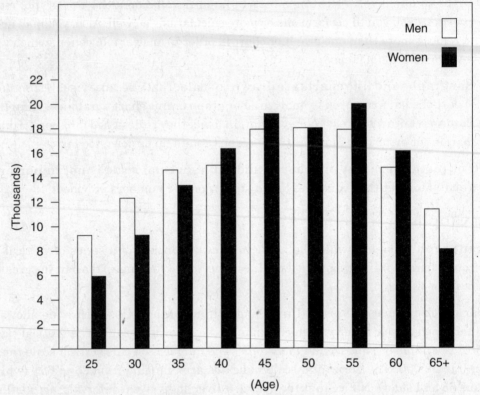

Dentists in Kansas by Age and Sex, 2003

But what do the "thousands" (vertical scale) and the ages (horizontal scale) involve? Examine the information above the illustration. This is the label, or title, for the graph. It tells you that the vertical scale indicates the number of *dentists* (in thousands), while the horizontal scale indicates *age* categories for dentists. It also tells you that these numbers involve one state during one year only: Kansas in 2003.

Finally, what is the distinction between a white bar and a black bar? Examine the **legend** in the upper-right corner. It tells you that for each age interval, the white bar represents the number of dentists who are men, and the black bar represents the number of dentists who are women.

So by examining the height of a white (or black) bar in each age category, you can "see" the approximate number of men (or women) dentists at each age interval. For example, in Kansas during 2003:

- Approximately 15,000 dentists were 40-year-old men

- Approximately 20,000 dentists were 55-year-old women

- Just over 8000 dentists were women 65 years of age or older

Notice that these numbers are approximations, or estimates. Remember: in analyzing GED® test bar graphs you won't need to provide precise values for numbers appearing on scales such as the vertical scale in this example.

Now answer a few questions involving a bit more than identifying a single value on the graph:

> *At what age were the number of male and female dentists equal?*

> Look at the graph and see where the white and black bars are the same, then look at the numbers at the bottom of the chart to see the age. The number of male and female dentists were equal at age 50.

> *How many more male dentists were there at age 30 than female dentists?*

> The bar for male dentists at age 30 reaches approximately 12,500, and the bar for female dentists reaches approximately 9500. So, of the dentists at age 30, there were approximately 3000 more men than women.

Now look at two GED® test-style questions referring to the same graph.

EXAMPLE 19 (EASIER):

Based on the graph, which statement is NOT accurate?

(A) Between ages 40 and 60, the total number of female dentists was greater than male dentists.

(B) Overall, there are more male dentists than female dentists.

(C) The number of female dentists decreased between ages 60 and 65+.

(D) The only time the number of male dentists is greater than female dentists is prior to age 40.

All of the statements are true according to the graph except choice (D). When examining the graph carefully, the number of male dentists is also greater than female dentists in the 65+ age group. **The correct answer is (D).**

EXAMPLE 20 (MORE CHALLENGING):

At which age did the number of male dentists increase the LEAST over the number of female dentists?

(A) age 30

(B) age 35

(C) age 45

(D) age 65+

First, notice that in the age 45 group, choice (C), there were more female dentists than male dentists. Therefore, you can eliminate choice (C) on this basis alone. No calculations are necessary when comparing choices (A), (B), and (D). For each of these age groups (30, 35, and 65+), examine the height difference between the two bars. The question asks for the *least* increase. At ages 30 and 65+, the differences in the heights of the bars is clearly greater than at age 35. Therefore, choices (A) and (D) can be eliminated.

The only remaining group is age 35, where the difference between the number of male and female dentists is small. **The correct answer is (B).**

Line Charts

A **line chart** consists of one or more lines running from left to right. Line charts are constructed by first plotting points at regular intervals, then connecting those points with **trend lines** (lines that suggest increases and decreases from one interval to the next). But the only data you know for sure are those indicated by the points themselves, and not by the lines. The higher the point on a line, the greater the number value the point represents.

Like bar graphs, line charts include a vertical axis and a horizontal axis, each showing a different measure or other variable. Examine the following line chart. The vertical scale indicates a number expressed in *thousands*. The numbers on this vertical scale range from 0 to 45,000. The horizontal scale indicates months of the years; all twelve months are represented.

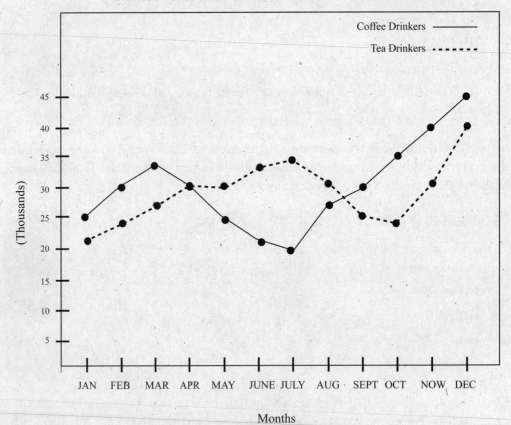

Number of Coffee and Tea Drinkers Over 12 Months

The chart's label, or title, above the illustration tells you that the vertical scale indicates the number of *coffee and tea drinkers* in thousands. The legend in the upper-right corner tells you that the solid line represents coffee drinkers, while the dotted line represents tea drinkers. By examining the height of the solid (or dotted) line at each point, you can "see" the approximate number of coffee (or tea) drinkers for that month. For example:

- The number of coffee drinkers in May was approximately 25,000.

- The number of tea drinkers in November was approximately 32,000.

These numbers are approximations, or estimates. As with bar graphs, analyzing GED® test line charts won't require identifying precise values for numbers appearing on scales such as the vertical scale in this example.

Now answer a few questions involving a bit more than identifying a single number value on the chart:

> *During what month was the number of coffee drinkers greatest?*

Look at the solid line and follow it to the highest point (dot) on the chart. Then look to the bottom of the chart to see the month. December saw the greatest number of coffee drinkers.

> *During what month were the number of coffee drinkers and tea drinkers most nearly the same?*

Look at the chart to see at what point the solid and dotted lines intersect, and then look to the bottom of the chart to identify the month. April was the month during which the number of coffee drinkers and tea drinkers were most nearly the same.

Now look at two GED® test-style questions referring to the same chart.

EXAMPLE 21 (EASIER):

During February, what was the approximate ratio of tea drinkers to coffee drinkers?

- **(A)** 2 to 5
- **(B)** 2 to 3
- **(C)** 4 to 5
- **(D)** 5 to 3

First, approximate both values: During February, there were about 24,000 tea drinkers and about 31,000 coffee drinkers. The *ratio* of tea to coffee drinkers is another way of expressing the fraction $\frac{24,000}{31,000}$. Since the numbers involved are approximations, you can safely round 31,000 down to 30,000, and then disregard the trailing zeroes. Factoring 24 and 30 leaves the simple fraction $\frac{4}{5}$, or a ratio of 4 to 5. **The correct answer is (C).**

EXAMPLE 22 (MORE CHALLENGING):

During which month was the total number of coffee drinkers and tea drinkers the lowest?

   (A) January

   (B) May

   (C) August

   (D) September

Your task here is to add together the number of coffee drinkers and tea drinkers. But there's no need to perform calculations for each of the months listed. Instead, focus on the months when the number of both coffee and tea drinkers were both low—in other words, where both points are low on the chart. January is a viable choice, and so is September. Combine *approximate* numbers for each of these two months:

   January: 21,000 (tea) + 25,000 (coffee) = 46,000

   September: 20,000 (tea) + 30,000 (coffee) = 50,000

Thus, January saw the lowest combined consumption. **The correct answer is (A).**

Circle Graphs

Circle graphs are sometimes referred to as **pie charts.** They show the parts, or segments, of a whole. Most often, the parts are expressed as percents of the whole. The parts of the whole add up to 100 percent. Reading circle graphs should not involve visual estimation. Rely only on the numbers provided, not on the visual size of any segment in relation to the whole. Here's an example of a circle graph:

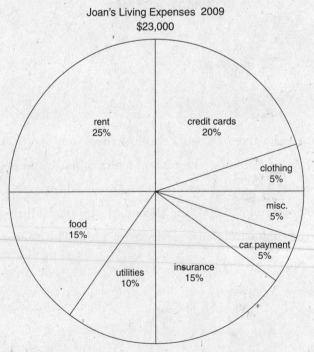

Joan's Living Expenses 2009
$23,000

The label, or title, above the graph tells you that each segment on the graph represents a percent of Joan's total living expenses ($23,000) for 2009. To determine her expenditures for each category, you would multiply the percent by her total salary.

Now answer a few simple questions involving the data in this graph:

> *How much did Joan spend for insurance?*

> Insurance accounted for 15% of Joan's living expenses. Convert 15% to a decimal number, then multiply: Joan spent $23,000 × 0.15 = $3450 on insurance.

> *How much did Joan spend on rent and utilities combined?*

> You can add the two percentages first: 25% (rent) + 10% (utilities) = 35%. Calculate the combined dollar amount: Joan spent $23,000 × 0.35 = $8050 on rent and utilities.

Now look at two GED® test-style questions referring to the same chart.

EXAMPLE 23 (EASIER):

How much more did Joan spend on food than on clothing?

- **(A)** $560
- **(B)** $1150
- **(C)** $2300
- **(D)** $3450

First, subtract 5% from 15%. Joan spent 10% more of her total expenses on food than on clothing. Then express 10% as a dollar amount: $23,000 × 0.10 = $2300. **The correct answer is (C).**

EXAMPLE 24 (MORE CHALLENGING):

Assume that Joan's total living expenses increase by 10 percent every year and that her credit card expenses increase by 5 percent every year. Approximately what portion of Joan's total 2010 living expenses went toward credit cards?

- **(A)** 18%
- **(B)** 19%
- **(C)** 20%
- **(D)** 21%

This question requires multiple steps, leaving ample opportunity for calculation errors. However, you can easily increase your odds by narrowing the choices. If Joan's *total* living expenses increase every year at a greater rate than her credit card expenses, the initial 20% that constitutes just the credit card portion will *decrease* with each passing year. So the correct answer must be less than 20%. Eliminate choices (C) and (D). To decide between choices (A) and (B), calculate Joan's 2010 credit card expenses and her 2010 total living expenses. This question would probably appear on Part I of the test, so you could use the calculator for the following computations.

2010 credit card expenses:

$$\$4600 + (0.05)(\$4600) = \$4830$$

2010 total living expenses:

$$\$23,000 + (0.10)(\$23,000) = \$25,300$$

To determine Joan's 2010 credit card expenses as a percentage of her total living expenses, divide. The question asks for an approximate percent, so you can round off your answer a bit:

$$\frac{4830}{25,300} \approx 0.19, \text{ or } 19\%.$$

The correct answer is (B).

Tables

A **table** consists of rows and columns of data. Beside each row and above each column is a heading that tells you what the numbers in the row or column signify. Most of us read tables every day: television, bus, and work schedules; menus; and even calendars are all everyday examples of tables. So you should have little trouble reading GED® test tables. Nevertheless, the tables on the test will be unfamiliar to you, and some of the questions can be a bit more challenging than you might expect. Look at the following table.

Resort	Snowfall (2009)	Snowfall (2010)	No. of Visitors (2009)	No. of Visitors (2010)
Blue Mountain	14.8 ft.	18.6 ft.	28,300	31,350
High Top	12.8 ft.	19.0 ft.	12,720	11,830
Crystal Hill	20.6 ft.	15.3 ft.	22,440	25,100
Snow Ridge	21.2 ft.	16.4 ft.	9580	12,360

Notice that for each of the four resorts, two pieces of data are provided for each of the two years: 2009 and 2010. This table does not come with a title or other explanatory information. But you don't need any to understand the table. Now answer a few simple questions involving the tabular data:

Which resort saw the least snowfall in 2009?

High Top saw only 12.8 feet of snowfall in 2009. All three other resorts saw more than that.

How much more snow fell in High Top than in Crystal Hill in 2010?

Subtract the amount at Crystal Hill (15.3) from the amount at High Top (19.0). The difference is 3.7 feet.

How many more visitors came to Crystal Hill in 2010 than in 2009?

Subtract the number in 2009 (22,440) from the number in 2010 (25,100). The difference is 2660.

Now look at two GED® test-style questions referring to the same table.

EXAMPLE 25 (EASIER):

Which resort experienced the greatest *percent* change in number of visitors from 2009 to 2010?

    (A) Blue Mountain

    (B) High Top

    (C) Crystal Hill

    (D) Snow Ridge

To answer the question, you don't need to calculate precise percent changes. Instead, compare changes among the resorts by rough estimation. Notice that for each of three resorts—Blue Mountain, Crystal Hill, and Snow Ridge—the change was roughly 3000. (For High Top, the change was far less, so you can rule out choice (B).) Also notice that the actual numbers are lowest for Snow Ridge, which means that the *percent* change at Snow Ridge was the highest. **The correct answer is (D).**

EXAMPLE 26 (MORE CHALLENGING):

Based on the 2009 and 2010 data, what can be inferred about the four resorts?

    (A) The higher a resort's elevation, the greater the snowfall at that resort.

    (B) The four resorts received more visitors altogether in 2009 than in 2010.

    (C) The numbers of visitors were not consistently related to snowfall amounts.

    (D) The four resorts received more snowfall altogether in 2010 than in 2009.

The data in the table contradict statements (B) and (D), and the table contains no data about elevation, choice (A). In contrast, the data strongly support choice (C). Only at Blue Mountain did the number of visitors vary directly with the amount of snowfall. (Both increased from 2009 to 2010.) At each of the other three resorts, the two variables varied *inversely*. At High Top, snowfall increased from 2009 to 2010, but the number of visitors decreased from one year to the next. At Crystal Hill and Snow Ridge, snowfall decreased from 2009 to 2010, but the number of visitors increased from one year to the next. **The correct answer is (C).**

ROUNDING, SIMPLIFYING, AND CHECKING YOUR CALCULATIONS

No GED® test-taker is immune to committing number-crunching errors—with or without a calculator. In this section, you'll learn how to approximate and round off numbers to help you solve problems quickly. You'll also learn how to simplify certain kinds of operations to make calculating numbers easier. Finally, you'll learn when it's best to use the calculator during Part I, as well as how best to check your calculations.

Approximations and Rounding

Some multiple-choice questions will clearly indicate that an approximate value will suffice. For example, a question might ask which choice is "most nearly equal to" a given expression. Or it might ask for "the approximate area" of a certain geometric figure. Read the question carefully for phrases such as these. If you see this sort of phrase, it tells you that you can *round off* some of your calculations yet work to a solution that is closest to the value provided as the correct answer.

How to Round Off a Number

When you round off a number, you eliminate one or more of the digits from the right end of the number. But this doesn't mean that you ignore those digits. Consider the number **4834.826.** If you simply ignore all digits to the right of the decimal point, you're left with 4834. But you have not rounded off the number to the nearest unit, because "**.826**" is closer to 1 than to 0. In this case, rounding off this number to the nearest unit requires increasing the "ones" digit from 4 to 5, so that the entire rounded number would be **4835.** For the record, here's the same number rounded off to all possible places:

4834.826 rounded to:	equals:	what we've done:
the nearest hundredth	4834.83	round .826 up to .830
the nearest tenth	4834.8	round .82 down to .80
the nearest unit	4835	round 4.8 up to 5.0
the nearest ten	4830	round 34 down to 30
the nearest hundred	4800	round 834 down to 800
the nearest thousand	5000	round 4834 up to 5000
the nearest ten thousand	0	round 4834 down to 0

But what about rounding the number 5, which lies midway between 0 and 10. Do you round it up or down? It doesn't matter. Don't worry: the correct response to a GED® test math question will *not* depend solely on whether you round the number 5 up or round it down. For example, if the solution to a problem is 4.5, you won't be asked to choose between 4 and 5 as the closest approximation.

Numbers with Non-repeating Decimal Places

Many numbers, especially square roots, include an infinite number of non-repeating decimal places. $\sqrt{2}$, $\sqrt{3}$, and π are three examples that appear frequently on the GED®

test because they are essential to certain geometry formulas. So how should you handle them? On the GED® test, answer choices often express such numbers "as is" rather than as their decimal or fractional equivalents, so that you won't have to deal with their values at all. But if a question should require you to estimate the values of such numbers, rounding them to the nearest tenth will usually suffice, unless the question tells you the approximate value you should use in your calculation. Here's a simple example involving the value of π.

EXAMPLE 27:

Which of the following most closely approximates the area of a circle whose radius is 3 centimeters?

    (A) 18 cm²

    (B) 28 cm²

    (C) 30 cm²

    (D) 36 cm²

The phrase "most closely approximates" tells you that you can round off some numbers and still narrow the choices to the correct answer. Notice that the answer choices are integers—a further clue that you can probably round off your calculation and work to the correct solution. The area of a circle is equal to πr^2, where r represents the circle's radius. To the nearest tenth, $\pi = 3.1$. Substituting 3.1 for π:

$$\text{Area} = 3.1 \times 3^2 = (3.1)(9) = 27.9$$

If you're uncomfortable with rounding π to just one decimal place, use a slightly more precise value for π. To the nearest hundredth, $\pi = 3.14$. Substitute 3.14 for π in the same equation:

$$\text{Area} = 3.14 \times 3^2 = (3.14)(9) = 28.26$$

As you can see, either rounded value (3.1 or 3.14) leads you to the closest approximation among the five choices. **The correct answer is (B).**

In the preceding example, what if the two closest values among the answer choices were 28 and 28.5? Using 3.1 as an approximate value of π would have resulted in the wrong answer. 27.9 is closer to 28 than to 28.5, while 28.26 is closer to 28.5 than to 28. Don't worry; you won't be required to slice the numbers this finely on the GED® test.

Rounding Off Numerators and Denominators

Nowhere is rounding more valuable than in dealing with fractions. Assume, for example, that a certain question for which you are not allowed to use the calculator requires you to divide 47 by 62. The quotient can be expressed as the fraction $\frac{47}{62}$. Since 47 is a prime number, you can't simplify the fraction or the division. And if you apply long division, you'll find it time consuming to find the precise quotient:

$$62\overline{)47} = 0.7580645$$

But this is not the sort of number that you'll be required to compute on the GED® test—with or without a calculator. If you face an operation such as this one, an approximation will almost always suffice to answer the question. If you're on a question for which the calculator may not be used, decide whether to round the numbers up or down, and by how far. But be sure to round both numbers *in the same direction* (either up or down), in order to minimize the change to the value of the overall fraction.

For example, in performing the operation $47 \div 62$, you can round 47 *down* to 45 and 62 *down* to 60, or you can round 47 *up* to 50 and 62 *up* to 65. Either method will result in a close enough approximation of the quotient 0.7580645:

$$\frac{47}{62} \approx \frac{45}{60} = \frac{3}{4} \text{ , or } 0.75$$

$$\frac{47}{62} \approx \frac{50}{65} = \frac{10}{13} \text{ , or approximately } 0.77$$

Whether you should round up or down depends on how easy it is to divide the revised numerator by the denominator. In the operation $47 \div 62$, rounding *up* is easier because you can simplify the resulting fraction. To underscore this idea, consider the fraction $\frac{42}{83.8}$. You can round both numbers *up*, and then simplify:

$$\frac{42}{83.8} \approx \frac{45}{85} = \frac{9}{17}$$

Better still, though, you can round both numbers *down*:

$$\frac{42}{83.8} \approx \frac{40}{80} = \frac{1}{2}$$

The second result is an easier fraction to work with and might suffice if the answer choices are expressed only to the nearest half unit.

Techniques for Combining Numbers

Here you'll learn some grouping techniques that can help you add, subtract, and multiply numbers efficiently. You'll also learn how to simplify multiplication and division of numbers that contain "trailing zeros." These techniques can be especially helpful for questions for which the use of the calculator is not allowed. But you can also apply them to calculator allowed questions in order to check your calculator work.

Cancel Numbers if Possible (Addition and Subtraction)

When combining a series of numbers by addition and/or subtraction, look for number pairs or larger groups that "cancel out"—in other words, that add up to 0 (zero). Consider this series of numbers:

$$17 + 10 - 14 - 3$$

The conventional method is to add each term to the next one, from left to right. But since $-14 - 3 = -17$, those two terms "cancel out" the number 17. In other words, the three numbers add up to 0 (zero). So you know that all four numbers must add up to 10.

Combine Similarly Signed Numbers First (Addition and Subtraction)

Another technique for combining by addition and subtraction is to add positive and negative numbers separately, and then subtract the second sum from the first. Consider this series of numbers:

$$23 - 12 - 14 + 7 - 8$$

The conventional method is to subtract 12 from 23, then subtract 14, then add 7, then subtract 8—in other words, to move from left to right. If pressed for time, it's remarkably easy to overlook minus signs and to add when you should be subtracting. So instead (or to check the work you performed the conventional way), combine the positive numbers and the negative numbers separately, then subtract the sums as follows:

$23 + 7 = 30$ (sum of positive terms)

$12 + 14 + 8 = 34$ (sum of negative terms)

$30 - 34 = -4$ (total sum)

Round One Number Up and Another Down (Addition and Subtraction)

Yet another method of combining by addition or subtraction is to round one number up and another one down by the same amount. For example, 89 is 11 *less* than 100, while 111 is 11 *greater* than 100. So 89 + 111 is the same as 100 + 100 = 200. Here's an example with four terms instead of just two:

$$251 + 423 + 749 + 77$$

Notice that 251 + 749 is the same as 250 + 750 = 1000. Also notice that 423 + 77 is the same as 425 + 75 = 500. So the calculation boils down to 1000 + 500 = 1500, which can be performed quickly yet accurately.

Multiply Numbers in the Easiest Sequence

You can multiply three or more numbers together most efficiently by looking for number pairs that combine easily. Consider the following expression:

$$25 \times 3\frac{1}{2} \times 16$$

To combine all three numbers, you can start with any pair. But the operation 25 × 16 is the easiest one to start with: 100 × 16 = 1600, and so 25 × 16 must equal one fourth of 1600, or 400. Now perform the second operation:

$$400 \times 3\frac{1}{2} = (400 \times 3) + (400 \times \frac{1}{2}) = 1400$$

Strip Away Trailing Zeros When Multiplying or Dividing

When facing multiplication involving large numbers ending in zeros, called "trailing zeros," many test-takers will include the zeros in their calculation (whether using the calculator or pencil and paper). But this method can easily result in a calculation error. Instead, strip away the trailing zeros before doing the math.

Consider the operation 4200×6000. Follow these three steps to make sure you handle the zeros correctly:

❶ Ignore all the trailing (consecutive) zeros at the end of the numbers.

❷ Multiply whatever numbers are left: $42 \times 6 = 252$.

❸ Add back the zeros to the end of your product. In this example, we ignored 5 zeros, so the answer is 252 with 5 zeros to the right: 25,200,000.

Now consider the same two numbers, except that the operation is division: $4200 \div 6000$. Follow these three steps to make sure you handle the zeros correctly:

❶ Ignore the zeros, and divide what's left: $42 \div 6 = 7$.

❷ Cancel (cross out) every trailing zero in the numerator for which there is also a trailing zero in the denominator. In this example, all zeros cancel out except for one zero in the denominator.

❸ For every extra zero in the denominator, move the decimal point in your quotient to the *left* one place. In this case, take the quotient, 7, and move the decimal point one place to the left. The answer is 0.7.

> *or*
>
> For each extra zero in the numerator, move the decimal point to the right one place. (This step doesn't apply to this particular example, but see below.)

Let's try this method again, this time reversing the numerator and the denominator ($6000 \div 4200$):

❶ Ignore the zeros, and divide what's left: $\frac{6}{42} = \frac{1}{7}$, or about 0.14.

❷ Cancel trailing zeros in the numerator and denominator.

❸ You're left with one extra zero in the numerator, so move the decimal point to the right *one* place. The answer is about 1.4. (To express the answer as a fraction, you would add the extra zero to the numerator: $\frac{10}{7}$.)

Remember: you can ignore trailing zeros, but only temporarily. You'll have to tag them back onto your final number. And you can't ignore zeros between non-zero numbers (like 308).

Using the Calculator to Your Advantage

As noted earlier you will have online access to the TI-30XS calculator and you should make sure you are thoroughly familiar with this calculator before taking the test.

For many questions, the calculator may be helpful. For some of these questions, however, using the calculator may be unnecessary or may actually slow you down. In any event, remember that a calculator is only a tool to avoid computing mistakes; it cannot take the place of understanding how to set up and solve a mathematical problem.

Here's a question for which a calculator might be helpful:

> *The price of one dozen roses is $10.80. At this rate, what is the price of 53 roses?*

The simplest way to approach this question is to divide $10.80 by 12, which gives you the price of one rose, then multiply that price by 53:

$$\$10.80 \div 12 = \$0.90$$

$$\$0.90 \times 53 = \$47.70$$

Although the arithmetic is fairly simple, using a calculator might improve your speed and accuracy. But in some questions involving numbers, using the calculator might actually slow you down because the question is set up to be solved in a quicker, more intuitive manner. Here's an example:

If $x = \dfrac{1}{2} \times \dfrac{1}{3} \times \dfrac{3}{2} \times \dfrac{4}{81}$, what is the value of $\sqrt{x}$?

To answer this question, you could use a calculator to perform all the steps:

1 Multiply the numerators.

2 Multiply the denominators.

3 Divide the product of the numerators by the product of the denominators.

4 Compute the square root.

But using a calculator is far more trouble than it's worth here. The problem is set up so that all numbers but 81 cancel out, so it's more quickly and easily solved this way (without a calculator):

$$x = \frac{1}{\cancel{2}} \times \frac{1}{\cancel{3}} \times \frac{\cancel{3}}{\cancel{2}} \times \frac{\cancel{4}}{81} = \frac{1}{81} \; ; \sqrt{\frac{1}{81}} = \frac{1}{9}$$

Checking Your Calculations

Computation errors are the leading cause of incorrect answers on the GED® Mathematical Reasoning Test. Take this fact as your cue to check your work on every question before proceeding to the next one. If answering a question involved only one simple calculation, then by all means perform that calculation again; it should only take a few seconds of your time.

For questions involving multiple calculations, checking your work does not necessarily mean going through all the steps in the same sequence a second time. You're less likely to repeat the same mistake if you use some other approach. Try reversing the computational process. If you've added two numbers together, check your work by subtracting one of the numbers from the sum:

$$56 + 233 = 289$$

$$289 - 233 = 56 \text{ (check)}$$

If you've subtracted one number from another, check your work by adding the result to the number you subtracted:

$$28.34 - 3.8 = 24.54$$

$$24.54 + 3.8 = 28.34 \text{ (check)}$$

If you've multiplied two numbers, check your work by dividing the product by one of the numbers:

$$11.3 \times 6.65 = 75.145$$

$$75.145 \div 11.3 = 6.65 \text{ (check)}$$

If you've divided one number by another, check your work by multiplying the quotient by the second number:

$$789 \div 3 = 263$$

$$263 \times 3 = 789 \text{ (check)}$$

And if you simply don't have time to recalculate, whether forward or in reverse, you may still have time to recalculate the *smallest digit* (the one farthest to the right) to make sure it's correct. This check is quick and easy since you don't have to think about carried numbers. For example:

$$289 - 233 + 4722 \text{ (the last digit should be 8)}$$

$$11.3 \times 6.65 \text{ (the last digit should be 5)}$$

GENERAL TEST-TAKING STRATEGIES

Here are some general strategies for tackling the GED® Mathematical Reasoning Test. Some of the points of advice encapsulate specific strategies you learned in the preceding pages. Apply all the strategies from this lesson to the Practice Tests in this book, and then review them again just before exam day.

Size up each question to devise a plan for handling it.

After reading a question, scan the answer choices (if any) and devise a plan of action for answering the question. Decide what operations or other steps are required to solve the problem. After some brief thought, if you still don't know where to start, try making a reasoned guess, and then move on to the next question. (Remember: you won't be penalized for incorrect answers.)

Be certain you know what the question is asking.

On the Mathematical Reasoning Test, careless reading is a leading cause of wrong answers. So be doubly sure you answer the precise question being asked. For example, does the question ask for the mean or the median? Circumference or area? A sum or a difference? A perimeter or a length of one side only? A total or an average? Feet or inches? Gallons or liters? Multiple-choice questions often bait you with incorrect answer choices that provide the *right* answer but to the *wrong* question. Don't fall for this ploy: know what the question is asking.

Look around for clues as to how to answer each question.

Be sure to read *all* information pertaining to the question. This includes not just the question itself, but also the answer choices and all information above, below, and beside a chart, graph, table, or geometry figure. Though you may not need every bit of information provided in order to answer the question at hand, reviewing it all helps ensure that you don't overlook what you need.

Don't hesitate to use your erasable note board.

You will be provided with an erasable note board, and by all means use it! Draw diagrams for geometry problems that don't supply them. Drawing a diagram often helps you visualize not only the problem but also the solution. Jot down any formulas or other equations needed to answer the question at hand. Remember also that you will not be allowed to use the calculator for 5 of the questions. For these, use the note board for all but the simplest calculations. (Immediately after the test, the test administrator will collect the note boards and erase your writing. So nothing you jot down on the note board will affect your score or be read by anyone.)

Save time by estimating and rounding.

If a question asks for an approximate value, you can safely round off your calculations. Just be sure not to round too far or in the wrong direction. Either the question itself or the answer choices should tell you how far you can round. Even if the question doesn't ask for an approximate value, you might be able to use estimation and rounding to zero-in on the correct answer—or at least eliminate choices that are too far off the mark.

Take the easiest route to the correct answer.

For some multiple-choice questions, it may be easier to work backward from the answer choices. For some algebra word problems, it might be easier to plug in numbers for variables instead of setting up and solving equations. When facing a long series of calculations, try to think of a shortcut. Avoid precise calculations when rough estimates will suffice. In short, be flexible in your approach: use whatever method reveals the answer.

Check your work before leaving any question.

The most common mistakes on math tests result not from lack of knowledge but from carelessness, and the GED® Mathematical Reasoning Test is no exception. So before recording any response on your answer sheet:

- Do a reality check. Ask yourself whether your solution makes sense for what the question asks. (This check is especially appropriate for word problems.)
- Make sure you used the same numbers as were provided in the question and that you didn't inadvertently switch numbers or other expressions.
- For questions where you solve algebraic equations, plug your solution into the equation(s) to make sure it works.

○ Confirm *all* your calculations. It's amazingly easy to commit errors in even the simplest calculations, especially under GED® test pressure. Using an eraser board the first time around makes this task easier.

Pace yourself properly.

You won't be penalized for incorrect answers, so don't spend too much time on any one question. Use your time to answer all the questions that are not difficult for you, and then go back and work on the tougher ones if there's time.

SUMMING IT UP

- You will have 90 minutes to answer the 37 questions of the Mathematical Reasoning Test. For 5 of these questions, you may not use a calculator. You may use a calculator when it's indicated by the clickable icon. The icon will not appear with questions for which you may not use a calculator.

- The calculator you will use during this test is the *TI-30XS* online calculator. It is highly recommended that you purchase or borrow one and become familiar with it *before* taking the test.

- The Mathematical Reasoning Test measures understanding and applying mathematical concepts and formulas, quantitative reasoning and problem solving, translating verbal language into mathematical terms, analyzing and interpreting graphical data, and computing, estimating, and rounding numbers.

- You will be given an erasable note board at the test site to jot down notes and calculations; however, it will be collected at the end of the test, and your handwritten calculations will not have any effect on your score. You will also receive a list of formulas that you may or may not need to refer to during the test.

- Twenty-five of the 37 questions on this test are multiple-choice questions. The remaining 12 questions will be graphic representations of the alternative format questions, such as drop-down items or fill-in-the-blank.

Math Review: Numbers

chapter 12

OVERVIEW

- What you'll find in this review
- Order and laws of operations
- Number signs and the four basic operations
- Integers and the four basic operations
- Factors, multiples, and divisibility
- Decimal numbers, fractions, and percentages
- Ratio and proportion
- Ratios involving more than two quantities
- Exponents (powers) and scientific notation
- Square roots (and other roots)
- Summing it up

WHAT YOU'LL FIND IN THIS REVIEW

In this review, you'll focus on:

- *Properties* of numbers (signs, integers, absolute value, and divisibility)

- *Forms* of numbers (fractions, mixed numbers, decimal numbers, percentages, ratios, exponential numbers, and radical expressions)

- *Operations* on numbers (the four basic operations and operations on exponential numbers and radical expressions)

Although this review is more basic than the next two in this part of the book, don't skip over it. The knowledge areas covered here are basic building blocks for all types of GED® test math questions.

The GED® test-style questions throughout this review are multiple-choice questions. The actual exam also includes questions in an alternative format, in which you supply the numerical answer to the question.

ORDER AND LAWS OF OPERATIONS

The following rules apply to all operations on numbers as well as on variables (such as x and y).

Order of operations

1 operations inside parentheses

2 operations with square roots and exponents

519

3 multiplication and division

4 addition and subtraction

Examples:

$(2 + 4) \times (7 - 2) = 6 \times 5$ (operate inside parentheses before multiplying)

$3 \times 4^2 = 3 \times 16$ (apply exponent before multiplying)

$5 + 7 \times 3 - 2 = 5 + 21 - 2$ (multiply before adding or subtracting)

$6 - 8 \div 2 + 3 = 6 - 4 + 3$ (divide before adding or subtracting)

The Commutative Law (addition and multiplication *only*)

$a + b = b + a$

$a \times b = b \times a$

Examples:

$3 + 4 = 4 + 3$

$3 \times 4 = 4 \times 3$

The Associative Law (addition and multiplication *only*)

$(a + b) + c = a + (b + c)$

$(ab)c = a(bc)$

Examples:

$(6 + 2) + 5 = 8 + 5 = 13$

$6 + (2 + 5) = 6 + 7 = 13$

$(3 \times 2) \times 4 = 6 \times 4 = 24$

$3 \times (2 \times 4) = 3 \times 8 = 24$

The Distributive Law

$a(b + c) = ab + ac$

$a(b - c) = ab - ac$

Examples:

$2(3 + 4) = 2 \times 7 = 14$

$(2)(3) + (2)(4) = 6 + 8 = 14$

$9(4 - 2) = 9 \times 2 = 18$

$(9)(4) - (9)(2) = 36 - 18 = 18$

NUMBER SIGNS AND THE FOUR BASIC OPERATIONS

A **positive number** is any number *greater than zero*, and a **negative number** is any number *less than zero*. The **sign** of a number indicates whether it is positive (+) or negative (–).

Be sure you know the sign—either positive or negative—of a non-zero number that results from combining numbers using the four basic operations (addition, subtraction, multiplication, and division). Here's a table that includes all the possibilities. A number's sign is indicated in parentheses. A question mark (?) indicates that the sign depends on which number is greater.

Addition:

(+) + (+) = +

(–) + (–) = –

(+) + (–) = ?

(–) + (+) = ?

Examples:

$5 + 3 = 8$

$-5 + (-3) = -8$

$5 + (-3) = 2$ but $3 + (-5) = -2$

$-5 + 3 = -2$ but $-3 + 5 = 2$

Subtraction:

(+) – (–) = (+)

(–) – (+) = (–)

(+) – (+) = ?

(–) – (–) = ?

Examples:

$6 - (-1) = 7$

$-6 - 1 = -7$

$6 - 1 = 5$ but $1 - 6 = -5$

$-6 - (-1) = -5$ but $-1 - (-6) = 5$

Multiplication:

(+) × (+) = +

(+) × (–) = –

(–) × (–) = +

Examples:

$7 \times 2 = 14$

$7 \times (-2) = -14$

$(-7) \times (-2) = 14$

Division:

(+) ÷ (+) = +

(+) ÷ (–) = –

(–) ÷ (+) = –

(–) ÷ (–) = +

Examples:

$8 \div 4 = 2$

$8 \div (-4) = -2$

$-8 \div 4 = -2$

$-8 \div (-4) = 2$

Multiplying and Dividing Negative Terms

Multiplication or division involving any *even* number of negative terms gives you a positive number. On the other hand, multiplication or division involving any *odd* number of negative terms gives you a negative number.

Examples (*even* number of negative terms):

$(5) \times (-4) \times (2) \times (-2) = +80$ (two negative terms)

$(-4) \times (-3) \times (-2) \times (-1) = +24$ (four negative terms)

Examples (*odd* number of negative terms):

$(3) \times (-3) \times (2) = -18$ (one negative terms)

$(-4) \times (-4) \times (2) \times (-2) = -64$ (three negative terms)

Absolute Value

A number's **absolute value** refers to its distance from zero (the origin) on the real-number line. The absolute value of x is indicated as $|x|$. The absolute value of any number other than zero is always a positive number. The concept of absolute value boils down to these two statements:

If $x \geq 0$, then $|x| = x$

Example: $|3| = 3$

Example: $|0| = 0$

If $x < 0$, then $|x| = -x$

Example: $|-2| = -(-2) = 2$

GED® test questions that involve combining signed numbers often focus on the concept of absolute value.

EXAMPLE 1 (EASIER):

What is the value of $|-2 - 3| - |2 - 3|$?

    (A) -2

    (B) -1

    (C) 1

    (D) 4

$|-2 - 3| = |-5| = 5$, and $|2 - 3| = |-1| = 1$. Performing subtraction: $5 - 1 = 4$. **The correct answer is (D).**

EXAMPLE 2 (MORE CHALLENGING):

The number M is the product of seven negative numbers. The number N is the product of six negative numbers and one positive number.

Which of the following holds true for all possible values of M and N?

   (A) $M - N > 0$

   (B) $M \times N < 0$

   (C) $N + M < 0$

   (D) $N \times M = 0$

The product of seven negative numbers is always negative (M is a negative number). The product of six negative numbers is always a positive number, and the product of two positive numbers is always a positive number (N is a positive number). Thus, the product of M and N must be a negative number. Choices (A) and (C) may or may not hold true, depending on the specific values of M and N. Choice (D) cannot hold true. **The correct answer is (B).**

INTEGERS AND THE FOUR BASIC OPERATIONS

An **integer** is any non-fraction number on the number line: $\{\ldots -3, -2, -1, 0, 1, 2, 3, \ldots\}$. Except for the number zero (0), every integer is either positive or negative and either even or odd. When you combine integers using a basic operation, whether the result is an odd integer, an even integer, or a non-integer depends on the numbers you combined. Here are the possibilities:

Addition and Subtraction:
integer $\pm$ integer = integer
even integer $\pm$ even integer = even integer (or possibly zero)
even integer $\pm$ odd integer = odd integer
odd integer $\pm$ odd integer = even integer (or possibly zero)

Multiplication and Division:
integer $\times$ integer = integer
integer $\div$ non-zero integer = integer, but only if the numerator is divisible by the denominator (if the result is a quotient with no remainder)
odd integer $\times$ odd integer = odd integer
even integer $\times$ non-zero integer = even integer
even integer $\div$ 2 = integer
odd integer $\div$ 2 = non-integer

GED® test questions that test you on the preceding rules sometimes look like algebra problems, but they're really not. Just apply the appropriate rule. If you're not sure of the rule, plug in simple numbers to zero-in on the correct answer.

EXAMPLE 3 (EASIER):

The numbers M and N are both integers. Without knowing the values of M and N, what formula would always determine the correct distance between M and N on a number line?

(A) $M - N$

(B) $N - M$

(C) $|M - N|$

(D) $|M| - |N|$

The distance between two points on a number line is expressed as a positive number. The distance is found by subtracting the lesser number from the greater number. Since the values of M and N are unknown, choices (A) and (B) provide no way to be certain that they will be subtracted in the correct order. Knowing that a positive value is required is an indication that you should apply absolute value. Choice (D) is not a good choice because it uses absolute value to make both numbers positive before subtracting them, which can result in a negative number if $|N| > |M|$. We know that distance must be positive. Choice (C) is the correct answer because it subtracts one value from the other, and then makes that value positive by taking the absolute value. **The correct answer is (C).**

EXAMPLE 4 (MORE CHALLENGING):

If P is an odd integer, and if Q is an even integer, which of the following expressions CANNOT represent an even integer?

(A) $3P - Q$

(B) $3P \times Q$

(C) $2Q \times P$

(D) $3Q - 2P$

Since 3 and P are both odd integers, their product $(3P)$ must also be an odd integer. Subtracting an even integer (Q) from an odd integer results in an odd integer in all cases except where $3Q = P$, in which case the result is 0 (zero). **The correct answer is (A).**

FACTORS, MULTIPLES, AND DIVISIBILITY

A **factor** (of an integer n) is any integer that you can multiply by another integer for a product of n. The factors of any integer n include 1 as well as n itself. Figuring out whether one number (f) is a factor of another (n) is simple: Just divide n by f. If the quotient is an integer, then f is a factor of n (and n is **divisible** by f). If the quotient is not an integer, then f is not a factor of n, and you'll end up with a **remainder** after dividing.

For example, 2 is a factor of 8 because $8 \div 2 = 4$, which is an integer. On the other hand, 3 is not a factor of 8 because $8 \div 3 = \frac{8}{3}$, or $2\frac{2}{3}$, which is a non-integer. (The remainder is 2, which you put over the divisor, 3, to form $\frac{2}{3}$.) Keep in mind these basic rules about factors, which are based on its definition:

- **RULE 1:** Any integer is a factor of itself.

- **RULE 2:** 1 and −1 are factors of all integers (except 0).

- **RULE 3:** The integer zero (0) has no factors and is not a factor of any integer.

- **RULE 4:** A positive integer's largest factor (other than itself) will never be greater than one half the value of the integer.

On the "flip side" of factors are **multiples.** If f is a factor of n, then n is a multiple of f. For example, 8 is a multiple of 2 for the same reason that 2 is a factor of 8: because $8 \div 2 = 4$, which is an integer.

A **prime number** is a positive integer that is divisible by only two positive integers: itself and 1. Zero (0) and 1 are not considered prime numbers; 2 is the first prime number. Here are all the prime numbers less than 50:

2 3 5 7

11 13 17 19

23 29

31 37

41 43 47

As you can see, factors, multiples, and divisibility are simply different aspects of the same concept. So, a GED® test question about factoring or prime numbers is also about multiples and divisibility.

EXAMPLE 5 (EASIER):

The number 24 is divisible by how many different positive integers other than 1 and 24?

- **(A)** three
- **(B)** four
- **(C)** five
- **(D)** six

The question asks for the number of different factors of 24 (other than 1 and 24). A good way to answer the question is to begin with 2 and work your way up to the largest possible factor, 12, which is half the value of 24:

$$2 \times 12 = 24$$

$$3 \times 8 = 24$$

$$4 \times 6 = 24$$

If you continue in this manner, you'll see that you've already accounted for all factors of 24, which include 2, 3, 4, 6, 8, and 12. **The correct answer is (D).**

EXAMPLE 6 (MORE CHALLENGING):

If $n > 6$, and if n is a multiple of 6, which of the following is always a factor of n ?

(A) $n + 6$

(B) $\frac{n}{3}$

(C) $\frac{n}{2} + 3$

(D) $\frac{n}{2} + 6$

Try the first multiple of 6 greater than 6, which is 12. This eliminates choices (A) and (C) because these are both greater than 12 and therefore cannot be factors. Finally, you can eliminate choice (D) because the largest factor of any positive number (other than the number itself) is half the number, which in this case is $\frac{n}{2}$. **The correct answer is (B).**

Every time you're dealing with fractions, you have to pay attention to the denominators. Because you cannot divide by zero, any expression that has zero in the denominator is considered undefined. For example, you may see a question that asks "For what values of x is the rational expression undefined?" What you are being asked to find is the values of x that will result in a denominator of 0. A fraction such as $\frac{x}{5}$ will always be defined, whereas $\frac{x}{0}$ will be undefined.

DECIMAL NUMBERS, FRACTIONS, AND PERCENTAGES

Any number can be expressed in the form of a decimal number, a fraction, or a percent. You use **decimal numbers** in your daily life every time you make a purchase at a store. Most of us are familiar with decimals in terms of money. When you have $5.87, you have 5 whole dollars, 8 dimes (or 8 tenths of a dollar), and 7 cents (or 7 hundredths of a dollar). When a number is written in decimal form, everything to the left of the decimal point is a whole number, and everything to the right of the decimal point represents a part of the whole (a tenth, hundredth, thousandth, and so on). Adding zeros to the *end* of a decimal number does not change its value. For example, the decimal number 0.5 is the same as 0.50 or 0.5000. But adding a zero to the *front* (the left) of the number *will* change the number's value. For example, 0.5 means "five tenths," but 0.05 means "five hundredths."

A **fraction** is a part of a whole. There are 10 dimes in each dollar, so one dime is one tenth of a dollar—one of ten equal parts. The fraction to represent one tenth is written $\frac{1}{10}$. The top number of a fraction is called the **numerator,** and the bottom number is called the **denominator.** A **proper fraction** is one in which the numerator is less than the denominator. An **improper fraction** is one in which the numerator is the same as or greater than the denominator. $\frac{1}{10}$ is a proper fraction, but $\frac{12}{10}$ is an improper fraction. Sometimes you will see a whole number and a fraction together. This is called a **mixed number.** $4\frac{3}{5}$ is an example of a mixed number.

A **percent (%)** is a fraction or decimal number written in a different form. 25% written as a decimal number is 0.25. A percent expressed as a fraction is the number divided by 100. For example, 25% written as a fraction is $\frac{25}{100}$. The number before the percent sign is the numerator of the fraction.

Converting One Number Form to Another

GED® test math questions involving fractions, decimal numbers, or percents often require you to convert one form to another as part of solving the problem at hand. You should know how to convert quickly and confidently. For percent-to-decimal conversions, move the decimal point two places to the *left* (and drop the percent sign). For decimal-to-percent conversions, move the decimal point two places to the *right* (and add the percent sign). Percents greater than 100 convert to numbers greater than 1.

Examples (converting percents to decimal numbers)
9.5% = 0.095
95% = 0.95
950% = 9.5

Examples (converting decimal numbers to percents)
0.004 = 0.4%
0.04 = 4%
0.4 = 40%
4.0 = 400%

For percent-to-fraction conversions, *divide* by 100 (and drop the percent sign). For fraction-to-percent conversions, *multiply* by 100 (and add the percent sign). Percents greater than 100 convert to numbers greater than 1.

Examples (converting percents to fractions)
$8.1\% = \frac{8.1}{100}$, or $\frac{81}{1000}$

$81\% = \frac{81}{100}$

$810\% = \frac{810}{100} = \frac{81}{10}$, or $8\frac{1}{10}$

Example (converting fractions to percents)

$$\frac{3}{8} = \frac{300}{8}\% = \frac{75}{2}\%, \text{ or } 37\frac{1}{2}\%$$

To convert a fraction to a decimal number, divide the numerator by the denominator, using long division or your calculator. Keep in mind that the result might be a precise value, or it might be an approximation with a never-ending string of decimal places. Compare these three examples:

$\frac{5}{8} = 0.625$ The equivalent decimal number is precise after three decimal places.

$\frac{5}{9} \approx 0.555$ The equivalent decimal number can only be approximated (the digit 5 repeats indefinitely).

$\frac{5}{7} \approx 0.714$ The equivalent decimal number can only be approximated; there is no repeating pattern by carrying the calculation to additional decimal places.

EXAMPLE 7 (EASIER):

What is the sum of $\frac{3}{4}$, 0.7, and 80% ?

(A) 1.59

(B) 1.62

(C) 2.04

(D) 2.25

Since the answer choices are expressed in decimal terms, express all terms to decimals:

$$\frac{3}{4} = 0.75 \text{ and } 80\% = 0.8.$$

Then add: $0.75 + 0.7 + 0.8 = 2.25$. **The correct answer is (D).**

EXAMPLE 8 (MORE CHALLENGING):

What is 150% of the product of $\frac{1}{8}$ and 0.4 ?

(A) 0.075

(B) 0.25

(C) 0.75

(D) 2.5

One way to solve the problem is to first express $\frac{1}{8}$ as its decimal equivalent 0.125. Next multiply: $0.125 \times 0.4 = 0.05$. Then, express 150% as the decimal number 1.5, and calculate the product: $1.5 \times 0.05 = 0.075$. **The correct answer is (A).**

Fraction-Decimal-Percent Equivalents

Certain fraction-decimal-percent equivalents appear on the GED® test more often than others. The numbers in the following tables are especially common. You should memorize this table, so that you can convert these numbers quickly during the test.

Percent	Decimal	Fraction	Percent	Decimal	Fraction
50%	0.5	$\frac{1}{2}$	$16\frac{2}{3}\%$	$0.16\frac{2}{3}$	$\frac{1}{6}$
25%	0.25	$\frac{1}{4}$	$83\frac{1}{3}\%$	$0.83\frac{1}{3}$	$\frac{5}{6}$
75%	0.75	$\frac{3}{4}$	20%	0.2	$\frac{1}{5}$
10%	0.1	$\frac{1}{10}$	40%	0.4	$\frac{2}{5}$
30%	0.3	$\frac{3}{10}$	60%	0.6	$\frac{3}{5}$
70%	0.7	$\frac{7}{10}$	80%	0.8	$\frac{4}{5}$
90%	0.9	$\frac{9}{10}$	$12\frac{1}{2}\%$	0.125	$\frac{1}{8}$
$33\frac{1}{3}\%$	$0.33\frac{1}{3}$	$\frac{1}{3}$	$37\frac{1}{2}\%$	0.375	$\frac{3}{8}$
$66\frac{2}{3}\%$	$0.66\frac{2}{3}$	$\frac{2}{3}$	$62\frac{1}{2}\%$	0.625	$\frac{5}{8}$
			$87\frac{1}{2}\%$	0.875	$\frac{7}{8}$

Decimal Numbers and Place Value

Place value refers to the specific value of a digit in a decimal number. For example, in the decimal number 682.793:

> The digit 6 is in the "hundreds" place.
> The digit 8 is in the "tens" place.
> The digit 2 is in the "ones" place.
> The digit 7 is in the "tenths" place.
> The digit 9 is in the "hundredths" place.
> The digit 3 is in the "thousandths" place.

So, you can express 682.793 as follows: $600 + 80 + 2 + \frac{7}{10} + \frac{9}{100} + \frac{3}{1000}$.

EXAMPLE 9 (EASIER):

The number 40.5 is 1000 times larger than which of the following numbers?

    (A) 0.405

    (B) 0.0405

    (C) 0.0450

    (D) 0.00405

To find the solution, divide 40.5 by 1000 by moving the decimal point 3 places to the left. **The correct answer is (B).**

EXAMPLE 10 (MORE CHALLENGING):

The letter M represents a digit in the decimal number 0.0M, and the letter N represents a digit in the decimal number 0.0N. Which expression is equivalent to 0.0M × 0.0N?

    (A) $\frac{1}{10,000} \times M \times N$

    (B) 0.000MN

    (C) 0.00MN

    (D) $\frac{1}{100} \times M \times N$

Suppose digits M and N are both 1. To find the product of 0.01 and 0.01, you multiply 1 by 1 (N × M), then add together the decimal places in the two numbers. There are four places altogether, so the product would be 0.0001, which is equivalent to $\frac{1}{10,000}$. Thus, whatever the values of N and M, $0.0M \times 0.0N = \frac{1}{10,000} \times (M \times N)$.

The correct answer is (A).

Simplifying Fractions

A fraction can be simplified to its *lowest terms* if its numerator number and denominator number share a common factor. Here are a few simple examples:

$$\frac{6}{9} = \frac{(3)(2)}{(3)(3)} = \frac{2}{3}$$ (you can "cancel" or "factor out" the common factor 3)

$$\frac{21}{35} = \frac{(7)(3)}{(7)(5)} = \frac{3}{5}$$ (you can "cancel" or "factor out" the common factor 7)

Before you perform any operation with a fraction, always check to see if you can simplify it first. By reducing a fraction to its lowest terms, you'll simplify whatever operation you perform on it.

Adding and Subtracting Fractions

To combine fractions by addition or subtraction, you combine numerators over a **common denominator.** If the fractions already have the same denominator, simply add (or subtract) numerators:

$$\frac{3}{4} + \frac{2}{4} = \frac{3+2}{4} = \frac{5}{4} \text{ (the two fractions share the common denominator 4)}$$

$$\frac{1}{7} - \frac{3}{7} = \frac{1-3}{7} = \frac{-2}{7}, \text{ or } -\frac{2}{7} \text{ (the two fractions share the common}$$

denominator 7)

If the fractions don't already have a common denominator, you'll need to find one. You can always multiply all of the denominators together to find a common denominator, but it might be a large number that's clumsy to work with. So instead, try to find the **least (or lowest) common denominator (LCD)** by working your way up in multiples of the largest of the denominators given. For denominators of 6, 3, and 5, for instance, try out successive multiples of 6 (12, 18, 24 . . .), and you'll hit the LCD when you get to 30.

When combining fractions by either addition or subtraction, pay close attention to the + and − signs. Also, don't let common numerators fool you into thinking you can add or subtract without a common denominator.

EXAMPLE 11 (EASIER):

The equation $\frac{5}{3} - \frac{5}{6} + \frac{5}{2}$ is equal to

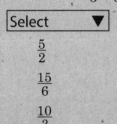

| Select ▼ |

$$\frac{5}{2}$$

$$\frac{15}{6}$$

$$\frac{10}{3}$$

$$\frac{15}{3}$$

On the online GED® Test, you will be asked to click on the drop-down menu to choose your answer. For this print version, circle the correct answer.

To find the LCD, try out successive multiples of 6 until you come across one that is also a multiple of both 3 and 2. The LCD is 6 itself. Multiply each numerator by the same number by which you would multiply the fraction's denominator to give you the LCD of 6.

$$\frac{5}{3} - \frac{5}{6} + \frac{5}{2} = \frac{5(2) - 5 + 5(3)}{6} = \frac{10 - 5 + 15}{6} = \frac{20}{6}, \text{ or } \frac{10}{3}$$

The correct answer is $\frac{10}{3}$.

Select ▼
$\frac{5}{2}$
$\frac{15}{6}$
$\frac{10}{3}$
$\frac{15}{3}$

EXAMPLE 12 (MORE CHALLENGING):

If $\frac{x}{3}$, $\frac{x}{7}$, and $\frac{x}{9}$ are all positive integers, what is the *least* possible value of x?

    (A) 42

    (B) 54

    (C) 63

    (D) 72

The answer to the question is the least value of x that is a multiple of all three denominators. In other words, the question asks for the least common denominator. Working your way up in multiples of the largest denominator, 9, you'll find that 63 is the lowest multiple that is also a multiple of both 7 and 3. Thus, $x = 63$.

The correct answer is (C).

Multiplying and Dividing Fractions

To combine fractions by multiplication, multiply the numerators, and multiply the denominators. The denominators need not be the same.

$$\frac{1}{2} \times \frac{5}{3} \times \frac{1}{7} = \frac{(1)(5)(1)}{(2)(3)(7)} = \frac{5}{42}$$

To divide one fraction by another, first invert the divisor (the number after the division sign) by switching its numerator and denominator. (This new fraction is called the **reciprocal** of the original one.) Then combine by multiplying.

$$\frac{\frac{2}{5}}{\frac{3}{4}} = \frac{2}{5} \times \frac{4}{3} = \frac{(2)(4)}{(5)(3)} = \frac{8}{15}$$

To simplify the multiplication or division, cancel factors common to a numerator and a denominator before combining fractions. You can cancel across fractions. Take, for instance, the operation $\frac{3}{4} \times \frac{4}{9} \times \frac{3}{2}$. Looking just at the first two fractions, you can factor out 4 and 3, so the operation simplifies to $\frac{\overset{1}{\cancel{3}}}{\underset{1}{\cancel{4}}} \times \frac{\overset{1}{\cancel{4}}}{\underset{3}{\cancel{9}}} \times \frac{3}{2}$. Now, looking just at the second and third fractions, you can factor out 3, and the operation becomes even simpler: $\frac{1}{1} \times \frac{1}{1\cancel{3}} \times \frac{\cancel{3}^1}{2} = \frac{1}{2}$.

Apply the same rules in the same way to variables (letters) as to numbers.

EXAMPLE 13 (EASIER):

Which expression is equal to $\frac{2}{a} \times \frac{b}{4} \times \frac{a}{5} \times \frac{8}{c}$?

- **(A)** $\frac{10b}{9c}$
- **(B)** $\frac{8}{5}$
- **(C)** $\frac{16b}{5ac}$
- **(D)** $\frac{4b}{5c}$

Since you're dealing only with multiplication, look for factors and variables (letters) in any numerator that match those in any denominator. Canceling common factors leaves $\frac{2}{1} \times \frac{b}{1} \times \frac{1}{5} \times \frac{2}{c}$.

Combining numerators and combining denominators gives you the answer $\frac{4b}{5c}$.

The correct answer is (D).

EXAMPLE 14 (MORE CHALLENGING):

Which is a simplified form of the complex fraction $\dfrac{\frac{3}{5} + \frac{3}{4}}{\frac{3}{4} - \frac{3}{5}}$?

- **(A)** $\frac{27}{10}$
- **(B)** 5
- **(C)** $\frac{27}{4}$
- **(D)** 9

Convert all four fractions to fractions with the least common denominator, 20. Then, add together the two numerator fractions and the two denominator fractions.

$$\frac{\frac{3}{5} + \frac{3}{4}}{\frac{3}{4} - \frac{3}{5}} = \frac{\frac{12}{20} + \frac{15}{20}}{\frac{15}{20} - \frac{12}{20}} = \frac{\frac{27}{20}}{\frac{3}{20}}$$

Then, multiply the resulting numerator fraction by the reciprocal of the resulting denominator fraction:

$$\frac{\frac{27}{20}}{\frac{3}{20}} = \left(\frac{27}{20}\right)\left(\frac{20}{3}\right) = \frac{27}{3} = 9$$

The correct answer is (D).

Mixed Numbers

As noted earlier, a *mixed number* consists of a whole number along with a simple fraction. The number $4\frac{2}{3}$ is an example of a mixed number. Before combining fractions, you might need to convert mixed numbers to improper fractions. To do so, follow these three steps:

1. Multiply the denominator of the fraction by the whole number.

2. Add the product to the numerator of the fraction.

3. Place the sum over the denominator of the fraction.

For example, here's how to convert the mixed number $4\frac{2}{3}$ to a fraction:

$$4\frac{2}{3} = \frac{(3)(4) + 2}{3} = \frac{14}{3}$$

To add or subtract mixed numbers, you can convert each one to a fraction, then find their LCD and combine them. Or, you can add together the whole numbers, and add together the fractions separately. To perform multiple operations, always perform multiplication and division before you perform addition and subtraction.

EXAMPLE 15 (EASIER):

What is the sum of $2\frac{1}{6}$, $3\frac{1}{5}$, and $2\frac{1}{15}$?

(A) $7\frac{13}{30}$

(B) $7\frac{4}{5}$

(C) $11\frac{3}{10}$

(D) $12\frac{17}{20}$

One way to combine these mixed numbers is to first convert the mixed numbers to fractions:

$$2\frac{1}{6} + 3\frac{1}{5} + 2\frac{1}{15} = \frac{13}{6} + \frac{16}{5} + \frac{31}{15}$$

But as you can see, to combine numerators over a LCD, you'll be dealing with large numbers. An easier method is to add together the whole numbers, and add together the fractions separately:

$$(2 + 3 + 2) + \frac{1}{6} + \frac{1}{5} + \frac{1}{15} = 7 + \frac{5 + 6 + 2}{30} = 7\frac{13}{30}$$

The correct answer is (A).

EXAMPLE 16 (MORE CHALLENGING):

If you subtract $3\frac{2}{3}$ from $\dfrac{4\frac{1}{2}}{1\frac{1}{8}}$, what is the resulting fraction?

(A) $\dfrac{1}{4}$

(B) $\dfrac{1}{3}$

(C) $\dfrac{11}{6}$

(D) $\dfrac{17}{6}$

First, convert all mixed numbers to fractions. Then, eliminate the complex fraction by multiplying the numerator fraction by the reciprocal of the denominator fraction (cancel across fractions before multiplying):

$$\frac{\frac{9}{2}}{\frac{9}{8}} - \frac{11}{3} = \left(\frac{9}{2}\right)\left(\frac{8}{9}\right) - \frac{11}{3} = \left(\frac{1}{1}\right)\left(\frac{4}{1}\right) - \frac{11}{3} = \frac{4}{1} - \frac{11}{3}$$

Then, express each fraction using the common denominator 3. Finally, subtract:

$$\frac{4}{1} - \frac{11}{3} = \frac{12-11}{3} = \frac{1}{3}$$

The correct answer is (B).

Problems Involving Percent

A GED® test question involving percent might involve one of these three tasks:

- Finding the percent of a number

- Finding a number when a percent is given

- Finding what percent one number is of another

Regardless of the task, four distinct numbers are involved: the part, the whole, the percent, and 100. The problem will give you three of the numbers, and your job is to find the fourth. An easy way to deal with percent problems is to set up a grid to decide which number is missing, and then solve for that missing number. Arrange the grid as follows:

part	percent
whole	100

The left column is actually a fraction that is equal to the right-column fraction. (Think of the middle horizontal line as a fraction bar.) The two fractions have the same value. Once you set up the problem in this way, you can solve it by these steps:

❶ Simplify the known fraction, if possible.

❷ Multiply the diagonally situated numbers that you know.

❸ Divide the product by the third number you know.

To see how this is done, study the following three examples.

Finding the Percent

30 is what percent of 50?

In this question, 50 is the whole, and 30 is the part. Your task is to find the missing percent:

30	?
50	100

First, simplify the left-hand fraction $\frac{30}{50}$ to $\frac{3}{5}$. Then, multiply the two diagonally situated numbers you know: $3 \times 100 = 300$. Finally, divide by the third number you know: $300 \div 5 = 60$. This is the answer to the question. *30 is 60% of 50.*

Finding the Part

What number is 25% of 80?

In this question, 80 is the whole, and 25 is the percent. Your task is to find the part:

?	25
80	100

First, simplify the right-hand fraction $\frac{25}{100}$ to $\frac{1}{4}$.

?	1
80	4

Then multiply the two diagonally situated numbers you know: $1 \times 80 = 80$. Finally, divide by the third number you know: $80 \div 4 = 20$. This is the answer to the question. *25% of 80 is 20.*

Finding the Whole

75% of what number is 150?

In this question, 150 is the part, and 75 is the percent. Your task is to find the whole:

150	75
?	100

First, simplify the right-hand fraction $\frac{75}{100}$ to $\frac{3}{4}$.

150	3
?	4

Then multiply the two diagonally situated numbers you know: $150 \times 4 = 600$. Finally, divide by the third number you know: $600 \div 3 = 200$. This is the answer to the question. *75% of 200 is 150.*

Percent Increase and Decrease

The concept of percent change is familiar to everyone. For example, investment interest, sales tax, and discount pricing all involve percent change. Here's the key to answering GED® test questions involving this concept: percent change always relates to the value *before* the change. Here are two simple examples:

10 increased by what percent is 12?

❶ The amount of the increase is 2.

❷ Compare the change (2) to the original number (10).

❸ The change in percent is $\frac{2}{10}$, or 20%.

12 decreased by what percent is 10?

❶ The amount of the decrease is 2.

❷ Compare the change (2) to the original number (12).

❸ The change is $\frac{2}{12}$, or $\frac{1}{6}$ (or $16\frac{2}{3}$%).

Notice that the percent increase from 10 to 12 (20%) is *not* the same as the percent decrease from 12 to 10 ($16\frac{2}{3}$%). That's because the original number (before the change) is different in the two questions.

GED® test percent-change problems typically involve tax, interest, profit, discount, or weight. In handling these problems, you might need to calculate more than one percent change.

EXAMPLE 17 (EASIER):

A computer originally priced at $500 is discounted by 10%, then by another 10%. What is the price of the computer after the second discount, to the nearest dollar?

(A) $400

(B) $405

(C) $425

(D) $450

After the first 10% discount, the price was $450 ($500 minus 10% of $500). After the second discount, which is calculated based on the $450 price, the price of the computer is $405 ($450 minus 10% of $450). **The correct answer is (B).**

EXAMPLE 18 (MORE CHALLENGING):

A merchant discounts an item priced at $80 by 25%. Later, the merchant discounts the item again, this time to $48. What *percent* was the second discount?

(A) 20

(B) 25

(C) 27.5

(D) 30

After the first discount, the price was $60 (the difference between $80 and 25% of $80 ($80 − $20). The second discount was $12 (the difference between $60 and $48). Calculate the discount rate using the price *before* the *second* discount: $\frac{12}{60} = \frac{1}{5}$, or 20%. **The correct answer is (A).**

RATIO AND PROPORTION

A **ratio** expresses proportion or comparative size—the size of one quantity *relative to* the size of another. Write a ratio by placing a colon (:) between the two numbers. Read the colon as the word "to." For example, read the ratio 3:5 as "3 to 5." As with fractions, you can reduce ratios to lowest terms by canceling common factors. For example, given a menagerie of 28 pets that includes 12 cats and 16 dogs:

- The ratio of cats to dogs is 12:16, or 3:4 ("3 to 4").

- The ratio of dogs to cats is 16:12, or 4:3 ("4 to 3").

- The ratio of cats to the total number of pets is 12:28, or 3:7 ("3 to 7").

- The ratio of dogs to the total number of pets is 16:28, or 4:7 ("4 to 7").

Another way of saying that two ratios (or fractions) are equivalent is to say that they are *proportionate*. For example, the ratio 12:16 is proportionate to the ratio 3:4. Similarly, the fraction $\frac{12}{16}$ is proportionate to the fraction $\frac{3}{4}$.

Determining Quantities from a Ratio

You can think of a ratio as parts adding up to a whole. In the ratio 5:6, for example, 5 parts + 6 parts = 11 parts (the whole). If the actual total quantity were 22, you'd multiply each element by 2: 10 parts + 12 parts = 22 parts (the whole). Notice that the ratios are the same. In other words, 5:6 is the same ratio as 10:12.

Another way to think about a ratio is as a fraction. Since you can express any ratio as a fraction, you can set two equivalent, or proportionate, ratios equal to each other, as fractions. So the ratio 16:28 is proportionate to the ratio 4:7 because $\frac{16}{28} = \frac{4}{7}$. If one of the four terms is missing from the equation (the proportion), you can solve for the missing term using the same method that you learned for solving percent problems:

1 Simplify the known fraction, if possible.

2 Multiply the diagonally situated numbers you know.

3 Divide the product by the third number you know.

For example, if the ratio 10:15 is proportionate to 14:?, you can find the missing number (?) by first setting up the following grid (which expresses an equation with two fractions):

10	14
15	?

Reading the ratio 10:15 as a fraction, simplify it to $\frac{2}{3}$.

2	14
3	?

Then, multiply the two diagonally situated numbers you know: $3 \times 14 = 42$. Finally, divide by the third number you know: $42 \div 2 = 21$. The ratio 10:15 is equivalent to the ratio 14:21.

In a GED® test ratio question, even if the quantities initially appear difficult to work with, it's a good bet that doing the math will be easier than it might seem.

EXAMPLE 19 (EASIER):

A class of students contains only freshmen and sophomores. 18 of the students are sophomores. If the ratio between the number of freshmen and the number of sophomores in the class is 5:3, how many students altogether are in the class?

(A) 30

(B) 40

(C) 48

(D) 56

Let's apply a part-to-whole analysis to answer this question. Look first at the ratio and the sum of its parts: 5 (freshmen) + 3 (sophomores) = 8 (total students). These aren't the actual quantities, but they're *proportionate* to those quantities. Given 18 sophomores altogether, sophomores account for 3 parts—each part containing 6 students. Accordingly, the total number of students must be 6 × 8 = 48. **The correct answer is (C).**

EXAMPLE 20 (MORE CHALLENGING):

If 3 miles are equivalent to 4.83 kilometers, then 11.27 kilometers are equivalent to how many miles?

(A) 8.4

(B) 7.0

(C) 5.9

(D) 1.76

The decimal numbers may appear daunting, but they simplify nicely. This feature is typical for the GED® Mathematical Reasoning Test. The question essentially asks: "a ratio of 3 to 4.83 is equivalent to a ratio of *what* to 11.27?" Set up a proportion grid (which expresses an equation with two fractions):

3	?
4.83	11.27

You might notice that the ratio (or fraction) $\frac{3}{4.83}$ simplifies to $\frac{1}{1.61}$. Using this simplified ratio might help you multiply and divide the numbers accurately. Otherwise, first multiply the diagonally situated numbers you know: 3 × 11.27 = 33.81. Then, divide by the third number you know: 33.81 ÷ 4.83 = 7. A ratio of 3 to 4.83 is equivalent to a ratio of 7 to 11.27. **The correct answer is (B).**

RATIOS INVOLVING MORE THAN TWO QUANTITIES

A more complex GED® test ratio problem might involve a ratio among three (or possibly more) quantities. The best way to handle these problems is with a part-to-whole approach, where the "whole" consists of more than two "parts."

EXAMPLE 21 (EASIER):

Machine X, Machine Y, and Machine Z each produce widgets. Machine Y's rate of production is one third that of Machine X, and Machine Z's production rate is twice that of Machine Y. If Machine Y can produce 35 widgets per day, how many widgets can the three machines produce per day working simultaneously?

   (A) 105

   (B) 180

   (C) 210

   (D) 224

The key to handling this question is to convert ratios to fractional parts that add up to 1. The ratio of X's rate to Y's rate is 3 to 1, and the ratio of Y's rate to Z's rate is 1 to 2. You can express the ratio among all three as 3:1:2 (X:Y:Z). Accordingly, Y's production accounts for $\frac{1}{6}$ of the total widgets that all three machines can produce per day. Given that Y can produce 35 widgets per day, all three machines can produce (35)(6) = 210 widgets per day. **The correct answer is (C).**

EXAMPLE 22 (MORE CHALLENGING):

Three lottery winners—Alan, Brenda, and Carl—are sharing a lottery jackpot. Alan's share is one fifth of Brenda's share and one seventh of Carl's share. If the total jackpot is $195,000, what is the dollar amount of Carl's share?

   (A) $15,000

   (B) $35,000

   (C) $75,000

   (D) $105,000

At first glance, this problem doesn't appear to involve ratios. (Where's the colon?) But it does. The ratio of Alan's share to Brenda's share is 1:5, and the ratio of Alan's share to Carl's share is 1:7. So you can set up the triple ratio: A:B:C = 1:5:7

Alan's winnings account for 1 of 13 equal parts (1 + 5 + 7) of the total jackpot. $\frac{1}{13}$ of $195,000 is $15,000. Accordingly, Brenda's share is 5 times that amount, or $75,000, and Carl's share is 7 times that amount, or $105,000. **The correct answer is (D).**

Proportion Problems Requiring Unit Conversions

GED® test ratio or proportion problems often involve units of measurement, such as inches, ounces, or gallons. These problems sometimes require that you convert one unit to another—for example, feet to inches, pounds to ounces, or quarts to gallons. The problem will provide the conversion rate if it is not commonly known.

The problem might ask for nothing more than a conversion. To solve this sort of problem, set up a proportion and then cross-multiply and divide. Here are two examples for review:

4.8 ounces is equivalent to how many pounds? [1 pound = 16 ounces]

Set up the proportion $\frac{4.8}{x} = \frac{16}{1}$. Cross-multiply (diagonally) what you know: $4.8 \times 1 = 4.8$. Then divide by the third number: $4.8 \div 16 = 0.3$. (4.8 ounces are equivalent to 0.3 pounds.)

If Trevor hiked 13.6 kilometers, how many miles did he hike?
[1 mile = 1.6 kilometers]

Set up the proportion $\frac{1}{1.6} = \frac{?}{13.6}$. Cross-multiply (diagonally) what you know: $13.6 \times 1 = 13.6$. Then divide by the third number: $13.6 \div 1.6 = 8.5$. (Trevor hiked 8.5 miles.)

Not all GED® test conversion-rate questions are so simple as the two preceding examples. A question might require *two* conversions, or it might use *letters* instead of numbers—in order to focus on the process rather than the result. Though these problems may seem intimidating, they are actually not very difficult. You can easily solve them by applying the same method you would use to solve simpler conversion-rate problems.

EXAMPLE 23 (EASIER):

The distance from City 1 to City 2 is 840 kilometers. On an accurate map showing both cities, 1 centimeter represents 75 kilometers. On the map, how many millimeters separate City 1 and City 2? [1 centimeter = 10 millimeters]

   (A) 11

   (B) 45

   (C) 89

   (D) 112

First, set up the proportion $\frac{1 \text{ cm}}{75 \text{ km}} = \frac{?}{840}$. Then cross-multiply (diagonally) what you know: $840 \times 1 = 840$. Then divide by the third number: $840 \div 75 = 11.2$. On the map, the distance from City 1 to City B = $840 \div 75 = 11.2$ centimeters. But 11.2 is *not* the answer to the question. Your final step is to convert centimeters to millimeters. The problem provides the conversion rate: $11.2 \times 10 = 112$. **The correct answer is (D).**

EXAMPLE 24 (MORE CHALLENGING):

A candy store sells candy only in half-pound boxes. At c cents per box, which of the following is the cost of a ounces of candy? [1 pound = 16 ounces]

(A) $\dfrac{ac}{8}$

(B) $\dfrac{a}{16c}$

(C) $\dfrac{c}{a}$

(D) $\dfrac{8c}{a}$

This question is asking: "c cents are to one box as *how many cents* are to a ounces?" Set up a proportion, letting "?" represent the cost of a ounces. Because the question asks for the cost of *ounces*, convert 1 box to 8 ounces (a half pound). $\dfrac{c}{8} = \dfrac{?}{a}$. Next, cross-multiply (diagonally) two terms that are provided (in this case, they are variables rather than numbers): $c \times a = ca$. Then divide by the third term that is provided: $\dfrac{ca}{8}$. (The expression ca, which signifies $c \times a$, is equal to ac, which signifies $a \times c$.) **The correct answer is (A).**

EXPONENTS (POWERS) AND SCIENTIFIC NOTATION

An **exponent** refers to the number of times that a number (referred to as the **base number**) is multiplied by itself. In the exponential number 2^4, the base number is 2 and the exponent is 4. To calculate the value of 2^4 means: $2^4 = 2 \times 2 \times 2 \times 2 = 16$. An exponent is also referred to as a **power.** So you can express the exponential number 2^4 as "2 to the 4th power."

On the GED® test, questions involving exponents usually require you to combine two or more exponential numbers using one of the four basic operations. To do so, you need to know certain rules. Can you combine base numbers *before* applying exponents to the numbers? The answer depends on which operation you're performing.

Combining Exponents by Addition or Subtraction

The rules for combining exponential numbers by addition or subtraction are very restrictive. You *can* combine exponential numbers *if* the base numbers and powers (exponents) are all the same. Here is the general rule, along with a simple example showing two ways to combine the numbers:

$$a^x + a^x + a^x = 3(a^x)$$

$$3^2 + 3^2 + 3^2 = (3)(3^2) = 3 \times 9 = 27$$

$$3^2 + 3^2 + 3^2 = 9 + 9 + 9 = 27$$

Otherwise, you cannot combine either base numbers or exponents. It's as simple as that. Here's the rule in symbolic form as it applies to different base numbers:

$$a^x + b^x \neq (a + b)^x$$

$$a^x - b^x \neq (a - b)^x$$

Substituting some simple numbers for a, b, and x illustrates the rule. In the following two examples, notice that you get a different result depending on which you do first: combine base numbers or apply each exponent to its base number.

Combining by addition:

$$(4 + 2)^2 = 6^2 = 36$$

$$4^2 + 2^2 = 16 + 4 = 20$$

Combining by subtraction:

$$(4 - 2)^2 = 2^2 = 4$$

$$4^2 - 2^2 = 16 - 4 = 12$$

EXAMPLE 25 (EASIER):

$a^7 + a^7 + a^7$ is equivalent to which of the following?

(A) a^{21}

(B) $3^7 \times a^7$

(C) $3 \times a^7$

(D) $21a$

You can combine terms here because base numbers and exponents are all the same. Adding together 3 of any quantity is the same as 3 *times* that quantity. **The correct answer is (C).**

EXAMPLE 26 (MORE CHALLENGING):

If $x = -2$, what is the value of $x^5 - x^2 - x$?

(A) -70

(B) -58

(C) -34

(D) 26

You cannot combine exponents here, even though the base number is the same in all three terms. Instead, you need to apply each exponent, in turn, to the base number, then subtract:

$$x^5 - x^2 - x = (-2)^5 - (-2)^2 - (-2) = -32 - 4 + 2 = -34$$

The correct answer is (C).

Combining Exponents by Multiplication or Division

Follow two basic rules for combining exponential numbers by multiplication and division.

RULE 1: You can combine base numbers first, but only if the exponents are the same. Here's the rule in symbolic form:

$$a^x \times b^x = (ab)^x$$

$$a^x \div b^x = (a \div b)^x \text{ or } \frac{a^x}{b^x} = \left(\frac{a}{b}\right)^x$$

Substituting some simple numbers for a, b, and x illustrates Rule 1. In the following two examples, notice that you get the same result whether or not you combine base numbers first.

Combining by multiplication:
$(4 \times 2)^2 = 8^2 = 64$
$4^2 \times 2^2 = 16 \times 4 = 64$

Combining by division:
$(10 \div 2)^2 = 5^2 = 25$
$10^2 \div 2^2 = 100 \div 4 = 25$

RULE 2: You can combine exponents first, but only if the base numbers are the same. When multiplying these terms, add the exponents. When dividing them, subtract the denominator exponent from the numerator exponent:

$$a^x \times a^y = a^{(x+y)}$$

$$a^x \div a^y = a^{(x-y)} \text{ or } \frac{a^x}{a^y} = a^{(x-y)}$$

Substituting some simple numbers for a, b, and x illustrates Rule 2. In the following two examples, notice that you get the same result whether or not you combine exponents first.

Combining by multiplication:
$2^3 \times 2^2 = 8 \times 4 = 32$
$2^{(3+2)} = 2^5 = 2 \times 2 \times 2 \times 2 \times 2 = 32$

Combining by division:
$2^5 \div 2^2 = 32 \div 4 = 8$
$2^{(5-2)} = 2^3 = 2 \times 2 \times 2 = 8$

When the same base number appears in a division problem, or in both numerator and denominator of a fraction, you can factor out (cancel) the number of powers common to both. To illustrate, consider the operation $9^6 \div 9^4$, or its equivalent fraction $\frac{9^6}{9^4}$. To find the quotient, you can either combine exponents, applying Rule 2, or you can factor out (cancel) 9^4 from each term:

Combining exponents first:
$\frac{9^6}{9^4} = 9^{(6-4)} = 9^2 = 81$

Canceling common factors first:

$$\frac{9^6}{9^4} = \frac{9^4 \times 9^2}{9^4} = \frac{9^2}{1} = 81$$

EXAMPLE 27 (EASIER):

When you divide $\frac{a^2b}{b^2c}$ by $\frac{a^2c}{bc^2}$, what is the result?

(A) $\frac{1}{b}$

(B) 1

(C) $\frac{b}{a}$

(D) $\frac{c}{b}$

First, cancel common factors in each term. Then you'll see that the numerator and denominator are the same, which means that the quotient must equal 1:

$$\frac{a^2b}{b^2c} \div \frac{a^2c}{bc^2} = \frac{a^2}{bc} \div \frac{a^2}{bc} = 1$$

The correct answer is (B).

EXAMPLE 28 (MORE CHALLENGING):

What is the value of $\frac{x^3 - y^4}{x^3y^4}$, where $x = 2$ and $y = -2$?

(A) $-\frac{1}{16}$

(B) $\frac{1}{32}$

(C) $\frac{1}{16}$

(D) 1

One way to answer this question is to simplify the fraction by distributing the denominator to each term in the numerator, then cancel common factors. But an easier way to solve the problem is to plug in the x and y values that are provided, and do the math:

$$\frac{x^3 - y^4}{x^3y^4} = \frac{2^3 - (-2)^4}{2^3 \times (-2^4)} = \frac{8 - 16}{8 \times 16} = \frac{-8}{128} = -\frac{1}{16}$$

The correct answer is (A).

Additional Rules for Exponents

For the GED® test, you should also keep in mind these three additional rules for exponents.

❶ When raising an exponential number to a power, multiply exponents:

Rule: $\left(a^x\right)^y = a^{xy}$

Example: $\left(2^2\right)^3 = 2^{(2)(3)} = 2^6 = 64$

2 Any number other than zero (0) raised to the power of 0 (zero) equals 1:

> **Rule:** $a^0 = 1$ $[a \neq 0]$

> **Example:** $13^0 = 1$

3 Raising a base number to a negative exponent is equivalent to 1 divided by the base number raised to the exponent's absolute value:

> **Rule:** $a^{-x} = \dfrac{1}{a^x}$

> **Example:** $4^{-2} = \dfrac{1}{4^2} = \dfrac{1}{16}$

These three rules are all fair game for the GED® test. In fact, a GED® test question might require you to apply more than one of these rules.

EXAMPLE 29 (EASIER):

What is the value of $5^{-2} \times 5^{-1} \times 5^0$?

   (A) -125

   (B) $-\dfrac{1}{25}$

   (C) 0

   (D) $\dfrac{1}{125}$

Rewrite each of the first two terms under the numerator 1, but with a positive exponent. Then multiply:

$$\frac{1}{5^2} \times \frac{1}{5} \times 1 = \frac{1}{25} \times \frac{1}{5} \times 1 = \frac{1}{125}$$

The correct answer is (D).

EXAMPLE 30 (MORE CHALLENGING):

What is the value of $\left(2^3\right)^2 \times 4^{-3}$?

   (A) $-\dfrac{1}{8}$

   (B) 1

   (C) $\dfrac{3}{2}$

   (D) 16

Multiply exponents in the first term. Rewrite the second term under the numerator 1, but with a positive exponent: $\left(2^3\right)^2 \times 4^{-3} = 2^{(2)(3)} \times \dfrac{1}{4^3} = \dfrac{2^6}{4^3} = \dfrac{2^6}{\left(2^2\right)^3} = \dfrac{2^6}{2^6} = 1$.

The correct answer is (B).

Exponents and the Real Number Line

Raising numbers to powers can have surprising effects on the size and/or sign (negative versus positive) of the number. You need to consider four separate regions of the real-number line.

For numbers greater than 1 (right of 1 on the number line):

Raising the number to a power greater than 1 gives a higher value. The greater the power, the greater the value. For example:

$$9^2 < 9^3 < 9^4 \text{ (and so on)}$$

For numbers less than –1 (left of –1 on the number line):

If the number is raised to an **even** power (such as 2, 4, or 6), the result is a number greater than 1. The greater the power, the greater the value. For example:

$$-3 < -3^2 < -3^4 < -3^6 \text{ (and so on)}$$

If the number is raised to an **odd** power (such as 3, 5, or 7), the result is a number less than –1. The greater the power, the smaller the value (the farther *left* on the number line). For example:

$$-2 > -2^3 > -2^5 > -2^7 \text{ (and so on)}$$

For fractional numbers between 0 and 1:

Raising the number to a power greater than 1 gives a *smaller positive* value. The greater the power, the smaller the value. For example:

$$\frac{2}{3} > \left(\frac{2}{3}\right)^2 > \left(\frac{2}{3}\right)^3 > \left(\frac{2}{3}\right)^4 \ldots > 0$$

For fractional numbers between –1 and 0:

Raising the fractional number to an **odd** power greater than 1 gives a *greater negative* value. The greater the power, the greater the value (approaching zero). For example:

$$-\frac{2}{3} < \left(-\frac{2}{3}\right)^3 < -\left(\frac{2}{3}\right)^5 \ldots < 0$$

Raising the fractional number to an **even** power greater than 1 gives a *positive fractional value* between 0 and 1. The greater the power, the lower the positive value (approaching zero). For example:

$$-\frac{2}{3} < 0, \text{ but} > \left(-\frac{2}{3}\right)^4 \ldots > 0$$

GED® test questions involving exponents and the number line can be confusing. Nevertheless, they can be quite manageable if you keep in mind the four different regions of the number line.

EXAMPLE 31 (EASIER):

If $-1 < x < 0$, which of the following must be true?

(A) $x^4 < -1$

(B) $x^4 > 1$

(C) $0 < x^4 < 1$

(D) $x^4 = 1$

This question tests you on the rule that a negative fractional value raised to an even power (in this case 4), results in a fractional positive number, between 0 and 1.
The correct answer is (C).

EXAMPLE 32 (MORE CHALLENGING):

If $x^2 > 1 > y^2$, which of the following must be true?

(A) $x > y$

(B) $x^3 < y^3$

(C) $x < y$

(D) $-1 < y^2 < 1$

Given $x^2 > 1$, we know that x is either greater than 1 or less than -1. We also know that y must be a fraction less than 1 if y^2 is less than 1, but y also has to be a negative fraction greater than -1 for y^2 to be > -1. There are several situations in which choice (A) would be false, such as if $x = -5$ and $y = -\frac{1}{2}$. Choice (B) and (C) would be false if $x = 2$ and $y = -\frac{1}{2}$. Choice **(D)** is the only answer that must be true.
The correct answer is (D).

Exponents You Should Know

For the GED® test, memorize the exponential values in the following table. These are the ones you're most likely to see on the exam.

Power and Corresponding Value

Base	2	3	4	5	6	7	8
2	4	8	16	32	64	128	256
3	9	27	81	243			
4	16	64	256				
5	25	125	625				
6	36	216					

Scientific Notation

Scientific notation is a system for writing extremely large or extremely small numbers. In scientific notation, an integer or decimal number between 1 and 10 is written to the power of 10. For example, the number 380,000,000 can be written as 3.8×10^8. The number between 1 and 10 that you are working with is 3.8. When you count the number of zeros plus the number to the right of the decimal point, you can see that there are 8 digits. That means that the exponent is 8. A negative exponent signifies a fractional number.

To illustrate further, here's a list of related decimal numbers and their equivalents in scientific notation:

$$837{,}000 \quad = 8.37 \times 10^5 \text{ (decimal point shifts 5 places to the left)}$$
$$8370 \quad = 8.37 \times 10^3 \text{ (decimal point shifts 3 places to the left)}$$
$$837 \quad = 8.37 \times 10^2 \text{ (decimal point shifts 1 place to the left)}$$
$$8.37 \quad = 8.37 \times 10^0 \text{ (decimal point unchanged in position)}$$
$$0.837 \quad = 8.37 \times 10^{-1} \text{ (decimal point shifts 1 place to the right)}$$
$$0.0837 \quad = 8.37 \times 10^{-2} \text{ (decimal point shifts 2 places to the right)}$$
$$0.000837 \quad = 8.37 \times 10^{-4} \text{ (decimal point shifts 4 places to the right)}$$

A GED® test question might ask you to simply convert a number to scientific notation form, or the other way around.

EXAMPLE 33 (EASIER):

A computer can process data at the rate of 3.9×10^8 bits per second. How many bits can the computer process in 0.02 seconds?

   (A) (1) 7.8×10^4

   (B) (2) 7.8×10^6

   (C) (3) 1.95×10^7

   (D) (4) 7.8×10^8

To answer the question, first multiply the rate by the number of seconds: $(0.02)(3.9 \times 10^8) = 0.078 \times 10^8$. Since the answer choices are in proper scientific notation, shift the decimal point to the right two places and lower the power accordingly: 7.8×10^6. **The correct answer is (B).**

> **EXAMPLE 34 (MORE CHALLENGING):**
>
> A particle travels at the rate of 52,500 meters per second. Expressed in millimeters, how far will the particle travel in 7×10^{-7} seconds?
> [1 meter = 1000 millimeters]
>
> **(A)** 0.3675
>
> **(B)** 3.675
>
> **(C)** 7.5
>
> **(D)** 36.75

Express 52,500 in scientific notation: 5.25×10^4. To convert this number from meters to millimeters, multiply by 1000 or 10^3:

$$(5.25 \times 10^4)(10^3) = 5.25 \times 10^7.$$

To answer the question, apply the following formula: distance = rate × time.

$$
\begin{aligned}
D &= (5.25 \times 10^7)(7.0 \times 10^{-7}) \\
&= (5.25)(7) \times 10^{(7-7)} \\
&= 36.75 \times 10^0 \\
&= 36.75 \times 1 \\
&= 36.75
\end{aligned}
$$

The correct answer is (D).

SQUARE ROOTS (AND OTHER ROOTS)

The **square root** of a number n is a number that you "square" (multiply it by itself, or raise to the power of 2), to obtain n. The **radical sign** signifies square root and looks like this: $\sqrt{}$. Here's a simple example of a square root:

$$2 = \sqrt{4} \text{ (the square root of 4) because } 2 \times 2 \text{ (or } 2^2) = 4$$

The **cube root** of a number n is a number that you raise to the power of 3 (multiply by itself twice) to obtain n. You determine higher roots (for example, the "fourth root") in the same way. Except for square roots, the radical sign will indicate the root to be taken. For example:

$$2 = \sqrt[3]{8} \text{ (the cube root of 8) because } 2 \times 2 \times 2 \text{ (or } 2^3) = 8$$

$$2 = \sqrt[4]{16} \text{ (the fourth root of 16) because } 2 \times 2 \times 2 \times 2 \text{ (or } 2^4) = 16$$

For the GED® test, you should know the rules for simplifying and for combining radical expressions.

Simplifying and Combining Radical Expressions

On the GED® test, look for the possibility of simplifying radicals by moving what's under the radical sign to the outside of the sign. Check inside square-root radicals for **perfect squares:** factors that are squares of nice tidy numbers or other terms. The same advice applies to perfect cubes, and so on. Study the following three examples:

$$\sqrt{4a^2} = 2a$$

4 and a^2 are both perfect squares. So you can remove them from under the radical sign, and change each one to its square root.

$$\sqrt[3]{27a^6} = 3a^2$$

27 and a^6 are both perfect cubes. So you can remove them from under the radical sign, and change each one to its cube root.

$$\sqrt{8a^3} = \sqrt{(4)(2)a^3} = 2a\sqrt{2a}$$

8 and a^3 both contain perfect-square factors; remove the perfect squares from under the radical sign, and change each one to its square root.

The rules for combining terms that include radicals are quite similar to those for exponents. Keep the following two rules in mind; one applies to addition and subtraction, while the other applies to multiplication and division.

RULE 1 (addition and subtraction): If a term under a radical is being added to or subtracted from a term under a different radical, you cannot combine the two terms under the same radical.

$$\sqrt{x} + \sqrt{y} \neq \sqrt{x + y}$$

$$\sqrt{x} - \sqrt{y} \neq \sqrt{x - y}$$

$$\sqrt{x} + \sqrt{x} = 2\sqrt{x} \text{ , not } \sqrt{2x}$$

RULE 2 (multiplication and division): Terms under different radicals can be combined under a common radical if one term is multiplied or divided by the other, but only if the radical is the same.

$$\sqrt{x}\sqrt{x} = \left(\sqrt{x}\right)^2 \text{, or } x$$

$$\sqrt{x}\sqrt{y} = \sqrt{xy}$$

$$\frac{\sqrt{x}}{\sqrt{y}} = \sqrt{\frac{x}{y}}$$

$$\sqrt[3]{x}\sqrt{x} = ? \text{ (you cannot combine)}$$

EXAMPLE 35 (EASIER):

$\left(2\sqrt{2a}\right)^2$ is equivalent to which of the following expressions?

(A) $4a$

(B) $4a^2$

(C) $8a$

(D) $8a^2$

Square each of the two terms, 2 and $\sqrt{2a}$, separately. Then combine their squares by multiplication: $\left(2\sqrt{2a}\right)^2 = 2^2 \times \left(\sqrt{2a}\right)^2 = 4 \times 2a = 8a$. **The correct answer is (C).**

EXAMPLE 36 (MORE CHALLENGING):

$\sqrt{24} - \sqrt{16} - \sqrt{6}$ simplifies to which of the following expressions?

(A) $\sqrt{6} - 4$

(B) $4 - 2\sqrt{2}$

(C) $\sqrt{6}$

(D) $2\sqrt{2}$

Although the numbers under the three radicals combine to equal 2, you cannot combine terms this way. Instead, simplify the first two terms, then combine the first and third terms:

$$\sqrt{24} - \sqrt{16} - \sqrt{6} = 2\sqrt{6} - 4 - \sqrt{6} = \sqrt{6} - 4$$

The correct answer is (A).

Roots You Should Know

Below is a list of common roots, for your reference. You don't need to memorize these roots for the GED® test. However, for those questions for which you may not use a calculator, it may be useful to commit to memory the first three roots in each column. Notice that the cube root of a positive number is positive, and the cube root of a negative number is negative.

Square roots of "perfect square" integers:	Cube roots of "perfect cube" positive integers:	Cube roots of "perfect cube" negative integers:	Other roots you should know:
$\sqrt{121} = 11$	$\sqrt[3]{8} = 2$	$\sqrt[3]{-8} = -2$	$\sqrt[4]{16} = 2$
$\sqrt{144} = 12$	$\sqrt[3]{27} = 3$	$\sqrt[3]{-27} = -3$	$\sqrt[4]{81} = 3$
$\sqrt{169} = 13$	$\sqrt[3]{64} = 4$	$\sqrt[3]{-64} = -4$	$\sqrt[5]{32} = 2$
$\sqrt{196} = 14$	$\sqrt[3]{125} = 5$	$\sqrt[3]{-125} = -5$	
$\sqrt{225} = 15$	$\sqrt[3]{216} = 6$	$\sqrt[3]{-216} = -6$	
$\sqrt{256} = 16$	$\sqrt[3]{343} = 7$	$\sqrt[3]{-343} = -7$	
$\sqrt{625} = 25$	$\sqrt[3]{512} = 8$	$\sqrt[3]{-512} = -8$	
	$\sqrt[3]{729} = 9$	$\sqrt[3]{-729} = -9$	
	$\sqrt[3]{1000} = 10$	$\sqrt[3]{-1000} = -10$	

SUMMING IT UP

- For the Mathematical Reasoning Test, it is important to review *properties* (signs, integers, absolute value, and divisibility), *forms* (fractions, mixed numbers, decimal numbers, percentages, ratios, exponential numbers, and radical expressions), and *operations* (the four basic operations and operations on exponential numbers and radical expressions). The knowledge areas that are covered here are basic building blocks for all types of GED® test math questions

- GED® test math questions involving fractions, decimal numbers, or percents often require you to convert one form to another as part of solving the problem at hand. Do your best to learn how to convert quickly and confidently.

- Certain fraction-decimal-percent equivalents appear on the GED® test more often than others. The numbers in the tables in this chapter are especially common. Try to memorize them so that you can convert these numbers quickly during the test.

- A GED® test question involving percent might involve one of the following tasks: finding the percent of a number, finding a number when a percent is given, or finding what percent one number is of another.

- GED® test ratio or proportion problems often involve units of measurement, such as inches, ounces, or gallons. These problems sometimes require that you convert one unit to another.

- An **exponent** refers to the number of times that a number (referred to as the **base number**) is multiplied by itself, *plus 1*. On the GED® test, questions involving exponents usually require you to combine two or more exponential numbers using one of the four basic operations.

- Remember these three rules for exponents: When raising an exponential number to a power, multiply exponents; any number other than zero (0) raised to the power of 0 (zero) equals 1; and raising a base number to a negative exponent is equivalent to 1 divided by the base number raised to the exponent's absolute value.

- For the GED® test, memorize the exponential values in the table that appears in this chapter. These are the ones you're most likely to see on the exam.

- On the GED® test, look for the possibility of simplifying radicals by moving what's under the radical sign to the outside of the sign. Check inside square-root radicals for **perfect squares:** factors that are squares of nice tidy numbers or other terms. The same advice applies to perfect cubes, and so on.

Math Review: Algebra and Descriptive Statistics

OVERVIEW

- What you'll find in this review
- Linear equations in one variable
- Linear equations in two variables
- Linear equations that can't be solved
- Solving algebraic inequalities
- Factorable quadratic expressions (one variable)
- Factorable quadratic expressions (two variables)
- Functions
- Measures of central tendency (mean, median, and range)
- Arithmetic series
- Probability
- Word problems involving formulas
- Summing it up

WHAT YOU'LL FIND IN THIS REVIEW

This review focuses on algebra and descriptive statistics. First you'll review the following algebra skills:

- Solving a linear equation in one variable

- Solving a system of two equations in two variables by substitution and addition-subtraction

- Recognizing unsolvable equations

- Handling algebraic inequalities

- Factoring quadratic expressions

- Finding the roots of quadratic equations by factoring

- Handling functions

- Solving formula word problems (weighted average, simple interest, and rate)

Later, you'll examine the concepts of mean, median, range, arithmetic series, and probability.

The GED® test-style questions throughout this review are multiple-choice questions. The actual exam also includes questions in an alternative format, in which you supply the numerical answer to the question.

LINEAR EQUATIONS IN ONE VARIABLE

Algebraic expressions are usually used to form **equations,** which set two expressions equal to each other. Equations contain at least one **variable:** a letter such as x or y that represents a number that can *vary.* Most equations you'll see on the GED® test are **linear equations,** in which the variables don't come with exponents.

To find the value of a linear equation's variable (such as x) is to **solve the equation.** To solve any linear equation containing only one variable, your goal is always the same: isolate the variable on one side of the equation. To accomplish this, you may need to perform one or more of the following operations on both sides, depending on the equation:

❶ Add or subtract the same term on both sides.

❷ Multiply or divide both sides by the same term.

❸ Clear fractions by cross-multiplication.

❹ Clear radicals by raising both sides to the same power (exponent).

Whatever operation you perform on one side of an equation you must also perform on the other side; otherwise, the two sides won't be equal. Performing any of these operations on *both* sides does not change the equality; it merely restates the equation in a different form.

Solving an Equation Using the Four Basic Operations

To find the value of the variable (to solve for x), you may need to either add a term to both sides of the equation or subtract a term from both sides. Here are two examples:

Adding the same number to both sides:

$$x - 2 = 5$$
$$x - 2 + 2 = 5 + 2$$
$$x = 7$$

Subtracting the same number from both sides:

$$\frac{3}{2} - x = 12$$

The objective is to isolate the variable x. To do this, like terms must be combined.

$$
\begin{array}{r}
\frac{3}{2} - x = \quad 12 \\
-\frac{3}{2} \qquad\quad -\frac{3}{2} \\
\hline
-x = 10\frac{1}{2} \quad \text{(divide by } -1 \text{ to make the variable positive)}
\end{array}
$$

$$x = -10\frac{1}{2}$$

The first system isolates x by adding 2 to both sides. The second system isolates x by subtracting $\frac{3}{2}$ from both sides. In some cases, solving for x requires that you either multiply or divide both sides of the equation by the same term. Here are two examples:

Multiplying both sides by the same number:

$$\frac{x}{2} = 14$$
$$2 \times \frac{x}{2} = 14 \times 2$$
$$x = 28$$

Dividing both sides by the same number:

$$3x = 18$$
$$\frac{3x}{3} = \frac{18}{3}$$
$$x = 6$$

The first system isolates x by multiplying both sides by 2. The second system isolates x by dividing both sides by 3. If the variable appears on both sides of the equation, first perform whatever operation is required to position the variable on just one side—either the left or the right. The next system positions both x-terms on the left side by subtracting $2x$ from both sides:

$$16 - x = 9 + 2x$$
$$16 - x - 2x = 9 + 2x - 2x$$
$$16 - 3x = 9$$

Now that x appears on just one side, the next step is to isolate it by subtracting 16 from both sides, and then dividing both sides by -3:

$$16 - 3x = 9$$
$$16 - 3x - 16 = 9 - 16$$
$$-3x = -7$$
$$\frac{-3x}{-3} = \frac{-7}{-3}$$
$$x = \frac{7}{3}$$

EXAMPLE 1 (EASIER):

For what value of x does $2x - 6$ equal $x - 9$?

(A) -6

(B) -3

(C) 2

(D) 6

First, write the verbal description as the equation $2x - 6 = x - 9$. Then position both x-terms on the same side. To place them both on the left side, subtract x from both sides. Then combine x-terms:

$$2x - 6 - x = x - 9 - x$$
$$x - 6 = -9$$

Finally, isolate x by adding 6 to both sides:

$$x - 6 + 6 = -9 + 6$$
$$x = -3$$

The correct answer is (B).

EXAMPLE 2 (MORE CHALLENGING):

If $12 = \dfrac{11}{x} - \dfrac{3}{x}$, then what is the value of x?

(A) $\dfrac{3}{11}$

(B) $\dfrac{1}{2}$

(C) $\dfrac{2}{3}$

(D) $\dfrac{11}{3}$

First, combine the x-terms: $12 = \dfrac{11 - 3}{x}$. Next, clear the fraction by multiplying both sides by x:

$$12x = 11 - 3$$
$$12x = 8$$

Finally, isolate x by dividing both sides by 12:

$$x = \frac{8}{12} \text{, or } \frac{2}{3}$$

The correct answer is (C).

Cross-multiplying and Clearing Radicals to Solve an Equation

If an equation equates two fractions, use **cross-multiplication** to eliminate the fractions. Combine each numerator with the denominator on the other side by multiplying diagonally across the equation. Then set one product equal to the other. (In effect, cross-multiplication is a shortcut method of multiplying both sides of the equation by both denominators.) Here's a simple example:

$$\frac{x}{3} = \frac{12}{2}$$
$$(2)(x) = (3)(12)$$
$$2x = 36$$
$$x = \frac{36}{2} \text{, or } 18$$

If the variable appears under the square-root radical sign $\sqrt{}$, eliminate ("clear") the radical sign by squaring both sides of the equation. Use the same method to clear cube roots and other roots:

$$\sqrt[3]{2x} = 4$$
$$\left(\sqrt[3]{2x}\right)^3 = 4^3$$
$$2x = 64$$
$$x = 32$$

Be careful when you square both sides of an equation. In some instances, doing so will produce a variable such as x^2, in which case the equation is *quadratic* rather than linear. This means that it might have more than one solution. You'll examine quadratic equations later in this review.

EXAMPLE 3 (EASIER):

If $3\sqrt{2x} = 2$, then what is the value of x?

(A) $\dfrac{1}{18}$

(B) $\dfrac{2}{9}$

(C) $\dfrac{1}{3}$

(D) $\dfrac{5}{4}$

First, clear the radical sign by squaring all items. In order to clear radicals, it is necessary to raise the radical to the index of the radical. Then the radical and its index cancel each other out.

$$3\sqrt{2x} = 2$$
$$9(2x) = 2^2$$
$$18x = 4$$
$$x = \frac{4}{18} = \frac{2}{9}$$

The correct answer is (B).

EXAMPLE 4 (MORE CHALLENGING):

For what value of a does $\dfrac{7a}{8}$ equal $\dfrac{a+1}{3}$?

(A) $\dfrac{8}{13}$

(B) $\dfrac{7}{8}$

(C) 2

(D) $\dfrac{7}{3}$

First, cross-multiply (multiply diagonally across the equation) and equate the two products:

$$(3)(7a) = (8)(a + 1)$$

Next, combine terms (distribute 8 to both a and 1):

$$21a = 8a + 8$$

Next, isolate a-terms on one side by subtracting $8a$ from both sides; then combine the a-terms:

$$21a - 8a = 8a + 8 - 8a$$
$$13a = 8$$

Finally, isolate a by dividing both sides by 13:

$$\frac{13a}{13} = \frac{8}{13}$$
$$a = \frac{8}{13}$$

The correct answer is (A).

LINEAR EQUATIONS IN TWO VARIABLES

In the preceding section, you examined linear equations in one variable only, and you saw that you can find the value of the variable by isolating it on one side of the equation. This is not so, however, for a linear equation in two (or more) different variables. Consider the following equation, which contains two variables:

$$x + 3 = y + 1$$

What is the value of x? It depends on the value of y, doesn't it? Similarly, the value of y depends on the value of x. Without more information about either x or y, you simply cannot find one of the other value. However, you *can* express x in terms of y, and you can express y in terms of x:

$$x = y - 2$$
$$y = x + 2$$

The two above equations are really the same. You can't solve it because it contains two variables. Look at a more complex example: $4x - 9 = \frac{3}{2}y$.

Solve for x in terms of y:

$$4x = \frac{3}{2}y + 9$$
$$x = \frac{3}{8}y + \frac{9}{4}$$

Solve for y in terms of x:

$$\frac{4x - 9}{\frac{3}{2}} = y$$

$$\frac{2}{3}(4x - 9) = y$$

$$\frac{8}{3}x - 6 = y$$

To determine numerical values of x and y, you need a system of two linear equations with the same two variables. Given this system, there are two different methods for finding the values of the two variables: the substitution method and the addition-subtraction method.

The Substitution Method

To solve a system of two equations using the **substitution method,** follow these steps (we'll use x and y here):

1 In *either* equation isolate one variable (x) on one side.

2 Substitute the expression that equals x in place of x in the other equation.

3 Solve that equation for y.

4 Now that you know the value of y, plug it into *either* equation to find the value of x.

Consider these two equations:

Equation A: $x = 4y$
Equation B: $x - y = 1$

In equation B, substitute $4y$ for x, and then solve for y:

$$4y - y = 1$$
$$3y = 1$$
$$y = \frac{1}{3}$$

To find x, substitute $\frac{1}{3}$ for y into either equation. The value of x will be the same in either equation.

Equation A: $x = 4\left(\frac{1}{3}\right) = \frac{4}{3}$

Equation B: $x - \frac{1}{3} = 1$; $x = \frac{4}{3}$

The Addition-Subtraction Method

Another way to solve for two variables in a system of two equations is with the **addition-subtraction** method. Here are the steps:

1 "Line up" the two equations by listing the same variables and other terms in the same order. Place one equation above the other.

2 Make the coefficient of *either* variable the same in both equations (you can disregard the sign) by multiplying every term in one of the equations. (A **coefficient** is a variable's number. For example, in the term $7x$, the coefficient of x is 7.)

3 Add the two equations (work down to a sum for each term), or subtract one equation from the other, to eliminate one variable.

Consider these two equations:

Equation A: $x = 3 + 3y$
Equation B: $2x + y = 4$

In equation A, subtract $3y$ from both sides, so that all terms in the two equations "line up":

Equation A: $x - 3y = 3$
Equation B: $2x + y = 4$

To solve for y, multiply each term in Equation A by 2, so that the x-coefficient is the same in both equations:

Equation A: $2x - 6y = 6$
Equation B: $2x + y = 4$

Subtract Equation B from Equation A, thereby eliminating x, and then isolate y on one side of the equation:

$$
\begin{aligned}
2x - 6y &= 6 \\
2x + y &= 4 \\
\hline
0x - 5y &= 2 \\
-5y &= 2 \\
y &= -\frac{2}{5}
\end{aligned}
$$

Which Method Should You Use?

Which method, substitution or addition-subtraction, you should use depends on what the equations look like to begin with. To understand this point, look at this system of two equations:

$$\frac{2}{5}p + q = 3q - 10$$
$$q = 10 - p$$

Notice that the second equation is already set up nicely for the substitution method. But you could use addition-subtraction instead; you'd just have to rearrange the terms in both the equations first:

$$\frac{2}{5}p - 2q = -10$$
$$p + q = 10$$

Now, look at the following system:

$$3x + 4y = -8$$
$$x - 2y = \frac{1}{2}$$

Notice that the x-term and y-term already line up nicely here. Also notice that it's easy to match the coefficients of either x or y: multiply both sides of the second equation by either 3 or 2. This system is an ideal candidate for addition-subtraction. To appreciate this point, try using substitution instead. You'll discover that it takes far more number crunching.

In short, to solve a system of two linear equations in two variables, use addition-subtraction if you can quickly and easily eliminate one of the variables. Otherwise, use substitution.

EXAMPLE 5 (EASIER):

If $q = \dfrac{p}{10}$ and $q = 4.4 - p$, what is the value of $\dfrac{p}{q}$?

(A) −4.4

(B) 1.1

(C) 2.2

(D) 10

Since the question asks for $\dfrac{p}{q}$ (rather than either p or q), you can answer it by applying just the first of the two equations:

$$q = \frac{p}{10}$$
$$10q = p$$
$$10 = \frac{p}{q}$$

The correct answer is (D).

EXAMPLE 6 (MORE CHALLENGING):

If $3x + 4y = -8$, and if $x - 2y = \dfrac{1}{2}$, what is the value of x ?

(A) −12

(B) $-\dfrac{7}{5}$

(C) $\dfrac{14}{5}$

(D) 9

To solve for x, you want to eliminate y. You can multiply each term in the second equation by 2, and then add the equations:

$$3x + 4y = -8$$
$$\underline{2x - 4y = 1}$$
$$5x + 0y = -7$$
$$x = -\frac{7}{5}$$

The correct answer is (B).

LINEAR EQUATIONS THAT CAN'T BE SOLVED

Never assume that one linear equation with one variable is solvable. If you can reduce the equation to $0 = 0$, then you can't solve it. In other words, the value of the variable could be any real number. Here's a simple example:

$$3x - 4 = 5x - 4 - 2x$$
$$3x - 4 = 3x - 4$$
$$0 = 0$$

In some cases, what appears to be a system of two equations in two variables might actually be the same equation expressed in two different ways. In other words, what you're really dealing with are two equivalent equations, which you cannot solve. Consider these two equations:

Equation A: $x + 4y = 16$
Equation B: $y = 4 - \dfrac{x}{4}$

If you multiply each term in Equation B by 4, you'll see that Equations A and B are the same:

Equation A: $x + 4y = 16$
Equation B: $4y = 16 - x$

On the GED® test, whenever you encounter a question that calls for solving one or more linear equations, and one answer choice provides something other than a numerical answer, size up the equation to see whether it's one of these two types of unsolvable problems. If so, then you have found your correct answer choice.

EXAMPLE 7 (EASIER):

If $-1 < x < 1$, and if $3x - 3 - 4x = x - 7 - 2x + 4$, then how many real numbers does the solution set for x contain?

   (A) 0

   (B) 1

   (C) 2

   (D) infinitely many

All terms on both sides cancel out:

$$3x - 3 - 4x = x - 7 - 2x + 4$$
$$-x - 3 = -x - 3$$
$$0 = 0$$

Thus, x could equal any real number between -1 and 1 (not just the integer 0). **The correct answer is (D).**

EXAMPLE 8 (MORE CHALLENGING):

$2b = 60 - 2a$, and $a + b = 30$. What is the value of a ?

(A) -10

(B) 10

(C) 12

(D) No solution is possible.

An unwary test-taker might assume that the values of both a and b can be determined with both equations together, because they appear at first glance to provide a system of two linear equations with two unknowns. But they don't. You can rewrite the first equation so that it is identical to the second:

$$2b = 60 - 2a$$
$$2b = 2(30 - a)$$
$$b = 30 - a$$
$$a + b = 30$$

As you can see, the equation $2b = 60 - 2a$ is identical to the equation $a + b = 30$. Thus, a and b could each be any real number. You can't solve one equation in two variables. **The correct answer is (D).**

SOLVING ALGEBRAIC INEQUALITIES

You solve algebraic inequalities in the same manner as equations. Isolate the variable on one side of the equation, factoring and canceling wherever possible. However, one important rule distinguishes inequalities from equations:

RULE: Whenever you multiply or divide by a negative number, you must *reverse* the inequality symbol. Expressed in symbolic form: if $a > b$, then $-a < -b$.

The following simple example demonstrates this important rule:

$$12 - 4x < 8 \text{ (original inequality)}$$
$$-4x < -4 \text{ (subtract 12 from both sides; inequality unchanged)}$$
$$x > 1 \text{ (both sides divided by } -4\text{; inequality reversed)}$$

Here are some additional rules for dealing with algebraic inequalities.

❶ Adding or subtracting unequal quantities to (or from) equal quantities:

If $a > b$, then $c + a > c + b$

If $a > b$, then $c - a < c - b$

❷ Adding unequal quantities to unequal quantities:

If $a > b$, and if $c > d$, then $a + c > b + d$

❸ Comparing three unequal quantities:

If $a > b$, and if $b > c$, then $a > c$

❹ Combining the same *positive* quantity with unequal quantities by multiplication or division:

If $a > b$, and if $x > 0$, then $xa > xb$

If $a > b$, and if $x > 0$, then $\dfrac{a}{x} > \dfrac{b}{x}$

If $a > b$, and if $x > 0$, then $\dfrac{x}{a} < \dfrac{x}{b}$

❺ Combining the same *negative* quantity with unequal quantities by multiplication or division:

If $a > b$, and if $x < 0$, then $xa < xb$

If $a > b$, and if $x < 0$, then $\dfrac{a}{x} < \dfrac{b}{x}$

If $a > b$, and if $x < 0$, then $\dfrac{x}{a} > \dfrac{x}{b}$

EXAMPLE 9 (EASIER):

If $-2x > -5$, then which of the inequalities holds true?

(A) $x > \dfrac{5}{2}$

(B) $x < \dfrac{5}{2}$

(C) $x > -\dfrac{2}{5}$

(D) $x < \dfrac{2}{5}$

Divide both sides of the equation by -2, and reverse the inequality:

$$-2x > -5$$

$$\frac{-2x}{-2} < \frac{-5}{-2}$$

$$x < \frac{5}{2}$$

The correct answer is (B).

EXAMPLE 10 (MORE CHALLENGING):

Dave has $150 to spend to buy tickets to go to a baseball game. The stadium charges a $12 fee for buying tickets. The inequality $12 + 30n \leq 150$ represents the number of tickets, n, Dave can afford. Graph all possible numbers of tickets that Dave can buy. On the online GED® test, click on the number line to plot the point(s).

To remove a point, place the arrow over the point and click the left mouse button. For this print version, write down your answer.

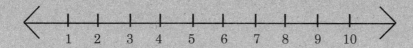

To solve the inequality $12 + 30n \leq 150$, the test-taker must subtract the one-time cost of 12 from both sides of the inequality. This results in a new inequality: $30n \leq 138$. Dividing both sides by 30 will result in $n \leq 4.6$. Since tickets can only be purchased in whole number quantities, the range of valid answers would be: 1, 2, 3, 4 and plotted on a number line like this:

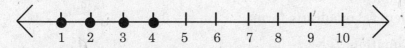

The correct answers are 1, 2, 3, and 4.

EXAMPLE 11 (MORE CHALLENGING):

Jennifer is moving from Boston to New York City, a distance of 220 miles. She needs to rent a truck one way to move her belongings. The rental of a truck is $100 and the cost for fuel for this trip is $75. Depending on where she rents the truck, there will be a varying fee per mile driven. If her moving budget is $400, which inequality below shows how big a fee per mile she will be able to afford when renting a truck?

   (A) $175x + 220 \geq 400$

   (B) $175x + 220 \leq 400$

   (C) $220x + 175 \geq 400$

   (D) $220x + 175 \leq 400$

The fixed costs of $175 (fuel + truck rental) are added to the variable cost per mile multiplied by x and put in a $\leq$ relationship with the total budget of $400. **The correct answer is (D).**

FACTORABLE QUADRATIC EXPRESSIONS (ONE VARIABLE)

A **quadratic expression** includes a "squared" variable, such as x^2. An equation is quadratic if you can express it in this general form: $ax^2 + bx + c = 0$, where:

> x is the variable
>
> a, b, and c are integers
>
> $a \neq 0$
>
> b can equal 0
>
> c can equal 0

Here are four examples (notice that the b-term and c-term are not essential; in other words, either b or c, or both, can equal zero):

> **Equation:** $2w^2 = 16$
> **General quadratic form:** $2w^2 - 16 = 0$ (no b-term)
>
> **Equation:** $x^2 = 3x$
> **General quadratic form:** $x^2 - 3x = 0$ (no c-term)
>
> **Equation:** $3y = 4 - y^2$
> **General quadratic form:** $y^2 + 3y - 4 = 0$
>
> **Equation:** $7z = 2z^2 - 15$
> **General quadratic form:** $2z^2 - 7z - 15 = 0$

Every quadratic equation has exactly two solutions, called **roots.** (But the two roots might be the same.) On the GED® test, you will probably be able to find the two roots by **factoring.**

To solve any factorable quadratic equation, follow these three steps:

❶ Put the equation into the standard form: $ax^2 + bx + c = 0$.

❷ Factor the terms on the left side of the equation into two linear expressions (with no exponents).

❸ Set each linear expression (root) equal to zero and solve for the variable in each one.

Some quadratic expressions are easier to factor than others. If either of the two constants b or c is zero, factoring is very simple. In fact, in some cases, no factoring is needed at all—as in the second equation below:

> **A factorable quadratic equation with no c-term:**
>
> $$2x^2 = x$$
> $$2x^2 - x = 0$$
> $$x(2x - 1) = 0$$
> $$x = 0, \quad 2x - 1 = 0$$
> $$x = 0, \frac{1}{2}$$

A factorable quadratic equation with no *b*-term:

$$2x^2 - 4 = 0$$
$$2(x^2 - 2) = 0$$
$$x^2 - 2 = 0$$
$$x^2 = 2$$
$$x = \sqrt{2}, -\sqrt{2}$$

In sum, when dealing with a quadratic equation, your first step is usually to put it into the general form $ax^2 + bx + c = 0$. But keep in mind: The only essential term is ax^2.

A **binomial** is an algebraic expression that contains *two* terms. You can rewrite the product of two binomials by multiplying each term in one binomial by each term in the other, adding together all four terms. To organize this task, apply the **FOIL** method:

(F) the product of the **first** terms of the two binomials

(O) the product of the **outer** terms of the two binomials

(I) the product of the **inner** terms of the two binomials

(L) the product of the **last** (second) terms of the two binomials

Here are two simple demonstrations of the **FOIL** method:

$$(x + 2)(x + 3) = x^2 \text{ (F)} + 3x \text{ (O)} + 2x \text{ (I)} + 6 \text{ (L)} = x^2 + 5x + 6$$

$$(2x - 1)(x + 1) = 2x^2 \text{ (F)} + 2x \text{ (O)} - x \text{ (I)} - 1 \text{ (L)} = 2x^2 + x - 1$$

In both examples, notice that the two middle terms, **(O)** and **(I)**, can be combined. The simplified result is a **trinomial,** which is an algebraic expression that contains *three* terms. On the GED® test, quadratic trinomials are generally *factorable* into two binomials.

Factoring trinomials often involves a bit of trial and error. You need to apply the **FOIL** method *in reverse*. To accomplish this task, keep in mind the following relationships between the general quadratic form $ax^2 + bx + c$ and the **FOIL** method:

(F) is the first term (ax^2) of the quadratic expression

(O + I) is the second term (bx) of the quadratic expression

(L) is the third term (c) of the quadratic expression

To factor the quadratic expression $x^2 + 3x + 2$, for example, first identify its components:

(F) $= x^2$

(O + I) $= 3x$

(L) $= 2$

Then create a binomial "shell" to fill in numbers as you determine them. Remember: in the general quadratic form, a, b, and c are all *integers*, and so all coefficients and other numbers in both binomial must be integers. In this example, since **(F)** is x^2, the first term in each binomial must be x:

$$(x + ?)(x + ?)$$

Since **(L)** is 2, the product of the two last terms (signified by "?") must be 2. The only possibilities are 2 and 1 or –2 and –1. Try them both:

$$(x + 2)(x + 1) = x^2 + 2x + x + 2$$

$$(x - 2)(x - 1) = x^2 - 2x - x + 2$$

As you can see, the first option is the one that simplifies to $x^2 + 3x + 2$.

Remember that on the GED® test, quadratic trinomials will probably be factorable into two binomials, so that you can apply the FOIL method to determine them.

EXAMPLE 12 (EASIER):

Which of the following is a factor of $x^2 - x - 6$?

   (A) $(x + 1)$

   (B) $(x - 3)$

   (C) $(x - 2)$

   (D) $(x + 3)$

Notice that x^2 has no coefficient. This makes the process of factoring into two binomials easier. Set up two binomial shells: $(x + ?)(x + ?)$. The product of the two missing second terms (the "L" term under the FOIL method) is –6. The possible integral pairs that result in this product are (1, –6), (–1, 6), (2, –3,), and (–2, 3). Notice that the second term in the trinomial is $-x$. This means that the sum of the two integers whose product is –6 must be –1. The pair (2, –3) fits the bill. Thus, the trinomial is equivalent to the product of the two binomials $(x + 2)$ and $(x - 3)$. To check your work, multiply the two binomials, using the FOIL method:

$$(x + 2)(x - 3) = x^2 - 3x + 2x - 6$$
$$= x^2 - x - 6$$

The correct answer is (B).

EXAMPLE 13 (MORE CHALLENGING):

How many different values of x does the solution set for the equation $4x^2 = 4x - 1$ contain?

   (A) none

   (B) one

   (C) two

   (D) four

First, express the equation in standard form: $4x^2 - 4x + 1 = 0$. Notice that the c-term is 1. The only two integral pairs that result in this product are (1,1) and (–1,–1). Since the b-term ($-4x$) is negative, the integral pair whose product is 1 must be ($-1,-1$). Set up a binomial shell:

$$(? - 1)(? - 1)$$

Notice that the a-term contains the coefficient 4. The possible integral pairs that result in this product are $(1,4)$, $(2,2)$, $(-1,-4)$, and $(-2,-2)$. A bit of trial-and-error reveals that only the pair $(2,2)$ works. Thus, in factored form, the equation becomes $(2x - 1)(2x - 1) = 0$.

To check your work, multiply the two binomials, using the FOIL method:

$$\begin{aligned}(2x - 1)(2x - 1) &= 4x^2 - 2x - 2x + 1 \\ &= 4x^2 - 4x + 1\end{aligned}$$

Since the two binomial factors are the same, the two roots of the equation are the same. In other words, x has only one possible value. **The correct answer is (B).**

(Although you don't need to find the value of x in order to answer the question, solve for x in the equation $2x - 1 = 0$; $x = \frac{1}{2}$.)

FACTORABLE QUADRATIC EXPRESSIONS (TWO VARIABLES)

In the world of math, solving nonlinear equations in two or more variables can be *very* complicated. But for the GED® test, all you need to remember are these three general forms:

Sum of two variables, squared:
$(x + y)^2 = x^2 + 2xy + y^2$

Difference of two variables, squared:
$(x - y)^2 = x^2 - 2xy + y^2$

Difference of two squares:
$x^2 - y^2 = (x + y)(x - y)$

You can verify these equations using the FOIL method:

$$\begin{aligned}(x + y)^2 \\ = (x + y)(x + y) \\ = x^2 + xy + xy + y^2 \\ = x^2 + 2xy + y^2\end{aligned} \qquad \begin{aligned}(x - y)^2 \\ = (x - y)(x - y) \\ = x^2 - xy - xy + y^2 \\ = x^2 - 2xy + y^2\end{aligned} \qquad \begin{aligned}(x + y)(x - y) \\ = x^2 + xy - xy - y^2 \\ = x^2 - y^2\end{aligned}$$

For the GED® test, memorize the three equation forms listed here. When you see one of these forms on the exam, you will probably need to convert it to another form.

EXAMPLE 14 (EASIER):

If $x^2 - y^2 = 100$, and if $x + y = 2$, then what is the value of $x - y$?

(A) –2

(B) 10

(C) 20

(D) 50

If you recognize the *difference of two squares* when you see the form, you can handle this question with ease. Use the third equation you just learned, substituting 2 for $(x + y)$, then solving for $(x - y)$:

$$x^2 - y^2 = (x + y)(x - y)$$
$$100 = (x + y)(x - y)$$
$$100 = (2)(x - y)$$
$$50 = (x - y)$$

The correct answer is (D).

EXAMPLE 15 (MORE CHALLENGING):

If $\dfrac{x + y}{x - y} = \dfrac{x + y}{x}$, which of the following expresses the value of x in terms of y?

(A) $-y$

(B) y^2

(C) $\dfrac{y}{2}$

(D) $y - 1$

Apply the cross-product method to eliminate fractions. Rewrite the equation in its unfactored form. (If you recognize the difference of two squares, you'll rewrite more quickly.) Simplify, and then solve for x:

$$x(x + y) = (x - y)(x + y)$$
$$x^2 + xy = x^2 - y^2$$
$$xy = -y^2$$
$$x = -y$$

The correct answer is (A).

FUNCTIONS

In a **function** or **functional relationship,** the value of one variable depends upon the value of, or is "a function of," another variable. In mathematics, the relationship is expressed in the form $y = f(x)$—where y is a function of x.

To find the value of the function for any value x, simply substitute the x-value for x wherever it appears in the function. In the following function, for example, the function of 2 is 14, and the function of −3 is 4.

$$f(x) = x^2 + 3x + 4$$
$$f(2) = 2^2 + 3(2) + 4 = 4 + 6 + 4 = 14$$
$$f(-3) = -3^2 + 3(-3) + 4 = 9 - 9 + 4 = 4$$

Determine the function of a variable expression the same way—just substitute the expression for x throughout the function. In the above function, here is how you would find $f(2 + a)$:

$$f(2 + a) = (2 + a)^2 + 3(2 + a) - 4$$
$$= 4 + 4a + a^2 + 6 + 3a - 4$$
$$= a^2 + 7a + 6$$

On the GED® test, a challenging function question might ask to apply the same function twice.

EXAMPLE 16 (EASIER):

If $f(a) = 9$, then for which function does $a = 6$?

(A) $f(a) = 9a$

(B) $f(a) = 3$

(C) $f(a) = a + 3$

(D) $f(a) = \dfrac{2}{3} a$

In each answer choice, substitute 9 for $f(a)$, and substitute 6 for a. Of the four functions listed, only the one in choice (C) holds true: $9 = 6 + 3$. **The correct answer is (C).**

EXAMPLE 17 (MORE CHALLENGING):

If $f(x) = 2x$, then $\dfrac{1}{f(x)} \times f\left(\dfrac{2}{x}\right)$ is equal to which of the following expressions?

(A) $\dfrac{1}{x}$

(B) 1

(C) $\dfrac{x^2}{2}$

(D) $\dfrac{2}{x^2}$

To rewrite the first term, simply substitute $2x$ for $f(x)$. To rewrite the second term, substitute $\frac{2}{x}$ for x in the function $f(x) = 2x$. Then combine the terms by multiplication:

$$\frac{1}{f(x)} \times f\left(\frac{2}{x}\right) = \left(\frac{1}{2x}\right)\left(2 \times \frac{2}{x}\right) = \frac{4}{2x^2} = \frac{2}{x^2}$$

The correct answer is (D).

MEASURES OF CENTRAL TENDENCY (MEAN, MEDIAN, AND RANGE)

Arithmetic mean (simple average), median, and range refer to different ways of describing a set of numbers with just one number. Each measures the *central tendency* of a set of numbers. Here's the definition of each one:

> **Arithmetic mean (simple average):** In a set of n terms, the sum of the terms divided by n.

> **Median:** The middle term in value, or the average (mean) of the two middle terms if the number of terms is even.

> **Range:** The difference in value between the greatest and the least term in a set.

For example, given a set of six numbers {8, –4, 8, 3, 2, and 7}:

> **mean = 4** $\left(\frac{8 - 4 + 8 + 3 + 2 + 7}{6} = \frac{24}{6} = 4\right)$

> **median = 5** (the average of 3 and 7, which are the two middle terms in value: {–4, 2, 3, 7, 8, 8}

> **range = 12** (the difference on the number line between 8 and –4)

The mean and median might be the same, or they might differ from each other (as in the previous example).

GED® test questions involving mean (simple average) usually involve calculating the mean by adding terms together ($a + b + c + \ldots$) and dividing the sum by the number of terms (n):

$$\text{mean} = \frac{(a + b + c + \ldots)}{n}$$

But a question might instead require you to find a missing term when the mean (average) of all the terms is known. To solve this type of problem, plug what you know into the arithmetic-mean formula. Then, use algebra to find the missing number. For example, if the average of 2 and another number (N) is 5, here's how you would find the value of N:

$$5 = \frac{2 + N}{2}$$
$$10 = 2 + N$$
$$8 = N$$

Approach arithmetic-mean problems that involve *variables* (such as *a* and *b*) the same way as those involving only numbers.

EXAMPLE 18 (EASIER):

What is the mean (simple average) of $\frac{1}{5}$, 25%, and 0.09 ?

(A) 0.18

(B) $\frac{1}{4}$

(C) 0.32

(D) $\frac{1}{3}$

Since the answer choices are not all expressed in the same form, first convert numbers into whichever form you think would be easiest to work with when you add the numbers together. In this case, the easiest form to work with is probably the decimal-number form. So, convert the first two numbers into decimal form, and then find the sum of the three numbers:

$$0.20 + 0.25 + 0.09 = 0.54$$

Finally, divide by 3 to find the average:

$$0.54 \div 3 = 0.18$$

The correct answer is (A).

EXAMPLE 19 (MORE CHALLENGING):

If *A* is the average of *P*, *Q*, and another number, which of the following represents the missing number?

(A) $\frac{1}{3}(A + P + Q)$

(B) $3A - P + Q$

(C) $A - P + Q$

(D) $3A - P - Q$

Let *x* = the missing number. Solve for *x* by the arithmetic-mean formula:

$$A = \frac{P + Q + x}{3}$$

$$3A = P + Q + x$$

$$3A - P - Q = x$$

The correct answer is (D).

ARITHMETIC SERIES

In an **arithmetic series** of numbers, there is a constant (unchanging) difference between successive numbers in the series. In other words, all numbers in an arithmetic series are evenly spaced on the number line. All of the following are examples of arithmetic series:

- Successive integers
- Successive even integers
- Successive odd integers
- Successive multiples of the same number
- Successive integers ending in the same digit

On the GED® test, an arithmetic-series question might ask for the *mean* (average) of a series, or it might ask for the *sum*. Since the numbers are evenly spaced, the mean and median of the series are the same. To find the mean, instead of adding all the terms and then dividing, you can find the median or, even easier, compute the average of the least number and the greatest numbers (the endpoints of the series). Faced with calculating the average of a series of evenly-spaced integers, you can shortcut the addition. Study the following examples:

The mean (and median) of all *even* integers 20 through 40 is $\frac{20+40}{2} = \frac{60}{2} = 30$.

The mean (and median) of all integers −11 through 20 is $\frac{-11+20}{2} = \frac{9}{2} = 4\frac{1}{2}$.

The mean (and median) of all positive two-digit numbers ending in the digit 5 is $\frac{15+95}{2} = \frac{110}{2} = 55$.

The mean (and median) of all integers greater than −100 but less than 100 is $\frac{-99+99}{2} = 0$. (The set's negative and positive numbers all cancel out.)

Finding the *sum* of an arithmetic (evenly spaced) series of numbers requires only one additional step: multiplying the average (which is also the median) by the number of terms in the series. When calculating the sum, be careful to count the number of terms in the series correctly. For instance, the number of positive *odd* integers less than 50 is 25, but the number of positive *even* integers less than 50 is only 24.

EXAMPLE 20 (EASIER):

What is the average of the first 20 positive integers?

(A) $7\frac{1}{2}$

(B) $10\frac{1}{2}$

(C) 15

(D) 20

Since the terms are evenly spaced (an arithmetic series), take the average of the first term (1) and the last term (20):

$$\frac{1+20}{2} = \frac{21}{2}, \text{ or } 10\frac{1}{2}$$

The correct answer is (B).

EXAMPLE 21 (MORE CHALLENGING):

What is the sum of all odd integers *between* 10 and 40?

(A) 250

(B) 325

(C) 375

(D) 400

The average of the described numbers is $\frac{11+39}{2} = \frac{50}{2}$, or 25. The number of terms in the series is 15. (The first term is 11, and the last term is 39.) The sum of the described series of integers = $25 \times 15 = 375$. **The correct answer is (C).**

PROBABILITY

Probability refers to the statistical chances, or "odds," of an event occurring (or not occurring). By definition, probability ranges from 0 to 1. Probability is never negative, and it's never greater than 1. Here's the basic formula for determining probability:

$$\text{Probability} = \frac{\text{number of ways the event can occur}}{\text{total number of possible occurrences}}$$

Probability can be expressed as a fraction, a percent, or a decimal number. The greater the probability, the greater the fraction, percent, or decimal number.

Determining Probability (Single Event)

Probability plays an integral role in games of chance, including many casino games. In the throw of a single die, for example, the probability of rolling a 5 is "one in six," or $\frac{1}{6}$, or $16\frac{2}{3}$%. Of course, the probability of rolling a certain other number is the same. A standard deck of 52 playing cards contains 12 face cards. The probability of selecting a face card from a full deck is $\frac{12}{52}$, or $\frac{3}{13}$. The probability of selecting a queen from a full deck is $\frac{4}{52}$, or $\frac{1}{13}$.

To calculate the probability of an event NOT occurring, just *subtract* the probability of the event occurring *from 1.*

EXAMPLE 22 (EASIER):

If you randomly select one candy from a jar containing two cherry candies, two licorice candies, and one peppermint candy, what is the probability of selecting a cherry candy?

(A) $\frac{1}{6}$

(B) $\frac{1}{3}$

(C) $\frac{2}{5}$

(D) $\frac{3}{5}$

There are two ways among five possible occurrences that a cherry candy will be selected. Thus, the probability of selecting a cherry candy is $\frac{2}{5}$. **The correct answer is (C).**

EXAMPLE 23 (MORE CHALLENGING):

A bag of marbles contains twice as many red marbles as blue marbles, and twice as many blue marbles as green marbles. If these are the only colors of marbles in the bag, what is the probability of randomly picking from the bag a marble that is NOT blue?

(A) $\frac{2}{9}$

(B) $\frac{2}{5}$

(C) $\frac{2}{7}$

(D) $\frac{5}{7}$

Regardless of the number of marbles in the bag, the red-blue-green marble ratio is 4:2:1. As you can see, blue marbles account for $\frac{2}{7}$ of the total number of marbles. Thus, the probability of picking a marble that is NOT blue is $1 - \frac{2}{7} = \frac{5}{7}$.

The correct answer is (D).

Determining Probability (Two Events)

To determine probability involving two or more events, it is important to distinguish probabilities involving **independent** events from an event that is **dependent** on another one.

Two events are *independent* if neither event affects the probability that the other will occur. The events may involve the random selection of one object from *each of two or more groups.* Or they may involve the random selection of one object from a group, then *replacing* it and selecting again (as in a "second round" or "another turn" of a game).

In either scenario, to find the probability of two events BOTH occurring, MULTIPLY together their individual probabilities:

probability of event 1 occurring

×

probability of event 2 occurring

=

probability of both events occurring

For example, assume that you randomly select one letter from each of two sets: {A, B} and {C, D, E}. The probability of selecting A and C $= \frac{1}{2} \times \frac{1}{3} = \frac{1}{6}$.

To calculate the probability that two events will *not both* occur, subtract the probability of both events occurring from 1.

Now let's look at *dependent* probability. Two distinct events might be related in that one event affects the probability of the other one occurring—for example, randomly selecting one object from a group, then selecting a second object from the same group *without replacing* the first selection. Removing one object from the group *increases the odds* of selecting any particular object from those that remain.

For example, assume that you randomly select one letter from the set {A, B, C, D}. Then, from the remaining three letters, you select another letter. What is the probability of selecting both A and B? To answer this question, you need to consider each of the two selections separately.

In the first selection, the probability of selecting either A or B is $\frac{2}{4}$. But the probability of selecting the second of the two is $\frac{1}{3}$. Why? Because after the first selection, only *three* letters remain from which to select. Since the question asks for the odds of selecting both A and B (as opposed to either one), multiply the two individual probabilities: $\frac{2}{4} \times \frac{1}{3} = \frac{2}{12}$, or $\frac{1}{6}$.

EXAMPLE 24 (EASIER):

A gaming die is a cube with numbers 1–6 on its faces, each number on a different face. In a roll of two dice, what is the probability that the two numbers facing up will total 12?

(A) $\frac{1}{64}$

(B) $\frac{1}{36}$

(C) $\frac{1}{12}$

(D) $\frac{1}{9}$

The only two-number combination on the dice that can total 12 is 6 + 6. The probability of rolling 6 on each die is $\frac{1}{6}$. Accordingly, the probability of rolling 6 on both die is $\frac{1}{6} \times \frac{1}{6} = \frac{1}{36}$. **The correct answer is (B).**

EXAMPLE 25 (MORE CHALLENGING):

Two pairs of socks are randomly removed from a drawer containing five pairs: two black, two white, and one blue. What is the probability of first removing a black pair and then, without replacement, removing a white pair from the drawer?

(A) $\frac{1}{10}$

(B) $\frac{1}{5}$

(C) $\frac{1}{3}$

(D) $\frac{2}{5}$

When removing the first pair, the probability that the pair removed will be black is $\frac{2}{5}$. Four pairs of socks remain, two of which are white. The probability of removing a white pair of socks from among those four is $\frac{2}{4}$. Combine the two probabilities by multiplying:

$$\frac{2}{5} \times \frac{2}{4} = \frac{4}{20}, \text{ or } \frac{1}{5}$$

The correct answer is (B).

WORD PROBLEMS INVOLVING FORMULAS

Certain types of GED® test word problems call for you to apply a formula. Here are the three types of formulas you can expect to apply during the GED® test:

- Weighted average (based on the formula for arithmetic mean)
- Simple interest (on a monetary investment)
- Rate

The formulas for simple interest and rate will be on the formulas sheet provided during the test.

In the next few pages, you'll learn how to handle these three types of word problems. Remember: for any type of word problem, including these three, you might be able to work backward from the answer choices as well. Even if not, you can often narrow down your choices by estimating the size of the answer.

Weighted-Average Problems

You solve *weighted-average* problems using the arithmetic-mean (simple average) formula, except you give the set's terms different weights. For example, if a final exam score of 90 receives *twice* the weight of each of two mid-term exam scores 75 and 85, think of the final-exam score as *two* scores of 90—and the total number of scores as 4 rather than 3:

$$WA = \frac{75 + 85 + (2)(90)}{4} = \frac{340}{4} = 85$$

Similarly, when some numbers among terms might appear more often than others, you must give them the appropriate "weight" before computing an average. A weighted-average problem might ask you to find the average, or it might provide the weighted average and ask for one of the terms. These questions sometimes require conversion from one unit of measurement to another.

EXAMPLE 26 (EASIER):

During an 8-hour trip, Brigitte drove 3 hours at 55 miles per hour and 5 hours at 65 miles per hour. What was her average rate, in miles per hour, for the entire trip?

(1) 58.5

(2) 60

(3) 61.25

(4) 62.5

Determine the total miles driven: $(3)(55) + (5)(65) = 490$. To determine the average over the entire trip, divide this total by 8, which is the number of total hours: $490 \div 8 = 61.25$. **The correct answer is (C).**

EXAMPLE 27 (MORE CHALLENGING):

A certain olive orchard produces 315 gallons of oil annually, on average, during four consecutive years. How many gallons of oil must the orchard produce annually, on average, during the next six years, if oil production for the entire ten-year period is to meet a goal of 378 gallons per year?

(A) 240

(B) 285

(C) 396

(D) 420

In the weighted-average formula, 315 annual gallons receives a weight of 4, while the average annual number of gallons for the next six years (x) receives a weight of 6:

$$378 = \frac{1260 + 6x}{10}$$
$$3780 = 1260 + 6x$$
$$3780 - 1260 = 6x$$
$$420 = x$$

This solution (420) is the average number of gallons needed per year, on average, during the next six years. **The correct answer is (D).**

Investment Problems

GED® test *investment* problems involve interest earned (at a certain percentage rate) on money over a certain time period (usually a year). To calculate interest earned, multiply the original amount of money by the interest rate:

amount of money × interest rate = amount of interest on money

For example, if you deposit $1000 in a savings account that earns 5% interest annually, the total amount in the account after one year will be $1000 + 0.05($1000) = $1000 + $50 = $1050.

A GED® test investment question might involve more than simply calculating interest earned on a given principal amount at a given rate. It might call for you to set up and solve an algebraic equation. When handling this sort of problem, it's best to eliminate percent signs.

EXAMPLE 28 (EASIER):

Gary wishes to have $2970 in a savings account at the end of the year. How much must Gary deposit in his account at the start of the year if the account pays him 8% interest per year?

(A) $2575

(B) $2732

(C) $2750

(D) $3208

Letting x equal the original amount deposited, set up the following equation: $x + 0.08x = 2970$. Combining terms on the left side of the equation: $1.08x = 2970$. Solve for x:

$$x = \frac{2970}{1.08} = 2750$$

Thus, Gary must invest $2750 at the start of the year to end with $2970. **The correct answer is (C).**

EXAMPLE 29 (MORE CHALLENGING):

Fiona deposits D dollars in a savings account that earns 10% interest per year. At the end of one year, she then deposits the total amount in another savings account, which earns 5% per year.

Which of the following represents the total amount in the account after the two-year period, in dollars?

(A) $1.05D$

(B) $1.155D$

(C) $1.10D$

(D) $1.5D$

The total dollar amount after the first year is $D + 0.10D$, or $1.1D$. Fiona deposits $1.1D$ in an account earning 5%. After one year, her total is $1.1D + 0.05(1.10)D$, which equals $1.10D + 0.055D$, or $1.155D$. **The correct answer is (B).**

Problems Involving Rate

A *rate* is a fraction that expresses a quantity per unit of time. For example, the rate of travel is expressed this way:

$$\text{rate of travel} = \frac{\text{distance}}{\text{time}}$$

Similarly, the rate at which a machine produces a certain product is expressed this way:

$$\text{rate of production} = \frac{\text{number of units produced}}{\text{time}}$$

A GED® test rate question will usually provide two of the three terms, and then it will ask you for the value of the third term. A rate question might also require you to convert a number from one unit of measurement to another.

EXAMPLE 30 (EASIER):

If a printer can print pages at a rate of 15 pages per minute, how many pages can it print in $2\frac{1}{2}$ hours?

(A) 1500

(B) 1750

(C) 2250

(D) 2500

Apply the following formula: $\text{rate} = \frac{\text{\# of pages}}{\text{time}}$. The rate is given in terms of minutes, so convert $2\frac{1}{2}$ hours to 150 minutes. Determine the number of pages by applying the formula to these numbers:

$$15 = \frac{\# \text{ of pages}}{150}$$
$$(15)(150) = \# \text{ of pages}$$
$$2250 = \# \text{ of pages}$$

The correct answer is (C).

EXAMPLE 31 (MORE CHALLENGING):

A passenger train and a freight train leave from the same station at the same time. Over 3 hours, the passenger train travels 45 miles per hour faster, on average, than the freight train.

Which of the following expresses the combined distance the two trains have traveled after 3 hours, where x represents the number of miles the freight train traveled per hour, on average?

(A) $3x + 45$

(B) $6x + 45$

(C) $3x + 120$

(D) $6x + 135$

Since x equals the rate (speed) of the freight train, you can express the rate of the passenger train as $x + 45$. Substitute these values for time and rate into the formula for each train:

Formula: rate × time = distance

Passenger: $(x + 45)(3) = 3x + 135$

Freight: $(x)(3) = 3x$

The combined distance that the two trains covered is $3x + (3x + 135) = 6x + 135$.

The correct answer is (D).

SUMMING IT UP

- For the GED® Mathematical Reasoning Test, be sure to review the following algebra skills: solving a linear equation in one variable, solving a system of two equations in two variables by the substitution method and the addition-subtraction method, recognizing unsolvable equations, handling algebraic inequalities, factoring quadratic expressions, finding the roots of quadratic equations by factoring, handling functions, and solving formula word problems (weighted average, simple interest, and rate).

- Most algebraic equations you'll see on the GED® test are linear. Remember the operations for isolating the unknown on one side of the equation. Solving algebraic inequalities is similar to solving equations: Isolate the variable on one side of the inequality symbol first.

- Weighted-average problems and currency problems can be solved in a similar manner by using the arithmetic mean (simple average) formula.

- Mixture and investment problems on the Mathematical Reasoning Test can be solved using what you've learned about proportion and percentage questions. Rates of production and travel questions can be solved using the strategies you've learned about fraction problems. GED® test *investment* problems involve interest earned (at a certain percentage rate) on money over a certain time period (usually a year).

- A GED® test rate question (*rate* is a fraction that expresses a quantity per unit of time) will usually provide two of the three terms, and then it will ask you for the value of the third term. A rate question might also require you to convert a number from one unit of measurement to another.

Math Review: Geometry

chapter 14

OVERVIEW

- What you'll find in this review
- Congruency and similarity
- Angles
- Triangles
- Quadrilaterals
- Polygons
- Circles
- Three-dimensional (3-D) geometric figures
- Right-triangle trigonometry
- Coordinate geometry
- Summing it up

WHAT YOU'LL FIND IN THIS REVIEW

In this review, you'll examine the areas of geometry covered on the Mathematical Reasoning Test. They include the following:

- Congruency and similarity

- Angles, parallel and perpendicular lines, and transversals

- Two-dimensional figures (triangles, quadrilaterals, polygons, and circles)

- Three-dimensional figures (cubes and other rectangular prisms, cylinders, cones, and square pyramids)

- Basic right-triangle trigonometry

- Coordinate geometry (points, lines, and other figures on the xy-coordinate plane)

The GED® test-style questions throughout this review are multiple-choice questions, as well as tech-enhanced items. The actual exam includes both types of questions.

CONGRUENCY AND SIMILARITY

Two geometric figures that have the same size and shape are said to be **congruent.** The symbol for congruency is $\cong$. Two angles are congruent if their degree measure (size) is the same. Two line segments are congruent if they are equal in length. Two triangles are congruent if the angle measures and sides are all identical in size. (The same applies to figures with more than three sides.)

If a two-dimensional geometric figure, such as a triangle or rectangle, has exactly the same shape as another one, then the two figures are **similar.** Similar figures share the same angle measures, and their sides are proportionate (though not the same length). Look at the figure below.

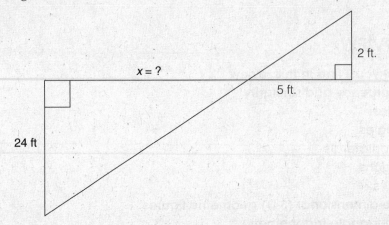

In order to find the length of the corresponding side of the larger triangle, you must set up a proportion. The triangles are similar, and so their sides are in proportion: $\frac{2}{5} = \frac{24}{x}$. To solve the proportion, cross multiply: $2x = 120$. Then, to find x, divide 120 by 2: $120 \div 2 = 60$. The unknown side is 60 feet in length. (You'll examine triangles in greater detail later in this review.)

ANGLES

Angles are indicated by the angle symbol ($\angle$). They are measured in degrees (°). The letter "m" is used to indicate the measure of an angle. The line that extends in only one direction from a point is called a **ray.** Lines, rays, or line segments meet at a point called the **vertex.** Angles are usually named by letters, as in the below figure.

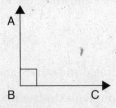

The name of the above angle is m $\angle ABC$. This angle is called a **right angle** because m $\angle ABC = 90°$. The small square drawn in the angle indicates that it is a right angle. When two lines meet to form a right angle, they are said to be **perpendicular** to each other, as indicated by the symbol $\perp$. In the above figure, $\overrightarrow{BA} \perp \overrightarrow{BC}$.

An angle that measures less than 90° is called an **acute** angle. $\angle VWX$ in the following figure is an acute angle. An angle that measures more than 90° but less than 180°, is called an **obtuse** angle. $\angle EFG$ in the following figure is an obtuse angle:

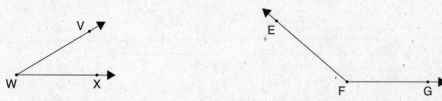

A **straight angle** measures 180°. ∠ *XYZ* below is a straight angle. Two or more angles whose measures add up to 180° are called **supplementary.** In the next figure, ∠ *DEG* forms a straight line and therefore measures 180°. ∠ *DEF* and ∠ *FEG* are supplementary angles; their measures add up to 180°.

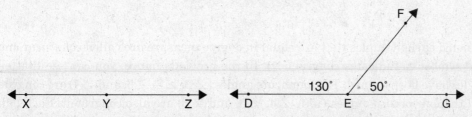

Two angles are called **complementary** angles when their measurements add up to 90° (a right angle). In the next figure, m∠ *ABC* = 90°. ∠ *ABE* and ∠ *CBE* are complementary because their measurements add up to 90°. You also know that m∠ *ABD* = 90° because ∠ *ABD* and ∠ *ABC* combine to form a straight line, which measures 180°.

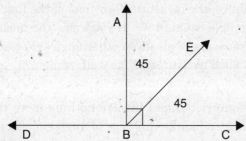

In geometry, the set of points that makes up a flat surface is referred to as a **plane.** When two lines in the same plane never meet, no matter how far they are extended, they are called **parallel lines** and are indicated by the symbol ‖. If two parallel lines are intersected by a third line, eight angles are formed. The line that intersects two parallel lines is called the **transversal.** If a transversal intersects two parallel lines perpendicularly (at a 90° angle), all eight angles that are formed are right angles (90°). Otherwise, some angles are acute, while others are obtuse. Look at the next figure.

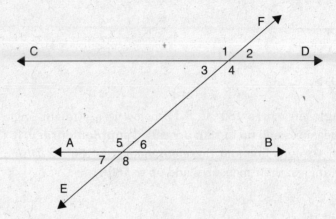

As noted earlier, angles that are equal in degree measure are called *congruent* angles (the symbol ≅ indicates congruency). In the previous figure, you can see that eight angles have been formed. The four acute angles (∠2, ∠3, ∠6, and ∠7) are congruent, and the four obtuse angles (∠1, ∠4, ∠5, and ∠8) are also congruent. Each pair of angles that are opposite each other in relation to a vertex (for example, ∠2 and ∠3) are called **vertical angles.** Vertical angles are always congruent.

Four angles formed by two intersecting lines add up to 360° in measure. In the preceding figure, m∠1 + m∠2 + m∠3 + m∠4 = 360°. (The same holds true for angles 5, 6, 7, and 8.) In the figure, the measure of any one of the four acute angles plus the measure of any obtuse angle equals 180°. If you know the measure of *any* one angle, you can determine the measure of all seven other angles. For example, if m∠2 = 30°, then ∠3, ∠6, and ∠7 each measures 30° as well, while ∠1, ∠4, ∠5, and ∠8 each measures 150°.

A GED® test geometry question might involve nothing more than intersecting lines and the angles they form. To handle this type of question, remember four basic rules about angles formed by intersecting lines:

❶ Vertical angles (angles across the vertex from each other and formed by the same two lines) are equal in degree measure, or congruent (≅). In other words, they're the same size.

❷ If adjacent angles combine to form a straight line, their degree measures total 180. In fact, a straight line is actually a 180° angle.

❸ If two lines are perpendicular (⊥) to each other, they intersect at right (90°) angles.

❹ The sum of all angles formed by the intersection of two (or more) lines at the same point is 360°, regardless of how many angles are involved.

EXAMPLE 1 (EASIER):

The figure below shows three intersecting lines.

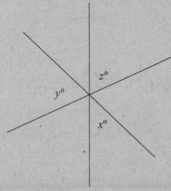

Which of the following expresses the value of $x + y$ in every case?

(A) $2z$

(B) $180 - z$

(C) $360 - z$

(D) $z + 90$

The angle vertical to the one whose measure is given as $z°$ must also measure $z°$. That angle and the angles whose measures are $x°$ and $y°$ combine to form a straight (180°) line. In other words, $x + y + z = 180$. Accordingly, $x + y = 180 - z$. **The correct answer is (B).**

EXAMPLE 2 (MORE CHALLENGING):

Line R intersects line P and line Q at a 45° angle. Which statement must be true?

(A) Line P is parallel to line Q.

(B) Line P intersects line Q at a 45° angle.

(C) Line P is perpendicular to line Q.

(D) Line Q intersects line R at a 135° angle.

Lines P and Q may or may not be parallel. But any two lines intersecting at a 45° angle also form a 135° at the vertex because adjacent angles combine to form a straight, 180° line. **The correct answer is (D).**

TRIANGLES

The **triangle** is a 3-sided shape. All triangles, regardless of shape or size, share the following four properties:

❶ **Length of the sides.** Each side is shorter than the sum of the lengths of the other two sides. (Otherwise, the triangle would collapse into a line.)

2 **Angle measures.** The measures of the three interior angles total 180°.

3 **Angles and opposite sides.** Comparative angle sizes correspond to the comparative lengths of the sides opposite those angles. For example, a triangle's largest angle is opposite its longest side. (The sides opposite two congruent angles are also congruent.)

4 **Area.** The area of any triangle is equal to one-half the product of its base and its height (or "altitude"): Area = $\frac{1}{2}$ × base × height. You can use any side as the base to calculate area.

The area formula for a triangle is NOT included on the Formula Sheet provided during the test.

The next figure shows three particular types of triangles. GED® test questions often involve these three types.

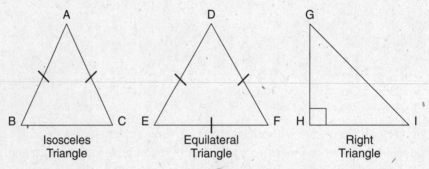

An **isosceles triangle** is one in which two sides (and two angles) are congruent. In the above figure, ∠B and ∠C are congruent, and the sides opposite those two angles, $\overline{AB}$ and $\overline{AC}$, are congruent. In an **equilateral triangle,** all three angles are congruent, and all three sides are congruent. In a **right triangle,** one angle is a right angle, and the other two angles are acute angles. The longest side of a right triangle (in this case, $\overline{GI}$) is called the **hypotenuse.** In the pages ahead, you'll examine each of these three types of triangles in greater detail.

EXAMPLE 3 (EASIER):

The length of one side of a certain triangular floor space is 12 feet. Which of the following CANNOT be the lengths of the other two sides?

   (A) 1 foot and 12 feet

   (B) 8 feet and 4 feet

   (C) 12 feet and 13 feet

   (D) 16 feet and 14 feet

The length of any two sides combined must be greater than the length of the third side. **The correct answer is (B).**

EXAMPLE 4 (MORE CHALLENGING):

In triangle T, the degree measure of one interior angle is three times that of *each* of the other two interior angles. What is the measure of triangle T's largest interior angle?

(A) 72°

(B) 90°

(C) 108°

(D) 120°

The ratio among the three angles is 3:1:1. Letting x = the length of either short side:

$$x + x + 3x = 180$$
$$5x = 180$$
$$x = 36$$

The largest angle measures $3 \times 36 = 108°$. **The correct answer is (C).**

Right Triangles and the Pythagorean Theorem

In a right triangle, one angle measures 90° and, of course, each of the other two angles measures less than 90°. The **Pythagorean theorem** involves the relationship among the sides of any right triangle and can be expressed by the equation $a^2 + b^2 = c^2$. As shown in the next figure, the letters a and b represent the lengths of the two **legs** (the two shortest sides) that form the right angle, and c is the length of the hypotenuse (the longest side, opposite the right angle).

Pythagorean theorem: $a^2 + b^2 = c^2$

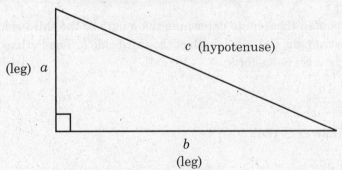

The Pythagorean theorem is included on the Formula Sheet provided during the test.

For any right triangle, if you know the length of two sides, you can determine the length of the third side by applying the Pythagorean theorem. Study the following two examples:

If the two shortest sides (the legs) of a right triangle are 2 and 3 inches in length, then the length of the triangle's third side (the hypotenuse) is $\sqrt{13}$ inches:

$$a^2 + b^2 = c^2$$
$$2^2 + 3^2 = c^2$$
$$4 + 9 = c^2$$
$$13 = c^2$$
$$\sqrt{13} = c$$

If a right triangle's longest side (hypotenuse) is 4 inches in length, and if another side (one of the legs) is 2 inches in length, then the length of the third side (the other leg) is $\sqrt{12}$ inches:

$$a^2 + b^2 = c^2$$
$$a^2 + 2^2 = 4^2$$
$$a^2 + 4 = 16$$
$$a^2 = 12$$
$$a = \sqrt{12}$$

EXAMPLE 5 (EASIER):

In a right triangle, one angle measures 90°. If the hypotenuse of a right triangle is c and one leg of the triangle is a, what is the length of the third side in terms of a and c?

(A) $\sqrt{a^2 + c^2}$

(B) $\dfrac{a + c}{2}$

(C) $\sqrt{a \times c}$

(D) $\sqrt{c^2 - a^2}$

Use the Pythagorean theorem to determine the length of the third side, which is the other leg of the triangle. Call the length of the third side b. The Pythagorean theorem says that $a^2 + b^2 = c^2$. Solve for b:

$$b^2 = c^2 - a^2$$
$$b = \sqrt{c^2 - a^2}$$

The correct answer is (D).

EXAMPLE 6 (MORE CHALLENGING):

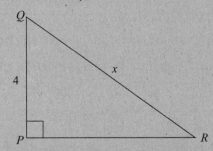

Which of the following expresses the unit length of $\overline{PR}$ in the above figure?

(A) $\sqrt{x^2 - 4}$

(B) $\sqrt{x + 16}$

(C) $x - 4$

(D) $\sqrt{x^2 - 16}$

The question asks for the length of leg $\overline{PR}$ in terms of the other two sides. Apply the Pythagorean theorem (let y = the length of $\overline{PR}$):

$$4^2 + y^2 = x^2$$
$$16 + y^2 = x^2$$
$$y^2 = x^2 - 16$$
$$y = \sqrt{x^2 - 16}$$

The correct answer is (D).

Pythagorean Side Triplets

A Pythagorean side triplet is a specific side ratio that satisfies the Pythagorean theorem. In each of the following triplets, the first two numbers represent the ratio between the lengths of the two legs (a and b), and the third, and largest, number represents the length of the hypotenuse (c) in relation to the two legs:

Side ratio	Pythagorean theorem
$(a{:}b{:}c)$	$(a^2 + b^2 = c^2)$
$1{:}1{:}\sqrt{2}$	$1^2 + 1^2 = (\sqrt{2})^2$
$1{:}\sqrt{3}{:}2$	$1^2 + (\sqrt{3})^2 = 2^2$
$3{:}4{:}5$	$3^2 + 4^2 = 5^2$
$5{:}12{:}13$	$5^2 + 12^2 = 13^2$
$8{:}15{:}17$	$8^2 + 15^2 = 17^2$
$7{:}24{:}25$	$7^2 + 24^2 = 25^2$

Each triplet above is expressed as a *ratio* because it represents a proportion among the triangle's sides. All right triangles with sides having the same proportion, or ratio, have the same shape. For example, a right triangle with sides of 5, 12, and 13 is smaller but exactly the same shape (proportion) as a triangle with sides of 15, 36, and 39.

To save valuable time on GED® test right-triangle problems, learn to recognize numbers (lengths of triangle sides) that are multiples of Pythagorean side triplets.

EXAMPLE 7 (EASIER):

Which of the following does NOT describe a right triangle?

A triangle with sides

(A) 3 inches, 4 inches, and 5 inches

(B) 5 inches, 12 inches, and 13 inches

(C) 10 inches, 24 inches, and 26 inches

(D) 6 inches, 10 inches, and 20 inches

Choice (A) describes a 3:4:5 triangle. Choices (B) and (C) describe 5:12:13 triangles. Choice (D) does not describe a right triangle ($6^2 + 10^2 \neq 20^2$). In fact, since the sum of the two sides (6 inches + 10 inches) is not greater in length than the third side (20 inches), this isn't even a triangle at all. **The correct answer is (D).**

EXAMPLE 8 (MORE CHALLENGING):

Two boats leave the same dock at the same time, one traveling due west at 30 miles per hour and the other due north at 40 miles per hour. If they maintain those speeds, how far apart are the boats after three hours?

(A) 90 miles

(B) 120 miles

(C) 150 miles

(D) 210 miles

The distance between the two boats after three hours forms the hypotenuse of a triangle in which the legs are the two boats' respective paths. The ratio of one leg to the other is 30:40, or 3:4. So you know you're dealing with a 3:4:5 triangle. The slower boat traveled 90 miles (30 mph × 3 hours). 90 corresponds to the number 3 in the 3:4:5 ratio, so the multiple is 30 (3 × 30 = 90). 3:4:5 = 90:120:150. **The correct answer is (C).**

Pythagorean Angle Triplets

In two (and only two) of the unique triangles identified in the preceding section as Pythagorean side triplets, all degree measures are *integers:*

The angles of a $1:1:\sqrt{2}$ triangle are 45°, 45°, and 90°.

The angles of a $1:\sqrt{3}:2$ triangle are 30°, 60°, and 90°.

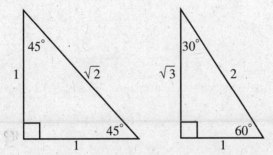

If one acute angle of a right triangle is given as 45°, and you know the length of one side, then you can find the lengths of the other sides. For example:

If one leg is 5, then the other leg must also be 5, while the hypotenuse must be $5\sqrt{2}$.

If the hypotenuse is 10, then each leg must be $\dfrac{10}{\sqrt{2}} = \dfrac{10}{\sqrt{2}} \times \dfrac{\sqrt{2}}{\sqrt{2}} = 5\sqrt{2}$ (divide hypotenuse by $\sqrt{2}$ and clear the radical from the denominator).

Similarly, if you know that one acute angle of a right triangle is either 30° or 60°, then given the length of any side you can find the lengths of the other sides. For example:

If the shortest leg (opposite the 30° angle) is 3, then the other leg (opposite the 60° angle) must be $3\sqrt{3}$, and the hypotenuse must be 6 units long (3×2).

If the hypotenuse is 10, then the shorter leg (opposite the 30° angle) must be 5, and the longer leg (opposite the 60° angle) must be $5\sqrt{3}$ (the length of the shorter leg multiplied by $\sqrt{3}$).

To save time on GED® test right-triangle problems, be on the lookout for either of the two Pythagorean angle triplets.

EXAMPLE 9 (EASIER):

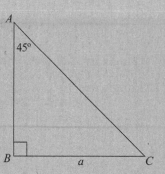

Which of the following expresses the length of $\overline{AC}$ in the above figure?

(A) $2a$

(B) $a\sqrt{2}$

(C) $a\sqrt{3}$

(D) $2\sqrt{a}$

The 45° angle tells you that $\overline{AB}$ and $\overline{BC}$ are congruent (equal in length). So the ratio of the three sides is $1{:}1{:}\sqrt{2}$. Given that each leg has a length of a, the ratio is $a:a:a\sqrt{2}$. **The correct answer is (B).**

EXAMPLE 10 (MORE CHALLENGING):

As shown in the figure below, $\overline{AC}$ is 5 units in length, m$\angle ABD = 45°$, and m$\angle DAC = 60°$.

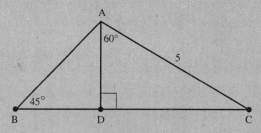

What is the unit length of $\overline{BD}$?

(A) $2\sqrt{2}$

(B) $\dfrac{5}{2}$

(C) $\dfrac{7}{2}$

(D) $\dfrac{7}{3}$

To find the length of $\overline{BD}$, you first need to find the length of $\overline{AD}$. Notice that $\triangle ADC$ is a 30°-60°-90° triangle. The ratio among its sides is $1{:}\sqrt{3}{:}2$. Given that $\overline{AC}$ is 5, $\overline{AD}$

must be $\frac{5}{2}$. (The ratio 1:2 is equivalent to a ratio of $\frac{5}{2}$ to 5.) Next, notice that $\triangle ABD$ is a 45°-45°-90° triangle. The ratio among its sides is $1:1:\sqrt{2}$. You know that $\overline{AD}$ is $\frac{5}{2}$ units in length. Thus, $\overline{BD}$ must also be $\frac{5}{2}$ units in length. **The correct answer is (B).**

Isosceles and Equilateral Triangles

An *isosceles* triangle has the following special properties:

1 Two of the sides are congruent (equal in length).

2 The two angles opposite the two congruent sides are congruent (equal in size or degree measure).

If you know any *two* angle measures of a triangle, you can determine whether the triangle is isosceles. Subtract the two angle measures you know from 180. If the result equals one of the other two measures, then the triangle is isosceles. For example:

> If two of the angles are 55° and 70°, then the third angle must be 55° (180 – 55 – 70 = 55). The triangle is isosceles, and the two sides opposite the two 55° angles are congruent.

> If two of the angles are 80° and 20°, then the third angle must be 80° (180 – 80 – 20 = 80). The triangle is isosceles, and the two sides opposite the two 80° angles are congruent.

In any isosceles triangle, lines bisecting the triangle's three angles each bisect its opposite side. The line bisecting the angle connecting the two congruent angles divides the triangle into two congruent right triangles.

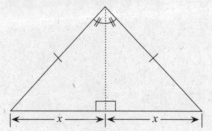

So, if you know the lengths of all three sides of an isosceles triangle, you can determine the area of the triangle by applying the Pythagorean theorem.

All **equilateral triangles** share the following three properties:

1 All three sides are congruent (equal in length).

2 The measure of each angle is 60°.

3 Area $= \dfrac{s^2\sqrt{3}}{4}$ (s = any side)

The area formula for an equilateral triangle will NOT appear on the Formula Sheet provided during the exam. If you need to find an equilateral triangle's area but don't recall the formula, you can bisect the triangle and combine the two smaller areas. As shown below, any line bisecting one of the 60° angles divides an equilateral triangle into two right triangles with angle measures of 30°, 60°, and 90° (one of the two Pythagorean angle triplets). Accordingly, the side ratio for each smaller triangle is $1:\sqrt{3}:2$. The area of this equilateral triangle is $\frac{1}{2}(2)\sqrt{3}$, or $\sqrt{3}$.

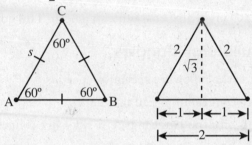

On the GED® test, equilateral triangles often appear in problems involving *circles*, which you'll examine later in this review.

EXAMPLE 11 (EASIER):

As shown in the figure, $\overline{BC}$ is 6 units in length, m$\angle A = 70°$, and m$\angle B = 40°$.

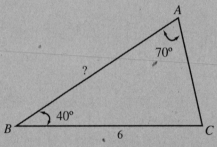

What is the unit length of $\overline{AB}$?

(A) 5

(B) 6

(C) 7

(D) $5\sqrt{2}$

Since m$\angle A$ and m$\angle B$ add up to 110°, m$\angle C = 70°$ (70 + 110 = 180), and you know the triangle is isosceles. Since m$\angle A = $ m$\angle C$, $\overline{AB} \cong \overline{BC}$. Given that $\overline{BC}$ is 6 units in length, $\overline{AB}$ must also be 6 units in length. **The correct answer is (B).**

EXAMPLE 12 (MORE CHALLENGING):

Two sides of a triangle are each 8 units in length, and the third side is 6 units in length. What is the area of the triangle, expressed in square units?

(A) 14

(B) $12\sqrt{3}$

(C) 18

(D) $3\sqrt{55}$

Bisect the angle connecting the two congruent sides ($\overline{BC}$ and $\overline{AC}$ in $\triangle ABC$ below). The bisecting line is the triangle's height (h), and $\overline{AB}$ is its base, which is 6 units long.

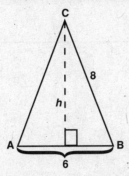

You can determine the triangle's height (h) by applying the Pythagorean theorem:

$$3^2 + h^2 = 8^2$$
$$h^2 = 64 - 9$$
$$h^2 = 55$$
$$h = \sqrt{55}$$

A triangle's area is half the product of its base and height. Thus, the area of $\triangle ABC = \frac{1}{2}(6)\sqrt{55} = 3\sqrt{55}$. **The correct answer is (D).**

QUADRILATERALS

A **quadrilateral** is any four-sided figure. The GED® test emphasizes four specific types of quadrilaterals: the square, the rectangle, the parallelogram, and the trapezoid.

Rectangles, Squares, and Parallelograms

A **parallelogram** is a quadrilateral in which opposite sides are parallel. A **rectangle** is a special type of parallelogram in which all four angles are right angles (90°). A **square** is a special type of rectangle in which all four sides are congruent (equal in length). Certain characteristics apply to all rectangles, squares, and parallelograms:

- The sum of the measures of all four interior angles is 360°.

- Opposite sides are parallel.

- Opposite sides are congruent (equal in length).

- Opposite angles are congruent (the same size, or equal in degree measure).

- Adjacent angles are supplementary (their measures total 180°).

For the GED® test, you should know how to determine the perimeter and area of each of these three types of quadrilaterals.

The Square

To find the perimeter of a square, multiply any side by 4. To find area, simply square any side.

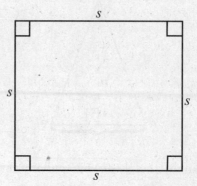

Perimeter = 4s [s = side]

Area = s^2

These formulas are NOT included on the Formula Sheet provided during the test.

GED® test questions involving squares come in many varieties. For example, you might need to determine an area based on a perimeter, or you might need to do just the opposite—find a perimeter based on a given area. For example:

The area of a square with a perimeter of 8 is 4.

$s = 8 \div 4 = 2; s^2 = 4$

The perimeter of a square with area 8 is $8\sqrt{2}$.

$s = \sqrt{8} = 2\sqrt{2}; 4s = 4 \times 2\sqrt{2}$

Or, you might need to determine a change in area resulting from a change in perimeter (or vice versa). These are just some of the possibilities.

EXAMPLE 13 (EASIER):

Nine square tiles, each with an area of 25 square centimeters, have been arranged to form a larger square. What is the perimeter of the large square?

(A) 60 centimeters

(B) 100 centimeters

(C) 150 centimeters

(D) 225 centimeters

The side of each square = $\sqrt{25}$ or 5 cm. Aligned to form a large square, the tiles form three rows and three columns, each column and row with side 5 × 3 = 15. The perimeter = 15 × 4 = 60. **The correct answer is (A).**

EXAMPLE 14 (MORE CHALLENGING):

If a square's sides are each increased by 50%, by what percent does the square's area increase?

(A) 100%

(B) 125%

(C) 150%

(D) 200%

The easiest way to answer this question is to plug in simple numbers. Assume that the square's original side length is 1. Its area is also 1. Increase the side length to 1.5, and then square it to find the new area: $1.5 \times 1.5 = 2.25$. Comparing 1 to 2.25, the percent increase is 125%. You can also solve the problem conventionally. Letting $s =$ the length of each side before the increase, area $= s^2$. Let $\frac{3}{2}s =$ the length of each side after the increase, the new area $= \left(\frac{3}{2}s\right)^2 = \frac{9}{4}s^2$. The increase from s^2 to $\frac{9}{4}s^2$ is $\frac{5}{4}$, or 125%.

The correct answer is (B).

The Rectangle

To find the perimeter of a rectangle, multiply width by 2, and multiply length by 2, and then add the two products. To find area, multiply length by width.

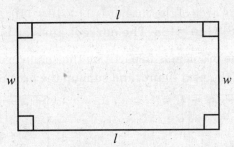

Perimeter $= 2l + 2w$

Area $= l \times w$

Neither of these formulas is included on the Formula Sheet provided during the test.

GED® test questions involving non-square rectangles also come in many possible varieties. For example, a question might ask you to determine area based on perimeter, or vice versa. Or, a question might require you to determine a combined perimeter or area of adjoining rectangles.

EXAMPLE 15 (EASIER):

In the figure below, all intersecting line segments are perpendicular.

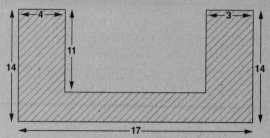

What is the area of the shaded region, in square units?

(A) 84

(B) 118

(C) 128

(D) 238

The figure provides the perimeters you need to calculate the area. One way to find the area of the shaded region is to consider it as what remains when a rectangular shape is cut out of a larger rectangle. The area of the entire figure without the "cut-out" is $14 \times 17 = 238$. The "cut-out" rectangle has a length of 11, and its width is equal to $17 - 4 - 3 = 10$. Thus, the area of the cut-out is $11 \times 10 = 110$. Accordingly, the area of the shaded region is $238 - 110 = 128$. **The correct answer is (C).**

Another way to solve the problem is to partition the shaded region into three smaller rectangles, as shown in the next figure, and sum up the area of each.

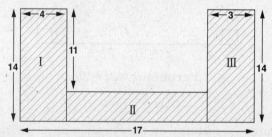

EXAMPLE 16 (MORE CHALLENGING):

The length of a rectangular closet with area 12 square meters is three times the closet's width. What is the perimeter of the closet?

(A) 10 meters

(B) 12 meters

(C) 14 meters

(D) 16 meters

The ratio of length to width is 3:1. The ratio 6:2 is equivalent, and $6 \times 2 = 12$ (the area). Thus, the perimeter $= (2)(6) + (2)(2) = 16$. **The correct answer is (C).**

The Parallelogram

To find the perimeter of a parallelogram, multiply the width by 2, multiply the length by 2, and then add the two products. To find area, multiply the base by the **altitude,** which is the parallelogram's *height*, not the length of any side.

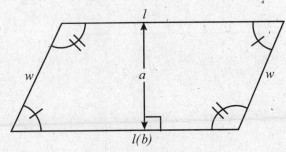

Perimeter $= 2l + 2w$

Area $=$ base $(b) \times$ altitude (a)

Of these two formulas, *only* the area formula is included on the Formula Sheet provided during the test.

A GED® test question about a non-rectangular parallelogram might focus on angle measures. These questions are easy to answer. In any parallelogram, opposite angles are congruent, and adjacent angles are supplementary. (Their measures total 180°.) So, if one of a parallelogram's angles measures 65°, then the opposite angle must also measure 65°, while the two other angles each measures 115°.

A more difficult question about a non-rectangular parallelogram might focus on area. To determine the parallelogram's altitude, you might need to apply the Pythagorean theorem (or one of the side or angle triplets).

EXAMPLE 17 (EASIER):

If one of a parallelogram's interior angles measures $a°$, which of the following expresses the combined measures of its two adjacent angles?

    (A) $2a + 90$

    (B) $180 - a$

    (C) $180 + a$

    (D) $360 - 2a$

$\angle a$ is supplementary to both its adjacent angles. Thus, the degree measure of each adjacent angle $= 180 - a$. Express their sum by adding: $(180 - a) + (180 - a) = 360 - 2a$. **The correct answer is (D).**

EXAMPLE 18 (MORE CHALLENGING):

In the figure below, $\overline{AB} \parallel \overline{CD}$, $\overline{AD} \parallel \overline{BC}$, and m $\angle B = 45°$.

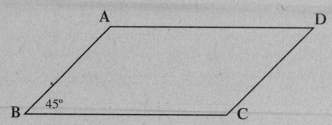

If $\overline{BC}$ is 4 units in length and $\overline{CD}$ is 2 units in length, what is the area of quadrilateral $ABCD$?

(A) $4\sqrt{2}$

(B) 6

(C) 8

(D) $6\sqrt{2}$

Since $ABCD$ is a parallelogram, its area = base (4) × altitude. To determine altitude (a), draw a vertical line segment connecting point A to $\overline{BC}$, which creates a 45°-45°-90° triangle.

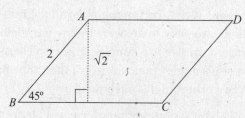

The ratio of the triangle's hypotenuse to each leg is $\sqrt{2}$:1. The hypotenuse $\overline{AB} = 2$. Thus, the altitude (a) of $ABCD$ is $\dfrac{2}{\sqrt{2}}$, or $\sqrt{2}$. Accordingly, the area of $ABCD = 4 \times \sqrt{2}$, or $4\sqrt{2}$. **The correct answer is (A).**

Trapezoids

A **trapezoid** is a quadrilateral with only one pair of parallel sides. All trapezoids share these four properties:

1 Only one pair of opposite sides is parallel.

2 The sum of all four angles is 360°.

3 Perimeter = the sum of the four sides.

4 Area = half the sum of the two parallel sides, multiplied by the altitude (a).

The next figure shows a trapezoid in which $\overline{BC} \parallel \overline{AD}$.

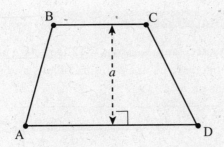

$$\text{Perimeter} = \overline{AB} + \overline{BC} + \overline{CD} + \overline{AD}$$

$$\text{Area} = \frac{\overline{BC} + \overline{AD}}{2} \times a$$

The area formula for a trapezoid is included on the Formula Sheet provided during the test.

GED® test trapezoid problems generally provide all but one of the values in the area formula, and then ask for the missing value.

EXAMPLE 19 (EASIER):

A metal sheet the shape of a trapezoid is to be assembled from a square piece and a triangular piece, as shown below.

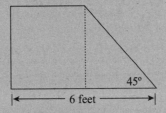

What is the area of the assembled product?

    (A) 12 square feet

    (B) $13\frac{1}{2}$ square feet

    (C) 15 square feet

    (D) $17\frac{1}{2}$ square feet

To answer this question, you don't need to apply the area formula. The 45° angle tells you that the triangle's two legs are the same length, which is also the height of the square. Since the two pieces together run 6 feet in length, each piece is half that length. Thus the altitude (dotted line) is 3. The area of the square = $3^2 = 9$. The area of the triangle $= \frac{1}{2} \times 3^2 = \frac{9}{2}$. The combined area is $13\frac{1}{2}$ square feet. **The correct answer is (B).**

EXAMPLE 20 (MORE CHALLENGING):

To cover the floor of an entry hall, a 1-foot × 12-foot strip of carpet is cut into two pieces, shown as the shaded strips in the figure below, and each piece is connected to a third carpet piece, as shown.

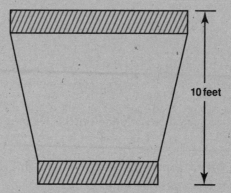

If the 1-foot strips run parallel to each other, what is the total area of the carpeted floor?

(A) 48 square feet

(B) 52.5 square feet

(C) 56 square feet

(D) 60 square feet

The altitude of the trapezoidal piece is 8. The sum of the two parallel sides of this piece is 12' (the length of the 1' × 12' strip before it was cut). You can apply the trapezoid formula to determine the area of this piece:

$$A = 8 \times \frac{12}{2} = 48$$

The total area of the two shaded strips is 12 square feet, so the total area of the floor is 60 square feet. **The correct answer is (D).**

POLYGONS

Polygons include all two-dimensional figures formed only by line segments. For the GED® test, the two most important points about polygons to remember are these two reciprocal rules:

1. If all angles of a polygon are congruent (equal in degree measure), then all sides are congruent (equal in length).

2. If all sides of a polygon are congruent (equal in length), then all angles are congruent (equal in degree measure).

A polygon in which all sides are congruent and all angles are congruent is called a **regular polygon.**

You can use the following formula to determine the sum of all interior angles of *any* polygon whose angles each measure less than 180° (n = number of sides):

$(n - 2)(180°)$ = sum of interior angles

This formula is NOT included on the Formula Sheet provided during the test. The test question will provide the formula if needed.

For *regular* polygons, the average angle size is also the size of every angle. But for *any* polygon (except for those with an angle exceeding 180°), you can find the average angle size by dividing the sum of the angles by the number of sides. One way to shortcut the math is to memorize the angle sums and averages for polygons with three to eight sides:

3 sides: $(3 - 2)(180°) = 180° \div 3 = 60°$

4 sides: $(4 - 2)(180°) = 360° \div 4 = 90°$

5 sides: $(5 - 2)(180°) = 540° \div 5 = 108°$

6 sides: $(6 - 2)(180°) = 720° \div 6 = 120°$

7 sides: $(7 - 2)(180°) = 900° \div 7 = 129°$

8 sides: $(8 - 2)(180°) = 1080° \div 8 = 135°$

You can add up known angle measures to find unknown angle measures.

EXAMPLE 21 (EASIER):

The measures of a polygon's interior angles total $(n - 2)(180°)$, where n = number of sides. If four of the interior angles of a five-sided polygon measure 100° each, what is the measure of the fifth interior angle?

(A) 40°

(B) 60°

(C) 90°

(D) 140°

The total number of degrees in the polygon = $(5 - 2)(180°) = 540°$. The four known angles total 400°, and so the fifth angle must be 140°. **The correct answer is (D).**

EXAMPLE 22 (MORE CHALLENGING):

The regular octagon pictured below is 12 inches on each side and has been divided into 9 smaller pieces.

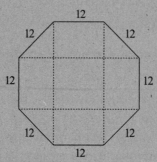

Which of the following most nearly approximates the area of the octagon?

(A) 660 square inches

(B) 790 square inches

(C) 860 square inches

(D) 1000 square inches

The center segment, a square, is 12 inches on each side and thus has an area of 144 square inches. Each of the four triangles is an isosceles right triangle, with the hypotenuse given as 12 inches. The ratio of the hypotenuse's length to the length of each leg is $\sqrt{2}:1$. To determine the length of each base, divide 12 by $\sqrt{2}$. Using 1.4 as an approximate value for $\sqrt{2}$, the length of each base is approximately 8 inches. The approximate area of each triangle $= \frac{1}{2}(8)(8) = 32$ square inches. The approximate area of each of the four non-square rectangles is $8 \times 12 = 96$. Combine the approximate areas of the octagon's nine pieces:

$$144 + 4(32) + 4(96) = 144 + 128 + 384$$

$$= 656 \text{ square inches}$$

Since the question asks for the closest approximation, the correct answer would then be choice (A), 670 square inches. **The correct answer is (A).**

CIRCLES

For the GED® test, you should be familiar with the following basic terminology involving circles:

- **circumference:** the distance around the circle (its "perimeter")

- **radius:** the distance from a circle's center to any point along the circle's circumference

- **diameter:** the greatest distance from one point to another on the circle's circumference (twice the length of the radius)

- **chord:** a line segment connecting two points on the circle's circumference (a circle's longest possible chord is its diameter, passing through the circle's center)

As noted above, a circle's diameter is twice the length of its radius. The next figure shows a circle with radius 6 and diameter 12.

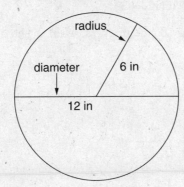

During the GED® test, you'll apply one, or possibly both, of two basic formulas involving circles (r = radius, d = diameter):

Circumference = $2\pi r$, or πd

Area = πr^2

Neither of these formulas is included on the Formula Sheet provided during the test. The value of π is approximately 3.14. A close fractional approximation of π is $\frac{22}{7}$.

With the circumference and area formulas, all you need is one value—area, circumference, diameter, or radius—and you can determine all the others. Referring to the circle shown above:

Given a circle with a diameter of 12:

radius = 6

circumference = 12π

area = $\pi(6)^2 = 36\pi$

For the GED® test, you won't need to work with a value of π any more precise than 3.14 or $\frac{22}{7}$. In fact, you might be able to answer a circle question using the symbol π itself, without approximating its value.

EXAMPLE 23 (EASIER):

If a circle with radius r has an area of 4 square feet, what is the area of a circle whose radius is $3r$?

(A) 6π square feet

(B) 36 square feet

(C) 12π square feet

(D) 48 square feet

The area of a circle with radius $r = \pi r^2$, which is given as 4. The area of a circle with radius $3r = \pi(3r)^2 = 9\pi r^2$. Since $\pi r^2 = 4$, the area of a circle with radius $3r = (9)(4) = 36$. **The correct answer is (B).**

EXAMPLE 24 (MORE CHALLENGING):

If a circle's circumference is 10 centimeters, what is the area of the circle?

(A) $\dfrac{25}{\pi}$ cm^2

(B) 5π cm^2

(C) 22.5 cm^2

(D) 25 cm^2

First, determine the circle's radius. Applying the circumference formula $C = 2\pi r$, solve for r:

$$10 = 2\pi r$$

$$\frac{5}{\pi} = r$$

Then, apply the area formula, with $\dfrac{5}{\pi}$ as the value of r:

$$A = \pi \left(\frac{5}{\pi}\right)^2$$

$$= \pi \left(\frac{25}{\pi^2}\right)$$

$$= \frac{25}{\pi^2} \cdot \frac{\pi}{1}$$

$$= \frac{25}{\pi}$$

The correct answer is (A).

Arcs and Degree Measures of a Circle

An **arc** is a segment of a circle's circumference. A **minor arc** is the shortest arc connecting two points on a circle's circumference. For example, in the next figure, minor arc $\overset{\frown}{AB}$ is the one formed by the 60° angle from the circle's center (O).

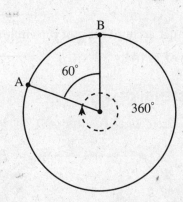

A circle, by definition, contains a total of 360°. The length of an arc relative to the circle's circumference is directly proportionate to the arc's degree measure as a fraction of the circle's total degree measure of 360°. For example, in the preceding figure, minor arc $\overset{\frown}{AB}$ accounts for $\frac{60}{360}$, or $\frac{1}{6}$, of the circle's circumference.

An arc of a circle can be defined either as a length (a portion of the circle's circumference) or as a degree measure. In the preceding figure, $\overset{\frown}{AB} = 60°$. If the circumference is 12π, then the length of minor arc $\overset{\frown}{AB}$ is $\frac{1}{6}$ of 12π, or 2π.

EXAMPLE 25 (EASIER):

Circle O has diameters $\overline{DB}$ and $\overline{AC}$, as shown in the figure below.

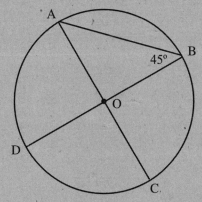

If the circumference of circle O is 12 inches, what is the length of minor arc $\overset{\frown}{BC}$?

   (A) 3 inches

   (B) $\frac{13}{4}$ inches

   (C) $\frac{11}{3}$ inches

   (D) 4 inches

Since $\overline{AO}$ and $\overline{BO}$ are both radii, $\triangle AOB$ is isosceles, and therefore $m\angle BAO = 45°$. It follows that $m\angle AOB = 90°$. That 90° angle accounts for $\frac{1}{4}$ of the circle's 360°.

Accordingly, minor arc $\overparen{BC}$ must account for $\frac{1}{4}$ of the circle's 12-inch circumference, or 3 inches. **The correct answer is (A).**

EXAMPLE 26 (MORE CHALLENGING):

A hexagon is inscribed in a circle whose center is O, as shown below.

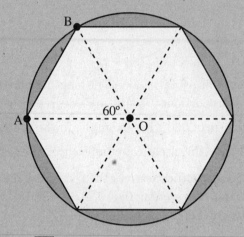

What is the unit length of $\overline{AB}$, expressed in terms of the diameter (d) of circle O?

(A) $\frac{d}{3}$

(B) $\frac{d}{\pi}$

(C) $\frac{d}{2}$

(D) $\frac{n}{d}$

Since $\overline{AO}$ and $\overline{BO}$ are both radii, the 60° central angle tells you that $\triangle ABO$ is equilateral. Accordingly, the length of $\overline{AB}$ must equal the circle's radius, which is half its diameter, or $\frac{d}{2}$. **The correct answer is (C).**

Circles and Tangent Lines

A circle is **tangent** to a line (or line segment) if the two intersect at one and only one point (called the **point of tangency**). Here's the key rule to remember about tangents: A line that is tangent to a circle is *always* perpendicular to the line passing through the circle's center and the point of tangency.

The next figure shows a circle with center O inscribed in a square. Point P is one of four points of tangency. By definition, $\overline{OP} \perp \overline{AB}$.

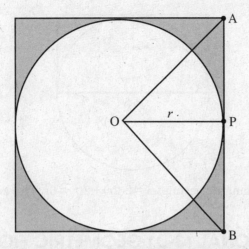

Also, notice the following relationships between the circle in the preceding figure and the inscribing square (r = radius):

Each side of the square is $2r$ in length.

The square's area is $(2r)^2$, or $4r^2$.

EXAMPLE 27 (EASIER):

Two parallel lines are tangent to the same circle. What is the shortest distance between the two lines?

  (A) the circle's radius

  (B) the circle's diameter

  (C) the circle's circumference

  (D) the product of the circle's radius and π

The two lines are both perpendicular to a chord that is the circle's diameter. Thus, the shortest distance between them is that diameter. **The correct answer is (B).**

EXAMPLE 28 (MORE CHALLENGING):

One side of a rectangle forms the diameter of a circle. The opposite side of the rectangle is tangent to the circle. In terms of the circle's radius (r), what is the perimeter of the rectangle?

  (A) $2r$

  (B) $4r$

  (C) $6r$

  (D) $8r$

The information in the problem describes the following figure:

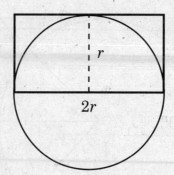

Given radius r, the rectangle's perimeter $= 2(2r) + 2(r) = 6r$. **The correct answer is (C).**

THREE-DIMENSIONAL (3-D) GEOMETRIC FIGURES

Three-dimensional (3-D) figures you might deal with on the GED® test include cubes and other rectangular prisms (box-shaped objects), cylinders, cones, and so-called "square" pyramids (pyramids that have a square base).

Rectangular Prisms

Rectangular prisms are box-shaped figures in which all corners are right angles. Any box-shaped figure has a total of six sides, or *faces*. The length of a side is generally referred to as an *edge*. A GED® test question about a rectangular prism will involve one or both of two basic formulas (p = perimeter of base, B = area of base ($l \times w$), h = height):

> **Volume** = Bh, or lwh
>
> **Surface Area** = $ph + 2B$

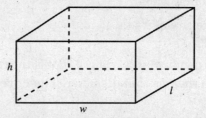

The volume formula is included on the Formula Sheet provided during the test.

To answer a GED® test question involving a rectangular prism, plug what you know into the appropriate formula—surface area or volume—and then solve for the missing term. Depending on the question, you might need to apply both formulas.

EXAMPLE 29 (EASIER):

Which of the following does NOT describe the dimensions of a rectangular box whose capacity is 120 cubic inches?

(A) 6 inches, 6 inches, and $3\frac{1}{3}$ inches

(B) 8 inches, 2 inches, and $7\frac{1}{2}$ inches

(C) 5 inches, 10 inches, and $2\frac{2}{5}$ inches

(D) 9 inches, 5 inches, and $2\frac{1}{2}$ inches

For each answer choice, multiply the three numbers. The only product not equal to 120 is choice (D), $9 \times 5 \times 2\frac{1}{2}$, which equals $112\frac{1}{2}$. **The correct answer is (D).**

EXAMPLE 30 (MORE CHALLENGING):

A closed rectangular box with a square base is 5 inches in height. If the volume of the box is 45 square inches, what is the box's surface area?

(A) 66 square inches

(B) 78 square inches

(C) 81 square inches

(D) 90 square inches

First, determine the dimensions of the square base. The box's height is given as 5. Accordingly, the box's volume (45) = $5lw$, and $lw = 9$. Since the base is square, the base is 3 inches long on each side. Now you can calculate the total surface area:

$$2lw + 2wh + 2lh = (2)(9) + (2)(15) + (2)(15) = 78.$$

The correct answer is (B).

Cubes

A **cube** is a rectangular prism whose length, width, and height are all the same—in other words, all six faces are squares. The volume and surface-area formulas are even simpler than for other rectangular prisms (let s = any edge):

volume $= s^3$, or $s = \sqrt[3]{\text{Volume}}$

surface area $= 6s^2$

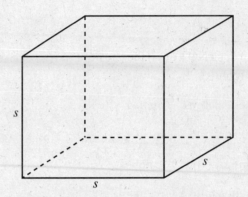

The volume formula is NOT included on the Formula Sheet provided during the test.

GED® test questions involving cubes (or other box shapes) are sometimes presented as "packing" problems. In this type of problem, your task is to determine how many small boxes fit into a larger, packing box. Another type of GED® test cube question focuses on the *ratios* among the cube's linear, square, and cubic measurements.

EXAMPLE 31 (EASIER):

How many cube-shaped boxes, each box 18 inches on a side, can be packed into a storage unit measuring 6 feet long, 6 feet wide, and 5 feet high?

(A) 36

(B) 42

(C) 48

(D) 64

First convert inches to feet: 18 inches $= 1\frac{1}{2}$ feet. You can pack 3 levels of 16 cube-shaped boxes, with a half-foot space left at the top of the storage unit. $3 \times 16 = 48$. **The correct answer is (C).**

EXAMPLE 32 (MORE CHALLENGING):

If the volume of one cube is 8 times greater than that of another, what is the ratio of any edge of the larger cube to any edge of the smaller cube?

(A) 2 to 1

(B) 4 to 1

(C) 8 to 1

(D) 16 to 1

The ratio of the two volumes is 8:1. The edge ratio is the cube root of this ratio: $\sqrt[3]{8}$ to $\sqrt[3]{1}$, or 2:1. **The correct answer is (A).**

Cylinders

A **cylinder** is a three-dimensional figure with a circular base. The only type of cylinder a GED® test question might involve is the *right* cylinder, in which the height and base are at 90° angles. The *surface area* of a right cylinder is the sum of three areas:

1 The circular base

2 The circular top

3 The rectangular surface around the cylinder's vertical face (visualize a rectangular label wrapped around a soup can)

The area of the vertical face is the product of the circular base's circumference (i.e., the rectangle's width) and the cylinder's height. The *volume* of a right cylinder is the product of the circular base's area and the cylinder's height. Given a radius r and height h of a cylinder:

Surface Area (SA) $= 2\pi r^2 + (2\pi r)(h)$

Volume $= \pi r^2 h$

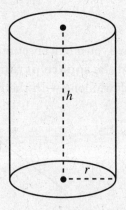

The volume formula is included on the Formula Sheet provided during the test.

A GED® test cylinder problem might require little more than a straightforward application of either the surface-area or the volume formula. As with rectangular-solid questions, just plug what you know into the formula, then solve for what the question asks. A more complex cylinder problem might require you to apply other math concepts, or require you to convert one unit of measurement to another.

EXAMPLE 33 (EASIER):

What is the volume of a cylinder whose circular base has a radius of 3 centimeters and whose height is 7 centimeters?

   (A) 21π cm³

   (B) 42π cm³

   (C) 63π cm³

   (D) 81π cm³

The cylinder's volume = $\pi(3)^2(7) = 63\pi$ cm^3. **The correct answer is (C).**

EXAMPLE 34 (MORE CHALLENGING):

A cylindrical can with diameter 14 inches and height 10 inches is filled to one-fourth its capacity with water. Which of the following most closely approximates the volume of water in the pail? [231 cubic inches = 1 gallon]

(A) 0.8 gallons

(B) 1.7 gallons

(C) 2.9 gallons

(D) 4.2 gallons

The volume of the pail = $\pi r^2 h \approx \frac{22}{7} \times 49 \times 10 = 22 \times 7 \times 10 = 1540$ cubic inches. The gallon capacity of the pail is approximately $1540 \div 231$, or about 6.7 gallons. One fourth of that amount is about 1.7 gallons. **The correct answer is (B).**

Cones and Pyramids

Two other three-dimensional figures you might encounter during the GED® Mathematical Reasoning Test are the **cone** and the **square pyramid** (a four-sided pyramid with a square base). Both are shown below, along with their volume formulas:

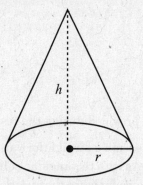 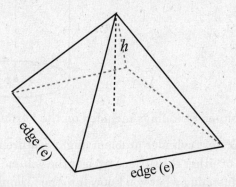

Volume of a cone: $\frac{1}{3} \times \pi \times$ radius$^2 \times$ height ($\pi \approx 3.14$)

Volume of a square pyramid: $\frac{1}{3} \times$ (base edge)$^2 \times$ height

The Formula Sheet provided during the exam includes both of these equations, so you do not need to memorize them. Notice that the volume of a cone is simply one-third that of a right cylinder, and that the volume of a square pyramid is simply one-third that of a rectangular prism.

EXAMPLE 35 (EASIER):

What is the volume of a pyramid whose height is 24 feet and whose square base measures 10 feet on each side?

    (A) 240 cubic feet

    (B) 480 cubic feet

    (C) 760 cubic feet

    (D) 800 cubic feet

The volume of the pyramid $= \frac{1}{3} \times \text{edge}^2 \times \text{height} = \frac{1}{3} \times 100 \times 24 = 800$ cubic feet. **The correct answer is (D).**

EXAMPLE 36 (MORE CHALLENGING):

Which of the following is nearest to the height of a cone with diameter 16 inches and volume 4480 cubic inches?

    (A) 36 inches

    (B) 44 inches

    (C) 56 inches

    (D) 70 inches

Given a diameter of 16, the radius is 8. Letting h = height, the cone's volume (4480) $= \frac{1}{3} \times \pi(8)^2(h) \approx \left(\frac{1}{3}\right)(3.14)(64)(h)$. Since the question asks for an approximation, try canceling out 3.14 and the denominator number 3. Solve for h:

$$4480 \approx 64h$$

$$\frac{4480}{64} \approx h$$

$$70 \approx h$$

The correct answer is (D).

RIGHT-TRIANGLE TRIGONOMETRY

Right-triangle trigonometry involves the ratios between sides of right triangles and the angle measures that correspond to these ratios. Refer to the following right triangle, in which the sides opposite angles A, B, and C are labeled a, b, and c, respectively (A and B are the two acute angles):

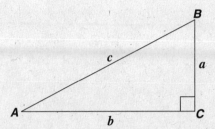

Referring to $\triangle ABC$, you express and define the six trigonometric functions sine, cosine, tangent, cotangent, secant, and cosecant for angle A as follows. Notice that each function in the right column is the *reciprocal*, or *multiplicative inverse*, of the function to the left of it.

$$\sin A = \frac{a}{c} \qquad \csc A = \frac{c}{a}$$

$$\cos A = \frac{b}{c} \qquad \sec A = \frac{c}{b}$$

$$\tan A = \frac{a}{b} \qquad \cot A = \frac{b}{a}$$

You would express and define the six functions for angle B similarly. The sine, cosine, and tangent functions are the most important ones. For the GED® test, you should memorize the following three general definitions:

$$\text{sine} = \frac{\text{opposite}}{\text{hypotenuse}}$$

$$\text{cosine} = \frac{\text{adjacent}}{\text{hypotenuse}}$$

$$\text{tangent} = \frac{\text{opposite}}{\text{adjacent}}$$

These definitions will NOT be included on the Formula Sheet provided during the exam.

On the GED® test you won't find any trigonometric tables, which list angle measures and their corresponding trigonometric function values. Though a question might provide specific angle measures, it's more likely that you'll express solutions to problems in terms of trigonometric functions. If the lengths of only two sides are given, you might need to use the Pythagorean theorem to find the length of the third side. For example, look at the next figure:

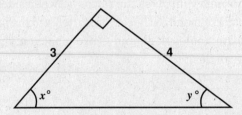

You should recognize the Pythagorean side triplet 3:4:5 in this figure ($3^2 + 4^2 = 5^2$). The length of the hypotenuse is 5. Applying the definitions of sine, cosine, and tangent to angles x and y, here are the results:

$$\sin x = \frac{4}{5} \qquad \sin y = \frac{3}{5}$$

$$\cos x = \frac{3}{5} \qquad \cos y = \frac{4}{5}$$

$$\tan x = \frac{4}{3} \qquad \tan y = \frac{3}{4}$$

For the GED® test, you should also keep in mind the following trigonometric identity:

$$\text{tangent} = \frac{\text{sine}}{\text{cosine}}$$

The relationships among the sine, cosine, and tangent functions result in the following three additional observations for a triangle with acute angles A and B:

1 By definition, $\tan A \times \tan B = 1$.

2 For all right triangles, $\sin A = \cos B$ (and $\sin B = \cos A$). For all other triangles, $\sin A \neq \cos B$ (and $\sin B \neq \cos A$).

3 In a right isosceles triangle (in which A and B each measures 45°), $\sin A = \sin B = \cos A = \cos B = \frac{\sqrt{2}}{2}$ (you can apply the Pythagorean theorem to show this fraction).

EXAMPLE 37 (EASIER):

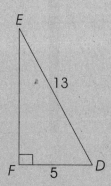

In $\triangle DEF$, what is the value of $\tan D$?

(A) $\frac{3}{5}$

(B) $\frac{12}{13}$

(C) $\frac{12}{5}$

(D) $\frac{13}{5}$

You can find the length of $\overline{EF}$ by applying the Pythagorean theorem. Notice that the sides conform to the Pythagorean side ratio 5:12:13 ($5^2 + 12^2 = 13^2$). The length of $\overline{EF}$ = 12. In $\triangle DEF$, $\tan D = \dfrac{\text{opposite}}{\text{adjacent}} = \dfrac{12}{5}$. **The correct answer is (C).**

EXAMPLE 38 (MORE CHALLENGING):

A 50-foot wire is attached to the top of a vertical electric pole and is anchored on the ground. If the wire rises in a straight line at a 70° angle from the ground, what is the height of the pole, in linear feet?

(A) $50\sin70°$

(B) $50\cos70°$

(C) $\dfrac{\cos70°}{50}$

(D) $\dfrac{50}{\cos70°}$

As shown in the next figure, the height of the pole (x) is opposite the 70° angle, and the triangle's hypotenuse (length of the wire) is 50.

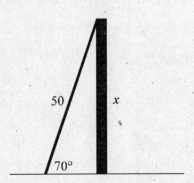

Apply the sine function: sine = opposite ÷ hypotenuse.

$$\frac{x}{50} = \sin70°$$
$$x = 50\sin70°$$

The correct answer is (A).

COORDINATE GEOMETRY

Finding points on a plane is the study of **coordinate geometry.** A grid is commonly used to do this. The grid is divided into four sections. Each section is called a **quadrant.** The two number lines that divide the grid into quadrants are called the **x-axis** (the horizontal axis) and the **y-axis** (the vertical axis). The center of the grid, where the two axes meet, is called the **origin.** The points that are drawn on the grid are identified by **ordered pairs.** The x-coordinate is always written first. Look at the grid below.

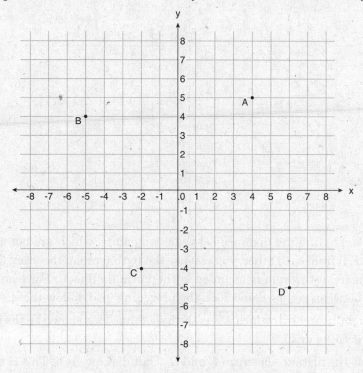

The ordered pair for the origin, in the middle of the grid, is (0, 0). To determine the ordered pair for point A, start at the origin, and count over four squares to the right on the x-axis. This gives you the coordinate for the first number of the pair. Now, count up 5 squares on the y-axis. The ordered pair for point A is (4, 5).

What ordered pair expresses point C's location? Because you must count two squares to the *left* of the origin (0, 0) and four squares *below* the origin, the ordered pair for point C is (–2, –4). The ordered pair for point B is (–5, 4), and the ordered pair for point D is (6, –5).

Finding the Distance Between Two Points

Finding the distance between two points that are directly horizontal or vertical from each other is simply a matter of counting the number of squares that separate the points. In the next grid, for example, the distance between points A(2, 3) and B(7, 3) is 5. The distance between points C(2, 1) and D(2, –4) is also 5.

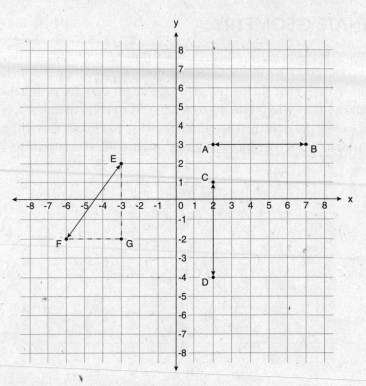

If you are asked to find the distance between two points, which are not directly horizontal or vertical from each other, you can use the Pythagorean theorem. (The formula for the Pythagorean theorem is included in the Formula Sheet.) For example, to find the distance between points E and F on the preceding grid, follow these steps:

1 Draw a right triangle in which $\overline{EF}$ is the hypotenuse (as shown by the broken lines on the preceding grid).

2 Determine the distance between E and G. That distance is 4. This is the length of one leg of right triangle EFG.

3 Determine the distance between F and G. That distance is 3. This is the length of the other leg of a right triangle EFG.

4 Apply the Pythagorean theorem to find the hypotenuse of $\triangle EFG$, which is the distance between E and F:

$$4^2 + 3^2 = c^2$$
$$16 + 9 = c^2$$
$$25 = c^2$$
$$5 = c$$

In applying the Pythagorean theorem to the coordinate grid, you may want to use the **distance formula,** which is a more specific way of expressing the theorem.

Distance between points $= \sqrt{\left(x_2 - x_1\right)^2 + \left(y_2 - y_1\right)^2}$, where the two points are (x_1, y_1) and (x_2, y_2)

The distance formula is NOT included on the Formula Sheet provided during the exam. Apply this formula to the preceding example, and you obtain the same result:

$$\sqrt{\left(-6-(-3)\right)^2 + \left(-2-2\right)^2} = \sqrt{\left(-3\right)^2 + \left(-4\right)^2} = \sqrt{9+16} = \sqrt{25} = 5$$

EXAMPLE 39 (EASIER):

On the coordinate plane, the distance between point A and point B is 8 units. If the coordinates of point A are (−4, 5), which of the following CANNOT be the coordinates of point B?

(A) (4, 5)

(B) (−4, −3)

(C) (−4, 13)

(D) (4, −3)

Point 1 is 8 units from point A, directly horizontal from point A. Points 2 and 3 are 8 units from point A, directly vertical from point A. Point 4 is diagonal to point 8 by more than 8 units. (Plotting the two points on the coordinate grid will show that the distance is greater than 8 units; there's no need to apply the distance formula.) **The correct answer is (D).**

EXAMPLE 40 (MORE CHALLENGING):

What is the distance between (−3,1) and (2,4) on the coordinate plane?

(A) 5

(B) $\sqrt{29}$

(C) $\sqrt{34}$

(D) 6

Apply the distance formula: $\sqrt{\left(-3-2\right)^2 + \left(1-4\right)^2} = \sqrt{25+9} = \sqrt{34}$. **The correct answer is (C).**

Finding the Midpoint of a Line Segment

To find the coordinates of the midpoint of a line segment, simply average the two endpoints' *x*-values and *y*-values:

$$x_M = \frac{x_1 + x_2}{2} \text{ and } y_M = \frac{y_1 + y_2}{2}$$

These formulas are NOT included on the Formula Sheet provided during the test.

A GED® test question might simply ask you to find the midpoint between two given points. Or, it might provide the midpoint and one endpoint, and then ask you to determine the other endpoint.

EXAMPLE 41 (EASIER):

Click on the graph to plot the point that represents the midpoint between (–3, 1) and (–7, 5) on the coordinate plane. For this print version, mark the graph to plot the point that represents the midpoint.

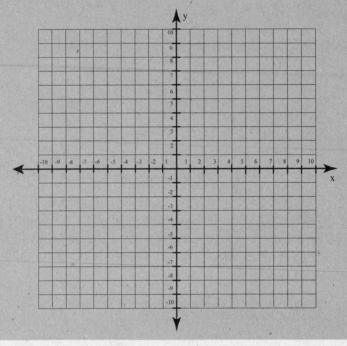

First apply the formula to the two x-values: $\dfrac{-3+(-7)}{2} = -\dfrac{10}{2} = -5$. Then apply the formula to the two y-values: $\dfrac{1+5}{2} = \dfrac{6}{2} = 3$. The midpoint is (–5, 3).

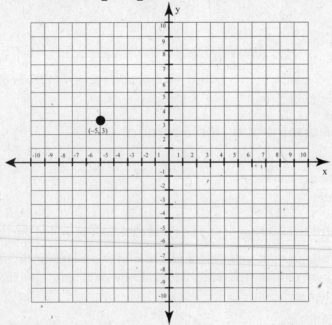

The correct answer is (–5, 3).

EXAMPLE 42 (MORE CHALLENGING):

On the coordinate plane, the point $M(-1, 3)$ is the midpoint of line segment whose endpoints are $A(2, -4)$ and B. What are the xy-coordinates of point B?

(A) $(-3, 8)$

(B) $(8, -4)$

(C) $(5, 12)$

(D) $(-4, 10)$

Apply the midpoint formula to find the x-coordinate of point B:

$$-1 = \frac{x + 2}{2}$$
$$-2 = x + 2$$
$$-4 = x$$

Apply the midpoint formula to find the y-coordinate of point B:

$$3 = \frac{y + (-4)}{2}$$
$$6 = y - 4$$
$$10 = y$$

Thus, the xy-coordinates of point B are $(-4, 10)$. **The correct answer is (D).**

Defining a Line on the Plane

You can define any line on the coordinate plane by the following general equation:

$$y = mx + b$$

In this equation:

The variable m is the slope of the line.

The variable b is the line's **y-intercept** (where the line crosses the y-axis).

The variables x and y are the coordinates of any point on the line. Any (x, y) pair defining a point on the line can substitute for the variables x and y.

Think of the **slope** of a line as a fraction in which the numerator indicates the vertical change from one point to another on the line (moving left to right) corresponding to a given horizontal change, which the fraction's denominator indicates. The common term used for this fraction is **rise-over-run**.

You can determine the slope of a line from any two pairs of (x, y) coordinates. In general, if (x_1, y_1) and (x_2, y_2) lie on the same line, calculate the line's slope according to the following formula:

$$\textbf{slope } (m) = \frac{y_2 - y_1}{x_2 - x_1}$$

This formula is included on the Formula Sheet provided during the test.

In applying the formula, be sure to subtract corresponding values. For example, a careless test-taker calculating the slope might subtract y_1 from y_2 but subtract x_2 from x_1. Also, be sure to calculate rise-over-run, and not run-over-rise.

A GED® test question might ask you to identify the slope of a line defined by a given equation, in which case you simply put the equation in the form $y = mx + b$, then identify the m-term. Or, it might ask you to determine the equation of a line, or just the line's slope (m) or y-intercept (b), given the coordinates of two points on the line.

EXAMPLE 43 (EASIER):

On the coordinate plane, what is the slope of the line defined by the two points $P(2, 1)$ and $Q(-3, 4)$?

(A) $-\dfrac{5}{3}$

(B) -1

(C) $-\dfrac{3}{5}$

(D) $\dfrac{1}{3}$

Apply the slope formula:

$$\text{slope } (m) = \frac{4-1}{-3-2} = \frac{3}{-5}, \text{ or } -\frac{3}{5}$$

The correct answer is (C).

EXAMPLE 44 (MORE CHALLENGING):

On the coordinate plane, at what point along the vertical axis (the y-axis) does the line passing through points (2, 4) and (–1, –5) cross the y-axis? Once you have calculated the answer, click on the intercept point on the coordinate grid. For the print book, mark the intercept point on the coordinate grid.

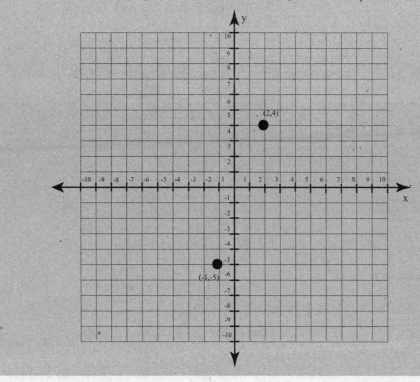

The question asks for the line's y-intercept (the value of b in the general equation $y = mx + b$). First, determine the line's slope:

$$\text{slope } (m) = \frac{y_2 - y_1}{x_2 - x_1} = \frac{-5 - 4}{-2 - 1} = \frac{-9}{-3} = 3$$

In the general equation ($y = mx + b$), $m = 3$. To find the value of b, substitute either (x, y) value pair for x and y, then solve for b. Substituting the (x, y) pair (2, 4):

$y = 3x + b$
$4 = 3(2) + b$
$4 = 6 + b$
$b = -2$

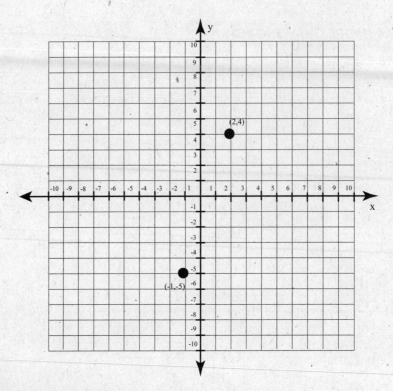

The correct answer is –2.

Graphing a Line on the Plane

You can graph a line on the coordinate plane if you know the coordinates of any two points on the line. Just plot the two points, and then draw a line connecting them. You can also graph a line from one point on the line, if you also know either the line's slope or its *y*-intercept.

A GED® test question might ask you to recognize the value of a line's slope (*m*) based on a graph of the line. If the graph identifies the precise coordinates of two points, you can determine the line's precise slope (and the entire equation of the line). Even without any precise coordinates, you can still estimate the line's slope based on its appearance.

Lines that slope *upward* from left to right:

- A line sloping *upward* from left to right has a positive slope (*m*).

- A line with a slope of 1 slopes upward from left to right at a 45° angle in relation to the *x*-axis.

- A line with a fractional slope between 0 and 1 slopes upward from left to right but at less than a 45° angle in relation to the *x*-axis.

- A line with a slope greater than 1 slopes upward from left to right at more than a 45° angle in relation to the *x*-axis.

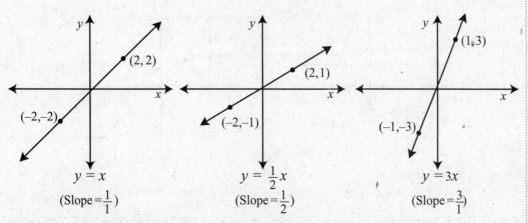

Lines that slope *downward* from left to right:

- A line sloping *downward* from left to right has a negative slope (*m*).

- A line with a slope of −1 slopes downward from left to right at a 45° angle in relation to the *x*-axis.

- A line with a fractional slope between 0 and −1 slopes downward from left to right but at less than a 45° angle in relation to the *x*-axis.

- A line with a slope less than −1 (for example, −2) slopes downward from left to right at more than a 45° angle in relation to the *x*-axis.

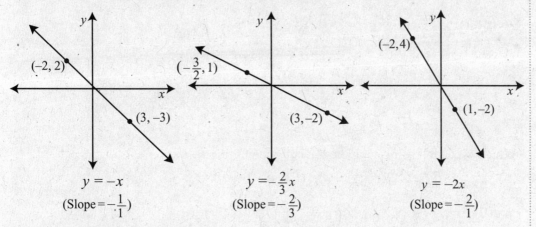

Horizontal and vertical lines:

- A *horizontal* line has a slope of zero (*m* = 0, and *mx* = 0).

- A *vertical* line has either an undefined or an indeterminate slope (the fraction's denominator is 0), so the *m*-term in the equation is ignored.

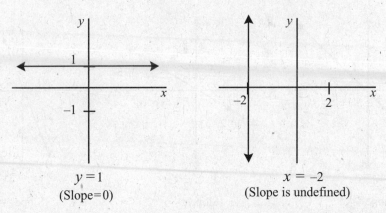

$y = 1$
(Slope$=0$)

$x = -2$
(Slope is undefined)

Parallel lines have the same slope (the same m-term in the general equation). The slope of a line perpendicular to another is the negative reciprocal of the other line's slope. The product of the two slopes is 1. For example, a line with slope $\frac{3}{2}$ is perpendicular to a line with slope $-\frac{2}{3}$.

EXAMPLE 45 (EASIER):

Line P is shown on the coordinate plane below.

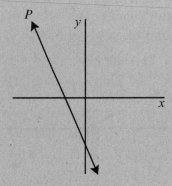

Which of the following could be the equation of line P?

(A) $y = -\frac{5}{2}x + \frac{5}{2}$

(B) $y = \frac{5}{2}x - \frac{5}{2}$

(C) $y = \frac{2}{5}x + \frac{2}{5}$

(D) $y = -\frac{5}{2}x - \frac{5}{2}$

Notice that line P slopes downward from left to right at an angle greater than 45° in relation to the x-axis. Thus, the line's slope (m in the equation $y = mx + b$) < -1. Also notice that line P crosses the y-axis at a negative y-value (below the x-axis). The line's y-intercept (b in the equation $y = mx + b$) is negative. Only choice (D) provides an equation that meets both conditions. **The correct answer is (D).**

EXAMPLE 46 (MORE CHALLENGING):

If the equation $x = \dfrac{y+5}{2}$ is graphed as a line on the coordinate plane, which statement about the line is accurate?

(A) The line crosses the y-axis at (3, 0).

(B) The line is vertical.

(C) The line crosses the x-axis at (0, −5).

(D) The line is horizontal.

Before rewriting the equation to find the slope, quickly test the statements of choices (A) and (C) by plugging the x-value and y-value of each ordered pair into the equation. You'll see that the equation holds true for the ordered pair (0, −5):

$$0 = \frac{-5+5}{2}$$

(0, −5) is a point on the line, and so statement (C) holds true. The point (3, 0) is not on the line because the equation does not hold true when these values are substituted. So, choice (A) is incorrect. If you want to test choices (B) and (D), rewrite the equation in standard form:

$$x = \frac{y+5}{2}$$
$$2x = y + 5$$
$$y = 2x - 5$$

The slope of the line is 2, and so choices (B) and (D) are not accurate. **The correct answer is (C).**

SUMMING IT UP

- Geometry questions on the Mathematical Reasoning Test cover the following areas: congruency and similarity; angles, parallel and perpendicular lines, and transversals; two-dimensional figures (triangles, quadrilaterals, polygons, and circles); three-dimensional figures (cubes and other rectangular prisms, cylinders, cones, and square pyramids); basic right-triangle trigonometry; and coordinate geometry (points, lines, and other figures on the xy-coordinate plane).

- Lines and line segments are the fundamental elements for most GED® test geometry problems, so it's important to be familiar with the basic rules of angles formed by intersecting lines.

- Most geometry formulas, such as the Pythagorean theorem, are included on the Formula Sheet that will be provided to you during the test. Other formulas, such as the definitions for the sine, cosine, and tangent functions, will NOT appear on the Formula Sheet, and you may want to memorize them before taking the test.

- Be sure you know the properties of all basic types of triangles. Not only will you encounter triangle problems on the GED® test, you'll also need these skills for solving problems with four-sided figures, three-dimensional figures, and circles.

- For the GED® test, know how to determine the perimeter and area of squares, rectangles, and parallelograms. GED® test questions involving non-square rectangles may ask you to determine the area based on the perimeter, or vice versa.

- You won't need to work with a value of π any more precise than 3.14 or $\frac{22}{7}$. In fact, you might be able to answer a circle question using the symbol π itself, without approximating its value.

- Become familiar with the following basic terminology involving circles: circumference, radius, diameter, and chord. GED® test circle problems typically involve other types of geometric figures as well, including triangles, squares, rectangles, and tangent lines. Learn the basics of circle problems, and you'll be a step ahead in solving the most advanced geometry problems.

- GED® test questions involving cubes (or other box shapes) are sometimes presented as "packing" problems, where you need to determine how many small boxes fit into a larger, packing box. Another type of GED® test cube question focuses on the *ratios* among the cube's linear, square, and cubic measurements.

- A GED® test cylinder problem might require little more than a straightforward application of either the surface-area or the volume formula. As with rectangular-solid questions, just plug what you know into the formula, then solve for what the question asks.

- GED® test coordinate questions involve the xy-plane defined by the horizontal x-axis and the vertical y-axis. You will need to know how to determine the slope of a line, so remember to calculate it as "rise over run" and not "run over rise."

PART VII

TWO PRACTICE TESTS

Practice Test 2

DIRECTIONS FOR TAKING THE PRACTICE TEST

Directions: The GED® Practice Test has four separate subtests: Reasoning Through Language Arts, Mathematical Reasoning, Science, and Social Studies.

- Read and follow the directions at the start of each test.

- Stick to the time limits.

- Enter your answers to the multiple-choice questions on the tear-out Answer Sheets provided. You will answer so-called technology-enhanced questions—like fill-in-the-blank, hot spot, drag-and-drop, and drop-down questions—directly in the test.

- When you have completed the entire test, compare your answers with the correct answers given in the Answer Key and Explanations at the end of this Practice Test.

- Remember to check the "Are You Ready to Take the GED® Test?" section to gauge how close you are to mastering the GED® test.

ANSWER SHEET PRACTICE TEST 2

Reasoning Through Language Arts

1. Ⓐ Ⓑ Ⓒ Ⓓ

2. Ⓐ Ⓑ Ⓒ Ⓓ

3. Ⓐ Ⓑ Ⓒ Ⓓ

4. Ⓐ Ⓑ Ⓒ Ⓓ

5. Ⓐ Ⓑ Ⓒ Ⓓ

6. Ⓐ Ⓑ Ⓒ Ⓓ

7. Ⓐ Ⓑ Ⓒ Ⓓ

8. Ⓐ Ⓑ Ⓒ Ⓓ

9. Ⓐ Ⓑ Ⓒ Ⓓ

10. Ⓐ Ⓑ Ⓒ Ⓓ

11. _____

12. Ⓐ Ⓑ Ⓒ Ⓓ

13. Ⓐ Ⓑ Ⓒ Ⓓ

14. Ⓐ Ⓑ Ⓒ Ⓓ

15. Ⓐ Ⓑ Ⓒ Ⓓ

16. Ⓐ Ⓑ Ⓒ Ⓓ

17. Ⓐ Ⓑ Ⓒ Ⓓ

18. Ⓐ Ⓑ Ⓒ Ⓓ

19. Ⓐ Ⓑ Ⓒ Ⓓ

20. Ⓐ Ⓑ Ⓒ Ⓓ

21. _____

22. Ⓐ Ⓑ Ⓒ Ⓓ

23. Ⓐ Ⓑ Ⓒ Ⓓ

24. Ⓐ Ⓑ Ⓒ Ⓓ

25. Ⓐ Ⓑ Ⓒ Ⓓ

26. Ⓐ Ⓑ Ⓒ Ⓓ

27. Ⓐ Ⓑ Ⓒ Ⓓ

28. _____

29. Ⓐ Ⓑ Ⓒ Ⓓ

30. _____

31. Ⓐ Ⓑ Ⓒ Ⓓ

32. Ⓐ Ⓑ Ⓒ Ⓓ

33. Ⓐ Ⓑ Ⓒ Ⓓ

34. _____

35. Ⓐ Ⓑ Ⓒ Ⓓ

36. Ⓐ Ⓑ Ⓒ Ⓓ

37. Ⓐ Ⓑ Ⓒ Ⓓ

38. Ⓐ Ⓑ Ⓒ Ⓓ

39. Ⓐ Ⓑ Ⓒ Ⓓ

40. Ⓐ Ⓑ Ⓒ Ⓓ

41. Ⓐ Ⓑ Ⓒ Ⓓ

42. Ⓐ Ⓑ Ⓒ Ⓓ

43. Ⓐ Ⓑ Ⓒ Ⓓ

44. Ⓐ Ⓑ Ⓒ Ⓓ

45. _____

46. Ⓐ Ⓑ Ⓒ Ⓓ

47. Ⓐ Ⓑ Ⓒ Ⓓ

48. Ⓐ Ⓑ Ⓒ Ⓓ

49. _____

ANSWER SHEET PRACTICE TEST 2

Mathematical Reasoning

1. _____
2. _____
3. Ⓐ Ⓑ Ⓒ Ⓓ
4. Ⓐ Ⓑ Ⓒ Ⓓ
5. Ⓐ Ⓑ Ⓒ Ⓓ
6. Ⓐ Ⓑ Ⓒ Ⓓ
7. _____
8. Ⓐ Ⓑ Ⓒ Ⓓ
9. Ⓐ Ⓑ Ⓒ Ⓓ
10. Ⓐ Ⓑ Ⓒ Ⓓ
11. _____
12. Ⓐ Ⓑ Ⓒ Ⓓ
13. Ⓐ Ⓑ Ⓒ Ⓓ
14. _____
15. Ⓐ Ⓑ Ⓒ Ⓓ

16. Ⓐ Ⓑ Ⓒ Ⓓ
17. _____
18. _____
19. _____
20. Ⓐ Ⓑ Ⓒ Ⓓ
21. Ⓐ Ⓑ Ⓒ Ⓓ
22. Ⓐ Ⓑ Ⓒ Ⓓ
23. Ⓐ Ⓑ Ⓒ Ⓓ
24. _____
25. _____
26. Ⓐ Ⓑ Ⓒ Ⓓ
27. Ⓐ Ⓑ Ⓒ Ⓓ

28. Ⓐ Ⓑ Ⓒ Ⓓ
29. Ⓐ Ⓑ Ⓒ Ⓓ
30. _____
31. Ⓐ Ⓑ Ⓒ Ⓓ
32. Ⓐ Ⓑ Ⓒ Ⓓ
33. Ⓐ Ⓑ Ⓒ Ⓓ
34. Ⓐ Ⓑ Ⓒ Ⓓ
35. _____
36. Ⓐ Ⓑ Ⓒ Ⓓ
37. Ⓐ Ⓑ Ⓒ Ⓓ

answer sheet

ANSWER SHEET PRACTICE TEST 2

Science

1. Ⓐ Ⓑ Ⓒ Ⓓ   11. _____   22. _____

2. _____   12. Ⓐ Ⓑ Ⓒ Ⓓ   23. _____

3. Ⓐ Ⓑ Ⓒ Ⓓ   13. _____   24. Ⓐ Ⓑ Ⓒ Ⓓ

4. Ⓐ Ⓑ Ⓒ Ⓓ   14. _____   25. Ⓐ Ⓑ Ⓒ Ⓓ

5. _____   15. Ⓐ Ⓑ Ⓒ Ⓓ   26. _____

6. Ⓐ Ⓑ Ⓒ Ⓓ   16. Ⓐ Ⓑ Ⓒ Ⓓ   27. Ⓐ Ⓑ Ⓒ Ⓓ

7. Ⓐ Ⓑ Ⓒ Ⓓ   17. _____   28. Ⓐ Ⓑ Ⓒ Ⓓ

8. Ⓐ Ⓑ Ⓒ Ⓓ   18. Ⓐ Ⓑ Ⓒ Ⓓ   29. Ⓐ Ⓑ Ⓒ Ⓓ

9. Ⓐ Ⓑ Ⓒ Ⓓ   19. Ⓐ Ⓑ Ⓒ Ⓓ   30. Ⓐ Ⓑ Ⓒ Ⓓ

10. Ⓐ Ⓑ Ⓒ Ⓓ   20. _____

21. Ⓐ Ⓑ Ⓒ Ⓓ

ANSWER SHEET PRACTICE TEST 2

Social Studies

1. Ⓐ Ⓑ Ⓒ Ⓓ   14. Ⓐ Ⓑ Ⓒ Ⓓ   24. Ⓐ Ⓑ Ⓒ Ⓓ

2. _____   15. Ⓐ Ⓑ Ⓒ Ⓓ   25. _____

3. Ⓐ Ⓑ Ⓒ Ⓓ   16. Ⓐ Ⓑ Ⓒ Ⓓ   26. Ⓐ Ⓑ Ⓒ Ⓓ

4. Ⓐ Ⓑ Ⓒ Ⓓ   17. Ⓐ Ⓑ Ⓒ Ⓓ   27. Ⓐ Ⓑ Ⓒ Ⓓ

5. Ⓐ Ⓑ Ⓒ Ⓓ   18. Ⓐ Ⓑ Ⓒ Ⓓ   28. Ⓐ Ⓑ Ⓒ Ⓓ

6. Ⓐ Ⓑ Ⓒ Ⓓ   19. Ⓐ Ⓑ Ⓒ Ⓓ   29. Ⓐ Ⓑ Ⓒ Ⓓ

7. Ⓐ Ⓑ Ⓒ Ⓓ   20. Ⓐ Ⓑ Ⓒ Ⓓ   30. Ⓐ Ⓑ Ⓒ Ⓓ

8. Ⓐ Ⓑ Ⓒ Ⓓ   21. Ⓐ Ⓑ Ⓒ Ⓓ   31. Ⓐ Ⓑ Ⓒ Ⓓ

9. _____   22. Ⓐ Ⓑ Ⓒ Ⓓ   32. Ⓐ Ⓑ Ⓒ Ⓓ

10. _____   23. Ⓐ Ⓑ Ⓒ Ⓓ   33. _____

11. Ⓐ Ⓑ Ⓒ Ⓓ   34. _____

12. Ⓐ Ⓑ Ⓒ Ⓓ

13. _____

answer sheet

Essay

_____

_____

_____

_____

_____

_____

_____

_____

_____

_____

_____

_____

_____

_____

_____

_____

_____

_____

_____

_____

_____

answer sheet

REASONING THROUGH LANGUAGE ARTS

150 Minutes • 49 Questions

Directions: The Reasoning Through Language Arts Test consists of passages of fiction and nonfiction reading material. Most questions are in multiple-choice format. Others are meant to prepare you for the electronically formatted questions that you will find on the test, such as drop-down, fill-in-the-blanks, and drag-and-drops. After you read a passage, answer the questions that follow it, referring back to the passage as needed. Answer all questions based on what is stated and implied in the passage. There is also an extended response question that requires you to read a paired passage that represents two views on a topic and write a well-organized essay supporting one of the view points. Record your answers on the Reasoning Through Language Arts section of the answer sheet provided.

QUESTIONS 1–6 REFER TO THE FOLLOWING PASSAGE.

A Citizen Is Entitled to Vote

The following speech has been adapted from A Citizen is Entitled to Vote by Susan B. Anthony, a nineteenth-century campaigner for women's rights. The speech was part of a speaking tour in 1872 across 29 towns in New York. At the time of the speech, women were not guaranteed the right to vote. Anthony's battle against the disenfranchisement of women, along with many other dedicated workers, earned women across the country the right to vote by 1920. The United States government granted women the right to vote by ratifying the 19ᵗʰ Amendment.

Friends and fellow citizens:—I stand before you tonight under indictment for the alleged crime of having voted at the last presi-
5 dential election, without having a lawful right to vote.

It shall be my work this evening to prove to you that in thus voting, I not only committed no crime, but
10 instead, simply exercised my *citizen's rights*, guaranteed to me and all United States citizens by the National Constitution, beyond the power of any State to deny.

15 The preamble of the Federal Constitution says: "We, the people of the United States, in order to form a more perfect union, establish justice, insure *domestic*
20 tranquility, provide for the common defense, promote the general welfare, and secure the blessings of liberty to ourselves and our posterity, do ordain and establish this
25 Constitution for the United States of America."

It was we, the people, not we, the white male citizens; but we, the whole people, who formed the
30 Union. And we formed it, not to give the blessings of liberty, but to secure them; not to the half of ourselves and the half of our posterity but to the whole people—women
35 as well as men. And it is a downright mockery to talk to women of their enjoyment of the blessings of liberty while they are denied the use of the only means of securing
40 them provided by this democratic-republican government—the ballot.

For any State to make sex a qualification that must ever result
45 in the disfranchisement of one entire half of the people is a violation of the supreme law of the land. By it the blessings of liberty are forever withheld from women

50 and their female posterity. To them this government has no just powers derived from the consent of the governed. To them this government is not a democracy. It is not a

55 republic. It is a hateful oligarchy of sex. An oligarchy of learning, where the educated govern the ignorant, might be endured; but this oligarchy of sex, which makes

60 father, brothers, husband, sons, the oligarchs or rulers over the mother and sisters, the wife and daughters of every household— which ordains all men sovereigns,

65 all women subjects, carries dissension, discord and rebellion into every home of the nation.

Webster's Dictionary defines a citizen as a person in the United

70 States, entitled to vote and hold office.

The only question left to be settled now is, Are women persons? And I hardly believe any of our

75 opponents will have the hardihood to say they are not. Being persons, then, women are citizens; and no State has a right to make any law, or to enforce any old law, that shall

80 abridge their privileges or immunities. Hence, every discrimination against women in the constitutions and laws of the several States is today null and void.

1. What is the main idea of this passage?

   (A) Women are not allowed to vote.

   (B) Because Susan B. Anthony was arrested, she lost the right to vote.

   (C) Men should give up their right to vote if women cannot vote.

   (D) Women should receive the same treatment and rights as men.

2. According to the passage, what does the word *disenfranchisement* mean?

   (A) denying someone the right to vote

   (B) segregating men and women

   (C) creating a new amendment

   (D) depriving someone of basic necessities

3. What most likely encouraged Anthony to deliver this speech?

   (A) She wanted to see how many people believed in women's rights.

   (B) She liked meeting people who also believed in women's rights.

   (C) She wanted to explain why she voted illegally in the election.

   (D) She wanted to convince people to vote for her in the next election.

4. Based on this passage, what most likely caused the United States government to allow women the right to vote?

   (A) England forced the United States to allow women to vote.

   (B) Women took over the government and changed the laws.

   (C) Activists like Susan B. Anthony convinced the populace to support women's suffrage.

   (D) There were fewer men than women in the country, so the government needed more people to vote.

5. What purpose did quoting the Preamble of the Constitution serve in Anthony's speech?

   (A) It was a way to teach the audience about the Constitution.

   (B) It reminded her audience that the founders of the U.S. declared independence because they lacked representation.

   (C) It showed that women were smart enough to understand the Constitution.

   (D) The quote emphasized the power possessed by the government.

6. "To them this government is not a democracy. It is not a republic. It is a hateful oligarchy of sex." What does this quote from the passage mean?

(A) The government of the U.S. does not treat women fairly because they are treated differently from men.

(B) Women are being forced to create their own republic within the U.S.

(C) Men do not care about the rights of women and treat them unfairly.

(D) Women should rewrite the constitution so that the country becomes a real democracy.

QUESTIONS 7–12 REFER TO THE FOLLOWING PASSAGE.

What Is Sleep?

Scientists have known for some years that sleep is important to human health. In fact, cases of long-term sleep deprivation has
5 even led to death. Yet, scientists are still studying this unique state in which humans spend a third of their lives.

It isn't only current scientists
10 who are intrigued with sleep. Throughout history, people have attempted to understand this remarkable experience. Many centuries ago, for example, sleep was
15 regarded as a type of anemia of the brain. Alcmaeon, a Greek scientist, believed that blood retreated into the blood vessels, and the partially starved brain went to sleep. Plato
20 supported the idea that the soul left the body during sleep, wandered through the world, and woke up the body when it returned.

Recently, more scientific explanations of sleep have been pro-
25 nations of sleep have been proposed. According to one theory, the brain is put to sleep by a chemical agent that accumulates in the body when it is awake. Another theory

30 is that weary branches of certain nerve cells break connections with neighboring cells. The flow of impulses required for staying awake is then disrupted. These
35 more recent theories have to be subjected to laboratory research.

Why do we sleep? Why do we dream? Modern sleep research is said to have begun in the 1920s
40 with the invention of a machine that could measure brain waves, the electroencephalograph (EEG). The study of sleep was further enhanced in the 1950s, when
45 Eugene Aserinsky, a graduate student at the University of Chicago, and Nathaniel Kleitman, his professor, observed periods of rapid eye movements (REMs) in
50 sleeping subjects. When awakened during these REM periods, subjects almost always remembered dreaming. On the other hand, when awakened during non-REM
55 phases of sleep, the subjects rarely could recall their dreams. Aserinsky and Kleitman used EEGs and other machines in an attempt to learn more about REMs and
60 sleep patterns.

Guided by REMs, it became possible for investigators to "spot" dreaming from outside and then awaken the sleeper to collect
65 dream stories. They could also alter the dreamers' experiences with noises, drugs, or other stimuli before or during sleep. Thankfully, it appears the body takes care of
70 itself by temporarily paralyzing muscles during REM sleep, preventing the dreamer from "acting out" dream activities.

Since the mid-1950s researchers
75 have been drawn into sleep laboratories. Initial studies attempted to answer questions about why people sleep and what happens in the brain and the body during
80 sleep. There, bedrooms adjoin other rooms that contain EEGs

and other equipment. The EEG amplifies signals from sensors on the face, head, and other parts
85 of the body, which together yield tracings of respiration, pulse, muscle tension, and changes of electrical potential in the brain that are sometimes called brain
90 waves. These recordings supply clues to the changes of the sleeping person's activities. These sleep studies have altered long-held beliefs that sleep was an inactive,
95 or passive, state only used for rest and recuperation. As scientists have learned more about the purpose of sleep and dreams during REM sleep, they are now turning to
100 the study of sleep disorders to learn more about problems during sleep.

7. What might be another title for this passage that summarizes its main ideas?

(A) REMs Through the Centuries

(B) Almcaeon, the Father of Sleep

(C) A History of the Study of Sleep

(D) The Story of Electroencephalographs

8. What does the phrase "anemia of the brain" in line 6 mean?

(A) The brain lacks functionality.

(B) There is a lack of red blood cells in the body.

(C) Anyone who sleeps regularly is anemic.

(D) The brain is very pale in color.

9. Drag and drop the ideas about sleep into the chart to show the order in which they occur in the passage. On the online GED® test, you will click and drag your answers into the correct spot. For this paper version, please write them in.

```
┌─────────────────────────────────────────────┐
│                                             │
└─────────────────────────────────────────────┘
┌─────────────────────────────────────────────┐
│                                             │
└─────────────────────────────────────────────┘
┌─────────────────────────────────────────────┐
│                                             │
└─────────────────────────────────────────────┘
┌─────────────────────────────────────────────┐
│                                             │
└─────────────────────────────────────────────┘
```

(A) REMs allow scientists a "window" into what is going on in a sleeper's brain.

(B) Modern sleep research includes studying sleep disorders.

(C) Sleep has been the subject of study for hundreds of years.

(D) Investigators have been able to alter dreams with noise, light, and other stimuli.

10. In the last paragraph, what is the best word or phrase used to describe how the detailed description of EEGs affects the understanding of the passage?

(A) It enhances it.

(B) It creates ambiguity.

(C) It muddles the concept.

(D) It negates it.

11. What led to the beginnings of sleep research in the 1920s? Type your answer in the box. On the online GED® test, you will type your answer. For this paper version, please write it in.

☐

12. If there were another paragraph in this passage, what would most likely be its subject?

(A) Greek scientists

(B) sleep laboratories

(C) Eugene Aserinsky

(D) sleep disorders

QUESTIONS 13–17 REFER TO THE FOLLOWING DOCUMENT.

IS IT RIGHT TO CONDUCT PERSONAL BUSINESS WHILE AT WORK?

County Policies for Use of the County Computer Network System (CCNS) and other Computerized Devices

A. Uses of the County Computer Network System (CCNS)
County employees should use the County's computer network system (CCNS) only to conduct official County business. However, brief and occasional use for personal reasons is permitted. Personal use of CCNS should not impede the conduct of County business; only incidental amounts of employee time, comparable to reasonable coffee breaks, should be used to attend to personal matters. Personal use of CCNS should not cause the County to incur a direct cost in addition to the costs of maintaining CCNS. Consequently, employees should not store or print personal material downloaded via CCNS.

B. Use of Personal Computer Devices
County employees shall not use their personal computer-hardware devices to conduct County business. Such devices include, but are not limited to, laptop, notebook and netbook computers, personal digital assistant (PDA) devices, and other handheld computing and communication devices. Connecting personal digital devices of any kind to the County's computer hardware is strictly prohibited. Employees who have been authorized to conduct County business from a remote location may do so only with equipment and software issued by the County.

C. Use of Other Personal Digital Devices
Notwithstanding the rules set forth in paragraph B, employees may bring personal cellular phones and similar communication devices with them to work, provided that they use these devices only to monitor incoming messages and to communicate with others in the event of an emergency.

D. Sharing Network Computing Resources
Use of the computer workstation assigned to another employee, whether with or without consent of that employee, is prohibited. However, in the presence of a supervising staff member for purposes such as project collaboration, training, or troubleshooting, two or more employees may briefly work at the same computer workstation.

E. No Privacy Expectation

County employees should have no expectation of privacy regarding their use of CCNS. All records created by CCNS use, including but not limited to Internet browsing history and cached data, are subject to inspection and audit by County administration or its representatives at any time, with or without notice. Use of CCNS by an employee indicates that the employee understands that the County has a right to inspect and audit all Internet use; and consents to any inspections following proper procedures and protocols.

13. Based on the document, how could an employee quickly understand the county's restrictions regarding computer use?

(A) by asking a co-worker

(B) by skimming the headings

(C) by calling the Personnel Department

(D) by checking e-mail

14. What is meant by "with or without notice" (paragraph E)?

(A) Employees are deemed to have read and understood the County's privacy policy.

(B) The County can inspect all e-mails sent and received by its employees.

(C) Employee Web-browsing history is recorded and monitored by the County.

(D) Employees need not be informed that their Internet use is being monitored.

15. If you were a County administrator and were hiring someone to ensure enforcement of the policies and procedures discussed in the document, which characteristic would you look for in that person?

(A) skill in interpersonal communications

(B) knowledge of computer networking

(C) skill in identifying suspicious behavior

(D) expertise in Internet privacy and security

16. Based on the document, which of the following is an example of what County employees either should or should not do?

County employees should

(A) access the Internet from work only while on coffee or meal breaks

(B) not conduct County business from home using their own computer

(C) print or save no more than a reasonable amount of data from the Internet

(D) maximize work efficiency by sharing computing resources with coworkers

17. Which of the following additional provisions would best support the ones in the document?

The best supporting provision would

(A) require employees to wear badges identifying their assigned workstation

(B) encourage employees to log out when leaving their workstations unattended

(C) discourage employees from troubleshooting computer problems on their own

(D) encourage employees to report observed rule violations to their supervisor

QUESTIONS 18-23 REFER TO THE FOLLOWING PASSAGE.

Henson and Peary

Matthew Henson was born in 1866 of free black parents in Maryland. He met Commander Robert Peary in 1888 and became first his servant, and then his assistant, on Peary's major expeditions to the Arctic. In these two passages, Henson and Peary describe the same area in Greenland, a place known as Karnah.

Passage 1—from Henson's Account of the 1908 Expedition

We stopped at Kookan, the most prosperous of the Esquimo settlements, a village of five tupiks (skin tents), housing twenty-four people,

5 and from there we sailed to the ideal community of Karnah.

Karnah is the most delightful spot on the Greenland coast. Situated on a gently southward

10 sloping knoll are the igloos and tupiks, where I have spent many pleasant days with my Esquimo friends and learned much of the folklore and history. Lofty moun-

15 tains, sublime in their grandeur, overtower and surround this place, and its only exposure is southward toward the sun. In winter its climate is not severe, as

20 compared with other portions of this country, and in the perpetual daylight of summer, life here is ideal. Rivulets of clear, cold water, the beds of which are grass- and

25 flower-covered, run down the sides of the mountain and, but for the lack of trees, the landscape is as delightful as anywhere on Earth.

Passage 2—from Peary's Account of the 1891 Expedition

From the eastern point of Academy Bay the main shore of the gulf extends, due east, to the face of the great Heilprin Glacier, and then

5 on beside the great ice-stream, until the crests of the cliffs disappear under the white shroud of the "Great Ice." From here on, the eastern and northern sides of

10 the head of the gulf are an almost continuous glacier face, six great ice-streams, separated by as many precipitous nunataks, flowing down from the interior ice-cap to dis-

15 charge an enormous fleet of bergs. As a result of this free discharge, the great white viscosity of the interior has settled down into a huge, and in clear weather easily discernible,

20 semi-circular basin, similar to those of Tossukatek, Great Kariak, and Jacobshavn. In this head of the gulf, situated some in the face of the glaciers, and others a short

25 distance beyond them, are seven or eight islands, most of which bear proof of former glaciation. Along the north-western shore of the gulf, the vertical cliffs resume

30 their sway, back of which rise the trio of striking peaks, Mounts Daly, Adams, and Putname. The cliffs continue westward for some little distance, then gradually merge into

35 a gentle slope, which is in turn succeeded by the face of the Hubbard Glacier. West of the glacier, cliffs of a different character (red and grey sandstone) occur, and extend

40 to the grand and picturesque red-brown Castle Cliffs at the entrance to Bowdoin Bay. At these cliffs, the shore takes an abrupt turn to the northward, into the now familiar

45 but previously unknown Bowdoin Bay, in which was located the headquarters of my last Expedition.

This bay has an extreme length of eleven miles, and an average

50 width of between three and four miles. What with its southern exposure, the protection from the wind afforded by the cliffs and bluffs which enclose it, and the

55 warmth of colouring of its shores, it presents one of the most desirable

locations for a house. The scenery is also varied and attractive, offering to the eye greater contrasts, with
60 less change of position, than any other locality occurring to me. Around the circuit of the bay are seven glaciers with exposures to all points of the compass, and varying
65 in size from a few hundred feet to over two miles in width.

The ice-cap itself is also in evidence here, its vertical face in one place capping and forming
70 a continuation of a vertical cliff which rises direct from the bay. From the western point of the bay, a line of grey sandstone cliffs—the Sculptured Cliffs of Karnah—inter-
75 rupted by a single glacier in a distance of eight miles, and carved by the restless arctic elements into turrets, bastions, huge amphitheatres, and colossal statues
80 of men and animals—extends to Cape Ackland, the Karnah of the natives. Here the cliffs end abruptly, and the shore trending north-westward to Cape Cleveland,
85 eighteen miles distant, consists of an almost continuous succession of fan-shaped, rocky deltas formed by glacier streams. Back of the shoreline is a gradually sloping
90 foreshore, rising to the foot of an irregular series of hills, which rise more steeply to the ice-cap lying upon their summits. In almost every depression between these
95 hills, the face of a glacier may be seen, and it is the streams from these that have made the shore what it is, and formed the wide shoals off it, on which every year a
100 numerous fleet of icebergs becomes stranded.

18. How does Henson support his opinion that "this is the most delightful spot on the Greenland coast"?
(A) with added drawings
(B) with quotes from natives
(C) with descriptions of the landscape
(D) with tales of nearby adventures

19. Based on the differing backgrounds and writing styles of the two men, as demonstrated in their accounts of Karnah, select which quotes from other expeditions belong to which explorer. Drag and drop the sentences into the correct location in the chart. On the online GED® test, you will click and drag the text into the correct place. For this paper version, please write them in.

Henson	Peary

(A) Here I am twenty-four years old and what have I done, what am I doing, or what am I in the way of doing? Nothing. . . . When I think of these things it makes me so restless that I can hardly keep quiet.

(B) I know it; the same old story, a man's work and a dog's life, and what does it amount to? What good is to be done? I am tired, sick, sore, and discouraged.

(C) If there ever was a job for a demon in Hades, that was it. I vividly recall it. At the same instant I was an imminent danger of freezng to death and being burned alive.

(D) These books, with a large assortment of novels and magazines, could be depended upon to relieve the tedium of the long arctic night, and very useful they were found for that purpose. Sitting up late at night means something when the night is some months long.

20. What might the reader infer as the cause of the difference between the descriptions by Henson and Peary?

 (A) a difference in travel experience

 (B) a difference in family size

 (C) a difference in religious training

 (D) a difference in education

21. Based on the descriptions, would Henson, Peary, both, or neither like to live in Karnah? Type your answer in the box provided. On the online GED® test, you will type in your answer. For this paper version, please write it in.

22. What does the phrase "carved by the restless arctic elements" in the last paragraph of Passage 2 suggest?

 (A) The natives enjoy making ice sculptures.

 (B) The weather is unpredictable.

 (C) The glaciers are moving.

 (D) The statues of men and animals are restless.

23. Based on context clues, what is Peary referring to when he mentions the "viscosity of the interior" in line 8 of the first paragraph of his account?

 (A) the thick inland formations

 (B) the depth of the sandstone rock formations

 (C) the water depth in the bay

 (D) the thick but still flowing glaciers

QUESTIONS 24–29 REFER TO THE FOLLOWING PASSAGE.

Passage 1

The future U.S. President Theodore Roosevelt, along with his close friend, Senator Henry Cabot Lodge, wrote a book entitled, Hero Tales from American History *(1895). This excerpt is taken from the chapter on George Washington.*

Washington

… [T]o sketch the life of Washington even in the barest outline is to write the history of the events which made the United States independent
5 and gave birth to the American nation…. We must look at him as he looked at life and the facts about him, without any illusion or deception, and no man in history
10 can better stand such a scrutiny. …

[H]e lived the life of a Virginia planter, successful in his private affairs and serving the public effectively but quietly as a member of
15 the House of Burgesses. When the troubles with the mother country began to thicken he was slow to take extreme ground, but he never wavered in his belief that
20 all attempts to oppress the colonies should be resisted, and when he once took up his position there was no shadow of turning. He was one of Virginia's delegates to the first Con-
25 tinental Congress, and, although he said but little, he was regarded by all the representatives from the other colonies as the strongest man among them. There was some-
30 thing about him even then which commanded the respect and the

confidence of everyone who came in contact with him. ...[H]e was the embodiment of the American
35 Revolution, and without him that revolution would have failed almost at the start. ...

After resigning his commission [in the Revolutionary Army] he
40 returned quietly to Mount Vernon, but he did not hold himself aloof from public affairs. On the contrary, he watched their course with the utmost anxiety. He saw the
45 feeble Confederation breaking to pieces, and he soon realized that that form of government was an utter failure.... [H]e stood at the head of the national movement,
50 and to him all men turned who desired a better union and sought to bring order out of chaos. With him Hamilton and Madison consulted in the preliminary stages which
55 were to lead to the formation of a new system. It was his vast personal influence which made that movement a success, and when the convention to form a constitution
60 met at Philadelphia, he presided over its deliberations, and it was his commanding will which, more than anything else, brought a constitution through difficulties and
65 conflicting interests which more than once made any result seem well-nigh hopeless. When the Constitution formed at Philadelphia had been ratified by the States, all
70 men turned to Washington to stand at the head of the new government. As he had borne the burden of the Revolution, so he now took up the task of bringing the government
75 of the Constitution into existence.

—Henry Cabot Lodge and
Theodore Roosevelt, *Hero Tales
from American History* (1895)

Passage 2

Moses Coit Tyler was an American historian, author, and professor. This excerpt is from his biography of Patrick Henry. Henry was a friend and colleague of George Washington in the days of the colonial government, and both men served in the Virginia House of Burgesses. Henry was a delegate to the Virginia Convention but lost the fight to reject ratification of the new Constitution.

It has been common to suppose that, even prior to the movement for the new Constitution, Patrick Henry had always been an extreme
5 advocate of the rights of the States as opposed to the central authority of the Union; and that the tremendous resistance which he made to the new Constitution
10 in all stages of the affair prior to the adoption of the first group of amendments is to be accounted for as the effect of an original and habitual tendency of his mind.
15 Such, however, seems not to have been the case.

In general it may be said that, at the very outset of the Revolution, Patrick Henry was one of the first of
20 our statesmen to recognize the existence and the imperial character of a certain cohesive central authority, arising from the very nature of the revolutionary act which the several
25 colonies were then taking. ... [A]s a leader in the Virginia House of Delegates from 1780 to 1784, he was in the main a supporter of the policy of giving more strength and dignity
30 to the general government. ...The great convention at Philadelphia, after a session of four months, came to the end of its noble labors on the 17th of September, 1787. Wash-
35 ington, who had been not merely its presiding officer but its presiding genius, then hastened back to Mt. Vernon, and, in his great anxiety to win over to the new Constitution

40 the support of his old friend Patrick Henry, he immediately dispatched to him a copy of that instrument, accompanied by a very impressive and conciliatory letter, …

45 But, now, what were Patrick Henry's objections to the new Constitution?

First of all, let it be noted that his objections did not spring from any
50 hostility to the union of the thirteen States, or from any preference for a separate union of the Southern States. … Then, in addition to his objections to the general character
55 of the Constitution, namely, as a consolidated government, unrestrained by an express guarantee of rights, he applied his criticisms in great detail, and with merciless
60 rigor, to each department of the proposed government,—the legislative, the executive, and the judicial; and with respect to each one of these he insisted that its intended functions
65 were such as to inspire distrust and alarm.

Patrick Henry's objections to the new Constitution, it may now be stated that they all sprang from a
70 single idea, and all revolved about that idea, namely, that the new plan of government, as it then stood, seriously endangered the rights and liberties of the people of the several
75 States. And in holding this opinion he was not at all peculiar. …

—Moses Coit Tyler, *Patrick Henry (c 1887)*

24. What can you infer was the author's intent in writing this biography of Patrick Henry (Passage 2)?

(A) to show that Henry was a patriot

(B) to show that Henry was misunderstood

(C) to show that Henry was a big proponent of states' rights

(D) to show that Henry favored the idea of federalism

25. Which sentence in Passage 1 describes why the authors thought Washington was successful in his role in creating the Constitution? Choose your answer from the drop-down menu. On the on-line GED® test, you will click to select your answer. For this paper version, please circle it.

Select ▼

(A) It was his commanding will which, more than anything else, brought a constitution through difficulties and conflicting interests which more than once made any result seem well-nigh hopeless.

(B) He was regarded by all the representatives from the other colonies as the strongest man among them.

(C) He did not hold himself aloof from public affairs.

(D) He was the embodiment of the American Revolution, and without him that revolution would have failed almost at the start.

26. What is the purpose of this sentence in Passage 2: "But, now, what were Patrick Henry's objections to the new Constitution?"

(A) to introduce the evidence in support of his argument

(B) to show that Henry's objections could be addressed

(C) to introduce Henry's ideas to amend the Constitution

(D) to show that Henry had no support for his ideas

27. According to Passage 1, what made Washington a great man?

    (A) He worked in the colonial government at every stage of its growth as the country moved toward independence.

    (B) His tireless contributions and dedication enabled the colonies to win independence and ensure success of the new government.

    (C) He risked his life fighting in the Revolution.

    (D) He gave up his land to help write a new Constitution.

28. Washington and Henry both wanted a new government and Constitution. Based on the passages, which of the following represents the best description of their differences? Choose your answer from the drop-down menu. On the online GED® test, you will click to select your answer. For this paper version, please circle it.

Select   ▼

    (A) Henry did not think the states should have so much power, while Washington thought the states needed more power.

    (B) Washington believed in the future of the country, while Henry thought the new republic would fail if the Constitution wasn't changed.

    (C) Henry thought the Constitution would put the nation at risk of tyranny, but Washington thought the Constitution would solve the problems of the Confederation.

    (D) Washington was more willing to compromise and Henry was stubborn.

29. What evidence does the text provide to suggest that Henry would not agree to vote to ratify the new Constitution (Passage 2)?

    (A) He was deeply critical of all aspects of the Constitution as it had been drafted.

    (B) He believed the Constitution seriously put the people's rights and liberties at risk.

    (C) Washington wrote him a letter to try to win him over.

    (D) He told Washington that he was against it when Washington showed him the new draft.

QUESTIONS 30–34 REFER TO THE FOLLOWING PASSAGE.

The Earth's Temperature Is a Balancing Act

Scientists have pieced together a picture of Earth's climate, dating back hundreds of thousands of years, by analyzing a number of
5 indirect measures of climate such as ice cores, tree rings, glacier lengths, pollen remains, and ocean sediments and by studying changes in Earth's orbit around the sun.
10   The historical record shows that the climate system varies naturally over a wide range of time scales. In general, climate changes prior to the Industrial Revolution in the
15 1700s can be explained by natural causes, such as changes in solar energy, volcanic eruptions, and natural changes in greenhouse gas (GHG) concentrations.
20   Recent climate changes, however, cannot be explained by natural causes alone. Research indicates that natural causes are very unlikely to explain most observed
25 warming, especially warming since the mid-twentieth century. Rather, human activities can very likely explain most of that warming.
     When sunlight reaches Earth's
30 surface, it can either be reflected

back into space or absorbed by Earth. Once absorbed, the planet releases some of the energy back into the atmosphere as heat (also
35 called infrared radiation). Greenhouse gases (GHGs) like water vapor (H_2O), carbon dioxide (CO_2), and methane (CH_4) absorb energy, slowing or preventing the loss of
40 heat to space. In this way, GHGs act like a blanket, making Earth warmer than it would otherwise be. This process is commonly known as the "greenhouse effect."

45 In the distant past (prior to about 10,000 years ago), CO_2 levels tended to track the glacial cycles. During warm "interglacial" periods, CO_2 levels have been higher. During
50 cool "glacial" periods, CO_2 levels have been lower. This is because the heating or cooling of Earth's surface can cause changes in greenhouse gas concentrations. These changes
55 often act as a positive feedback (an initial process that triggers changes in a second process that in turn influences the initial process), amplifying existing temperature
60 changes.

Since the Industrial Revolution began around 1750, human activities have contributed substantially to climate change by adding CO_2
65 and other heat-trapping gases to the atmosphere. These greenhouse gas emissions have increased the greenhouse effect and caused Earth's surface temperature to rise. The
70 primary human activity affecting the amount and rate of climate change is greenhouse gas emissions from the burning of fossil fuels.

The most important GHGs
75 directly emitted by humans include CO_2, CH_4, nitrous oxide (N_2O), and several others.

Carbon dioxide is the primary greenhouse gas that is contributing
80 to recent climate change. CO_2 is absorbed and emitted naturally as part of the carbon cycle, through animal and plant respiration, volcanic eruptions, and ocean-
85 atmosphere exchange. Human activities, such as the burning of fossil fuels and changes in land use, release large amounts of carbon to the atmosphere, causing CO_2
90 concentrations in the atmosphere to rise.

Atmospheric CO_2 concentrations have increased by almost 40% since pre-industrial times, from approxi-
95 mately 280 parts per million by volume (ppmv) in the eighteenth century to 390 ppmv in 2010. The current CO_2 level is higher than it has been in at least 800,000 years.
100 Some volcanic eruptions released large quantities of CO_2 in the distant past. However, the U.S. Geological Survey (USGS) reports that human activities now emit
105 more than 135 times as much CO_2 as volcanoes each year.

Human activities currently release over 30 billion tons of CO_2 into the atmosphere every year.
110 This buildup in the atmosphere is like a tub filling with water, where more water flows from the faucet than the drain can take away.

—epa.gov/climatechange

30. When did human behavior begin to have an impact of the Earth's climate? Write your answer in the box.

[   ]

On the online GED® test, you type in your answer. For this paper version, please write it in.

31. What evidence does the passage provide to support the conclusion that human activity is largely responsible for climate change?

(A) The levels of carbon dioxide in the atmosphere have increased by almost 40 percent since pre-industrial times.

(B) The measurement of ice cores shows an increase in atmospheric carbon.

(C) Volcanic eruptions have added carbon dioxide to the atmosphere, accumulating over time.

(D) Greenhouse gases prevent the loss of heat into space and make the Earth warmer.

32. Why are carbon dioxide, methane, and water vapor called greenhouse gases?

(A) These gases all act like a greenhouse by keeping heat in the Earth's atmosphere.

(B) These gases all reflect light from the sun.

(C) These gases are all useful in growing plants in a greenhouse.

(D) These gases are all part of the natural carbon cycle, which mimics plant respiration in a greenhouse.

33. Some people say that climate change is a result of natural phenomena like volcanic eruptions. What scientific studies cited in the passage show that this argument is not valid?

(A) studies of the role of feedback in temperature changes

(B) studies of changes in the temperature of the sun

(C) studies of the carbon cycle

(D) historical records of changes to the Earth's atmosphere

34. If you were to draw a picture of the word *feedback* as it is used in the passage, it would look like

[   ].

On the online GED® test, you type in your answer. For this paper version, please write it in.

QUESTIONS 35–40 REFER TO THE FOLLOWING PASSAGE.

Should May and Newland Elope?

Newland Archer was speaking with his fiancée, May Welland.

"Sameness—sameness!" he muttered, the word running through
5 his head like a persecuting tune as he saw the familiar tall-hatted figures lounging behind the plate glass; and because he usually dropped in at the club at that hour,
10 he had passed by instead. And now he began to talk to May of their own plans, their future, and Mrs. Welland's insistence on a long engagement.
15 "If you call it long!" May cried. "Isabel Chivers and Reggie were engaged for two years, Grace and Thorley for nearly a year and a half. Why aren't we very well off
20 as they are?"

"We might be much better off. We might be truly together—we might travel."

Her face lit up. "That would
25 be lovely," she admitted; she would love to travel. But her mother would not understand their wanting to do things so differently.

"As if the fact that it is different
30 doesn't account for it!" Archer insisted.

"Newland! You're so original!" she exulted.

His heart sank. He saw that
35 he was saying all the things that young men in the same situation were expected to say, and that she was making the answers that

instinct and tradition taught her to
40 make—even to the point of calling
him original.

"Original! We're all as like each
other as those dolls cut out of the
same folded paper. We're like pat-
45 terns stenciled on a wall. Can't
you and I strike out for ourselves,
May?"

"Goodness—shall we elope?" she
laughed.

50 "If you would—"

"You do love me, Newland! I'm
so happy."

"But then—why not be happier?"

"We can't behave like people in
55 novels, though, can we?"

"Why not—why not—why not?"
She looked a little bored by his
insistence. She knew very well
why they couldn't, but it was
60 troublesome to have to produce a
reason. "I'm not clever enough to
argue with you. But that kind of
thing is rather—vulgar, isn't it?"
she suggested, relieved to have
65 hit on a word that would certainly
extinguish the whole subject.

"Are you so much afraid, then,
of being vulgar?"

She was evidently staggered by
70 this. "Of course I should hate it—
and so would you," she rejoined, a
trifle irritably.

Feeling that she had indeed
found the right way of closing
75 the discussion, she went on light-
heartedly, "Oh, did I tell you
that I showed cousin Ellen my
engagement ring?"

—from *The Age of Innocence*,
by Edith Wharton

35. As revealed in the passage, what does
Newland Archer most yearn for?

(A) personal wealth

(B) May Welland's respect

(C) a stable marriage

(D) variety in life

36. When Newland mentions Mrs.
Welland's insistence on a long engagement, what does May's reaction
suggest about her?

May's reaction suggests that she

(A) considers the engagement
period planned by her mother to
be brief.

(B) feels that Newland Archer has
insulted her mother.

(C) disagrees with her mother about
when she and Newland should
marry.

(D) believes that her friends'
engagements periods were too
long.

37. How does May Welland put an end to
the discussion that Newland Archer
starts?

(A) She asserts that what he has
said during their discussion is
pointless.

(B) She denounces elopement as too
distasteful for her and Newland.

(C) She reminds him that their
friends would disapprove of an
elopement.

(D) She accuses him of trying to go
against her mother's wishes.

38. What would Newland probably conclude about May's responses to him?

He would conclude that they are influenced mainly by

(A) her educational background.

(B) social customs and expectations.

(C) her friends Isabel, Grace, and
Ellen.

(D) what her mother has told her
to say.

39. Edith Wharton wrote *The Age of Innocence* largely as a panorama of New York's upper middle-class society during the 1870s. What does the passage suggest about the prevailing attitude among that society toward leisure travel?

Leisure travel was considered to be

(A) traditional.

(B) a privilege.

(C) dangerous.

(D) uncommon.

40. What does the passage suggest about women from the era and culture that are the setting for *The Age of Innocence*?

(A) They were discouraged from thinking for themselves.

(B) They had high expectations of friends and family.

(C) They enjoyed long engagements.

(D) They liked to travel.

QUESTIONS 41–48 REFER TO THE FOLLOWING PASSAGE.

Kate Williams
15 Lake Street
Dorchester, MA 02122
508-122-1234
kwilliams@google.com

April 27, 2013
(1) Ms. Patricia Powell
(2) Personnel Department
(3) Acme publishing company
(4) 421 Main Street
(5) Alexandria, Virginia 01597
(6) Dear Ms. Powell,

(A)

(7) My name is Kate Williams and I am interested in the Assistant Editor position at your company. (8) While I do not have editing experience, I have worked in the publishing industry and have other relevant experience that could be helpful in this position. (9) Actually, I believe that the requirements you are seeking in an employee and my related experience and skills is an ideal match.

(B)

(10) For two summers during high school I was employed by Network Cable Services as a secretary where I answered the phone and did data entry. (11) I learned much about phone etiquette and dealing with the public. (12) The data entry work was assigned as I had time between telephone calls and greeting any customers as they came into the office. (13) The data entry work required great attention to detail and proofreading skills to ensure accuracy.

(C)

(14) While a college student, I worked as a Publicity and Marketing Intern for UNC Press from 2007-2009, where I researched authors and sent in press packets for books as well as completed clerical duties. (15) Again, accuracy and attention to detail was critical.

(D)

(16) Nevertheless, I was also an executive assistant intern for the NAACP, where I was responsible for many types of duties in 2010. (17) I researched and wrote articles for the national newsletter, learning much about the printing processes during this

internship. (18) He was always pleased with my work. (19) In this position I did some writing of speeches for the assistant director and designed brochures explaining some of the NAACP functions and programs for the staff in the Development Office.

(E)

(19) I am confident my skill set will exceed the expectations of this position. (20) Yet, I am still seeking more knowledge and experience within this field. (21) I believe my education and experience would make me an ideal candidate for your advertised opening. (22) I am convinced that I could be a positive addition to your staff. (23) I have references from each of my past positions. (24) There included with this letter of application. (25) I would greatly appreciate the opportunity for an interview.

(F)

(26) I can't wait to hear from you—soon I hope!

Sincerely,

Kate Williams

41. Sentence 3: Acme publishing company

    Which of the following is the correct version of sentence 3?

    (A) Acme publishing company

    (B) Acme Publishing company

    (C) acme publishing company

    (D) Acme Publishing Company

42. Sentence 6: Dear Ms. Powell,

    Which of the following corrections should be made to sentence 6?

    (A) Keep it as is

    (B) Replace the comma with a semicolon

    (C) Replace the comma with a colon

    (D) Delete the comma

43. Sentence 9: Actually, I believe that the requirements you are seeking in an employee and my related experience and skills is an ideal match.

    Which of the following corrections should be made to sentence 9?

    (A) keep it as is

    (B) change *is* to *was*

    (C) change *is* to *are*

    (D) change *is* to *were*

44. Sentence 10: For two summers during high school I was employed by Network Cable Services as a secretary where I answered the phone and did data entry.

    Which of the following corrections should be made to sentence 10?

    (A) insert a comma after *summers* and a comma after *school*

    (B) insert a comma after *school*

    (C) keep it as is

    (D) insert a semicolon after *school*

45. The sentences in Paragraph D appear below as they are in the letter. Put them in the order that makes the most sense. If the order is correct as shown, do not change it. On the online GED® test, you will click and drag the sentences into the correct order. For this paper version, please number them to indicate the correct order.

____ (16) Nevertheless, I was also an executive assistant intern for the NAACP, where I was responsible for many types of duties in 2010.

____ (17) I researched and wrote articles for the national newsletter, learning much about the printing processes during this internship.

____ (18) He was always pleased with my work.

____ (19) In this position I did some writing of speeches for the assistant director and designed brochures explaining some of the NAACP functions and programs for the staff in the Development Office.

46. Sentence 18: He was always pleased with my work.

Which of the following corrections should be made to sentence 18?

(A) keep it as is

(B) replace *He was* with *He were*

(C) replace *He was* with *They were*

(D) replace *He was* with *We were*

47. Sentence 24: There included with this letter of application.

Which of the following corrections should be made to sentence 24?

(A) replace *There* with *They're*

(B) replace *There* with *There is*

(C) replace *There* with *There*

(D) replace *There* with *Their*

48. Sentence 26: I can't wait to hear from you—soon I hope!

Which of the following would be the best replacement for sentence 26?

(A) I sure hope you'll call soon.

(B) I look forward to hearing from you in the near future.

(C) I can't wait to hear from you—soon I hope.

(D) Maybe I should drop by your office and hope you will see me.

49. *The following passages present two views of a Supreme Court decision. Take 45 minutes to choose which of the positions you wish to support and use the paper provided to write a well-organized essay. Use reasons and examples to support your position.*

One of the major issues debated in the 2010 Supreme Court decision known as Citizens United centered on free speech related to political campaigns. Federal laws prohibit corporations from making direct contributions to political candidates and to spending corporate monies on activities that expressly advocate the election or defeat of specific candidates.

Case Background:
In January 2008, Citizens United, a nonprofit corporation, released a 90-minute documentary film entitled *Hillary: The Movie.* The film is critical
5 of then-Senator Hillary Clinton, who was a candidate in the Democratic Party's 2008 presidential primary elections. The film was released in theaters and on DVD, but Citizens
10 United also wanted to make it available through video-on-demand and was prepared to pay the cable companies so that the public could watch it free of charge. In addition,
15 Citizens United planned to air ads about the film on network TV and cable channels. The FEC (Federal Election Commission) stepped in to stop the broadcast, claiming
20 that federal law prohibited such

advertising to the public within 30 days of the primary. In a 5–4 decision, the Court ruled that such advertising is Constitutionally protected speech, and corporations cannot be barred from making these types of political contributions.

The following excerpts are from 1.) Justice Kennedy, who wrote an opinion for the majority, and 2.) Justice Stevens, who wrote an opinion for the minority.

1. Justice Kennedy for the majority:

Federal law prohibits corporations and unions from using their general treasury funds to make independent expenditures for speech defined as an "electioneering communication" or for speech expressly advocating the election or defeat of a candidate. ... Speech is an essential mechanism of democracy, for it is the means to hold officials accountable to the people. ... The right of citizens to inquire, to hear, to speak, and to use information to reach consensus is a precondition to enlightened self-government and a necessary means to protect it. ... For these reasons, political speech must prevail against laws that would suppress it, whether by design or inadvertence. ...

Speech restrictions based on the identity of the speaker are all too often simply a means to control content. Quite apart from the purpose or effect of regulating content, moreover, the Government may commit a constitutional wrong when by law it identifies certain preferred speakers. By taking the right to speak from some and giving it to others, the Government deprives the disadvantaged person or class of the right to use speech to strive to establish worth, standing, and respect for the speaker's voice. The Government may not by these means deprive the public of the right and privilege to determine for itself what speech and

speakers are worthy of consideration. The First Amendment protects speech and speaker, and the ideas that flow from each. ... [I]t is inherent in the nature of the political process that voters must be free to obtain information from diverse sources in order to determine how to cast their votes. ... We find no basis for the proposition that, in the context of political speech, the Government may impose restrictions on certain disfavored speakers. Both history and logic lead us to this conclusion. ... [P]olitical speech does not lose First Amendment protection "simply because its source is a corporation." ... The Court has thus rejected the argument that political speech of corporations or other associations should be treated differently under the First Amendment simply because such associations are not "natural persons." ...

2. Justice Stevens for the minority wrote:

The real issue in this case concerns how, not if, the appellant [organization appealing to the Court] may finance its electioneering. Citizens United is a wealthy nonprofit corporation that runs a political action committee (PAC) with millions of dollars in assets. ... [I]t could have used those assets to televise and promote *Hillary: The Movie* wherever and whenever it wanted to. It also could have spent unrestricted sums to broadcast *Hillary* at any time other than the 30 days before the last primary election. Neither Citizens United's nor any other corporation's speech has been "banned." ... All that the parties dispute is whether Citizens United had a right to use the funds in its general treasury to pay for broadcasts during the 30-day period.

The notion that the First Amendment dictates an affirmative answer to that question is, in my judgment, profoundly misguided. ...

The basic premise underlying the Court's ruling is its iteration, and constant reiteration, of the propo-
30 sition that the First Amendment bars regulatory distinctions based on a speaker's identity, including its "identity" as a corporation. While that glittering generality has rhetorical
35 appeal, it is not a correct statement of the law. ...

In the context of election to public office, the distinction between corporate and human speakers is signif-
40 icant. Although they make enormous contributions to our society, corporations are not actually members of it. They cannot vote or run for office. Because they may be managed and
45 controlled by nonresidents, their interests may conflict in fundamental respects with the interests of eligible voters. ...

It might also be added that cor-
50 porations have no consciences, no beliefs, no feelings, no thoughts, no desires. Corporations help structure and facilitate the activities of human beings, to be sure, and their "per-
55 sonhood" often serves as a useful legal fiction. But they are not themselves members of "We the People" by whom and for whom our Constitution was established. ...

60 In a democratic society, the long-standing consensus on the need to limit corporate campaign spending should outweigh the wooden application of judge-made rules.

MATHEMATICAL REASONING

90 Minutes • 37 Questions

General Directions: The Mathematical Reasoning Test consists of 37 questions intended to measure your general mathematics skills, including your ability to solve math problems. The test consists of 5 questions that you will not have access to a calculator to answer and 32 questions that you will have use of a calculator to solve.

Disclaimer: The Mathematical Reasoning Test will have calculator-allowed questions mixed with calculator-prohibited questions, with the calculator tool available to use when it is an option. However, for this test, the calculator-prohibited questions are grouped together as the first 5 questions.

To answer some questions you will need to apply one or more mathematics formulas. The formulas provided on the next page will help you to answer those questions. Some questions refer to charts, graphs, and figures. Unless otherwise noted, charts, graphs, and figures are drawn to scale.

Answering Alternative-format Questions

Most questions are multiple choice, but to answer some questions, you will be required to select from a drop-down menu, fill an answer in a blank, drag and drop correct answers, and select answers on a given graphic.

practice test

Mathematics Formula Sheet & Explanation

The 2014 GED® Mathematical Reasoning test contains a formula sheet, which displays formulas relating to geometric measurement and certain algebra concepts. Formulas are provided to test-takers so that they may focus on *application*, rather than the *memorization*, of formulas.

Area of a:

parallelogram	$A = bh$
trapezoid	$A = \frac{1}{2}h(b_1 + b_2)$

Surface Area and Volume of a:

rectangular/right prism	$SA = ph + 2B$	$V = Bh$
cylinder	$SA = 2\pi rh + 2\pi r^2$	$V = \pi r^2 h$
pyramid	$SA = \frac{1}{2}ps + B$	$V = \frac{1}{3}Bh$
cone	$SA = \pi rs + \pi r^2$	$V = \frac{1}{3}\pi r^2 h$
sphere	$SA = 4\pi r^2$	$V = \frac{4}{3}\pi r^3$

(p = perimeter of base B; $\pi \approx 3.14$)

Algebra

slope of a line	$m = \dfrac{y_2 - y_1}{x_2 - x_1}$
slope-intercept form of the equation of a line	$y = mx + b$
point-slope form of the equation of a line	$y - y_1 = m(x - x_1)$
standard form of a quadratic equation	$y = ax^2 + bx + c$
quadratic formula	$x = \dfrac{-b \pm \sqrt{b^2 - 4ac}}{2a}$
Pythagorean Theorem	$a^2 + b^2 = c^2$
simple interest	$I = prt$

(I = interest, p = principal, r = rate, t = time)

The use of a calculator is prohibited for questions 1–5.

1. The figure below shows a solid cube 3 inches on a side but with a 1-inch square hole cut through it.

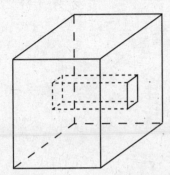

The resulting surface area of the solid figure is [   ] square inches. *Hint:* Remember to include surfaces inside the hole. On the online GED® test, you type your answer in the box. For this paper test, please write it in.

2. The result of the following operation is [   ]

   $13 + 7 \times 17 \div 4$

   The answer should be expressed as a decimal number. On the online GED® test, you type your answer in the box. For this paper test, please write it in.

3. David and Steven work together in the shipping-and-handling department of the same company. David can pack a total of 48 boxes in 5 hours. Steven can pack two-thirds the number of boxes each hour as David. How many boxes can Steven pack in 3 hours?

   (A) 19
   (B) 28
   (C) 32
   (D) 36

4. The equation of a circle is $x^2 + y^2 = r^2$, where r is the radius and x and y are the coordinates of the circle's center. A circle has a center at $(x, 12)$ and a radius of 13. What is the value of x?

   (A) 1
   (B) 5
   (C) 12
   (D) 25

5. There are five flavors of ice cream at the ice cream shop: vanilla, cherry, blueberry, pistachio, and mint. In how many ways can you combine three different scoops of ice cream?

   (A) 10
   (B) 30
   (C) 60
   (D) 120

The use of a calculator is allowed for questions 6–37.

QUESTIONS 6 AND 7 REFER TO THE FOLLOWING GRAPH.

XY Lumber Co. Budget, 2011
$200,000

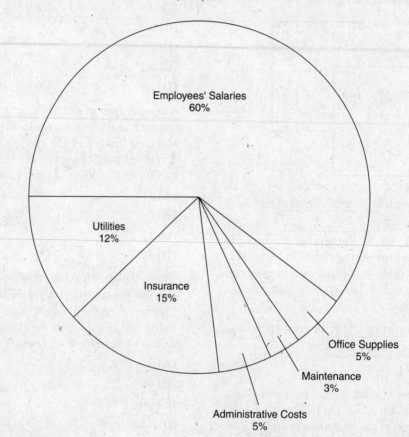

6. How much money was budgeted for administrative costs?

   (A) $1000
   (B) $10,000
   (C) $20,000
   (D) $100,000

7. The budget for insurance exceeds the budget for utilities by

   | Select ▼ |

   $300

   $600

   $3000

   $6000

   On the online GED® test, you click on the correct answer. For this paper version, please circle it.

8. The degree sum of the interior angles of any polygon can be expressed as $(n - 2)(180°)$, where n = the number of sides. If four of the five interior angles of a pentagon measure 110°, 60°, 120°, and 100°, what is the measure of the fifth interior angle?

   (A) 110°
   (B) 125°
   (C) 135°
   (D) 150°

QUESTIONS 9 AND 10 REFER TO THE FOLLOWING TABLE.

ELECTRICITY USAGE AT FOUR HOUSES: A, B, C, and D

(Month of June)

House	Interior area (square area)	Interior volume (cubic feet)	Electricity usage in kilowatt hours (kWh)
A	1300	10,400	960
B	1500	12,000	1044
C	2000	16,200	1125
D	2300	18,400	1205

9. The month of June consists of 30 days. During June, how much more electricity was used at house C per day than at house A per day, on average?

   (A) 2.8 kWh
   (B) 4.0 kWh
   (C) 4.8 kWh
   (D) 5.5 kWh

10. Assuming each house has a flat ceiling, which house has the greatest ceiling height?

    (A) House A
    (B) House B
    (C) House C
    (D) House D

11. A cone-shaped doll hat has a radius of 2 inches and the height of 5 inches. If the hat is turned upside down and filled with water, it will hold [   ] of water, to the nearest cubic inch. On the online GED® test, you type your answer in the box. For this paper test, please write it in.

12. Which of the following simplifies to an integer?

    (A) $\dfrac{5}{3} + \dfrac{3}{4}$
    (B) $\dfrac{5}{4} + \dfrac{3}{2}$
    (C) $\dfrac{3}{5} + \dfrac{4}{3}$
    (D) $\dfrac{3}{4} + \dfrac{5}{4}$

13. Which of the following expressions is a simplified form of $(-2x^2)^4$?

    (A) $-16x^6$
    (B) $-8x^8$
    (C) $8x^6$
    (D) $16x^8$

14. The graph of the equation $y = 7x - 3$ is a straight line. The y-intercept of this line is at point P.

On the online GED® test, you click on the grid point to plot point P. For this paper test, please draw point P.

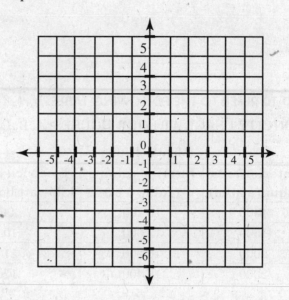

15. How many distinct values of x satisfy the function $f(x) = \left(6x - \dfrac{4}{3} \right)$?

(A) 0

(B) 1

(C) 2

(D) infinitely many

16. The figure below shows the end of a packing box that holds six identical tubes.

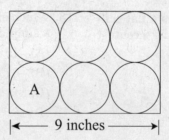

What is the circumference of tube A?

(A) 2π inches

(B) 3π inches

(C) 3.5π inches

(D) 4.5π inches

17. A legislature passed a bill into law by a 5:3 margin. No legislator abstained, and therefore [Select ▼] of the votes cast were in favor of the bill.

$$\frac{3}{8}$$

$$\frac{5}{8}$$

$$\frac{3}{5}$$

$$\frac{5}{3}$$

On the online GED® test, you click on the correct answer. For this paper version, please circle it.

18. A vending machine contains only dimes (*d*) and nickels (*n*). Complete a linear expression that represents the total dollar amount of all coins in the vending machine. In the online GED® test, you will drag and drop the numbers, variables, and operands into the appropriate box. For this paper test, please write in the correct answer.

$0.05	$0.15	$0.10	*n*	*d*

$(n + d)$	+	−	×	÷

19. Identify the x- and y-intercepts of the line: $y = \dfrac{2}{3}x - 2$. On the online GED® test,
you will click on the grid to mark the points. For this paper version, please write
in the points.

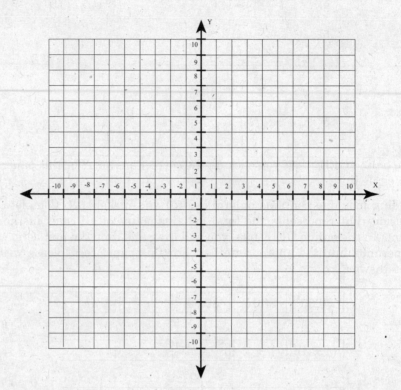

20. Which of the following is NOT equal
to 4.23×10^{-2} ?

(A) 4230×10^{-4}

(B) 0.00423×10^{1}

(C) 0.423×10^{-1}

(D) 42.3×10^{-3}

21. Two square rugs, R and S, have a
combined area of 20 square feet. If the
area of rug R is four times the area of
rug S, what is the perimeter of rug S?

(A) 4 feet

(B) 8 feet

(C) 10 feet

(D) 12 feet

22. In which of the following forms can
the quadratic expression $x^2 - 2x - 3$ be
written?

(A) $(x - 3)(x + 1)$

(B) $(x - 3)(x - 2)$

(C) $(x + 3)(x - 1)$

(D) $(x - 2)(x + 1)$

23. The figure below shows a wire (represented by the dashed line) connecting the outer edge of a porch roof to the base of the building's wall. The height of the building is 12 feet and the width of the porch roof is 5 feet.

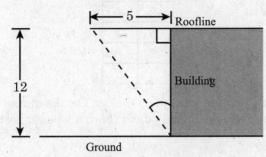

Not drawn to scale.

Which of the following represents the length of wire, in feet?

(A) 12

(B) 13

(C) 17

(D) 144

24. The surface area of a right prism is the sum of the area of its faces.

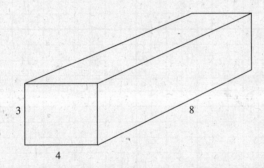

Create an equation to calculate the surface area of prism *P*. On the online GED® test, you will drag and drop the numbers and operands into the appropriate boxes. For this paper test, please write in the correct answers.

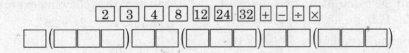

25. The table of xy values below shows values for the line $y = 2x - 1$.

x	y
-2	-5
0	-1
2	3
4	7

Graph the line on the coordinate plane below. On the online GED® test, you will click on the grid to plot two of the points. For this paper test, write down two of the points.

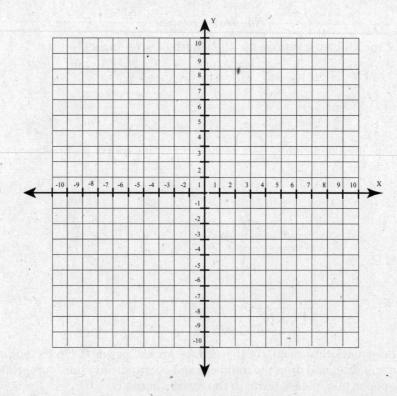

26. Kieran is calculating the percent growth, P, in an algae population. He is using the formula $P = \dfrac{a_2 - a_1}{a_1} \times 100$, where $a_1 = 1250$ and $a_2 = 1480$. What is the percent growth in the algae population, P?

(A) 230%

(B) 184%

(C) 84.5%

(D) 18.4%

27. Which of the following expressions is equal to $x^2 - 12x + 36$?

(A) $(x - 6)^2$

(B) $(x + 6)^2$

(C) $(x + 6)(x - 6)$

(D) $(x + 3)(x - 12)$

28. Movie tickets are $12.00 for adults and $8.00 for children aged 12 and under. On Tuesday, 180 tickets are sold. Which expression can be used to represent the total revenues from Tuesday's ticket sales if A is the number of adult tickets sold and C is the number of children's tickets sold?

(A) $A + C$

(B) $12A + 8C$

(C) $180(A + C)$

(D) $12A \times 8C$

29. What is the value of x if $\dfrac{Ax - Bx}{2} = 2$?

(A) $\dfrac{A - B}{4}$

(B) $\dfrac{4}{A - B}$

(C) $\dfrac{2}{A - B}$

(D) $Ax - Bx$

30. If $2y \le \dfrac{y + 3}{-2}$, then it must be true that $5y$ ▼ Select ▼ Select

=	3
≤	−3
≥	$\dfrac{3}{5}$
<	
>	$-\dfrac{3}{5}$

On the online GED® test, you will click on the correct answers. For this paper version, circle them.

31. To cater a brunch, Food-to-Go charges a $115 set-up fee plus $9.75 per person. Miranda has to comply with a budget, b, from her company and wants to plan a holiday brunch using Food-to-Go. Which of the following inequalities will help Miranda calculate how much money she needs for brunch for p people?

(A) $115p > b - 9.75$

(B) $9.75b \le b - 115 + p$

(C) $9.75p + 115 \le b$

(D) $115 + 9.75p > b$

practice test

32. Fresh produce should be kept at temperatures between 41° and 45° Fahrenheit. The formula $F = \frac{9}{5}C + 32$ can be used to convert Celsius temperatures, C, to Fahrenheit temperatures, F. Which inequality indicates the best Celsius temperatures for fresh produce?

(A) $7.2 \leq C \geq 5$

(B) $5 \leq C \leq 7.2$

(C) $9 \leq C \leq 13$

(D) $41 \leq C \leq 45$

33. What number should be added to $x^2 - \frac{1}{2}x = 4$ to complete the square?

(A) $-\frac{1}{16}$

(B) $-\frac{1}{4}$

(C) $\frac{1}{16}$

(D) $\frac{1}{4}$

34. An industrial mower has 140 gallons of gasoline in the gas tank. After mowing for 6 hours, the mower has 35 gallons of gasoline left in the tank. The graph below shows the amount of gas in the mower during its route. What is the average hourly rate at which the mower uses gasoline?

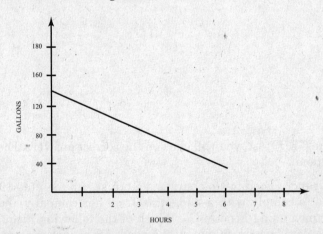

(A) 95 gallons per hour

(B) 40 gallons per hour

(C) 17.5 gallons per hour

(D) 3.8 gallons per hour

35. The equation of a line with a slope of m is $y = mx + b$, where x and y are two points on the line, m is the slope, and b is the y-intercept. The equation of a line with a slope of $-\frac{1}{3}$ that goes through the point (2, –2) is $y = \boxed{}x + \boxed{}$. Click on the numbers below and drag them into the correct position to form the equation of the line.

For the print version of the book draw arrows from the blank boxes to the correct numbers.

$$-2, \ -\frac{4}{3}, \ -\frac{1}{3}, \ \frac{2}{3}, \ \frac{4}{3}, \ 2$$

36. Which pair of equations represents two lines that are perpendicular to each other?

(A) $y = 2x + 4$; $y = -2x + 4$

(B) $\frac{1}{2}y = x - 2$; $-2y = x - 2$

(C) $-y = 4x - 1$; $y = \frac{1}{4}x + 1$

(D) $y = \frac{2}{3}x - 5$; $y = \frac{3}{2}x - 5$

37. In which of the following functions is it true that each element in the domain has exactly one element in the range?

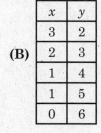

(A)

x	y
0	−1
0	1
1	−2
1	2
2	−3

(C)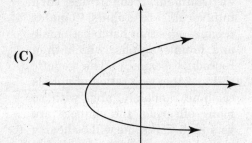

(B)

x	y
3	2
2	3
1	4
1	5
0	6

(D)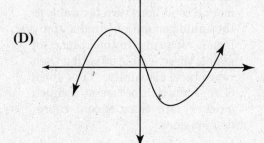

SCIENCE

90 Minutes • 30 Questions

Directions: The Science Test consists of questions in several formats designed to measure your knowledge of general science concepts. The questions are based on brief passages of text and visual information (charts, graphs, diagrams, and other figures). Some questions are based on both text and visual information. Study the information provided, and answer the question(s) that follow, referring back to the information as needed.

You will have 90 minutes to answer all 30 questions. Record your answers on the answer sheet provided.

QUESTION 1 IS BASED ON THE FOLLOWING INFORMATION.

Aphids are a family of insects that are considered to be destructive pests. During autumn, when environmental conditions turn unfavorable to aphids, females produce eggs that hatch both male and female aphids, which then reproduce sexually. The genetic traits of this generation of aphids combine randomly, and, with so many offspring, the chances are very high that some will be hearty enough to survive the harsh fall and winter seasons. Eggs that are laid during the winter and that hatch in the spring, when environmental conditions turn favorable to the aphid population, produce only female offspring. In the absence of males, these female offspring then reproduce asexually. This form of reproduction occurs at a much quicker rate than sexual reproduction does.

1. Which is the best explanation for why aphids have evolved to reproduce asexually during the spring season?

   (A) Most of the eggs produced during the winter season never hatch offspring.

   (B) Environmental conditions during the spring and summer support a large aphid population.

   (C) Male aphids typically survive a harsh winter season, whereas female aphids do not.

   (D) Spring is the only season of the year during which aphids can reproduce.

QUESTIONS 2 AND 3 REFER TO THE FOLLOWING CHART.

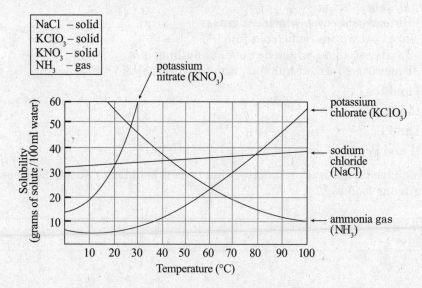

NaCl – solid
KClO₃ – solid
KNO₃ – solid
NH₃ – gas

2. A 20°C solution containing 100 ml of water and 15 grams of potassium nitrate (KNO₃) is heated to 25°C. Approximately how much more KNO₃ must be added to reach the saturation point—at which no more KNO₃ can be dissolved? Mark your answer on the line below. On the GED® test, you will be asked to click on the correct point.

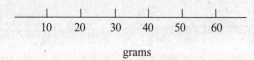

grams

3. Which conclusion is best supported by the chart?

   (A) The solubility of a solid increases as temperature decreases.

   (B) Ammonia is soluble at any temperature.

   (C) The solubility of a gas varies inversely with temperature.

   (D) Solids are soluble, but gases are not.

QUESTIONS 4 AND 5 REFER TO THE FOLLOWING INFORMATION.

A food web is made up of linking food chains. The two basic types of food webs are the grazing web and the detrital web. In the grazing web, the chain begins with plants that are eaten by herbivores (plant eaters) and then by carnivores (flesh eaters) or omnivores (those that eat both plants and animals). The detrital web begins with plant and animal matter that become decomposers (bacteria and fungi). The decomposers then pass to detritivores (organisms that feed on decomposed matter) and then to carnivores.

4. Among the following statements, which provides evidence that the grazing and detrital webs overlap?

    I. Humans eat cows, which eat grass.

    II. Birds eat worms, which eat fungi.

    III. Snails eat algae, which do not eat anything else.

    IV. Tapeworms feed off humans, who eat vegetables.

(A) I and II

(B) II and III

(C) I and IV

(D) II and IV

5. Tigers have no natural predators. What does this indicate about their position in the grazing food web?

_____

_____

QUESTION 6 REFERS TO THE FOLLOWING GRAPHIC.

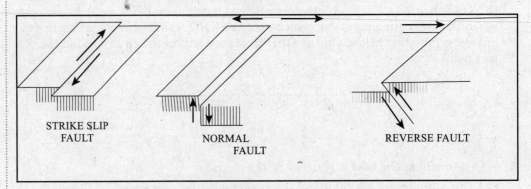

6. Which of the three types of faults can create a mountain range?

(A) only a normal fault

(B) either a normal or reverse fault

(C) only a reverse fault

(D) either a normal or strike-slip fault

QUESTIONS 7 AND 8 REFER TO THE FOLLOWING INFORMATION.

Scientists today can modify the genetic makeup of plants and animals in order to produce desirable traits and eliminate undesirable ones. Genetically modified organisms, or GMOs, are widely used today by large, corporate-owned farms in the production of crops to enhance their color, size, and vitamin content, as well as to make crops more resistant to pests, disease, and severe weather conditions. Opponents of these so-called "Frankenfoods" point out that farm and migratory animals will often refuse to eat genetically altered feed, and they fear that GMO foods may cause cancer in humans. A large agribusiness company behind the development of many GMOs reports, however, that its own scientific studies show no incidence of cancer in humans or other animals resulting from the ingestion of genetically modified foods.

7. What is a possible criticism of the GMO studies conducted by the agribusiness corporations?

(A) They had a vested interest in a particular outcome of the study.

(B) They failed to account for other possible causes of cancer in humans.

(C) They did not compare the health effects of genetically modified foods to those of organic foods.

(D) They had no control over independent variables.

8. GMO critics also worry that modified genes could spread to other plants, with potentially disastrous consequences for their ecosystems. In making this criticism, what sort of scenario might these critics have in mind?

(A) a genetically mutated "superweed" that comes to dominate an entire biome

(B) small farmers in impoverished countries driven to ruin by agribusiness

(C) contamination of water supplies needed to support human communities

(D) the spread of disease that a GMO was intentionally engineered to prevent

QUESTION 9 REFERS TO THE FOLLOWING INFORMATION.

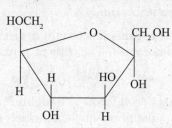

GLUCOSE   FRUCTOSE

| O – OXYGEN |
| C – CARBON |
| H – HYDROGEN |
| LEGEND |

9. What is the main difference between a glucose molecule and a fructose molecule?

(A) The placement of the carbon atoms is different.

(B) Glucose has fewer oxygen atoms.

(C) Fructose has more carbon atoms.

(D) They have a different total number of atoms.

QUESTION 10 REFERS TO THE FOLLOWING INFORMATION.

An individual human has about 35,000 genes, each of which occupies a certain position on a molecule of DNA, called a chromosome, inside the nucleus of every cell. Genes direct the production of proteins that result in all the specific physical traits of the individual. During sexual reproduction, the parent's chromosomes pair up and join to be passed on to the child, who inherits the DNA of both parents.

10. Which best explains the wide variation in physical traits that you see among the thousands of people at a crowded festival or sporting event?

(A) Each pair of corresponding genes from two parents blends together in the child.

(B) The parents' genes combine randomly to form the child's DNA structure.

(C) Children inherit only the traits of the parent whose genes are dominant.

(D) Many physical traits disappear after the first generation of offspring.

QUESTION 11 REFERS TO THE FOLLOWING INFORMATION.

THE 5-KINGDOM
CLASSIFICATION SYSTEM

Monera (bacteria): Single-celled prokaryotic organisms; reproduce by binary fission (simple cell division); found in every habitat

Protista (protists): Single-celled eukaryotic organisms; include plantlike, animal-like, and fungi-like organisms; reproduce by binary fission

Fungi: Single-celled and multicellular eukaryotic organisms; cells reproduce by either budding (forming a string of cells) or binary fission

Plantae (plants): Multicellular eukaryotic organisms with cell walls; make their own food from the Sun's energy

Animalia (animals): Multicellular eukaryotic organisms without cell walls; ingest food and process it internally

The cells of eukaryotic organisms contain a distinct nucleus, and their DNA is organized into chromosomes. The cells of prokaryotic organisms lack these features.

11. In reproduction of yeast, a cell forms a "daughter" cell, and then the nucleus of the parent cell splits into a daughter nucleus, which migrates into the daughter cell.

Yeast belongs to the | Select ▼ | kingdom.

monera

protista

fungi

plantae

animalia

On the online GED® test, you will click to select your answer. For this paper version, please circle it.

12. When a source emits sound energy, sound waves spread out over an ever-enlarging sphere, decreasing in intensity as they travel. Also, some sound energy is absorbed by the air (or other medium) along the way.

Which of the following do these phenomena best help to explain?

(A) how a cheerleader's megaphone works

(B) why acoustic tiling is used in opera houses

(C) how an echo chamber works

(D) why audio speakers should face the listener

QUESTION 13 REFERS TO THE FOLLOWING ILLUSTRATION.

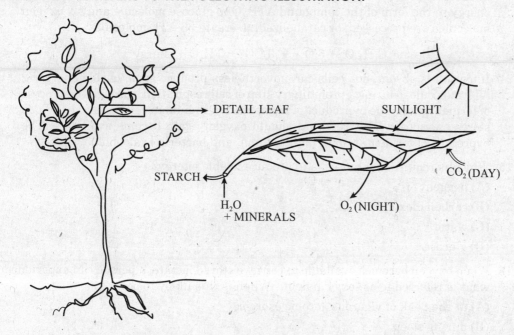

13. A green plant manufactures the carbohydrates it needs to grow and survive by combining [   ] molecules and [   ] molecules. On the online GED® test, you will type your answers in the box. For this paper test, please write them in.

QUESTION 14 REFERS TO THE FOLLOWING INFORMATION.

Most heart attacks occur as a result of coronary artery disease (CAD). CAD is the buildup over time of a material called plaque on the inner walls of the coronary arteries. Eventually, a section of plaque can break open, causing a blood clot to form at the site. A heart attack occurs if the clot becomes large enough to cut off most or all of the blood flow through the artery. The blocked blood flow prevents oxygen-rich blood from reaching the part of the heart muscle fed by the artery. The lack of oxygen damages the heart muscle. If the blockage isn't treated quickly, the damaged heart muscle begins to die. Common signs that a person is having a heart attack are chest pain and upper body discomfort in one or both arms, the back, neck, jaw, or stomach.

14. Based on the above information, which organ do coronary arteries carry blood from and which organ do the coronary arteries carry it to?

_____

_____

QUESTIONS 15 AND 16 REFER TO THE FOLLOWING INFORMATION.

Most of the food humans consume is processed by our cells into usable energy through cell respiration, in which glucose and other molecules are broken down in the presence of oxygen into carbon dioxide and water to release chemical energy in the form of the compound ATP. One glucose molecule and six oxygen molecules are processed, or catabolized, to create 36 ATP molecules:

$$C_6H_{12}O_6 + 6\,O_2 \rightarrow 6\,CO_2 + 6\,H_2O + energy$$

If oxygen is absent, our cells can nevertheless produce some usable energy (2 ATP molecules) during a preliminary step of cell respiration, through the process of fermentation. The byproduct of fermentation in human cells is lactate, which stores energy for later retrieval should oxygen again become available. (The byproduct of fermentation in plants, fungi, and bacteria is alcohol.)

15. Which is required for our cells to produce usable energy?
    (A) oxygen
    (B) carbon dioxide
    (C) water
    (D) glucose

16. When oxygen becomes available to retrieve stored lactate, a person can experience what is referred to as "oxygen debt." When is this likely to occur?
    (A) at the peak of vigorous aerobic exercise
    (B) during sleep
    (C) after a large meal
    (D) shortly after vigorous exercise

QUESTION 17 IS BASED ON THE FOLLOWING ILLUSTRATION.

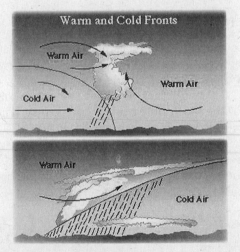

17. The border between two air masses is referred to as a *front*. An advancing front can be either warm or cold. When the air in a warm front rises above an approaching cold front, water vapor in the air

    [   ]. On the online GED® test, you will type your answer in the box. For this paper test, please write it in.

18. An object of mass, *m*, is at rest until a force, *F*, acts on it for a period of 10 seconds. Which expression shows the average velocity of the object during those 10 seconds?

    (A) $5F$

    (B) $10Fm$

    (C) $\dfrac{5F}{m}$

    (D) $\dfrac{10F}{m}$

QUESTION 19 REFERS TO THE FOLLOWING TABLE.

	Potassium	Sodium	Calcium	Magnesium	Aluminum	Zinc	Iron	Tin	Lead	Copper	Mercury	Silver	Gold	Platinum
Reaction— air or oxygen	Burns								Converts to oxide		No reaction			
Reaction— water	Reacts with cold water		Reacts with steam	No reaction										
Reaction— acids	Displaces hydrogen from acids									Reacts only with oxidizing axids		No reaction		

19. The more reactive a metal to oxygen, the more it tends to corrode. The table would be useful in the production of any of the following EXCEPT which one?

    (A) oil rigs

    (B) a boat hull

    (C) fine jewelry

    (D) cooking pans

QUESTION 20 REFERS TO THE FOLLOWING INFORMATION.

Each human gene can come in one or more varieties, called *alleles*. For each gene type, we inherit one allele from each parent. Each corresponding pair of alleles defines a unique physical or other trait. Either allele in a pair can be dominant or recessive. Two recessive alleles for one trait can actually mask the expression of alleles located at certain other sites on the chromosome that define different but closely related traits. On the online GED® test, you will click to select your answer. For this paper version, please circle it.

20. A good example of a trait that is expressed in this way is

    [Select   ▼]

    height

    hair color

    gender

    intelligence

    foot size

QUESTION 21 REFERS TO THE FOLLOWING ILLUSTRATION.

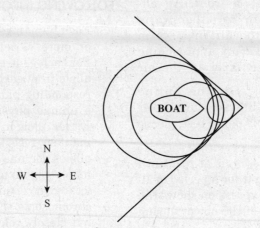

As a fast-moving boat skims along the water surface, it creates ring-shaped waves that extend away from the path of the boat. In the illustration above, the boat is moving faster than the waves it creates, and the waves form a larger *bow wave*.

21. Referring to the illustration, why do the circles become smaller from west to east?

    (A) The western-most waves were created first.

    (B) The bow wave loses energy over time.

    (C) The wind direction is east to west.

    (D) The bow wave is traveling east.

22. A solar eclipse depends on the alignment of the Sun, Moon, and Earth. During a solar eclipse, the Sun appears in the sky as a large dark circle surrounded by a bright ring. On the online GED® test, drag the circles representing Earth, the Moon, and the Sun into the position they must be in for people on Earth to witness a solar eclipse. For this paper version, please write the correct order below.

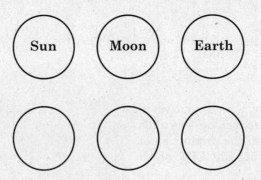

QUESTION 23 IS BASED ON THE FOLLOWING ILLUSTRATION.

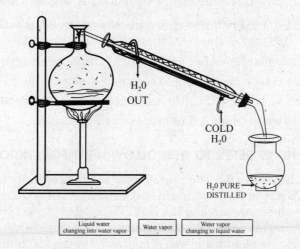

| Liquid water changing into water vapor | Water vapor | Water vapor changing to liquid water |

23. The laboratory apparatus shown can be used to purify water by separating it from other substances. On the online GED® test, you will be asked to show how this is done by dragging the labeled boxes to the appropriate locations in the apparatus. For this print test, please draw a line from the boxes to the spot on the diagram where they should be located.

QUESTION 24 REFERS TO THE FOLLOWING INFORMATION.

Certain types of red-colored flowers produce nectar that is chemically ideal as food for a hummingbird. The hummingbird can easily locate these flowers because it can see the color red especially well. The recurved petals of these flowers remain out of the hummingbird's way while it extracts nectar with its long beak, which is perfectly suited for the task. While gathering nectar, the hummingbird's head feathers brush against the flowers, collecting pollen that it carries away and disperses.

24. Which chart depicts the evolutionary relationship between the hummingbirds and flowers described above?

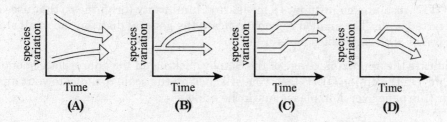

25. A botanist observes that the leaves of tomato plant A are beginning to wrinkle and mottle. Plant B, which sits directly next to plant A, appears healthy.

What experiment might help determine whether plant B has evolved an adaptation that makes it resistant to the virus that is infecting plant A?

(A) Move the two plants farther apart, and continue to observe their leaves.

(B) Infect plant B with the virus and continue to observe plant B.

(C) Compare the number of healthy-looking tomatoes on the two plants.

(D) Continue to water plant A, but stop watering plant B.

QUESTIONS 26 AND 27 REFER TO THE FOLLOWING INFORMATION.

About 10 billion years after the Sun's birth, the hydrogen fuel in the core will be exhausted, and the core will begin to contract and heat up. Hydrogen fusion will begin in a shell surrounding the core. The surface layers will then begin to expand in size and luminosity until, after several billion years, the Sun becomes a Red Giant, a state at which it will remain for a mere 250 million years, while its core contracts and heats up.

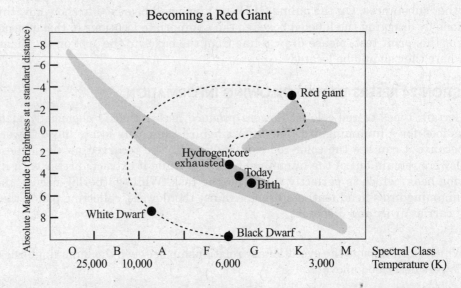

Becoming a Red Giant

NOTE: Absolute magnitude is a measure of luminosity (brightness) that uses an inverted scale. The shaded regions indicate the general distribution of all stars in terms of the variables measured.

26. Indicate the approximate age of the Sun by clicking on the appropriate spot on the scale. On the online GED® test, you will click on the scale to indicate your answer. For this paper version, please mark the scale.

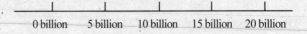

27. During the remainder of its life, the Sun will
    (A) experience two more cooling cycles.
    (B) darken as its surface continues to expand.
    (C) expand and heat up, then contract and cool.
    (D) grow brighter even as it shrinks in size.

QUESTION 28 REFERS TO THE FOLLOWING INFORMATION.

Within the phylum *chordata*, the sub-phylum *vertebrata* includes mammals, birds, reptiles, amphibians, and fish. All vertebrates share in common four characteristics during the embryonic stage of their life cycle:

- a hollow, dorsal (rear) nerve cord
- a notochord (backbone)
- gill slits (which develop into other structures in terrestrial vertebrates)
- a post-anal tail

28. Which part of the human anatomy shows that it belongs to the same sub-phylum as a lizard?
    (A) outer skin
    (B) spinal cord
    (C) toes and fingers
    (D) lungs

QUESTION 29 REFERS TO THE FOLLOWING CHART.

The pH Scale

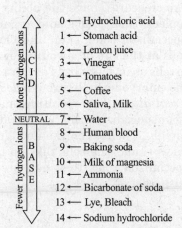

The pH scale is a compressed scale. Each level (0–14) represents a tenfold change from the next level up or down.

29. Which statement does the information in the pH scale support?
    (A) Bleach and lye burn your skin because they are highly acidic.
    (B) Milk is more effective than water in reducing the acidity of coffee.
    (C) It is easier to float in water high in hydrogen ions than in other water.
    (D) Drinking a carbonated beverage reduces the acidity inside your stomach.

QUESTION 30 REFERS TO THE FOLLOWING INFORMATION.

Urodeles, a class of small, lizard-like creatures, have the ability to replace their limbs and organs. Specialized bone, skin, and blood cells at the site of a wound revert to cells as unspecialized as those in the embryonic limb through *dedifferentiation*. The resulting mass of unspecialized cells proliferates rapidly. Then when the new limb takes shape, the cells take on the specialized roles they had previously cast off.

30. Which is the best term for the process described above?
   (A) cloning
   (B) random reproduction
   (C) cell regeneration
   (D) genetic mutation

SOCIAL STUDIES

70 Minutes • 34 Questions

> **Directions:** The Social Studies Test consists of a series of questions involving general social studies concepts. The questions are based on brief passages of text and visual information (graphs, charts, maps, cartoons, and other figures). Some questions are based on both text and visual information. Study the information provided, and answer the question(s) that follow it, referring back to the information as needed. Most questions are in multiple-choice format. Others are meant to prepare you for the electronically formatted questions that you will find on the test, such as drop-down questions, hot spot maps, and fill-in-the-blanks. The extended response question requires you to write an essay in which you analyze certain documents. Record your answers on the Social Studies section of the answer sheet provided.

QUESTION 1 REFERS TO THE FOLLOWING INFORMATION.

Following the conclusion of the French and Indian War in 1763, Great Britain and the American Colonies enjoyed a brief period of friendly relations. But soon Britain began to enforce restrictions on American trade, and taxes were levied on the colonists. After Americans protested, most taxes—with the exception of a few, including the tax on tea—were lifted. Tensions continued, however, and in 1770, British troops fired on a crowd in Boston, killing 5 people. On December 16, 1773, a group of colonists dressed as Indians boarded British ships and dumped chests of tea into the sea at Boston Harbor.

1. Colonists dumped chests of tea into Boston's harbor because

   (A) the British had put restrictions on American trade.

   (B) there was a tax on tea.

   (C) Britain had raised the tax on tea.

   (D) Britain had lifted the tax on tea.

QUESTION 2 IS BASED ON THE FOLLOWING EXCERPT.

Robert Kennedy played a key role in the resolution of the Cuban Missile Crisis. A close advisor to his brother, President John F. Kennedy, Robert Kennedy became a key liaison between his brother, U.S. military leaders, and the Soviet Ambassador. Yet RFK's role might have been drastically different if certain key aspects about the U.S. response to a Soviet presence in Cuba hadn't changed.

In April of 1961, with support from U.S. government's armed forces, a U.S.-trained force of Cuban exiles invaded Cuba to overthrow Fidel Castro's government but was quickly defeated by Soviet-bloc trained Cuban forces. Days after the failed "Bay of Pigs" invasion, U.S. Attorney General Robert Kennedy stated that longstanding U.S. neutrality laws "clearly . . . were not designed for the kind of situation which exists in the world today." As a result of the invasion, Castro sought protection against the Unites States from the Soviet Union, which suggested placing nuclear weapons in Cuba to ensure its security.

In May 1962, Soviet Premier Nikita Kruschev proposed to Cuban leader Fidel Castro the idea of placing Soviet nuclear missiles on the island, and by the following October, U.S. reconnaissance aircraft detected the construction of these bases. A nuclear war seemed inevitable.

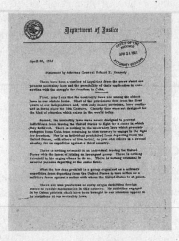

On October 21, Robert Kennedy once again modified his position. During a discussion with the president and a few other officials, he reiterated his support for the blockade on the grounds that it was preferable to a Pearl Harbor-style attack on Cuba that would cause the Soviet Union to respond militarily, thus making nuclear war a possibility. Elaborating, he said "we should start with the initiation of the blockade and thereafter 'play for the breaks.'" The day before he had said the quarantine should be followed shortly afterwards by an air strike, if the Russians did not halt work on the missile sites. Now he was suggesting that the administration should keep its options open once the blockade had been implemented. Even after promoting the quarantine so ardently on October 19, therefore, there were elements of vacillation in his position thereafter.

—Excerpt from "Robert Kennedy and the Cuban Missile Crisis: A Reinterpretation" by Mark White

2. Read the excerpt provided. How would you describe the change in key aspects about the U.S. response and the factors that contributed to it?

_____

_____

_____

_____

_____

_____

_____

_____

_____

_____

QUESTION 3 IS BASED UPON THE FOLLOWING EXCERPT.

The North, in an unrestrained intercourse with the South, protected by the equal laws of a common government, finds in the productions of the latter great additional resources of maritime and commercial enterprise and precious materials of manufacturing industry. The South, in the same intercourse, benefiting by the agency of the North, sees its agriculture grow and its commerce expand. Turning partly into its own channels the seamen of the North, it finds its particular navigation invigorated; and, while it contributes, in different ways, to nourish and increase the general mass of the national navigation, it looks forward to the protection of a maritime strength, to which itself is unequally adapted. The East, in a like intercourse with the West, already finds, and in the progressive improvement of interior communications by land and water, will more and more find a valuable vent for the commodities which it brings from abroad, or manufactures at home. The West derives from the East supplies requisite to its growth and comfort, and, what is perhaps of still greater consequence, it must of necessity owe the secure enjoyment of indispensable outlets for its own productions to the weight, influence, and the future maritime strength of the Atlantic side of the Union, directed by an indissoluble community of interest as one nation. Any other tenure by which the West can hold this essential advantage, whether derived from its own separate strength, or from an apostate and unnatural connection with any foreign power, must be intrinsically precarious.

—From George Washington's "Farewell Address to
the People of the United States"

3. According to the passage, Washington perceives a potential threat from the West because it

(A) is largely unknown.

(B) is populated by Native Americans.

(C) could develop an alliance with a foreign power.

(D) is populated by religious fanatics.

QUESTION 4 REFERS TO THE FOLLOWING INFORMATION.

The War Powers Act of 1973 placed the following limits on the president's use of the military:

- The president must report in writing to Congress within 48 hours after sending troops into any conflict.
- Congress then has sixty days to declare war or provide for the continued use of those troops.
- If Congress fails to provide such authorization, the president must remove the troops.

4. What is a result of the passage of the War Powers Act of 1973?

(A) The president gained the power to declare war.

(B) The president can commit troops to a long overseas war without the explicit approval of Congress.

(C) Congress can only approve combat operations lasting longer than sixty days if war is declared.

(D) The president cannot send troops into combat overseas for more than sixty days without the approval of Congress.

QUESTIONS 5 AND 6 REFER TO THE FOLLOWING INFORMATION.

Studies report that, since 1980, gang membership in the United States has risen considerably. In 1980, nearly 2000 gangs were reported, with nearly 100,000 gang members. By 1996, 31,000 gangs with 846, 000 members were reported. Sadly, membership included the very young. Of a survey of eighth-graders from 11 cities, 9 percent of the students surveyed reported that they were gang members and a disturbing 17 percent stated that they had belonged to a gang at some point in their younger lives.

The reasons and motives for gang membership are many and varied. Studies report that many members join to gain prestige among peers, especially peers of the opposite sex. In addition, many see gangs as exciting and an opportunity for gaining power and protection. Most gang members are from impoverished backgrounds and see gangs as a way to bypass conventional means of social advancement and attain wealth and status. Still others join for a sense of identity and membership in a kind of pseudo family. Some are born into families who are gang members and face a dangerous path if they attempt to escape.

—from the Office of Juvenile Justice and Delinquency Prevention

5. According to recent studies, most youth gang members

   (A) are usually born into families who are already gang members.

   (B) are usually introduced to gang membership while in prison.

   (C) are attracted to the possibility of gaining wealth and status.

   (D) are often discouraged after their first year of membership.

6. The author reports that studies show that gang membership even appeals to

   (A) college students.

   (B) college graduates.

   (C) grade school students.

   (D) law enforcement officials.

7. When your dollar buys less in goods and services than it used to, you are experiencing the effects of monetary inflation. Among the following people, who would most immediately experience an adverse effect of inflation?

   (A) an investor in enterprises involving real estate

   (B) an individual whose capital is mainly invested in common stock

   (C) a recent college graduate with little or no savings or assets

   (D) a retired individual living on a fixed pension

QUESTION 8 IS BASED ON THE FOLLOWING INFORMATION.

In the landmark Supreme Court case of *Marbury* v. *Madison* (1803), the Court held that an act of Congress in conflict with the Constitution was void and that it is the function of the Court to determine whether such a conflict exists.

8. What was the implication of *Marbury* v. *Madison*?

   (A) The Supreme Court could overrule the Constitution.

   (B) The Constitution had to be amended.

   (C) The Constitution was no longer valid.

   (D) The Supreme Court could override acts of Congress.

QUESTIONS 9–11 ARE BASED UPON THE FOLLOWING PASSAGE.

Following the War for American Independence, the United States was in debt to several foreign governments for aid they had provided during the war. France had provided loans of over two million dollars. John Adams obtained a loan from Dutch bankers in 1782, and loans were also obtained from Spain. Following the War, the Government established under the Articles of Confederation needed to find a way to pay off these loans, even thought it was prohibited by the Articles to levy taxes to do so. The government stopped payments off interest to France in 1785 and 1787, and instead focused on paying of their debts to Dutch bankers, as they remained a potential source of future loans despite the unpromising state of American financial affairs.

9. During the War for American Independence, | Select ▼ | provided financial assistance to the United States.

> France, Spain, and Dutch bankers
>
> France, Spain, and British anarchists
>
> France, Spain, and Russia
>
> France, Austria, and Russia

On the online GED® test, you click to select the correct answer. For this paper version, please circle it.

10. Following the War, the U.S. Government was hindered in its efforts to pay off its debts because [   ].
On the online GED® test, you type your answer into the space provided. For this paper version, please write it in.

11. Which of the following best describes the philosophy of repayment practiced by the United States?
(A) Pay off the source that loaned the most money.
(B) Pay off the source that loaned the least money.
(C) Pay off the source that could provide additional loans.
(D) Pay off the source that might pose a military threat.

QUESTION 12 REFERS TO THE FOLLOWING INFORMATION.

After World War I, President Wilson proposed the establishment of an international organization to help settle international disputes and prevent future wars. Wilson was successful in establishing the League of Nations as part of the peace treaty negotiated at the end of the war. Although the League of Nations was established in 1919, Wilson's dream was blocked when Congress refused to ratify the treaty and blocked U.S. involvement in the League. Without the United States, perhaps the world's most powerful nation at the time, the League of Nations proved ineffective and was unable to stop World War II from breaking out only 20 years later.

12. The author of the passage implies that

(A) the Senate should not have the power to reject treaties.

(B) the Senate should not be involved in foreign affairs.

(C) the League of Nations would have been more successful had the United States joined.

(D) Wilson was out of touch with the American people who did not want to become involved in European disputes.

QUESTIONS 13 AND 14 REFER TO THE FOLLOWING INFORMATION.

Farmers add fertilizer to improve their crops. But, if a farmer keeps increasing the amount of fertilizer, the improvement in yield will slow, and continuing to add more and more fertilizer will not help much. In fact, at some point, if too much fertilizer is used, the yield will decline because too much fertilizer will actually stunt growth or kill the crop. This pattern applies to all factors of production (the inputs that go into the production process). This relationship is called the Law of Diminishing Returns. The point at which the average output per unit of fertilizer starts to decline is the point of diminishing return on the investment in fertilizer.

The chart below shows how output is affected by changes in the number of workers hired at an automobile factory. Hiring more workers will increase output, but at some point simply hiring more and more workers, without expanding the factory, does not have much effect and may even cause output to fall.

XYZ AUTO FACTORY

Number of Workers	Autos Produced Weekly	Production per Worker
100	30	0.3
200	100	0.5
300	210	0.7
400	300	0.75
500	360	0.72
600	400	0.67
700	390	0.56

13. Click on the number of workers hired that shows the point when the XYZ Auto Factory begins to see diminishing returns in productivity. On the online GED® test, you click to select the correct answer. For this paper version, please circle it.

14. Which statement best explains the law of diminishing returns as applied to this factory?

   (A) Since the production capacity of the factory is limited by the equipment and space available, at some point simply hiring more workers doesn't do much to increase output.

   (B) Hiring more workers will always increase automobile production.

   (C) Automobile companies maximize profits if they always keep workers at a minimum.

   (D) Automobile factories should never hire more than 600 workers.

QUESTION 15 REFERS TO THE FOLLOWING PASSAGE.

The men who wrote the U.S. Constitution divided the authority of the federal government into three independent branches of government: the legislative branch makes laws, the executive branch carries out the laws, and the judicial branch interprets the laws. This separation of powers prevents any one branch from gaining power over the entire federal government. Besides separating government into independent branches, the authors of the Constitution also established a system of checks and balances whereby each branch, under certain circumstances, can check the power of the other branches.

15. Which of the following is NOT an example of the system of checks and balances?

   (A) The president can veto a law passed by Congress.

   (B) State governments can overturn actions of the federal government in their states.

   (C) The Supreme Court can declare a law passed by Congress to be unconstitutional and invalidate it.

   (D) The Senate must approve top officials appointed by the president.

QUESTION 16 REFERS TO THE FOLLOWING INFORMATION.

The 2000 presidential election required a Supreme Court ruling to declare a winner. After other states had declared their results, the outcome of the election depended upon Florida, where then Governor George W. Bush led by about 1800 votes. Florida law required that a margin that narrow necessitated a recount. The recount only narrowed the margin to a mere 327-vote lead for Bush, at which point Vice President Gore exercised his right per Florida law to ask for a manual recount in four counties of his choice. Gore chose counties where there had been widespread complaints of voting machine malfunction: Miami-Dade, Broward, Volusia, and Palm Beach. The recount was complicated by another Florida law that required votes to be certified by the Florida Secretary of State within seven days of the election. Secretary of State Harris stated that she would only entertain requests for extensions if a request was made in writing by 2 p.m. the following day. When

practice test

three of the four counties filed such a request, they were rejected. Secretary of State Harris declared that the result would be announced on Saturday, November 18. Vice President Gore and Palm Beach County filed for an injunction by the Florida Supreme Court. The Florida Supreme Court issued the injunction and declared that the counties had until November 26.

Miami-Dade stopped counting, stating that it could not meet the extended deadline and Secretary Harris certified the election for Bush who held a 537-vote lead. Gore again appealed to the Florida Supreme Court, which ruled that ballots needed to be manually recounted because voting machines sometimes failed to count ballots where "chads," the portion of the ballot that should have been punched when the vote was cast, had remained hanging on the ballot. Vice President Bush appealed to the United States Supreme Court, which ruled, in a landmark decision, that the ruling of the Florida

Supreme Court was unconstitutional and that Secretary Harris's declaration of Bush as the winner should stand.

16. Why did Vice President Gore call for a manual recount of Florida votes in four specific counties, even after an initial recount had been taken?

(A) The results showed a difference of less than 500 votes between candidates.

(B) There were widespread reports of voting machine malfunctions.

(C) The results showed a difference of less than 300 votes between candidates.

(D) The counties had a large population of registered democrats.

QUESTIONS 17 AND 18 ARE BASED ON THE FOLLOWING CHARTS.

The Economy Before and After the New Deal, 1929-1941

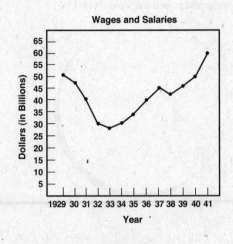

Wages and Salaries

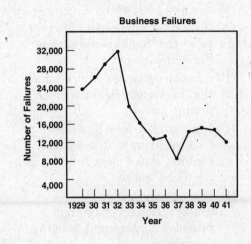

Business Failures

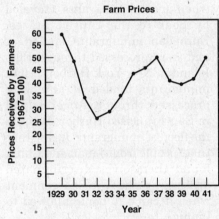

Farm Prices

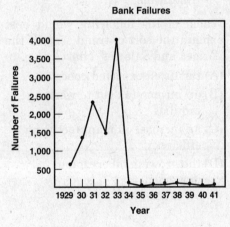

Bank Failures

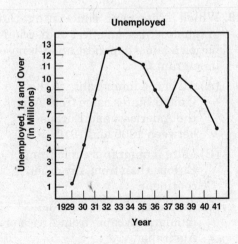

Unemployed

17. Based on the charts, which of the following was probably a feature of the Roosevelt Administration's New Deal policies and programs?

   (A) It established a cap on interest rates that banks could charge their customers.

   (B) It broke up large corporations that previously held too much pricing power.

   (C) It diverted federal assistance from rural areas to industrial centers, where most Americans lived and worked.

   (D) It established a land-conservation program that provided employment to many Americans.

18. Which of the following would best explain the sort of trend seen in the "Wages and Salaries" chart?

   (A) tariffs on exported goods

   (B) an income-tax cut to working families

   (C) an increase in manufacturing efficiency

   (D) the growing labor-union movement

QUESTIONS 19–21 ARE BASED ON THE FOLLOWING GRAPH AND TEXT.

Immigration to the United States, 1900–1910

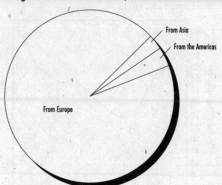

The early 1900s were a time when most immigrants traveled by boat to the United States. European immigrants landed at and were processed through Ellis Island in New York Harbor. Asian immigrants landed at and were processed through Angel Island in San Francisco Harbor. Despite the flood of immigrants during that time, people from Japan and China found themselves discriminated against by the U.S. government when it came to being allowed to immigrate.

19. Which statement concerning the graph describes an effect of discrimination against Japanese and Chinese immigrants?

   (A) All of the immigrants to the United States came from Asia, the Americas, and Europe between 1900 and 1910.

   (B) More immigrants came from Europe than from any other continent.

   (C) According to the graph, no immigrants came from Africa or Australia.

   (D) Only a very small percentage of the total number of immigrants to the United States came from Asia, which includes China and Japan.

20. Based on the information in the graph and text, which of the following statements is true?

(A) Many more immigrants were processed through Ellis Island than through Angel Island in the early 1900s.

(B) Asian immigrants were often forced to live at Angel Island for several months when they first arrived.

(C) Ellis Island was the port of entry for passengers who did not travel first class.

(D) Immigrants at both Ellis Island and Angel Island had to pass brief medical examinations.

21. Racial tensions that characterized the aftermath of the Civil War in the United States probably had what effect on immigration to the United States between 1900 and 1910?

(A) They led to the United States' foreign policy of isolationism.

(B) They led to a near complete absence of immigration from Africa.

(C) They led to a reluctance by Asian immigrants to move to the United States.

(D) They led to more extensive immigration from Northern Europe.

QUESTION 22 REFERS TO THE TABLE BELOW.

U.S. Federal Spending, Fiscal Year (FY) 2011
(in billions of dollars)

Category	Amount	Percentage of Total
Social Security	$ 725	20%
Medicare and Medicaid	$ 835	23%
Student Loans, Veteran's Benefits, and Other Mandatory Spending	$ 465	13%
Defense Spending	$ 700	19%
All Other Federal Programs	$ 646	18%
Interest on the Federal Debt	$ 227	6%
TOTAL	$3598	

[Note: Due to rounding to the nearest whole percentage point, breakdowns by percentage often don't add up to exactly 100%.]

22. Which one of the following categories accounted for the most spending by the federal government in FY 2011?

(A) Social Security

(B) defense spending

(C) interest on the federal debt

(D) Medicare and Medicaid

QUESTIONS 23 AND 24 REFER TO THE FOLLOWING INFORMATION

Parole violation is a serious problem in our corrections system. It is estimated that nearly half of the prison population consists of parole violators. Some of these have committed new crimes. Others are guilty of violating parole conditions. Their offenses include missing meetings or failing drug tests.

Specialists advise that corrections officials revise current procedures to include a more focused and strategic approach to handling parole supervision and violation. These procedures should include greater communication between the releasing authority and supervising agency. The releasing authority is either a judge or parole board, but that authority needs to communicate concerns and suggestions to the appropriate agency that can act on those concerns. Secondly, the supervising agency needs to remember that its responsibility is to provide for the safety of the community. Therefore, it should have appropriate research-based risk assessment tools at their disposal for use during hearings and judgments. For those who do violate the terms of their parole, officials should consider a graduated response system, with community service for lighter infractions and incarceration of repeat offenders. For those who meet the conditions, parole supervisors should always be aware of the value of positive reinforcement.

23. Recent studies indicate that parole violations could be improved if

   (A) even minor infractions were severely punished.

   (B) releasing authorities and supervising agencies communicate more effectively.

   (C) supervising agencies could also punish offenders.

   (D) releasing authorities were held accountable for parole violations.

24. An effective strategy to respond to parole violators should include

   (A) increased drug tests.

   (B) longer prison terms.

   (C) transfer to a different supervisor.

   (D) lighter punishments for lesser infractions.

25. The 1930s saw the migration of hundreds of thousands from the U.S. prairie states, such as Texas and Oklahoma, westward, especially to California.

   | Select ▼ | without taking adequate precautions against erosion had turned millions of acres to dust, and severe drought conditions trans-

   Mineral mining   formed the entire prairie into a great "Dust Bowl" for much of the decade.

   Oil drilling

   Over-farming

   Urban construction

   On the online GED® test, you click to select the correct answer. For this paper version, please circle it.

QUESTION 26 IS BASED ON THE FOLLOWING INFORMATION.

At the height of the civil rights movement in the 1960s, Dr. Martin Luther King, Jr., as head of the Southern Christian Leadership Conference, delivered a speech in which he stated:

"The whirlwinds of revolt will continue to shake the foundation of our nation until the bright day of justice emerges. But there is something that I must say to my people who stand on the warm threshold which leads into the palace of justice. In the process of gaining our rightful place we must not be guilty of wrongful deeds. Let us not seek to satisfy our thirst for freedom by drinking from the cup of bitterness and hatred."

26. What did Dr. Martin Luther King, Jr. recommend as a means of attaining civil rights?

(A) establishing black-only communities

(B) relying on one's faith in God

(C) passive resistance

(D) inciting social upheaval

QUESTION 27 REFERS TO THE FOLLOWING GRAPH.

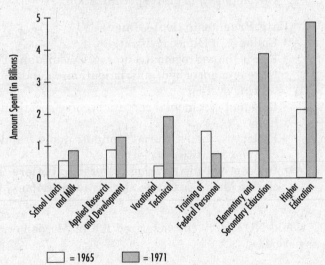

Federal Spending on Education, 1965 and 1971

□ = 1965   ▨ = 1971

27. According to the graph, for which category did spending decline between 1965 and 1971?

(A) school lunch and milk

(B) applied research and development

(C) vocational technical

(D) training of federal personnel

QUESTIONS 28 AND 29 REFER TO THE FOLLOWING INFORMATION.

MESOAMERICA: PRECLASSIC (FORMATIVE) PERIOD

(2500 BC–1 AD)

3000 BC	Major volcanic eruption destroys life in southern regions
2500 BC–1250 BC	**Early Preclassic (Pre-Olmec)** • Cultivation and control of plant life • Settled villages established in highlands and lowlands • Highland maize (corn) transmitted to lowlands becomes staple food and allows for population growth • Development of refined grinding tools • Pottery and root-crop agriculture appear (possibly from South America)
1250 BC–400 BC	**Middle Preclassic (Olmec Horizon)** • Rise of Olmec civilization in lowlands • Development of interregional exchange networks to circulate ritual items, foodstuffs, and utilitarian goods • Development of wealth, power, and well-defined class structure • Development of craft specialization
400 BC–1 AD	**Late Preclassic (Epi-Olmec)** • Collapse of Olmec civilization • Rise of the two regional centers of Cuicuico and Teotihuacan • Development of hydraulic irrigation, calendar system, and writing system • Regional ceremonial centers become social and religious hubs • Elaborate tombs, burial mounds, and pyramids suggest complex stratified society • Widespread distribution of ceramic pottery (features of classic Mayan art style already identifiable)

---

28. Which activity would NOT have characterized life in Mesoamerican during the early Preclassic period?

    (A) grinding corn

    (B) making simple pottery

    (C) regional travel

    (D) building pyramids

29. When did the rise of the Mayan civilization in Mesoamerica occur?

    (A) before the Preclassic period

    (B) during the Early Preclassic period

    (C) during the Middle Preclassic period

    (D) following the Late Preclassic period

QUESTION 30 IS BASED ON THE
FOLLOWING INFORMATION.

One role of the Federal Reserve
Bank (called the "Fed") is to keep
the banking system healthy. The
Federal Reserve clears checks
between banks, provides short-
term loans to banks, and serves
as a lender-of-last resort if a bank
is in danger of collapse. Through
the interest rates the Federal
Reserve charges for its loans to
banks (called the "discount rate"),
it strongly influences the interest
rates banks charge on loans to
their customers.

30. What would be an effect of the Fed
lowering the discount rate?

(A) More banks would fail.

(B) Banks would increase the rates
of interest they pay on savings
accounts.

(C) The interest rate the bank
charges on loans to its
customers would decrease.

(D) Banks would make fewer loans
to their customers.

QUESTION 31 IS BASED ON THE
FOLLOWING INFORMATION.

In American history, the majority
of conflicts between Native Americans and European settlers and
their descendents developed as a
result of U.S. government attempts
to move Native Americans to
reservations. The battle at South
Dakota's Wounded Knee (1890),
during which nearly 200 Sioux
Indians were killed, is generally
considered the last major battle in
this long series of conflicts.

For seventy days in 1973,
200 members of the American
Indian Movement (AIM) occupied
Wounded Knee, which is located
near the Pine Ridge reservation,
consistently one of the poorest
counties in the nation. A standoff

between U.S. marshals and the
occupiers turned bloody. In support
of the protesters, actor Marlon
Brando famously refused to appear
at the Academy Awards that year
to accept his best-actor award. In
his place, a Native American Sioux
woman made a speech calling the
world's attention to the protesters'
cause.

31. Based on the information provided,
what assumption can reasonably be
made regarding the occupation at
Wounded Knee?

(A) The protestors wanted to return
to the days before the Sioux
were defeated in the Battle of
Wounded Knee.

(B) The protestors wanted to expand
the Pine Ridge Reservation.

(C) The protesters wanted to
establish Wounded Knee as a
national historic site in order to
encourage tourism.

(D) The protesters wanted to
get media attention to draw
attention to the unjust
treatment of Native Americans.

QUESTION 32 REFERS TO THE
FOLLOWING INFORMATION.

The beginning of the twentieth
century saw more reform in many
areas of life in the United States.
Under the administration of Teddy
Roosevelt, trusts, or combinations
of companies that reduced competition, came under increasing
government scrutiny.

32. The scrutiny described in the previous paragraph was a response to
which of the following?

(A) an era of big business

(B) a time of war and strife

(C) a constitutional amendment

(D) a series of natural disasters

QUESTIONS 33 AND 34 ARE BASED ON THE FOLLOWING MAP.

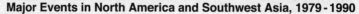

Major Events in North America and Southwest Asia, 1979-1990

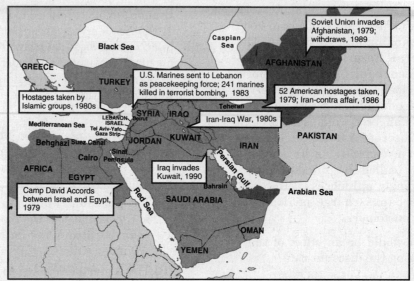

33. Click on the label on the map that identifies the event that is associated with the beginning of Operation Desert Storm. On the online GED® test, you click to select the correct answer. For this paper version, please circle it.

34. Click on the label on the map that identifies an event that took place during the administration of President Jimmy Carter. On the online GED® test, you click to select the correct answer. For this paper version, please circle it.

ANSWER KEY AND EXPLANATIONS

Reasoning Through Language Arts

1. (D)	17. (B)	33. (D)
2. (A)	18. (C)	34. circle
3. (C)	19. See explanation below.	35. (D)
4. (C)	20. (D)	36. (A)
5. (B)	21. See explanation below.	37. (B)
6. (A)	22. (B)	38. (B)
7. (C)	23. (D)	39. (D)
8. (A)	24. (B)	40. (A)
9. See explanation below.	25. (A)	41. (D)
10. (A)	26. (A)	42. (C)
11. See explanation below.	27. (B)	43. (C)
12. (D)	28. (D)	44. (B)
13. (B)	29. (C)	45. See explanation below.
14. (D)	30. See explanation below.	46. (C)
15. (B)	31. (A)	47. (A)
16. (B)	32. (A)	48. (B)
		49. See explanation below.

1. **The correct answer is (D).** Her main point is that in a democracy, there is no way to justify denying the right to vote to half the citizens, purely on the basis of gender.

2. **The correct answer is (A).** Anthony speaks about how unreasonable it is to have half the population disenfranchised. Through context, we know that disenfranchisement must mean not having voting rights.

3. **The correct answer is (C).** Since she was thrown in jail for voting illegally, she is explaining what motivated her to take such a strong stand.

4. **The correct answer is (C).** With continued pressure from Anthony and others like her, the women's suffrage movement would be likely to convince others to support their cause. In turn, the politicians would be influenced by their constituencies that voting for women's suffrage was in their best interests.

5. **The correct answer is (B).** The reference to the Constitution was a reminder that without being allowed to participate in the government, women could not change laws that affected them, so the first step in improving women's lives was

convincing others that women should be allowed to vote. It also was a reminder of the reason the United States was created in the first place—to break free from the control of a country in which they had no voting rights.

6. **The correct answer is (A).** A democracy and republic are supposed to grant equal rights to its citizens. In an oligarchy, only a small group of people have power.

7. **The correct answer is (C)** A History of the Study of Sleep is the only option that covers the entire passage. All other responses are limited to topics within paragraphs.

8. **The correct answer is (A).** This is the only reasonable figurative answer. The other responses are all too literal and generally erroneous.

9. **The correct order is (C), (A), (D), (B).** The passage begins with the history of humans' interest in sleep, choice (C); then continues with the importance of REMs, choice (A), and how investigators can influence dreams, choice (D); and ends with modern sleep research, choice (B).

10. **The correct answer is (A).** The description of EEGs provides details that support the purpose of the machine and its uses.

11. **The correct answer is the invention of the electroencepholograph (EEG).** The machine could record sleep patterns, and thus ushered in a new era of sleep research.

12. **The correct answer is (D).** The last sentence makes reference to sleep disorders, which would be a good lead-in to a new paragraph on that topic. All other responses make reference to topics mentioned earlier in the passage.

13. **The correct answer is (B).** The structure of the passage with its headings emphasizes the details under the headings. Noting the headings would be a good way to determine the basic contents.

14. **The correct answer is (D).** Reading paragraph E as a whole, its main point seems to be that employees should *not* expect to be notified if and when their Internet browsing is being monitored. In the context of the paragraph, choice (D) is the only one that provides a reasonable interpretation of the phrase "with or without notice." The other options are true but not related to the phrase.

15. **The correct answer is (B).** The person hired must know how to store and retrieve data processed through the County's computer network, and he or she must know how to identify the specific computer stations that are the source of that data. However, that person would probably not need expertise in monitoring employee behaviors that can be observed visually (for example, eavesdropping, printing, connecting personal-computing devices to County equipment, and so forth) or in protecting the privacy or security of employees who use CCNS.

16. **The correct answer is (B).** Paragraph B indicates that employees conducting County business from a remote location may do so "only with equipment and software issued by the County."

17. **The correct answer is (B).** Urging employees to logout when leaving their computer workstations unattended would help ensure compliance with the rule in paragraph D, prohibiting the use of another employee's workstation.

18. **The correct answer is (C).** Henson placed a series of descriptive phrases together that describes the scenery and supports his contention that Karnah "is the most delightful spot on the Greenland coast."

19. **The correct answer is Peary wrote the passages that begin "Here I am..." and "These books..."** The others were written by Henson. Peary's role as leader of the expedition, plus his ambitions as an explorer, make him the logical choice for the first passage. The reference to extensive reading is likely to have come from a person with more education. The tone and the simpler language of the second and third passages correspond to Henson's background and character.

20. **The correct answer is (D).** The reader will definitely have to infer the more verbose passage is due to more education, since the other choices are not covered. Since the other choices are not really covered, it should not be too difficult.

21. **The correct answer is both men would like to live in Karnah.** Since Henson describes Karnah as "the most delightful spot on the Greenland coast" and says that "the landscape is as delightful as anywhere on Earth," it can be assumed that he wouldn't mind living there. Peary describes a spot by the bay that would be a "desirable location for a house." Thus, he would probably like living there as well.

22. **The correct answer is (B).** The elements refer to weather events of snow, rain, sleet, and so forth, with the term arctic referring to the most likely types of weather elements. "Restless" refers to the fact that the weather changes, and it is probable that the wind blows often.

23. **The correct answer is (D).** This is a figurative term that refers to the moving and changing glaciers. It is the only response that could be thought of as thick and slow moving.

24. **The correct answer is (B).** The opening paragraph describes the commonly held idea that Henry objected to the Constitution because of his belief in states' rights, but it explains that this "seems not to have been the case" and goes on to explain why.

25. **The correct answer is (A).** This sentence summarizes the overall work that Washington did for the Constitution—navigating its negotiations to get agreement. The authors say it was his "commanding will" that got the job done. In other words, his persistence and ability to persuade people allowed the delegates to finally agree on the Constitution.

26. **The correct answer is (A).** This question is a transition the author uses to begin citing the evidence that supports his position that Henry's objections to the Constitution were based on his advocacy of states' rights. The rest of the text after this sentence supports this idea.

27. **The correct answer is (B).** The overall tone of the passage shows Washington as a humble man who dedicated a part of his life to working tirelessly to secure independence for the colonies and skillfully work with others to form a new country. These qualities made him stand out from the rest.

28. **The correct answer is (D).** Passage 1 implies that Washington was willing to compromise or he would not have been able to make sure the men reached agreement. However, Henry had strong beliefs that prevented him from agreeing to the Constitution.

29. **The correct answer is (C).** After the Constitution had been completed, Washington headed home. He wanted to persuade Henry to accept the new Constitution, so he sent him a copy along with a letter to try to win him over. The fact that Washington knew Henry needed to be persuaded tells us that Henry had not approved of the Constitution.

30. **The correct answer is since the Industrial Revolution, or since the middle of the eighteenth century.** With the start of the Industrial Revolution came the use of fossil fuels to propel the machines that increased production but also increased the carbon released into the atmosphere.

31. **The correct answer is (A).** The passage explains why carbon levels have increased and then states that concentration has increased by almost 40 percent since pre-industrial times. This connection shows that human activity—burning the fossil fuels used in industry—has been the largest contributor to rising carbon concentrations in the atmosphere.

32. **The correct answer is (A).** Carbon dioxide, methane, and water vapor are the major gases that absorb energy from the sun and prevent the loss of heat to space, warming the Earth's atmosphere.

33. **The correct answer is (D).** Various studies have been made of the Earth's climate over the millennia, and the passage lists a few. However, the main tool for showing that natural phenomena are not responsible for the greatly increased carbon in the atmosphere is the historical records of the Earth's atmosphere. The data from these records indicate that earlier fluctuations in carbon concentrations closely paralleled natural events like volcanoes but it has only been since the mid-eighteenth century that the carbon concentrations have steadily increased over time.

34. **The correct answer is a circle.** Feedback is a continuous loop in which one process triggers another, which then affects the original process. This process would look like a circle. Any other shapes are incorrect.

35. **The correct answer is (D).** The passage suggests that Newland is afraid his life is becoming too much of a routine. He repeatedly mutters the word "sameness," which he obviously dislikes. His longing for variety reveals itself in almost every aspect of his life, from the change in his daily routine to his suggesting that he and May strike out on their own simply because it would be something different from what is expected of them.

36. **The correct answer is (A).** May's response ("If you call it long") strongly suggests that she considers her mother's proposed engagement period to be short, especially compared to the engagement periods of some of her acquaintances.

37. **The correct answer is (B).** May tells Newland that his ideas are "rather vulgar." Then, speaking for both of them, she says, ". . . I should hate it—and so would you." May then changes the topic of discussion.

38. **The correct answer is (B).** Newland concludes that May was "making the answers that instinct and tradition taught her to." The context of this narrative suggests that what Newland means by "tradition" are the conventional behaviors, attitudes, and values of a culture.

39. **The correct answer is (D).** The passage tells us of May's belief that her mother—who, in context, symbolizes "society"—would consider May and Newland's desire to travel as different. In other words, leisure travel was not very common at that time.

40. **The correct answer is (A).** The passage reveals Newland's realization that his fiancée, who is typical of young women of the time, was spouting responses that simply parroted what she has been taught. The clear implication here is that she, like most young women of that time, had not been encouraged to think for herself or to speak her own mind.

41. The correct answer is (D). All words in the name of a business should be capitalized, especially when used formally in an address.

42. The correct answer is (C). This is a business letter, which requires a colon after the salutation.

43. The correct answer is (C). The subject and verb need to agree. Because of the intervening material, matching the correct verb and subject may be confusing.

44. The correct answer is (B). The introductory prepositional phrase (For two summers during high school) should have a comma after it.

45. The correct order is (16), (17), (19), (18). This is the only order that clarifies who "He" in sentence (18) is.

46. The correct answer is (C). The pronoun needs to agree with its antecedent. In this case, the pronoun should refer to both the assistant director and the staff.

47. The correct answer is (A). This is a frequently confused word. The contraction needs to be broken into two words to determine the correct meaning and agreement.

48. The correct answer is (B). Since the letter is formal, the summarizing statement should balance with the rest of the letter and maintain a tone of formality rather than familiarity.

49. Extended response. Answers will vary. You will find two sample essays on pages 728-729.

answers practice test 2

Mathematical Reasoning

1. 64	16. (B)	27. (A)
2. 42.75	17. $\frac{5}{8}$	28. (B)
3. (A)	18. $0.10d + $0.05n$	29. (B)
4. (B)		30. ≥; 3
5. (A)	19. points marked on (0, −2), (3, 0)	31. (C)
6. (B)	20. (A)	32. (B)
7. $6000	21. (B)	33. (C)
8. (D)	22. (A)	34. (C)
9. (D)	23. (B)	35. $y = -\frac{1}{3}x + \left(-\frac{4}{3}\right)$
10. (C)	24. 2(3 × 4) + 2(8 × 3) + (8 × 4)	36. (C)
11. 21		37. (D)
12. (D)	25. a line between any two of the following points: (−2, −5), (0, −1), (2, 3), (4, 7)	
13. (D)		
14. point P at (0, −3)		
15. (D)	26. (D)	

1. **The correct answer is 64.** Without the square hole, each of the cube's six outer surfaces contains 9 square inches, for a total of 54 square inches of outer surface area. The square hole reduces that total by 2 square inches, to 52. Each of the four inner surfaces (inside the hole) accounts for an additional 3 square inches—for a total of 12 square inches of inner surface area. The solid's total surface area = 52 + 12 = 64 square inches.

2. **The correct answer is 42.75.** Multiply and divide (in either order) before adding. Starting with division:

$$13 + 7 \times (17 \div 4) = 13 + (7 \times 4.25)$$
$$= 13 + 29.75$$
$$= 42.75$$

3. **The correct answer is (A).** In 5 hours, Steven can pack $\frac{2}{3} \times 48 = 32$ boxes. Therefore, in 3 hours he can pack $0.6 \times 32 = 19.2$ boxes, or 19 *complete* boxes.

4. **The correct answer is (B).** Substitute 12 for y and 13 for r in the equation of the circle:

$$x^2 + 12^2 = 13^2$$
$$x^2 + 144 = 169$$
$$x^2 = 169 - 144$$
$$x^2 = 25$$
$$x = 5$$

5. **The correct answer is (A).** Use the formula for combinations, because the order doesn't matter. In other words, cherry, cherry, pistachio is the same as cherry, pistachio, cherry. The combination formula is: $C(n,k) = \dfrac{n!}{(n-k)!\,k!}$ where $n = 5$ and $k = 3$.

$$C(5,3) = \frac{5!}{(5-3)!\,3!} = \frac{5 \times 4 \times 3 \times 2 \times 1}{2 \times 1 \times 3 \times 2 \times 1} = \frac{5 \times 4}{2 \times 1} = 10$$

6. **The correct answer is (B).** Administrative costs were 5% of the total budget:

$0.05 \times \$200{,}000 = \$10{,}000$.

7. **The correct answer is $6000.** The budget for insurance (15%) exceeds the budget for utilities (12%) by 3%: $0.03 \times \$200{,}000 = \$6{,}000$.

8. **The correct answer is (D).** Since the figure has 5 sides, it contains 540°: $180(5 - 2) = 540$. To find the fifth angle (x), set up and solve an equation:

$540 = x + 110 + 60 + 120 + 100$

$540 = x + 390$

$150 = x$

9. **The correct answer is (D).** The June usage difference between houses C and A was $1125 - 960 = 165$ kWh. Divide this monthly difference by 30 to find the average per-day difference:

$165 \div 30 = 5.5$ kWh.

10. **The correct answer is (C).** The interior volume of each house is the product of its square-foot area and its ceiling height (volume = area × height). To determine a house's ceiling height, divide its volume by its square-foot area. For Houses A, B, and D, the quotient (ceiling height) is exactly 8.0 linear feet. For house C, however, the quotient is greater than 8.0 linear feet.

11. **The correct answer is 21.** The formula for the volume of a cone is $\dfrac{1}{3}\pi r^2 \times h$. Letting $r = 2$ and $h = 5$, first find the volume in terms of π:

$$\frac{1}{3}\pi 2^2 \times 5 = \frac{1}{3}\pi(4)(5) = \frac{20\pi}{3}$$

Then, using 3.14 as the approximate value of π, calculate the volume:

$$\frac{(20)(3.14)}{3} = \frac{62.8}{3} \approx 20.9$$

The nearest cubic inch is 21.

12. **The correct answer is (D).** Since the two fractions in choice (D) share the same denominator, you can simply add the numerators to find the sum:

$$\frac{3}{4} + \frac{5}{4} = \frac{8}{4} = 2$$

13. **The correct answer is (D).** Raise both the coefficient -2 and variable x^2 to the power of 4. When raising an exponent to a power, multiply:

$(-2x^2)^4 = -2^4 x^{(2)(4)} = 16x^8$

14. **The correct answer is point *P* at (0, –3).** The *y*-intercept of the equation $y = 7x - 3$ is the point at which the line crosses the *y*-axis. At this point, the value of *x* is 0. Substitute 0 for *x* in the equation, and then solve:

$$y = 7(0) - 3; \; y = -3$$

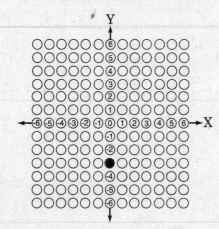

The *y*-intercept is at point (0, –3).

15. **The correct answer is (D).** A linear equation in two variables, regardless of the number of terms or values of coefficients, allows an infinite number of combinations for the two variables.

16. **The correct answer is (B).** Each tube has a diameter of 3 inches. The circumference of any of the tubes (including A) = πd (where d = diameter). Given a diameter of 3, the circumference of circle A = 3π.

17. **The correct answer is $\frac{5}{8}$.** Think of the legislature as containing 8 voters divided into two parts: $\frac{5}{8} + \frac{3}{8} = \frac{8}{8}$. For every 5 votes in favor, 3 were cast against the bill. Thus, 5 out of every 8 votes, or $\frac{5}{8}$, were cast in favor of the motion.

18. **The correct answer is $\$0.10d$ + $\$0.05n$.** A dime = $0.10, and a nickel = $0.05. The total value of the dimes = ($0.10)(*d*), and the total value of the nickels =

($0.05)(*n*). Together, ($0.10)(*d*) + ($0.05)(*n*) represents the dollar value of all coins in the vending machine.

19. **The correct answers are the points (0, –2) and (3, 0).** In the equation, $\frac{2}{3}$ is the slope and 2 is the *y*-intercept.

Using the slope–intercept equation $y = mx + b$, for the *x*-intercept:

$$y = \frac{2}{3}\,0 - 2$$
$$y = 0 - 2$$
$$y = -2$$
$$(0, -2)$$

For the *y*-intercept:

$$0 = \frac{2}{3}x - 2$$
$$\frac{2}{3}x = 2$$
$$x = 3$$
$$(3, 0)$$

20. **The correct answer is (A).** $4230 \times 10^{-4} = 4.23 \times 10^{-1}$

21. **The correct answer is (B).** Rug R must be 4' × 4', and rug S must be 2' × 2'. The perimeter of Rug S is 8 feet.

22. **The correct answer is (A).** Multiply each term of a binomial by each term of the other binomial, then add the four products: $(x - 3)(x + 1) = x^2 - 3x + x - 3 = x^2 - 2x - 3$.

23. **The correct answer is (B).** The length of wire can be seen as the hypotenuse of a right triangle. Using the Pythagorean theorem $a^2 + b^2 = c^2$:

$$25 + 144 = c^2$$
$$c^2 = \sqrt{169}$$
$$c = 13$$

24. **The correct answer is $2(3 \times 4) + 2(8 \times 3) + 2(8 \times 4)$.** Each of the smaller end faces of the prism measures 3 by 4. There are two of these faces,

so we need to multiply: $2(3 \times 4)$. Two of the four longer sides measure 8×3, so we multiply: $2(8 \times 3)$. The other two longer sides measure 8×4, so that's $2(8 \times 4)$. Then we add these three expressions together: $2(3 \times 4) + 2(8 \times 3) + 2(8 \times 4)$.

25. **The correct answer is the line formed by any of the points (–2, –5), (0, –1), (2, 3), and (4, 7).**

26. **The correct answer is (D).** Substitute 1250 for a_1 and 1480 for a_2 into the equation:

$$P = \frac{1480 - 1250}{1250} \times 100 = 18.4$$

27. **The correct answer is (A).** The equation is $(x-6)^2 = (x-6)(x-6)$. Use the FOIL method to multiply: $x^2 - 6x - 6x + 36 = x^2 - 12x + 36$.

28. **The correct answer is (B).** To find the revenues for the adult tickets, multiply A by 12, which is $12(A)$. To find the revenue for the children's tickets, multiply C by 8, which is $8C$. Add $12A + 8C$ to find total revenues.

29. **The correct answer is (B).** Simplify by factoring x out of $Ax - Bx$: $\frac{(A-B)x}{2} = 2$. Multiply both sides of the equation by 2: $(A-B)x = 4$. Divide both sides of the equation by $A - B$: $\frac{(A-B)x}{(A-B)} = \frac{4}{(A-B)}$, $x = \frac{4}{(A-B)}$.

30. **The correct answers are ≥ and 3.** First, multiply both sides of the inequality by −2 to eliminate the fraction. When you multiply or divide an inequality by a negative number, change the direction of the inequality:

$$(-2)2y \le \left(\frac{y+3}{-2}\right)(-2) = -4y \ge y + 3$$

Next, subtract y from both sides: $-4y - y \ge y - y + 3$, so you get $5y \ge 3$.

31. **The correct answer is (C).** Each person, p, will cost \$9.75, so the expression for total cost based on the number of people is $9.75p$. The set-up fee is \$115, so that has to be added to the total cost: $9.75p + 115$. This total must be less than or equal to the budget b, so $9.75p + 115 \le b$.

32. **The correct answer is (B).** Calculate the lower end of the range, using 41°F: $41 = \frac{9}{5}C + 32$, $9 = \frac{9}{5}C$, $C = 5$. The higher end of the range is $45 = \frac{9}{5}C + 32$, $13 = \frac{9}{5}C$, $C \approx 7.2$. C must be at least 5 and at most 7.2. Written in math terms: $5 \le C \le 7.2$.

33. **The correct answer is (C).** To complete the square, take $\frac{1}{2}$ of the coefficient of x and square it. The coefficient of x is $-\frac{1}{2}$, so multiply by $\frac{1}{2}$: $-\frac{1}{2} \times \frac{1}{2} = -\frac{1}{4}$ and square it: $\left(-\frac{1}{4}\right)^2 = \frac{1}{16}$.

34. **The correct answer is (C).** Calculate the slope of the line to get the rate using the two points (0, 140) and (6, 35) in the slope formula:

$$slope = \frac{y_1 - y_2}{x_1 - x_2} = \frac{140 - 35}{0 - 6} = \frac{105}{6} = -17.5$$

The slope is the rate at which the amount of gasoline is decreasing; the tank is losing 17.5 gallons per hour.

35. The correct answer is
$y = -\frac{1}{3}x + \left(-\frac{4}{3}\right)$. First, insert the
given slope as the coefficient of x:
$y = -\frac{1}{3}x + b$. Substitute the given
x and y values into the equation:
$-2 = -\frac{1}{3}(2) + b$. Solve for b:
$-2 = -\frac{2}{3} + b$, $b = -2 + \frac{2}{3} = -\frac{4}{3}$.

36. The correct answer is (C). Start
by converting the first equation into
standard format by dividing through
by -1: $\frac{-y}{-1} = \frac{4x}{-1} + \frac{-1}{-1} = y = -4x + 1$.
Since -4, the x-coefficient in the first

equation, is the negative reciprocal
of $\frac{1}{4}$, the x-coefficient in the second
equation, and the equations are
otherwise identical, these two lines
are perpendicular.

37. The correct answer is (D). Only
this graph shows a function in which
there is a unique y-value for every
x-value. In the functions in choices
(A), (B), and (C), there is at least
one x-value that corresponds to two
different y-values, so only the graph in
(D) has a one-to-one correspondence
of x-values to y-values.

Science

1. (B)	13. Water and carbon dioxide, in either order.	23. See explanation below.
2. 30 grams	14. from the lungs to the heart	24. (C)
3. (C)	15. (D)	25. (B)
4. (C)	16. (D)	26. 5 billion
5. Tigers are at the top of a grazing food web, or chain.	17. condenses	27. (A)
6. (C)	18. (C)	28. (B)
7. (A)	19. (C)	29. (D)
8. (A)	20. Hair color	30. (C)
9. (A)	21. (A)	
10. (B)	22. Earth-Moon-Sun	
11. fungi		
12. (A)		

1. The correct answer is (B). The
fact that aphids rely on sexual
reproduction during the harsh winter
months is to ensure, through natural
selection, that some of the population
is hearty enough to survive. But
during the gentler spring, when

environmental conditions support a
much larger population, their main
goal is to generate as many offspring
as possible, as quickly as possible.
This goal is better achieved by
asexual reproduction.

2. **The correct answer is 30 grams.** At 20°C, all 15 grams are dissolved (the point lies below the KNO_3 solubility curve). From 25°C on the chart's horizontal axis, trace up to the solubility curve, and you'll find that about 45 grams of KNO_3 are soluble at that temperature. Thus, 30 more grams of KNO_3 must be added to saturate the water with KNO_3.

3. **The correct answer is (C).** Ammonia is the only gas among the four substances represented in the chart. For all three other substances, there is a direct relationship between temperature and solubility. In contrast, there is an inverse relationship for ammonia: as the temperature increases, solubility decreases. Choice (C) provides the only conclusion that is supported by the data in the chart.

4. **The correct answer is (C).** Statement I shows that humans are part of a grazing web, while statement IV shows that humans are part of a detrital web. Since humans are a part of both web types, the two must overlap.

5. **The correct answer is: Tigers are at the top of a grazing food web, or chain.** All species of animals consume plants and/or animals, and so tigers must be part of a food chain. Since they prey on other animals but no other animals prey on them, they must be at the top of a grazing food chain. (Tigers are also part of a detrital chain, since their bodies are eventually consumed by decomposers and detritivores, such as vultures, that are farther up that chain.)

6. **The correct answer is (C).** Only the figure on the right (reverse fault) shows two bedrock masses compressing along a fault plane. This compression, or pushing together, forces one of the two masses upward (the right-hand rock in the figure), creating a mountain range.

7. **The correct answer is (A).** Although formulating a hypothesis is a proper initial step in a scientific experiment, in order for the results to be credible (believable), the experiment must be carried out objectively. In this case, the corporation clearly has a financial interest in showing that GMOs are safe to humans, and so the results of its studies are not credible.

8. **The correct answer is (A).** It is easy enough to imagine an out-of-control weed that can resist all of its natural survival threats because it has become genetically altered in the same way that crops are. Such a weed could easily overrun its ecosystem.

9. **The correct answer is (A).** Glucose and fructose both have the same chemical formula: $C_6H_{12}O_6$. The main difference is the placement of carbon in the molecular structure.

10. **The correct answer is (B).** If each pair of corresponding genes—for example, the one that determines hair color—"blended" together, as choice (A) suggests, every child of the same two parents would appear as a similar "blend" of the parent's physical traits; and so, with each subsequent generation, people would appear more and more the same. But what you see at a crowded festival is a broad diversity of physical traits. This suggests that the genes of two parents combine unpredictably, or randomly, to form the child's unique genetic structure, or DNA.

11. **The correct answer is fungi.** Since a yeast cell contains a nucleus, it is a eukaryotic organism. The formation of a daughter cell describes budding, and so yeast matches the description of one sort of fungi.

12. **The correct answer is (A).** A megaphone funnels sound at its source, so instead of spreading spherically, the energy is all concentrated in one direction.

13. **The correct answers are water and carbon dioxide, in either order.** As the illustration shows, carbon dioxide enters a plant's leaf through its underside, while water (hydrogen combined with oxygen) enters from the plant's roots. The plant then separates the hydrogen from the oxygen, expels the oxygen as waste, and combines the hydrogen and carbon dioxide molecules to form glucose (carbohydrates).

14. **The correct answer is: from the lungs to the heart.** Blood in the coronary arteries is "oxygen-rich," which means it has just come from the lungs, and the clot blocks that blood from reaching the part of the heart muscle fed by the artery.

15. **The correct answer is (D).** Glucose is the fuel that cells process into useable energy.

16. **The correct answer is (D).** If all available oxygen is depleted while exercising, your cells can continue to provide useable energy but will now produce and store lactate. When you stop exercising, oxygen will again become available and will retrieve the store of lactate. (Some will be converted into glucose, and some will be broken down into water and carbon dioxide.) Heavy breathing to "catch your breath" is the tell-tale sign that this is occurring.

17. **The correct answer is condenses.** The illustrations show a cold front meeting a warm front. When the moisture in the warm air condenses, water vapor turns to liquid. (Both illustrations show condensation, in the form of rain where cold air meets warmer air.)

18. **The correct answer is (C).** $F = ma$, so $a = \dfrac{F}{m}$. $v = at$, and $t = 10$, so final $v = 10a = \dfrac{10F}{m}$. Because acceleration

is constant, average v = final $\dfrac{v}{2} = \left(\dfrac{1}{2}\right)\dfrac{10F}{m} = \dfrac{5F}{m}$.

19. **The correct answer is (C).** Gold and silver, which are used in fine jewelry, do not react with oxygen. In making this sort of jewelry, there would be no need to protect the metal from oxygen's corrosive effects.

20. **The correct answer is hair color.** Hair color makes the most sense. A pair of recessive alleles for skin color can mask the expression of alleles governing hair and eye color located at other sites on the chromosome. Albinos (animals with albinism) are characterized by a lack of pigment, which provides color, in the hair *and* eyes *and* skin, even though each of these three features is governed by alleles at different sites on the chromosome. A lack of pigment is the result of a congenital, or inherited, absence of melanin.

21. **The correct answer is (A).** The boat is moving from west to east. The waves farther west were created earlier than those that are farther east and have had more time to travel away from the boat's path.

22. **The correct answer is order is Earth-Moon-Sun.** During a solar eclipse, the Moon is positioned directly between Earth and the Sun. To witness the solar eclipse, one must be standing on Earth within the shadow cast by the moon.

23. **The correct answer is first box in or near the top of the liquid in the flask, 2nd box in the space above the surface of the liquid in the flask, 3rd box anywhere in the condenser.** The illustrated lab setup shows undistilled water heated to its boiling point (left). Substances whose boiling points are higher than that of the water remain in the flask. As more water vapor accumulates,

it is forced down the cooling tube (condenser), where it cools back down to the boiling point, condenses to liquid, and collects in the beaker (right).

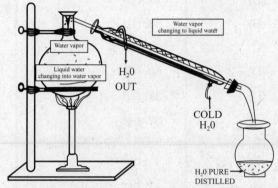

24. **The correct answer is (C).** The figure in choice (C) illustrates the concept of co-evolution, in which two different species that interact with each other evolve in tandem as a result of that relationship.

25. **The correct answer is (B).** After infecting plant B with the virus, if its leaves also begin wrinkling and mottling, this evidence would support the hypothesis that it is the virus that is causing the wrinkling and mottling in plant A's leaves and that plant B has not developed a resistance to it.

26. **The correct answer is 5 billion.** The Sun is about midway to the time when its hydrogen core will be exhausted, at the age of 10 billion years.

27. **The correct answer is (A).** Following the Sun's life path (the broken line), you can see that after its hydrogen core is exhausted, the Sun will go through a cooling period until it becomes a Red Giant, then a longer warming period, followed by a final cooling period.

28. **The correct answer is (B).** The hollow, dorsal (rear) nerve cord, which is common to all vertebrates, refers to the spinal cord.

29. **The correct answer is (D).** Bicarbonate of soda is a base with a pH of 12—at the opposite end of the pH scale as stomach acid. Thus drinking a soda (a carbonated beverage) serves to reduce the pH of your stomach acid.

30. **The correct answer is (C).** The term "cell regeneration" aptly describes the development of a new limb consisting of the same types of specialized cells that were lost. Choice (A) is incorrect because to clone is to create a duplicate of a cell or group of cells, but not to regenerate the original cells(s) that were lost.

Social Studies

1. (B)	13. 400	25. Over-farming
2. See explanation below.	14. (A)	26. (C)
	15. (B)	27. (D)
3. (C)	16. (B)	28. (D)
4. (D)	17. (D)	29. (D)
5. (C)	18. (D)	30. (C)
6. (C)	19. (D)	31. (D)
7. (D)	20. (A)	32. (A)
8. (D)	21. (B)	33. See explanation below.
9. France, Spain, Dutch bankers	22. (D)	
10. It was not allowed to raise taxes	23. (B)	34. See explanation below.
	24. (D)	
11. (C)		
12. (C)		

1. **The correct answer is (B).** The Boston Tea Party protested the tax on tea. The tax had not been raised, choice (C), but neither had it been lifted (eliminated), choice (D). Choice (A) contributed to tensions between British and Americans but was not directly responsible for the protest against the tea tax.

2. As you review your essay, check for the following:

   - Do I have a clear thesis statement that responds exactly to what the prompt asks?

   - Is my essay well organized?

   - Have I analyzed the evidence carefully? Do I use evidence to support my ideas rather than just summarize what the documents are about?

   - Do I provide effective transitions between sections by noting how each section relates to the one before it (e.g., further clarification, contrast)?

   - Do I provide a thoughtful conclusion to my essay?

   You will find two sample essays on pages 730–731.

3. **The correct answer is (C).** Because of its "separate strength," the West could secure an "apostate and unnatural connection with any foreign power."

4. **The correct answer is (D).** The purpose of the War Powers Act was to limit the power of the president to involve the country in wars without the approval of Congress. The Constitution gives Congress the power to declare war, but in today's world, formal declarations of war are no longer usually made. Korea, Vietnam, Iraq, Afghanistan, etc. were all "undeclared" wars.

5. The correct answer is (C). Most youth gang members are attracted to the possibility of gaining wealth and status. While the other choices describe attributes of gang membership that are sometimes true, the most pervasive attribute about membership that the article describes is an attraction to wealth and status.

6. The correct answer is (C). The article states that a survey of eighth-graders from 11 cities indicated that 9 percent of the students surveyed were already gang members and a disturbing 17 percent stated that they had belonged to a gang at some point in their younger lives.

7. The correct answer is (D). A retired individual living on a fixed pension would see the value of his or her income depreciate in terms of what it can purchase. The other three choices would experience little or no immediate adverse effect from inflation.

8. The correct answer is (D). The *Marbury* v. *Madison* decision gave the Supreme Court the power to nullify an act of Congress if it violates the Constitution, as determined by the Court.

9. The correct answer is: France, Spain, and Dutch bankers. The Americans received financial aid from France, Spain, and Dutch bankers.

10. The correct answer is: it was not allowed to raise taxes. Following the War, the Americans were hindered in repaying their debt because the government, under the Articles of Confederation, lacked the authority to raise taxes.

11. The correct answer is (C). The Americans repaid Dutch bankers first because they were willing to provide additional loans despite the Americans' precarious financial situation.

12. The correct answer is (C). To imply something is to strongly suggest something without actually stating it. The last sentence of the passage strongly suggests that the League of Nations would have been more successful had the United States joined. The passage does not provide clues as to the author's views on choices (A), (B), or (D).

13. The correct answer is 400. When more than 400 workers are hired, the average production per worker begins to decline.

14. The correct answer is (A). Hiring more workers will not always increase production, choice (B), which is shown by the last line in the table. Profits are not maximized by keeping labor at a minimum, choice (C); the level of workers needed to maximize profits depends on the size and equipment of the factory and the demand for the product. Although the table demonstrates this factory should not hire more than 600 workers, it's wrong to state that all auto factories should never hire more than 600 workers, choice (D), since factories vary in size and types of equipment.

15. The correct answer is (B). State governments do not have the power to check the federal government since, under the Constitution, federal law is supreme over state law. Of course, a federal law may be unconstitutional, but only the Supreme Court can make that determination, not a state government. All the other answer choices are examples of one branch of the federal government checking the power of another branch.

16. The correct answer is (B). There were widespread reports of voting machine malfunctions. The decision proved to be problematic, in that it slowed down the recount process. Still, even when Gore appealed to the Florida Supreme Court when Secretary of State Harris announced that she would declare a winner even though not all of the votes had been tallied, the Court remained concerned that voting machines had indeed malfunctioned because the ballots did not register the vote because they had not been completely perforated when voters cast their votes.

17. **The correct answer is (D).** The "Unemployed" chart shows that the unemployment rate declined in the years after the New Deal policies were initiated. This trend is consistent with the establishment of a federal program that employed many Americans.

18. **The correct answer is (D).** A strong labor union has the power to negotiate higher wages and salaries for its member-workers. (The first half of the twentieth century saw a growing labor-union movement in the United States.)

19. **The correct answer is (D).** This is the only one that describes the situation regarding immigration from Japan and China to America.

20. **The correct answer is (A).** The large number of immigrants from Europe were processed through Ellis Island, so choice (A) is the correct answer.

21. **The correct answer is (B).** The great racial tensions between African Americans and whites of European descent were probably what caused immigration from Africa to be almost nonexistent.

22. **The correct answer is (D).** Of all the categories in the table, Medicare and Medicaid is the largest.

23. **The correct answer is (B).** Increased communication would provide for effective strategizing based upon risk assessments and other factors.

24. **The correct answer is (D).** Non-prison term responses could enhance rehabilitation and would create needed prison space of more serious offenders.

25. **The correct answer is Over-farming.** Students should consult context clues such as "erosion" and "drought."

26. **The correct answer is (C).** King referred to the "whirlwind of revolt" that must continue until justice prevails. Yet, he urged his followers not to resort to aggression, as "we must not be guilty of wrongful deeds" or drink "from the cup of bitterness and hatred."

27. **The correct answer is (D).** Between 1965 and 1971, spending declined for only one category: training of federal personnel.

28. **The correct answer is (D).** Building pyramids would have suggested that a small number of wealthy, powerful individuals could organize and exploit the labor of many lower-class workers. However, a stratified socioeconomic system did not appear in Mesoamerica until the Middle Preclassic period.

29. **The correct answer is (D).** In the Late Preclassic period, pottery had begun to show some features of classic Mayan art. This information suggests that the Mayan civilization was still to come. (Indeed, the Mayan civilization helps define the Classic Period of Mesoamerica.)

30. **The correct answer is (C).** If the Fed lowers the interest rate it charges banks (the discount rate), then banks will also begin to lower the rates they charge their loan customers. This would also generally cause the interest paid on savings accounts to go down, not up as in choice (B). It's likely that banks would make more loans, not fewer as in choice (D). A change in the discount rate would not normally affect the number of banks that fail, choice (A).

31. **The correct answer is (D).** The occupation and the speech given at the Academy Awards showed that the protesters wanted to draw media attention to the unjust treatment of Native Americans. There is nothing to suggest they somehow wanted to return to the days before the Sioux were defeated, choice (A); to expand the Pine Ridge Indian Reservation, choice (B); or to establish a national historic site, choice (C).

32. **The correct answer is (A).** As the paragraph implies, the preceding period was marked by the emergence of large companies that wielded too much power.

33. **The correct answer is: Iraq invades Kuwait, 1990.** The First Gulf War began when Iraq invaded Kuwait.

34. **The correct answer is: Camp David Accords between Israel and Egypt, 1979.** The Camp David Accords between Israel and Egypt occurred during the administration of President Jimmy Carter.

Reasoning Through Language Arts Extended Response Sample Essays

High-Scoring Response

In these excerpts from the 2008 Supreme Court case *Citizens United v. Federal Election Commission*, I found the minority opinion written by Justice Stevens to be much more compelling than Justice Kennedy's majority opinion, because the former discusses the impetus for the case and directly addresses the matter at hand, while the latter waxes poetic about the First Amendment and the Government's abuse of power.

While the majority opinion takes a popular stance against speech restrictions, it fails to address the fact that Citizens United was breaking federal law in the way that the corporation was promoting their anti-Hillary ideology. The minority opinion correctly identifies the "real issue" right away, which "concerns how, not if, the appellant may finance its electioneering"—that is, the corporation cannot advertise their political agenda in a broadcast that airs within 30 days of the primary. Justice Stevens importantly comments that "[n]either Citizens United's nor any other corporation's speech has been 'banned.'" Furthermore, he says, the majority opinion's focus on the First Amendment stirs the pot but fails to distinguish between human speakers and corporations in its zeal against speech restrictions. Corporations can help build up a society, but they cannot participate in it the ways that humans can, by running for office or voting—and they may even be controlled by noncitizens who cannot contribute themselves, so that "their interests may conflict in fundamental respects with the interests of eligible voters." Justice Stevens also acknowledges that we "need to limit corporate campaign spending," which means that rather than banning corporate speech, we must place limitations on it so that the voices of the people can still be heard over the voices of corporations. I think that Justice Kennedy's opinion completely neglects this central distinction in this case.

I feel the minority opinion is much more effective as an argument than the majority opinion in this case, because Justice Stevens makes the important distinction that the case involves the manner in which the corporation exercised its free speech. His opinion was thoughtful and precise, while Justice Kennedy's lingered on the crowd-pleasing invocation of the First Amendment. As every American knows, the First Amendment covers almost all speech but does not represent an unlimited privilege—there are a few things we are not allowed to say. Our government created these rules to preserve the safety of all Americans. If individual people abide by the rules, why shouldn't corporations like Citizens United?

EXPLANATION

This response would receive a high score because it generates a text-based argument and uses relevant evidence from the passage to support it, contains ideas that are organized and well-developed, and demonstrates a command of standard English conventions. Specifically, this essay defends the minority opinion in the *Citizens United* Supreme Court case. It shows a logical and thoughtful progression of ideas, and demonstrates fluency in Standard English and uses varied sentence structure.

Low-Scoring Response

I believe the second opinion is the better of these passages because it shows that corporations are evil and can spend their money doing other things than advertising against Hillary Clinton. The other passage is more concerned with saying corporations are speakers with the same rights as humans, which they aren't.

So the second passage makes an argument about the facts of the case, that Citizens United is quite wealthy and has the opportunity to promote its new movie. However it could have done that at another point because it has so much money. It also says that corporations have no identity like people so they cannot be judged the same way.

Corporations also can be evil if they have non-Americans as their CEOs because they might try to take over the US by their monetary power. However corporations like these and their CEOs are not able to vote, so they must manipulate everyone's votes locally, not in a national Hillary Clinton movie. "In a democratic society, the longstanding consensus on the need to limit corporate campaign spending should outweigh the wooden application of judge-made rules." So the second opinion finishes a discussion that judges are not the best for the job and should agree about campaign spending.

In this way the second opinion of Justice Stevens is the more argumentative because it is structured like a debate and uses the Constitution.

EXPLANATION

This response would receive a low score because it neglects to answer the question and is far too short, with an argument that is convoluted and uses little to no evidence from the passage to support it. It contains ideas that are confusing and not clearly organized, and demonstrates minimal command of Standard English conventions with only some varied sentence structure.

Social Studies Extended Response Sample Essays

High-Scoring Response

The excerpt reproduced here demonstrates Robert Kennedy's role in moving the United States away from a position of neutrality in the mid-twentieth century. This key change in foreign policy allowed the US to respond to the potential threat of nuclear war from the Soviet bloc, and to maintain a position of power on the world stage.

This change came about after the threat emerged following the infamous "Bay of Pigs" invasion, a bungled attempt to overthrow the regime of Fidel Castro, conducted by US-trained Cuban exiles against Soviet-trained Cuban forces. This incident made it clear that the Soviet bloc was declaring its allegiance with Castro, in direct opposition to US sympathies. Robert Kennedy, as US Attorney General and one of his President John F. Kennedy's (his brother) closest advisers, possessed the political clout to declare that "longstanding U.S. neutrality laws 'clearly…were not designed for the kind of situation which exists in the world today.'" A year later, when Soviet Premier Nikita Kruschev suggested that Cuba host some of the bloc's nuclear weapons as a security measure, the US was further catapulted from its neutral origins by the immediacy of the threat.

Despite all of the impetus for this policy adjustment, Robert Kennedy wavered at times in his position, as shown in the excerpt. He decisively urged the country's leaders to construct a blockade, but was apparently unable to decide whether the US should refrain from an attack that might incite nuclear war, one day calling for an air strike and the next cautioning against use of force. This could be attributed to the fact that he believed that the US had a responsibility to act but still felt that moving too quickly could be highly detrimental.

In any case, Robert Kennedy's influence in the tense situation now known as the Cuban Missile Crisis, along with the Bay of Pigs debacle and the construction of Soviet military bases in Cuba, without a doubt contributed to the US's switch in foreign policy from a position of neutrality to an interventionist stance.

EXPLANATION

This response would receive a high score because it generates a text-based argument and uses relevant evidence from the passage to support it, contains ideas that are organized and well-developed, and demonstrates a command of standard English conventions. Specifically, this essay describes the role of Robert Kennedy and contemporary events in bringing about a change in US foreign policy during the Cuban Missile Crisis. It shows a logical and thoughtful progression of ideas, and demonstrates fluency in Standard English and uses varied sentence structure.

Low-Scoring Response

The US response to the Bay of Pigs changed because they thought the soldiers they trained would win against the Soviets but they did not succeed. Furthermore, Robert Kennedy changed his response several times about whether he wanted to attack Cuba.

In the beginning of the Cuban Missile Crisis Robert Kennedy did not want to attack Cuba. Then the Cubans who were friends of the Soviets and Nikita Kruschev won the Bay of Pigs so Kennedy tried to get his brother the president to attack them. However, the next day he changed his mind. He asked for a blockade around the Bay of Pigs to protect the next attack from failure. Then he had a quarantine of the Cubans so that they would no longer be allies of the Soviets.

So, we can see from Robert Kennedy's example that the US policy changed significantly from the Bay of Pigs, and was constantly changing how it would deal with the Cubans.

EXPLANATION

This response would receive a low score because it neglects to answer the question and is far too short, with an argument that is convoluted and uses little to no evidence from the passage to support it. It contains ideas that are confusing and not clearly organized, and demonstrates minimal command of Standard English conventions with only some varied sentence structure.

ARE YOU READY TO TAKE THE GED® TEST?

Now that you have spent a great deal of time and effort studying for the GED® and taking this Practice Test, hopefully you are well-prepared to take the GED® test. But, it's best to make sure that you are completely ready. Check your scores from this Practice Test on the table below to see where you stand.

	All Set— Well- Prepared	Possibly Ready	Need More Preparation
Reasoning Through Language Arts	37–49	25–36	0–24
Mathematical Reasoning	26–34	17–25	0–16
Science	22–30	17–21	0–16
Social Studies	28–37	18–27	0–17

If your scores are in the "All Set—Well-Prepared" column, you are probably ready to take the actual GED® test, and you should apply to take the test soon. If some of your scores are in the "Possibly Ready" column, you should focus your study on those areas where you need to improve most. "Possibly Ready" means that you are probably ready enough to earn a GED® diploma, but it's not a bad idea to spend a little more time brushing up and improving your chances to pass the actual GED® test.

If any of your scores fell in the lowest category, take more time to review the pertinent chapters in this book—and in any high school text books, if necessary. Good luck!

Practice Test 3

DIRECTIONS FOR TAKING THE PRACTICE TEST

Directions: The GED® Practice Test has four separate subtests: Reasoning Through Language Arts, Mathematical Reasoning, Science, and Social Studies.

- Read and follow the directions at the start of each test.

- Stick to the time limits.

- Enter your answers to the multiple-choice questions on the tear-out Answer Sheets provided. You will answer so-called technology-enhanced questions—like fill-in-the-blank, hot spot, drag-and-drop, and drop-down questions—directly in the test.

- When you have completed the entire test, compare your answers with the correct answers given in the Answer Key and Explanations at the end of this Practice Test.

- Remember to check the "Are You Ready to Take the GED® Test?" section to gauge how close you are to mastering the GED® test.

x

practice test 3

733

ANSWER SHEET PRACTICE TEST 3

Reasoning Through Language Arts

1. Ⓐ Ⓑ Ⓒ Ⓓ

2. Ⓐ Ⓑ Ⓒ Ⓓ

3. Ⓐ Ⓑ Ⓒ Ⓓ

4. Ⓐ Ⓑ Ⓒ Ⓓ

5. Ⓐ Ⓑ Ⓒ Ⓓ

6. _____

7. Ⓐ Ⓑ Ⓒ Ⓓ

8. Ⓐ Ⓑ Ⓒ Ⓓ

9. _____

10. Ⓐ Ⓑ Ⓒ Ⓓ

11. Ⓐ Ⓑ Ⓒ Ⓓ

12. Ⓐ Ⓑ Ⓒ Ⓓ

13. Ⓐ Ⓑ Ⓒ Ⓓ

14. Ⓐ Ⓑ Ⓒ Ⓓ

15. _____

16. Ⓐ Ⓑ Ⓒ Ⓓ

17. Ⓐ Ⓑ Ⓒ Ⓓ

18. Ⓐ Ⓑ Ⓒ Ⓓ

19. _____

20. Ⓐ Ⓑ Ⓒ Ⓓ

21. _____

22. _____

23. Ⓐ Ⓑ Ⓒ Ⓓ

24. _____

25. _____

26. _____

27. _____

28. _____

29. Ⓐ Ⓑ Ⓒ Ⓓ

30. _____

31. Ⓐ Ⓑ Ⓒ Ⓓ

32. _____

33. Ⓐ Ⓑ Ⓒ Ⓓ

34. _____

35. Ⓐ Ⓑ Ⓒ Ⓓ

36. Ⓐ Ⓑ Ⓒ Ⓓ

37. Ⓐ Ⓑ Ⓒ Ⓓ

38. Ⓐ Ⓑ Ⓒ Ⓓ

39. _____

40. Ⓐ Ⓑ Ⓒ Ⓓ

41. Ⓐ Ⓑ Ⓒ Ⓓ

42. _____

43. _____

44. _____

45. _____

46. _____

47. _____

48. _____

49. _____

ANSWER SHEET PRACTICE TEST 3

Mathematical Reasoning

1. Ⓐ Ⓑ Ⓒ Ⓓ
2. Ⓐ Ⓑ Ⓒ Ⓓ
3. Ⓐ Ⓑ Ⓒ Ⓓ
4. Ⓐ Ⓑ Ⓒ Ⓓ
5. _____
6. _____
7. Ⓐ Ⓑ Ⓒ Ⓓ
8. _____
9. Ⓐ Ⓑ Ⓒ Ⓓ
10. Ⓐ Ⓑ Ⓒ Ⓓ
11. _____
12. Ⓐ Ⓑ Ⓒ Ⓓ
13. _____
14. _____
15. Ⓐ Ⓑ Ⓒ Ⓓ

16. Ⓐ Ⓑ Ⓒ Ⓓ
17. Ⓐ Ⓑ Ⓒ Ⓓ
18. Ⓐ Ⓑ Ⓒ Ⓓ
19. Ⓐ Ⓑ Ⓒ Ⓓ
20. Ⓐ Ⓑ Ⓒ Ⓓ
21. Ⓐ Ⓑ Ⓒ Ⓓ
22. Ⓐ Ⓑ Ⓒ Ⓓ
23. Ⓐ Ⓑ Ⓒ Ⓓ
24. Ⓐ Ⓑ Ⓒ Ⓓ
25. Ⓐ Ⓑ Ⓒ Ⓓ
26. Ⓐ Ⓑ Ⓒ Ⓓ
27. Ⓐ Ⓑ Ⓒ Ⓓ

28. Ⓐ Ⓑ Ⓒ Ⓓ
29. Ⓐ Ⓑ Ⓒ Ⓓ
30. _____
31. _____
32. _____
33. _____
34. _____
35. _____
36. Ⓐ Ⓑ Ⓒ Ⓓ
37. Ⓐ Ⓑ Ⓒ Ⓓ

answer sheet

ANSWER SHEET PRACTICE TEST 3

Science

1. Ⓐ Ⓑ Ⓒ Ⓓ   11. Ⓐ Ⓑ Ⓒ Ⓓ   22. _____

2. Ⓐ Ⓑ Ⓒ Ⓓ   12. Ⓐ Ⓑ Ⓒ Ⓓ   23. _____

3. Ⓐ Ⓑ Ⓒ Ⓓ   13. Ⓐ Ⓑ Ⓒ Ⓓ   24. Ⓐ Ⓑ Ⓒ Ⓓ

4. _____   14. Ⓐ Ⓑ Ⓒ Ⓓ   25. _____

5. Ⓐ Ⓑ Ⓒ Ⓓ   15. Ⓐ Ⓑ Ⓒ Ⓓ   26. Ⓐ Ⓑ Ⓒ Ⓓ

6. _____   16. Ⓐ Ⓑ Ⓒ Ⓓ   27. Ⓐ Ⓑ Ⓒ Ⓓ

7. _____   17. _____   28. Ⓐ Ⓑ Ⓒ Ⓓ

8. _____   18. Ⓐ Ⓑ Ⓒ Ⓓ   29. _____

9. Ⓐ Ⓑ Ⓒ Ⓓ   19. Ⓐ Ⓑ Ⓒ Ⓓ   30. Ⓐ Ⓑ Ⓒ Ⓓ

10. Ⓐ Ⓑ Ⓒ Ⓓ   20. _____

                  21. Ⓐ Ⓑ Ⓒ Ⓓ

ANSWER SHEET PRACTICE TEST 3

Social Studies

1. Ⓐ Ⓑ Ⓒ Ⓓ

2. Ⓐ Ⓑ Ⓒ Ⓓ

3. _____

4. Ⓐ Ⓑ Ⓒ Ⓓ

5. Ⓐ Ⓑ Ⓒ Ⓓ

6. Ⓐ Ⓑ Ⓒ Ⓓ

7. Ⓐ Ⓑ Ⓒ Ⓓ

8. Ⓐ Ⓑ Ⓒ Ⓓ

9. Ⓐ Ⓑ Ⓒ Ⓓ

10. Ⓐ Ⓑ Ⓒ Ⓓ

11. _____

12. Ⓐ Ⓑ Ⓒ Ⓓ

13. Ⓐ Ⓑ Ⓒ Ⓓ

14. Ⓐ Ⓑ Ⓒ Ⓓ

15. Ⓐ Ⓑ Ⓒ Ⓓ

16. Ⓐ Ⓑ Ⓒ Ⓓ

17. _____

18. _____

19. _____

20. _____

21. Ⓐ Ⓑ Ⓒ Ⓓ

22. Ⓐ Ⓑ Ⓒ Ⓓ

23. Ⓐ Ⓑ Ⓒ Ⓓ

24. _____

25. _____

26. _____

27. Ⓐ Ⓑ Ⓒ Ⓓ

28. Ⓐ Ⓑ Ⓒ Ⓓ

29. Ⓐ Ⓑ Ⓒ Ⓓ

30. Ⓐ Ⓑ Ⓒ Ⓓ

31. Ⓐ Ⓑ Ⓒ Ⓓ

32. Ⓐ Ⓑ Ⓒ Ⓓ

33. _____

34. Ⓐ Ⓑ Ⓒ Ⓓ

answer sheet

Essay

_____

_____

_____

_____

_____

_____

_____

_____

_____

_____

_____

_____

_____

_____

_____

_____

_____

_____

_____

_____

answer sheet

REASONING THROUGH LANGUAGE ARTS

150 Minutes • 49 Questions

Directions: The Reasoning Through Language Arts Test consists of passages of fiction and nonfiction reading material. Most questions are in multiple-choice format. Others are meant to prepare you for the electronically formatted questions that you will find on the test, such as drop-down, fill-in-the-blanks, and drag-and-drops. After you read a passage, answer the questions that follow it, referring back to the passage as needed. Answer all questions based on what is stated and implied in the passage. There is also an extended response question that requires you to read a paired passage that represents two views on a topic and write a well-organized essay supporting one of the view points. Record your answers on the Reasoning Through Language Arts section of the answer sheet provided.

QUESTIONS 1 TO 9 REFER TO THE FOLLOWING PASSAGE.

Edna still felt dazed when she got outside in the open air. The Doctor's coupe [horse drawn carriage] had returned for him and
5 stood before the porte cochere [driveway]. ...She told Doctor Mandelet she would walk; she was not afraid, and would go alone. ... He started to walk home with her.
10   Up—away up, over the narrow street between the tall houses, the stars were blazing. They walked slowly, the Doctor with a heavy, measured tread and his hands
15 behind him; Edna, in an absent-minded way, as she had walked one night at Grand Isle, as if her thoughts had gone ahead of her and she was striving to overtake them.
20   "You shouldn't have been there, Mrs. Pontellier," he said. "That was no place for you. Adele is full of whims at such times. There were a dozen women she might have had
25 with her, unimpressionable women. ... You shouldn't have gone."
    "Oh, well!" she answered, indifferently. "I don't know that it matters after all. One has to think
30 of the children some time or other; the sooner the better."
    "When is Leonce coming back?"

    "Quite soon. Some time in March."
35   "And you are going abroad?"
    "Perhaps—no, I am not going. I'm not going to be forced into doing things. I don't want to go abroad. I want to be let alone. Nobody has any
40 right—except children, perhaps—and even then, it seems to me—or it did seem—" She felt that her speech was voicing the incoherency of her thoughts, and stopped abruptly.
45   "The trouble is," sighed the Doctor, grasping her meaning intuitively, "that youth is given up to illusions. It seems to be a provision of Nature; a decoy to secure mothers
50 for the race. And Nature takes no account of moral consequences, of arbitrary conditions which we create, and which we feel obliged to maintain at any cost."
55   "Yes," she said. "The years that are gone seem like dreams—if one might go on sleeping and dreaming—but to wake up and find—oh! well! perhaps it is better
60 to wake up after all, even to suffer, rather than to remain a dupe to illusions all one's life."
    "It seems to me, my dear child," said the Doctor at parting, holding
65 her hand, "you seem to me to be in trouble. ..."

"Some way I don't feel moved to speak of things that trouble me. Don't think I am ungrateful or that
70 I don't appreciate your sympathy. There are periods of despondency and suffering which take possession of me. But I don't want anything but my own way. That is wanting a good
75 deal, of course, when you have to trample upon the lives, the hearts, the prejudices of others—but no matter—still, I shouldn't want to trample upon the little lives. Oh! I
80 don't know what I'm saying, Doctor. Good night. Don't blame me for anything."

"Yes, I will blame you if you don't come and see me soon. ... It will do
85 us both good. I don't want you to blame yourself, whatever comes. Good night, my child."

She let herself in at the gate, but instead of entering she sat
90 upon the step of the porch. The night was quiet and soothing. All the tearing emotion of the last few hours seemed to fall away from her like a somber, uncomfortable
95 garment, which she had but to loosen to be rid of. She went back to that hour before Adele had sent for her; and her senses kindled afresh in thinking of Robert's words, the
100 pressure of his arms, and the feeling of his lips upon her own. She could picture at that moment no greater bliss on earth than possession of the beloved one. His expression of
105 love had already given him to her in part. When she thought that he was there at hand, waiting for her, she grew numb with the intoxication of expectancy. It was so late; he
110 would be asleep perhaps. She would awaken him with a kiss. She hoped he would be asleep that she might arouse him with her caresses.

Still, she remembered Adele's
115 voice whispering, "Think of the children; think of them." She meant to think of them; that determination had driven into her soul like a

death wound—but not to-night.
120 To-morrow would be time to think of everything.

Robert was not waiting for her in the little parlor. He was nowhere at hand. The house was empty. But
125 he had scrawled on a piece of paper that lay in the lamplight:

"I love you. Good-by—because I love you."

Edna grew faint when she read
130 the words. She went and sat on the sofa. Then she stretched herself out there, never uttering a sound. She did not sleep. She did not go to bed. The lamp sputtered and went
135 out. She was still awake in the morning, when Celestine unlocked the kitchen door and came in to light the fire.

—From Kate Chopin,
The Awakening

1. What conclusion can you draw from the passage about Edna's marriage?

   (A) She is happily married but lonely because her husband is away.

   (B) She wants to leave her husband and run off with Robert.

   (C) She was married when she was very young.

   (D) She thinks her husband is unreasonable, and she quarrels with him a lot.

2. How does Edna react to the Doctor's invitation to visit him?

   (A) She brushes it off and says she doesn't want to talk about her troubles.

   (B) She expresses her appreciation for his friendship and promises to call on him.

   (C) She gets confused and ends the conversation.

   (D) She gets upset because he is blaming her for her behavior.

3. What does Edna seem to be deluding herself about?

(A) That she can leave her life and run off with Robert.

(B) That she can support her children by herself.

(C) That she can travel with her husband and leave the children at home.

(D) That Robert loves her.

4. What is Edna's relationship to the Doctor?

(A) The Doctor lives next door to Edna, and they enjoy one another's company.

(B) The Doctor is a friend who Edna confides in.

(C) They are casual acquaintances who don't know one another very well.

(D) The Doctor is her family physician and worries about her behavior.

5. Which figure of speech in the passage conveys Edna's desire to be free?

(A) "as if her thoughts had gone ahead of her"

(B) "the intoxication of expectancy"

(C) "like a somber, uncomfortable garment"

(D) "youth is given up to illusions"

6. In the drop-down menu, click on the answer that best completes the sentence. Edna's struggle shows that she feels [Select ▼].

guilty about leaving her children

guilty about betraying her husband

angry that she can't travel abroad

sad that she has lost her youth

On the online GED® test, you will click to select your answer. For this paper version, please circle it.

7. What does the Doctor mean when he describes the women who were among the guests at Adele's house as "unimpressionable."

(A) resistant to conforming to the social mores

(B) hard to please

(C) stubborn and unlikeable

(D) socially important for maintaining appearances

8. What does the Doctor do that indicates he might be aware of Edna's plan?

(A) He tells her not to blame herself.

(B) He offers her sympathy.

(C) He tells her he thinks she's in trouble.

(D) He tries to reinforce her guilt about leaving her children.

9. In the drop-down menu, click on the answer that best completes the sentence. As she is walking to the house, Edna is most concerned that [Select ▼].

the children will hear her coming into the house

Robert awaits her and her life will change forever

her husband will find her out and he will leave her

she will be forced to do things she doesn't want to do

On the online GED® test, you will click to select your answer. For this paper version, please circle it.

QUESTIONS 10-15 REFER TO THE FOLLOWING PASSAGE FROM A LETTER.

WHY IS THE AUTHOR WRITING A NEW BOOK?

I had two little curly-headed twin daughters to begin with, and my stock in this line was gradually increased, till I have been the
5 mother of seven children, the most beautiful and the most loved of whom lies buried near my Cincinnati residence. It was at his dying bed and at his grave that I
10 learned what a poor slave mother may feel when her child is torn away from her. In those depths of sorrow which seemed to me immeasurable, it was my only prayer to
15 God that such anguish might not be suffered in vain. There were circumstances about his death of such peculiar bitterness, of what seemed almost cruel suffering, that I felt
20 that I could never be consoled for it unless this crushing of my own heart might enable me to work out some great good to others.

I allude to this here because I
25 have often felt that much that is in that book ("Uncle Tom's Cabin") had its root in the awful scenes and bitter sorrows of that summer. It has left now, I trust, no trace on
30 my mind except a deep compassion for the sorrowful, especially for mothers who are separated from their children.

I am now writing a work which
35 will contain, perhaps, an equal amount of matter with "Uncle Tom's Cabin." It will contain all the facts and documents upon which that story was founded, and
40 an immense body of facts, reports of trial, legal documents, and testimony of people now living South, which will more than confirm every statement in "Uncle Tom's Cabin."

45 I must confess that till I began the examination of facts in order to write this book, much as I thought I knew before, I had not begun to measure the depth of
50 the abyss. The law records of courts and judicial proceedings are so incredible as to fill me with amazement whenever I think of them. It seems to me that the book
55 cannot but be felt, and, coming upon the sensibility awaked by the other, do something.

I suffer exquisitely in writing these things. It may be truly said
60 that I suffer with my heart's blood. Many times in writing "Uncle Tom's Cabin" I thought my heart would fail utterly, but I prayed earnestly that God would help me
65 till I got through, and still I am pressed beyond measure and above strength.

—Harriet Beecher Stowe

10. To what does the author trace her compassion for slave mothers?

   (A) her writing of "Uncle Tom's Cabin"

   (B) her hatred of injustice

   (C) the loss of her own son

   (D) her reading of legal documents and testimony

11. What does the author disclose about the new book she is writing?

   The new book will be

   (A) at least as long as "Uncle Tom's Cabin."

   (B) based on the lives of her parents.

   (C) more successful than "Uncle Tom's Cabin."

   (D) a call to abolish slavery.

12. To what does the author refer by her words "the depth of the abyss" (lines 49–50)?

    (A) the cruelty of the judicial process

    (B) the suffering of young mothers

    (C) the horrors of slavery

    (D) the immeasurable intensity of grief

13. What effect does the author believe her new book will have on its readers?

    (A) It will prompt readers to read her last book.

    (B) It will arouse empathy and prompt them to act.

    (C) It will cause readers intense suffering.

    (D) It will help readers of "Uncle Tom's Cabin" understand why some people had slaves.

14. What does the passage reveal about its author?

    (A) She was unable to conduct the research needed for her book.

    (B) She became active in the abolitionist movement.

    (C) She wrote with little effort.

    (D) She was deeply and emotionally involved in her work.

15. Which of the following things will be in Harriet Beecher Stowe's new work? On the online GED® test, you will click and drag your choices into the blank circles. For this paper version, please write them in.

    reports of trial

    legal documents

    sequel to "Uncle Tom's Cabin"

    testimony of Southerners

    information about Stowe's children

    Stowe's autobiography

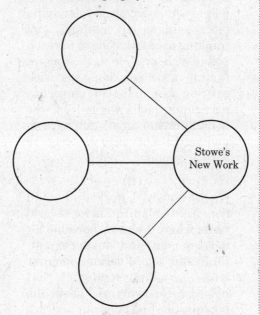

QUESTIONS 16–23 REFER TO THE FOLLOWING PASSAGE.

Cover Letter

(A)

(1) To Whom It May Concern:
(2) Please consider this application for the Marketing and Communications Internship at your company. (3) At my previous employments, I have gained valuable marketing and sales experience that I am looking forward to building upon. (4) While working at my last job, I improved my editorial, writing, and management skills, as well as working with clients and problem solving issues we had. (5) I also worked with the Marketing department on there regular campaigns—this involved managing blogs, sending out mailings, and thinking of creative ideas to reach possible clients—as well as maintaining good relationships with existing clients. (6) One project in particular that I worked on was helping create small gift bags to male out, one of which we designed with a "summer" theme.

(B)

(7) Previously, I worked at small non-profit organization for several years where I was responsible for development and advancement. (8) In this role, I became familiar with marketing strategies that helped raise awareness about the organization and build our network of supporters. (9) In addition, I was in charge of planning several of our yearly fundraising events in which we successfully raised millions of dollars, from which I personally gained communications and management skills. (10) Because of my position at this company, I also have extensive organizational experience and am able to balance many tasks.

(C)

(11) From my work in marketing, I believe that I am well qualified to you're position because I have experience in marketing, research, editorial, and social media. (12) In addition, I can organize and manage multiple projects or task at once, as well as problem solving and communicating effectively with clients and coworkers. (13) I also know how to conduct research, report, and present information in a concise, clear manner. (14) I also have experience working with various social media outlets and am proficient at Microsoft Office programs.

(D)

(15) If I am given the opportunity to join the company, I look forward to advancing the visibility and goals through my work with the marketing department. (16) Particularly, I am skilled at social media, community relations outreach, and campaign development and I look forward to bringing what I know to the company.

(E)

(17) I think I am a strong applicant for your position because of my diverse background and experiences, but also because I am eager to try new things. (18) I am a very quick learner, dedicated, innovative, and a natural problem-solver. (19) My boss told me she couldn't of finished so much work this summer without my help. (20) Furthermore, I am interested in learning more about marketing because its applicable to many different industries. (21) I look forward to hearing from you, please let me know if you require any additional information.

Sincerely,

Kelly Smith

16. Choose the best option for improving sentence 12.

(12) In addition, I can organize and manage multiple projects or task at once, as well as problem solving and communicating effectively with clients and coworkers.

(A) In addition, I can organize and manage multiple projects or tasks at the same time, as well as problem solving and communicating effectively with clients and coworkers.

(B) In addition, I can organize and manage several projects or tasks at one time, as well as problem-solve and communicate effectively with clients and coworkers.

(C) In addition, I can organize and manage multiple projects or task at once, as well as problem solve and communicating effectively with clients and coworkers.

(D) In addition, I can organize and manage multiple projects or tasks at once, as well as problem solve and communicate effectively with clients and coworkers.

17. What is the best way to improve sentence 20?

(20) I look forward to hearing from you, please let me know if you require any additional information.

(A) Replace the comma after the first you with a semi-colon.

(B) Replace the comma after the first you with a colon.

(C) Delete the comma after the first you.

(D) Add the word *and* after the comma.

18. Which sentence pairs seem to repeat some of the same points?

(A) sentence 11 and sentence 14

(B) sentence 4 and sentence 7

(C) sentence 8 and sentence 18

(D) sentence 6 and sentence 19

19. Which of the following skills does Kelly have experience doing? On the online GED® test, you will click and drag our choices into the blank circles. For this paper version, please write them in.

balancing budgets

planning fundraising events

creating client gifts

doing research

speaking Spanish

designing print products

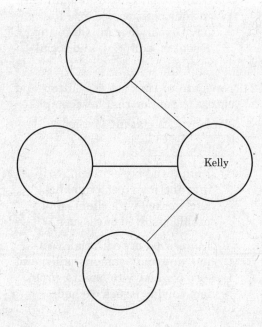

20. Which of the following is the best reworking of sentence 11? If the sentence is fine as is, choose (D).

Sentence 11: From my work in marketing, I believe that I am well qualified to your position because I have experience in marketing, research, editorial, and social media.

(A) From my work in marketing, I believe that I am well qualified to your position because I have experience in marketing, research, editorial, and social media and knowing how to use a copy machine.

(B) From my work in marketing, I believe that I am well qualified for your position because I have experience in marketing, research, editorial, and social media.

(C) I believe that I am well qualified for your position because I have experience in marketing, research, editorial, and social media.

(D) From my work in marketing, I believe that I am well qualified to your position because I have experience in marketing, research, editorial, and social media.

21. Navigate to the "select" button and choose the option that best completes

While working at my last job,

Select ▼

I improved my editorial, writing, and management skills, and worked with clients and problem-solved our issues.

I improved my editorial, writing, and management skills, and also worked with clients, problem solving issues we had.

I improved my editorial, writing, and management skills by working with clients and problem solving.

I improved my editorial, writing, and management skills, as well as working with clients and problem solving issues we had.

22. Consider sentence 9 in the context of the entire cover letter. Then navigate to the "select" button and choose the best revision of the sentence. On the online GED® test, you will click on your answer. For this paper version, please circle it.

Sentence 9: In addition, I was in charge of planning several of our yearly fundraising events in which we successfully raised millions of dollars, from which I personally gained communications and management skills.

Select ▼

I personally gained communication and management skills when I was in charge of planning several of our yearly fundraising events when we successfully raised millions of dollars.

I was in charge of planning several of our yearly fundraising events, during which we successfully raised millions of dollars.

Being in charge of several of our yearly fundraising events and successfully raising millions of dollars gave me additional communication and management skills.

The fact that I was in charge of several yearly fundraising events and successfully raising millions of dollars meant that I gained communication and management skills.

23. Choose the best choice to correct the following run-on (or fused) sentence.

Sentence 17: I think I am a strong applicant for your position because of my diverse background and experiences also because I am eager to try new things.

(A) I think I am a strong applicant for your position, because of my diverse background and experiences also because, I am eager to try new things.

(B) I think I am a strong applicant for your position because of my diverse background and experiences. Also because I am eager to try new things.

(C) I think I am a strong applicant for your position not only because of my diverse background and experiences, also because I am eager to try new things.

(D) I think I am a strong applicant for your position because of my diverse background and experiences, and also because I am eager to try new things.

Directions: The following words appear in Kelly's cover letter. These words are homonyms—they sound the same as other words that have different meanings. For Questions 23–28, if the word is spelled correctly based on the context in which it appears, type "ok" in the box. If it is not, type the correct spelling in the box. On the online GED® test, you will type your answer into the spaces provided. For this paper version, please write them in.

24. [sentence 5] there ⬚

25. [sentence 6] male ⬚

26. [sentence 9] our ⬚

27. [sentence 11] you're ⬚

28. [sentence 19] its ⬚

QUESTIONS 29–35 REFER TO THE FOLLOWING PAIR OF PASSAGES.

Love Letters

Among the great loves in history are those of the composer Robert Schumann for his wife, Clara, and of Napoleon Bonaparte for his wife, Josephine. Their love is public knowledge due to the hundreds of love letters they left behind. The excerpts that follow are from their letters. The first one is from Schumann to his then-fiancée, and the second is from Napoleon, written on the battlefield to his wife at home.

Passage 1—Robert Schumann to Clara Wieck (1838)

I have a hundred things to write to you, great and small, if only I could do it neatly, but my writing grows more and more indistinct, a sign, I
5 fear, of heart weakness. There are terrible hours when your image forsakes me, when I wonder anxiously whether I have ordered my life as wisely as I might, whether
10 I had any right to bind you to me, my angel, or can really make you as happy as I should wish. These doubts all arise, I am inclined to think, from your father's attitude
15 towards me. It is so easy to accept other people's estimate of oneself. Your father's behaviour makes me ask myself if I am really so bad— of such humble standing—as to
20 invite such treatment from anyone. Accustomed to easy victory over difficulties, to the smiles of fortune, and to affection, I have been spoiled by having things made too easy for
25 me, and now I have to face refusal, insult, and calumny. I have read of many such things in novels, but I thought too highly of myself to imagine I could ever be the hero of
30 a family tragedy of the Kotzebue sort myself. If I had ever done your father an injury, he might well hate me; but I cannot see why he should despise me and, as you say, hate me
35 without any reason. But my turn

will come, and I will then show him how I love you and himself; for I will tell you, as a secret, that I really love and respect your father for his many
40 great and fine qualities, as no one but yourself can do. I have a natural inborn devotion and reverence for him, as for all strong characters, and it makes his antipathy for me
45 doubly painful. Well, he may some time declare peace, and say to us, "Take each other, then."

You cannot think how your letter has raised and strengthened
50 me . . . You are splendid, and I have much more reason to be proud of you than of me. I have made up my mind, though, to read all your wishes in your face. Then you will
55 think, even though you don't say it, that your Robert is a really good sort, that he is entirely yours, and loves you more than words can say. You shall indeed have cause
60 to think so in the happy future. I still see you as you looked in your little cap that last evening. I still hear you call me *du*. Clara, I heard nothing of what you said but that
65 *du*. Don't you remember?

Passage 2—Napoleon Bonaparte to Josephine Bonaparte (1796)

I have not spent a day without loving you; I have not spent a night without embracing you; I have not so much as drunk a single cup of
5 tea without cursing the pride and ambition which force me to remain separated from the moving spirit of my life. In the midst of my duties, whether I am at the head of my
10 army or inspecting the camps, my beloved Josephine stands alone in my heart, occupies my mind, fills my thoughts. If I am moving away from you with the speed of
15 the Rhône torrent, it is only that I may see you again more quickly. If I rise to work in the middle of the night, it is because this may hasten by a matter of days the arrival of
20 my sweet love. Yet in your letter of the 23rd and 26th Ventôse, you call me *vous*. *Vous* yourself! Ah! wretch, how could you have written this letter? How cold it is! And then
25 there are those four days between the 23rd and the 26th; what were you doing that you failed to write to your husband? . . . Ah, my love, that vous, those four days make me
30 long for my former indifference. Woe to the person responsible! May he, as punishment and penalty, experience what my convictions and the evidence (which is in your friend's
35 favour) would make me experience! Hell has no torments great enough! *Vous! Vous!* Ah! How will things stand in two weeks? . . . My spirit is heavy; my heart is fettered and
40 I am terrified by my fantasies . . . You love me less; but you will get over the loss. One day you will love me no longer; at least tell me; then I shall know how I have come to
45 deserve this misfortune . . .

29. What type of figurative language does Napoleon use in the first sentence of his letter?

(A) simile

(B) onomatopoeia

(C) hyperbole

(D) cliché

30. Which of the following devices is NOT used in BOTH passages? On the on-line GED® test, you will click on your answer. For this paper version, please circle it.

| Select ▼ |

foreign phrases

third-person

recollection

simile

31. How would you best describe the tone of the latter half of Napoleon's letter?

(A) depressed

(B) teasing

(C) ecstatic

(D) angry

32. Select ▼

Kotzebue and Ventôse

Ventôse and Kotzebue

du and vous

vous and du

are foreign phrases used in passages 1 and 2 respectively, that both mean

 Select ▼

lover

darling

you

him

On the online GED® test, you will click on your answer. For this paper version, please circle it.

33. What is the major obstacle to Schumann's relationship with Clara?

(A) His heart disease

(B) Their difference in fortune

(C) Her father's disapproval

(D) The distance between them

34. Based on their letters, fill in the Venn diagram to show the differences between the two men, as well as what they have in common. On the online GED® test, you will click and drag your answers into the Venn diagram. For this paper version, please write them in.

married

poor

musician

long-distance relationship

at war

focusing on memories

uneducated

expresses self-doubt

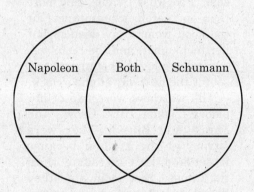

35. What word most closely describes Schumann's use of "reverence" (line 42)?

(A) respect

(B) tolerance

(C) love

(D) acceptance

QUESTIONS 36–41 REFER TO THE FOLLOWING PASSAGE.

"Miss Tempy's Watchers"

The following is an excerpt from a short story, "Miss Tempy's Watchers," by Sarah Orne Jewett, a novelist and short-story writer who lived from 1849–1909. In the story, two women watch over their deceased friend on the evening before her funeral and share their memories of her.

The time of year was April; the place was a small farming town in New Hampshire, remote from any railroad. One by one the lights
5 had been blown out in the scattered houses near Miss Tempy Dent's, but as her neighbors took a last look out of doors, their eyes turned with instinctive curiosity
10 toward the old house where a lamp burned steadily. They gave a little sigh. "Poor Miss Tempy!" said more than one bereft acquaintance; for the good woman lay dead in her
15 north chamber, and the lamp was a watcher's light. The funeral was set for the next day at one o'clock.

The watchers were two of her oldest friends. Mrs. Crowe and
20 Sarah Ann Binson. They were sitting in the kitchen because it seemed less awesome than the unused best room, and they beguiled the long hours by steady
25 conversation. One would think that neither topics nor opinions would hold out, at that rate, all through the long spring night, but there was a certain degree of excitement
30 just then, and the two women had risen to an unusual level of expressiveness and confidence. Each had already told the other more than one fact that she had determined
35 to keep secret; they were again and again tempted into statements that either would have found impossible by daylight. Mrs. Crowe was knitting a blue yarn stocking for
40 her husband; the foot was already

so long that it seemed as if she must have forgotten to narrow it at the proper time. Mrs. Crowe knew exactly what she was about,
45 however; she was of a much cooler disposition than Sister Binson, who made futile attempts at some sewing, only to drop her work into her lap whenever the talk was most
50 engaging.

Their faces were interesting— of the dry, shrewd, quick-witted New England type, and thin hair twisted neatly back out of the way.
55 Mrs. Crowe could look vague and benignant, and Miss Binson was, to quote her neighbors, a little too sharp-set, but the world knew that she had need to be, with the
60 load she must carry supporting an inefficient widowed sister and six unpromising and unwilling nieces and nephews. The eldest boy was at last placed with a
65 good man to learn the mason's trade. Sarah Ann Binson, for all her sharp, anxious aspect never defended herself, when her sister whined and fretted. She was told
70 every week of her life that the poor children would never have had to lift a finger if their father had lived, and yet she had kept her steadfast way with the little
75 farm, and patiently taught the young people many useful things for which, as everybody said, they would live to thank her. However pleasureless her life appeared to
80 outward view, it was brimful of pleasure to herself.

Mrs. Crowe, on the contrary, was well-to-do, her husband being a rich farmer and an easy-going
85 man. She was a stingy woman, but for all of that she looked kindly; and when she gave away anything, or lifted a finger to help anybody, it was thought a great piece of benefi-
90 cence, and a compliment, indeed, which the recipient accepted with twice as much gratitude as double

the gift that came from a poorer and more generous acquaintance.

95 Everybody liked to be on good terms with Mrs. Crowe. Socially, she stood much higher than Sarah Ann Binson.

36. From whose point of view do we learn the information given at the beginning of the excerpt?

(A) Mrs. Crowe

(B) Sarah Ann Binson

(C) an omniscient narrator

(D) the townspeople

37. Mrs. Crowe and Sarah Ann Binson feel comfortable sharing secrets because

(A) Miss Tempy is dead.

(B) they are close friends.

(C) it is night time.

(D) no one else is with them.

38. Mrs. Crowe's donations are greatly appreciated because they

(A) are so substantial.

(B) are well-thought-out.

(C) are so rare.

(D) give her pleasure.

39. Drag and drop the phrases that describe the characters into the correct location on the chart. On the online GED® test, you will click and drag your answers into the spaces provided. For this paper version, please write them in.

Mrs. Crowe	Sarah Ann Binson

supports widowed sister	well-to-do
sharp-set	stingy

40. Sarah Ann Binson can best be described as

(A) assertive.

(B) skillful.

(C) timid.

(D) impatient.

41. What do Sarah Ann Binson and Mrs. Crowe NOT have in common?

(A) their friendship with Miss Tempy

(B) their wealth

(C) their appearance

(D) their place of origin

42. *The following passages present two views on children's vacation time. Take 45 minutes to choose which of the two viewpoints you wish to support and use the paper provided to write a well-organized essay. Use reasons and examples to support your position.*

WHAT YOUR CHILD DID LAST SUMMER

Let's Keep School Out for the Summer

Many see a summer vacation being built into a school calendar as a necessity, one that they never thought to question. Others—

5 parents, teachers, and students alike—have questioned summer break, claiming the academic benefits of year-round school outweigh any of the pros long associated with

10 the vacation time.

While support for a full-calendar year of school often relies heavily on studies showing students retain knowledge better with shorter

15 breaks between learning periods, they are not the only modes of research regarding learning efficiency. Other academic studies have shown that the same loss

20 of knowledge happens annually, regardless of whether students are in school or not. What matters most about knowledge retention is the application of what was learned,

25 which cannot be guaranteed for all subjects even in school. Not to mention, a strict school setting is not the only atmosphere a child can learn in. Students may refresh the

30 knowledge acquired from a previous school year countless ways over the summer: from camps to classes to simple workbooks and reading refreshers.

35 Further arguments for a more spread out school year include the cost savings for childcare. This may be the case for many who cannot take off the summer months from

40 work, but the costs associated with keeping a school open and up-to-date year round have to be met by someone. And who would be paying for such costs? Most likely the tax-

45 payers of the town, including the couple thinking they were saving from childcare. In a similar vein, many working parents struggle enough with planning family time

50 (be it vacations, parties, etc.) in the summer, but that problem only increases with the schedules of year-round schools. Oftentimes the new breaks introduced to make

55 up for the lack of summer vacation do not overlap with other schools, including those of different levels in the same district. So planning for an effective time with children spread

60 out at different schools would be even more difficult, particularly when factoring in, say cousins who live in a different town. The schedules simply would likely not

65 match up.

Beyond the fact that it has been the most common approach to a school calendar, the most persuasive argument for maintaining

70 summer vacation is that schools that have year-round trials simply have not chosen the newer option. Whether it be because of cost or scheduling issues, a majority of the

75 cases have found the approach to simply not work well enough, and returned to the traditional decision to allow students to have a summer break.

Year-Round School Solution to "Summer Learning Loss"

In a generation where U.S. academics are lacking compared to those worldwide, adding days to the academic calendar seems like the

5 only solution. Administrators and government officials are pressing to keep students in the classroom while others suggest this isn't the best solution. Although the school

10 calendar might be up for debate,

it's clear extended summers are responsible for putting students behind.

Johns Hopkins University con-
15 ducted a twenty-year-long study that tracked the learning progress of a group of students, following them from kindergarten to high school. The results showed that
20 although there is even-keeled learning throughout the school year, disadvantaged students suffered huge learning losses once summer hit. By the end of grammar
25 school, these low-income students were up to three grade levels behind their peers.

This "summer learning loss," otherwise nicknamed "summer
30 brain drain" or "the summer slide," is detrimental. Because some low-income students lack the means to attend summer programs, take family vacations, or reside
35 in safe neighborhoods in which they can freely play, their mental and physical exercise slow to a mere crawl—the students become isolated and bored. According to
40 experts at Duke University, low-income students can lose anywhere from one to three months of progress in math and reading skills each summer. Although higher income
45 students may be performing better than their lower income peers, their learning patterns are still slacking when compared to those around the globe.
50 If school districts, cities, and parents take the initiative to promote learning year-round, whether it be through adjusting the calendar—spreading out vacation
55 days so that no break extends more than a few weeks—or through hosting summer enrichment programs, students may not only maintain their scores, but improve
60 them. Some states that rely on volunteer programs have still managed to host enrichment programs

that resulted in full letter grade improvements for their students
65 in the following year. Others, with government funding, showed scores that started in the bottom 30th percentile increase to reach the 70th percentile in math and reading.
70 Despite the approach, it is clear that students need more academic involvement throughout the year, rather than the three-month summer "vacation" they've become
75 accustomed to. By promoting year-round learning, students will be more likely to maintain classroom knowledge while making themselves academically competitive
80 around the globe.

QUESTIONS 43–48 REFER TO THE FOLLOWING E-MAIL.

Subject: Beta version of our website
From: Shannon McDougal
To: Adrian Webster <adrian.webster@ websterswebdesign.net>

Mr. Webster:

(A)

(1) I finally found time to try out the website beta version submitted to our company last week by you. (2) The navigation buttons, using the pull-down menus, and the product ordering page are all intuitive and user-friendly. (3) Overall, you've done a great job designing the site. (4) But I do have a few points of constructive criticism:

(B)

(5) Is it possible to use a three-column format instead of two columns? (6) That way, more information is visible "above the fold" on each page.

(C)

(7) The subheadings can be hard to distinguish from the text, at least for me. (8) Can you use a larger size or a contrasting color for these headings?

(D)

(9) Can you change the orientation of the menu buttons to horizontal, across the top of each page, instead of vertically (down the left side of the screen)? (10) I asked my boss, and me and her both like the horizontal design better.

(E)

(11) We have a new company logo that we wish to use on every page of the Web site. (12) We can e-mail an image of the logo to you. (13) Please let me know if you have any particular file format or size requirements.

(F)

(14) I'd like the site to include a site map. (15) I didn't see one in this beta version, but maybe that's something that will automatically be generated once the site design will be complete.

(G)

(16) We have not yet decided on a Web hosting service. (17) Do you have any recommendations, given our data and functionality requirements? (18) Of utmost importance is our customers' security and privacy, who will be entering credit card information at the site.

(H)

(19) Everyone here hopes to see the final product vary soon because we're anxious to "go live" with our new website by the end of this month.

Regards,
Shannon McDougal

43. Sentence 1: I finally found time to try out the website beta version

| Select ▼ |

submitted to our company last week by you

you submitted to our company last week

for our company. You submitted it last week

by you, submitted last week to our company

On the online GED® test, you will click to select your answer. For this paper version, please circle it.

44. Sentence 2: The navigation buttons, using the pull-down menus, and the product ordering page are all intuitive and user-friendly.

Which correction should be made to sentence 2?

| Select ▼ |

remove the comma after <u>buttons</u>

remove the word <u>using</u>

remove the comma after <u>menus</u>

change <u>are all</u> to <u>is</u>

On the online GED® test, you will click to select your answer. For this paper version, please circle it.

45. Sentence 5 and Sentence 6: Is it possible to use a three-column format instead of two columns? That way, more information is visible "above the fold" on each page.

An effective combination of sentences 5 and 6 would include which of the following groups of words?

Select   ▼

so that more information is visible

the more visible the information is

on each page, use a three-column format

Is it possible instead of two columns

On the online GED® test, you will click to select your answer. For this paper version, please circle it.

46. Sentence 9: Can you change the orientation of the menu buttons to horizontal, across the top of each page, instead of vertically (down the left side of the screen)?

Which correction should be made to sentence 9?

Select   ▼

change Can to Can't

replace to with from

replace across to a cross

change vertically to vertical

On the online GED® test, you will click to select your answer. For this paper version, please circle it.

47. Sentence 10: I asked my boss, and me and her both like the horizontal design better.

Which is the best way to write the underlined portion of sentence 10?

Select   ▼

and me and her both

and her and I each

she and I both

and she and I both

On the online GED® test, you will click to select your answer. For this paper version, please circle it.

48. Sentence 19: Everyone here hopes to see the final product vary soon because we're anxious to "go live" with our new website by the end of this month.

Which correction should be made to sentence 19?

Select   ▼

replace Everyone with Every one

change hopes to hope

replace vary with very

replace month with Month

On the online GED® test, you will click to select your answer. For this paper version, please circle it.

49. Paragraph E is not in the most logical order. Drag and drop the sentences into the order that makes the most sense. On the online GED® test, you will click and drag your answers into the space provided. For this paper version, please write them in.

```
┌─────────────────────────────┐
│                             │
│                             │
│                             │
└─────────────────────────────┘
              ↓
┌─────────────────────────────┐
│                             │
│                             │
│                             │
└─────────────────────────────┘
              ↓
┌─────────────────────────────┐
│                             │
│                             │
│                             │
└─────────────────────────────┘
```

MATHEMATICAL REASONING

90 Minutes • 37 Questions

General Directions: The Mathematics Test consists of 37 questions intended to measure your general mathematics skills, including your ability to solve math problems. The test consists of five questions that you will not have access to a calculator to answer and 32 questions that you will have use of a calculator to solve.

Disclaimer: The Math test will have calculator allowed questions mixed with calculator prohibited questions, with the calculator tool available to use when it is an option. However, for this test, the calculator prohibited questions are grouped together as the first five questions.

To answer some questions you will need to apply one or more mathematics formulas. The formulas provided on the next page will help you to answer those questions. Some questions refer to charts, graphs, and figures. Unless otherwise noted, charts, graphs, and figures are drawn to scale.

Answering Alternative-format Questions

Most questions are multiple choice, but to answer some questions, you will be required to select from a drop down menu, fill an answer in a blank, drag and drop correct answers, and select answers on a given graphic.

Mathematics Formula Sheet & Explanation

TESTING SERVICE®

The 2014 GED® Mathematical Reasoning test contains a formula sheet, which displays formulas relating to geometric measurement and certain algebra concepts. Formulas are provided to test-takers so that they may focus on *application*, rather than the *memorization*, of formulas.

Area of a:

parallelogram $A = bh$

trapezoid $A = \frac{1}{2}h(b_1 + b_2)$

Surface Area and Volume of a:

rectangular/right prism	$SA = ph + 2B$	$V = Bh$
cylinder	$SA = 2\pi rh + 2\pi r^2$	$V = \pi r^2 h$
pyramid	$SA = \frac{1}{2}ps + B$	$V = \frac{1}{3}Bh$
cone	$SA = \pi rs + \pi r^2$	$V = \frac{1}{3}\pi r^2 h$
sphere	$SA = 4\pi r^2$	$V = \frac{4}{3}\pi r^3$

(p = perimeter of base B; $\pi \approx 3.14$)

Algebra

slope of a line $m = \dfrac{y_2 - y_1}{x_2 - x_1}$

slope-intercept form of the equation of a line $y = mx + b$

point-slope form of the equation of a line $y - y_1 = m(x - x_1)$

standard form of a quadratic equation $y = ax^2 + bx + c$

quadratic formula $x = \dfrac{-b \pm \sqrt{b^2 - 4ac}}{2a}$

Pythagorean Theorem $a^2 + b^2 = c^2$

simple interest $I = prt$

(I = interest, p = principal, r = rate, t = time)

The use of a calculator is prohibited for questions 1–5.

1. A pair of athletic shoes priced originally at $75 is sold for $65. What is the approximate rate of the discount?

   (A) 10 percent

   (B) 13.3 percent

   (C) 15.4 percent

   (D) 18.5 percent

2. When Felicia checked out at the grocery store, she gave the clerk $20.00 and received $3.80 as the correct amount of change. Which of the following could Felicia have bought?

   (A) eight cans of olives at $2.15 each

   (B) four frozen dinners at $3.95 each

   (C) six bags of apples at $2.70 each

   (D) seven cans of dog food at $2.30 each

3. If $a = 3$, $b = -3$, and $c = \frac{1}{3}$, then what is the value of ab^2c^2 ?

   (A) -27

   (B) -1

   (C) 3

   (D) 9

4. $52x(31x + 27x)$ has the same value as which of the following?

   (A) $31x(52x + 27x)$

   (B) $31x + 52x + 27x$

   (C) $(52x)(27x) + (31x)(27x)$

   (D) $(52x)(31x) + (52x)(27x)$

5. Joe earns $13.50 an hour when he works on weekdays and time-and-a-half per hour when he works on the weekend. Last week, he worked 40 hours Monday through Friday and 6 hours on Saturday. How much did he earn for the week?

The use of a calculator is allowed for questions 6–37.

6. What is the midpoint *M* of a line segment connecting points (5, 2) and (–11, 6) on the *xy*-coordinate plane?

   On the online GED® test, you will click the coordinate grid to mark the location of point *M* by clicking the coordinate grid. For this paper version, please write in point *M*.

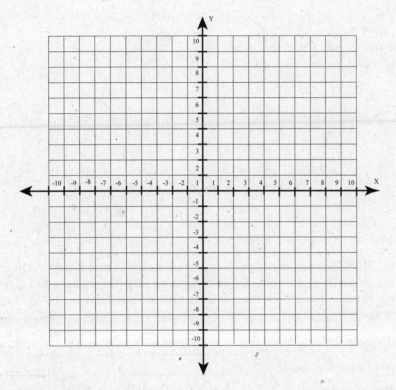

7. A pyramid with a square base has a volume of 125 cubic feet and a height (*h*) of 15 feet, as shown in the below figure.

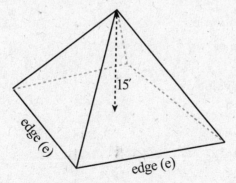

   What is the area of the pyramid's square base?

   (A) 15 square feet

   (B) 25 square feet

   (C) 36 square feet

   (D) 54 square feet

8. Jason ate one third of a pizza for dinner, and his brother ate one sixth of the same pizza. What portion of the pizza was left over? On the online GED® test, you will type your answer. For this paper version, please write it in.

$$\boxed{\dfrac{}{}}$$

9. What is the slope of the line represented by the equation $5y - 13 = 4x$?

(A) $-\dfrac{5}{4}$

(B) $-\dfrac{2}{3}$

(C) $\dfrac{4}{5}$

(D) $\dfrac{3}{2}$

10. What is the value of m in the following system of two equations?

$$4m = 12 - 3n$$

$$\dfrac{3n}{4} = 3 - m$$

(A) -6

(B) -3

(C) 2

(D) any real number

11. Create the BEST inequality describing distributions D and E below. On the online GED® test, you will create the inequality by dragging the phrases and symbols into the boxes. For this paper version, please write in your answer.

Choices are:

PHRASES:

range of distribution D

median of distribution E

arithmetic mean of distribution D

range of distribution E

arithmetic mean of distribution E

any of the other values

SYMBOLS:

\>

\<

Phrase	Symbol	Phrase

Distribution D: {2, 5, 9, 9}

Distribution E: {3, 6, 9, 10}

12. If $x < -1$, which of the following is greatest in value?

 (A) x^3

 (B) $x + 1$

 (C) x^2

 (D) $| x |$

13. $\frac{x}{3}$, $\frac{x}{7}$, and $\frac{x}{9}$ are all positive integers. Drag and drop the fractions to create a correct comparison. On the online GED® test, you will click and drag the fractions into the correct blank spaces. For this paper version, write in the fractions.

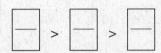

14. The two parallel sides of trapezoid T have a combined length of 14 centimeters. If the height of trapezoid T is 14 centimeters, what is the area of trapezoid T?

15. A certain function is defined as $f(x) = \dfrac{a}{x^2}$, where a and x are both positive numbers. Which of the following graphs best depicts this function?

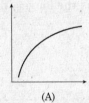
(A)
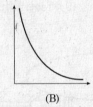
(B)
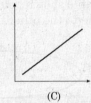
(C)
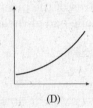
(D)

16. For what value of m is the following expression undefined?

$$\frac{m^2 - 4}{m^3 - 1}$$

 (A) -2

 (B) -1

 (C) 1

 (D) 2

17. An architect's plans for a living room and kitchen area are shown below. The scale of the drawing is 1:20 centimeters. Looking at the length of the kitchen in the architect's rendering, what is the actual length of the kitchen?

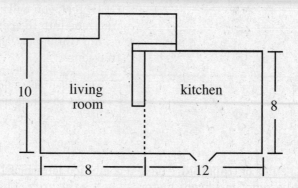

(A) 10 cm

(B) 15 cm

(C) 150 cm

(D) 300 cm

18. The area of the picnic table shown below is 49π feet. What is the longest distance from one end of the table to the other?

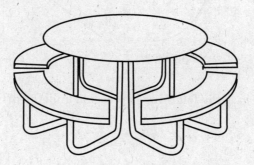

(A) 7 feet

(B) 14 feet

(C) 25 feet

(D) 49 feet

19. The shape below is comprised of an equilateral triangle and a semi-circle. The diameter of the semi-circle is 4 cm. What is the area of the whole shape?

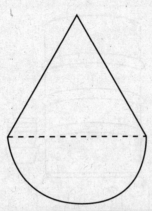

Area of an equilateral triangle: $\frac{s^2\sqrt{3}}{4}$

Area of a circle: πr^2

(A) $4\sqrt{3} + 2\pi$

(B) $4\sqrt{3} + 4\pi$

(C) $4\sqrt{3} + 8\pi$

(D) $2\sqrt{3} + 8\pi$

20. The oil drum below has to be painted. In order to determine how much paint is needed, the surface area (*SA*) must be calculated. The height of the drum is 8 feet and the radius is 2.5 feet. What is the surface area?

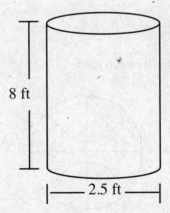

(A) $12.5\,\pi$

(B) $40\,\pi$

(C) $52.5\,\pi$

(D) $500\,\pi$

21. Each cone-shaped cup in a water dispenser holds 4π cubic inches of water. If the radius of each cup is 2 inches, what is the height of each cup?

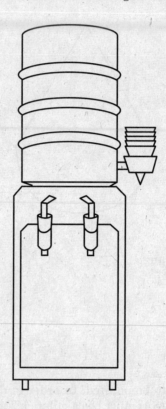

    (A) 4 inches
    (B) 3 inches
    (C) 2 inches
    (D) 1 inch

22. The volume of the basketball is 466 cubic inches.

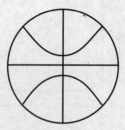

Which is the closest approximation of the radius of the basketball?
    (A) 10 inches
    (B) 6.5 inches
    (C) 5.1 inches
    (D) 4.8 inches

23. People coming out of a movie were asked their ages. The data collected appears in the histogram below.

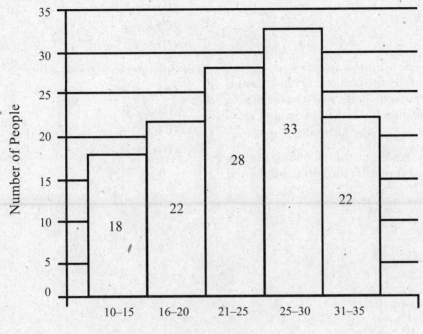

Age Range

How many people surveyed were at least 21 years old?

(A) 28

(B) 40

(C) 55

(D) 83

24. In a standard deck of 52 playing cards, there are 4 cards with a picture of a queen on them. What is the probability of randomly selecting a queen?

(A) $\frac{1}{52}$

(B) $\frac{1}{13}$

(C) $\frac{1}{4}$

(D) $\frac{1}{2}$

25. What is $\frac{3x - 4}{4x}$ when $x = -1$?

(A) $-\frac{7}{4}$

(B) $-\frac{1}{4}$

(C) $\frac{1}{4}$

(D) $\frac{7}{4}$

26. What is the value of the expression $2xy^2 - x + 4$ when $x = -1$ and $y = 0$?

    (A) 3

    (B) 5

    (C) 7

    (D) 9

27. Normally the cost of a toy boat rental at a pond includes a $10 base fee plus $2.50 per hour, h. Maria and José have a coupon for $\frac{1}{2}$ off the hourly rate. Which of the following expressions represents the cost to Maria and José?

    (A) $\dfrac{10 + 2.5h}{2}$

    (B) $5 + \dfrac{2.5h}{2}$

    (C) $10 + \dfrac{2.5h}{2}$

    (D) $\dfrac{(10 + 2.5h)}{\frac{1}{2}}$

28. Simplify: $\dfrac{x^2 + x - 6}{x + 3}$

    (A) $x - 2$

    (B) $x + 2$

    (C) $x - 3$

    (D) $x + 3$

29. Solve for x: $-2x + 6 \geq 0$.

    (A) $x \leq 3$

    (B) $x \geq 3$

    (C) $x \leq -3$

    (D) $x \geq -3$

30. Click on a point in the graph below that satisfies the inequality $2x - 4 > y$.

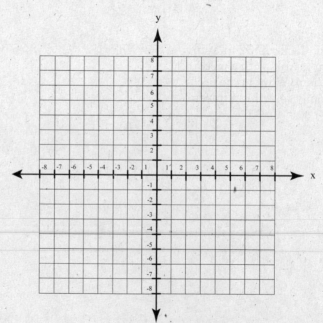

31. Carmen has a budget of $430 for renting a car during a business trip. She has determined that it will cost $48 for gas and $37.50 per day to rent the car. _____ is an inequality that shows how to find the number of days, d, Carmen can rent the car.

Select ▼

37.5	+	37.5d	=	37.5
48	×	48d	<	48
430	−	430d	>	430
48	+	37.5d	≤	430
48d	×	37.5	≥	37.5d

32. A company is manufacturing a batch of 400 square steel frames for shipping containers. To comply with space constraints, the area of each frame will be 196 square inches. Create an equation to determine what the side of each frame, s, must measure. On the online GED® test, you will click on the variables and numbers and drag them to the blank boxes. For this paper version, please write in the answers in the correct order.

| 196 | 400 | s | s^2 |

| | = | |

33. Click on two points on the graph below to create the line that represents the equation $2y + 4x = -6$. On the online GED® test, you will click on the coordinate grid to mark your answer. For this paper version, please write in your answer.

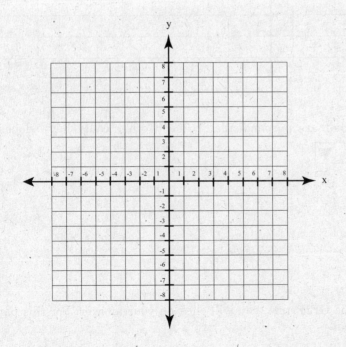

34. In the graph below, $f(x)$ is [Select ▼] along the interval [Select ▼]

increasing	$-3 < x < 0$
decreasing	$-3 < x < 5$
flat	$0 < x < 12$
	$5 < x < 13$

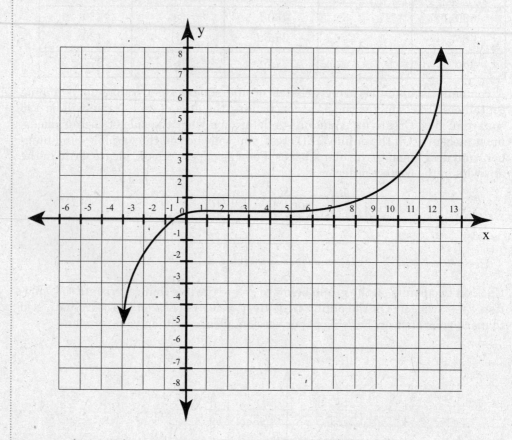

35. Two lines that are perpendicular to each other could have slopes of $\frac{1}{2}$ and

[Select ▼] .

-2

$-\dfrac{1}{2}$

$\dfrac{1}{2}$

2

On the online GED® test, you will click on your answer. For this paper version, please circle it.

36. Which of the following functions has exactly one output for each input?

(A)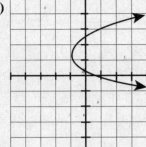

(C)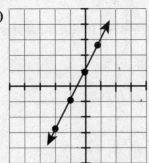

(B)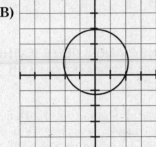

(D)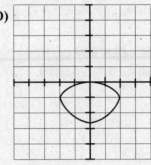

37. Which of the following is true about the two functions shown below, *f(x)* and *f(a)*?

x	f(x)
0	−3
1	5
2	13
3	21
4	29

$f(a) = 8a + 2$

(A) *f(x)* is linear and *f(a)* is quadratic.

(B) *f(x)* is quadratic and *f(x)* is linear.

(C) The rate of change of *f(x)* is greater than the rate of change of *f(a)*.

(D) The graph of *f(a)* is parallel to the graph of *f(x)*.

SCIENCE

90 Minutes • 30 Questions

Directions: The Science Test consists of questions in several formats designed to measure your knowledge of general science concepts. The questions are based on brief passages of text and visual information (charts, graphs, diagrams, and other figures). Some questions are based on both text and visual information. Study the information provided, and answer the question(s) that follow, referring back to the information as needed.

You will have 90 minutes to answer all 30 questions. Record your answers on the answer sheet provided.

QUESTION 1 REFERS TO THE FOLLOWING ILLUSTRATION.

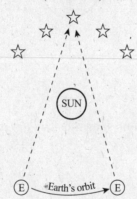

(STARFIELD)

1. The diagram shows why stars appear to move across the night sky during the course of a year. What explains this misperception?

   (A) In an expanding universe, all objects are moving away from Earth.

   (B) Our solar system is mistakenly taken to be a fixed point of reference.

   (C) Because of the tilt of Earth's axis, star positions change with the seasons.

   (D) Because the stars are so far away, their positions have changed by the time their light reaches us.

QUESTIONS 2 AND 3 REFER TO THE FOLLOWING INFORMATION AND CHART.

Cell metabolism, the creation of energy by the processing of glucose and other sugars at the cellular level, can be accomplished either (A) in the presence of oxygen, through the process of aerobic respiration, or (B) without oxygen, through the process of anaerobic respiration.

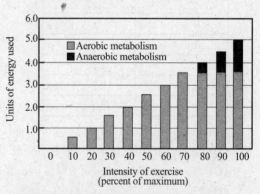

Intensity of exercise
(percent of maximum)

2. During which of these activities would the ratio of anaerobic energy to aerobic energy be greatest?

   (A) running up 10 flights of stairs

   (B) climbing a 1000-foot vertical cliff

   (C) walking 15 miles carrying a backpack

   (D) falling at 120 miles per hour during a sky dive

3. Referring to the chart, which activity is most likely to require 4.0 arbitrary units of energy?

   (A) swimming four laps of a full-length pool

   (B) lifting a very heavy weight once

   (C) running two laps around the high-school track

   (D) cycling up a short but steep hill

4. Some species have learned to exploit one single, abundant resource, resulting in their suddenly developing a very large population. If environmental conditions change, these so-called "strategists" can quickly run out of resources needed to grow, or even sustain, their population.

   A good example of such strategists are

   | Select ▼ |.

   fungi

   termites

   weeds

   rabbits

   algae

   On the online GED® test, you will click on the correct answer. For this paper version, please circle it.

QUESTION 5 REFERS TO THE FOLLOWING INFORMATION.

The hereditary patterns of a plant species can be seen by observing the physical traits of two individual "parent" plants and then noting the traits of the "daughter" plants. Though many plants can be studied in this way, some are more useful than others in drawing predictive conclusions.

5. Which type of plant species would a botanist be MOST interested in studying for this purpose?

   A plant species that

   (A) reproduces at a slow rate

   (B) can be easily controlled in a greenhouse

   (C) exhibits many different traits

   (D) exhibits many subtle variations of just one trait

QUESTION 6 REFERS TO THE FOLLOWING ILLUSTRATION.

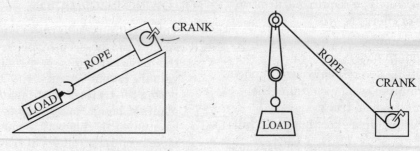

Incline Plane   Simple Pulley

6. Both of these machines change the way work is done on a load. Both machines change work in the same way. Explain how the machines change the applied force needed, and how they change the distance over which the force must be applied?

_____

QUESTION 7 REFERS TO THE FOLLOWING DIAGRAM AND INFORMATION.

VIRAL INFECTION

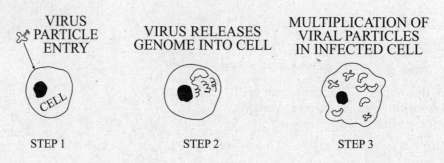

VIRUS PARTICLE ENTRY   VIRUS RELEASES GENOME INTO CELL   MULTIPLICATION OF VIRAL PARTICLES IN INFECTED CELL

STEP 1   STEP 2   STEP 3

Step 1: A virus particle attaches to a receptor site on the cell wall, from where it penetrates the cell wall.

Step 2: The virus particle sheds its protein shell and releases its genome into the cell.

Step 3: The viral genome creates new virus particles within the cell, causing the cell to swell in size.

7. Based on steps 1–3 of a viral infection, as shown above, explain what is likely to occur next? On the online GED® test, you will type your answer in the space provided. For this paper version, please write it in.

_____

QUESTIONS 8 AND 9 REFER TO THE FOLLOWING INFORMATION.

Sometimes when two or more atoms or molecules come in contact they react chemically with each other, resulting in the formation of one or more new substances (products). If the formation of the products requires <u>more</u> energy than is available from the original substances (the reactants), external energy, usually heat or light, must be absorbed for this purpose. This type of reaction is referred to as *endothermic*. On the other hand, if the formation of the products requires <u>less</u> than all of the energy available from the reactants, energy is released in an *exothermic* reaction. In order to start either type of reaction in the first place, however, the energy of the reactants must be raised by some external energy source. For example, you need to heat paper before it will react by burning, which is what releases heat in an exothermic reaction.

The following two charts represent an endothermic reaction and an exothermic reaction, but not necessarily in that order.

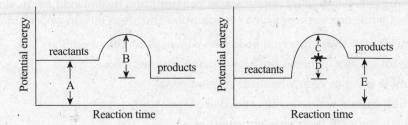

8. The amount of energy absorbed by an endothermic reaction is indicated by arrow

   [Select   ▼] .

   A

   B

   C

   D

   E

   On the online GED® test, you will click on the correct answer. For this paper version, please circle it.

9. Based on the passage and the diagrams, which of the following is an endothermic reaction?

   (A) Heat + $NH_4NO_3(s) \rightarrow NH_4NO_3(l)$

   (B) $C_3H_8 + 5 O_2 \rightarrow 3 CO_2 + 4 H_2O + Heat$

   (C) $FE_2O_3 + 2 Al \rightarrow 2 Fe + Al_2O_3 + Heat$

   (D) $CO_2(s) \rightarrow CO_2(g)$

10. A transverse wave is one in which the oscillating (cyclical) motion of particles is perpendicular to the direction of the wave's motion. A longitudinal wave is one in which oscillation occurs along the same axis, or in the same direction, as the wave's motion.

Which of the following creates transverse waves?

(A) snapping the string of a bow to shoot an arrow

(B) bouncing on a coiled spring mattress

(C) striking a drumhead with a drumstick

(D) vigorously shaking out a dusty blanket

QUESTION 11 REFERS TO THE FOLLOWING INFORMATION.

When a person faces sudden stress, he or she may experience an "adrenaline rush," during which the adrenal glands secrete hormones that work to increase blood-sugar levels and increase oxygen consumption and blood flow in skeletal muscles, while decreasing oxygen consumption and blood flow in smooth muscles.

11. The purpose of these internal bodily responses is to help a person

(A) maintain steady blood pressure during emergencies

(B) inhale more oxygen when it is needed most

(C) think calmly when facing crucial decisions under stress

(D) escape quickly from dangerous situations

12. Covalent bonding occurs when two atoms share a pair of electrons, one from each atom's outer shell.

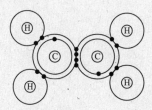

What can you conclude from the above information and diagram?

(A) Carbon has one electron in its outer shell.

(B) Hydrogen has one electron in its outer shell.

(C) Carbon has eight electrons in its outer shell.

(D) Hydrogen has two electrons in its outer shell.

QUESTION 13 REFERS TO THE FOLLOWING ILLUSTRATIONS.

MITOSIS

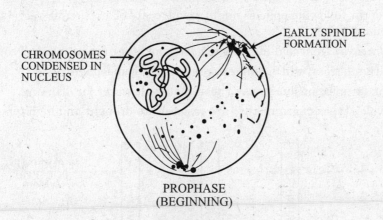

CHROMOSOMES CONDENSED IN NUCLEUS

EARLY SPINDLE FORMATION

PROPHASE
(BEGINNING)

CHROMOSOMES

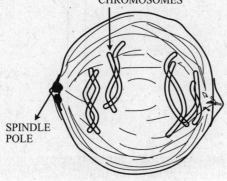

SPINDLE POLE

METAPHASE
(WALLS OF NUCLEUS DISAPPEAR)

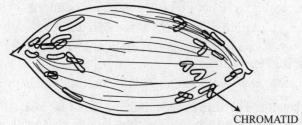

CHROMATID

ANAPHASE
(ALIGNMENT OF CHROMATIDS TO OPPOSITE POLES)

13. What process is the sequence of three illustrations showing?

   (A) A healthy cell is mutating into a cancerous one.

   (B) A cell is creating an identical matching cell.

   (C) A virus created inside a cell is destroying the cell.

   (D) A cell's damaged nucleus is repairing itself.

14. Advocates of a "no-regrets" attitude toward climate change and increased levels of air and water pollution recommend adapting to such developments rather than attempting to halt or reverse them.

Which of the following policies might an advocate of a strict "no-regrets" approach recommend?

(A) Move away from coal-burning to solar and other renewable fuel sources.

(B) Cultivate trees, which emit oxygen into the atmosphere.

(C) Look for inexpensive ways to desalinate salt water for drinking.

(D) Develop types of grains that are resistant to drought and high temperatures.

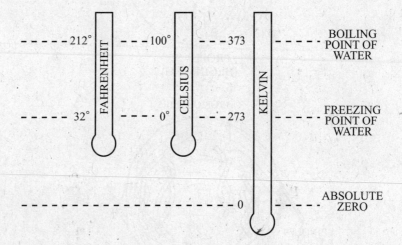

15. Three different systems for measuring temperature are shown above. The Kelvin scale was developed more recently than the other two. The Kelvin scale is favored by scientists making thermodynamic calculations.

Which best explains why the Kelvin scale was developed?

(A) The other scales were not precise enough for science.

(B) The other scales did not have the same size units.

(C) The new scale was based on the accepted understanding that temperature had an actual lower limit.

(D) The new scale gave exact values for the melting and boiling points of water.

16. Energy can be stored or transferred, but it cannot be lost. Allison and Brian are holding the two ends of a rope. Allison then begins shaking her end of the rope up and down to create waves, which travel one after another toward Brian. If Brian holds his end of the rope still without allowing his arm to move, what will occur when the first wave reaches Brian?

(A) The wave's energy will be absorbed into Brian's body.

(B) Some wave energy will be reflected back toward Allison.

(C) Each successive wave will carry more energy.

(D) Allison will receive the same wave force that Brian received.

QUESTIONS 17–19 REFER TO THE FOLLOWING CHART.

TEMPERATURES AND SNOW ACCUMULATION—NORTHERN GREENLAND

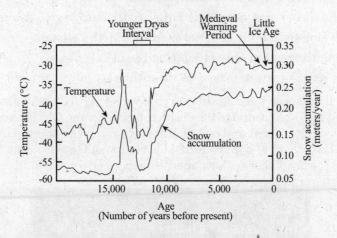

Age
(Number of years before present)

17. Put a mark on the scale to show about how much temperature varied from the Medieval Warming Period through the Little Ice Age. On the online GED® test, you will click on the correct spot on the graphic. For this paper version, please write in your mark.

10° ——————
9° ——————
8° ——————
7° ——————
6° ——————
5° ——————
4° ——————
3° ——————
2° ——————
1° ——————
0° ——————

18. The Younger Dryas Interval began about 12,800 years ago and ended about 11,000 years ago. What can you infer from the chart about Greenland during this time interval?

The Younger Dryas time interval was generally characterized by

(A) gradually cooling temperatures.

(B) wet and hot weather.

(C) cold and dry weather.

(D) a rising sea level.

19. Scientists gleaned the chart data from tree rings, ice cores, and rock sediments in Greenland. When these data are reconciled, it is possible to create graphs like the one shown here.

Scientists can then use this combined information to

(A) prove the theory that human activities contribute to global warming

(B) identify long-term cyclical patterns in the Earth's climate

(C) predict the amount of snowfall during the next century

(D) show how temperature extremes affect the rate of tree growth

20. The visible light spectrum contains varying wavelengths, each appearing as a distinct color. White light contains the entire color spectrum. Objects around us absorb some wavelengths of light and reflect others. Click on the point in the graphic that shows the wavelength of light reflected by a banana. On the online GED® test, you will click on the graphic. For this paper version, please write in the correct answer.

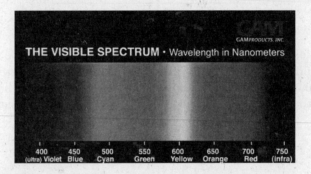

QUESTIONS 21 AND 22 REFER TO THE FOLLOWING DIAGRAM.

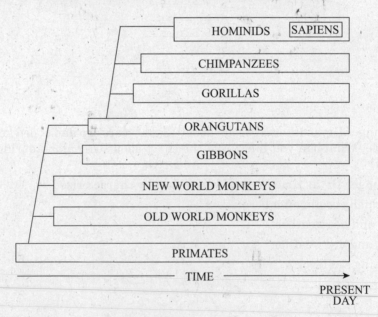

21. Which is the best title for the chart?
   (A) "Early Anthropoids by Category"
   (B) "The Missing Evolutionary Link"
   (C) "What All Apes Have in Common"
   (D) "Our Branch on the Primate Tree"

22. Show which species Gorillas descended from by dragging **GORILLAS** to their most recent ancestors. On the online GED® test, you will click and drag the word to the correct spot. For this paper version, please write it in.

QUESTION 23 REFERS TO THE FOLLOWING INFORMATION.

In a plant, water tends to move toward areas with the lowest water and water-vapor concentration. When water reaches a leaf from the root system and xylem, it moves through the spongy mesophyll to the stomata, which are small openings in the leaf's surface that open and close to allow the exchange of gases.

23. The amount of water reaching the leaf's surface will be reduced if the air is

[   ]. On the online GED® test, you will type your answer in the space provided. For this paper version, please write it in.

QUESTION 24 REFERS TO THE FOLLOWING ILLUSTRATION.

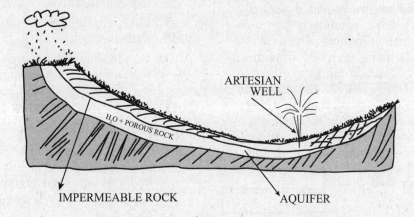

24. Underground water stored in aquifers is a valuable resource that has sometimes been over-exploited. Sometimes this water is brought up with pumps, and sometimes it rises through the surface spontaneously as an artesian well. What allows water to rise through an artesian well without the aid of a pump?

   (A) pressure on the aquifer from an impermeable rock layer just above it
   (B) atmospheric pressure on the water table
   (C) the downward pressure of water within the aquifer
   (D) boiling temperatures of the water within an aquifer

QUESTION 25 REFERS TO THE FOLLOWING INFORMATION.

In an ecological food chain, tertiary consumers eat secondary consumers, which in turn eat primary consumers, which in turn eat producers. In this chain, the producers are plants that generate their own food through photosynthesis: a process of using light energy and carbon to create glucose.

Although lichens are fungi and corals are animals, both use the energy that photosynthesizing algae produce for their sustenance and growth. Lichens rely solely on algae for their energy. As for corals, while some species can exist solely by capturing food, most receive energy by hosting millions of single-celled algae organisms known as *zooxanthellae*. The *zooxanthellae* are provided not only safety from predation but also certain by-products of the coral's metabolism, such as ammonia, which *zooxanthellae* require to grow and reproduce. In return, the corals use a portion of the energy *zooxanthellae* produce through photosynthesis for their own sustenance, growth, and reproduction.

25. In this food chain, [   ] are producers, [   ] are primary consumers, and [   ] are both primary and secondary consumers.

On the online GED® test, you will type your answers in the spaces provided. For this paper version, please write them in.

QUESTION 26 REFERS TO THE FOLLOWING DIAGRAM.

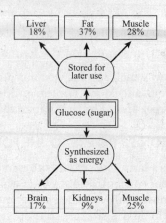

26. Which conclusion does the diagram best support?
    (A) Eating the right foods can improve your intelligence.
    (B) Athletes typically must eat a lot to be competitive.
    (C) Eating foods high in sugar can damage the liver.
    (D) People should not exercise immediately after eating.

QUESTIONS 27 AND 28 REFER TO THE FOLLOWING INFORMATION.

Humans can hear sound-wave frequencies ranging from about 20 Hz (20,000 kHz) to about 20,000 Hz. We experience a wave's frequency as "pitch."

Animal	Range of Hearing (Hertz = 1 cycle/sec.)
dog	30 Hz – 30,000 Hz
cat	15 Hz – 40,000 Hz
bat	2000 Hz – 100,000 Hz
porpoise	30 Hz – 150,000 Hz
elephant	3 Hz – 10,000 Hz
human	20 Hz – 20,000 Hz

27. Many species of animals rely heavily on their sense of hearing for survival and communication. What might this fact, along with the data in the table, help explain?

(A) why elephants have large ears

(B) how blind bats can navigate dark caves

(C) why porpoises are so easily trained

(D) why cats don't respond to human commands

28. To monitor activities beneath the ocean surface, sonar devices used on navy ships emit sound waves with frequencies ranging from about 1000 kHz to 100,000 kHz that are intense enough to interfere with the ability of porpoises to communicate and navigate. What refinement in the frequency range on these devices might remedy this problem?

(A) Reduce the upper range limit to 20,000 kHz.

(B) Raise the lower range limit to 50,000 kHz.

(C) Limit the range size to 10,000 kHz.

(D) Extend the range size to 200,000 kHz.

QUESTION 29 REFERS TO THE FOLLOWING ILLUSTRATION.

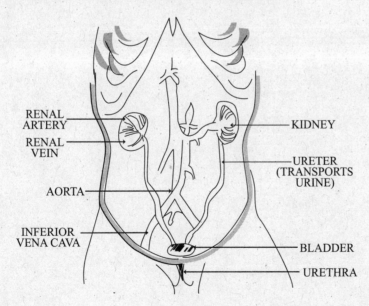

29. The renal (urinary) system is illustrated here. Drag **PRODUCED** to the organ or organs where urine is produced. Drag **STORED** to the organ or organs where urine is stored. On the online GED® test, you will click and drag the words to the correct spot on the graphic. For this paper version, please write them in.

QUESTION 30 REFERS TO THE FOLLOWING INFORMATION.

Positively charged particles and negatively charged particles attract each other. An oxygen atom is highly electromagnetic, which means that it attracts electrons from atoms with which it has bonded—for example, hydrogen atoms—toward its nucleus. The result is a polar bond in which the oxygen atom takes a slightly negative charge, while the other atoms take a slightly positive charge, reinforcing the bond.

30. The diagram shows the partial charges and the attraction between separate water molecules. Which does the discussion and diagram help to explain?

(A) why we breathe air instead of water

(B) why ice cracks but water doesn't

(C) why some water is "softer" than other water

(D) why water has a much higher boiling point than most molecules its size

SOCIAL STUDIES

70 Minutes • 34 Questions

Directions: The Social Studies Test consists of a series of questions involving general social studies concepts. The questions are based on brief passages of text and visual information (graphs, charts, maps, cartoons, and other figures). Some questions are based on both text and visual information. Study the information provided, and answer the question(s) that follow it, referring back to the information as needed. Most questions are in multiple-choice format. Others are meant to prepare you for the electronically formatted questions that you will find on the test, such as drop-down questions, hot spot maps, and fill-in-the-blanks. The extended response question requires you to write an essay in which you analyze certain documents. Record your answers on the Social Studies section of the answer sheet provided.

QUESTION 1 REFERS TO THE FOLLOWING INFORMATION.

A *bill of attainder* is a legislative act declaring a person or group of persons guilty of a crime and punishing them without benefit of a trial. During the eighteenth century, England applied bills of attainder to its colonies in America. Declaration of guilt usually meant, among other consequences, that the guilty party forfeited all of their property to the Crown. The U.S. Constitution forbids both the federal and state governments to enact bills of attainder.

1. The Fifth Amendment to the U.S. Constitution provides: "In all criminal prosecutions, the accused shall enjoy the right to a speedy and public trial, by an impartial jury. . . ." How does this amendment relate to the prohibition of bills of attainder as provided in the Constitution?

The Fifth Amendment

(A) extends that prohibition to the states.

(B) requires that bills of attainder be applied in a speedy manner.

(C) legalizes bills of attainder issued by the courts.

(D) reinforces that prohibition.

QUESTION 2 IS BASED ON THE FOLLOWING MAP AND INFORMATION.

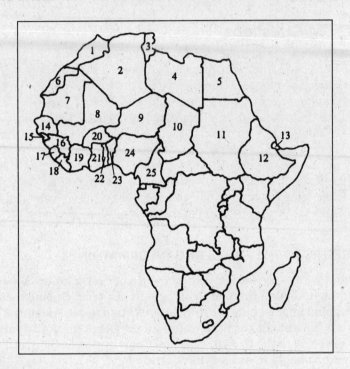

1. Morocco
2. Algeria
3. Tunisia
4. Libya
5. Egypt
6. Western Sahara
7. Mauritania
8. Mali
9. Niger
10. Chad
11. Sudan
12. Ethiopia
13. Djibouti
14. Senegal
15. Guinea-Bissau
16. Guinea
17. Sierra Leone
18. Liberia
19. Cote d'lvoire
20. Burkina Faso
21. Ghana
22. Togo
23. Benin
24. Nigeria
25. Cameroon

Except where Egypt's northeast corner adjoins Saudi Arabia, the entire African continent is surrounded by seas and oceans: to the east are the Red Sea and, farther south, the Indian Ocean; to the west is the Atlantic Ocean; and to the north is the Mediterranean Sea. At Morocco's northern-most point is the Strait of Gibraltar, which separates Morocco from southern Europe and which marks the entrance to the Mediterranean Sea.

The Sahara Desert extends from the Atlantic Ocean to Egypt and the Red Sea. The Mediterranean Sea and the Atlas Mountains in central Algeria and Morocco mark the desert's northern boundary, while Sudan and the valley of the Niger River (in the country of Niger) mark its southern boundary. The desert's highest sand dunes are in southern Morocco, and its highest mountain peak—Emi Kousi (3415 meters)—is in northern Chad.

2. How many of the *numbered* countries are situated at least partially along the coastline of the Atlantic Ocean?

(A) five

(B) nine

(C) twelve

(D) fourteen

QUESTION 3 IS BASED ON THE FOLLOWING INFORMATION.

Following the adoption of the Constitution by the convention in Philadelphia, the document needed to be ratified by each of the individual states before it could be officially adopted. Key to the debate surrounding ratification was the Constitution's lack of a specific bill of rights. Opponents, using pseudonyms such as "Brutus," published editorials—now known as the Anti-Federalist Papers—*denouncing the document as a threat to the liberties of individual states. Alexander Hamilton and James Madison, writing under the pseudonym "Publius," responded with their own series of editorials.*

It is therefore not only necessarily implied thereby, but positively expressed, that the different State Constitutions are repealed and entirely done away, so far as they are inconsistent with this, with the laws which shall be made in pursuance thereof, or with treaties made, or which shall be made, under the authority of the United States. Of what avail will the Constitutions of the respective States be to preserve the rights of its citizens? Should they be pled, the answer would be, the Constitution of the United States, and the laws made in pursuance thereof, is the supreme law, and all legislatures and judicial officers, whether of the General or State governments, are bound by oath to support it. No privilege, reserved by the bills of rights, or secured by the State governments, can limit the power granted by this, or restrain any laws made in pursuance of it. It stands, therefore, on its own bottom, and must receive a construction by itself, without any reference to any other. And hence it was of the highest importance, that the most precise and express declarations and reservations of rights should have been made.

"Brutus"

Anti-Federalist 84

The most considerable of the remaining objections is that the plan of the convention contains no bill of rights. Among other answers given to this, it has been upon different occasions remarked that the constitutions of several of the States are in a similar predicament. I add that New York is of the number. And yet the opposers of the new system, in this State, who profess an unlimited admiration for its constitution, are among the most intemperate partisans of a bill of rights. To justify their zeal in this matter, they allege two things: one is that, though the constitution of New York has no bill of rights prefixed to it, yet it contains, in the body of it, various provisions in favor of particular privileges and rights, which, in substance amount to the same thing; the other is, that the Constitution adopts, in their full extent, the common and statute law of Great Britain, by which many other rights, not expressed in it, are equally secured.

To the first I answer, that the Constitution proposed by the convention contains, as well as the constitution of this State, a number of such provisions. . . .

I go further, and affirm that bills of rights, in the sense and to the extent in which they are contended for, are not only unnecessary in the proposed Constitution, but would even be dangerous. They would contain various exceptions to powers not granted; and, on this very account, would afford a colorable pretext to claim more than were granted. For why declare that things shall not be done which there is no power to do? Why, for instance, should it be said that the liberty of the press shall not be restrained, when no power is given by which restrictions may be imposed? I will not contend that such a provision would confer a regulating power; but it is evident that it would furnish, to men disposed to usurp, a plausible pretense for claiming that power. They might urge with a semblance of reason, that the Constitution ought not to be charged with the absurdity of providing against the abuse of an authority which was not given, and that the provision against restraining the liberty of the press afforded a clear implication, that a power to prescribe proper regulations concerning it was intended to be vested in the national government. This may serve as a specimen of the numerous handles which would be given to the doctrine of constructive powers, by the indulgence of an injudicious zeal for bills of rights.

Publius (Alexander Hamilton)

Federalist 84

3. Both Brutus and Publius believe strongly that individual liberties must be protected, but they differ as to how or if the proposed constitutional government can provide and foster that protection. Compare and contrast how each author understands the relationship between rights and government. Note particularly how each understands the role that the proposed constitution will play in shaping a government that may or may not guarantee the rights of its citizens.

_____

_____

_____

_____

_____

_____

_____

_____

_____

_____

_____

_____

4. The 100-mile Suez Canal in northeastern Egypt was constructed in the mid-nineteenth century and links the Mediterranean Sea and the Gulf of Suez, which becomes the Red Sea.

Which makes most sense as a reason for the canal's construction?

(A) to allow water transportation from Europe to Asia without navigating around Africa

(B) to provide water to the eastern Egyptian desert for agricultural purposes

(C) to fortify African military defenses against European incursions

(D) to symbolize Egyptian independence from Libyan rule

QUESTIONS 5–7 ARE BASED ON THE FOLLOWING INFORMATION.

Andrew Jackson was the first president of the United Sates not from a wealthy family and without an extensive education. Born to a poor family on the frontier, he rose to become a general and a wealthy plantation owner with 150 slaves. He became a war hero for his crushing defeat of a larger British force in the Battle of New Orleans (1815) and then entered politics. As president (1829–1837), he supported slavery but also a strong national union. He promoted westward expansion and removed Native Americans to territory farther west.

The period from 1830–1850 is known as the Age of Jacksonian Democracy, which was characterized by growing democracy in America. The right to vote was extended to all white males, rather than just property owners. Jackson even proposed the election of judges and the president by a popular vote. Jackson promoted himself as a "common man" and railed against the wealthy, well-educated elite that held economic and political power.

5. What fact about Andrew Jackson is inconsistent with the image of Jackson as a "common man"?

(A) Jackson was not well educated.

(B) Jackson supported the extension of the right to vote to white males who did not own property.

(C) Jackson was a wealthy plantation owner who had many slaves.

(D) Jackson criticized Eastern elites.

6. From the previous passage, we can infer that, although Jackson supported the extension of democracy, he would NOT have supported the extension of the right to vote to

(A) Native Americans and slaves.

(B) women.

(C) white males under age 21.

(D) white males who were not landowners.

7. Based on the passage, what value strongly influenced Jackson?

(A) a belief in equal rights for all adult citizens

(B) a belief in the importance of education

(C) support of the established order

(D) a hatred of special privilege based on class, education, or wealth

QUESTIONS 8 AND 9 REFER TO THE FOLLOWING INFORMATION.

By 1970, opposition to the American military involvement in Vietnam was gaining momentum. While the so-called Tet Offensive of 1968 had brought about widespread losses for the North Vietnamese, it became a political loss for President Lyndon Johnson, who chose not to seek reelection. Johnson's successor, Richard M. Nixon, announced a policy of "Vietnamization," in which South Vietnamese forces would replace American troops. At the same time, however, the U.S. military reinstituted the draft to provide personnel for remaining troop coverage.

For the first time since 1942, the U.S. military reinstituted the draft to conscript young American men for military service. The first lottery drawing for the draft was held on December 1, 1969, at Selective Service Headquarters in Washington, D.C. Three hundred and sixty-six blue plastic capsules held the birthdates for men born between 1944 and 1950. The order of the date drawn determined where those born on that date stood in line for conscription. Thus, the first date to be drawn, September 14, meant that men born on that date stood first in line to be called for military service for 1970. Subsequent lotteries were held for men born in 1951 and 1952. Those born in 1953 were not conscripted, as the draft ended in 1973.

8. Which of the following best describes "Vietnamization"?

   (A) an offensive against North Vietnam ordered by President Johnson

   (B) a policy of resistance to the American military presence on the part of the South Vietnamese

   (C) a policy of replacement of American military by South Vietnamese troops ordered by President Nixon

   (D) the adoption of Vietnamese customs on the part of the American military

9. Despite Nixon's promise for troop withdrawal, however, the American military began

   (A) covertly increasing the amount of American troops in Vietnam.

   (B) reinstituting the draft to conscript American men for military service.

   (C) discouraging South Vietnamese participation in defense efforts.

   (D) encouraging allied troops to support American military efforts.

QUESTION 10 REFERS TO THE FOLLOWING INFORMATION.

In order for a bill to become law in the United States, it must be passed in identical form by both the House of Representatives and the Senate and signed by the president. If the president vetoes the bill instead of signing it, the bill can still become law if two thirds of each house of Congress approves the bill in a new vote, overriding the president's veto. If the president neither signs nor vetoes a bill passed by Congress, the bill becomes law ten days later, unless Congress is no longer is session. If Congress has adjourned, the unsigned bill does not become law; this is known as a pocket veto.

10. Which statement best summarizes the previous passage?

(A) The president plays the key role in passing a new law.

(B) The president has the power to block Congress from passing a law.

(C) The president, by simply not signing a law, can keep it from taking effect.

(D) The president can sometimes check the power of Congress to pass new laws.

11. From the ninth through the eleventh centuries, the fearsome Germanic Scandinavian seafarers known as [   ] raided and settled many regions of Northern Europe. Denmark and Scandinavia were well outside the borders of the Roman Empire, and by the end of the eighth century the region contained many small tribal kingdoms, where farm-ing and fishing accounted for most of the economy. However, a growing population found that its fertile land was in limited supply and inhabitants journeyed elsewhere in search of food and land. On the online GED® test, you will type your answer into the space provided. For this paper version, please write it in.

QUESTION 12 REFERS TO THE FOLLOWING INFORMATION.

In the aftermath of the Civil War, the South struggled to rebuild destroyed cities, railroads, bridges, and farms. Perhaps even more difficult for the South was estab-lishing a new economic system not based on slavery. Meanwhile, the North moved rapidly forward, undergoing rapid industrial devel-opment. Factories were expanding and modernizing, farms were becoming more mechanized, and new resources—coal, iron ore, copper, and petroleum—were being developed. It was also during this time that the telephone and electric lighting were invented and cross-country railroads completed.

12. Which statement best compares the North and the South during this time?

(A) The North and the South were facing the same challenges.

(B) The North was advancing much more rapidly than the South.

(C) The North and the South were both struggling to rebuild after the Civil War.

(D) The differences between North and South were diminishing.

QUESTIONS 13–17 ARE BASED ON THE FOLLOWING GRAPHS.

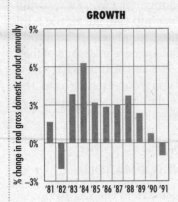

GROWTH

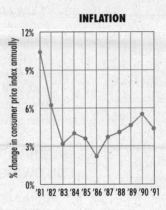

INFLATION

UNEMPLOYMENT

13. The greatest *decrease* in the growth of the gross domestic product was during which time period?
    - **(A)** 1981–1982
    - **(B)** 1985–1987
    - **(C)** 1988–1990
    - **(D)** 1988–1991

14. Which statement best describes the relationship between the gross domestic product and the rate of unemployment?
    - **(A)** A low rate of GDP growth is associated with high or rising unemployment.
    - **(B)** A high rate of GDP growth often comes with high or rising unemployment.
    - **(C)** A low or falling rate of unemployment is a sign of a low GDP growth rate.
    - **(D)** A high or rising rate of unemployment is a sign of moderate GDP growth.

15. Based on the graphs, when is the best time to look for a new job?
    - **(A)** when inflation is rising, unemployment is falling, and economic growth is rising
    - **(B)** when inflation is falling, unemployment is rising, and economic growth is falling
    - **(C)** when inflation is falling, unemployment is falling, and economic growth is rising
    - **(D)** when inflation is falling, unemployment is falling, and economic growth is falling

16. During the years shown in the graphs, the U.S. economy never achieved full employment, which economists define as an unemployment rate of 4 percent or lower among working-age adults.

    Which statement best helps explain this definition of "full employment"?
    - **(A)** The government is reluctant to acknowledge unemployment above the 4-percent rate.
    - **(B)** Teenagers who are employed typically hold part-time rather than full-time jobs.
    - **(C)** Older workers often refuse to accept low-wage employment.
    - **(D)** At any given time, many people are in transition between jobs.

QUESTIONS 17–18 ARE BASED ON THE FOLLOWING MAP.

The first thirteen colonies were founded between 1607 and 1733. The first British settlement in Jamestown later became Virginia Colony. Plymouth Colony later merged with other settlements in the area and became Massachusetts Bay Colony. The last incorporated colony was originally founded as a way for the "worthy poor" from England to avoid prison and make a new life.

The First 13 Colonies

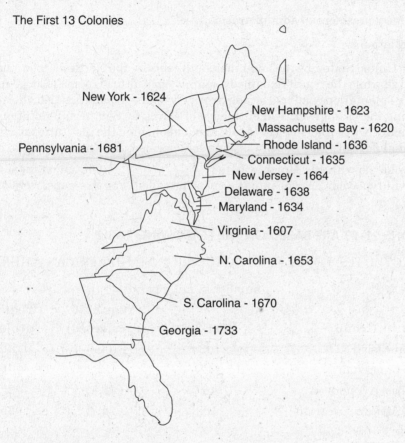

New York - 1624

New Hampshire - 1623

Massachusetts Bay - 1620

Rhode Island - 1636

Pennsylvania - 1681

Connecticut - 1635

New Jersey - 1664

Delaware - 1638

Maryland - 1634

Virginia - 1607

N. Carolina - 1653

S. Carolina - 1670

Georgia - 1733

17. Click on the colony that had initial settlements at Plymouth and later at Salem and Boston. On the online GED® test, you click on the colony in the graphic. For this paper version, please circle the name.

18. Click on the colony that was founded by James Oglethorpe as an agrarian refuge for those held in British debtors' prisons. On the online GED® test, you click on the colony in the graphic. For this paper version, please circle the name.

19. Increasing money supply, increasing government spending, and lowering taxes are measures usually taken in response to

| Select   ▼ |

    a war.

    a recession.

    a new presidential administration.

    inflation.

20. In the United States, by the mid-nineteenth century, the North was becoming industrialized while the South remained a mainly agricultural region of large cotton and tobacco plantations and had a comparatively sparse population. Northerners were growing increasingly critical of the use of slaves by Southern plantation owners, and many Northerners began to talk about abolishing the institution of slavery. By the final days of 1860, South Carolina had decided that the best way to deal with its problems with the Union was to [   ]. On the online GED® test, you will type your answer into the space provided. For this paper version, please write it in.

QUESTIONS 21–23 ARE BASED ON THE FOLLOWING TABLE.

PROJECTED U.S. POPULATION: CAUCASIANS AND AFRICAN AMERICANS

(number in millions)

Group	Year 2010	Year 2050 (projected)	Year 2080 (projected)
Male, Caucasian	108.8	105.6	103.6
Female, Caucasian	112.7	116.2	108.7
Male, African American	16.7	22.4	22.6
Female, African American	18.3	24.7	25.0

21. Which statement best summarizes the information in the table?

(A) The number of African Americans in the United States will increase between the years 2010 and 2080.

(B) The number of African Americans in the United States will show the greatest percentage increase between the years 2010 and 2050.

(C) The number of Caucasians in the United States will be greater than the number of African Americans in the years between 2010 and 2080.

(D) The total number of African Americans in the United States will increase between the years 2010 and 2080, both in actual numbers and in relation to the total number of Caucasians.

22. In the United States, the combined Hispanic and African American population is expected to surpass the Caucasian population by the year 2050. If that projection turns out to be accurate, what would this development suggest about the projections in the table?

    (A) This development would have no effect on the projections in the table.

    (B) The African American population will be higher than projected in the table.

    (C) The Hispanic population will be higher than projected in the table.

    (D) The Caucasian population will be lower than projected in the table.

23. Which expectation best supports the projections in the table?

    (A) Average life expectancies in the United States are anticipated to increase steadily.

    (B) An increasing number of African Americans is expected to obtain college degrees.

    (C) The birthrate among U.S. Caucasians is expected to continue declining.

    (D) More women than men are expected to immigrate to the United States during the twenty-first century.

24. The Consumer Price Index (CPI) is used as a measure of inflation, or a general rise in prices in terms of a specific currency, such as the U.S. dollar. The index measures the prices of a "typical consumer's market basket" of goods and services.

    | Select   ▼ | would NOT be included in this market basket.

    Rent

    Meat

    Automobiles

    Wages

QUESTIONS 25–27 REFER TO THE FOLLOWING MAP.

Expansion of the Continental United States

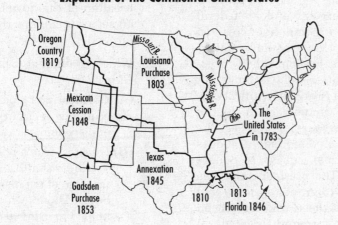

25. The largest and earliest land acquisition after 1783 was ⬚. On the online GED® test, you will type your answer into the space provided. For this paper version, please write it in.

26. The Mexican War of 1846–1848 was ended by the Treaty of Guadalupe Hidalgo. Circle the area of land given to the United States by that treaty. On the online GED® test, you will click and circle the area on the map. For this paper version, please write in the circle.

27. Based on the map, which statement is LEAST accurate?

(A) Texas was annexed before the Gadsden Purchase was made.

(B) The Louisiana Purchase extended from the Gulf of Mexico to the Canadian border.

(C) The expansion of the continental United States occurred entirely during the nineteenth century.

(D) The entire region east of the Mississippi River was annexed before the areas west of that river.

QUESTION 28 REFERS TO THE FOLLOWING INFORMATION.

Under the U.S. Constitution, the president's job includes the task of enforcing all federal laws as the chief executive of all federal departments and agencies. In addition, the president determines U.S. foreign policy, negotiates treaties (which must get Senate approval for ratification), and is the commander in chief of the nation's armed forces. The president appoints federal judges (to life terms), subject to Senate approval. The president also has the power to grant reprieves and pardons to those who have been convicted of committing federal crimes.

28. Which presidential action below is within the scope of the presidential powers described in this passage?

(A) The president pardons a person a state court has convicted of murder.

(B) The president pardons a person who has been accused, but not yet convicted, of passing top-secret documents to another country.

(C) The president begins secret negotiations between the United States and Russia.

(D) The president fires a justice of the Supreme Court.

QUESTIONS 29 AND 30 REFER TO THE FOLLOWING INFORMATION.

In 1985, Mikhail Gorbachev became the Soviet Union's leader. He introduced a policy of economic reform known as *Perestroika* as well as *Glasnost,* a policy of openness between the Soviet government and its people. These policies were intended to spur economic growth and revitalize the government of the Soviet Union. Although Gorbachev considered himself a Communist, the policies he introduced opened the door to free expression, economic reform, and nationalism that ended with the fall of Communism and the breakup of the Soviet Union into 15 separate nations (Russia is the largest).

29. Which statement best summarizes *Glasnost*?

(A) *Glasnost* was a policy of economic reform that failed to end economic stagnation.

(B) *Glasnost* was a policy of openness that brought greater freedom of expression in the Soviet Union, which ultimately helped to bring about the fall of the Communist Party and the breakup of the Soviet Union.

(C) *Glasnost* refers to the growth of nationalistic identities within the Soviet Union that led to its breakup into 15 separate nations.

(D) *Glasnost* refers to the general lack of government transparency and openness in Russian government.

30. Which of the following is a statement of fact rather than an opinion or value judgment?

(A) Gorbachev failed in his goal of reforming communism and revitalizing the Soviet Union.

(B) Gorbachev would have been more successful had he tried more gradual reform rather than introducing far-reaching political and economic reforms all at once.

(C) To accomplish his reform goals, Gorbachev should have only introduced *Glasnost* or *Perestroika* one at a time, rather than together.

(D) Gorbachev followed the right policies, but it was too late to save communism or the Soviet Union.

QUESTION 31 REFERS TO THE FOLLOWING INFORMATION.

Businesses generally try to provide just enough supply of goods and services to meet the demand for them. If too high a price is set, businesses won't be able to sell their entire supply. On the other hand, setting too low a price leaves businesses without enough supply to meet demand.

31. If the demand for automobiles increases, but the supply does not change, what will most likely happen to the price and the quantity exchanged?

(A) The price and the quantity will both stay the same.

(B) The price and the quantity exchanged will increase.

(C) The price will increase and the quantity exchanged will decrease.

(D) The price will decrease and the quantity exchanged will increase.

QUESTION 32 REFERS TO THE FOLLOWING INFORMATION.

Listed below are several policies and programs established by various Democratic U.S. presidents.

New Deal: The social and economic programs under President Franklin D. Roosevelt in the 1930s that reformed the U.S. banking system and created the Agricultural Adjustment Administration, the Civilian Conservation Corps, the Public Works Administration, the Tennessee Valley Authority, the Social Security system, and the National Labor Relations Board, as well as establishing minimum wage and hours laws.

Fair Deal: A continuation of the New Deal. Under President Harry Truman, the Fair Deal brought a public housing bill.

New Frontier: Under President John F. Kennedy, the program included government aid for education, housing, mass transportation, equal-opportunity employment, tax reform, and the Peace Corps.

Great Society: President Johnson's program that concentrated on antipoverty, health (Medicare), education, conservation, and urban-planning measures.

Recovery and Reinvestment Act: President Obama's program focused on creating jobs in infrastructure development and new technologies, providing funding for education and health care, and providing tax credits, subsidies, and other aid to middle-class families and small businesses.

32. Which of the following would LEAST likely be an outgrowth of the listed policies and programs?

(A) a rental housing subsidy

(B) a reduction in capital gains taxes

(C) a college loan or scholarship program

(D) a national food bank for the homeless

QUESTIONS 33 AND 34 ARE BASED ON THE FOLLOWING INFORMATION.

In the Supreme Court's landmark case, *Brown* v. *The Board of Education of Topeka* (1954), an earlier decision was overturned. In the earlier case, *Plessy* v. *Ferguson* (1896), the doctrine of "separate but equal" was established with regard to education. In the *Brown* case, the Court decided that public school segregation, which had been a state-prescribed issue, was a violation of the equal-protection clause of the Fourteenth Amendment to the Constitution.

33. One of the first results of the Court's decision in the *Brown* case was

 Select ▼ .

imposing quotas on prestigious private colleges to ensure admission of racial minorities

redrawing voting districts to include racial minority groups in as many districts as possible

opening private country club memberships to racial minorities

mandatory bussing of schoolchildren to public schools in other districts

On the online GED® test, you will click to select your answer. For this paper version, please circle it.

34. *Brown* v. *The Board of Education of Topeka* was an important case in the fight for

(A) women's suffrage.

(B) civil rights.

(C) white supremacy.

(D) private school education.

ANSWER KEY AND EXPLANATIONS

Reasoning Through Language Arts

1. (B)	19. See explanation below.	34. See explanation below.
2. (A)	20. (C)	35. (A)
3. (A)	21. See explanation below.	36. (D)
4. (D)	22. See explanation below.	37. (C)
5. (C)	23. (D)	38. (C)
6. See explanation below.	24. their	39. See explanation below.
7. (A)	25. mail	40. (C)
8. (D)	26. "ok"	41. (B)
9. See explanation below.	27. your	42. See explanation below.
10. (C)	28. it's	43. (B)
11. (A)	29. (C)	44. (B)
12. (C)	30. simile	45. (A)
13. (B)	31. (B)	46. (D)
14. (D)	32. See explanation below.	47. (D)
15. See explanation below.	33. (C)	48. (C)
16. (D)		49. See explanation below.
17. (A)		
18. (A)		

1. **The correct answer is (B).** The last part of the passage tells us that she was going to see Robert. His note shows that he had decided not to continue their relationship, though he loves her.

2. **The correct answer is (A).** The Doctor observed that Edna has been in the company of women who he does not think are a good influence (he calls them "unimpressionable women") and he notices how distracted she is. He tries to get her to confide in him, but she rejects his offers saying she doesn't want to talk about her troubles.

3. **The correct answer is (A).** The plan, which is revealed when Edna arrives at the house, is that Robert was to be there and they would begin a new life together.

4. **The correct answer is (D).** The Doctor seems to know Edna and her family fairly well and has been observing her behavior. Although he disapproves, he takes a somewhat objective position and offers to listen to her troubles. Although he is clearly concerned, his attitude is more detached than that of a friend.

5. **The correct answer is (C).** As Edna sits outside the house, she contemplates her new life with Robert and says she finally feels "like a somber, uncomfortable garment" has been removed. The simile compares her pent-up feelings to a tight and uncomfortable piece of clothing that she has been carrying around and can't wait to remove.

6. **The correct answer is guilty about leaving her children.** Edna makes numerous references to her children, saying that only children might have a right to force her to do things she might not like. This concept creates a conflict: she doesn't want to stay in spite of the pull the children have because of her duties and love as a mother, yet she wants to follow her heart, which means leaving them behind.

7. **The correct answer is (A).** "Impressionable" means open to being impressed or influenced; unimpressionable, the opposite, refers to not being subject to outside influence. In the context of the story, the women the Doctor refers to are outside of the influence of others—they will do what they want and will not necessarily conform. The Doctor worries that the reputation of these women is not suitable and disapproves of Edna's association with them

8. **The correct answer is (D).** The Doctor is suspicious that Edna is going to take some action, though he doesn't knows the specifics. He talks about the obligations of motherhood and how Nature ties mothers to their children so that they feel obligated. This reinforces Edna's guilty feelings about the idea of leaving her children, an idea the Doctor raises hoping that it will prevent her from doing anything foolish.

9. **The correct answer is Robert awaits her and her life will change forever.** Edna is obsessed with the freedom represented by a new life with Robert. It is what makes her nervous when talking to the Doctor and it is why she feels incoherent.

10. **The correct answer is (C).** In the first paragraph, the author indicates that through her son's death she learned "what a poor slave mother may feel when her child is torn away from her," and in the second paragraph she writes that this sorrowful event instilled in her "deep compassion for . . . mothers who are separated from their children."

11. **The correct answer is (A).** The book will "contain all the facts and documents upon which that story was founded." This statement indicates that this information will inform readers of the horrors and realities of slavery.

12. **The correct answer is (C).** A careful reading of the third and fourth paragraphs makes it clear that the author is referring to the horrors of slavery, which she thought she knew, but now finds she "had not begun to measure."

13. **The correct answer is (B).** In the third paragraph, the author writes, "It seems to me that the book cannot but be felt, and, coming upon the sensibility awaked by the other, do something," suggesting that her readers will feel the pain she documents and act to remedy the institution of slavery.

14. **The correct answer is (D).** The passage vividly conveys the sense of emotion with which the author approaches her writing. Although Stowe did become an abolitionist, that information is not in the passage.

15. **The correct answer is reports of trial, legal documents, testimony of Southerners.** In the passage, Stowe lists all the elements she feels she must include.

16. **The correct answer is (D).** The writer tends to repeat herself and gets wordier than is necessary for the purpose of a cover letter.

17. **The correct answer is (A).** Sentence 20 consists of two complete sentences, which should be separated by a semicolon, not just a comma.

18. **The correct answer is (A).** In both sentences she mentions her experience with social media.

19. **The correct answers are planning fundraising events, creating client gifts, and doing research.** The passage states that Kelly has done each of these three things in the past and does not mention anything related to budgets or foreign languages or to designing print products herself.

20. **The correct answer is (C).** The sentence suffers from two main problems: a dangling modifier and an error in pronoun-antecedent agreement. It's not clear to whom "skilled in social media . . ." applies. It is also unclear to whom "they" refers.

21. **The correct answer is "I improved my editorial, writing, and management skills by working with clients and problem-solving."** This choice is the least awkward, and the writer avoids the lack of parallel structure that makes some of the other choices confusing.

22. **The correct answer is "I was in charge of planning several of our yearly fundraising events, during which we successfully raised millions of dollars."** The first and fourth sentences are awkward and confusing. The third sentence is weak because the verbs don't emphasize Kelly's actions; words such as "gave me" make it sound as if she were a bystander.

23. **The correct answer is (D).** Choice (A) is a run-on sentence, and choices (B) and (C) contain fragments.

24. **The correct answer is *their*.**

25. **The correct answer is *mail*.**

26. **The correct answer is "ok."**

27. **The correct answer is *your*.**

28. **The correct answer is *it's*.**

29. **The correct answer is (C).** In the foreword to the two passages, it is stated that Napoleon and his wife are currently in separate places. Napoleon therefore must have spent at least some time away from his wife, and he is thus exaggerating the fact that he has "not spent a day without loving [. . .] without embracing" Josephine.

30. **The correct answer is simile.** Both writers use a foreign translation of "you," refer to themselves in the third person ("your Robert," "your husband"), and recall memories of their lovers. Neither passage, however, compares two things using "like" or "as."

31. **The correct answer is (B).** Napoleon is exaggerating how long it takes his wife to write to him and what that means and teases her that this means she no longer, or will soon no longer, love him.

32. **The correct answers are *du* and *vous* and *you*.** Answers must be chosen in the order they are used in the passages, so *du* and *vous* are respectively used in passages 1 and 2. Using context clues and perhaps background knowledge, the best logical meaning of both words is *you*.

33. **The correct answer is (C).** While the distance between Schumann and Clara is unknown and must be causing some strain, it appears that the main problem is the lack of approval from her father.

34. **The correct answers are *Napoleon*: married, at war; *Both*: long-distance relationship, focusing on memories; *Schumann*: musician, expresses self-doubt.** From the foreword, we know that Napoleon is

married when writing his letter, but Schumann is not; that Napoleon is at war, and that Schumann is a composer, which would categorize him as a musician. Neither letter provides evidence that either man is uneducated or poor, but both depict men who are loving from a distance and focusing on memories of their lovers. Schumann "expresses self-doubt" about whether he "had any right to bind you to me" and several other concerns in the first paragraph.

35. **The correct answer is (A).** Schumann describes the desire to have a good relationship with Clara's father, so merely by context, the answer would not be a neutral term. The choices are then narrowed down to "respect" and "love," and as Schumann describes his reverence existing "for all strong characters," "respect" would be a much more logical definition than "love."

36. **The correct answer is (D).** Although the excerpt is being told by an omniscient narrator, the point of view from which we learn information about Miss Tempy comes from the townspeople's point of view who notice, for instance, that her house is the one home left with a lamp on.

37. **The correct answer is (C).** While each of the answer choices could be a possible reason for sharing secrets, the passage directly states that the women "told the other more than one fact that she had determined to keep secret…that either would have found impossible by daylight."

38. **The correct answer is (C).** The background knowledge of Mrs. Crowe does not specify whether her acts of charity are large in scope, but makes it clear that she is "stingy" and if she so much as "lifted a finger to help anybody" it was appreciated more than it normally would be. Therefore, one can assume that she does not often make donations or aid those in need.

39. **The correct answers are Sarah Ann Binson supports widowed sister and is sharp-set and Mrs. Crowe is well-to-do and stingy.**

40. **The correct answer is (C).** In paragraph 3, where we learn about Sarah Ann's life. She is described as having "never defended herself" against her sister, who seems to treat her like a pushover.

41. **The correct answer is (B).** From the beginning, we know that the two women were both close friends to Miss Tempy, and both women are described as having a similar appearance and as coming from New England. The end of the passage states that Mrs. Crowe has a higher social standing, which, when combined with the exaggerated gratitude for her charity, leads one to believe she has more money than Sarah Ann. It is also more likely that she should have more wealth as she is married, whereas Sarah Ann is not.

42. **Extended Response. Answers will vary.** You will find two sample essays on pages 815-818.

43. **The correct answer is (B).** To make the sentence clearer, either *submitted* and *by you* should be positioned together (*submitted by you*), or the active phrase *you submitted* should be used.

44. **The correct answer is (B).** The three list items should be grammatically parallel, but they're not. Removing the word *using* from the second item corrects the problem. The sentence would then read: *The navigation buttons, the pull-down menus, and the product ordering page are all intuitive and user-friendly.*

45. **The correct answer is (A).** Choice (A) provides a good way to transform the second sentence into a dependent clause beginning with *so that.* Here's a complete revised version: *Is it possible to use a three-column format instead of two columns so that more informa-*

tion is visible "above the fold" on each page?

46. The correct answer is (D). The words *horizontal* and *vertical* should be parallel in the sentence. Changing *vertically* to *vertical* clarifies the sentence and corrects the construction. None of the other options correct this error.

47. The correct answer is (D). This sentence contains two independent clauses, each of which can stand alone as a complete sentence. The second clause contains the compound subject *me and her*, which incorrectly employs object pronoun cases.

48. The correct answer is (C). The word *vary* (differ or fluctuate) doesn't make sense here. The writer probably intended to use the word *very* (extremely). The other options introduce new errors into the sentence.

49. The correct order is We have a new company logo that we wish to use on every page of the website. We can e-mail an image of it to you. Please let me know if you have any particular file format or size requirements. It makes more sense to bring up the logo before mentioning that they can mail it. The use of "it" in the first sentence is unclear, because the reader doesn't yet know that "it" refers to the logo.

Mathematical Reasoning

1. (B)	14. 98	28. (A)
2. (C)	15. (B)	29. (A)
3. (C)	16. (C)	30. Any point in the shaded area of the graph of $2x - 4 = y$
4. (D)	17. (D)	
5. $661.50	18. (B)	
6. (−3, 4)	19. (A)	31. $48 + 37.5 \leq 430$
7. (B)	20. (C)	32. $s^2 = 196$
8. $\frac{1}{2}$	21. (B)	33. (0, −3), (1, −1)
9. (C)	22. (D)	34. Increasing along the interval $-3 < x < 0$
10. (D)	23. (D)	35. −2
11. See explanation below.	24. (B)	36. (C)
	25. (D)	37. (D)
12. (C)	26. (B)	
13. $\frac{x}{3} > \frac{x}{7} > \frac{x}{9}$	27. (C)	

1. The correct answer is (B). Calculate the discount rate using the original price: $\frac{10}{75} = 13\frac{1}{3}$% or, rounding to the nearest tenth of a percent, 13.3.

2. The correct answer is (C). Felicia paid $16.20 for the items she bought ($20.00 − $3.80). At $2.70 each, six bags of apples cost $16.20.

3. **The correct answer is (C).**

$$ab^2c^2 = 3 \times 9 \times \frac{1}{9}$$
$$= \frac{27}{9}$$
$$= 3$$

4. **The correct answer is (D).** There's no need to perform any calculations. This problem illustrates the distributive law: $a(b + c) = ab + ac$. Choice (D) correctly applies this property (you can ignore the variable x):

$$52(31 + 27) = (52)(31) + (52)(27).$$

5. **The correct answer is \$661.50.** First, calculate Joe's regular pay by multiplying his regular rate by 40. Then determine Joe's time-and-a-half rate and multiply that by his 6 hours of overtime pay. Finally, add those two figures together.

$$\$13.50 \times 40 = \$540$$
$$\left(\frac{\$13.50}{2} + \$13.50\right) \times 6 = \$121.50$$
$$\$540 + \$121.50 = \$661.50$$

6. **The correct answer is (–3, 4).** You can express the midpoint's coordinates using the midpoint formula:

$$M = \left(\frac{x_1 + x_2}{2}, \frac{y_1 + y_2}{2}\right)$$
$$= \left(\frac{5 + (-11)}{2}, \frac{2 + 6}{2}\right)$$
$$= \left(\frac{-6}{2}, \frac{8}{2}\right)$$
$$= (-3, 4)$$

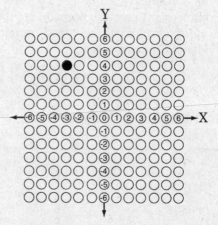

7. **The correct answer is (B).** The volume of a pyramid with a square base $= \frac{1}{3} \times$ edge$^2 \times$ height. Given a volume of 125 and height of 15, here is how you can solve for e^2:

$$125 = \frac{1}{3}e^2 \times 15$$
$$375 = 15e^2$$
$$25 = e^2$$

8. **The correct answer is $\frac{1}{2}$.** First, add the fractions: $\frac{1}{3} + \frac{1}{6} = \frac{2+1}{6} = \frac{3}{6}$, or $\frac{1}{2}$. Subtracting the total from 1 (the whole pizza) leaves one half of the pizza.

9. **The correct answer is (C).**

$$5y - 13 = 4x$$
$$5y - 13 + 13 = 4x + 13$$
$$\frac{5y}{5} = \frac{4x}{5} + \frac{13}{5}$$
$$y = \frac{4}{5}x + \frac{13}{5}$$

The line has a slope of $\frac{4}{5}$.

10. **The correct answer is (D).** If you multiply the second equation by 4, and then isolate the m-term, it reveals that the two equations are the same:

$$4 \times \frac{3n}{4} = 4(3 - m)$$
$$3n = 12 - 4m$$
$$4m = 12 - 3n$$

Given one linear equation with two variables, there are an infinite number of possible values for each variable.

11. **The correct answer is arithmetic mean of distribution D < any of the other value and any of the other value > arithmetic mean of distribution D.** The arithmetic mean of distribution D is 6.25. All the other values are equal to 7. Any inequality that shows that the mean of distribution D is less than any of the other values is correct.

12. **The correct answer is (C).** The quantities described in choices (A) and (B) are both negative (less than 0). Choice (D) describes a positive value greater than 1, but x^2 is the square of $|x|$ and therefore must be greater in value.

13. **The correct answer is $\frac{x}{3} > \frac{x}{7} > \frac{x}{9}$.**

The key to the question is the least value of x that is a multiple of all three denominators. In other words, the question asks for the least common denominator. Work your way up in multiples of the largest denominator, 9. You'll find that 63 is the lowest multiple that is also a multiple of both 7 and 3. Thus, $x = 63$.

14. **The correct answer is 98.** Apply the formula for the area of a trapezoid:

$$\frac{1}{2}(\text{base}_1 + \text{base}_2) \times \text{height} = \frac{1}{2}(14) \times 14$$
$$= 7 \times 14 = 98 \text{ square centimeters.}$$

15. **The correct answer is (B).** $f(x)$ varies inversely with x. In other words, as the value of x increases, the value of y decreases. Since x is squared, the relationship is exponential, and the graph must be curved (not a straight line). Only choice (B) provides a graph that fits this functional relationship.

16. **The correct answer is (C).** An expression is undefined when the denominator is equal to 0, or when $m^3 - 1 = 0$.

17. **The correct answer is (D).** Set up a proportion: where l is the actual length of the kitchen. Solve for l by cross-multiplying: $l = (15)(20) = 300$.

18. **The correct answer is (B).** The area of a circle is determined by the formula $A = \pi r^2$, where r is the radius. In this case $r^2 = 49$, so $r = 7$. If the radius is 7, the diameter is 14, or $2r$, which is the longest distance from one end of the table to the other.

19. **The correct answer is (A).** Calculate the area of the triangle using 4 for s because the diameter of the circle is also the side of the triangle: $\frac{4^2\sqrt{3}}{4} = \frac{16\sqrt{3}}{4} = 4\sqrt{3}$. Divide the area of the circle by 2 to get the area of the semi-circle, using 2 as the radius (half the diameter): $\frac{\pi 2^2}{2} = \frac{4\pi}{2} = 2\pi$.

20. The correct answer is (C). Substitute 2.5 for r and 8 for h in the formula given for surface area:

$$SA = 2\pi(2.5)^2 + 2\pi(2.5) \times (8)$$
$$= 12.5\pi + 40\pi$$
$$= 52.5\pi$$

21. The correct answer is (B). Substitute the values given into the formula for the volume of a cone:

$$4\pi = \frac{1}{3}\pi(2^2)h$$

$$4\pi = \frac{4}{3}\pi h$$

$$3 = h$$

22. The correct answer is (D). Insert the values given into the formula for the volume of a sphere: $466 = \frac{4}{3}\pi r^3$.

Isolating the r term gives us:

$111 \approx r^3$. The closest approximation for r is 4.8.

23. The correct answer is (D). Add up the numbers in the columns representing the age ranges 21–25, 26–30, and 31–35: $28 + 33 + 22 = 83$.

24. The correct answer is (B). There are a total of 52 cards and 4 queens in a standard deck. Put the total number of ways to select a queen, which is 4, over the total number of ways to select any card, which is 52:

$$\frac{4}{52} = \frac{1}{13}.$$

25. The correct answer is (D). Replace x with −1 in the expression:

$$\frac{3(-1)-4}{4(-1)} = \frac{-7}{-4} = \frac{7}{4}.$$

26. The correct answer is (B). Replace x with −1 and y with 0 in the expression:

$$2(-1)(0)^2 - (-1) + 4 = 0 + 1 + 4 = 5.$$

27. The correct answer is (C). The base fee is not discounted, so that is $10. The hourly rate, $2.5h$, is divided by 2 because of the coupon.

28. The correct answer is (A). The numerator can be factored into: $(x + 3)(x - 2)$. Putting this back into

the expression: $\dfrac{(x+3)(x-2)}{x+3}$, the

factor $(x + 3)$ factors out, leaving $(x - 2)$.

29. The correct answer is (A). First subtract 6 from both sides of the inequality: $-2x \geq -6$. Next divide both sides of the equation by −2. When dividing or multiplying an inequality by a negative number, the inequality

sign changes direction: $x \leq \dfrac{-6}{-2} = 3$

30. The correct answer is any point in the shaded area of the graph of $2x - 4 = y$.

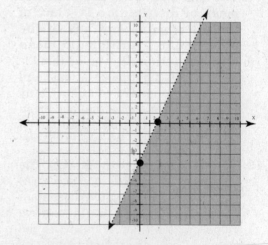

31. The correct answer is 48 + 37.5d ≤ 430. Add the cost of the gas, 48, and the cost of d days, which is the daily rate, 37.50, times d: $48 + 37.5d$. This sum must be less than or equal to Carmen's budget of $430, so the inequality is $48 + 37.5d \leq 430$.

32. **The correct answer is $s2 = 196$.** If the area of a square is 196, then the length of each side is the square root of 196.

33. **The correct answer is (0, –3) and (1, –1).** First isolate y to put the equation given into point-slope form $y = mx + b$:

$$2y = 4x - 6$$
$$y = 2x - 3$$

The line must cross the y-axis at –3, because $b = -3$. So one point is (0, –3). Choose another x-value such as 1 and calculate the value of y at $x = 1$: $y = 2(1) - 3 = -3$. Another point is (1, –1). Plot these two points on the graph and connect them with the line.

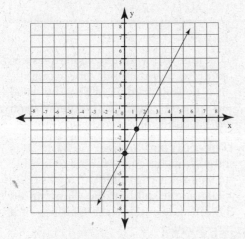

Note that hot spots can be anywhere along this line. The line will form when you click on the second point. Any point along this line that satisfies the x- and y-values in the equation is correct.

34. **The correct answer is that $f(x)$ is increasing along the interval $-3 < x < 0$.** Looking at the graph, the function increases until it gets to about $x = 0.5$, when it starts to flatten until about $x = 5$, and then increases until about $x = 12$.

35. **The correct answer is –2.** Perpendicular lines have slopes that are negative reciprocals of each other. To find the reciprocal of a fraction, divide 1 by the fraction: $\dfrac{1}{\frac{1}{2}} = 1 \times \dfrac{2}{1} = 2$. The reciprocal is 2, so the negative reciprocal is –2.

36. **The correct answer is (C).** Only in the graph of the function shown in (C) is there one unique output, or y-value, for each input, or x-value. The graphs of the functions in (A), (B), and (D) all show functions for which there are two possible y-values for each x-value.

37. **The correct answer is (D).** The graphs of these two functions are parallel because their slopes are equivalent. You can quickly determine the slope of $f(a)$ by seeing that the slope m, from the point-slope format $y = mx + b$, is equal to 8. From the table for $f(x)$, you can see that for every 1-unit change in x, there is a positive change of 8 in $f(x)$. That means the slope of this line is also equal to 8 and the two lines are parallel.

Science

1. (B)	11. (D)	22. Orangutans
2. (A)	12. (B)	23. humid
3. (D)	13. (B)	24. (C)
4. termites	14. (D)	25. algae, lichens, and corals (in that order)
5. (B)	15. (C)	
6. apply less force over a greater distance	16. (B)	26. (B)
	17. 2°C	27. (B)
7. the virus will break out of the cell and infect other cells	18. (C)	28. (A)
	19. (B)	29. PRODUCED to both kidneys, STORED to bladder
8. arrow D	20. yellow (about 580 nm)	
9. (A)		30. (D)
10. (D)	21. (D)	

1. **The correct answer is (B).** There are no fixed points in the universe, and there is no center. Whenever a point or region is used as a reference point, all other points appear to move in relation to it.

2. **The correct answer is (A).** Only intensity of exercise affects the anaerobic : aerobic ratio. Some of the other forms burn more energy overall, but they do not reach the level of intensity of running up stairs. Do not confuse psychologically intense with physically intense exercise.

3. **The correct answer is (D).** 4.0 arbitrary units of energy are used when exercise intensity is at 80 percent. Cycling up a short but steep hill involves strenuous, intense exertion (mainly involving your leg muscles), which does not require oxygen. Even so, your cells will probably process quite a bit of oxygen, which is why you might be short of breath by the time you reach the top.

4. **The correct answer is termites.** It is common knowledge that a termite population can grow dramatically to consume all available wood in its immediate environment (for example, in a house's frame). When the wood disappears, the termite population will decline very quickly.

5. **The correct answer is (B).** It is important for such studies to be able to isolate the test plants from outside pollen and pollinators. This would be difficult outside the confines of a greenhouse.

6. **The correct answer is apply less force over a greater distance.** Both the incline plane (left) and the pulley (right) reduce the magnitude, or intensity, of effort required to move the load from one level up to another. The total force required is still the same, but that force is spread out over a greater distance. (In the case of the incline plane, the increase in distance is the length of the ramp in excess of the vertical distance; in the case of the pulley, the increase in distance is the extra length of the rope that the pulley requires.)

7. **The correct answer is the virus will break out of the cell and in-**

fect other cells. The cell has swollen due to the reproduction of the virus within the cell. At some point, the virus particles are likely to breach (break through) the cell wall, releasing themselves to spread to other cells, where the process will repeat itself.

8. **The correct answer is arrow D.** In the right-hand graph, some energy in addition to what was available from the reactants has been absorbed during the formation of the products. The amount is the difference between the energy of the reactants and the energy of the products, arrow D.

9. **The correct answer is (A).** Choices (B) and (C) release heat, making them exothermic. Furthermore, choice (D) is a physical process, not a chemical reaction. Choice (A) is the only reaction that absorbs heat during the course of the reaction.

10. **The correct answer is (D).** Each shake of a blanket creates a wave of energy emanating from where you are gripping the blanket. The wave travels outward, toward the far end of the blanket, while the oscillation is up and down—perpendicular to the outward direction of the wave.

11. **The correct answer is (D).** An increase in blood flow and oxygen consumption in skeletal muscles facilitates the sort of muscle activity needed for bursts of strength, agility, and energy. The adrenal glands' response is an evolutionary survival mechanism—for fighting or fleeing from predators and other dangers.

12. **The correct answer is (B).** The diagram shows each hydrogen atom bonded with one of the two carbon atoms. This can only occur because each hydrogen atom has one electron in its outer shell, which is paired with one electron in the outer shell of a carbon atom. Each carbon atom has four electrons altogether in its outer shell.

13. **The correct answer is (B).** The first illustration shows poles forming in the cell, connected by spindles. The next illustration shows the cell's nucleus broken down, allowing the chromosomes to line up across the center of the spindle. The third illustration shows each chromosome splitting apart into two identical chromatids, as one half of the cell pulls the matching sets of chromosomes apart. It appears that the cell is attempting to reproduce itself.

14. **The correct answer is (D).** Developing types of grains that are resistant to drought and high temperatures does not depend at all on what occurs here on Earth in terms of climate change. It is focussed on adjusting to what is happening rather than changing it. Each of the other three policies seeks to slow or halt pollution or climate change.

15. **The correct answer is (C).** The Kelvin scale starts at "absolute zero," which is −273° on the Celsius scale. Starting with the lowest possible temperature makes temperature proportional to average kinetic energy of particles and simplifies many thermodynamic calculations.

16. **The correct answer is (B).** If Brian's arm were relaxed, the wave energy would work to move his arm up and down, thereby absorbing the energy. But since Brian is not allowing himself to absorb the wave energy, that energy will reflect back toward Allison.

17. **The correct answer is 2°C.** During the period in question, the temperature varied over the range of −28 to −30°C.

18. **The correct answer is (C).** The chart shows the Younger Dryas Interval as a period of comparatively low temperatures (cold weather) and low amounts of snow accumulation.

Snow accumulation can decrease due to either a decrease in precipitation (specifically, snow) or a sufficient rise in temperature that melts snow (or both). Since the chart tells us that temperatures were low during the Younger Dryas Interval, the best explanation for the low snow accumulation is that precipitation was low—in other words, the weather was relatively dry.

19. **The correct answer is (B).** The chart shows a continual series—going back 20,000 years—of warming-cooling cycles, accompanied by cycles in the amount of snow accumulation.

20. **The correct answer is yellow (about 580 nm).** The skin of a banana reflects the wavelengths for yellow while absorbing all other wavelengths, including blue.

21. **The correct answer is (D).** The chart shows all hominids, including *Homo sapiens* (humans), branching from "Primates" (the trunk at the bottom of the chart).

22. **The correct answer is Orangutans.** The chart shows the "Gorilla" branch as an offshoot of the "Orangutan" branch, which means that gorillas are direct descendants of orangutans.

23. **The correct answer is humid.** Humid air contains more water vapor than dry air. The moister air will attract less water to the leaf's surface, which is where transpiration occurs.

24. **The correct answer is (C).** The only explanation as to why the water in the aquifer would be forced up through the well is that there is pressure on the water toward the opening. The illustration shows an aquifer extending downward and at an angle from the surface (the recharge area). The volume of water above the aquifer's deeper waters can exert significant pressure on those deeper waters—

pressure that a properly positioned artesian well can release.

25. **The correct answer is algae, lichens, and corals (in that order).** The first sentence of the second paragraph tells us that corals and lichen both maintain a mutually beneficial relationship with photosynthesizing algae. So we know that both corals and lichen are primary consumers, while algae are producers. But the paragraph also tells us that some corals eat other animals, while other corals rely on algae for their food. So some corals are secondary consumers, while others are primary consumers.

26. **The correct answer is (B).** As the illustration shows, about half of the glucose manufactured by eating food is directed to the muscles, either for immediate use as energy or for storage to be converted to energy later. Competitive athletes burn more fuel for energy than most people, and therefore they must produce more glucose by eating more.

27. **The correct answer is (B).** A bat can make high-frequency sounds (some of which humans can't hear) that it listens to as they echo off the walls of a dark cave. By processing this information, the bat is able to map the logistics of the cave and fly around its interior without colliding with the cave walls.

28. **The correct answer is (A).** The table shows that the lowest frequency that a porpoise can hear is *higher* than the lowest frequency that humans can hear, which is given as 20 Hz, or 20,000 kHz. (1 Hz = 1000 kHz.) So, by eliminating all sonar frequencies above 20,000 kHz, the sonar would no longer interfere with the ability of porpoises to hear other sounds.

29. **The correct answers are PRODUCED to both kidneys and STORED to bladder.** As your cells metabolize glucose for energy, they

leave by-products (waste) in the fluids in and around your body's cells. These by-products must be filtered out of this "interstitial" fluid and removed from the body. As the diagram shows, this is the function of the renal system.

30. **The correct answer is (D).** Positively charged particles and negatively charged particles are attracted

to each other. Hence the positively charged hydrogen atoms in a water molecule and the negatively charged oxygen atoms in other water molecules will form hydrogen bonds, as the illustration shows. These intermolecular bonds have the effect of holding molecules together, resisting leaving the liquid phase and raising the boiling point.

Social Studies

1. (D)	13. (D)	24. wages
2. (D)	14. (A)	25. Louisiana Purchase
3. See explanation below.	15. (C)	26. Mexican Cession
	16. (D)	27. (D)
4. (A)	17. Massachusetts Bay	28. (C)
5. (C)		29. (B)
6. (A)	18. Georgia	30. (A)
7. (D)	19. a recession	31. (B)
8. (B)	20. secede or withdraw	32. (B)
9. (C)		33. See explanation below.
10. (D)	21. (D)	
11. Vikings or Norse	22. (A)	34. (B)
12. (B)	23. (C)	

1. **The correct answer is (D).** The Fifth Amendment protects citizens from being convicted in a criminal court without trial. This protection is similar to, and hence reinforces, the protection provided in the Constitution against a legislature doing the same thing.

2. **The correct answer is (D).** Western Morocco (identified on the map by the number 1) lies along the Atlantic coastline, as do either the western or southern boundaries of the countries numbered 6, 7, 14, 15, 16, 17, 18, 19, 21, 22, 23, 24, and 25.

3. As you review your essay, check for the following:

   - Do I have a clear thesis statement that responds exactly to what the prompt asks?
   - Is my essay well organized?
   - Have I analyzed the evidence carefully? Do I use evidence to support my ideas rather than just summarize what the documents are about?
   - Do I provide effective transitions between sections by noting how each section relates to the one

before it (e.g., further clarification, contrast)?

- Do I provide a thoughtful conclusion to my essay?

You will find two sample essays on pages 815-818.

4. **The correct answer is (A).** Europe is to the north of Africa, across the Mediterranean Sea. A waterway connecting that sea to the Red Sea (east of Egypt, Sudan, and Ethiopia) facilitated global trade by allowing water transport between Europe and Asia (to the east) without going around the African continent.

5. **The correct answer is (C).** The fact that Jackson was a wealthy plantation owner is inconsistent with his image as a "common man" rather than a member of the wealthy elite. The others facts all helped Jackson promote the image of himself as a "common man" and friend of ordinary citizens.

6. **The correct answer is (A).** We can infer that Jackson would not have supported the extension of the right to vote to Native Americans and slaves since he ordered the removal of Indians and supported slavery. From the reading, we know he supported extending the right to all adult, white males, choice (D). However, the passage doesn't provide enough information to make inferences regarding his position on voting rights for women, choice (B), or his position on what age males become adults, choice (C).

7. **The correct answer is (D).** A value is a deep-seated belief that helps determine a person's ideas and outlook on life. Jackson hated the fact that many wealthy, better educated people looked down on him and often were able to advance ahead of him due to special privilege. Much of his political life is defined by criticism of the political and economic elite and the positions he took in support of ordinary citizens (the "common man"). Since the right to vote was extended to only white males, we know he did not value equal rights for all, choice (A). In addition, formal education, choice (B), and the established order, choice (C), were not values that strongly influenced him.

8. **The correct answer is (B).** The draft used a lottery system and the first was held on December 1, 1969.

9. **The correct answer is (C).** Nixon had run for office on the promise of ending American involvement in Vietnam.

10. **The correct answer is (D).** Congress, not the president, choice (A), plays the key role in debating, writing, and passing a new law. The president cannot always block Congress, choice (B), which can override his veto,. Not signing a law, choice (C), will not keep it from taking effect, unless Congress has adjourned.

11. **The correct answer is Vikings or Norse.** Context clues indicate that the persons lived in northern locations. Wherever they were not welcome, they saw little practical choice but to seize land by force.

12. **The correct answer is (B).** The statement in choice (B) captures the main difference between North and South. Choice (A) is incorrect since the North and South faced different challenges: the South had to rebuild and reform, and the North did not. The North, unlike the South, was not destroyed during the Civil War and did not have to rebuild, choice (C). The passage explained that regional differences between the North and South were continuing, not diminishing, choice (D).

13. **The correct answer is (D).** The greatest decrease—from about 4% growth to about a 1% contraction (negative growth)—occurred from 1988–1991.

14. **The correct answer is (A).** The left-hand and right-hand charts show an inverse relationship overall between GDP and unemployment: when the economy is growing, unemployment declines. Conversely, when economic growth slows, unemployment increases. This observation makes sense. A low rate of economic growth typically means that employers are not expanding their businesses and therefore, are not hiring additional employees, and employers may actually be laying off workers in response to sluggish business.

15. **The correct answer is (C).** The best time to look for a job would be when the economy is growing (which is when businesses are more likely to need additional workers), unemployment is falling (which means fewer available workers for employers to choose from), and inflation is falling (which is when businesses are more confident about investing for their future).

16. **The correct answer is (D).** Common sense tells you that, at any given time, some portion of the working-age population will be experiencing a brief lapse in employment while transitioning from one job to another. It makes sense to take such factors into account when defining *full employment.*

17. **The correct answer is Massachusetts Bay.** The colony was originally founded as the Plymouth Colony by English Pilgrims in 1620. When the Massachusetts Bay company established settlements at Salem in 1628 and Boston in 1630, the colonies merged as the Massachusetts Bay Colony.

18. **The correct answer is Georgia.** James Oglethorpe had served on a Parliamentary commission convened to study prison reform for debtors prisons. Oglethorpe believed that growing urbanization was responsible for growing poverty. In 1732, he founded the colony, named for George II, as a place where "worthy poor" could cultivate farms and avoid prison. In fact, few debtors actually settled there.

19. **The correct answer is a recession.** A recession is a business cycle contraction characterized by a marked decrease in economic spending. A recession may be caused by a financial crisis or an adverse supply shock. The measures noted are meant to restore spending and increase economic activity.

20. **The correct answer is secede or withdraw.** Use knowledge of the time period to determine your answer.

21. **The correct answer is (D).** Choice (D) gives the most complete description of the relationship between the African American population and the Caucasian population. Each of the other choices describes only one portion of the facts presented in the table.

22. **The correct answer is (A).** Proportionate changes among the three demographic groups would have no effect on the number of people in each group.

23. **The correct answer is (C).** The table shows a declining Caucasian population from 2010 to 2080. An expected decline in the birthrate among Caucasians would lead to this projection. Choice (A) runs contrary to the projected decline in the Caucasian population. Choice (B) is not directly related to the information in the table. Choice (D) runs contrary to the projected decline in the Caucasian female population.

24. **The correct answer is wages.** Rent, food, and transportation (automobiles) are all goods or services purchased by typical consumers. Wages are not.

25. **The correct answer is Louisiana Purchase.** In looking at the map, the other land acquisitions are smaller and were acquired after 1803.

26. **The correct answer is Mexican Cession.** The Mexican Cession was added to the United States in 1848 as a result of the Mexican War, which ended that year.

27. **The correct answer is (D).** No part of Florida, which lies east of the Mississippi River, was annexed by the United States until after the Louisiana Purchase (west of the river).

28. **The correct answer is (C).** The president's power to conduct foreign affairs and negotiate treaties means opening talks with a foreign power, such as Russia, clearly falls within the scope of presidential powers. The president can only pardon people convicted of federal crimes, choice (A), and can only issue a pardon if the person is convicted, choice (B). Also, the president cannot fire Supreme Court justices, choice (D), who are appointed for life.

29. **The correct answer is (B).** Only this statement defines *Glasnost* and correctly states the results of the policy. *Perestroika,* not *Glasnost,* was a policy of economic reform, choice (A). The term does not refer to the breakup of the Soviet Union into 15 separate nations, choice (C), although the policy may have helped cause this. *Glasnost* means "openness," not the lack thereof, choice (D).

30. **The correct answer is (A).** Since communism, and the Soviet Union itself, came to an end, it is an undisputed fact that Gorbachev failed in his goal to revitalize them. Statements of what "should" have happened are statements of opinion, choice (C).

Statements of right or wrong, choice (D), are value judgments rather than facts. Statements of what "would have happened if…," choice (B), are opinions rather than statements of fact since they can never be proven or disproven.

31. **The correct answer is (B).** An increase in demand means that more automobiles will be purchased at any given price. So the number of automobiles exchanged will increase. Also, since demand exceeds supply, sellers will be able to set higher prices for their automobiles—at least until excess demand has been met.

32. **The correct answer is (B).** An income-tax reduction for the middle and lower classes might further the sorts of goals of these programs, but a capital gains tax cut mainly helps wealthier investors, who are not the people that these policies and programs are aimed at helping.

33. **The correct answer is mandatory bussing of schoolchildren to public schools in other districts.** Though the Brown decision may have led to integration with respect to other aspects of American society as well, the most direct result of the decision was to impose integration requirements on public schools. One common way to meet the requirements was to transport white school students to predominantly African-American schools, and vice versa.

34. **The correct answer is (B).** The Brown decision was an important stride in addressing civil rights concerns because it struck down the long-held idea of "separate but equal."

Reasoning Through Language Arts Extended Response Sample Essays

High-Scoring Essay

I find the argument in Passage 2 supporting year-round schooling in the United States is more compelling because it provides a clear stance with evidence cited from reputable experts and studies, while Passage 1 takes a side but neglects to defend it with specific research or statistics.

The second passage begins with a strong global statement that compels Americans to be concerned about the decline in strength of our academic system as compared to other Western systems, and follows up with evidence from studies from the prestigious Johns Hopkins and Duke, providing the proof for the correlation between summer vacations and learning losses. The most compelling evidence showed the disparities in summer learning losses between disadvantaged and higher-income students in the twenty-year-long study at Johns Hopkins. Our schools should work to minimize differences in education, especially those due to socioeconomic status. That lower-income students could end up three grade levels behind their well-off peers at the end of secondary school is highly alarming. It makes sense to implement some form of year-round learning that makes educational activities accessible to all young minds, so as to prevent lower-income students from falling behind because of a lack of resources and safe spaces. Additionally, as the second passage says, higher-income students might have an advantage, but even "their learning patterns are still slacking when compared to those around the globe."

Passage 2 provides not only the research behind the need for year-round schooling, but also different options for implementing such a program, including "spreading out vacation days" and "hosting summer enrichment programs." These alternatives demonstrate that we can explore many ways of encouraging students to maintain their education all year, rather than the traditional single option of simply extending school through the summer.

The argument of Passage 1 is weaker because it provides an oversimplified logic for clinging to the summer vacation, which boils down to the conviction that things should stay the same because of tradition. Its supporting arguments about childcare costs, conflicting schedules, and the trouble of maintaining schools throughout the summer seem feeble compared to the statistics offered in Passage 2.

For all of the reasons previously noted, I support the argument that American schools should implement year-round learning initiatives. The evidence and argument is compelling and it appears to be a reasonable solution to the very real problem of "summer learning loss."

EXPLANATION

This response would receive a high score because it generates a text-based argument and uses relevant evidence from the passage to support it, contains ideas that are organized and well-developed, and demonstrates a command of standard English conventions. Specifically, this essay supports the argument for year-round schooling by citing information and organization in the passages to show effectiveness of language and argument. The passage shows a logical and thoughtful progression of ideas. The essay demonstrates fluency in standard English and uses varied sentence structure.

Low-Scoring Essay

I think that Passage 2 has the better argument because it shows why having school all year is really important for American students, plus evidence from University studies.

Passage 2 starts off with blaming summer vacation for US academics being less educated. I think that this argument is powerful for many who are afraid of China beating the US in education. It follows this with evidence from studies of experts who say that low-income students suffer more from not having a family vacation or a place to play in the summer, so they fall behind when school starts again. They also probably cannot go to summer camps or education programs to learn in the summer because their parents can't afford it. Passage 2 is therefore the clear winner in using statistics.

Passage 2 has a twenty-year-long study in it supporting its argument, plus the facts that even higher-income students don't do as well as students in other countries, so we need to have school in the summer. However, there are some options for doing this, which the passage then describes.

Passage 1 is not as good for it does not have the same statistical facts and it only argues about childcare and cost of school in the summer, it does not say anything about benefits except that they may not be so beneficial. It also does not say anything about the lower-income students or their care. So Passage 2 is the one I support.

EXPLANATION

This response would receive a low score because it is far too short, with an argument that is convoluted and uses little to no evidence from the passage to support it. It contains ideas that are confusing and not clearly organized, and demonstrates minimal command of Standard English conventions with several mistakes and only some varied sentence structure.

Social Studies Extended Response Sample Essays

High-Scoring Essay

The excerpts provided demonstrate the two poles of the argument surrounding the embryonic Constitution and its protection of citizens' rights. The Anti-Federalist interpretation, represented here under the name of "Brutus," views the Constitution as a threat to individual liberties because it would trump State Constitutions in the event of a contradiction. The Federalist viewpoint, represented as "Publius," argues that the threat is nonexistent because the Constitution does not give the federal government the power to violate the individual rights that the Anti-Federalists seek to defend.

Brutus's concern for individual rights seems highly reasonable because the federal laws would take precedence over state laws. However, from his declaration that no "privilege, reserved by the bills of rights, or secured by the State governments, can limit the power granted by this, or restrain any laws made in pursuance of it," it is clear that he perceives the Constitution as a document granting the federal government unequivocal and unlimited powers and privileges. Therefore, to take this conviction to its logical end, any individual right not explicitly protected in the Constitution may be trampled with impunity under the new government.

Publius, on the other hand, points out that many states at that point have a Constitution lacking a bill of rights – including those, such as New York, with a large number of outspoken Anti-Federalists advocating for a federal bill of rights. He acknowledges their arguments of New Yorkers that their Constitution contains "various provisions in favor of particular privileges and rights," besides adopting "the common and statute law of Great Britain, by which many other rights, not expressed in it, are equally secured." Publius counters that the proposed federal Constitution does contain many of these protections, so that individual rights cannot be infringed upon with impunity. Furthermore, the proposed Constitution purposely grants the federal government rather narrow powers, so that an explicit protection of certain rights could end up implicitly giving the government claim to powers that it had not previously been granted.

Ultimately, for Brutus and the Anti-Federalists, the Constitution made citizens vulnerable to attack from an overly large and powerful federal government, while Publius and the Federalists conceived of the Constitution instead as an attempt to develop a uniform central government that could be kept on a very tight rein.

EXPLANATION

This response would receive a high score because it generates a text-based argument and uses relevant evidence from the passage to support it, contains ideas that are organized and well-developed, and demonstrates a command of standard English conventions.

Specifically, this essay develops a comparison between the Anti-Federalist and Federalist conceptions of the Constitution. It shows a logical and thoughtful progression of ideas, and demonstrates fluency in Standard English and uses varied sentence structure.

Low-Scoring Essay

Brutus and Publius are clear opposites on the topic of the Constitution's bill of rights. They both have a different idea of how the government will work to protect people's rights so that they have differing views on the usefulness of a bill of rights.

Brutus, for whom Publius thinks is wrong, thinks that the bill of rights is essential to protecting people from the government because it will have so much more power than the states. He sees that the government will take away rights by the Constitution because it will have no protection in it. The Constitution therefore must say what rights people have and tell the government not to take them away. Also he says that the Constitution is going to repeal the state constitutions but he warns that it might not be the best one possible. In the end time tells that our government has a bill of rights, so Brutus was of course correct in his opinion.

But according to Publius, Brutus is wrong because of all the state's constitutions have no bill of rights but some parts do protect the rights of citizens. Therefore the Constitution will have some of this protection in it. But he also says that a bill of rights is dangerous because people could take the power for themselves. They will read about how the government is supposed to protect people and try to do it on their own, so the government will have to take over and fix their mistakes. The liberty of the press is one of these examples, where the press might not restrain themselves but the government cannot do it so the people will. So you can see that a bill of rights will only give the press more power than it deserves.

This is how the opinion of Brutus and Publius on the subject of the Constitution is different vastly.

EXPLANATION

This response would receive a low score because it is far too short, with an argument that is convoluted and uses little to no evidence from the passage to support it. It contains ideas that are confusing and not clearly organized, and demonstrates minimal command of Standard English conventions with only some varied sentence structure. There are also several run on sentences and other mistakes.

ARE YOU READY TO TAKE THE GED® TEST?

Now that you have spent a great deal of time and effort studying for the GED® and taking this Practice Test, hopefully you are well-prepared to take the GED® test. But, it's best to make sure that you are completely ready. Check your scores from this Practice Test on the table below to see where you stand.

	All Set— Well-Prepared	Possibly Ready	Need More Preparation
Reasoning Through Language Arts	37–49	25–36	0–24
Mathematical Reasoning	26–34	17–25	0–16
Science	22–30	17–21	0–16
Social Studies	28–37	18–27	0–17

If your scores are in the "All Set—Well-Prepared" column, you are probably ready to take the actual GED® test, and you should apply to take the test soon. If some of your scores are in the "Possibly Ready" column, you should focus your study on those areas where you need to improve most. "Possibly Ready" means that you are probably ready enough to earn a GED® diploma, but it's not a bad idea to spend a little more time brushing up and improving your chances to pass the actual GED® test.

If any of your scores fell in the lowest category, take more time to review the pertinent chapters in this book—and in any high school text books, if necessary. Good luck!

Word List

A

abbreviate (verb) to make briefer, to shorten. *Because time was running out, the speaker had to abbreviate his remarks.* **abbreviation** (noun).

abrasive (adjective) irritating, grinding, rough. *The manager's rude, abrasive way of criticizing the workers was bad for morale.* **abrasion** (noun).

abridge (verb) to shorten, to reduce. *The Bill of Rights is designed to prevent Congress from abridging the rights of Americans.* **abridgment** (noun).

absolve (verb) to free from guilt, to exonerate. *The criminal jury absolved Mr. Callahan of the murder of his neighbor.* **absolution** (noun).

abstain (verb) to refrain, to hold back. *After his heart attack, William was warned by his doctor to abstain from smoking, drinking, and overeating.* **abstinence** (noun), **abstemious** (adjective).

accentuate (verb) to emphasize, to stress. *The overcast skies and chill winds only accentuate our gloomy mood.* **accentuation** (noun).

acrimonious (adjective) biting, harsh, caustic. *The election campaign became acrimonious, as the candidates traded insults and accusations.* **acrimony** (noun).

adaptable (adjective) able to be changed to be suitable for a new purpose. *Some scientists say that the mammals outlived the dinosaurs because they were more adaptable to a changing climate.* **adapt** (verb), **adaptation** (noun).

adulation (noun) extreme admiration. *The young actress received great adulation from critics and fans following her performance in the Broadway play.* **adulate** (verb), **adulatory** (adjective).

adversary (noun) an enemy or opponent. *When the former Soviet Union became an American ally, the United States lost a major adversary.* **adversarial** (adjective).

adversity (noun) misfortune. *It's easy to be patient and generous when things are going well; a person's true character is revealed under adversity.* **adverse** (adjective).

aesthetic (adjective) relating to art or beauty. *Mapplethorpe's photos may be attacked on moral grounds, but no one questions their aesthetic value—they are beautiful.* **aestheticism** (noun).

affected (adjective) false, artificial. *At one time, Japanese women were taught to speak in an affected high-pitched voice, which was thought girlishly attractive.* **affect** (verb), **affectation** (noun).

aggressive (adjective) forceful, energetic, and attacking. *Some believe that a football player needs a more aggressive style of play than a soccer player.* **aggression** (noun).

alacrity (noun) promptness, speed. *Thrilled with the job offer, he accepted with alacrity—"Before they can change their minds!" he thought.* **alacritous** (adjective).

allege (verb) to state without proof. *Some have alleged that Foster was murdered, but all the evidence points to suicide.* **allegation** (noun).

alleviate (verb) to make lighter or more bearable. *Although no cure for AIDS has been found, doctors are able to alleviate the suffering of those with the disease.* **alleviation** (noun).

ambiguous (adjective) having two or more possible meanings. *The phrase, "Let's table that discussion" is ambiguous; some think it means, "Let's discuss it now," while others think it means, "Let's save it for later."* **ambiguity** (noun).

ambivalent (adjective) having two or more contradictory feelings or attitudes; uncertain. *She was ambivalent toward her impending marriage; at times she was eager to go ahead, while at other*

821

times she wanted to call it off. **ambivalence** (noun).

amiable (adjective) likable, agreeable, friendly. *He was an amiable lab partner, always smiling, on time, and ready to work.* **amiability** (noun).

amicable (adjective) friendly, peaceable. *Although they agreed to divorce, their settlement was amicable and they remained friends afterward.*

amplify (verb) to enlarge, expand, or increase. *Uncertain as to whether they understood, the students asked the teacher to amplify his explanation.* **amplification** (noun).

anachronistic (adjective) out of the proper time. *The reference, in Shakespeare's Julius Caesar to "the clock striking twelve" is anachronistic, since there were no striking timepieces in ancient Rome.* **anachronism** (noun).

anarchy (noun) absence of law or order. *For several months after the Nazi government was destroyed, there was no effective government in parts of Germany, and anarchy ruled.* **anarchic** (adjective).

anomaly (noun) something different or irregular. *Tiny Pluto, orbiting next to the giants Jupiter, Saturn, and Neptune, had long appeared to be an anomaly.* **anomalous** (adjective).

antagonism (noun) hostility, conflict, opposition. *As more and more reporters investigated the Watergate scandal, antagonism between Nixon and the press increased.* **antagonistic** (adjective), **antagonize** (verb).

antiseptic (adjective) fighting infection; extremely clean. *A wound should be washed with an antiseptic solution. The all-white offices were bare and almost antiseptic in their starkness.*

apathy (noun) lack of interest, concern, or emotion. *Tom's apathy toward his job could be seen in his lateness, his sloppy work, and his overall poor attitude.* **apathetic** (adjective).

arable (adjective) able to be cultivated for growing crops. *Rocky New England has relatively little arable farmland.*

arbiter (noun) someone able to settle disputes; a judge or referee. *The public is the ultimate arbiter of commercial value; it decides what sells and what doesn't.*

arbitrary (adjective) based on random or merely personal preference. *Both*

computers cost the same and had the same features, so in the end I made an arbitrary decision about which one to buy.

arcane (adjective) little-known, mysterious, obscure. *Eliot's Waste Land is filled with arcane lore, including quotations in Latin, Greek, French, German, and Sanskrit.* **arcana** (noun, plural).

ardor (noun) a strong feeling of passion, energy, or zeal. *The young revolutionary proclaimed his convictions with an ardor that excited the crowd.* **ardent** (adjective).

arid (adjective) very dry; boring and meaningless. *The arid climate of Arizona makes farming difficult. Some find the law a fascinating topic, but for me it is an arid discipline.* **aridity** (noun).

ascetic (adjective) practicing strict self-discipline for moral or spiritual reasons. *The so-called Desert Fathers were hermits who lived an ascetic life of fasting, study, and prayer.* **asceticism** (verb).

assiduous (adjective) working with care, attention, and diligence. *Although Karen is not a naturally gifted math student, by assiduous study she managed to earn an A in trigonometry.* **assiduity** (noun).

astute (adjective) observant, intelligent, and shrewd. *The reporter's years of experience in Washington and his personal acquaintance with many political insiders made him an astute commentator on politics.*

atypical (adjective) not typical; unusual. *In Hyde Park on Hudson, Bill Murray, best known as a comic actor, gave an atypical dramatic performance.*

audacious (adjective) bold, daring, adventurous. *Her plan to cross the Atlantic single-handed in a 12-foot sailboat was audacious, if not reckless.* **audacity** (noun).

audible (adjective) able to be heard. *Although she whispered, her voice was picked up by the microphone, and her words were audible throughout the theater.* **audibility** (noun).

auspicious (adjective) promising good fortune; propitious. *The news that a team of British climbers had reached the summit of Everest seemed an auspicious sign for the reign of newly crowned Queen Elizabeth II.*

authoritarian (adjective) favoring or demanding blind obedience to leaders. *Despite Americans' belief in democracy,* the American government has supported authoritarian regimes in other countries. **authoritarianism** (noun)

B

belated (adjective) delayed past the proper time. *She called her mother on January 5th to offer her a belated "Happy New Year."*

belie (verb) to present a false or contradictory appearance. *Lena Horne's youthful appearance belied her long, distinguished career in show business.*

benevolent (adjective) wishing or doing good. *In old age, Carnegie used his wealth for benevolent purposes, donating large sums to found libraries and schools.* **benevolence** (noun).

berate (verb) to scold or criticize harshly. *The judge angrily berated the two lawyers for their unprofessional behavior.*

bereft (adjective) lacking or deprived of something. *Bereft of parental love, orphans sometimes grow up to be insecure.*

bombastic (adjective) inflated or pompous in style. *Old-fashioned bombastic political speeches don't work on television, which demands a more intimate style of communication.* **bombast** (noun).

bourgeois (adjective) middle class or reflecting middle-class values. *The Dadaists of the 1920s produced art deliberately designed to offend bourgeois art collectors, with their taste for respectable, refined, uncontroversial pictures.* **bourgeois** (noun).

buttress (noun) something that supports or strengthens; a projecting structure of masonry or wood. *The endorsement of the American Medical Association is a powerful buttress for the claims made about this new medicine. The buttress on the south wall of the Medieval castle was beginning to crumble.* **buttress** (verb).

camaraderie (noun) a spirit of friendship. *Spending long days and nights together on the road, the members of a traveling theater group develop a strong sense of camaraderie.*

candor (noun) openness, honesty, frankness. *In his memoir about the Vietnam War, former defense secretary McNamara described his mistakes with remarkable candor.* **candid** (adjective).

capricious (adjective) unpredictable, whimsical. *The pop star Madonna has changed her image so many times that each new transformation now appears capricious rather than purposeful.* **caprice** (noun).

carnivorous (adjective) meat-eating. *The long, dagger-like teeth of the Tyrannosaurus make it obvious that this was a carnivorous dinosaur.* **carnivore** (noun).

carping (adjective) unfairly or excessively critical; querulous. *New York is famous for its demanding critics, but none is harder to please than the carping John Simon, said to have single-handedly destroyed many acting careers.* **carp** (verb).

catalytic (adjective) bringing about, causing, or producing some result. *The conditions for revolution existed in America by 1765; the disputes about taxation that arose later were the catalytic events that sparked the rebellion.* **catalyze** (verb).

caustic (adjective) burning, corrosive. *No one was safe when the satirist H. L. Mencken unleashed his caustic wit.*

censure (noun) blame, condemnation. *The news that the senator had harassed several women brought censure from many feminists.* **censure** (verb).

chaos (noun) disorder, confusion, chance. *The first few moments after the explosion were pure chaos: no one was sure what had happened, and the area was filled with people running and yelling.* **chaotic** (adjective).

circuitous (adjective) winding or indirect. *We drove to the cottage by a circuitous route so we could see as much of the surrounding countryside as possible.*

circumlocution (noun) speaking in a roundabout way; wordiness. *Legal documents often contain circumlocutions that make them difficult to understand.*

circumscribe (verb) to define by a limit or boundary. *Originally, the role of the executive branch of government was clearly circumscribed, but that role has greatly expanded over time.* **circumscription** (noun).

circumvent (verb) to get around. *When James was caught speeding, he tried to circumvent the law by offering the police officer a bribe.*

clandestine (adjective) secret, surreptitious. *As a member of the underground,*

Balas took part in clandestine meetings to discuss ways of sabotaging the Nazi forces.

cloying (adjective) overly sweet or sentimental. *The deathbed scenes in the novels of Dickens are famously cloying: as Oscar Wilde said, "One would need a heart of stone to read the death of Little Nell without dissolving into tears . . . of laughter."*

cogent (adjective) forceful and convincing. *The committee members were won over to the project by the cogent arguments of the chairman.* **cogency** (noun).

cognizant (adjective) aware, mindful. *Cognizant of the fact that it was getting late, the master of ceremonies cut short the last speech.* **cognizance** (noun).

cohesive (adjective) sticking together, unified. *An effective military unit must be a cohesive team, all its members working together for a common goal.* **cohere** (verb), **cohesion** (noun).

collaborate (verb) to work together. *To create a truly successful movie, the director, writers, actors, and many others must collaborate closely.* **collaboration** (noun), **collaborative** (adjective).

colloquial (adjective) informal in language; conversational. *Some expressions from Shakespeare, such as the use of thou and thee, sound formal today but were colloquial English in Shakespeare's time.*

competent (adjective) having the skill and knowledge needed for a particular task; capable. *Any competent lawyer can draw up a will.* **competence** (noun).

complacent (adjective) smug, self-satisfied. *Until recently, American auto makers were complacent, believing that they would continue to be successful with little effort.* **complacency** (noun).

composure (noun) calm, self-assurance. *The company's president managed to keep his composure during his speech even when the teleprompter broke down, leaving him without a script.* **composed** (adjective).

conciliatory (adjective) seeking agreement, compromise, or reconciliation. *As a conciliatory gesture, the union leaders agreed to postpone a strike and to continue negotiations with management.* **conciliate** (verb), **conciliation** (noun).

concise (adjective) expressed briefly and simply; succinct. *Less than a page long, the Bill of Rights is a concise statement of the freedoms enjoyed by all Americans.* **concision** (noun).

condescending (adjective) having an attitude of superiority toward another; patronizing. *"What a cute little car!" she remarked in a condescending style. "I suppose it's the nicest one someone like you could afford!"* **condescension** (noun).

condolence (noun) pity for someone else's sorrow or loss; sympathy. *After the sudden death of Princess Diana, thousands of messages of condolence were sent to her family.* **condole** (verb).

confidant (noun) someone entrusted with another's secrets. *No one knew about Jane's engagement except Sarah, her confidant.* **confide** (verb), **confidential** (adjective).

conformity (noun) agreement with or adherence to custom or rule. *In my high school, conformity was the rule: everyone dressed the same, talked the same, and listened to the same music.* **conform** (verb), **conformist** (noun, adjective).

consensus (noun) general agreement among a group. *Among Quakers, voting traditionally is not used; instead, discussion continues until the entire group forms a consensus.*

consolation (noun) relief or comfort in sorrow or suffering. *Although we miss our dog very much, it is a consolation to know that she died quickly, without suffering.* **console** (verb).

consternation (noun) shock, amazement, dismay. *When a voice in the back of the church shouted out, "I know why they should not be married!" the entire gathering was thrown into consternation.*

consummate (verb) to complete, finish, or perfect. *The deal was consummated with a handshake and the payment of the agreed-upon fee.* **consummate** (adjective), **consummation** (noun).

contaminate (verb) to make impure. *Chemicals dumped in a nearby forest had seeped into the soil and contaminated the local water supply.* **contamination** (noun).

contemporary (adjective) modern, current; from the same time. *I prefer old-fashioned furniture rather than contemporary styles. The composer Vivaldi was roughly contemporary with Bach.* **contemporary** (noun).

contrite (adjective) sorry for past misdeeds. *The public is often willing to forgive celebrities who are involved in some scandal, as long as they appear contrite.* **contrition** (noun).

conundrum (noun) a riddle, puzzle, or problem. *The question of why an all-powerful, all-loving God allows evil to exist is a conundrum many philosophers have pondered.*

convergence (noun) the act of coming together in unity or similarity. *A remarkable example of evolutionary convergence can be seen in the shark and the dolphin, two sea creatures that developed from different origins to become very similar in form.* **converge** (verb).

convoluted (adjective) twisting, complicated, intricate. *Tax law has become so convoluted that it's easy for people to accidentally violate it.* **convolute** (verb), **convolution** (noun).

corroborating (adjective) supporting with evidence; confirming. *A passerby who had witnessed the crime gave corroborating testimony about the presence of the accused person.* **corroborate** (verb), **corroboration** (noun).

corrosive (adjective) eating away, gnawing, or destroying. *Years of poverty and hard work had a corrosive effect on her beauty.* **corrode** (verb), **corrosion** (noun).

credulity (noun) willingness to believe, even with little evidence. *Con artists fool people by taking advantage of their credulity.* **credulous** (adjective).

criterion (noun) a standard of measurement or judgment. *In choosing a design for the new taxicabs, reliability will be our main criterion.* **criteria** (plural).

critique (noun) a critical evaluation. *The editor gave a detailed critique of the manuscript, explaining its strengths and its weaknesses.* **critique** (verb).

culpable (adjective) deserving blame, guilty. *Although he committed the crime, because he was mentally ill he should not be considered culpable for his actions.* **culpability** (noun).

cumulative (adjective) made up of successive additions. *Smallpox was eliminated only through the cumulative efforts of several generations of doctors and scientists.* **accumulation** (noun), **accumulate** (verb).

curtail (verb) to shorten. *The opening round of the golf tournament was curtailed by the severe thunderstorm.*

D

debased (adjective) lowered in quality, character, or esteem. *The quality of TV journalism has been debased by the many new tabloid-style talk shows.* **debase** (verb).

debunk (verb) to expose as false or worthless. *Magician James Randi loves to debunk psychics, mediums, clairvoyants, and others who claim supernatural powers.*

decorous (adjective) having good taste; proper, appropriate. *Prior to her visit to Buckingham Palace, the young woman was instructed to demonstrate the most decorous behavior.* **decorum** (noun).

decry (verb) to criticize or condemn. *The workers continued to decry the lack of safety in their factory.*

deduction (noun) a logical conclusion, especially a specific conclusion based on general principles. *Based on what is known about the effects of greenhouse gases on atmospheric temperature, scientists have made several deductions about the likelihood of global warming.* **deduce** (verb).

delegate (verb) to give authority or responsibility. *The president delegated the vice president to represent the administration at the peace talks.* **delegate** (noun).

deleterious (adjective) harmful. *About thirty years ago, scientists proved that working with asbestos could be deleterious to one's health, producing cancer and other diseases.*

delineate (verb) to outline or describe. *Naturalists had long suspected the fact of evolution, but Darwin was the first to delineate a process—natural selection—through which evolution could occur.* **delineation** (noun)

demagogue (noun) a leader who plays dishonestly on the prejudices and emotions of his followers. *Senator Joseph McCarthy was a demagogue who used the paranoia of the anti-Communist 1950s as a way of seizing fame and power in Washington.* **demagoguery** (noun).

demure (adjective) modest or shy. *The demure heroines of Victorian fiction have given* *way to today's stronger, more opinionated, and more independent female characters.*

denigrate (verb) to criticize or belittle. *The firm's new president tried to explain his plans for improving the company without appearing to denigrate the work of his predecessor.* **denigration** (noun).

depose (verb) to remove from office, especially from a throne. *Iran was once ruled by a monarch called the Shah, who was deposed in 1979.*

derelict (adjective) neglecting one's duty. *The train crash was blamed on a switchman who was derelict, having fallen asleep while on duty.* **dereliction** (noun).

derivative (adjective) taken from a particular source. *When a person first writes poetry, her poems are apt to be derivative of whatever poetry she most enjoys reading.* **derivation** (noun), **derive** (verb).

desolate (adjective) empty, lifeless, and deserted; hopeless, gloomy. *Robinson Crusoe was shipwrecked and had to learn to survive alone on a desolate island. The murder of her husband left Mary Lincoln desolate.* **desolation** (noun).

destitute (adjective) very poor. *Years of rule by a dictator who stole the wealth of the country had left the people of the Philippines destitute.* **destitution** (noun).

deter (verb) to discourage from acting. *The best way to deter crime is to ensure that criminals will receive swift and certain punishment.* **deterrence** (noun), **deterrent** (adjective).

detractor (noun) someone who belittles or disparages. *Neil Diamond has many detractors who consider his music boring, inane, and sentimental.* **detract** (verb).

deviate (verb) to depart from a standard or norm. *Having agreed upon a spending budget for the company, we mustn't deviate from it; if we do, we may run out of money soon.* **deviation** (noun).

devious (adjective) tricky, deceptive. *The CEO's devious financial tactics were designed to enrich his firm while confusing or misleading government regulators.*

didactic (adjective) intended to teach, instructive. *The children's TV show Sesame Street is designed to be both entertaining and didactic.*

diffident (adjective) hesitant, reserved, shy. *Someone with a diffident personality should pursue a career that involves little public contact.* **diffidence** (noun).

diffuse (verb) to spread out, to scatter. *The red dye quickly became diffused through the water, turning it a very pale pink.* **diffusion** (noun).

digress (verb) to wander from the main path or the main topic. *My high school biology teacher loved to digress from science into personal anecdotes about his college adventures.* **digression** (noun), **digressive** (adjective).

dilatory (adjective) delaying, procrastinating. *The lawyer used various dilatory tactics, hoping that his opponent would get tired of waiting for a trial and drop the case.*

diligent (adjective) working hard and steadily. *Through diligent efforts, the townspeople were able to clear away the debris from the flood in a matter of days.* **diligence** (noun).

diminutive (adjective) unusually small, tiny. *Children are fond of Shetland ponies because their diminutive size makes them easy to ride.* **diminution** (noun).

discern (verb) to detect, notice, or observe. *I could discern the shape of a whale off the starboard bow, but it was too far away to determine its size or species.* **discernment** (noun).

disclose (verb) to make known; to reveal. *Election laws require candidates to disclose the names of those who contribute large sums of money to their campaigns.* **disclosure** (noun).

discomfit (verb) to frustrate, thwart, or embarrass. *Discomfited by the interviewer's unexpected question, Peter could only stammer in reply.* **discomfiture** (noun).

disconcert (verb) to confuse or embarrass. *When the hallway bells began to ring halfway through her lecture, the speaker was disconcerted and didn't know what to do.*

discredit (verb) to cause disbelief in the accuracy of some statement or the reliability of a person. *Although many people still believe in UFOs, among scientists the reports of "alien encounters" have been thoroughly discredited.*

discreet (adjective) showing good judgment in speech and behavior. *Be discreet when discussing confidential business* matters— *don't talk among strangers on the elevator, for example.* **discretion** (noun).

discrepancy (noun) a difference or variance between two or more things. *The discrepancies between the two witnesses' stories show that one of them must be lying.* **discrepant** (adjective).

disdain (noun) contempt, scorn. *The professor could not hide his disdain for those students who were perpetually late to his class.* **disdain** (verb), **disdainful** (adjective).

disingenuous (adjective) pretending to be candid, simple, and frank. *When Texas billionaire H. Ross Perot ran for president, many considered his "jest plain folks" style disingenuous.*

disparage (verb) to speak disrespectfully about, to belittle. *Many political ads today both praise their own candidate and disparage his or her opponent.* **disparagement** (noun), **disparaging** (adjective).

disparity (noun) difference in quality or kind. *There is often a disparity between the kind of high-quality television people say they want and the low-brow programs they actually watch.* **disparate** (adjective).

disregard (verb) to ignore, to neglect. *If you don't write a will, when you die, your survivors may disregard your wishes about how your property should be handled.* **disregard** (noun).

disruptive (adjective) causing disorder, interrupting. *When the senator spoke at our college, angry demonstrators picketed, heckled, and engaged in other disruptive activities.* **disrupt** (verb), **disruption** (noun).

dissemble (verb) to pretend, to simulate. *When the police questioned her about the crime, she dissembled innocence.*

dissipate (verb) to spread out or scatter. *The windows and doors were opened, allowing the smoke that had filled the room to dissipate.* **dissipation** (noun).

dissonance (noun) lack of music harmony; lack of agreement between ideas. *Most modern music is characterized by dissonance, which many listeners find hard to enjoy. There is a noticeable dissonance between two common beliefs of most conservatives: their faith in unfettered free markets and their preference for traditional social values.* **dissonant** (adjective).

diverge (verb) to move in different directions. *Frost's poem* The Road Less Traveled *tells of the choice he made when "Two roads diverged in a yellow wood."* **divergence** (noun), **divergent** (adjective).

diversion (noun) a distraction or pastime. *During the two hours he spent in the doctor's waiting room, the game on his cell phone was a welcome diversion.* **divert** (verb).

divination (noun) the art of predicting the future. *In ancient Greece, people wanting to know their fate would visit the priests at Delphi, supposedly skilled at divination.* **divine** (verb).

divisive (adjective) causing disagreement or disunity. *Throughout history, race has been the most divisive issue in American society.*

divulge (verb) to reveal. *The people who count the votes for the Oscar awards are under strict orders not to divulge the names of the winners.*

dogmatic (adjective) holding firmly to a particular set of beliefs with little or no basis. *Believers in Marxist doctrine tend to be dogmatic, ignoring evidence that contradicts their beliefs.* **dogmatism** (noun).

dominant (adjective) greatest in importance or power. *Turner's Frontier Thesis suggests that the existence of the frontier had a dominant influence on American culture.* **dominate** (verb), **domination** (noun).

dubious (adjective) doubtful, uncertain. *Despite the chairman's attempts to convince the committee members that his plan would succeed, most of them remained dubious.* **dubiety** (noun).

durable (adjective) long lasting. *Denim is a popular material for work clothes because it is strong and durable.*

duress (noun) compulsion or restraint. *Fearing that the police might beat him, he confessed to the crime, not willingly but under duress.*

E

eclectic (adjective) drawn from many sources; varied, heterogeneous. *The Mellon family art collection is an eclectic one, including works ranging from ancient Greek* sculptures to modern paintings. **eclecticism** (noun).

efficacious (adjective) able to produce a desired effect. *Though thousands of people today are taking herbal supplements to treat depression, researchers have not yet proved them efficacious.* **efficacy** (noun).

effrontery (noun) shameless boldness. *The sports world was shocked when a professional basketball player had the effrontery to choke his head coach during a practice session.*

effusive (adjective) pouring forth one's emotions very freely. *Having won the Oscar for Best Actress, Sally Field gave an effusive acceptance speech in which she marveled, "You like me! You really like me!"* **effusion** (noun).

egotism (noun) excessive concern with oneself; conceit. *Robert's egotism was so great that all he could talk about was the importance—and the brilliance—of his own opinions.* **egotistic** (adjective).

egregious (adjective) obvious, conspicuous, flagrant. *It's hard to imagine how the editor could allow such an egregious error to appear.*

elated (adjective) excited and happy; exultant. *When the Washington Redskins' last, desperate pass was intercepted, the elated fans of the Philadelphia Eagles began to celebrate.* **elate** (verb), **elation** (noun).

elliptical (adjective) very terse or concise in writing or speech; difficult to understand. *Rather than speak plainly, she hinted at her meaning through a series of nods, gestures, and elliptical half sentences.*

elusive (adjective) hard to capture, grasp, or understand. *Though everyone thinks they know what "justice" is, when you try to define the concept precisely, it proves to be quite elusive.*

embezzle (verb) to steal money or property that has been entrusted to your care. *The church treasurer was found to have embezzled thousands of dollars by writing phony checks on the church bank account.* **embezzlement** (noun).

emend (verb) to correct. *Before the letter is mailed, please emend the two spelling errors.* **emendation** (noun).

emigrate (verb) to leave one place or country to settle elsewhere. *Millions of Irish emigrated to the New World in the wake of*

the great Irish famines of the 1840s. **emigrant** (noun), **emigration** (noun).

eminent (adjective) noteworthy, famous. *Vaclav Havel was an eminent author before he was elected president of the Czech Republic.* **eminence** (noun).

emissary (noun) someone who represents another. *In an effort to avoid a military showdown, former President Jimmy Carter was sent as an emissary to Korea to negotiate a settlement.*

emollient (noun) something that softens or soothes. *She used a hand cream as an emollient on her dry, work-roughened hands.* **emollient** (adjective).

empathy (noun) imaginative sharing of the feelings, thoughts, or experiences of another. *It's easy for a parent to have empathy for the sorrow of another parent whose child has died.* **empathetic** (adjective).

empirical (adjective) based on experience or personal observation. *Although many people believe in ESP, scientists have found no empirical evidence of its existence.* **empiricism** (noun).

emulate (verb) to imitate or copy. *The British band Oasis admitted their desire to emulate their idols, the Beatles.* **emulation** (noun).

encroach (verb) to go beyond acceptable limits; to trespass. *By quietly seizing more and more authority, Robert Moses continually encroached on the powers of other government leaders.* **encroachment** (noun).

enervate (verb) to reduce the energy or strength of someone or something. *The extended exposure to the sun along with dehydration enervated the shipwrecked crew, leaving them almost too weak to spot the passing vessel.*

engender (verb) to produce, to cause. *Countless disagreements over the proper use of national forests have engendered feelings of hostility between ranchers and environmentalists.*

enhance (verb) to improve in value or quality. *New kitchen appliances will enhance your house and increase the amount of money you'll make when you sell it.* **enhancement** (noun).

enmity (noun) hatred, hostility, ill will. *Long-standing enmity, like that between the*

Protestants and Catholics in Northern Ireland, is difficult to overcome.

enthrall (verb) to enchant or charm. *The Swedish singer Jenny Lind enthralled American audiences in the nineteenth century with her beauty and talent.*

ephemeral (adjective) quickly disappearing; transient. *Stardom in pop music is ephemeral; many of the top acts of ten years ago are forgotten today.*

equanimity (noun) calmness of mind, especially under stress. *FDR had the gift of facing the great crises of his presidency—the Depression and the Second World War—with equanimity and even humor.*

eradicate (verb) to destroy completely. *American society has failed to eradicate racism, although some of its worst effects have been reduced.*

espouse (verb) to take up as a cause; to adopt. *No politician in America today will openly espouse racism, although some behave and speak in racially prejudiced ways.*

euphoric (adjective) a feeling of extreme happiness and well-being; elation. *One often feels euphoric during the earliest days of a new love affair.* **euphoria** (noun).

evanescent (adjective) vanishing like a vapor; fragile and transient. *As she walked by, the evanescent fragrance of her perfume reached me for just an instant.*

exacerbate (verb) to make worse or more severe. *The roads in our town already have too much traffic; building a new shopping mall will exacerbate the problem.*

exasperate (verb) to irritate or annoy. *Because she was trying to study, Sharon was exasperated by the yelling of her neighbors' children.*

exculpate (verb) to free from blame or guilt. *When someone else confessed to the crime, the previous suspect was exculpated.* **exculpation** (noun), **exculpatory** (adjective).

exemplary (adjective) worthy to serve as a model. *The Baldrige Award is given to a company with exemplary standards of excellence in products and service.* **exemplar** (noun), **exemplify** (verb).

exonerate (verb) to free from blame. *Although the truck driver was suspected at first of being involved in the bombing, later evidence exonerated him.* **exoneration** (noun), **exonerative** (adjective).

expansive (adjective) broad and large; speaking openly and freely. *The LBJ Ranch is located on an expansive tract of land in Texas. Over dinner, she became expansive in describing her dreams for the future.*

expedite (verb) to carry out promptly. *As the flood waters rose, the governor ordered state agencies to expedite their rescue efforts.*

expertise (noun) skill, mastery. *The software company was eager to hire new graduates with programming expertise.*

expiate (verb) to atone for. *The president's apology to the survivors of the notorious Tuskegee experiments was his attempt to expiate the nation's guilt over their mistreatment.* **expiation** (noun).

expropriate (verb) to seize ownership of. *When the Communists came to power in China, they expropriated most businesses and turned them over to government-appointed managers.* **expropriation** (noun).

extant (adjective) currently in existence. *Of the seven ancient Wonders of the World, only the pyramids of Egypt are still extant.*

extenuate (verb) to make less serious. *Jeanine's guilt is extenuated by the fact that she was only twelve when she committed the theft.* **extenuating** (adjective), **extenuation** (noun).

extol (verb) to greatly praise. *At the party convention, speaker after speaker rose to extol their candidate for the presidency.*

extricate (verb) to free from a difficult or complicated situation. *Much of the humor in the TV show* I Love Lucy *comes in watching Lucy try to extricate herself from the problems she creates by fibbing or trickery.* **extricable** (adjective).

extrinsic (adjective) not an innate part or aspect of something; external. *The high price of old baseball cards is due to extrinsic factors, such as the nostalgia felt by baseball fans for the stars of their youth, rather than the inherent beauty or value of the cards themselves.*

exuberant (adjective) wildly joyous and enthusiastic. *As the final seconds of the game ticked away, the fans of the winning team began an exuberant celebration.* **exuberance** (noun).

F

facile (adjective) easy; shallow or superficial. *The one-minute political commercial favors a candidate with facile opinions rather than serious, thoughtful solutions.* **facilitate** (verb), **facility** (noun).

fallacy (noun) an error in fact or logic. *It's a fallacy to think that "natural" means "healthful"; after all, the deadly poison arsenic is completely natural.* **fallacious** (adjective).

felicitous (adjective) pleasing, fortunate, apt. *The sudden blossoming of the dogwood trees on the morning of Matt's wedding seemed a felicitous sign of good luck.* **felicity** (noun).

feral (adjective) wild. *The garbage dump was inhabited by a pack of feral dogs that had escaped from their owners and become completely wild.*

fervent (adjective) full of intense feeling; ardent, zealous. *In the days just after his religious conversion, his piety was at its most fervent.* **fervid** (adjective), **fervor** (noun).

flagrant (adjective) obviously wrong; offensive. *Nixon was forced to resign the presidency after a series of flagrant crimes against the U.S. Constitution.* **flagrancy** (noun).

flamboyant (adjective) very colorful, showy, or elaborate. *At Mardi Gras, partygoers compete to show off the most wild and flamboyant outfits.*

florid (adjective) flowery, fancy; reddish. *The grand ballroom was decorated in a florid style. Years of heavy drinking had given him a florid complexion.*

foppish (adjective) describing a man who is foolishly vain about his dress or appearance. *The foppish character of the 1890s wore bright-colored spats and a top hat; in the 1980s, he wore fancy suspenders and a shirt with a contrasting collar.* **fop** (noun).

formidable (adjective) awesome, impressive, or frightening. *According to his plaque in the Baseball Hall of Fame, pitcher Tom Seaver turned the New York Mets "from lovable losers into formidable foes."*

fortuitous (adjective) lucky, fortunate. *Although the mayor claimed credit for the falling crime rate, it was really caused by several fortuitous trends.*

fractious (adjective) troublesome, unruly. *Members of the British Parliament are often fractious, shouting insults and sarcastic questions during debates.*

fragility (noun) the quality of being easy to break; delicacy, weakness. *Because of their fragility, few stained-glass windows from the early Middle Ages have survived.* **fragile** (adjective).

fraternize (verb) to associate with on friendly terms. *Although baseball players aren't supposed to fraternize with their opponents, players from opposing teams often chat before games.* **fraternization** (noun).

frenetic (adjective) chaotic, frantic. *The floor of the stock exchange, filled with traders shouting and gesturing, is a scene of frenetic activity.*

frivolity (noun) lack of seriousness; levity. *The frivolity of the Mardi Gras carnival is in contrast to the seriousness of the religious season of Lent that follows.* **frivolous** (adjective).

frugal (adjective) spending little. *With our last few dollars, we bought a frugal dinner: a loaf of bread and a piece of cheese.* **frugality** (noun).

fugitive (noun) someone trying to escape. *When two prisoners broke out of the local jail, police were warned to keep an eye out for the fugitives.* **fugitive** (adjective).

G

gargantuan (adjective) huge, colossal. *The building of the Great Wall of China was one of the most gargantuan projects ever undertaken.*

genial (adjective) friendly, gracious. *A good host welcomes all visitors in a warm and genial fashion.*

grandiose (adjective) overly large, pretentious, or showy. *Among Hitler's grandiose plans for Berlin was a gigantic building with a dome several times larger than any ever built.* **grandiosity** (noun).

gratuitous (adjective) given freely or without cause. *Since her opinion was not requested, her harsh criticism of his singing seemed a gratuitous insult.*

gregarious (adjective) enjoying the company of others; sociable. *Naturally gregarious, Emily is a popular member of several clubs and a sought-after lunch companion.*

guileless (adjective) without cunning; innocent. *Deborah's guileless personality and complete honesty make it hard for her to survive in the harsh world of politics.*

gullible (adjective) easily fooled. *When the sweepstakes entry form arrived bearing the message, "You may be a winner!" my gullible neighbor tried to claim a prize.* **gullibility** (noun).

H

hackneyed (adjective) without originality, trite. *When someone invented the phrase, "No pain, no gain," it was clever, but now it is so commonly heard that it seems hackneyed.*

haughty (adjective) overly proud. *The fashion model strode down the runway, her hips thrust forward and a haughty expression, like a sneer, on her face.* **haughtiness** (noun).

hedonist (noun) someone who lives mainly to pursue pleasure. *Having inherited great wealth, he chose to live the life of a hedonist, traveling the world in luxury.* **hedonism** (noun), **hedonistic** (adjective).

heinous (adjective) very evil, hateful. *The massacre by Pol Pot of more than a million Cambodians is one of the twentieth century's most heinous crimes.*

hierarchy (noun) a ranking of people, things, or ideas from highest to lowest. *A cabinet secretary ranks just below the president and vice president in the hierarchy of the executive branch.* **hierarchical** (adjective).

hypocrisy (noun) a false pretense of virtue. *When the sexual misconduct of the television preacher was exposed, his followers were shocked at his hypocrisy.* **hypocritical** (adjective).

I

iconoclast (noun) someone who attacks traditional beliefs or institutions. *Comedian Stephen Colbert enjoys his reputation as an iconoclast, though people in power often resent his satirical jabs.* **iconoclasm** (noun), **iconoclastic** (adjective).

idiosyncratic (adjective) peculiar to an individual; eccentric. *Cyndi Lauper sings pop music in an idiosyncratic style, mingling high-pitched whoops and squeals with throaty gurgles.* **idiosyncrasy** (noun).

idolatry (noun) the worship of a person, thing, or institution as a god. *In Communist China, Chairman Mao was the subject of idolatry; his picture was displayed everywhere, and millions of Chinese memorized his sayings.* **idolatrous** (adjective).

impartial (adjective) fair, equal, unbiased. *If a judge is not impartial, then all of her rulings are questionable.* **impartiality** (noun).

impeccable (adjective) flawless. *The crooks printed impeccable copies of the Super Bowl tickets, making it impossible to distinguish them from the real ones.*

impetuous (adjective) acting hastily or impulsively. *Stuart's resignation was an impetuous act; he did it without thinking, and he soon regretted it.* **impetuosity** (noun).

impinge (verb) to encroach upon, touch, or affect. *You have a right to do whatever you want, so long as your actions don't impinge on the rights of others.*

implicit (adjective) understood without being openly expressed; implied. *Although most clubs had no rules excluding minorities, many had an implicit understanding that no member of a minority group would be allowed to join.*

impute (verb) to credit or give responsibility to; to attribute. *Although Helena's comments embarrassed me, I don't impute any ill will to her; I think she didn't realize what she was saying.* **imputation** (noun).

inarticulate (adjective) unable to speak or express oneself clearly and understandably. *A skilled athlete may be an inarticulate public speaker, as demonstrated by many post-game interviews.*

incisive (adjective) clear and direct expression. *Franklin settled the debate with a few incisive remarks that summed up the issue perfectly.*

incompatible (adjective) unable to exist together; conflicting. *Many people hold seemingly incompatible beliefs: for example, supporting the death penalty while believing in the sacredness of human life.* **incompatibility** (noun).

inconsequential (adjective) of little importance. *When the flat screen TV was delivered, it was a different shade of gray* *than I expected, but the difference was inconsequential.*

incontrovertible (adjective) impossible to question. *The fact that Alexandra's fingerprints were the only ones on the murder weapon made her guilt seem incontrovertible.*

incorrigible (adjective) impossible to manage or reform. *Lou is an incorrigible trickster, constantly playing practical jokes no matter how much his friends complain.*

incremental (adjective) increasing gradually by small amounts. *Although the initial cost of the Medicare program was small, the incremental expenses have grown to be very large.* **increment** (noun).

incriminate (verb) to give evidence of guilt. *The fifth amendment to the Constitution says that no one is required to reveal information that would incriminate him or her in a crime.* **incriminating** (adjective).

incumbent (noun) someone who occupies an office or position. *It is often difficult for a challenger to win a seat in Congress from the incumbent.* **incumbency** (noun), **incumbent** (adjective).

indeterminate (adjective) not definitely known. *The college plans to enroll an indeterminate number of students; the size of the class will depend on the number of applicants and how many accept offers of admission.* **determine** (verb).

indifferent (adjective) unconcerned, apathetic. *The mayor's small proposed budget for education suggests that he is indifferent to the needs of our schools.* **indifference** (noun).

indistinct (adjective) unclear, uncertain. *We could see boats on the water, but in the thick morning fog their shapes were indistinct.*

indomitable (adjective) unable to be conquered or controlled. *The world admired the indomitable spirit of Nelson Mandela; he remained courageous despite years of imprisonment.*

induce (verb) to cause. *The doctor prescribed a medicine that was supposed to induce a lowering of the blood pressure.* **induction** (noun).

ineffable (adjective) difficult to describe or express. *He gazed in silence at the sunrise over the Taj Mahal, his eyes reflecting an ineffable sense of wonder.*

inevitable (adjective) unable to be avoided. *Once the Japanese attacked Pearl Harbor, American involvement in World War II was inevitable.* **inevitability** (noun).

inexorable (adjective) unable to be deterred; relentless. *It's difficult to imagine how the mythic character of Oedipus could have avoided his evil destiny; his fate appears inexorable.*

ingenious (adjective) showing cleverness and originality. *The Post-it note is an ingenious solution to a common problem—how to mark papers without spoiling them.* **ingenuity** (noun).

inherent (adjective) naturally part of something. *Compromise is inherent in democracy, since everyone cannot get his or her way.* **inhere** (verb), **inherence** (noun).

innate (adjective) inborn, native. *Not everyone who takes piano lessons becomes a fine musician, which shows that music requires innate talent as well as training.*

innocuous (adjective) harmless, inoffensive. *I was surprised that Melissa took offense at such an innocuous joke.*

inoculate (verb) to prevent a disease by infusing with a disease-causing organism. *Pasteur found he could prevent rabies by inoculating patients with the virus that causes the disease.* **inoculation** (noun).

insipid (adjective) flavorless, uninteresting. *Some TV shows are so insipid that you can watch them while reading without missing a thing.* **insipidity** (noun).

insolence (noun) an attitude or behavior that is bold and disrespectful. *Some feel that news reporters who shout questions at the president are behaving with insolence.* **insolent** (adjective).

insular (adjective) narrow or isolated in attitude or viewpoint. *Americans are famous for their insular attitudes; they seem to think that nothing important has ever happened outside of their country.* **insularity** (noun).

insurgency (noun) uprising, rebellion. *The angry townspeople had begun an insurgency bordering on downright revolution; they were collecting arms, holding secret meetings, and refusing to pay certain taxes.* **insurgent** (adjective).

integrity (noun) honesty, uprightness; soundness, completeness. *"Honest Abe" Lincoln is considered a model of political* integrity. *Inspectors examined the building's support beams and foundation and found no reason to doubt its structural integrity.*

interlocutor (noun) someone taking part in a dialogue or conversation. *Annoyed by the constant questions from someone in the crowd, the speaker challenged his interlocutor to offer a better plan.* **interlocutory** (adjective).

interlude (noun) an interrupting period or performance. *The two most dramatic scenes in King Lear are separated, strangely, by a comic interlude starring the king's jester.*

interminable (adjective) endless or seemingly endless. *Addressing the United Nations, Castro announced, "We will be brief"—then delivered an interminable 4-hour speech.*

intransigent (adjective) unwilling to compromise. *Despite the mediator's attempts to suggest a fair solution, the two parties were intransigent, forcing a showdown.* **intransigence** (noun).

intrepid (adjective) fearless and resolute. *Only an intrepid adventurer is willing to undertake the long and dangerous trip by sled to the South Pole.* **intrepidity** (noun).

intrusive (adjective) forcing a way in without being welcome. *The legal requirement of a search warrant is supposed to protect Americans from intrusive searches by the police.* **intrude** (verb), **intrusion** (noun).

intuitive (adjective) known directly, without apparent thought or effort. *An experienced chess player sometimes has an intuitive sense of the best move to make, even if she can't explain it.* **intuit** (verb), **intuition** (noun).

inundate (verb) to flood; to overwhelm. *As soon as the playoff tickets went on sale, eager fans inundated the box office with orders.*

invariable (adjective) unchanging, constant. *When writing a book, it was her invariable habit to rise at 6 a.m. and work at her desk from 7 to 12.* **invariability** (noun).

inversion (noun) a turning backwards, inside-out, or upside-down; a reversal. *Latin poetry often features inversion of word order; for example, the first line of Virgil's Aeneid: "Arms and the man I sing."* **invert** (verb), **inverted** (adjective).

inveterate (adjective) persistent, habitual. *It's very difficult for an inveterate gambler to give up the pastime.* **inveteracy** (noun).

invigorate (verb) to give energy to, to stimulate. *As her car climbed the mountain road, Lucinda felt invigorated by the clear air and the cool breezes.*

invincible (adjective) impossible to conquer or overcome. *For three years at the height of his career, boxer Mike Tyson seemed invincible.*

inviolable (adjective) impossible to attack or trespass upon. *In the president's remote hideaway at Camp David, guarded by the Secret Service, his privacy is, for once, inviolable.*

irrational (adjective) unreasonable. *Richard knew that his fear of insects was irrational, but he was unable to overcome it.* **irrationality** (noun).

irresolute (adjective) uncertain how to act, indecisive. *The line in the ice cream shop grew as the irresolute child wavered between her two favorite ice cream flavors before finally choosing one.* **irresolution** (noun).

J

jeopardize (verb) to put in danger. *Terrorist attacks jeopardize the fragile peace in the Middle East.* **jeopardy** (noun).

juxtapose (verb) to put side by side. *Juxtaposing the two editorials revealed the enormous differences in the writers' opinions.* **juxtaposition** (noun).

L

languid (adjective) without energy; slow, sluggish, listless. *The hot, humid weather of late August can make anyone feel languid.* **languish** (verb), **languor** (noun).

latent (adjective) not currently obvious or active; hidden. *Although he had committed only a single act of violence, the examining psychiatrist said it's likely he always had a latent tendency toward violence.* **latency** (noun).

laudatory (adjective) giving praise. *The ads for the movie are filled with laudatory comments from critics.*

lenient (adjective) mild, soothing, or forgiving. *The judge was known for his lenient disposition; he rarely imposed long jail sentences on criminals.* **leniency** (noun).

lethargic (adjective) lacking energy; sluggish. *Visitors to the zoo are surprised that the lions appear so lethargic, but, in the wild, lions sleep up to 18 hours a day.* **lethargy** (noun).

liability (noun) an obligation or debt; a weakness or drawback. *The insurance company had a liability of millions of dollars after the town was destroyed by a tornado. Slowness afoot is a serious liability in an aspiring basketball player.* **liable** (adjective).

lithe (adjective) flexible and graceful. *The ballet dancer was almost as lithe as a cat.*

longevity (noun) length of life; durability. *The reduction in early deaths from infectious diseases is responsible for most of the increase in human longevity over the past two centuries.*

lucid (adjective) clear and understandable. *Hawking's* A Short History of the Universe *is a lucid explanation of modern scientific theories about the origin of the universe.* **lucidity** (noun).

lurid (adjective) shocking, gruesome. *While the serial killer was on the loose, the newspapers were filled with lurid stories about his crimes.*

M

malediction (noun) curse. *In the fairy tale "Sleeping Beauty," the princess is trapped in a death-like sleep because of the malediction uttered by an angry witch.*

malevolence (noun) hatred, ill will. *Critics say that Iago, the villain in Shakespeare's* Othello, *seems to exhibit malevolence with no real cause.* **malevolent** (adjective).

malinger (verb) to pretend incapacity or illness to avoid a duty or work. *During the labor dispute, hundreds of employees malingered, forcing the company to slow production and costing it millions in profits.*

malleable (adjective) able to be changed, shaped, or formed by outside pressures. *Gold is a very useful metal because it is so malleable. A child's personality is malleable and deeply influenced by the things his or her parents say and do.* **malleability** (noun).

mandate (noun) order, command. *The new policy of using only organic produce in the restaurant went into effect as soon as the manager issued his mandate about it.* **mandate** (verb), **mandatory** (adjective).

maturation (noun) the process of becoming fully grown or developed. *Free markets in the former Communist nations are likely to operate smoothly only after a long period of maturation.* **mature** (adjective and verb), **maturity** (noun).

mediate (verb) to act to reconcile differences between two parties. *During the baseball strike, both the players and the club owners were willing to have the president mediate the dispute.* **mediation** (noun).

mediocrity (noun) the state of being middling or poor in quality. *The New York Mets finished in ninth place in 1968 but won the world's championship in 1969, going from horrible to great in a single year and skipping mediocrity.* **mediocre** (adjective).

mercurial (adjective) changing quickly and unpredictably. *The mercurial personality of Robin Williams, with his many voices and styles, made him perfect for the role of the ever-changing genie in* Aladdin.

meticulous (adjective) very careful with details. *Repairing watches calls for a craftsperson who is patient and meticulous.*

mimicry (noun) imitation, aping. *The continued popularity of Elvis Presley has given rise to a class of entertainers who make a living through mimicry of "The King."* **mimic** (noun and verb).

misconception (noun) a mistaken idea. *Columbus sailed west with the misconception that he would reach the shores of Asia.* **misconceive** (verb).

mitigate (verb) to make less severe; to relieve. *Wallace certainly committed the assault, but the verbal abuse he'd received helps to explain his behavior and somewhat mitigates his guilt.* **mitigation** (noun).

modicum (noun) a small amount. *The plan for your new business is well designed; with a modicum of luck, you should be successful.*

mollify (verb) to soothe or calm; to appease. *Samantha tried to mollify the angry customer by promising him a full refund.*

morose (adjective) gloomy, sullen. *After Chuck's girlfriend dumped him, he lay* around the house for a couple of days, feeling morose.

mundane (adjective) everyday, ordinary, commonplace. *Moviegoers in the 1930s liked the glamorous films of Fred Astaire because they provided an escape from the mundane problems of life during the Great Depression.*

munificent (adjective) very generous; lavish. *Ted Turner's billion-dollar donation to the United Nations was one of the most munificent acts of charity in history.* **munificence** (noun).

mutable (adjective) likely to change. *A politician's reputation can be highly mutable, as seen in the case of Harry Truman—mocked during his lifetime, revered afterward.*

N

narcissistic (adjective) showing excessive love for oneself; egoistic. *Andre's room, decorated with photos of himself and the sports trophies he has won, suggests a narcissistic personality.* **narcissism** (noun).

nocturnal (adjective) of the night; active at night. *Travelers on the Underground Railroad escaped from slavery to the North by a series of nocturnal flights. The eyes of nocturnal animals must be sensitive in dim light.*

nonchalant (adjective) appearing to be unconcerned. *Unlike the other players on the football team who pumped their fists when their names were announced, John ran on the field with a nonchalant wave.* **nonchalance** (noun).

nondescript (adjective) without distinctive qualities; drab. *The bank robber's clothes were nondescript; none of the witnesses could remember their color or style.*

notorious (adjective) famous, especially for evil actions or qualities. *Warner Brothers produced a series of movies about notorious gangsters such as John Dillinger and Al Capone.* **notoriety** (noun).

novice (noun) beginner. *Lifting your head before you finish your swing is a typical mistake committed by the novice at golf.*

nuance (noun) a subtle difference or quality. *At first glance, Monet's paintings of water lilies all look much alike, but the more you study them, the more you appreciate the nuances of color and shading that distinguish them.*

nurture (verb) to nourish or help to grow. *The money given by the National Endowment for the Arts helps nurture local arts organizations throughout the country.* **nurture** (noun).

O

obdurate (adjective) unwilling to change; stubborn, inflexible. *Despite the many pleas he received, the governor was obdurate in his refusal to grant clemency to the convicted murderer.*

objective (adjective) dealing with observable facts rather than opinions or interpretations. *When a legal case involves a shocking crime, it may be hard for a judge to remain objective in his rulings.*

oblivious (adjective) unaware, unconscious. *Karen practiced her oboe with complete concentration, oblivious to the noise and activity around her.* **oblivion** (noun), **obliviousness** (noun).

obscure (adjective) little known; hard to understand. *Mendel was an obscure monk until decades after his death when his scientific work was finally discovered. Most people find the writings of James Joyce obscure; hence the popularity of books that explain his books.* **obscure** (verb), **obscurity** (noun).

obsessive (adjective) haunted or preoccupied by an idea or feeling. *His concern with cleanliness became so obsessive that he washed his hands twenty times every day.* **obsess** (verb), **obsession** (noun).

obsolete (adjective) no longer current; old-fashioned. *W. H. Auden said that his ideal landscape would include water wheels, wooden grain mills, and other forms of obsolete machinery.* **obsolescence** (noun).

obstinate (adjective) stubborn, unyielding. *Despite years of effort, the problem of drug abuse remains obstinate.* **obstinacy** (noun).

obtrusive (adjective) overly prominent. *Philip should sing more softly; his bass is so obtrusive that the other singers can barely be heard.* **obtrude** (verb), **obtrusion** (noun).

ominous (adjective) foretelling evil. *Ominous black clouds gathered on the horizon, for* *a violent storm was fast approaching.* **omen** (noun).

onerous (adjective) heavy, burdensome. *The hero Hercules was ordered to clean the Augean Stables, one of several onerous tasks known as "the labors of Hercules."* **onus** (noun).

opportunistic (adjective) eagerly seizing chances as they arise. *When Princess Diana died suddenly, opportunistic publishers quickly released books about her life and death.* **opportunism** (noun).

opulent (adjective) rich, lavish. *The mansion of newspaper tycoon Hearst is famous for its opulent decor.* **opulence** (noun).

ornate (adjective) highly decorated, elaborate. *Baroque architecture is often highly ornate, featuring surfaces covered with carving, sinuous curves, and painted scenes.*

ostentatious (adjective) overly showy, pretentious. *To show off his wealth, the millionaire threw an ostentatious party featuring a full orchestra, a famous singer, and tens of thousands of dollars' worth of food.*

ostracize (verb) to exclude from a group. *In Biblical times, those who suffered from the disease of leprosy were ostracized and forced to live alone.* **ostracism** (noun).

P

pallid (adjective) pale; dull. *Working all day in the coal mine had given him a pallid complexion. The new musical offers only pallid entertainment: the music is lifeless, the acting dull, the story absurd.*

parched (adjective) very dry; thirsty. *After two months without rain, the crops were shriveled and parched by the sun.* **parch** (verb).

pariah (noun) outcast. *Accused of robbery, he became a pariah; his neighbors stopped talking to him, and people he'd considered friends no longer called.*

partisan (adjective) reflecting strong allegiance to a particular party or cause. *The vote on the president's budget was strictly partisan: every member of the president's party voted yes, and all others voted no.* **partisan** (noun).

pathology (noun) disease or the study of disease; extreme abnormality. *Some people believe that high rates of crime are symptoms of an underlying social pathology.* **pathological** (adjective).

pellucid (adjective) very clear; transparent; easy to understand. *The water in the mountain stream was cold and pellucid. Thanks to the professor's pellucid explanation, I finally understand relativity theory.*

penitent (adjective) feeling sorry for past crimes or sins. *Having grown penitent, he wrote a long letter of apology, asking forgiveness.*

penurious (adjective) extremely frugal; stingy. *Haunted by memories of poverty, he lived in penurious fashion, driving a 12-year-old car and wearing only the cheapest clothes.* **penury** (noun).

perceptive (adjective) quick to notice, observant. *With his perceptive intelligence, Holmes was the first to notice the importance of this clue.* **perceptible** (adjective), **perception** (noun).

perfidious (adjective) disloyal, treacherous. *Although he was one of the most talented generals of the American Revolution, Benedict Arnold is remembered today as a perfidious betrayer of his country.* **perfidy** (noun).

perfunctory (adjective) unenthusiastic, routine, or mechanical. *When the play opened, the actors sparkled, but by the thousandth night their performance had become perfunctory.*

permeate (verb) to spread through or penetrate. *Little by little, the smell of gas from the broken pipe permeated the house.*

persevere (adjective) to continue despite difficulties. *Although several of her teammates dropped out of the marathon, Gail persevered.* **perseverance** (noun).

perspicacity (noun) keenness of observation or understanding. *Journalist Murray Kempton was famous for the perspicacity of his comments on social and political issues.* **perspicacious** (adjective).

peruse (verb) to examine or study. *Caroline perused the contract carefully before she signed it.* **perusal** (noun).

pervasive (adjective) spreading throughout. *As news of the disaster reached the town, a pervasive sense of gloom could be felt.* **pervade** (verb).

phlegmatic (adjective) sluggish and unemotional in temperament. *It was surprising* *to see Tom, who is normally so phlegmatic, acting excited.*

placate (verb) to soothe or appease. *The waiter tried to placate the angry customer with the offer of a free dessert.* **placatory** (adjective).

plastic (adjective) able to be molded or reshaped. *Because it is highly plastic, clay is an easy material for beginning sculptors to use.*

plausible (adjective) apparently believable. *According to the judge, the defense attorney's argument was both powerful and plausible.* **plausibility** (noun).

polarize (verb) to separate into opposing groups or forces. *For years, the abortion debate has polarized the American people, with many people voicing extreme views and few trying to find a middle ground.* **polarization** (noun).

portend (verb) to indicate a future event; to forebode. *According to folklore, a red sky at dawn portends a day of stormy weather.*

potentate (noun) a powerful ruler. *The Tsar of Russia was one of the last hereditary potentates of Europe.*

pragmatism (noun) a belief in approaching problems through practical rather than theoretical means. *Roosevelt's approach to the Great Depression was based on pragmatism: "Try something," he said. "If it doesn't work, try something else."* **pragmatic** (adjective).

preamble (noun) an introductory statement. *The preamble to the Constitution begins with the famous words, "We the people of the United States of America..."*

precocious (adjective) mature at an unusually early age. *Picasso was so precocious as an artist that, at nine, he is said to have painted far better pictures than his teacher.* **precocity** (noun).

predatory (adjective) living by killing and eating other animals; exploiting others for personal gain. *The tiger is the largest predatory animal native to Asia. Microsoft has been accused of predatory business practices that prevent other software companies from competing with it.* **predation** (noun), **predator** (noun).

predilection (noun) a liking or preference. *To relax from his presidential duties, Kennedy had a predilection for spy novels featuring James Bond.*

predominant (adjective) greatest in numbers or influence. *Although hundreds of religions are practiced in India, the predominant faith is Hinduism.* **predominance** (noun), **predominate** (verb).

prepossessing (adjective) attractive. *Smart, lovely, and talented, she has all the prepossessing qualities that mark a potential movie star.*

presumptuous (adjective) going beyond the limits of courtesy or appropriateness. *The senator winced when the presumptuous young staffer addressed him as "Chuck."* **presume** (verb), **presumption** (noun).

pretentious (adjective) claiming excessive value or importance. *For a shoe salesman to call himself a "Personal Foot Apparel Consultant" seems awfully pretentious.* **pretension** (noun).

procrastinate (verb) to put off, to delay. *If you habitually procrastinate, try this technique: never touch a piece of paper without either filing it, responding to it, or throwing it out.* **procrastination** (noun).

profane (adjective) impure, unholy. *It is inappropriate and rude to use profane language in a church.* **profane** (verb), **profanity** (noun).

proficient (adjective) skillful, adept. *A proficient artist, Louise quickly and accurately sketched the scene.* **proficiency** (noun).

proliferate (verb) to increase or multiply. *Over the past twenty-five years, high-tech companies have proliferated in northern California, Massachusetts, and Seattle.* **proliferation** (noun).

prolific (adjective) producing many offspring or creations. *With more than 300 books to his credit, Isaac Asimov was one of the most prolific writers of all time.*

prominence (noun) the quality of standing out; fame. *Barack Obama rose to political prominence after his keynote address to the 2004 Democratic National Convention.* **prominent** (adjective).

promulgate (verb) to make public, to declare. *Lincoln signed the proclamation that freed the slaves in 1862, but he waited several months to promulgate it.*

propagate (verb) to cause to grow; to foster. *John Smithson's will left his fortune for the founding of an institution to propagate knowledge, without saying whether that meant a university, a library, or a museum.* **propagation** (noun).

propriety (noun) appropriateness. *The principal questioned the propriety of the discussion the teacher had with her students about another instructor's gambling addiction.*

prosaic (adjective) everyday, ordinary, dull. *"Paul's Case" tells the story of a boy who longs to escape from the prosaic life of a clerk into a world of wealth, glamour, and beauty.*

protagonist (noun) the main character in a story or play; the main supporter of an idea. *Leopold Bloom is the protagonist of James Joyce's great novel* Ulysses.

provocative (adjective) likely to stimulate emotions, ideas, or controversy. *The demonstrators began chanting obscenities, a provocative act that they hoped would cause the police to lose control.* **provoke** (verb), **provocation** (noun).

proximity (noun) closeness, nearness. *Neighborhood residents were angry over the proximity of the sewage plant to the local school.* **proximate** (adjective).

prudent (adjective) wise, cautious, and practical. *A prudent investor will avoid putting all of her money into any single investment.* **prudence** (noun), **prudential** (adjective).

pugnacious (adjective) combative, bellicose, truculent; ready to fight. *Ty Cobb, the pugnacious outfielder for the Detroit Tigers, got into more than his fair share of brawls, both on and off the field.* **pugnacity** (noun).

punctilious (adjective) very concerned about proper forms of behavior and manners. *A punctilious dresser like James would rather skip the party altogether than wear the wrong color tie.* **punctilio** (noun).

pundit (noun) someone who offers opinions in an authoritative style. *The Sunday morning talk shows are filled with pundits, each with his or her own theory about the week's political news.*

punitive (adjective) inflicting punishment. *The jury awarded the plaintiff one million dollars in punitive damages, hoping to teach the defendant a lesson.*

purify (verb) to make pure, clean, or perfect. *The new plant is supposed to purify the drinking water provided to everyone in the nearby towns.* **purification** (noun).

Q

quell (verb) to quiet, to suppress. *It took a huge number of police officers to quell the rioting.*

querulous (adjective) complaining, whining. *The nursing home attendant needed a lot of patience to care for the three querulous, unpleasant residents on his floor.*

R

rancorous (adjective) expressing bitter hostility. *Many Americans are disgusted by recent political campaigns, which seem more rancorous than ever before.* **rancor** (noun).

rationale (noun) an underlying reason or explanation. *Looking at the sad faces of his employees, it was hard for the company president to explain the rationale for closing the business.*

raze (verb) to completely destroy; demolish. *The old Coliseum building will soon be razed to make room for a new hotel.*

reciprocate (verb) to give and take mutually. *If you'll watch my children tonight, I'll reciprocate by taking care of yours tomorrow.* **reciprocity** (noun).

reclusive (adjective) withdrawn from society. *During the last years of her life, actress Greta Garbo led a reclusive existence, rarely appearing in public.* **recluse** (noun).

reconcile (verb) to make consistent or harmonious. *FDR's greatness as a leader can be seen in his ability to reconcile the demands and values of the varied groups that supported him.* **reconciliation** (noun).

recrimination (noun) a retaliatory accusation. *After the governor called his opponent unethical, his opponent angrily replied with recriminations that the governor was a hypocrite.* **recriminate** (verb), **recriminatory** (adjective).

recuperate (verb) to regain health after an illness. *Although Marie left the hospital two days after her operation, it took her a few weeks to fully recuperate.* **recuperation** (noun), **recuperative** (adjective).

redoubtable (adjective) inspiring respect, awe, or fear. *Johnson's knowledge, experience, and personal clout made him a redoubtable political opponent.*

refurbish (verb) to fix up; renovate. *It took three days' work by a team of carpenters, painters, and decorators to completely refurbish the apartment.*

refute (verb) to prove false. *The company invited reporters to visit their plant in an effort to refute the charges of unsafe working conditions.* **refutation** (noun).

relevance (noun) connection to the matter at hand; pertinence. *Testimony in a criminal trial may be admitted only if it has clear relevance to the question of guilt or innocence.* **relevant** (adjective).

remedial (adjective) serving to remedy, cure, or correct some condition. *Affirmative action can be justified as a remedial step to help minority members overcome the effects of past discrimination.* **remediation** (noun), **remedy** (verb).

remorse (noun) a painful sense of guilt over wrongdoing. *In Poe's story* The Tell-Tale Heart, *a murderer is driven insane by remorse over his crime.* **remorseful** (adjective).

remuneration (noun) pay. *In a civil lawsuit, the attorney often receives part of the financial settlement as his or her remuneration.* **remunerate** (verb), **remunerative** (adjective).

renovate (verb) to renew by repairing or rebuilding. *The television program* This Old House *shows how skilled craftspeople renovate houses.* **renovation** (noun).

renunciation (noun) the act of rejecting or refusing something. *King Edward VII's renunciation of the British throne was caused by his desire to marry an American divorcee, something he couldn't do as king.* **renounce** (verb).

replete (adjective) filled abundantly. *Graham's book is replete with wonderful stories about the famous people she has known.*

reprehensible (adjective) deserving criticism or censure. *Although Pete Rose's misdeeds were reprehensible, not all fans agree that he deserves to be excluded from the Baseball Hall of Fame.* **reprehend** (verb), **reprehension** (noun).

repudiate (verb) to reject, to renounce. *After it became known that Duke had been a leader of the Ku Klux Klan, most Republican leaders repudiated him.* **repudiation** (noun).

reputable (adjective) having a good reputation; respected. *Find a reputable auto mechanic by asking your friends for recommendations based on their own experiences.* **reputation** (noun), **repute** (noun).

resilient (adjective) able to recover from difficulty. *A professional athlete must be resilient, able to lose a game one day and come back the next with confidence and enthusiasm.* **resilience** (noun).

resplendent (adjective) glowing, shining. *In late December, midtown New York is resplendent with holiday lights and decorations.* **resplendence** (noun).

responsive (adjective) reacting quickly and appropriately. *The new director of the Internal Revenue Service has promised to make the agency more responsive to public complaints.* **respond** (verb), **response** (noun).

restitution (noun) return of something to its original owner; repayment. *Some Native American leaders are demanding that the U.S. government make restitution for the lands taken from them.*

revere (verb) to admire deeply, to honor. *Millions of people around the world revered Mother Teresa for her saintly generosity.* **reverence** (noun), **reverent** (adjective).

rhapsodize (verb) to praise in a wildly emotional way. *That critic is such a huge fan of Toni Morrison that she will surely rhapsodize over the writer's next novel.* **rhapsodic** (adjective).

S

sagacious (adjective) discerning, wise. *Only a leader as sagacious as Nelson Mandela could have united South Africa so successfully and peacefully.* **sagacity** (noun).

salvage (verb) to save from wreck or ruin. *After the hurricane destroyed her home, she was able to salvage only a few of her belongings.* **salvage** (noun), **salvageable** (adjective).

sanctimonious (adjective) showing false or excessive piety. *The sanctimonious prayers of the TV preacher were interspersed with requests that the viewers send him money.* **sanctimony** (noun).

scapegoat (noun) someone who bears the blame for others' acts; someone hated for no apparent reason. *Although Buckner's error was only one reason the Red Sox lost, many fans made him the scapegoat, booing him mercilessly.*

scrupulous (adjective) acting with extreme care; painstaking. *Disney theme parks are famous for their scrupulous attention to small details.* **scruple** (noun).

scrutinize (verb) to study closely. *The lawyer scrutinized the contract, searching for any sentence that could pose a risk for her client.* **scrutiny** (noun).

secrete (verb) to emit; to hide. *Glands in the mouth secrete saliva, a liquid that helps in digestion. The jewel thieves secreted the necklace in a tin box buried underground.*

sedentary (adjective) requiring much sitting. *When Officer Samson was given a desk job, she had trouble getting used to sedentary work after years on the street.*

sequential (adjective) arranged in an order or series. *The courses for the chemistry major are sequential; you must take them in order, since each course builds on the previous ones.* **sequence** (noun).

serendipity (noun) the act of lucky, accidental discoveries. *Great inventions sometimes come about through deliberate research and hard work, sometimes through pure serendipity.* **serendipitous** (adjective).

servile (adjective) like a slave or servant; submissive. *The tycoon demanded that his underlings behave in a servile manner, agreeing quickly with everything he said.* **servility** (noun).

simulated (adjective) imitating something else; artificial. *High-quality simulated gems must be examined under a magnifying glass to be distinguished from real ones.* **simulate** (verb), **simulation** (noun).

solace (verb) to comfort or console. *There was little the rabbi could say to solace the husband after his wife's death.* **solace** (noun).

spontaneous (adjective) happening without plan. *When the news of Kennedy's assassination broke, people everywhere gathered in a spontaneous effort to share their shock and grief.* **spontaneity** (noun).

spurious (adjective) false, fake. *The so-called Piltdown Man, supposed to be the fossil of a primitive human, turned out to be spurious, although who created the hoax is still uncertain.*

squander (verb) to use up carelessly, to waste. *Those who had made donations to the charity were outraged to learn that its director had squandered millions on fancy dinners and first-class travel.*

stagnate (verb) to become stale through lack of movement or change. *Having had no contact with the outside world for generations, Japan's culture gradually stagnated.* **stagnant** (adjective), **stagnation** (noun).

staid (adjective) sedate, serious, and grave. *This college is definitely not a "party school"; the students all work hard, and the campus has a reputation for being staid.*

stimulus (noun) something that excites a response or provokes an action. *The arrival of merchants and missionaries from the West provided a stimulus for change in Japanese society.* **stimulate** (verb).

stoic (adjective) showing little feeling, even in response to pain or sorrow. *A soldier must respond to the death of his comrades in stoic fashion, since the fighting will not stop for his grief.* **stoicism** (noun).

strenuous (adjective) requiring energy and strength. *Hiking in the foothills of the Rockies is fairly easy, but climbing the higher peaks can be strenuous.*

submissive (adjective) accepting the will of others; humble, compliant. *At the end of Ibsen's play* A Doll's House, *Nora leaves her husband and abandons the role of submissive housewife.*

substantiate (verb) verified or supported by evidence. *The charge that Nixon had helped to cover up crimes was substantiated by his comments about it on a series of audio tapes.* **substantiated** (adjective), **substantiation** (noun).

sully (verb) to soil, stain, or defile. *Nixon's misdeeds as president did much to sully the reputation of the American government.*

superficial (adjective) on the surface only; without depth or substance. *Her wound was superficial and required only a light bandage. His superficial attractiveness hides the fact that his personality is lifeless and his mind is dull.* **superficiality** (noun).

superfluous (adjective) more than is needed, excessive. *Once you've won the debate,* *don't keep talking; superfluous arguments will only bore and annoy the audience.*

suppress (verb) to put down or restrain. *As soon as the unrest began, thousands of helmeted police were sent into the streets to suppress the riots.* **suppression** (noun).

surfeit (noun) an excess. *Most American families have a surfeit of food and drink on Thanksgiving Day.* **surfeit** (verb).

surreptitious (adjective) done in secret. *Because Iraq avoided weapons inspections, many believed it had a surreptitious weapons development program.*

surrogate (noun) a substitute. *When the congressman died in office, his wife was named to serve the rest of his term as a surrogate.* **surrogate** (adjective).

sustain (verb) to keep up, to continue; to support. *Because of fatigue, he was unable to sustain the effort needed to finish the marathon.*

T

tactile (adjective) relating to the sense of touch. *The thick brush strokes and gobs of color give the paintings of van Gogh a strongly tactile quality.* **tactility** (noun).

talisman (noun) an object supposed to have magical effects or qualities. *Superstitious people sometimes carry a rabbit's foot, a lucky coin, or some other talisman.*

tangential (adjective) touching lightly; only slightly connected or related. *Having enrolled in a class on African-American history, the students found the teacher's stories about his travels in South America of only tangential interest.* **tangent** (noun).

tedium (noun) boredom. *For most people, watching the Weather Channel for 24 hours would be sheer tedium.* **tedious** (adjective).

temerity (noun) boldness, rashness, excessive daring. *Only someone who didn't understand the danger would have the temerity to try to climb Everest without a guide.* **temerarious** (adjective).

temperance (noun) moderation or restraint in feelings and behavior. *Most professional athletes practice temperance in their personal habits; too much eating or drinking, they know, can harm their performance.* **temperate** (adjective).

tenacious (adjective) clinging, sticky, or persistent. *Tenacious in pursuit of her goal, she applied for the grant unsuccessfully four times before it was finally approved.* **tenacity** (noun).

tentative (adjective) subject to change; uncertain. *A firm schedule has not been established, but the Super Bowl in 2019 has been given the tentative date of February 3.*

terminate (verb) to end, to close. *The Olympic Games terminate with a grand ceremony attended by athletes from every participating country.* **terminal** (noun), **termination** (noun).

terrestrial (adjective) of the Earth. *The movie* Close Encounters of the Third Kind *tells the story of the first contact between beings from outer space and terrestrial humans.*

therapeutic (adjective) curing or helping to cure. *Hot-water spas were popular in the nineteenth century among the sickly, who believed that soaking in the water had therapeutic effects.* **therapy** (noun).

timorous (adjective) fearful, timid. *The cowardly lion approached the throne of the wizard with a timorous look on his face.*

toady (noun) someone who flatters a superior in hopes of gaining favor; a sycophant. *"I can't stand a toady!" declared the movie mogul. "Give me someone who'll tell me the truth—even if it costs him his job!"* **toady** (verb).

tolerant (adjective) accepting, enduring. *San Franciscans have a tolerant attitude about lifestyles: "Live and let live" seems to be their motto.* **tolerate** (verb), **toleration** (noun).

toxin (noun) poison. *DDT is a powerful toxin once used to kill insects but now banned in the United States because of the risk it poses to human life.* **toxic** (adjective).

tranquillity (noun) freedom from disturbance or turmoil; calm. *She moved from New York City to rural Vermont seeking the tranquillity of country life.* **tranquil** (adjective).

transgress (verb) to go past limits; to violate. *No one could fathom why the honor student transgressed by shoplifting hundreds of dollars of merchandise from his favorite clothing store.* **transgression** (noun).

transient (adjective) passing quickly. *Long-term visitors to this hotel pay a* *different rate than transient guests who stay for just a day or two.* **transience** (noun).

transitory (adjective) quickly passing. *Public moods tend to be transitory; people may be anxious and angry one month but relatively content and optimistic the next.* **transition** (noun).

translucent (adjective) letting some light pass through. *Panels of translucent glass let daylight into the room while maintaining privacy.*

transmute (verb) to change in form or substance. *In the Middle Ages, the alchemists tried to discover ways to transmute metals such as iron into gold.* **transmutation** (noun).

treacherous (adjective) untrustworthy or disloyal; dangerous or unreliable. *Nazi Germany proved to be a treacherous ally, first signing a peace pact with the Soviet Union, then invading. Be careful crossing the rope bridge; parts are badly frayed and treacherous.* **treachery** (noun).

tremulous (adjective) trembling or shaking; timid or fearful. *Never having spoken in public before, he began his speech in a tremulous, hesitant voice.*

trite (adjective) boring because of over-familiarity; hackneyed. *Her letters were filled with trite expressions, like "All's well that ends well" and "So far so good."*

truculent (adjective) aggressive, hostile, belligerent. *Hitler's truculent behavior in demanding more territory for Germany made it clear that war was inevitable.* **truculence** (noun).

truncate (verb) to cut off. *The poor copying job truncated the playwright's manuscript: the last page ended in the middle of a scene, halfway through the first act.*

turbulent (adjective) agitated or disturbed. *The night before the championship match, Serena Williams was unable to sleep, her mind turbulent with fears and hopes.* **turbulence** (noun).

U

unheralded (adjective) little known, unexpected. *In a year of big-budget, much-hyped, mega-movies, this unheralded foreign film has surprised everyone with its popularity.*

unpalatable (adjective) distasteful, unpleasant. *Although I agree with the candidate on many issues, I can't vote for her because I find her position on capital punishment unpalatable.*

unparalleled (adjective) with no equal; unique. *Tiger Woods's victory in the Masters golf tournament by a full twelve strokes was an unparalleled accomplishment.*

unstinting (adjective) giving freely and generously. *Eleanor Roosevelt was much admired for her unstinting efforts on behalf of the poor.*

untenable (adjective) impossible to defend. *The theory that this painting is a genuine van Gogh became untenable when the artist who actually painted it came forth.*

untimely (adjective) out of the natural or proper time. *The untimely death of a youthful Princess Diana seemed far more tragic than Mother Teresa's death of old age.*

unyielding (adjective) firm, resolute, obdurate. *Despite criticism, Mario Cuomo was unyielding in his opposition to capital punishment; he vetoed several death penalty bills as governor.*

usurper (noun) someone who takes a place or possession without the right to do so. *Kennedy's most devoted followers tended to regard later presidents as usurpers, holding the office they felt he or his brothers should have held.* **usurp** (verb), **usurpation** (noun).

utilitarian (adjective) purely of practical benefit. *The design of the Model T car was simple and utilitarian, lacking the luxuries found in later models.*

utopia (noun) an imaginary, perfect society. *Those who founded the Oneida community dreamed that it could be a kind of utopia— a prosperous state with complete freedom and harmony.* **utopian** (adjective).

V

validate (verb) to officially approve or confirm. *The election of the president is validated when the members of the Electoral College meet to confirm the choice of the voters.* **valid** (adjective), **validity** (noun).

variegated (adjective) spotted with different colors. *The brilliant, variegated* appearance of butterflies makes them popular among collectors. **variegation** (noun).

venerate (verb) to admire or honor. *In Communist China, Chairman Mao Zedong was venerated as an almost god-like figure.* **venerable** (adjective), **veneration** (noun).

verdant (adjective) green with plant life. *Southern England is famous for its verdant countryside filled with gardens and small farms.* **verdancy** (noun).

vestige (noun) a trace or remainder. *Today's tiny Sherwood Forest is the last vestige of a woodland that once covered most of England.* **vestigial** (adjective).

vex (verb) to irritate, annoy, or trouble. *It vexes me that she never helps with any chores around the house.* **vexation** (noun).

vicarious (adjective) experienced through someone else's actions by way of the imagination. *Great literature broadens our minds by giving us vicarious participation in the lives of other people.*

vindicate (verb) to confirm, justify, or defend. *Lincoln's Gettysburg Address was intended to vindicate the objectives of the Union in the Civil War.*

virtuoso (noun) someone very skilled, especially in an art. *Vladimir Horowitz was one of the great piano virtuosos of the twentieth century.* **virtuosity** (noun).

vivacious (adjective) lively, sprightly. *The role of Maria in* The Sound of Music *is usually played by a charming, vivacious young actress.* **vivacity** (noun).

volatile (adjective) quickly changing; fleeting, transitory; prone to violence. *Public opinion is notoriously volatile; a politician who is very popular one month may be voted out of office the next.* **volatility** (noun).

W

whimsical (adjective) based on a capricious, carefree, or sudden impulse or idea; fanciful, playful. *Dave Barry's* Book of Bad Songs *is filled with the kind of goofy jokes that are typical of his whimsical sense of humor.* **whim** (noun).

Z

zealous (adjective) filled with eagerness, fervor, or passion. *A crowd of the candidate's most zealous supporters greeted her at the airport with banners, signs, and a marching band.* **zeal** (noun), **zealot** (noun), **zealotry** (noun).